THE
WAGNER
COMPENDIUM

THE WAGNER COMPENDIUM

A GUIDE TO WAGNER'S LIFE AND MUSIC

EDITED BY BARRY MILLINGTON

SCHIRMER BOOKS
An Imprint of Macmillan Publishing Company
New York

Maxwell Macmillan International
New York Oxford Singapore Sydney

First American edition published in 1992 by Schirmer Books, An Imprint of Macmillan
Publishing Company

Schirmer Books   Maxwell Macmillan Canada, Inc.
An Imprint of Macmillan Publishing Company   1200 Eglinton Avenue East
866 Third Avenue   Suite 200
New York, NY 10022   Don Mills, Ontario M3C 3N1

First published in Great Britain by
Thames and Hudson Ltd.
30-34 Bloomsbury Street
London WC1B 3QP

Macmillan Publishing Company is part of the Maxwell Communication Group of
Companies.

Library of Congress Catalog Card Number: 92-32214

PRINTED IN THE UNITED STATES OF AMERICA

Printing number
1 2 3 4 5 6 7 8 9 10

Designed by Lis Rudderham

Frontispiece: Lorenz Geddon, bronze cast of Wagner, 1880-83.

Library of Congress Cataloging-in-Publication Data

The Wagner compendium : a guide to Wagner's life and music / edited by Barry Millington.
   — 1st American ed.
   p. cm.
"First published in Great Britain by Thames and Hudson, Ltd."—Verso t.p.
Includes bibliographical references and index.
ISBN 0-02-871359-1
1. Wagner, Richard, 1813-1883. I. Millington, Barry.
ML410.W13W122 1992
782.1'092—dc20   92-32214
[B]   CIP
                                                                  MN

CONTENTS

Reader's Guide   9

Section 1   *CALENDAR OF WAGNER'S LIFE, WORKS*
             AND RELATED EVENTS BARRY MILLINGTON   12

Section 2   *WHO'S WHO OF WAGNER'S*
             CONTEMPORARIES BARRY MILLINGTON   22

Section 3   *HISTORICAL BACKGROUND*

             The Holy Roman Empire from 1618 to 1789   36
             The French Revolution and the Wars of Liberation:
                1789–1815   39
             Reaction and revolution: 1815–1849   41
             German unification 'from above': 1850–1871   45
             The Reich in Europe: 1871–1883   47
                KONRAD BUND

Section 4   *INTELLECTUAL BACKGROUND*

             Philosophy ROGER HOLLINRAKE   52
             Literature RAYMOND FURNESS   55
             Religion ROGER HOLLINRAKE   58

Section 5   *MUSICAL BACKGROUND AND*
             INFLUENCES

             Formation of the earlier style   64
             The music drama and its antecedents   79
             Patronage, commissions and royalties in Wagner's day 88
                THOMAS S. GREY

Section 6   *WAGNER AS AN INDIVIDUAL*

    Paternity BARRY MILLINGTON   94
    Family BARRY MILLINGTON   95
    Appearance and character BARRY MILLINGTON   97
    Wagner as a conductor DAVID BRECKBILL   99
    Wagner's working routine THOMAS S. GREY   102

    THE PORTRAITS (plates 1–20)   104

    Wagner as polemicist WILLIAM WEBER   114
    Finances and attitude to money BARRY MILLINGTON   116
    Wagner and women BARRY MILLINGTON   118
    Relationship with King
      Ludwig II BARRY MILLINGTON   121
    Dealings with publishers RONALD TAYLOR   124
    Dealings with critics RONALD TAYLOR   126
    Wagner as scapegoat BARRY MILLINGTON   128

Section 7   *MYTHS AND LEGENDS* BARRY MILLINGTON   132

Section 8   *OPINIONS AND OUTLOOK*

    Social and political attitudes ROGER HOLLINRAKE   140
    Philosophical outlook ROGER HOLLINRAKE   143
    Religious beliefs ROGER HOLLINRAKE   146
    Literary tastes STEWART SPENCER   149
    The Beethoven legacy THOMAS S. GREY   151
    Opera and social reform WILLIAM WEBER   153
    Wagner and the Greeks HUGH LLOYD-JONES   158
    Wagner and the Jews BARRY MILLINGTON   161
    Wagner's Middle Ages STEWART SPENCER   164
    Bayreuth and the idea of a festival
      theatre STEWART SPENCER   167
    Contemporary composers THOMAS S. GREY   170
    Wagner, animals and modern scientific
      medicine JOACHIM THIERY and ULRICH TRÖHLER   174
    Wagner's critique of science and technology
      JOACHIM THIERY and ULRICH TRÖHLER   177

Section 9   *SOURCES*

    Autobiographical writings STEWART SPENCER   182
    Diaries STEWART SPENCER   186

Letters STEWART SPENCER   190

Collected writings STEWART SPENCER   193

Autograph manuscripts:

  Sketches/drafts (text)   196

  Sketches/drafts (music)   203

  Scores   219

  WARREN DARCY

WAGNER'S HAND (plates 21–30)   208

Printed editions:

  Breitkopf edition   221

  Sämtliche Werke (Schott)   223

  Miscellaneous   225

  WARREN DARCY

Section 10   *A WAGNERIAN GLOSSARY* THOMAS S. GREY   230

Section 11   *MUSICAL STYLE*

  Compositional process WARREN DARCY   244

  Musical language ARNOLD WHITTALL   248

Section 12   *WAGNER AS LIBRETTIST* STEWART SPENCER   264

Section 13   *THE MUSIC*   270

  Operas   271

  Orchestral music   309

  Choral music   313

  Chamber music   315

  Works for solo voice and orchestra   315

  Works for solo voice and piano   316

  Piano music   318

  Projected or unfinished dramatic works   320

  Editions and arrangements   322

  BARRY MILLINGTON

Section 14   *THE PROSE WORKS*

  A list of Wagner's writings, speeches, open letters and reviews   326

  BARRY MILLINGTON

Section 15   *ORCHESTRATION* JONATHAN BURTON   334

Section 16   *PERFORMANCE PRACTICE*
                  The orchestra   350
                  Conducting   352
                  Singing   354
                  Wagner and the early music movement   358
                     DAVID BRECKBILL

Section 17   *WAGNER IN PERFORMANCE*
                  Singing DAVID BRECKBILL   362
                  Conducting DAVID BRECKBILL   368
                  Staging BARRY MILLINGTON   374

Section 18   *RECEPTION*
                  Contemporary assessments DAVID C. LARGE   380
                  Posthumous reputation and
                     influence DAVID C. LARGE   384
                  The Bayreuth legacy DAVID C. LARGE   389
                  The birth of modernism:
                     Wagner's impact on the history of
                        music ARNOLD WHITTALL   393
                     Wagner's impact on literature RAYMOND FURNESS 396
                     Wagner's impact on the visual
                        arts MICHAEL HALL   398
                  Wagner literature:
                     Biographies STEWART SPENCER   402
                     Analysis and criticism CHRISTOPHER WINTLE 404
                     Miscellaneous STEWART SPENCER   408

                  Select Bibliography   412

                  List of Illustrations   419

                  The Contributors   420

                  Index   422

Reader's Guide

THE AIM OF THIS BOOK is to provide a compendium of information on every significant aspect of Wagner and his music. The entire range of subject matter has been covered: the historical, intellectual and musical background; his acquaintances and contemporaries; his character and personality; his opinions and outlook; the sources from which our knowledge about him and his works is derived; his musical and literary style; orchestration and the performing of his music; and the impact of Wagner on both his contemporaries and posterity. There is also a chronological survey of his life, a full list of his prose writings, a comprehensive listing and discussion of the works, a glossary of Wagnerian terms and a section devoted to the mythmaking that has surrounded Wagner ever since he himself began to make notes for his future autobiography.

Within each section and sub-section of the *Compendium* we have endeavoured to present a digest of information representing the most up-to-date and authoritative thinking on the subject; the book is thus intended to be a handy reference tool rather than a work of literature. The emphasis throughout is on clarity and accessibility: the hope is that the *Compendium* (like its predecessors on Mozart and Beethoven) will prove to be useful to any general reader interested in Wagner or his music, as well as to the student and scholar, who will find information assembled here which would otherwise have to be culled from a variety of recondite sources.

With eighteen different authors writing on a subject as controversial, contradictory and multivalent as Wagner, a unified, consistent point of view is unlikely to be projected. Nor should it be. I have made no attempt to suppress opinions with which I disagree, or which conflict with views expressed elsewhere in the *Compendium*; rather the plurality of opinion should be seen as a reflection of the richness of the subject. This should not be taken, however, as an abdication of the editor's responsibilities. Indeed, an overall pattern does emerge from the various contributions which I hope will enable Wagner to be seen in a new perspective. What is common to all the contributions is a healthy scepticism about the Wagner cult, and a refusal to indulge in sentimental mythmaking, neither of which is necessarily inconsistent with affection and admiration for the music, or even with respect for the man and his achievement. The latter point is important, because it is my belief that for all the desanctification, cynicism and critical reappraisal to which the composer has been subjected over recent decades, the Wagner phenomenon remains more susceptible to dubious Pavlovian responses than that of any composer born outside Salzburg. It would be good to think that we might be ready for a more dispassionate, better-informed approach to Wagner that located him more objectively in the historical context of the 19th-century Germany of which he was, according to Thomas Mann, the 'perfect epitome'.

No composer's life and work – least of all Wagner's – lends itself to convenient pigeon-holing. A description of Wagner's indebtedness to Otto Wesendonck, for example, could equally occur in the Who's Who or in the sections under patronage, character, finances or publishers. Each such subject receives fullest treatment in the most appropriate section, with cross-references from subsidiary discussions elsewhere. It is hoped that the list of contents, the index and the system of cross-references will guide the reader swiftly to the desired information.

Bibliographical references have been kept to a minimum. They have not generally been included where an opinion has been generally accepted; rather they serve to indicate controversial opinions, or recently discovered, and as yet little-known, scholarly facts. Such references are shown as follows: 'Coleman, 1991', or, in cases where two or more publications emanate from the same year, 'Dahlhaus, 1989a'.

Quotations from sources such as Wagner's writings have with one or two exceptions (where they are revised versions of the standard Ashton Ellis translation) been freshly translated by the contributors themselves; again no attempt has been made to impose a monolithic unity on either the translation of oft-quoted phrases, such as 'ersichtlich gewordene Taten der Musik', or on the style of translation in general.

I would like to extend my warmest thanks to my seventeen co-authors for their patience and generous co-operation in the project and not least for their splendid contributions. In particular, I would like to thank Stewart Spencer, from whose unrivalled knowledge of matters Wagnerian the *Compendium* has immensely benefited: his punctilious reading of the entire manuscript has greatly enhanced its accuracy. Grateful thanks are also due to Ingrid Grimes, whose multifaceted skills make her the most sought-after proofreader in the business, and to all my friends and former colleagues at Thames and Hudson for their enthusiastic support and unsurpassed professionalism at all stages of the book's production.

Barry Millington
LONDON 1991

Section 1

CALENDAR OF WAGNER'S LIFE, WORKS AND RELATED EVENTS

CALENDAR OF WAGNER'S LIFE, WORKS AND RELATED EVENTS

1813
22 May Born in the Brühl, Leipzig, the son of Johanna Rosine Wagner and (probably) Carl Friedrich Wagner: the rival claim of the actor and painter Ludwig Geyer has never been conclusively proved or disproved.
Jul–Aug Johanna, presumably with the baby, travels 100 miles from Leipzig to Teplitz and stays with Geyer.
16 Aug Baptized in the Thomaskirche, Leipzig.
Oct Napoleon defeated at Leipzig in the Battle of the Nations.
23 Nov Carl Friedrich Wagner dies; Geyer offers family assistance.

1814
Feb Johanna visits Geyer in Dresden; they become engaged.
28 Aug Johanna and Geyer are married.
Sep Congress of Vienna meets until Jun 1815, creating the German Confederation.

1817
Attends (probably briefly) the school of Karl Friedrich Schmidt, the royal vice-Kantor.
Oct Wartburg Festival organized by German students' association.

1819
Metternich, the Austrian chancellor, imposes the Carlsbad Decrees suppressing liberal ideas in Germany.

1820
Enters care of Pastor Christian Wetzel at Possendorf, near Dresden; has some piano lessons.

1821
30 Sep Geyer dies.

1822
26 Jan Weber's *Der Freischütz* first performed in Dresden. The young Wagner soon shares the general enthusiasm.
Dec Enters Dresden Kreuzschule as Richard Geyer.

1824
7 May Premiere of Beethoven's Ninth Symphony in Vienna.

1826
Enthusiasm for ancient Greece demonstrated in his translation of twelve books of the *Odyssey* and in the attempt to write an epic poem entitled *The Battle of Parnassus*. Five-act tragedy *Leubald* probably also begun at this time.
Dec Family moves to Prague, where sister Rosalie has post at theatre. Wagner stays in Dresden, with the family of some schoolfriends, to continue studies at the Kreuzschule.

1827
8 Apr Confirmation in Kreuzkirche, Dresden.
Spring In company of schoolfriend, undertakes journey from Dresden to Prague on foot.
Summer School trip to Leipzig; stimulated by scholarly, free-thinking uncle Adolf and demeanour of university students.
Dec Moves to Leipzig, to where most of family now returned.

1828
21 Jan Enters Nicolaischule in Leipzig, now called Richard Wagner.
Spring/summer Finishes *Leubald*, and in order to write incidental music for it, studies J.B. Logier's *Thorough-Bass*.
Autumn Begins harmony lessons with Christian Gottlieb Müller.

1829
First compositions: two piano sonatas and a string quartet (all lost).
Summer Alone in Leipzig; then undertakes journey on foot to Magdeburg to visit his sister Klara.

1830
Easter Leaves Nicolaischule.
16 Jun Enrols at Thomasschule, Leipzig.
Jul Revolution in Paris; inspires unrest elsewhere in Europe. Poles rebel against Russians.
Summer Short period of violin tuition.
Summer/autumn Composes three overtures and another one (in C major) at the end of the year (all lost).
6 Oct Offers piano transcription of Beethoven's Ninth Symphony to Schott's.
25 Dec 'Drum-beat Overture' performed in Leipzig under Heinrich Dorn.

1831
(**Early 1831**) Composes seven pieces for Goethe's *Faust* (voice and piano) and Piano Sonata in B♭ for four hands.
23 Feb Matriculates at Leipzig University.
Autumn Studies with new teacher, Christian Theodor Weinlig, and composes the Piano Sonata in B♭ (published as op.1) and a Fantasia, also for piano.

1832
(**Early 1832**) Composes Grosse Sonate in A major.
Apr–Jun Composes Symphony in C major (performed in Prague in Nov).
Sep–Oct Brief infatuation with daughter of Count Pachta, on whose estate at Pravonin, near Prague, he stays. Conceives ?three-act opera, *Die Hochzeit*, while at Pravonin; composition of music abandoned the following Mar.

1833
End Jan/Feb Moves to Würzburg to take up post of chorus master at theatre there. Writes text for *Die Feen*; music completed 6 Jan 1834. Rehearses works by Marschner, Meyerbeer, Hérold, Auber and others. Private singing lessons for chorus soprano, Therese Ringelmann, develop into short-lived love affair.

1834
21 Jan Returns to Leipzig, where he comes under the influence of Heinrich Laube and Young Germany.
Mar Wilhelmine Schröder-Devrient makes guest appearance in Leipzig as Romeo in Bellini's *I Capuleti e i Montecchi*.
10 Jun First essay on aesthetics of opera, *On German Opera*, published in Laube's journal.
Jun–Jul Holiday in Bohemia with Theodor Apel; inspiration for *Das Liebesverbot*, elaborated over following eighteen months.
End Jul Becomes musical director of Heinrich Bethmann's travelling theatre company, based in Magdeburg.
2 Aug Début as opera conductor with *Don Giovanni* in Bad Lauchstädt. Engagement brings about meeting with Minna Planer, with whom he falls in love.

1835
Jan Completes music for Apel's play *Columbus*. Begins composition of *Das Liebesverbot*.
Apr Wilhelmine Schröder-Devrient arrives in Magdeburg for series of performances under Wagner; financial disaster.
Summer Tours Bohemia and south Germany in search of vocal talent. Bavarian town of Bayreuth makes favourable impression; witnesses street brawl in Nuremberg (later to be recalled in *Meistersinger*).
Aug Begins notes in Red Pocketbook for future autobiography.

Nov Minna leaves to take up engagement at Königstadt Theatre in Berlin; hysterical stream of letters from Wagner obliges her to return within fortnight.

1836
29 Mar Premiere of *Das Liebesverbot* in Magdeburg. Bethmann company subsequently collapses (Apr).
May Travels to Berlin in vain bid to secure performance of *Das Liebesverbot*; impressed by Spontini's grand opera *Fernand Cortez*.
May–Jul Composes *Polonia* Overture.
7 Jul Follows Minna to Königsberg, where she has been offered another engagement. Sketches prose scenario for *Die hohe Braut* and sends it to Scribe.
24 Nov Marries Minna in the little church at Königsberg-Tragheim.

1837
Mar Composes *Rule Britannia* Overture; performed ?19 Mar in Riga.
1 Apr Appointed musical director at Königsberg Theatre.
31 May Minna leaves him for merchant called Dietrich. He pursues her and they stay for a time in lodgings at Blasewitz, near Dresden. There he reads Bulwer-Lytton's novel *Rienzi*; sketches opera on subject (Jun/Jul).
Jun Appointed musical director at theatre in Riga.
1 Sep First conducting engagement in Riga.
24 Dec Cosima Liszt born at Como.

1838
Summer Begins composition of Singspiel *Männerlist grösser als Frauenlist*, but breaks off after two numbers.
5/6 Aug Completes poem of *Rienzi*; begins music (7 Aug).
15 Nov Beginning of new season in Riga, in which Wagner is to conduct six of Beethoven's symphonies, among other works.

1839
Mar Contract not renewed at Riga.
Jun/Jul Endeavours to learn French and leaves Riga clandestinely (to elude creditors) with Minna but no passport. Minna suffers miscarriage. Stormy sea crossing to London (arrives 12 Aug).
20 Aug Journey completed to France; received by Meyerbeer at Boulogne.
17 Sep Arrives in Paris.
24 Nov First performance of Berlioz's *Roméo et Juliette* in Paris; Wagner present either then or 1 Dec and deeply impressed.
Dec Drafts first movement of a 'Faust Symphony' (to become the *Faust* Overture).

1840
6 May Prose sketch of *Der fliegende Holländer* sent to Scribe and (Jun) to Meyerbeer.

1840 (*cont.*)
May–Jul Music of the *Holländer* begun.
12 Jul Publication of Wagner's first essay for Schlesinger's *Revue et Gazette Musicale* entitled *De la musique allemande*.
Oct/Nov Dire financial straits but narrowly avoids the debtors' gaol.
19 Nov Completes *Rienzi*.

1841
Mar Begins to file reports for the Dresden *Abend-Zeitung*.
18–28 May Poem of the *Holländer* written.
Nov Score of the *Holländer* completed.

1842
Feb–Mar Prose draft for opera on E.T.A. Hoffmann's story *Die Bergwerke zu Falun*; the project was abandoned.
7 Apr Wagner and Minna leave Paris and make for Dresden, where *Rienzi* is to be performed.
Jun–Jul Holiday in Teplitz; sketches for *Tannhäuser*.
20 Oct Immense success of Dresden premiere of *Rienzi* under Reissiger establishes Wagner's reputation.

1843
2 Jan Premiere, in Dresden, of the *Holländer*, under Wagner.
1 and 8 Feb Publishes *Autobiographical Sketch* in Laube's *Zeitung für die elegante Welt*.
2 Feb Appointed Kapellmeister (with Reissiger) at King of Saxony's court in Dresden.
Apr Completes poem of *Tannhäuser*.
6 Jul Conducts *Das Liebesmahl der Apostel* in Frauenkirche, Dresden.
Summer Begins composition of *Tannhäuser*.
1 Oct Moves to relatively expensive apartment in the Ostra-Allee, where he assembles a library of classical, medieval and contemporary literature and source material on the Germanic epics.

1844
7 Jan Conducts first Berlin performance of the *Holländer*.
Autumn Spontini invited to Dresden to conduct his *La Vestale*.
14 Dec Ceremony for transferral of Weber's remains from London to Dresden; Wagner's *Trauermusik* played.
15 Dec Delivers oration at Weber's graveside; his *An Webers Grabe* for male-voice ensemble then performed.

1845
13 Apr Completes score of *Tannhäuser*.
3 Jul To Marienbad, with Minna, dog and parrot, to take waters; immerses himself simultaneously in Parzival and Lohengrin legends.

16 Jul Prose draft for *Die Meistersinger* completed.
3 Aug Prose draft for *Lohengrin* completed.
19 Oct Premiere of *Tannhäuser* under Wagner in Dresden.

1846
2 Mar Submits report about reorganization of royal orchestra.
5 Apr Conducts Beethoven's Ninth at traditional Palm Sunday concert.
30th Jul Finishes first complete draft of *Lohengrin*.
Oct Prose sketch for a five-act work (probably an opera) on the Friedrich Barbarossa legend.

1847
22 Feb Conducts his own version of Gluck's *Iphigénie en Aulide*.
29 Aug Finishes second complete draft of *Lohengrin*.
24 Oct Berlin premiere of *Rienzi* under Wagner.
(1847) Reads Greek authors in translation, including Aeschylus (the *Oresteia*) and Aristophanes.

1848
9 Jan Death of mother in Leipzig.
Feb Uprising in Paris.
Mar Uprising in Vienna, heralded by Wagner with a signed poem of enthusiastic approbation: 'Greeting from Saxony to the Viennese'.
8 Mar Performs Palestrina's Stabat Mater in his own edition.
28 Apr Completes score of *Lohengrin*.
May German National Assembly convenes in Frankfurt. Wagner submits his *Plan for the Organization of a German National Theatre for the Kingdom of Saxony*.
14 Jun Delivers address to the republican Vaterlandsverein, published the following day as *How do Republican Endeavours Stand in Relation to the Monarchy?*
4 Oct Original prose résumé for *Ring: Der Nibelungen-Mythus*.
Autumn Above turned into libretto, called *Siegfrieds Tod*; read to group of friends (Dec).
Winter Further sketch (for second act) of *Friedrich I*.

1849
Jan–Apr Scenario for five-act drama (?opera), *Jesus von Nazareth*.
?Mid-Feb Speculative connections between Friedrich I and Nibelung hoard formulated in the essay *Die Wibelungen*.
28 Mar Frankfurt Parliament offers imperial crown to Friedrich Wilhelm IV, the King of Prussia; he rejects it.
8 Apr Anarchistic essay *The Revolution*, possibly by Wagner, published in Röckel's *Volksblätter*.
Apr–May Active in revolutionary struggle, possibly involved in manufacture of hand-grenades.

5 May Climbs tower of Kreuzkirche to report on troop movements.

9 May Retreat of insurrectionists begins.

16 May Warrant for Wagner's arrest issued (published in *Dresdner Anzeiger* on 19th).

24–28 May Flees to Switzerland, with Liszt's help, and thence to Paris (2 Jun).

Jul Settles down in Zurich; writes *Art and Revolution*.

4 Nov Completes *The Artwork of the Future*.

Dec Begins prose draft for *Wieland der Schmied*.

1850

Jan Julie Ritter and Jessie Laussot propose annual allowance of 3000 francs.

14 Mar Visits Jessie and Eugène Laussot in Bordeaux.

Mar–May Affair with Jessie Laussot; plan evolved to 'elope' to Greece or Asia Minor – thwarted by Jessie's husband.

3 Jul Returns to Zurich and Minna.

Summer Preliminary musical sketches for *Siegfrieds Tod*.

28 Aug Premiere of *Lohengrin* in Weimar, under Liszt.

Sep Publishes anti-Semitic essay *Jewishness in Music*.

Winter Writes *Opera and Drama* (completed 10 Jan 1851).

1851

May Sketches *Der junge Siegfried*, then writes poem (Jun).

Jul–Aug Writes *A Communication to my Friends*.

15 Sep Submits himself to rigorous regimen at hydropathic establishment at Albisbrunn, near Zurich, in the hope of alleviating erysipelas and constipation.

Autumn Receives allowance of 800 thalers from Julie Ritter (continued until 1859). Prose sketches for *Rheingold* and *Walküre*.

Dec Wagner, still hoping for revolution, starting in France, refuses to acknowledge 1852.

1852

Feb Meets Otto and Mathilde Wesendonck, and subsequently Georg Herwegh and François and Eliza Wille.

Apr–May Conducts four performances of revised version of the *Holländer* in Zurich.

1 Jul Verse draft of *Walküre* completed.

3 Nov Verse draft of *Rheingold* completed.

Nov–Dec Revisions of texts for *Der junge Siegfried* and *Siegfrieds Tod*.

(1852) Suffers depression and contemplates suicide; these moods continue until 1857.

1853

Feb Publishes fifty copies of complete *Ring* poem, and reads it to an invited audience at the Hôtel Baur au Lac in Zurich.

15 Apr Moves with Minna into larger apartment on second floor of 13 Zeltweg (Zurich).

May Conducts three concerts of music from his earlier works.

May–Jun Writes piano sonata for Mathilde Wesendonck.

Jul Liszt visits and impresses Wagner with his *Faust* Symphony and symphonic poems.

Aug–Sep Holiday in Italy, during which inspiration for opening music of *Rheingold* supposedly occurs in a dream experience in a hotel room in La Spezia.

10 Oct Meets the fifteen-year-old Cosima Liszt and her sister Blandine while dining with Liszt in Paris.

1 Nov Begins complete draft of *Rheingold*.

1854

Jan–Jun Minna's heart condition deteriorates, as does the Wagners' marriage. Minna takes whey cure at Seelisberg on Lake Lucerne (Jun).

28 Jun Begins complete draft of *Walküre*.

Sep Supporting Minna, her daughter Natalie and her parents, his debts total 10,000 francs; Otto Wesendonck settles these in part and provides regular allowance in exchange for receipts from future performances of Wagner's works. Minna addresses petition for clemency to new Saxon king, Johann; it is rejected.

Sep/Oct Herwegh introduces him to philosophy of Schopenhauer. Conceives *Tristan*, presumably under pressure of infatuation for Mathilde Wesendonck.

1855

Jan Revises work now known as *Faust* Overture for publication.

Mar–Jun In England, conducting series of eight concerts for the Philharmonic Society; describes his existence as like that of 'a damned soul in hell'. Is savaged by the press but received respectfully by Queen Victoria and Prince Albert. Makes closer acquaintance of Berlioz, also conducting in London.

Autumn Frequent attacks of erysipelas.

1856

23 Mar Finishes fair copy of full score of *Walküre*.

16 May Further plea to King Johann; later rejected. Prose sketch for projected Buddhist opera *Die Sieger*.

Summer New Schopenhauer-inspired ending for the *Ring*; later rejected.

Sep Begins composition of *Siegfried*.

Oct–Nov During visit from Liszt, becomes intimately acquainted with latter's symphonic poems.

19 Dec First dated musical sketches for *Tristan*.

1857

Apr Occupies the Asyl, adjoining the Wesendoncks' villa in the Zurich suburb of Enge. Conceives *Parsifal*.

1857 (*cont.*)
9 Aug Breaks off composition of *Siegfried* at end of Act II.
Sep Hans von Bülow and his bride Cosima stay with the Wagners on their honeymoon.
(1857) Passion for Mathilde Wesendonck reciprocated; works on *Tristan* and sets five of Mathilde's poems to music.

1858
Marital tensions on the Green Hill necessitate Wagner's temporary removal to Paris. There Berlioz reads him text of *Les Troyens*.
7 Apr Back in Zurich, Minna intercepts 'Morning Confession' letter to Mathilde; resulting scenes eventually force Wagner to leave the Asyl for good (17 Aug).
29 Aug Arrives in Venice with Karl Ritter; stays in apartment in Palazzo Giustiniani on Grand Canal. Continues to work on Act II of *Tristan*. Prevented from communication with Mathilde, he confides his feelings to the 'Venice Diary'.

1859
(Early 1859) Stay in Venice marred by bad health (including dysentery and leg ulcer) and police harassment.
24 Mar Leaves Venice for Lucerne, where he completes Act III of *Tristan*.
6 Aug Completes full score of *Tristan*.
Sep Revisits Wesendoncks in Zurich; concludes business deal with Otto, by which latter buys copyright in four *Ring* scores for 6000 francs each.
10 Sep Settles in Paris (where he remains until Jul 1861) in the hope of bringing about performances of *Tannhäuser*, *Lohengrin* and *Tristan*.
17 Nov Minna arrives with dog and parrot; some attempt made to salvage marriage.

1860
Winter Schott negotiates for rights in Wagner's music; is offered *Rheingold* for 10,000 francs.
Jan–Feb Conducts three concerts of his music in Paris.
12 Aug Partial amnesty allows him to return to Germany, but not yet Saxony.
24 Sep Rehearsals begin for *Tannhäuser* at Paris Opéra.

1861
Mar *Tannhäuser* reaches stage of Opéra; politically inspired demonstration by aristocratic Jockey Club causes fiasco and necessitates withdrawal of production after three performances.
Apr–May Hopes of bringing *Tristan* to stage in Karlsruhe (not realized).
Nov Visits Wesendoncks in Venice. Embarks on *Die Meistersinger*.

1862
25 Jan Poem of *Die Meistersinger* completed.

5 Feb Public reading of *Die Meistersinger* poem at Schott's house in Mainz.
Feb Takes lodgings in Biebrich, across Rhine from Mainz, and works there on *Die Meistersinger*.
21 Feb Minna arrives uninvited; their marital strife described by Wagner as 'ten days in hell'. Unable to propose divorce, on account of Minna's poor health, but suggests setting her up in Dresden with a room put aside for him to make occasional visits.
28 Mar Full amnesty enables him to re-enter Saxony, but no wish to return permanently to Dresden. Meanwhile, encounters Mathilde Maier, to whom he feels greatly attracted, and Friederike Meyer, an actress.
Jul Hans and Cosima von Bülow visit him in Biebrich. Coaches Ludwig Schnorr von Carolsfeld and his wife Malvina in the roles of Tristan and Isolde, with Bülow at the piano.
Nov Last meeting with Minna in Dresden.
23 Nov Reading of *Die Meistersinger* at Dr Standhartner's house in Vienna, in which city he is now staying; the critic Hanslick, perceiving himself caricatured in Beckmesser, makes his excuses and leaves.

1863
Jan–Apr Travels to Prague, St Petersburg and Moscow to give concerts of his music.
May Moves to new apartment in Penzing, near Vienna; with help of Viennese seamstress Bertha Goldwag, furnishes it in luxurious style.
Jul–Dec Further concerts in Budapest, Prague, Karlsruhe, Breslau and Vienna.
Nov Wagner and Cosima von Bülow commit themselves to each other 'with sobs and tears' (*Mein Leben*).

1864
Mar Mounting debts force Wagner to leave Vienna to escape arrest; takes refuge with Eliza Wille at Mariafeld.
10 Mar Eighteen-year-old Wagner enthusiast becomes King Ludwig II of Bavaria. He immediately summons Wagner, pays off his debts and houses him near the royal castle Schloss Berg, overlooking Lake Starnberg, near Munich,.
Jun Cosima arrives at Starnberg with two daughters; union with Wagner consummated.
Oct Moves into spacious house at 21 Briennerstrasse in Munich, provided by king, who also authorizes generous annual stipend.
Autumn Bülow, at Wagner's instigation, appointed performer to the king; Gottfried Semper summoned to design a festival theatre for the *Ring* in Munich.

1865
Feb Suffers first ill-treatment at hands of courtiers and local press.
10 Apr His and Cosima's first child, Isolde, born.

10 Jun Premiere of *Tristan* in Munich under Bülow.

17 Jul Begins to dictate autobiography *Mein Leben* to Cosima, using notes from the Red Pocketbook.

Aug Prose draft for *Parsifal*.

Oct Hostility to Wagner mounts, both in court circles and among people of Munich at large. Wagner negotiates annual stipend of 8000 gulden and additional payment of 40,000 gulden to discharge pressing debts.

Dec Campaign to have Wagner banished from Munich finally successful. Ludwig compelled to give order, and Wagner leaves Munich (10 Dec).

1866

Jan Seeks congenial place to live in south of France.

25 Jan Minna dies in Dresden.

8 Mar Cosima joins Wagner in Geneva; they decide to make the house Tribschen, on Lake Lucerne, their home.

22 May Receives secret birthday visit from King Ludwig, announcing himself as 'Walther von Stolzing'; the latter accepts explanation that Cosima there as composer's amanuensis.

Jun Public scandal over the liaison with Cosima (the '*Volksbote* affair') drives the couple to outright mendacity with the king.

June Austro-Prussian War, in which Bavaria sides with Austria.

3 Jul Battle of Königgrätz decides war in Prussia's favour.

1867

17 Feb Birth of second daughter, Eva.

Mar–Jun Visits to Munich.

Apr Bülow appointed court Kapellmeister to Ludwig and director of proposed music school.

24 Oct Full score of *Die Meistersinger* finished.

Dec Hans Richter appointed répétiteur at Court Theatre, Munich.

23 Dec Returns to Munich and stays there until 9 Feb 1868.

1868

Mar Semper threatens legal proceedings over decision to drop plan for festival theatre; Wagner lukewarm about the project in view of difficulties in Munich.

21 Jun Triumphant premiere of *Die Meistersinger* in Munich under Bülow.

Aug *Luthers Hochzeit* project reflects problems with Cosima's marriage and Catholicism.

Sep–Oct Travels to Italy with Cosima.

8 Nov Meets Nietzsche in Leipzig.

16 Nov Cosima finally moves into Tribschen with Isolde and Eva; Ludwig officially informed.

1869

1 Mar Resumes work on the *Ring* with composition of Act III.

Spring *Jewishness in Music* reprinted with new preface complaining of alleged persecution by Jews.

6 Jun Birth of son, Siegfried; Nietzsche present at Tribschen and visits frequently thereafter.

Jul Visited by three French admirers: Judith Mendès-Gautier, her husband Catulle, and the poet Villiers de l'Isle-Adam.

22 Sep *Rheingold* performed in Munich under Franz Wüllner, despite Wagner's strenuous efforts to prevent it.

Christmas Reads *Parsifal* sketch to Nietzsche.

1870

Mar The Upper Franconian town of Bayreuth considered as venue for festival.

26 Jun Premiere of *Walküre* in Munich under Wüllner.

Jul The Bülows' marriage legally dissolved. Outbreak of Franco-Prussian War. A French entourage, consisting of the Mendès couple and Villiers, together with the composers Saint-Saëns, Duparc and others, arrives at Tribschen at the very time war is declared; a reading by Villiers on the last day of their visit provokes an insulting outburst from Wagner.

25 Aug Marriage of Wagner and Cosima in the Protestant church in Lucerne.

7 Sep Completes essay *Beethoven* in celebration of composer's centenary.

Nov Text for *Eine Kapitulation*, a 'comedy in the antique style', written.

25 Dec *Siegfried Idyll* performed on staircase at Tribschen in honour of Cosima's birthday.

1871

5 Feb Work on *Siegfried* completed.

14 Apr First performance of *Kaisermarsch* in Berlin.

Apr Wagners visit Bayreuth. They decide that the Markgräfliches Opernhaus is too small to accommodate the *Ring* and that a new theatre will have to be built.

12 May In Leipzig, Wagner announces that the first Bayreuth Festival will be held in 1873.

13 May In Darmstadt, Wagner discusses the technical direction of the Festival with Carl Brandt.

22 May Writes the foreword for the complete edition of his writings. He supervises the publication of the first nine volumes (1871–3), and the tenth is published posthumously (1883).

Nov Informs Friedrich Feustel, banker and chair of town council of Bayreuth, of his desire to locate his Festival there. Feustel secures authority of council and offers any site he chooses.

1872

Feb Acquires site adjoining the palace gardens in Bayreuth for his future home, Wahnfried. 'Green Hill' of Bürgerreuth chosen for theatre itself. Society of Patrons of the Bayreuth Festival established.

1872 (*cont.*)

22 May Laying of foundation stone of new theatre, followed by speeches and performance of Beethoven's Ninth Symphony.

Sep Writes essay *On Actors and Singers*.

End Sep The Wagners move into a temporary home in Bayreuth: Dammallee 7.

Oct Liszt makes first visit to Bayreuth. Cosima converts to Protestantism.

Nov–Dec Wagner and Cosima undertake tour of Germany's opera houses in search of singers.

1873

Jan–Feb (**also Apr**) Further tours to scout for artists for the Festival; Wagner also conducts fundraising concerts.

3 May Begins full score of *Götterdämmerung*.

24 Jun Sends Bismarck his report on the laying of the foundation stone of the Festspielhaus, including his nationalistic speech; no offer of financial aid is forthcoming.

30 Aug Announces that Festival must be postponed until 1875.

Sep Bruckner visits Wagner in Bayreuth and requests permission to dedicate symphony to him.

Nov In view of threat to Festival enterprise through lack of funds, Wagner asks King Ludwig for help.

1874

Jan King Ludwig initially refuses help, but subsequently extends loan of 100,000 thalers.

28 Apr Wagners move into new home, Wahnfried.

Jun–Sep Rehearsals for *Ring* with conductor Hans Richter (stays until 25 Jul) and singers.

21 Nov Finishes score of *Götterdämmerung*, and thus of entire *Ring*.

1875

Feb–May Concert tours of Vienna, Budapest and Berlin; travels also to Leipzig, Hanover and Brunswick.

Jul–Aug Rehearsals for the *Ring* with soloists and orchestra. All energies directed towards realization of Festival the following year.

1876

Feb–Mar Composes *Grosser Festmarsch* to a commission to celebrate the hundredth anniversary of the American Declaration of Independence.

3 Jun Rehearsals for *Ring* begin.

13–30 Aug First Bayreuth Festival: three complete cycles under Richter, attended by luminaries and musicians from all over Europe. Nietzsche is present but leaves before end of Festival in severe physical pain; he and Wagner meet for last time in Sorrento in October. The deficit for the Festival is 148,000 Marks. Following the contrived proximity to Judith Gautier (now separated from her husband) at the Festival (Wagner had arranged to be seated next to

her), an intimate and clandestine correspondence begins and continues until February 1878, when Cosima, having recently discovered the truth, resolutely brings it to an end.

1877

23 Feb Second prose draft of *Parsifal* completed.

19 Apr *Parsifal* text completed.

7–29 May Series of eight concerts given in the recently opened Royal Albert Hall in London; the profits of £700 do little to reduce the deficit for the Festival.

Sep Begins composition of *Parsifal*.

Oct Hans von Wolzogen invited to Bayreuth to edit the *Bayreuther Blätter*, a new monthly journal devoted to Wagner and his work.

1878

Jan First issue of *Bayreuther Blätter* published.

12 Mar Finishes *Modern*, the first of the series of so-called 'regeneration writings'.

31 Mar Question of Bayreuth deficit settled by agreement with King Ludwig, whereby king's right to produce Wagner's works is confirmed in exchange for a 10 per cent royalty which is set against the debt.

1879

Apr Finishes drafts of music for *Parsifal*.

Jul Antivivisectionists appeal to him to lend his voice to their campaign. After reading Ernst von Weber's book *The Torture Chambers of Science*, he publishes an open letter on the subject to Weber (Oct).

31 Dec Advised by his doctor to seek a milder climate, Wagner leaves Bayreuth with his family *en route* for Italy.

1880

4 Jan The family take up residence in the Villa d'Angri, overlooking the Bay of Naples, and remain there until 8 Aug. Joined there by Paul von Joukowsky, the future stage designer for *Parsifal*.

May The Moorish-style castle and exotic garden of the Palazzo Rufolo at Ravello provide the model for the stage setting of Act II of *Parsifal*: 'Klingsor's magic castle is found!', he writes in the visitors' book.

21 Aug The cathedral in Siena similarly provides the inspiration for the Hall of the Grail. Joukowsky makes sketches of both stage pictures.

12 Nov Wagner conducts private performance for King Ludwig of *Parsifal* Prelude in the Court Theatre in Munich. Last meeting with the king.

17 Nov Returns to Bayreuth.

1881

5–9 May First complete performance of the *Ring* in Berlin, given in the presence of the composer by Angelo Neumann's company.

11 May The French writer Count Gobineau, whose acquaintance Wagner has made previously, comes to Bayreuth, where he spends several weeks in animated conversation with the composer on the subject of the supposed degeneration of the human species.

25–29 May The Wagners, with Gobineau and Joukowsky, attend the fourth cycle of the *Ring* in Berlin.

Aug–Sep Writes essay *Heroism and Christianity*.

5 Nov The family arrive in Palermo, where they stay at the Hôtel des Palmes until 2 Feb 1882.

Dec Suffers chest spasms which his doctor fails to diagnose as a heart condition.

1882

13 Jan Finishes score of *Parsifal*.

15 Jan Portrait sketched by Renoir.

End Mar First major heart attack, after continuing chest spasms.

Apr The family travel through Messina, Naples and Venice, arriving back in Bayreuth on 1 May.

May Gobineau visits Wagner in Bayreuth. Bayreuth scholarship fund set up.

26 Jul Premiere of *Parsifal* in Bayreuth under Hermann Levi. Sixteen performances given in July and August under Levi and Franz Fischer. At last performance, Wagner takes baton from Levi and conducts conclusion.

14 Sep Departure from Bayreuth for Venice, where the family and entourage occupy the mezzanine floor of the Palazzo Vendramin.

24 Dec Conducts his youthful C major Symphony in celebration of Cosima's birthday.

1883

11 Feb Begins essay entitled *On the Feminine in the Human* (uncompleted).

13 Feb After furious row with Cosima, apparently over a Flowermaiden called Carrie Pringle, Wagner suffers fatal heart attack; he dies some time after 3 o'clock in Cosima's arms.

18 Feb Following procession through the town of Bayreuth, to where the coffin has been conveyed, the burial takes place privately in the garden of Wahnfried.

BARRY MILLINGTON

Section 2

WHO'S WHO OF WAGNER'S CONTEMPORARIES

WHO'S WHO OF WAGNER'S CONTEMPORARIES

Anders, Gottfried Engelbert (1795–1866). Of aristocratic lineage, Anders' original surname was Bettendorf (or Bethendorf); his adopted name means 'Otherwise'. From 1832 he was an employee of the Bibliothèque Royale in Paris. He was one of Wagner's closest friends in the Paris years (1839–42).

Apel, Theodor (1811–67). German poet and dramatist and contemporary of Wagner's, both at the Nicolaischule and then at the University in Leipzig; the two were close friends. Apel lost his sight after falling from his horse in 1836, in which year the friendship all but terminated as a result of Wagner's departure from Magdeburg. Wagner wrote an overture and incidental music for Apel's play about Christopher Columbus, as well as setting a poem of his to music (*Glockentöne*, 1832).

Auber, Daniel-François-Esprit (1782–1871). French composer, chiefly of *opéras comiques*. Auber and his principal librettist, Eugène Scribe, dominated the *opéra comique* for nearly half a century, although only *Fra Diavolo* (1831) remains in the repertory today. *La Muette de Portici* (1828), an early performance of which in Brussels precipitated the uprising of the Belgians against the Dutch, ushered in the era of grand opera, but Auber remained most closely identified with the lighter *opéra comique*.

Avenarius, Eduard (1809–85). German publisher who for a time acted as the Paris agent of the Leipzig firm Brockhaus. On Wagner's arrival in Paris in 1839 his half-sister Cäcilie was engaged to Avenarius; they were married the following year.

Bakunin, Mikhail (1814–76). Russian anarchist who arrived in Dresden in 1849 and there made Wagner's acquaintance. Bakunin's espousal of violent struggle and individual acts of terrorism, in order to bring about the replacement of existing institutions by more equitable forms of social organization, made some appeal to the Wagner of the revolutionary period.

Bellini, Vincenzo (1801–35). Italian composer whose music made a profound impression on the youthful Wagner. The assumption of the role of Romeo in Bellini's *I Capuleti e i Montecchi* by the soprano Wilhelmine Schröder-Devrient affected him deeply, and his essay *Bellini* (1837) was an enthusiastic endorsement of the Italianate bel canto line. Bellini's technique of melodic sequence has been traced in *Tristan*.

Benedictus, Louis [Ludwig] (d. 1921). Amateur composer, the son of a Dutch diamond merchant. After the separation of Judith Gautier (q.v.) from her husband Catulle Mendès in 1874, Benedictus became her close companion. The relationship survived Wagner's intimacy with her in 1876–8.

Berlioz, (Louis-) Hector (1803–69). French composer, regarded today – but not in his time – as the leading French musician of his era. The misunderstanding and neglect Berlioz endured, not least in his frustrated dealings with the Paris Opéra, helped him and Wagner to identify each other as fellow-sufferers, though they failed to sustain an intimate friendship. Berlioz's music contains a number of interesting pre-echoes of Wagner.

Betz, Franz (1835–1900). German baritone. Though he initially sang largely Italian and French roles, he later acquired a considerable reputation in Wagner roles, not least those of Hans Sachs, which he sang more than 100 times in Berlin alone, and Wotan/Wanderer, which he sang at the first performance of the *Ring* in Bayreuth (1876).

Bilz (-Planer), (Ernestine) Natalie (1826–?98). Illegitimate daughter of Minna Planer (later Wagner's wife) and a guards captain, Ernst Rudolph von Einsiedel. Minna was seduced and abandoned by Einsiedel at the age of 15. The ensuing child, Natalie, was brought up as Minna's sister, an understandable deception which was sustained throughout Natalie's life. Indeed, for most of it, Natalie also believed the fiction, though she lived with Minna and Wagner intermittently for many years. Natalie did little to improve the already tense marital atmosphere in the household, but both Wagner, and after his death Cosima, made over an allowance to her.

Bismarck, Otto Eduard Leopold, Prince von (1815–98). Prussian statesman. His career in politics reached its peak when he was appointed chancellor and foreign secretary (September and October 1862 respectively) under Wilhelm I, and subsequently prime minister. The aggressive policies of Bismarck – whose autocratic, ruthless character earned him the nickname the 'Iron Chancellor' – led to the Austro-Prussian War of 1866, which established Prussian hegemony once and for all. Her victory in the Franco-Prussian War of 1870 was followed directly by the foundation of the Second German Empire: Wilhelm I was proclaimed Emperor on 18 January 1871. Though initially repelled by Bismarck and his policies, Wagner came to appreciate, after 1866 – as did many of his compatriots – that their end result would be the long-sought national unification of Germany.

Brahms, Johannes (1833–97). German composer and pianist. After signing the ill-advised manifesto of 1860 opposing the New German School of Wagner and Liszt, Brahms came to be regarded as a figurehead for the conservative, Classically orientated strain of German music. This predisposition for 'absolute music', reinforced by his alignment with the anti-Wagnerite critic Hanslick, gave rise to a grudging and distant relationship with Wagner.

Brandt, Carl (1828–81). As technical director of the theatre in Darmstadt, Brandt had a high reputation for his abilities, which Wagner drew on in the construction both of the machinery for the *Ring* and of the Festspielhaus itself. Neither Doepler, the costume designer, nor Fricke, the director of movement, found Brandt easy to work with, but like Wagner they recognized his exceptional talents and he was invited back to Bayreuth to stage-manage *Parsifal* in 1882.

Brendel, (Karl) Franz (1811–68). German music historian, writer and critic. He assumed the editorship of Schumann's periodical *Neue Zeitschrift für Musik* from 1 January 1845 and continued in the post until his death. An influential figure in German musical circles, Brendel used his position to campaign for the New German School of Wagner and Liszt and for the cultural and political unification of Germany.

Brockhaus, Friedrich (1800–65). German publisher. With his brother Henrich he directed the family firm until 1850. In 1828 he married Wagner's sister Luise.

Brockhaus, Luise, *née* Wagner (1805–72). Sister of Wagner who gave up her career as an actress on marrying Friedrich Brockhaus in 1828.

Brockhaus, Ottilie, *née* Wagner (1811–83). Elder sister of Wagner; she married the philologist Hermann Brockhaus in 1836.

Brückner, Gotthold (1844–92) and Max (1836–1919). The Brückner brothers were employed by the Coburg Court Theatre when Wagner commissioned them to execute the sets for the first Bayreuth *Ring* (1876) from the designs made by Josef Hoffmann. They similarly prepared the sets for the first *Parsifal* in 1882 from the designs of Paul von Joukowsky.

Bülow, Cosima von. See Wagner, Cosima.

Bülow, Baron Hans (Guido) von (1830–94). German conductor and pianist. Abandoning his legal studies for a career as a musician, he became an enthusiastic and sometimes aggressive advocate of the New German School. His mentors were Wagner and Liszt, with whom he studied the piano from 1851. Bülow also composed at this time, his works earning praise from both senior composers. But it was as a pianist and conductor that he made his reputation, directing the premieres of *Tristan* (1865) and *Die Meistersinger* (1868). Bülow's admiration for Wagner remained undiminished by his wife Cosima's liaison with, and eventual marriage to, him.

Cornelius, (Carl August) Peter (1824–74). German composer, related to the celebrated artist Peter (von) Cornelius. He lived and taught in Vienna from 1859 to 1865 and it was there that he first came into close contact with Wagner. He struggled against Wagner's inclination to swamp him, both emotionally and artistically, and only reluctantly accepted his invitation to join him in Munich at the end of 1864, initially becoming his musical assistant and then a teacher at the music school re-established by Wagner and Bülow.

Dannreuther, Edward (1844–1905). English pianist, writer and teacher. Of German origin, he gradually established himself as a leading figure in English musical life. He was the founder of the Wagner Society in London (1872), was instrumental in obtaining the dragon and other stage props for the first *Ring* in Bayreuth (1876), and then assisted in the organization of Wagner's London tour the following year. His writings and lectures frequently featured Wagner and he also translated three of his essays.

Devrient, Eduard Philipp (1801–77). German theatre historian, librettist and singer. His career as a baritone was cut short by his partial loss of voice after 1831. He became chief producer and actor at the Dresden Court Theatre (1844–6) and director of the Karlsruhe Court Theatre (1852–70). His reminiscences of Mendelssohn (1869) provoked a spiteful essay from Wagner, entitled *Herr Eduard Devrient und sein Stil.* The soprano Wilhelmine Schröder-Devrient (q.v.) was his sister-in-law.

Dietsch, (Pierre-) Louis (-Philippe) (1808–65). French conductor and composer. He became chorus master at the Paris Opéra in 1840 and conductor at the Opéra in 1860. His and Wagner's paths crossed on two notable occasions. In November 1842 Dietsch's opera *Le Vaisseau fantôme* was given at the Opéra. Wagner's misinformed claim (see 'Myths and Legends', p. 134) that the libretto, by Foucher and Révoil, was based on Wagner's own scenario for *Der fliegende Holländer*, has often been repeated. It was again Dietsch who was conducting *Tannhäuser* at the Opéra in 1861 when the performances were sabotaged by the Jockey Club. Although he was not responsible for the fiasco, Dietsch had already driven Wagner to despair by his incompetent handling of the score.

Doepler, Carl Emil (1824–1905). Costume designer, born in Warsaw. From 1860 to 1870 he was costume designer for the Court Theatre in Weimar, following which he was based in Berlin as a professor of costume design. In commissioning costumes from Doepler for the first production of the *Ring* in 1876, Wagner made clear his distaste for the traditional pseudo-Nordic attempts to represent characters from the *Nibelungenlied*. But he did not make his intentions clear enough, and Doepler's costumes were later notoriously described by Cosima as 'reminiscent throughout of Red Indian chiefs'.

Dorn, Heinrich Ludwig Egmont (1804–92). German composer, conductor and writer. As Kapellmeister of the Leipzig Municipal Theatre, he did the young Wagner the dubious favour of bringing about the humiliating performance of his ill-conceived 'Drum-beat Overture' in B♭ (1830). Their paths crossed again in 1839 when, after a contractual wrangle, Dorn succeeded Wagner as musical director of the theatre in Riga. His many operas include one based on the Nibelung legend (1854).

Düfflipp, Lorenz von (1820–86). Court Secretary to Ludwig II from 1866 to 1877. Though well disposed towards Wagner he had a firmer grasp of political realities than his successor Bürkel was to display.

Eiser, Otto (1834–98). German physician, resident in Frankfurt, where Nietzsche consulted him in 1877, Wagner offering Eiser his own diagnosis of Nietzsche's malaise. Eiser was also a faithful adherent to the Wagnerian cause, being a representative of the Society of Patrons in Frankfurt, and contributing to the *Bayreuther Blätter*.

Feuerbach, Ludwig Andreas (1804–72). German philosopher who exerted a profound influence on 19th-century German thought by turning attention away from the abstract metaphysics of Hegel (by whom he was nevertheless influenced) and towards the moral, religious and social issues of everyday life. His *Das Wesen des Christentums* (*The Essence of*

Christianity) of 1841 proclaimed a new religion of humanity, that is, a theological outlook in which God was perceived as a projection of the hopes and needs of men and women themselves, and asserted the supremacy of love over the law. Wagner's Feuerbachian acknowledgment of 'the glorious necessity of love' continued to inform his outlook even after the discovery of Schopenhauer (q.v.)

Feustel, Friedrich (1824–91). Banker and chair of the town council of Bayreuth. Wagner informed him in November 1871 that he had chosen Bayreuth as the venue for his festival enterprise, and Feustel responded with alacrity, immediately securing the authority of his council to offer Wagner any site he should select. Feustel remained a loyal supporter of Wagner and was a pallbearer at his funeral.

Franck, Hermann (d.1855). German writer. Admired by Wagner for his extensive knowledge and discriminating judgment, an opinion not diminished by Franck's complimentary article on *Tannhäuser* published in the Augsburg *Allgemeine Zeitung* in November 1845. It was shortly before this that Wagner became acquainted with him while Franck was teaching in Dresden. The circumstances of Franck's death in Brighton aroused much interest in the British press. He leapt to his death from a hotel window after, it was alleged, murdering his son. Many felt him to have been incapable of murder, and the inquest left the cause of the son's death open.

Frantz, Constantin Gustav Adolph (1817–91). German political theorist. Frantz's conservative pan-Germanic views were warmly embraced by Wagner when he encountered them in 1865. Wagner recommended Frantz's writings to King Ludwig, especially his exposition of the principle of federalism, in *Der Föderalismus* (1879).

Fritzsch, Ernst Wilhelm (1840–1902). Publisher in Leipzig, where he edited the journal *Musikalisches Wochenblatt* and published Wagner's collected writings.

Fröbel, Julius (1805–93). He made the acquaintance of Wagner while working as a journalist in Dresden in the late 1840s. Returning from exile in the 1860s (he had been sympathetic to the democratic cause) he was engaged in an advisory capacity by the Austrian government. In 1867 he became, at Wagner's suggestion, the first editor of the *Süddeutsche Presse*.

Frommann, Alwine (1800–75). German artist who held the post of reader to the Princess Augusta of Prussia (later Queen of Prussia and Empress of Germany). She first wrote to Wagner after hearing *Der fliegende Holländer* in Berlin in February 1844, and again after travelling to Dresden to hear *Rienzi* in October of that year. She continued throughout her life to bring what influence she had to bear on the court at Berlin on behalf of Wagner.

Gaillard, Karl (1813–51). German writer. Like Alwine Frommann (q.v.), Gaillard was fired by the Berlin production of the *Holländer* in 1844. He too wrote to Wagner in enthusiastic terms, and further promoted the cause in the journal he had established, the *Berliner Musikalische Zeitung* (1844–7). The journal foundered for lack of capital, as did his small music shop. His health declined and within a few years he was dead, much mourned by Wagner who, notwithstanding the slightness of Gaillard's poems and dramas, had a sincere affection for him.

Gasperini, Auguste de (1825–69). French doctor and writer on music. An early enthusiast for Wagner's music in France, Gasperini befriended Wagner when he arrived in Paris for the series of three concerts early in 1860 and the production of *Tannhäuser* at the Opéra the following year. He provided much valued moral support and advice, though his plea that Wagner abandon the new music composed for the Paris *Tannhäuser* – on account of the resulting stylistic disparity – was not heeded.

Gautier, Judith (1845–1917). French author and writer on music; brilliant and gifted daughter of the writer Théophile Gautier. An enthusiast for Wagner's work from an early age, she met the equally devoted Catulle Mendès in the early 1860s, marrying him on 17 April 1866. Together with the poet Villiers de l'Isle-Adam they visited Wagner at Tribschen in 1869 and again the following year. In 1874 the Mendès couple made a decision to separate, and by the time of the first Bayreuth Festival two years later Judith was enjoying the serious attentions of an amateur composer called Louis Benedictus (q.v.) This, however, did not discourage Wagner (now married to Cosima) from attempting to give vent to his infatuation for her. Their relationship may or may not have been consummated, but they continued to conduct an intimate and clandestine correspondence until February 1878. Wagner claimed that he needed the intoxication of at least her spiritual presence, as well as the silks, satins and exotic perfumes she sent, in order to compose *Parsifal*. She also made an intellectual contribution to Wagnerism, however, with a translation of *Parsifal* into French, various writings on Wagnerian topics, and a three-volume memoir of the composer.

Geyer, Ludwig (1779–1821). German actor and painter; a close friend of the family and from 1814 Wagner's step-father (see 'Paternity', pp. 94–5). From 1809 until his death he was an actor in Dresden (from 1814 with the title 'Court Actor').

Glasenapp, Carl Friedrich (1847–1915). German writer on music. His biography of Wagner was begun while Glasenapp was still a student, and completed in its two-volume version in 1876–7 (it was subsequently enlarged and eventually republished in six volumes). The biography was 'authorized' in that Glasenapp enjoyed the confidence of Wagner and Cosima and was granted access to much material of significance. However, the merits of its overall factual accuracy were diminished by the 'protectionist' approach typical of the inner Bayreuth circle.

Gobineau, Count Joseph-Arthur de (1816–82). French diplomat, novelist and historian. Gobineau's significance for Wagner consisted not in his stylish short stories and other literary works but in his views on miscegenation, particularly as expounded in his *Essai sur l'inégalité des races humaines* (1853–5). The supposed 'degeneration' of the human species' was an outlook the two men shared, though Gobineau believed that a certain degree of inter-breeding – the cause of degeneration – was necessary for the survival of civilization, whereas Wagner held that the pure blood of Christ provided an agent of redemption. The two men met in November 1876. Gobineau visited Wahnfried in 1881–2 and his works were much discussed there; his views continued to be espoused for long after his death.

Goldwag, Bertha. Viennese milliner and seamstress, who supplied Wagner's wardrobe and furnishings first for his apartment in Penzing (1863–4) and then in Munich (1864–5). In view of the extravagance of the exotic fabrics requested by Wagner, Goldwag travelled to Munich incognito, informing customs officials that her silks and perfumes were for a countess in Berlin. The luxury of Wagner's interiors soon became common knowledge, however, and his embarrassment was maximized when his letters to the *Putzmacherin* were published in 1877, after an unsavoury chain of transactions involving Brahms, among others. According to one source, the letters were offered at one stage to Wagner himself, for a price, but he refused to be blackmailed.

Gutzkow, Karl Ferdinand (1811–78). German novelist and dramatist. Associated with the Young German group of writers, his radical outlook was expressed in various articles and novels until the federal decree of December 1835 caused him to be charged and imprisoned the following year. Turning subsequently to the theatre, he produced a series of plays on social and political themes, and from 1846 to 1848 was dramaturg at the Dresden Court Theatre.

Halévy, Jacques-François-Fromental (1799–1862). French composer. A fluent composer, especially of *opéras comiques*, he was also an active teacher and administrator in a succession of posts in France. His best-known work is *La Juive* (1835), his first attempt at a serious grand opera, which was an instant success at the Opéra. Another popular work was *La Reine de Chypre* (1841), which Wagner reviewed favourably the following year, having laboured over the score in Paris to produce arrangements.

Hanslick, Eduard (1825–1904). German writer on music and aesthetics. A powerfully influential force in 19th-century music criticism, Hanslick was for most of his life implacably hostile to the Wagnerian cause. Hanslick's conservative aesthetic outlook led him to espouse the absolute music of Brahms and his followers as against the progressive notions of music drama and programme music associated with Wagner, Liszt and the New German School.

Heckel, Emil (1831–1908). Music dealer in Mannheim, who was energetic in raising money for the establishment of the Bayreuth Festival. His scheme for a network of Wagner Societies, whose members might combine to make a joint subscription to the fund, was adopted, and Heckel himself founded a society in Mannheim.

Heim, Ignaz (1813–80). The conductor of a local choral society, the Harmonie, in Zurich, where he and his wife Emilie, a singer, were friends of Wagner.

Heine, Ferdinand (1798–1872). As costume designer and wardrobe manager at the Dresden Court Theatre from 1819 to 1850, Heine was involved in the first performances there of *Rienzi* (1842), *Holländer* (1843) and *Tannhäuser* (1845). He was an enthusiastic advocate of Wagner's works and one of his firmest friends during the Dresden years.

Heine, Heinrich (1797–1856). German writer and poet. As one of the inspirational figures of Young Germany, Heine may be said to have made an indirect contribution to the conception of *Das Liebesverbot*. But greater debts date from after their first meeting in Paris: Wagner drew on stories by Heine for *Holländer* and *Tannhäuser*. Less often observed is the fact that Heine's *Elementargeister* (*Elemental Spirits*) of 1837 prefigures much of the mythical world of the *Ring*.

Herwegh, Georg (1817–75). German poet and political activist. In 1839 he escaped court-martial during military service by deserting to Switzerland. There he quickly established a reputation with the first volume of the revolutionary *Gedichte eines Lebendigen* (*Poems of a Living Man*, 1841), the collection containing his celebrated broadside against Freiligrath: *Die Partei*. He was active in the 1848–9 uprisings and subsequently gave shelter to many political refugees in his house in Zurich. It was there that Herwegh introduced Wagner to the philosophy of Schopenhauer.

Hey, Julius (1831–1909). German singing teacher, at the school of music in Munich. Wagner made his acquaintance at Starnberg in 1864 and subsequently called upon him for advice on vocal matters during the rehearsals for the *Ring* in Bayreuth. When Hey gave his opinion that the prospective Siegfried, Georg Unger, was technically defective, Wagner commissioned Hey with the task of coaching him for the part.

Hill, Karl (1831–93). German bass-baritone. A postal official prior to his engagement at Schwerin in 1868. It was his 'demonic passion' as the Dutchman there in 1873 that persuaded Wagner to cast him as Alberich in the first Bayreuth *Ring*, and he subsequently sang Klingsor in the first *Parsifal* (1882). He died insane.

Hoffmann, Josef (1831–1904). An academic painter in Vienna who accepted Wagner's commission to design the scenery for the first Bayreuth *Ring* (1876). Although the sketches he submitted were eminently satisfactory, Hoffmann had neither studio nor assistants to effect their execution, and the task was entrusted to the Brückner brothers. A dispute subsequently broke out when Hoffmann objected to changes made, for technical reasons, in his scenic designs. Wagner was thereafter obliged to minimize Hoffmann's personal involvement in the preparations.

Hülsen, Botho von (1815–86). German theatre director. In June 1851 he succeeded Küstner as intendant at the Berlin Opera. From 1866 he was responsible also for the theatres at Hanover, Cassel and Wiesbaden.

Jenkins, Newell Sill. American dentist practising in Dresden. Jenkins, who treated Wagner in Basle and Bayreuth on several occasions, was entrusted with the negotiations involved in his proposed emigration to America (1880).

Joukowsky, Paul von (1845–1912). Russian painter. He entered Wagner's circle in January 1880 by presenting himself at the Villa d'Angri in Naples. Wagner responded favourably to him and in due course invited him to design the sets and costumes for *Parsifal*. Joukowsky was regarded as a member of the family and stayed with them, accompanied by his adoptive son Pepino.

Kietz, Ernst Benedikt (1815–92). German painter. He was in Paris, finishing his art studies, at the time Wagner and Minna were there (1839–42). He became a regular visitor at their house and in 1858 (when Kietz was 43) they even offered to 'adopt' him. Wagner humorously asserted that Kietz never completed a commission, but his various sketches and portraits of the composer in his early years are invaluable.

Kirchner, Theodor Fürchtegott (1823–1903). German organist and composer. From 1843 to 1862 he played, taught and organized the musical life in Winterthur and came to the attention of Wagner and Liszt, both of whom admired his talent. During Wagner's years in Zurich, Kirchner was called upon to provide the piano accompaniment for informal play-throughs of his works.

Klindworth, Karl (1830–1916). German pianist, conductor and teacher. From 1852 he was part of Liszt's circle in Weimar and it was through Liszt's enthusiastic advocacy that Klindworth met Wagner in London in 1855. Klindworth undertook the arrangement of vocal scores for each opera of the *Ring,* as well as those for *Die Meistersinger* and *Tristan* (a simpler version than Bülow's). His adoptive daughter, Winifred Williams, became the wife of Siegfried Wagner.

Laube, Heinrich (1806–84). German writer, critic and latterly theatre director. His writing, notably in the three-volume social and political novel *Das junge Europa* (1833–7), was radical in outlook, and as a leading member of Young Germany he was constantly persecuted by the authorities. The strength of his convictions made an impression on the young Wagner (Laube was a family friend) and as editor of the *Zeitung für die elegante Welt* he published some of Wagner's earliest essays; in later years, however, they were estranged. From 1840 Laube was a theatre critic in Leipzig; subsequently he was director of the Vienna Burgtheater (1849–67), Leipzig Stadttheater (1869–71) and Vienna Stadttheater (from 1872).

Laussot, Jessie, *née* Taylor (*c.* 1829–1905). The English-born wife of the Bordeaux wine merchant Eugène Laussot. Her passion for Wagner's music and commitment to his ideals led her to offer him, together with Julie Ritter, an annual allowance of 3000 francs. Wagner's visit to Bordeaux in March 1850 led to a brief affair with Jessie, but a plan to 'elope' to Greece or Asia Minor was thwarted by the intervention of her mother and husband. Jessie was talented musically, and in later life was active as a conductor and administrator in Florence.

Lehrs, Samuel (1806–43). German philologist. One of the group of Wagner's close friends in Paris (1839–42). Wagner was indebted to Lehrs for providing him with background material on the Tannhäuser and Lohengrin legends, and for introducing him to intellectual ideas current at the time.

The deprivation Lehrs suffered in Paris led to his early death, shortly after Wagner had left for Dresden.

Lenbach, Franz von (1836–1904). German artist. From 1868 he devoted himself to portraiture and became the leading exponent of the genre in the Germany of his day. He became acquainted both with Cosima and subsequently with Wagner himself, drawing and painting them on several occasions, though not always from life.

Levi, Hermann (1839–1900). German conductor. After study in Mannheim and Leipzig, he held conducting posts in Saarbrücken, Mannheim, Rotterdam and Karlsruhe, before becoming chief conductor of the Munich Court Opera (1872–90). Despite his Jewishness and his association with Brahms and his followers, Levi was welcomed by Wagner as a distinguished interpreter of his works, notably *Parsifal,* which he conducted at its premiere in 1882 and for several years thereafter. Levi's assumption that he would have to undergo baptism in order to conduct *Parsifal* was encouraged by Wagner, but after a disagreeable exchange on the subject, the idea was dropped.

Liszt, Franz (1811–86). Hungarian composer and pianist. The two men first encountered each other in Paris, in March 1841, when Liszt was already at the height of his fame. But it was not until Liszt had retired from the concert platform to devote himself to composition and to the promotion of other musicians that their friendship blossomed. Their extraordinary but sincere relationship was based on profound mutual admiration and understanding; as the acknowledged leaders of the New German School, each was particularly fascinated by the other's progressive traits, and in terms of influence it is difficult to determine who was the greater beneficiary. The friendship survived occasional periods of coolness, the most serious estrangement being caused by Wagner's liaison with Liszt's daughter Cosima.

Ludwig II, King of Bavaria (1845–86). The son of Maximilian II and grandson of Ludwig I, he ascended the throne of Bavaria in 1864 at the age of 18. His passion for Wagner's music resulted in generous subsidies which transformed the composer's life style. However, public opinion was scandalized by Wagner's affair with Cosima, and by the supposed exploitation of the king's munificence; in December 1865 Ludwig was forced to ask Wagner to leave Munich. His support continued and even though the relationship was strained to breaking-point over the following years, Ludwig made a timely contribution to the Bayreuth enterprise and remained fanatically devoted to Wagner's art. His penchant for building fantastic castles of monumental extravagance, combined with his erratic behaviour and progressive lack of interest in his subjects or affairs of state, eventually led to an official declaration of insanity and to his deposition on 10 June 1886. The king and an escorting psychiatrist were found drowned in Lake Starnberg three days later; the precise events of their deaths have never been conclusively established.

Lüttichau, Baron (Wolf Adolf) August von (1786–1863). He began his career as a forestry official, joining the Dresden Court Theatre in 1824, where he remained intendant until shortly before his death. Despite the tensions and disagreements brought about by the disparity in their professional status, he and Wagner each had a certain underlying respect for the other.

Maier, Mathilde (1833–1910). Wagner met Mathilde Maier, the daughter of a notary, at Franz Schott's house in Mainz in March 1862. His overtures to her were discouraged on grounds of incipient deafness. He urged her to join him at Haus Pellet (June 1864) as housekeeper and companion, but hurriedly withdrew the invitation on learning of Cosima's imminent arrival there. A number of passages – probably of a compromising nature – in Wagner's letters to Mathilde of this period have been irrecoverably deleted in the autographs.

Marbach, Rosalie, *née* Wagner (1803–37). Elder sister of Wagner. She made her stage début in her stepfather's play *Das Erntefest* (December 1818), joining the company of the Royal Court two years later. After notable successes in Prague and elsewhere, from 1826, she took up an appointment at Leipzig in 1829. She died prematurely, little more than a year after her marriage to the university professor Oswald Marbach.

Marschner, Heinrich (August) (1795–1861). German composer. After a period as musical director at Dresden (1824–6) and Kapellmeister at Leipzig (1827–30), he was appointed Court Kapellmeister at Hanover in 1830, remaining there until 1859. As one of the leading figures in the development of German Romantic opera, Marschner inevitably made a considerable impact on the maturing Wagner, who was exposed to his works in the 1820s and 1830s. Many similarities of technique and content between especially Marschner's *Der Vampyr* and *Hans Heiling* and Wagner's *Holländer*, *Tannhäuser* and *Lohengrin* may be discerned.

Materna, Amalie (1844–1918). Austrian soprano. Despite her early career in operetta, she became one of the first of the new breed of dramatic sopranos demanded by Wagner's music dramas. She sang Brünnhilde in the first complete *Ring* (1876) and Kundry in 1882, both at Bayreuth.

Mendelssohn (-Bartholdy), Felix (1809–47). German composer, pianist, organist and conductor. After extraordinary early successes as a child prodigy, he eventually took up posts as conductor of the Leipzig Gewandhaus Orchestra (1835–47) and as first director of the newly opened conservatory in that city (from 1843). A handful of operas, including the unfinished *Loreley* (1847), bear witness to Mendelssohn's lifelong struggle for mastery in the medium. But it is primarily for his instrumental and choral works that he is now remembered. The popular view that Mendelssohn's works too rarely rise above superficiality has, over recent years, undergone reappraisal. Wagner's prejudice against him, partly anti-Semitic in origin, did not prevent him from echoing Mendelssohn in his own earlier works.

Mendès, Catulle (-Abraham) (1841–1909). French poet, librettist and critic. He was the founder and editor of the journal *La Revue Fantaisiste*, to which he invited Wagner to contribute an article following the *Tannhäuser* débâcle at the Paris Opéra in 1861. His enthusiasm for Wagner was shared by his first wife, Judith Gautier, and they visited Wagner at Tribschen in 1869 (twice) and 1870. Mendès' friendship with Wagner survived the tensions of the last visit (which coincided precisely with the declaration of the Franco-Prussian War), but not the publication, in 1873, of Wagner's crudely jingoistic farce *Eine Kapitulation*. However, Mendès' continuing admiration for Wagner the artist was demonstrated in his full-length biography of him (1886), as well as various other writings, some for the *Revue Wagnérienne*, which he co-founded in 1885.

Mendès-Gautier, Judith. *See* Gautier, Judith.

Metternich, Princess Pauline (1836–1921). Granddaughter of the Austrian statesman; she also married one of his sons, Richard, Prince von Metternich-Winneburg, who became the Austrian ambassador in Paris. It was primarily her influence at the court of Napoleon III that brought about the performance of *Tannhäuser* in Paris in 1861, but it was also her unpopularity in certain court circles that was largely responsible for the political demonstration by the Jockey Club on that occasion.

Meyerbeer, Giacomo [orig. Jakob Liebmann Beer] (1791–1864). German composer. Meyerbeer began his career as a child prodigy on the piano, but after a series of Italian operas he made his home in Paris, where for many years he dominated French grand opera. Meyerbeer's works are irrevocably associated with triumphal processions and *Grand Guignol*, aspects which made them hugely popular in the Paris of his day, but which are less fashionable today. There have been too few opportunities in recent times to judge these works adequately –

especially in the theatre. Nevertheless, his influentially imaginative orchestration has been appreciated. Wagner's hostile opinion of Meyerbeer was partly a result of anti-Semitism but was also in tune with the prevailing critical consensus in Germany, according to which Meyerbeer's works displayed rhythmic monotony and undue eclecticism, elevating contrived effect above genuine dramatic tension.

Meysenbug, Baroness Malwida von (1816–1903). German writer and political activist; a prominent democrat and campaigner for women's rights. Following the 1848–9 uprisings, she was banned from Berlin in 1852 on account of her associations with revolutionaries. As a result she moved first to London, where she became a governess and a newspaper correspondent, and in 1862 to Italy. She was an admirer and friend of Wagner, as well as Nietzsche, Liszt and a number of radicals such as Garibaldi and Mazzini.

Mitterwurzer, Anton (1818–76). Baritone at the Dresden Opera. He sang Wolfram in the first performance of *Tannhäuser* (1845) and Kurwenal in that of *Tristan* (1865).

Monnais, Edouard (1798–1868). French theatre official. For a short period (1839–41) he was associate director of the Paris Opéra, but he continued to wield influence as Commissaire royal près le Théâtre de l'Opéra. He was also editor of and (under the pseudonym 'Paul Smith') contributor to various journals.

Mrazéck, Anna (c.1834–1914). Housekeeper to Wagner first in Vienna (1863–4) and then in Munich and Starnberg. It was largely Anna Mrazéck's testimony in 1914 that deprived Isolde Beidler of a court ruling that she was indeed Wagner's daughter; she testified that when Bülow visited Wagner at Starnberg in July 1864, Cosima occupied the same room as her husband, not that of Wagner.

Mrazéck, Franz (d.1874). Bohemian who acted as manservant to Wagner in Vienna, Munich and Starnberg. He was subsequently employed at the music school in Munich. In her diary entry for 6 August 1874, Cosima records his death, attributing it to ill-treatment by the school's directors in revenge for his loyalty to Wagner.

Müller, Christian Gottlieb (1800–63). German instrumentalist and conductor. From 1826 he was a member of the Leipzig Gewandhaus Orchestra, after which he became, in 1831, conductor of the (largely amateur) Euterpe Society in that city. In 1836 he became music director in Altenburg. Wagner studied harmony with Müller for the best part of three years (1828–31).

Muncker, Theodor (1823–1900). Mayor of Bayreuth from 1863. He supported the Bayreuth venture when Wagner first solicited the town's help in 1871, and became a friend as well as a member of the management committee for the festival.

Neumann, Angelo (1838–1910). Austrian baritone and theatrical producer. From 1876 to 1880 he was director of the Leipzig Opera and he obtained permission from Wagner to mount the *Ring* cycle there in 1878. He contemplated the possibility of a permanent Wagner theatre in Berlin, to which the composer was willing to lend his name. In August 1882 a contract was concluded enabling Neumann to take the *Ring* on tour with his travelling theatre; in the following years it was performed by them all over Europe.

Niemann, Albert (1831–1917). German tenor. Made his début in Dessau in 1849, and after engagements in Stuttgart, Hanover and elsewhere, became a member of the Berlin Opera (1866–89). He sang Tannhäuser in the Paris performances of 1861 and Siegmund in the first Bayreuth *Ring*. He made his London début also in the latter role (1882) and was the first American Tristan and Siegfried (in *Götterdämmerung*).

Nietzsche, Friedrich (1844–1900). German philosopher. In 1869, at the age of 24, he was appointed Professor of Classical Philology at Basle University. From the time of his first visit to Tribschen the same year, he was a frequent and welcome guest at Wagner's house. His literary works were admired by Wagner and Cosima, especially *Die Geburt der Tragödie*, not least because it appeared to celebrate Wagner's central position in Western culture. For his part, Nietzsche was fascinated by what he regarded as the insidious power of Wagner's music, and overwhelmed by the 'horrible, sweet infinitude' of *Tristan*. The ambivalence of Nietzsche's response began to be reflected in his essay 'Richard Wagner in Bayreuth' (1875–6), and in subsequent years, as his mental and physical health deteriorated, he took up a bitterly hostile stance towards Wagner's 'decadent' art.

Ollivier, Blandine (1835–62). Elder sister of Cosima Wagner, born to Liszt and the Countess Marie d'Agoult. She married the French politician Emile Ollivier in 1857, and died in childbirth. Fond as Wagner was of her, there is no evidence to substantiate the rumours that they engaged in an affair.

Perfall, Baron Karl von (1824–1907). Intendant of the Munich Court Theatre from 1867 to 1893. Perfall was an influential administrator and his long period of tenure accommodated the musical directorships of Lachner, Bülow, Wüllner and Levi.

Pfistermeister, Franz Seraph von (1820–1912). King Ludwig II's cabinet secretary until October 1866, when he submitted his resignation. This was apparently precipitated by his frustration at Wagner's interference in affairs of state. Wagner, for his part, accused Pfistermeister – not unjustly – of scheming against him.

Pfordten, Baron Ludwig von der (1811–80). German lawyer and politician. He served as the foreign minister and president of the Bavarian council from 1849 to 1859, and as prime minister from 1864 to 1866. He and Pfistermeister (q.v.) were Wagner's chief antagonists at the Munich court.

Pillet, Léon (1803–68). Pillet succeeded Duponchel and Monnais as director of the Paris Opéra officially in 1841 (though in effect the previous year). He was thus the chief administrator with whom Wagner had to deal during his Paris years. He was forced to resign the directorship in 1847.

Planer, Minna. *See* Wagner, Minna.

Planer, Natalie. *See* Bilz (-Planer), Natalie.

Porges, Heinrich (1837–1900). German editor and writer on music. From 1863 co-editor of the *Neue Zeitschrift für Musik*, and from 1867 responsible, with the editor, Fröbel, for the arts pages of the *Süddeutsche Presse*. He came to Wagner's attention in Vienna in 1863, and although he declined to accept Wagner's summons the following year to join him in Munich, he did later act as his assistant, most notably at the rehearsals for the first *Ring* at Bayreuth, which, at Wagner's request, he recorded in detail.

Praeger, Ferdinand Christian Wilhelm (1815–91). German composer, pianist and writer. He settled in London in 1834, where he was much in demand as a teacher. Works by him were performed in France, Germany and England. He befriended Wagner and gave him hospitality during his London visit in 1855, later claiming, falsely, to have been responsible for the invitation. This was only one of countless fabrications in his notorious publication *Wagner as I knew him* (1892).

Pusinelli, Anton (1815–78). Wagner's family doctor, and one of his most intimate and trusted friends, from the time of their first acquaintance in Dresden. In the early 1860s, when Wagner's marriage to Minna was on the brink of collapse, Pusinelli was entrusted with the delicate task of acting as intermediary.

Reissiger, Karl Gottlieb (1798–1859). German composer, conductor and teacher. Kapellmeister at the court of Dresden from 1828 until his death, Reissiger was present, if sometimes less than fully active, throughout Wagner's time there. In his earlier years Reissiger had justly taken the credit for putting the Dresden Opera in the front rank of German theatres. By the 1840s, however, he was allowing his junior colleague to occupy much of the gap left by his own creeping inertia. Reissiger's compositions, which are competent rather than creatively original, include eight operas.

Richter, Hans (1843–1916). Austro-Hungarian conductor. After study in Vienna, and experience as a horn player in the Kärntnerthor Theatre there (1862–6), he joined Wagner at Tribschen as a copyist, 1866–7, producing a fair copy of the *Meistersinger* score. He then assisted Bülow in Munich, 1868–9, and went on to conduct Wagner and other operas in various cities, including Brussels, Budapest and Vienna. He conducted the first complete *Ring* at Bayreuth (1876) and maintained a distinguished career thereafter, both in Bayreuth and in England, where he conducted the Hallé Orchestra (1899–1911) and the London Symphony Orchestra (1904–11), as well as giving the first English-language performance of the *Ring* (1908).

Ritter, Julie, *née* Momma (1794–1869). After the death of her husband, the merchant Karl Ritter, she took up residence in Dresden, where she became a friend and benefactress of Wagner. In 1850, together with Jessie Laussot (q.v.), she promised him an annual allowance of 3000 francs. Even after the ignominious 'Bordeaux affair', she made over 800 thalers to him annually from 1851 to 1859.

Ritter, Karl (1830–91). Son of Julie Ritter and her husband Karl. It was not until towards the end of Wagner's years in Dresden that he made the acquaintance of the Ritter family. Karl accompanied him into exile in Switzerland and in 1858 went with him to Venice after Wagner was obliged to leave the Asyl.

Röckel, August (1814–76). German conductor and composer. Röckel held posts at Bamberg (1838) and Weimar (1839–43) before being appointed assistant conductor to Wagner in Dresden (1843–9). Their joint involvement in the revolutionary *Volksblätter* (edited by Röckel) and in the uprisings of 1848–9 led to exile for Wagner and a thirteen-year term of imprisonment for Röckel (his death sentence having been commuted). Wagner's letters to Röckel dating from these years contain some revealing passages on his intentions in the *Ring*.

Rubinstein, Joseph (1847–84). Pianist born into an affluent Russian Jewish family. He approached Wagner seeking deliverance from his 'Jewish deficiencies', and became a regular visitor to Wahnfried. Described as 'Wahnfried's supreme court pianist', he played music of all kinds to the Wagners, notably Bach preludes and fugues, and also made piano arrangements of some of Wagner's works. He did not long survive Wagner, committing suicide in Lucerne.

Sayn-Wittgenstein, Princess Carolyne von (1819–87). Benefactress and companion of Liszt for many years. After separating from Prince Nikolaus von Sayn-Wittgenstein soon after their arranged marriage, the princess joined Liszt in Weimar where she exercised a dominant influence over his artistic and emotional life. Her initially warm relationship with Wagner cooled when each began to regard the other as a rival for Liszt's friendship.

Schleinitz, Baroness Marie von, *née* von Buch (1842–1912). Wife of Baron Alexander von Schleinitz, a minister of the Royal Household in Berlin. As Marie von Buch, she has been a friend and confidante of Cosima's at the time of Starnberg (1864). During the years of fundraising for the Bayreuth enterprise, she proved to be an immensely energetic campaigner.

Schlesinger, Maurice [Moritz] (1797–1871). German music publisher. In 1821 he established a branch of his father's Berlin business in Paris, and was also proprietor and editor of the journal *Gazette Musicale de Paris* (from 1835 *Revue et Gazette Musicale de Paris*). Wagner earned a modest income from Schlesinger during his Paris years (1839–42).

Schnorr von Carolsfeld, Ludwig (1836–65). German tenor. Son of the painter Julius Schnorr von Carolsfeld. After settling in Dresden in 1860, he consolidated his reputation with such roles as Tannhäuser and Lohengrin, subsequently creating that of Tristan opposite his wife Malvina (Munich, 1865). His death only three weeks after the first run of *Tristan* performances was a severe personal blow to Wagner.

Schnorr von Carolsfeld, Malvina, *née* Garrigues (1825–1904). Daughter of the Brazilian consul in Copenhagen, where she was born. She began her career as a soprano in *Robert le diable*, after which she sang in Coburg, Gotha, Hamburg and (from 1854) Karlsruhe. She caused severe embarrassment to Wagner and Cosima by denouncing their liaison to King Ludwig.

Schopenhauer, Arthur (1788–1860). German philosopher. Wagner was profoundly influenced by Schopenhauer's ideas as expounded in *Die Welt als Wille und Vorstellung* and *Parerga und Paralipomena*. In fact, some of these ideas were already being discussed within Wagner's circle of Zurich friends (notably Herwegh and François Wille) before Wagner himself first read Schopenhauer's *magnum opus* in October 1854. Schopenhauer's elevation of

music over the other arts and his pessimistic philosophy of renunciation had a decisive impact on Wagner's works from the *Ring* onwards. A letter to Schopenhauer on the question of suicide was drafted by Wagner but not sent. The two never met.

Schröder-Devrient, Wilhelmine (1804–60). German soprano. Her reputation as one of the leading singers of her day was based on the conviction with which she invested her dramatic portrayals rather than on security of technique. She was particularly acclaimed for her assumption of the role of Leonore in *Fidelio*; among the roles she created were Wagner's Adriano (in *Rienzi*), Senta and Venus. Her marriage to the actor Karl Devrient (brother of Eduard, q.v.) was dissolved in 1828.

Schumann, Robert (1810–56). German composer, pianist and critic. A founder and first editor of the *Neue Zeitschrift für Musik*, his voice carried some weight in contemporary music criticism. He was encouraging and sympathetic to the young Wagner, though he professed to be perplexed by the through-composed approach to opera. More predisposed to the Classically inclined, absolute music of Brahms, whom he met and befriended in 1853, Schumann would doubtless, had he lived, have been a partisan for him rather than the New German School. However, following a deterioration in his mental health, he spent the last couple of years of his life in an asylum.

Seidl, Anton (1850–98). Austro-Hungarian conductor. After studying at Leipzig Conservatory, he assisted in Bayreuth as a member of the 'Nibelung Chancellery', copying parts and scores. He helped in the production of the 1876 *Ring*, after which, on Wagner's recommendation, he joined Neumann at Leipzig (1879–82), conducting the *Ring* on his European tour, beginning the following year. He made his début at the Metropolitan, New York, in 1885, returning to conduct 340 performances, including the American premieres of *Die Meistersinger*, *Tristan* and all the *Ring* operas except *Die Walküre*. His premature death deprived New York of a vigorous champion of Wagner and an authoritative conductor of his scores.

Semper, Gottfried (1803–79). German architect. Celebrated as the builder of the Dresden Opera House (the first, opened in 1841, was burnt down in 1869 and eventually replaced by a second Semper building in 1878). He was acquainted with Wagner during his Dresden period and they took part together in the uprising of 1849, Semper taking responsibility for the construction of barricades. To escape arrest he made first for London and then Zurich, where he taught and renewed his acquaintance with Wagner. His designs for a festival theatre in Munich – commissioned by King Ludwig in the 1860s – were never realized.

Spohr, Louis [Ludwig] (1784–1859). German composer, violinist and conductor. After a brilliantly successful early career as a travelling virtuoso violinist, Spohr settled at the court of Cassel (Kapellmeister from 1822, Generalmusikdirektor from 1847). There he was responsible for the productions of the *Holländer* (1843) and *Tannhäuser* (1853). In spite of his popular success as a composer, Spohr has generally been regarded – both in his own time and in the present day – as fluent in technique rather than original in inspiration. Nevertheless, his music anticipated that of Wagner in a number of ways: in his use of chromaticism and leitmotif, in the through-composed construction of his operas, and even in specific chords and modulations.

Standhartner, Joseph (1818–92). Physician resident in Vienna, where he served various members of the court, including the empress, and where he made the acquaintance of Wagner. He invited Wagner to occupy his house for six weeks in 1861, while he was away. Standhartner was to remain a firm friend of Wagner's.

Stocker, Jakob (1827–1909). Wagner's manservant, who joined the household on his marriage to Vreneli Weidmann (January 1867).

Stocker, Vreneli. *See* Weidmann, Vreneli.

Sulzer, (Johann) Jakob (1821–97). From 1847 he was cantonal secretary of Zurich; thereafter, a series of influential posts established him as a leading figure in local and national governmental affairs. He befriended Wagner in his Swiss exile in the 1850s, and provided much valued moral and pecuniary support.

Tausig, Carl (1841–71). Polish pianist and composer. A prodigious pupil of Liszt in Weimar, he was sent by him in May 1858 to Wagner in Zurich, who was as delighted as he was astonished by Tausig's extrovert playing and personality. He assumed the administration of the scheme of Bayreuth Patrons' certificates in 1871, but fell victim to typhus only a few weeks later.

Tichatschek, Joseph (Aloys) (1807–86). Bohemian tenor. In 1830 he joined the chorus of the Kärntnerthor Theatre in Vienna; he made his début as a principal in Graz in 1837 and in Dresden the same year. In 1838 he took up an appointment at the Dresden Court opera, where he helped to elevate the vocal standards to the highest in Germany. He took both lyric tenor and *Spieltenor* roles, but was also widely regarded as an ideal Wagnerian *Heldentenor*, creating and frequently repeating the roles of Rienzi and Tannhäuser. He continued to perform until 1870.

Uhlig, Theodor (1822–53). German violinist, theorist, critic and composer. Illegitimate son of Friedrich August II of Saxony. After joining the Dresden Court orchestra in 1841 he became eventually, though not at first, one of Wagner's closest friends and most dependable supporters. Their friendship, sustained by their similar political outlook, continued into the early years of Wagner's Swiss exile and produced some correspondence revealing as to Wagner's views at that time. Uhlig's writings were admired by Wagner and others, and he had produced an oeuvre of 84 opus numbers by the time of his early death.

Unger, Georg (1837–87). German tenor. He made his début in Leipzig in 1867 and was subsequently heard at Mannheim by Richter, who recommended him to Wagner. In order to undertake the role of Siegfried in the first Bayreuth *Ring* in 1876, he had to be coached specially by Julius Hey, on account of his technical deficiencies.

Villiers de l'Isle-Adam, Count Philippe-Auguste (1834–89). French poet. From a family of noble lineage but reduced to impoverishment. His works, written against a background of indigence, are by turns Romantic, mystical, idealistic, and always sensitive to the more visionary tendencies of his age. A friend of Mallarmé, he was influenced by Baudelaire and Poe, and was an admirer of Wagner.

Vogl, Heinrich (1845–1900). German tenor. He studied in Munich where in 1865 he made his début as Max in *Der Freischütz*. He remained attached to Munich for the remainder of his career, creating the roles of Loge and Siegmund there (1869 and 1870 respectively). Having sung Loge at Bayreuth in 1876, he returned in 1886 as Tristan and Parsifal, appearing also in Berlin (1881), London (1882), Vienna (1884/5) and New York (1890). He sang all the major Wagner tenor roles with the exception of Walther. His wife, Therese Thoma (1845–1921), created the role of Sieglinde at Munich in 1870 and sang Brünnhilde in the first complete London *Ring* (1882).

Wagner, Albert (1799–1874). Elder brother of Wagner. From 1819 he held appointments as a tenor and actor in various German theatres. From 1857 to 1865 he was a director at the Berlin Court Theatre.

Wagner, Clara. *See* Wolfram, Clara.

Wagner, Cosima (1837–1930). Daughter of Franz Liszt and the Countess Marie d'Agoult. In 1857 she married the conductor and pianist Hans von Bülow, bearing him two daughters, Daniela and Blandine. In 1863 she began a liaison with Wagner, which eventually resulted in three children, Isolde, Eva and Siegfried – all born out of wedlock. In 1870 her marriage to Bülow was finally dissolved and she married Wagner the same year. Cosima was well educated but narrow-minded, superficially self-confident but in fact haunted by guilt and psychological insecurity. Nevertheless, she had both the intellect and the aptitude to make an ideal companion for Wagner: his sexual relationship with her was the only enduring one of his life. After Wagner's death, Cosima, though not regarded as the natural successor, took over the direction of the Bayreuth Festival, with an assurance born of utter devotion to the wishes of her husband. She remained in charge until 1906.

Wagner, Franziska (1829–95). Wagner's niece; daughter of Albert Wagner (q.v.) An actress at the Schwerin Court Theatre, she married Julie Ritter's son, Alexander.

Wagner, Luise. *See* Brockhaus, Luise.

Wagner, Christine Wilhelmine ('Minna'), *née* Planer (1809–66). German actress and Wagner's first wife. She made his acquaintance in 1834 when Wagner was offered the job of musical director of Heinrich Bethmann's theatre company (of which she was at the time one of the leading actresses). They married in 1836 but the years of Wagner's Kapellmeistership in Dresden (1843–9) charted an irreversible decline in their relationship. Minna had no sympathy for his progressive views about either art or politics, and his enforced exile in the 1850s dealt the final blow to their marriage. Wagner's subsequent infidelities could only exacerbate matters, but he could not bring himself to divorce Minna, fearing that her weak heart condition might prove fatal.

Wagner, Ottilie. *See* Brockhaus, Ottilie.

Wagner, Rosalie. *See* Marbach, Rosalie.

Wagner, Siegfried (Helferich Richard) (1869–1930). German composer and conductor; son of Richard Wagner. The birth of his son and heir, regarded as a highly auspicious event by Wagner, was retrospectively celebrated by the composition of the *Siegfried Idyll* (1870). Wagner was anxious not to impose a musical career on his son, and in fact Siegfried pursued architecture for a short time. Then from 1892 to 1896 he became an assistant at Bayreuth, conducting his first performance there in the latter year (*Ring*), and producing *Der fliegende Holländer* in 1901. Assuming directorship of the Festival on the retirement of his mother Cosima in 1906, Siegfried was constrained to a considerable extent in the early years by her conservationist instincts. In his five post-war festivals, however (1924–30), some cautious innovations were made.

Weber, Ernst von (1830–1902). Naturalist and founder of an international Anti-Vivisection Society. His pamphlet *Die Folterkammern der Wissenschaft* (*The Torture Chambers of Science*) met with Wagner's wholehearted approval. Wagner's letter to Weber on the subject of vivisection was developed into an article for the *Bayreuther Blätter* (October, 1879).

Weidmann, Vreneli [Verena] (1832–1906). Vreneli Weidmann first entered Wagner's service in Lucerne in 1859. He appreciated her so much that he re-engaged her, as housekeeper, in Munich (1864), and she remained in his service after his move to Tribschen. She became Vreneli Stocker on her marriage in January 1867.

Weinlig, Christian Theodor (1780–1842). German organist and composer. Kantor of the Dresden Kreuzschule (1814–17) and of the Thomaskirche, Leipzig, from 1823. Wagner studied counterpoint and composition with him for about six months, beginning in the autumn of 1831. Weinlig's compositions consisted mostly of sacred choral works; he also published a significant treatise on fugue.

Weissheimer, Wendelin (1838–1910). German conductor and composer. Attended the Leipzig Conservatory in 1856 and subsequently studied with Liszt in Weimar. He became Kapellmeister in various cities, including Mainz, Würzburg, Strasbourg, Baden-Baden and Milan. His friendship with Wagner began in 1862 when the latter was staying in Biebrich. Occasional tensions in their relationship reached a peak in 1868 when Wagner refused to recommend Weissheimer's opera *Theodor Körner* for performance in Munich.

Wesendonck, Mathilde, *née* Luckemeyer (1828–1902). German poet and author. The friendship of Wagner and Mathilde Wesendonck that began in 1852 developed subsequently into a sexual relationship which may or may not have been consummated. The impossible passion of Tristan and Isolde was enacted simultaneously by the composer with Mathilde, until eventually (August, 1858) social propriety dictated his removal. Five of Mathilde's poems were set by Wagner (the *Wesendonck Lieder*); her other works include the five-act drama *Gudrun* (1868), the five-act tragedy *Edith oder die Schlacht bei Hastings* (1872) and the dramatic poem *Odysseus* (1878).

The Wesendoncks spelt their name thus; it was not until after 1900 that their son reverted to what was probably the original spelling of the Dutch-derived name – Wesendonk.

Wesendonck, Otto (1815–96). German businessman. After a short but lucrative career as a partner in a New York firm of silk importers, he retired to

Zurich in 1851 to enjoy his wealth. Wagner had no scruples about assisting him in this; indeed, it could be argued that Wesendonck needed a struggling artist to patronize as much as Wagner required a generous benefactor. They thus continued to oblige each other even after the marital crisis of 1858.

Wille, Eliza, *née* Sloman (1809–93). German novelist. From the years of Wagner's Swiss exile, his friend and confidante. She and her husband François made Wagner's acquaintance after they retired to a small estate at Mariafeld, near Zurich, in 1851. Wagner became a regular visitor to their home.

Wolfram, Clara, *née* Wagner (1807–75). Elder sister of Wagner; she married the singer Heinrich Wolfram in 1828. Clara herself began an operatic career in a performance of Rossini's *La Cenerentola* in Dresden in 1824, but retired from the stage a few years after her marriage.

Wolzogen, Hans (Paul), Baron von (1848–1938). German writer on music. After studying comparative philology and philosophy in Berlin (1868–70), he came to Wagner's attention and was invited to Bayreuth in October 1877 as editor of the newly founded *Bayreuther Blätter*. Wolzogen remained editor from the first issue (published at the beginning of 1878) until his death 60 years later, during which period he became identified as one of the chief guardians of the 'Holy Grail' of Bayreuth. He also produced a series of thematic guides to the *Ring* and other works, and edited three volumes of Wagner's letters.

BARRY MILLINGTON

Section 3
HISTORICAL BACKGROUND

The Holy Roman Empire from 1618 to 1789   36
The French Revolution and the Wars of
    Liberation: 1789–1815   39
Reaction and revolution: 1815–1849   41
German unification 'from above': 1850–1871   45
The Reich in Europe: 1871–1883   47

THE HISTORICAL BACKGROUND

'THE FUTURE IS CONCEIVABLE only in terms of the past': these are the words of a man whose cradle was rocked by the sound of booming cannons during the Battle of Nations, as it raged round Leipzig on 18 October 1813. They sum up Wagner's thinking and his whole approach to life, deriving, as they do, from his bitter first-hand experience of the collapse of a seemingly stable world, which he saw in terms of the dialectics of liberation and deprivation. Voluntaristic revolt against the limitations of historical tradition is just as much a part of Wagner's spiritual makeup as his instinctive empathy for historical conditionality and permanence beyond all change. The 19th century as a whole is typified by the antinomy between revolutionary intellectual, social and political change and the compensatory wish to ensure a continuity that would go on reproducing the same unchanging structures. It is a contradiction which left its mark on states and societies, cultures and economies. In Wagner's works, will and creative ability produced an enforced synthesis of that contradiction that turns him into what Thomas Mann described as the 'perfect epitome' of his age. All the more important is it, therefore, to cast an orientational glance at 19th-century history, and German history in particular.

IN EUROPE A SYSTEM of states had evolved from the High Middle Ages onwards consisting of powers which had each developed at noticeably different rates. Located at the heart of Europe, Germany or, to give it its official name, the 'Holy Roman Empire of the German Nation' consisted of over 300 secular and ecclesiastical principalities and imperial cities. Its overlord, the Roman Emperor, was elected by seven Electors from among the German princes. (After 1692 there were nine.) Although he 'reigned' over the Empire, his practical power as territorial sovereign was limited to his own inherited principalities. The Empire remained at the level of development of a medieval feudal state held together by merely personal feudal ties, while the territories governed by the Empire's princes gradually assumed many of the characteristics associated with modern territorial states, the main distinguishing feature of which is exclusive and indivisible sovereignty.

Notwithstanding their individual constitutional differences, the states which bordered the Empire's boundary (and especially those to the west) represented this modern type of state. The Reformation, moreover, had left Germany denominationally divided, the

The Holy Roman Empire from 1618 to 1789

principle of *cuius regio, eius religio* meaning that each territorial sovereign, including even the meanest princeling, determined his subjects' faith. Only the Emperor had to be Catholic.

German princes waged wars and concluded treaties not only among themselves and with foreign powers but even against the Emperor. The Thirty Years War (1618–48) began as a domestic dispute between German Catholics and Protestants but soon became a struggle of all the major European powers for hegemony fought out, in the main, on German soil. When hostilities finally ceased, half the German population lay dead and the country was ravaged and destitute, a traumatic experience which, centuries later, still marked the German consciousness. As yet, however, resentment was not directed at any one particular neighbour, since the confessional aspect overrode all others.

The Peace of Westphalia of 1648 gave the King of Sweden territories within the Empire, so that, like the King of Denmark, he, too, became a member of the Empire, France and Sweden guaranteeing a constitution which, although it ensured the Empire's survival, effectively clipped its wings. Impractical in its political structure, it did not conform to any existing state theory and was therefore described as a 'monstrosity' (*monstro simile*) by the jurist Samuel Pufendorf (1632–94).

In such circumstances the sense of German national identity was bound to be different from that of other nations, especially those of western Europe, inasmuch as it was based on the idea of the Empire, on German culture and the German language but not on any well-defined territory or reasons of state.

From a psychological point of view, 1689 was to prove of crucial importance in European history: under a series of absolute monarchs France, the most modern and powerful western European state, had gradually evolved a policy of imperialist expansion, extending her territories at the expense of her neighbours, regardless of their nationality, especially those which were members of the Holy Roman Empire. In 1681 Louis XIV had used force to capture the imperial city of Strassburg and seven years later began a war of conquest against the Palatinate which provoked an alliance between the German princes and the whole of the rest of Europe with the aim of resisting French aggression. Risking losing all it had conquered, the government in Paris resolved on a course of wholesale devastation of an entire region – the first occasion in modern history when such a policy had been pursued: on Whitmonday 1689, at 4 o'clock in the afternoon, the imperial cities of Speyer, Worms and Oppenheim, which had declared their neutrality and peacefully opened their gates to the French, were systematically set on fire by members of the French army; Speyer's imposing Romanesque cathedral was partially blown up, the tombs of the German emperors desecrated and the inhabitants driven out of the town. During the months that followed a similar fate was meted out to Heidelberg (whose famous castle ruins are wholly unromantic in origin), while dozens of towns and thousands of villages between the French border and the Rhine were routinely laid waste and depopulated.

This pseudo-rational, precisely calculated and methodically executed scorched-earth policy produced a state of psychic shock in those affected by it, a shock which released a potential for fear, hatred and moral unscrupulousness which, for the next two and half centuries, had devastating consequences for the social psyche not only of its victims but of those who had been responsible for it. The 'hereditary enmity' between the Germans and French dates from 1689, an enmity which was to become a dominant obsession of the 19th century as a whole.

Throughout the following two centuries every major European conflict was fought on German soil, the instability of the Empire's power structure almost literally inviting invaders, while Austria and Prussia, the two leading German powers, vied for hegemony. German and non-German states – Austria and Hungary, Saxony and Poland, Hanover and England, Holstein and Denmark, Pomerania and Sweden – formed monarchical personal unions with a tendency towards a real and permanent union. The many small German states could survive only by forming alliances with other German or foreign states.

By the end of the 18th century, the majority of these states were notable, in terms of social reality, for the enlightened absolutism of their rulers and even for their anti-clerical rationalism, but chiefly for their feudalistic legal and property structures. Power was often vested in bureaucratic, rigidly structured administrative bodies and in military institutions run by the aristocracy. Germany was still an agrarian country. Out of a population of some 23 millions, less than a quarter lived in towns, of which only two, Vienna and Berlin, had more than 100,000 inhabitants. Most of the rural population lived in a state of feudal dependency, crafts were protected – prohibitively so – by the system of guilds and their constitutions, and although these latter could not prevent manufacturing industry from evolving, they succeeded in holding back its growth thanks to the feudal links which bound the peasantry to the soil. A precondition for economic and social progress was freedom of trade and the emancipation of the peasants (who made up most of the population) from their feudal bonds. The middle class, slowly emerging as a social group on the international scene, was still unable to exercise any decisive influence in largely agrarian countries where the towns were generally small in size. Relying defensively on traditional 'good old rights', including the rights of the towns and the privileges of the patricians and guilds, it attempted instead to counter the levelling claims to power of the absolutist principality, without being able to rid itself of a basically backward-looking outlook.

The culture of the leading social class, in other words the princes and aristocracy, was entirely subject to French and Italian influence, so that the bourgeoisie, with its emergent cultural awareness, saw princes such as Friedrich the Great, who wrote better French than German, as representatives of a cultural imperialism described as *welsch*, in other words, Romance. Schiller refers to this attitude in his poem *Die deutsche Muse*:

> Kein Augustisch Alter blühte,
> Keines Medicäers Güte,
>   Lächelte der deutschen Kunst;
> Sie ward nicht gepflegt vom Ruhme,
> Sie entfaltete die Blume
>   Nicht am Strahl der Fürstengunst.
>
> Von dem grössten deutschen Sohne,
> Von des grossen Friedrichs Throne
>   Ging sie schutzlos, ungeehrt.
> Rühmend darf's der Deutsche sagen,
> Höher darf das Herz ihm schlagen:
>   *Selbst* erschuf er sich den Werth.
>
> No blossoming Augustan Age,
> No Medicean patronage
>   On German art has ever smiled.
> No fame and glory e'er she knew,
> Though fair as any flower that grew,
>   By princely grace was ne'er beguiled.
>
> The Germans' greatest son has shown
> It scant respect; great Frederick's throne
>   Left German art defiled, alone;
> And yet each German heart may beat
> With pride. Let each to each repeat:
>   The German's merit is his own!

In January 1867 Wagner gave expression to this same idea when versifying these lines from Sachs's final address to the populace of Nuremberg:

> in falscher wälscher Majestät
> kein Fürst bald mehr sein Volk versteht;
> und wälschen Dunst mit wälschem Tand
> sie pflanzen uns in's deutsche Land, (GS VII, 270)

literally, 'in false, Romance majesty no prince will soon understand his people; they will implant Romance vapidity with Romance dross in our German land'.

The French Revolution and the Wars of Liberation: 1789–1815

THE FRENCH REVOLUTION of 1789 – an anti-feudal uprising on the part of the bourgeoisie – initially met with committed support among members of the German middle classes, especially in the western parts of the Empire, although even the Saxon peasants rose up in revolt and had to be put down by military force. However, when the new French revolutionary government demanded 'natural frontiers' in 1792, adopting a strategy of 'liberation through armed missionaries' and annexing Germany west of the Rhine, German memories were stirred of the shock that the country had suffered in 1689. The Napoleonic empire, with its claims to world domination, finally destroyed the structure of the Holy Roman Empire between 1804 and 1806, replacing its system of myriad states, in those areas of Germany which had not been directly annexed, by the so-called *Rheinbund*, a group of newly formed, dependent 'middle' states, while Austria and Prussia were driven away to the east: Germany was divided, constitutionally, into four parts and was now no more than a geographical concept. Feudalism was formally abolished in the areas ceded to France. In 1803, under the terms of the final decree of a special deputation of the Imperial Diet, the dispossessed German princes west of the Rhine were compensated for their losses by grants of secularized church properties, while the smaller secular territories were mediatized and deprived of their governmental rights, thus undermining the political basis of feudalism in the rest of Germany, too. One consequence of this was the emancipation of the peasantry in Prussia, where personal feudal ties were abolished, thereby opening up the way to the growth of a class of 'free' wage-labourers and hence to the process of industrialization.

Although the French Revolution roused the German middle class to a sense of national and political consciousness, the imperialistic degeneration of the Revolution forced them into a fatal alliance with the ruling aristocratic powers in Austria and Prussia, both of which were feudal states undergoing a process of reform under the pressure of circumstances. But not only did French imperialism make a union of democratic and national aspirations politically impossible, it also rendered it ideologically suspect. Thus German attitudes were affected throughout the whole of the 19th century, causing large sections of the German educated classes to renounce the struggle for political responsibility. Around 1802 Schiller wrote in his unfinished draft, 'German Greatness':

> The German Empire and the German nation are two different things. The majesty of the German never rested on the head of his princes. The German has established his own independent worth, quite apart from any political worth, and even if the Holy Roman Empire were to vanish into dust, German dignity would still remain unchallenged. [. . .] It is a moral entity, dwelling in the culture and character of the nation, which is independent of all political vicissitudes.

This same idea recurs at the end of Wagner's 1845 draft for *Die Meistersinger von Nürnberg*. (The lines in question were added at some date between July 1845 and December 1848.)

> Zerging' das heil'ge röm'sche Reich in Dunst,
> Uns bliebe doch die heil'ge deutsche Kunst.

In Newman's translation:

> though should depart the might of holy Rome,
> no harm will come to holy German art!

From here there is a direct line to what Thomas Mann called the 'turning-inwards under the protection of a powerful state' ('machtgeschützte Innerlichkeit') on the part of 'unpolitical' German cultural philistines of the early 20th century.

The War of Liberation of 1813–14 thus became not only a struggle for German national survival but, by implication, a struggle for survival of the neo-absolutist princedom. The Vienna Congress held by the victorious European powers, Russia, England, Austria and Prussia, sanctioned the supremacy of conservative, reactionary forces. The demands of the middle-class democratic national liberation movement, which had helped to overthrow French hegemony, were ignored, and the Holy Roman Empire was supplanted by a 'German Confederation' of thirty-nine sovereign German states, while the democrats were promised 'constitutions' – though not representative ones ('landständische Verfassungen'). State absolutism, however, remained largely unaffected. France had been defeated but was by no means done for as a major power and, although she had to give up the majority of her German conquests, she renewed her revisionist demands for 'natural frontiers'.

Reaction and revolution: 1815–1849

THE LEADING POWER in the German Confederation was the Austrian monarchy, the larger, non-German part of which did not, however, belong to the Confederation. Having formed a 'Holy Alliance' with Prussia and Russia, the Austrian Chancellor, Clemens Metternich, proceeded to adopt a policy of repression towards the emergent opposition, the principal supporters of which were to be found among the nationally and liberally inclined bourgeoisie, whose watchword was 'Honour, Freedom, Fatherland': the Wartburg Festival organized by the German students' association or *Burschenschaft* in October 1817 led to the 1819 Carlsbad Decrees of the German Confederation and to the suppression of liberal aspirations throughout the whole of Germany. Censorship, stringent policing and a network of informers were the means to which German governments stooped.

The defeat of Napoleon and the resultant lifting of the 'Continental Blockade' caused a major decline in trade and industry, since mainland Europe was unable to compete economically with the more efficient manufacturing system which obtained at this time in England. Crop failures in 1816–17 added to the country's difficulties and provoked a political crisis.

The 'hepp-hepp riots' of 1819 began among manual workers and were directed above all at the association of aristocrats and Jews, although not even this alleged allegiance prevented a Hohenzollern prince from heaping anti-Jewish abuse on the head of the ten-year-old Felix Mendelssohn-Bartholdy and spitting on the ground when they passed each other in a street in Berlin.

Jewish emancipation in the years leading up to 1789 had been supported by intellectuals and enlightened civil servants in Prussia and elsewhere: suffice it to recall the friendship between Gotthold Ephraim Lessing and Moses Mendelssohn. One of the consequences of the French Revolution was that all citizens were now treated as equals, irrespective of their denomination: in Prussia, too, the Jews who were resident there were granted Prussian citizenship in 1812.

The July Revolution which broke out in Paris in 1830 led to unrest all over Europe, including Germany, where local insurgents sought to topple reactionary princedoms. In 1832 intellectuals, manual workers and peasants met at Hambach in the Palatinate for a great popular assembly, demanding the abolition of the monarchy, the unification of Germany and the liberation of Poland, Italy and Hungary. The *Hambacher Fest* provoked federal decrees suspending the right of assembly and extending censorship and repression. Among the songs sung at this time was *Fürsten zum Land hinaus!* (*Princes, get out!*), each federal state taking a verse in turn, including the lines:

Juste Milieu, träges Tier,	Juste Milieu, sluggish beast,
Rothschild und Staatspapier!	Rothschild and government bonds!
Hepp!	Hepp!

The anti-Jewish battle cry of 1819 appears here in the context of a freedom song, the singing of which brought with it a mandatory prison sentence. Emancipatory hatred of the country's princely rulers and popular anti-Jewish sentiments thus became associated, a combination which was to have fatal consequences for the future.

German particularism, with its numerous customs borders and independent currencies, weights and measures, had turned out to be a major obstacle to economic progress. In 1834, therefore, eighteen of the thirty-nine German states formed the German Customs Union or *Zollverein* under Prussian leadership. Among notable absentees were Hanover, which was bound by dynastic ties to England, and Austria, which remained in a state of archaic ossification.

None the less, the creation of a national market extending over much of Germany was a starting signal for the Industrial Revolution, while at the same time providing an economic lever for uniting the country as a whole: within ten years, industrial production had risen by 50 per cent, the number of steam-driven engines in Prussia had trebled and 2500 kilometres of railway tracks had been laid.

In 1840 the Levant Treaty was signed by Russia and England. Intended to curtail France's expansionist designs in the Mediterranean, it led to a change of direction in French foreign policy, encouraging France to arm herself for war with the aim of overturning the Final Act of the Vienna Congress of 1815 and of enforcing the Rhine as the 'natural' border with Germany.

This latter demand, noisily bruited abroad, stirred up memories of 1689 and 1806 in a country which, although suffering political repression and undergoing a period of economic change, was becoming conscious of its growing power: fear and hatred of the 'hereditary' enemy produced an undercurrent of nationalism which affected the German psyche for the whole of the rest of the century. Written in 1840 by the poet Max Schneckenburger, the popular song, *Die Wacht am Rhein* (*The Watch on the Rhine*) sums up to perfection the spirit of the times. It remained an unofficial national anthem until 1914, a sort of German *Rule, Britannia*:

> Es braust ein Ruf wie Donnerhall,
> Wie Schwertgeklirr und Wogenprall,
> Zum Rhein, zum Rhein, zum deutschen Rhein!
> Wer will des Stromes Hüter sein?
> Lieb' Vaterland, magst ruhig sein,
> Fest steht und treu die Wacht am Rhein.

> Like pounding seas, the cry rings out
> Mid clash of arms, a thunderous shout:
> The Rhine, the Rhine, the German Rhine,
> O who will go and guard its line?
> Dear fatherland, no more ado:
> The watch that guards the Rhine is true.

Nikolaus Becker's *Rheinlied*, set to music by Robert Schumann in 1840 as *Patriotisches Lied*, was not without influence on Wagner's works:

> Sie sollen ihn nicht haben,
> Den freien, deutschen Rhein,
> Und wenn sie auch wie Raben
> Sich heiser danach schrei'n!

> They'll never claim it as their own:
> The German Rhine is free for aye;
> Though they may croak like ravens till
> They're hoarse, it's ours until we die.

The same image recurs in Walther's Trial Song in *Die Meistersinger*, with its 'hoarse chorus of ravens' and a 'wondrous bird', described in German as a 'Vogel wunderbar', the words automatically suggesting a rhyme with 'Aar', meaning 'eagle', the Empire's heraldic bird.

The following year, 1841, the liberal poet Hoffmann von Fallersleben wrote his *Lied der Deutschen*, directed against the German princes and particularism (its opening words, 'Deutschland, Deutschland über alles', originally had nothing to do with expansionist pretensions) and appealing to national solidarity in the hour of need ('as long as we always stand together like brothers'). The Prussian king dismissed Hoffmann from his professorship in Breslau; the princes banned the song but concluded a military treaty against France, thereby showing a better understanding of its words than many others since.

Economic changes brought a series of crises and led not only to the gradual emergence of a proletariat but, in 1844, to the Weavers' Uprising in Silesia. Starting out from Königsberg, the erstwhile home of Immanuel Kant, a civic movement sprang up, aimed at bringing about democratic reforms within the Prussian state. Its first success was the summoning of the 'United Diet' of all the Prussian provinces to Berlin in 1847.

Meanwhile, Karl Marx was working on his political and economic analysis of bourgeois society. During the winter of 1847–8, while living in exile in London, he collaborated with Friedrich Engels on the *Communist Manifesto*: as a result of the change in production relations, the labour movement now developed alongside, and distinct from, the bourgeois movement for greater democracy.

By the beginning of 1848 the masses were no longer willing to tolerate the old régime, while the rulers themselves were no longer capable of sustaining it, so that conditions were now ripe for a democratic bourgeois revolution, a revolution sparked off by events in France in February 1848, when the monarchy was overthrown. Peasant uprisings and civil unrest followed throughout southern Germany, until finally, in March 1848, the revolution triumphed in Vienna and Berlin. The Austrian Chancellor, Metternich, was driven into exile, as was Wilhelm, Prince of Prussia, later the German emperor, who was known at this time as 'the Grapeshot Prince' following his remark that 'only grenades are of use against democrats'. His brother, King Friedrich Wilhelm IV, was made to remove his hat in the presence of the black, red and gold national flag as it fluttered over the coffins of the Berliners shot by the military on the barricades. He was allowed, however, to keep his head, a concession which robbed the revolutionaries of their ultimate victory.

As long as the state and military machinery concentrated in the hands of the aristocracy was temporarily paralysed, the civic movement was able to install reform governments and to hold elections throughout Germany for a National Assembly. The Assembly duly met in St Paul's Church in Frankfurt on 18 May 1848 and set about the task of creating a democratic constitution.

The republican left, supporting the idea of a united Germany that would include all the German-speaking territories, argued over their country's future organization with the right-wing supporters of a federal constitutional monarchy (German unification was possible only if Austria's monarchical ties with non-German territories such as Hungary and Italy were severed), while the aristocratic counter-revolutionaries in Austria and Prussia reorganized their armies in the autumn of 1848 and proceeded to reinstate the former power structures by means of military force, imposing new constitutions on their subjects from above. In this they were supported by Russia and England, two major powers with a long-standing hostility to revolution, but also by a part of the propertied bourgeoisie, which observed with horror the movement for democracy, which would not only threaten their class privileges but even give political power to the mass of the people.

Attempts to include the German-speaking parts of the Habsburg Empire in a unified Germany were frustrated by Austria's internal reorganization. This *grossdeutsch* solution was therefore replaced by a *kleindeutsch* alternative in the form of a federalist constitutional monarchy led by Prussia, a plan proposed by the moderate and right-wing majority in the National Assembly but thwarted in April 1849 when the King of Prussia refused to accept the imperial crown and rejected the new constitution, even though it had already been accepted by twenty-eight states, since he wished to avoid forfeiting the divine right of princes to the sovereignty of the people. An attempt by the democratic left to implement the constitution by revolutionary means led to armed insurrection on the part of the people in May 1849, an insurrection of which the battles which raged on the barricades in Dresden were only one small part. After a series of bloody battles, military force prevailed: the counter-revolution had triumphed and the struggle for a democratic, united Germany was lost for generations to come.

The constitution thrashed out in St Paul's Church in Frankfurt separated civic rights from religious denomination, thereby granting equal rights to the Jews, the vast majority of whom were willing to be integrated into the rest of the population. In doing so, it adopted the pro-emancipatory stance of the upper-middle classes and intellectuals but not that of the majority of the country's population, made up of lower-middle-class craftsmen and peasants, for whom 'the Jews' were part of the hated 'rich', who had sided with the counter-revolution.

German unification 'from above': 1850–1871

WAGNER'S ANTI-JEWISH PAMPHLET of 1850 is a typical product of the mood which obtained in Germany following the failure of the revolution. In its argumentation, it sets out, empirically, from the 'profound aversion to all things Jewish' which Wagner found among the population at large, while sharing with Marx the goal of 'emancipating society from the Jews'. In other words, it demands the 'disappearance of Judaism as a religion and as a religious group' and does so, moreover, for reasons which, as Hermann Greive has argued, are ultimately 'religious'.

The German Confederation was reratified in 1850 in the Treaty of Olmütz. Although reactionary forces triumphed inside Germany with the reestablishment of a police state, the Industrial Revolution continued on its course, increasing the economic strength of the bourgeoisie and encouraging the growth of the proletariat. The economic arguments for German unification remained as compelling as ever and received further support from developments in European power politics at this time: in the war which the two western powers, France and England, waged against Russia in their attempts to drive the latter back from the Bosporus, the two major German powers found themselves in a precarious state of political isolation when, in 1854–6, they attempted to pursue a policy of 'armed neutrality'. The Italian War of Unification of 1859 weakened Austria's position and, for a time, threatened to result in a war on two fronts against France and Russia. In the end, however, it served only to intensify the clash of interests between Austria and Prussia. All attempts at peaceful reconciliation came to a definite end at the Congress of Princes (*Fürstentag*) held in Frankfurt in 1863.

In 1864, the new Prussian prime minister Otto von Bismarck, acting in league with Austria, forcibly prevented Denmark from making the duchy of Schleswig an integrated part of the Danish state. Although it owed allegiance to the Danish crown, the predominantly German-speaking duchy had been constitutionally linked with Holstein since 1386, Holstein itself being part of the German Confederation. ('Up ewig ungedeelt' – 'forever undivided' – was a guaranteed constitutional right.) It was the question of the future of the two duchies which, in 1866, enabled Bismarck to launch his decisive offensive against Austria and to settle the issue of supremacy in Germany once and for all. The German War of 1866 and the defeat of the Austrian Empire resulted in the second division of Germany since 1806: the German Confederation was disbanded, Austria was forced to go its own way and Prussia, newly enlarged through a series of vast annexations, formed the North German Confederation (*Norddeutscher Bund*) comprising the states north of the Main. Military and customs treaties were concluded with the southern German states. Bismarck was helped in all this by renewed French claims to the Bavarian and Hessian Palatinate, the aggressive demands made by Napoleon III's Second Empire driving the allies into the arms of a victorious Prussia.

The German middle class had proved itself incapable, in 1848, of implementing the sovereignty of the people at the expense of the divine right of princes. The result was that Germany was now divided into three. Since 1862 the civic liberal majority in the Prussian diet had been embroiled with the royalist government over the question of which of them had the right to fix the budget and had declined to settle the army bills. The victory of the Prussian military monarchy now robbed that majority of its political basis, the reactionary Prussian state triumphing not only politically but psychologically, too, over both the liberal middle class and the industrial and commercial bourgeoisie thanks to Bismarck's doctrine that problems could be solved 'by iron and blood'. The bourgeoisie forfeited its claim to any decisive role in the affairs of state, a refusal to become involved which not even the demonstrable opposition to Bismarck's policy of unification, more especially on the part of legitimist and conservative groupings of the Old Prussian school, can allow us to ignore. The organized workers' movement founded in 1863 by Ferdinand Lassalle and known as the General German Workers' Union (*Allgemeiner deutscher Arbeiterverein*) was no more in a position to compensate for this failure on the part of the bourgeoisie than August Bebel's Social Democratic Workers' Party which, founded in 1869, was modelled on Marx's analysis of society. (Marx's main work, *Das Kapital*, had appeared in 1867.) They remained opposition parties, unable to influence events in the short term. Their goal was still a *grossdeutsch* democratic republic, including the German-speaking parts of

Austria, within the framework of international working-class solidarity.

The final spur to German unification (albeit of the *kleindeutsch* kind) was given by Napoleon III, who, seeing his government under threat at home, sought territorial gains at Germany's expense, even going so far as to declare war on Prussia in order to prevent the formation of a national German state. France's swift defeat had two immediate consequences: the King of Prussia was proclaimed German emperor on 18 January 1871 and the German Reich was refounded, but refounded from above, not from below by the people. None the less, for the first time since 1648 Germany was no longer at the mercy of the other major European powers, but, with a population of some 41 millions, a major power in its own right.

German annexation of Alsace-Lorraine, two territories in eastern France which, predominantly German-speaking, had been part of the Holy Roman Empire until the 17th and 18th centuries, was intended to end two hundred years of repeated French invasions by cutting off the French army's route to the heart of Germany, but it failed to end the trauma of 1689, inaugurating instead a new round of 'hereditary' hostility between Germany and France. The German concept of nationality, founded on language and culture, prevented the Germans from seeing that the inhabitants of Alsace and Lorraine, although culturally 'German', had become politically 'French' as a result of the process of political emancipation ushered in by the French Revolution, and that their reannexation *à la* Louis XIV violated their right of self-determination, even if, at the time, this right had yet to be recognized under international law. The German labour movement was therefore solidly against this decision.

The Reich in Europe: 1871–1883

THE NEW GERMAN REICH was constituted as a 'perpetual alliance' of twenty-five German princes and free cities under the presidency of the King of Prussia as the hereditary German emperor. It was they, rather than the nation, who jointly safeguarded the sovereignty which they exercised in the Bundesrat or Federal Council. The Reichstag or Imperial Diet, whose members were elected by secret ballot in accordance with the principle of universal male suffrage, retained control of the budget but could not call the *Reichskanzler* to account. The Reich was a federal authoritarian state with a central democratic core but, as Karl Marx noted, it also contained many elements of a 'military despotism bolstered up by the police'.

In the politico-economic field, the Industrial Revolution came of age, freedom of trade having been introduced in 1869. By 1871 as much as 36 per cent of the population of the Reich (excluding Austria) lived in towns (in 1789 it had been less than 25 per cent, by

1910 it was 60 per cent); of these, one had more than 500,000 inhabitants, five more than 100,000. Between 1870 and 1872 alone, industrial production rose by more than 30 per cent (production of pig-iron went up 40 per cent, that of steel by 80 per cent). A brief post-war boom (the *Gründerzeit*) was followed by a rapid and critical concentration of capital on a previously unknown scale (the *Gründerkrach*). Monetary and fiscal union helped to consolidate the new structure, while a national policy of protective tariffs replaced free trade and international competition. Price increases and housing shortages affected the lower classes most of all, who reacted by going on strike. A slump ensued, from which the country recovered only slowly.

On a wider front, Bismarck attempted to bolster up the German Reich by a virtuoso policy of alliances (*Bündnispolitik*) aimed at preventing the country from becoming isolated, which he feared would happen if an alliance were to be struck between the defeated French, on the one hand, and one of Germany's powerful neighbours on the other (the 'cauchemar des coalitions'). At the same time he sought to prevent a general war (the 1873 *Dreikaiser-Abkommen* with Austria and Russia, and the Berlin Congress of 1878 were part of this general policy), fearing that any such war would inevitably lead to revolution 'in more than one country' in Europe.

On the domestic front, Bismarck enjoyed the support of the National Liberals in his fight against two 'enemies of the Reich': on the one hand, there was Church interference in the affairs of state and the insistently federalist, *grossdeutsch* opposition of the Catholic Centre Party to a Reich which, since the exclusion of Austria, had become more Protestant and more northern, and, on the other, the German Social Democratic Party which, following its unification in 1875, had gone from strength to strength.

The attempt to reorganize the relationship between the established Churches and the State (including disbandment of the Church inspectorate of schools, a ban on politically inspired pulpit oratory and the introduction of civil marriage and state-run registry offices) led to a period of bitter conflict known as the *Kulturkampf* (1871–6), involving the arrest or expulsion of all Catholic bishops in Prussia and the abolition of ecclesiastical orders. Only gradually could a compromise be worked out and for many years German Catholics were branded as being 'nationally unreliable', since they had stood up in support of Catholic and national minorities such as the Poles and the people of Alsace-Lorraine.

As for social democracy and its rising tide of influence, Bismarck feared that it posed an immediate threat to the conservative monarchical state structures which obtained in Europe, while its internationalist aspirations were regarded as a danger to the newly founded national state. The attempt to suppress the Social Democrats by means of special laws (the 'Socialist Laws' of 1878) served only to encourage them, although one of its long-term effects was the party's propagandist exclusion from national solidarity and its members being stigmatized as 'comrades without a fatherland'.

In 1875 the stock exchange crash and *Kulturkampf* conspired to encourage the 'formation of a Catholic and Protestant united front against the Jews' (to quote Hermann Greive), a conservative grouping directed against the National Liberals and their 'Jewish economic liberalism'. The agricultural crisis which first made itself felt in 1876 increased opposition to free trade and lent widespread support to anti-Jewish agitation especially among the rural population. By around 1880, 'modern', racist anti-Semitism had emerged as a force to be reckoned with in Germany.

Bismarck's political allegiance with the National Liberals came to grief over the question of customs and fiscal reform. In 1879 he succeeded in passing a law through the Reichstag implementing a neo-mercantile policy of protective tariffs and in bringing off a new political merger between the agrarian and militaristic Junkers and heavy industry representing upper-middle-class armaments capital. Politically and economically, it was a decision sparked off by parallel events in France, Russia and England, as the world economy fragmented into a series of national economies, each of which was cut off from the others; the result was economic warfare, a free-for-all, which, given the world's immense capacity for economic growth, only slowly gave rise to critical confrontation between the major powers.

Even by 1883, the year of Wagner's death, new alignments were already beginning to emerge across the political face of Europe, persuading contemporaries such as Bismarck's son Herbert that his father's system of safeguarding the nation's security could be sustained 'for only a few more years' and that the danger of political isolation ('Einkreisung'), with all its consequences, would then become a very real threat. Militaristic thinking and massive rearmament left their mark, in turn, on Germany's domestic policy, ushering in a period of anti-liberal, ultraconservative thinking inspired by the Junkers' anti-democratic master-ideology, an ideology encouraged by the state, supported by suitably equipped state-run machinery and summed up in Nietzsche's 'will to power' (1888). Meanwhile, on the international scene, a European crisis was initiated by a French campaign of rearmament, aimed at exacting revenge for 1871 and at reestablishing the 'natural Rhine frontier'. The subsequent degeneration of international relations culminated in 1914 with the unleashing, by Germany, Russia and Austria, of the First World War.

KONRAD BUND
translated by Stewart Spencer

Section 4
INTELLECTUAL BACKGROUND

Philosophy   52

Literature   55

Religion   58

INTELLECTUAL BACKGROUND

THE PARTICULAR BRAND of optimism associated with 19th-century Idealist philosophy achieved early celebrity through Voltaire's *Candide* (1759) and Pangloss's dictum 'All is for the best in the best of all possible worlds' – a précis of the thesis of Leibniz's *Essais de théodicée sur la bonté de Dieu* (1710). Voltaire's satire might have been heeded had not Kant, the founder of Idealism, developed a penchant for the works of Jean-Jacques Rousseau (whose open letter in defence of Providence was directly implicated in Voltaire's attack). Paradoxically, it was through Kant's *Kritik der reinen Vernunft* (*Critique of Pure Reason*) and its sequels that around the turn of the century Romantic irrationality began to supplant the rationalism of the Enlightenment and Empfindsamkeit.

Philosophy

From the outset, the Idealists displayed an unbounded confidence in the capacity of the human mind to encompass the totality of experience by means of introspection. When, inspired by Rousseau's *Discours*, Kant dispensed with the alleged scholastic proofs of God's existence, he asserted the wider jurisdiction of philosophy through the Categorical Imperative, which in *Zur Metaphysik der Sitten* (*On the Metaphysics of Morals*) of 1785 he represented as an ethical criterion, innate rather than inherited or acquired: 'The maxim of my action is moral only if I can will that it should become a universal law.'

A similar emphasis on subjectivity characterized the writings of Kant's numerous disciples: Fichte, the early advocate of atheism and nationalism, whose *Versuch einer Kritik aller Offenbarung* (*Attempt at a Critique of All Revelation*) of 1792 advanced a theory of the absolute ego known only by intuition; Schelling, whose *System des transzendentalen Idealismus* (*System of Transcendental Idealism*) of 1800 linked the duality of the ego and the non-ego, as conceived by Fichte, in synthesis in art; and the theologian Schleiermacher, whose famous *Reden über die Religion* (*On Religion: Speeches to its Cultured Despisers*) of 1799 and subsequent works reflecting his Pietist upbringing reduced religion to intuition and feeling ('Anschauung und Gefühl') independent of doctrine and dogma.

The extent of the danger inherent in a school of philosophy of a subjective cast impressively institutionalized in a department of the Prussian civil service became apparent only with Hegel's appointment as professor at Berlin University (1818–31).

In the beginning, Hegel's emphasis on rationality, notably in the preface to the *Philosophie des Rechts* (*Philosophy of Right*), suggested a reaction against the cult of inwardness favoured by his colleagues; and, indeed, while applauding Rousseau's teaching as the basis of

Kant's moral philosophy, Hegel attacked the glorification of natural instinct as the epitome of hedonistic irresponsibility. In Hegel's own writings, however, reason at times was pressed to irrational, not to say hedonistic extremes. When in his lectures on the philosophy of history he described the dialectical progress of the 'Weltgeist' (world-spirit) from the state of pure being towards the absolute idea, he bestowed a Teutonic identity, intelligence, will and purpose on the world-historical process whose recent achievements he commemorated in a series of ominous aphorisms, contending that 'the state [of modern Prussia] is the Divine Idea [i.e., God] as it exists on earth.'

For Hegel, be it said, the state also represented a collective conscience so inexorable as to overrule almost any notion of individual responsibility or freedom of choice: 'Men are so foolish that, blinded by their ideal vision of unselfish conceptions of freedom of conscience and of political liberty, and by the inward ardour of enthusiasm, they do not see the truth that lies in power.' The presumption of such statements, more blatant than anything even Fichte had perpetrated in his patriotic discourses, was only compounded by an occasional perfunctory nod in the direction of a Christianity fully assimilated into and, Hegel believed, superseded by his philosophy: 'The destiny of the German peoples is to be the bearer of the Christian principle.'

In the second half of the century, Hegel's dynastic claims – made long before Prussia had risen to prominence within the German Empire – were to be endorsed with a ruthlessness that Hegel himself could not possibly have envisaged.

For the moment, the torch passed to a group of dissenters from optimistic orthodoxy, the Young Hegelians, who were inevitably stigmatized as fanatics and renegades despite the comparative sanity of the views they expressed in many cases. Unlike the Hegelian vanguard, the Old Hegelians, whose names are mostly forgotten, the Young Hegelians were inspired by precisely that inward ardour of enthusiasm which Hegel had deplored. To this end, they initiated a comprehensive programme of reform, replacing metaphysical abstraction and (ostensible) rationality with personal experience (Feuerbach's 'Sinnlichkeit') and something like an appeal to common sense. With the possible exception of Karl Marx, who under the influence of Proudhon, La Mettrie, and other French and English materialists had become engrossed in an attempt to reduce history to the economics of class, these writers directed their best efforts to undermining what they saw as the last obstacle to progress: established religion. To this end, they applied the forensic techniques of historiography and emergent psychology to considerable effect. This may be said of David Friedrich Strauss, whose *Das Leben Jesu* (*The Life of Jesus*), pronounced heretical by its judges, can be seen as a pioneering work of textual criticism; of Arnold Ruge, whose *System der Religion unserer Zeit* (*System of Contemporary Religion*), rejecting belief in transcendence, attempted to derive a scientific humanism from the study of religion; Bruno Bauer, whose *Entdecktes Christentum* (*The Truth About Christianity*) represented Christianity as a disaster to be redressed only by total de-Christianization; and, not least, Max Stirner, whose onslaught on Feuerbach in *Der Einzige und sein Eigentum* (*The Ego and His Own*) transformed the humanist doctrine into a charter for uncompromising and stoical egoism, if not for anarchy in the style of Bakunin.

The fate of Feuerbach, whose *Das Wesen des Christentums* (*The Essence of Christianity*) of 1841 (see 'Religion', pp. 59–60) had been received as the definitive statement of the humanist creed by the radicals of the *Vormärz* (1815–48), was typical of that of the Young Hegelians, all of whom suffered eclipse with the political *débâcle* of 1848–9. Of their original number, only Marx toiling in obscurity in London until 1883 went on to develop an effective strategy: a strategy that in the guise of scientific socialism would erupt with devastating consequences as one of the dominant ideologies of the 20th century.

Despite his dismissal of Idealism as a monstrous charade and betrayal of the purpose of philosophy as represented by Kant (whom he admired), Arthur Schopenhauer had much in common with his system-building contemporaries. In particular, his noumenal 'will', evolved from Kant's metaphysical 'Ding an sich' (thing in itself) and Fichte's conception of the will, had an affinity with Hegel's 'world-spirit': except that the 'will' appeared as a blind, irrational demiurge, indifferent alike to the interests of Prussian hegemony and German supremacy (Schopenhauer, whose gift of sarcasm was notable, had denounced Hegel's mythology of power as the last refuge of the philosophically destitute). The emphasis on the primacy of unreasoning instinct – Schopenhauer's most modern trait – anticipated the ideas of the Young Hegelians in their opposition to Hegel's cult of rationality. Yet, while the Young Hegelians may have questioned the role of reason, like Hegel they passionately believed in the efficacy of political action as the instrument of progress. For Schopenhauer, strongly influenced by the thought of the Orient, a different view was possible. According to the inflexible determinism of *Die Welt als Wille und Vorstellung* (*The World as Will and Representation*), any attempt to temporize with the life force was inherently futile. The goal, prefigured in the disinterested contemplation of art and in the (Buddhist) ethics of compassion, consisted in the act of renunciation: the only authentic act of free (i.e., 'will'-less) will. In describing the bliss of deliverance, Schopenhauer's divergence from Hegel – and from the philosophical tradition of the West – was total.

The thirty-five years' neglect of *The World as Will and Representation* (1818), rescued by an article by John Oxenford in *The Westminster Review* in 1853, was hardly surprising at the time of Hegel's ascendancy; nor was Schopenhauer's inability to avert Hegel's posthumous triumph any more surprising with the resurgence of optimism in the second half of the century. For discerning intellectuals, however, his posthumous prestige had a more than symbolic value as, with a frightening inevitability, the best of all possible worlds began to come into being.

Although extremely precocious, Friedrich Nietzsche, too, was little read by the contemporaries he addressed with such rhetorical eloquence and urgency; his admission to the pantheon of the 19th century is almost a contemporary phenomenon (the collected edition begun in 1977 is still incomplete).

Modern philosophy, indeed, has been hard put to it to dispose of the legacy of German Idealism which by the turn of the century had entered a period of international conquest. In Germany, too, the theory of historical progress which had distinguished the movement in its formative stages was invoked to great effect by a group of outstanding historians in the footsteps of Ranke – Droysen, Dahlmann, Sybel, the extreme nationalist Treitschke and, initially at least, the finally disillusioned and isolated Mommsen – who interpreted the rising tide of political optimism in the 1860s as positive proof of the validity of the Idealist position. In this fatefully altered guise, Idealism was to continue to haunt the political imagination well into the 20th century. The revolution in thought in these years, then, was inaugurated neither by the neo-Hegelians who sought to perpetuate an intellectual *status quo*, nor by the radicals who saw themselves as Hegel's potential successors. Its leaders had recourse to a more drastic yet far simpler strategy in redrawing the map of philosophy itself, and excluding as irrelevant almost all the areas of concern that had claimed the attention of their predecessors: Comte, the inventor of positivism and precursor of the philosophy of science; Bergson, with his theory of creative evolution; Mach, the moving spirit behind the Vienna Circle of logical positivists; Brentano, the pioneer of empirical psychology; Frege, whose research in mathematical logic led to advances in the philosophy of language; Freud, the founder of psychoanalysis and with Marx a pioneer of structuralism; and Husserl, who promoted the movements known as phenomenology and hermeneutics.

ROGER HOLLINRAKE

Literature

'NO MUSICIAN HAS READ or written more' (Lloyd-Jones, 1976). Wagner is unique in musical history in his knowledge of literature, both of past ages and of his own time. As an adolescent he absorbed the works of the German classics (and Shakespeare), together with the fascinating world of the Romantics; he had close links with the writers known as *Junges Deutschland* (Young Germany) and shared many of their beliefs; he moved into the shadow of Schopenhauerian pessimism and endorsed Nietzsche's criticism of cultural values; his last years were enacted against the background of the Wilhelminian expansionism. His libraries were no mere ostentation but bore witness to a remarkable desire to remain abreast of literary and philosophical developments, and Cosima Wagner's *Diaries* record many evenings' discussions and readings. (For an alternative perspective, see 'Literary tastes', pp. 149–51.)

Two early influences, Ludwig Geyer and Adolf Wagner, were of great importance. Geyer's theatrical ambitions and talents made the young adolescent aware of the greatness of the German Classical writers, Goethe above all. The young Wagner was surrounded by theatre, with several of his siblings associated in one way or another with the stage. He was able to see Shakespeare performed, that playwright whose influence on German literature (via the Wieland, and later the more famous Schlegel–Tieck translations) cannot be over-emphasized. Wagner's *Leubald* may be seen as a juvenile attempt to emulate Goethe's *Götz von Berlichingen* and other plays of knights, chivalry and intrigue which Shakespeare had been deemed to inspire. Shakespeare was regarded by many as a liberator, a writer who was closer to the German spirit than to the French; this is how the young Goethe and the young Wagner saw him. The mature Wagner never ceased to admire the genius of the English dramatist, seeing in Shakespeare the supreme mentor. 'He is my only spiritual friend', he later claimed (CT, 22 May 1882).

The other important influence was that of his uncle, Adolf Wagner. This eccentric was not only an expert on Shakespeare and the Greeks: he was steeped in the writings of the Romantics and had been an associate of E.T.A. Hoffmann. Wagner has been called German Romanticism's most favoured beneficiary and he responded with enthusiasm to the world of spirits, medievalism, artist-figures and outsiders which that movement delighted in portraying. Romanticism in Germany lasted some thirty years, and Wagner absorbed it as no other musician. Hoffmann, Tieck and Fouqué impressed him deeply, Hoffmann being a most potent influence. In *Der Dichter und der Komponist* (*The Writer and the Composer*) Wagner learned of the need for an indissoluble link between libretto and music; *Meister Martin der Küfner und seine Gesellen* (*Master Martin the Cooper and his Apprentices*) spoke of late-medieval Nuremberg and its mastersingers; *Die Bergwerke zu Falun* (*The Mines at Falun*) fascinated him by its description of mines and subterranean spirits; *Der Kampf der Sänger* (*The Minstrels' Contest*) described a song-contest.

Hoffmann's admiration for Carlo Gozzi led Wagner to use the latter's *La donna serpente* (*The Serpent Woman*) as a libretto for *Die Feen*. And Hoffmann was also a composer of some repute: his opera *Undine*, based on Fouqué's captivating story of the elemental water-sprite (a story from which Wagner read aloud the night before his death) was performed in Berlin in 1816. Wagner also read a great deal of Tieck, admiring the *Phantasus* collection particularly, which contained the story *Der getreue Eckart und der Tannenhäuser* (*Faithful Eckart and Tannenhäuser*); his Dresden library later contained the first twenty volumes of Tieck's *Schriften* (Berlin, 1828–54). Themes of love, death and night may well have been derived from Friedrich Schlegel and Novalis. Of great importance to Wagner would also be Jacob Grimm's *Deutsche Mythologie*, of which he possessed the second edition (Göttingen, 1844), Wilhelm Grimm's *Die deutsche Heldensage* (Göttingen, 1829) and the three-volume edition of the brothers' *Kinder- und Hausmärchen* (Berlin, 1819–22).

Romanticism was superseded by *Junges Deutschland*, a loose grouping of young writers who sought to reject the fantastic and portray contemporary problems: the Paris revolution of 1830 had been symptomatic of the attempt to achieve greater emancipation and political freedom. The appearance in 1835 of Karl Gutzkow's novel *Wally die Zweiflerin* (*The Woman who Doubted*) had caused an uproar and his works, together with those of Heine, Wienbarg, Mundt and Laube, were banned by the censor. Wagner arrived in Paris in 1839 and met Heine there (he would glean the idea for *Der fliegende Holländer* from Heine). The latter's journalistic skills Wagner greatly admired, and these he sought to emulate in his newspaper articles; he also sympathized with many of the new ideas. Metternich's conservative régime (the time known as the *Vormärz*) had ensured political stability in Germany and Austria, but the tremors of 1830 prefigured the greater explosion of revolutionary activity in 1848 in Paris and other European cities.

In Dresden Wagner, now Kapellmeister, had thrown himself into intensive study for the *Nibelungen* project, reading the secondary literature, translations, and other versions of the sagas; his reading of the Greeks and of Feuerbach concentrated his thinking on a vision of emancipated humanity, free from restraints both political and sexual. The ideas of Heinse (*Ardinghello*) and of *Junges Deutschland* had prepared the way: Wagner also knew his Proudhon (he read *Qu'est-ce que la propriété* in the summer of 1849) and, with Bakunin, exulted in the revolutionary fervour of that year. The drama fragments of *Jesus von Nazareth* and *Achilleus* were meant to portray natural freedom and morality as opposed to stifling constraints: early drafts of the *Ring* also are indebted to Wagner's vision of liberated humanity.

The materialistic philosophies of Feuerbach and Ludwig Büchner corresponded to an outlook fostered by an anti-Romantic, more socially orientated *Weltanschauung*, but Schopenhauer's *Die Welt als Wille und Vorstellung* (*The World as Will and Representation*), first published in 1818 and ignored until the 1850s, represented a counter-tendency which, in its pessimism, appealed to many who were disillusioned with the failure of the 1848–9 revolutions. Wagner's writings in Zurich were originally inspired by a desire to reform German culture and to get back to the mythical entities of Greek antiquity: his reading of Schopenhauer in 1854 deflected his thinking into other channels. Schopenhauer's doctrine of the negation of the will, and the disillusionment felt at the failure of the 1848–9 revolutions led to a cult of withdrawal amongst many German writers and an emphasis not on urban sophistication but on provincialism. Wagner's work on *Tristan und Isolde* exemplified the tendency to concentrate on rapt inwardness; *Die Meistersinger von Nürnberg* extols that city during the late Middle Ages.

As regards Wagner's contact with literary figures, the meetings with Ludwig Tieck in Dresden, Gottfried Keller in Zurich and the dramatists Franz Grillparzer and Friedrich Hebbel in Vienna are significant, although Wagner did not take Hebbel's *Nibelungen* trilogy seriously, and was most scathing about Grillparzer's *Sappho*. The most important of his friendships was that with Friedrich Nietzsche. Nietzsche was astonished by Wagner's knowledge of Greek antiquity and was moved to see in his work a rebirth of the Greek mythical tradition. Wagner's fame was spreading: the successes of *Tristan* and *Meistersinger* made him a European phenomenon. Nietzsche's later apostasy is notorious, and writers of the stature of Grillparzer, Paul Heyse, F.Th. Vischer and Theodor Fontane indulged frequently in satire and mockery *vis-à-vis* the Wagner 'problem'. Gottfried Keller may well have detected a 'sense of antique tragedy' in the *Nibelungen* poem, but others saw Wagner as a typical example of the *Gründerzeit*, that time of Prussian commercial expansionism. Monumentalism and grandiloquent gestures characterize much of the art of the 1870s: the second Reich, proud of its conquests on the field of battle and secure in its industrial might, demanded self-glorification, a literature of sycophantic praise for the Hohenzollerns such as was provided by Ernst von Wildenbruch. Prussia's conquest of France called forth much nationalistic fervour and writing which commended German power and 'Nibelungentreue': the ending of Felix Dahn's *Ein Kampf um Rom* (*The Battle for Rome*), a novel which rapidly became a bestseller on its appearance in 1876, creates an obvious set-piece reminiscent of the historical tableaux of Conrad Ferdinand Meyer. Very popular were the novels of Friedrich Spielhagen, whose portrayals of the opulence, material values and predatory ambitions of those years make exemplary reading. But Wagner is not of this ilk: *Der Ring des Nibelungen* may seem redolent of the *Gründerzeit* but is both atavistic and ultra-modern in its fusion of myth and psychology, as Thomas Mann well understood. And *Parsifal* is already a work which adumbrates the refinements of French Symbolism and *décadence*, providing the contributors of the *Revue Wagnérienne* with a mystical prism to reflect their own effulgence. From the literature of past ages and his own he gained much: to the literature of the coming century he gave incomparably more.

RAYMOND FURNESS

THE 19TH CENTURY in Germany was a period of secularization in which the structure of society succumbed to the forces of science, industrialization and power politics on an unprecedented scale.

Since the Lutheran Reformation, the Christian religion had been imperilled by a lack of cohesion within the ecclesiastical

Religion

establishment: a danger recognized in the aftermath of the Peace of Westphalia by Leibniz's *Systema theologicum* (1686), with its appeal for reconciliation among the warring religious denominations.

At the turn of the century, Christianity was represented by a large Catholic adherence in the south and west centring on the Munich of Ludwig I and bordering on Catholic Austria and France. The north and east, centring on Protestant Berlin, even after the Holy Alliance of 1815–16 and the precarious equilibrium of the Evangelical Union imposed by Friedrich Wilhelm III of Prussia on the tercentenary of the Reformation in 1817, continued to be split into competing Protestant sects with Lutherans and Calvinists in sharp contention. To these major rivals were added minority groups of dissidents: Pietists, Herrnhuter, Saint-Simonians, Ebelian Muckers, free thinkers and agnostics – a legacy of the Enlightenment with its noble plea for tolerance, and of the northern preoccupation since the age of Friedrich the Great with the fruits of (predominantly atheistic) French culture.

Philosophy, promoted by the Protestant universities of Prussia alongside theology and the study of comparative religion, which grew in importance, retained a nominally Christian allegiance as well as a conservative political orientation (in 1841, Friedrich Wilhelm IV invited Schelling to Berlin in an attempt to curb the proliferation of agnosticism). In the moral philosophy of Kant, however, the notion of a secular theodicy had been implanted, which despite official censure would engender a formidable corpus of literature in which the critique of religion would hold a strategic position. Not implausibly, Schelling attributed the rise of philosophy to a sense of insecurity which made it necessary to seek to answer religious questions on an intellectual plane.

By the mid-1840s, the nominally Christian philosophical systems constructed on Kantian foundations by Hegel and his Idealist associates, Fichte, Schelling, and the enormously influential theologian Schleiermacher, were challenged by an uncoordinated group of radical thinkers, the Young Hegelians: so called on the basis of a distinction drawn by David Friedrich Strauss. In what was to become a bestseller of the period, *Das Leben Jesu (The Life of Jesus)* of 1835–6, Strauss applied the myth theory to the life of Christ and denied any historical foundation for the supernatural elements in the Gospels (the ensuing furore put an end to Strauss's academic career; only much later was it recognized that many of his tenets had been anticipated by Hegel himself in a series of frequently vitriolic theological essays, including a *Leben Jesu*, written before the end of the 18th century).

Still more disturbing was the impact of the embryonic psychology unleashed in Feuerbach's *Das Wesen des Christentums (The Essence of Christianity)* of 1841, in which religion was explained as a reification of human values and aspirations. The humanist revolt of the 40s was short-lived; but its implications were far-reaching. Even in the writings of such an essentially conservative Christian apologist as Kierkegaard, who purchased a copy of *The Essence of*

Christianity in Copenhagen on 24 March 1844, it was assumed that religious insight was to be obtained almost anywhere but in the dogmatic teachings of the Church. Theology, Feuerbach had argued, in so far as it contrived to demean man as a base, dependent creature and to confer perfection only on God, was the embodiment of a conspiracy against Christianity, an expression of hate rather than of love; an attack on the religious establishment, accordingly, was a prime religious duty.

The insurrection against ecclesiastical orthodoxy was carried to the heights of passion in the second half of the century by two thinkers whose concern, by and large, was the total destruction of religion as such. However far removed from the Young Hegelians' vision of an emancipated society, the Godless, religionless state conjured up by Marx came as an extension of the ideals which Feuerbach had enunciated (indeed, in *Die Heilige Familie* (*The Holy Family*) of 1844, Marx went to some lengths to acknowledge the debt, more fully discharged in the eleven *Thesen über Feuerbach* (*Theses on Feuerbach*) of 1845: according to Engels, the starting-point for what came to be known as Marxism). To an even greater extent, perhaps, the hybristic philosophy of the self-styled Antichrist, Nietzsche, had its roots in an instinctive aversion to modern bourgeois Christian society. In the vehement prose-poetry of *Also sprach Zarathustra* (*So Said Zarathustra*) – the 'Bible of the future', as Nietzsche dubbed it – the joyful tidings of the death of God were represented as the ultimate challenge to creativity in open defiance of Christian teaching: 'Dionysos *versus* the Crucified'. (Intellectually, Nietzsche's Dionysian man of the future or superman (*Übermensch*) is distanced from the free individual of Feuerbach's philosophy of the future by Darwin's *On the Origin of Species* (1859) and *The Descent of Man* (1871): scientific studies whose value at the time was assessed almost exclusively from the point of view of their theological consequences.)

Meanwhile, following the shameful indecisions of the Frankfurt Parliament of 1848 and reimposition of the German Confederation in 1850 – a triumph for Austrian diplomacy at Olmütz – the surrogate religion of nationalism personified in the Hohenzollern dynasty of Prussia was invoked to provide the focus for the spiritual aspirations of the nation dissipated by more than three centuries of religious conflict.

In the atmosphere of euphoria and relief that ensued upon Bismarck's victories in 1866, the resurgence of Catholic Ultramontanism was singularly inopportune. On his return to Rome from exile in 1850, the authoritarian Pope Pius IX embarked on a crusade against the subversive spirit of the age. The strengthening of the Jesuit order, the mainstay of the Curia; the issuing of the Syllabus of Errors of 1864 attacking the doctrines of progress, liberalism and modern civilization; and the First Vatican Council of 1870 with its definition of Papal Primacy and Infallibility – all these did nothing to heal the rift between German Protestants and Catholics, or to deter the Chancellor and his henchmen, Field-

Marshals Moltke and Roon, poised in readiness for war with France, from their policy of 'iron and blood' ('Eisen und Blut').

Retaliation in the form of the *Kulturkampf* (Cultural Purge) of the 70s was swift and even by Bismarck's standards drastic (with only partial success did the Chancellor attempt to pass these excesses off on his colleague Adalbert Falk). The suppression of the Catholic department of the Ministry of Public Worship and Education in 1871; the expulsion of the Jesuits in 1872; the enforcing of the May Laws of 1873 which limited the disciplinary powers of the Church and brought all seminaries under state supervision; the recalling of the German Ambassador to the Holy See; and the legislation of 1875 which deprived the Catholic Church of support from the imperial exchequer were all parts of a ruthless strategy aimed at asserting the primacy of the state and a mystical conception of nationhood.

Afterwards, the Peace Laws enacted during the pontificate of the conciliatory Leo XIII undid most of the illiberal and vindictive legislation of the *Kulturkampf* (except for the laws relating to the Jesuits). Not that the denominational dispute was at an end; for the late 1880s were to see the emergence of Beyschlag's Evangelischer Bund (Evangelical League) which, to the dismay of conservative intellectuals, would carry the isolationism, de-Westernization and de-Christianization of the Wilhelminian era forward into the 20th century. There was an outstanding irony in the fact that in 1890 Bismarck himself would be swept from office by his own protégé, the young Kaiser Wilhelm II, overcome by a manic sense of his divine prerogative.

ROGER HOLLINRAKE

Section 5

MUSICAL BACKGROUND AND INFLUENCES

Formation of the earlier style   64

The music drama and its antecedents   79

Patronage, commissions and royalties in Wagner's
*   day*   88

MUSICAL BACKGROUND AND INFLUENCES

In his mid-life autobiographical retrospective, *Eine Mitteilung an meine Freunde* (*A Communication to my Friends*, 1851), Wagner attributes all artistic creativity to 'the power of one's receptive capacity'. 'The first creative impulse', he continues, 'is nothing other than the satisfaction of an instinctive drive to imitate that which most strongly attracts us.' (GS IV, 246) It could be maintained, paradoxically, that the astounding originality of Wagner the mature musician is a direct consequence of the voracious appetite with which he consumed and digested the instrumental and operatic fare he encountered as a youth. As Carl Dahlhaus has suggested (1986), Wagner's career has provided music history with one of its classic biographical paradigms: an early phase of stylistic assimilation (the alternating influences of German Romantic opera, Italian bel canto, French *opéra comique* and grand opera) is followed by a period of concentrated, original development of internal resources (especially the period encompassing the composition of *Das Rheingold* up to *Tristan und Isolde*), culminating in the composer's own long-term influence on following generations. With Wagner, all three phases are especially pronounced. A discussion of 'background and influences' is primarily concerned with the first of these 'phases': the creative imagination responsible for the startlingly original 'music dramas' of the mature composer was, if we are to take Wagner at his word, heavily indebted to early impressions. The following section therefore focuses on the earlier stages of Wagner's career, up to about 1860, while also attempting to consider ways in which earlier models and influences continue to shape the later works.

Early years and musical training (1821–33)

Wagner's account of his earliest musical impressions in *Mein Leben* is at once entertaining and highly insightful. He clearly delighted in the artistic and theatrical milieu of his [step-?] father Ludwig Geyer, his uncle Adolf Wagner, his older brother Albert and his sisters Rosalie, Luise and Clara. The theatre and all its components attracted him: role-acting and expressive gesture, costumes, scenery and music all contributed to the representation of imaginary worlds. Music was at first merely an adjunct to such magical representations, but one whose potential power quickly dawned on the young boy. Initially attracted by the Romantically 'spooky' atmosphere of *Der Freischütz* as a drama, his fascination

Formation of the earlier style

64

with Weber's overture soon impelled him to acquire a rudimentary command of the piano. Similarly, it was the desire to deck out his grisly revenge tragedy *Leubald* with suitable incidental music (after the model of Beethoven's *Egmont*) that spurred him to the study of J.B. Logier's popular thoroughbass method in the hope of rapidly mastering the art of composition. Instruction in the fundamentals of harmony from a member of the Leipzig theatre orchestra, Gottlieb Müller, achieved little, as the pupil was too much immersed in the fantastic musical realm of E.T.A. Hoffmann's Kapellmeister Kreisler and the *Fantasiestücke* to submit to the sober rigours of conventional theory.

His reactions to the sustained unison C opening the *Freischütz* Overture or the famous oscillating open fifths beginning Beethoven's Ninth Symphony are further evidence of this thoroughly Romantic state of mind: these elemental sonorous effects inspired in the young enthusiast an awestruck admiration for the mysterious and 'demonic' powers of tone. One might accuse Wagner of self-conscious posing in such autobiographical descriptions, but the carefully copied piano arrangement of the Ninth Symphony (WWV 9, 1830–31) provides incontestable proof of this early enthusiasm, atypical of contemporary musical tastes at large. Elements of these two works and of Beethoven's *Coriolan* Overture were to resurface in the darkly brooding introduction and agitated main section (*sehr bewegt*) of the *Faust* Overture (WWV 59, 1839–40) and the Overture to *Der fliegende Holländer* (1841), with its open-fifth tremolo in the upper strings, as well as in an earlier Concert Overture in D minor (WWV 20, 1831).

Wagner himself might be partly to blame for the myth propagated by Nietzsche and others that he was essentially a musical dilettante, if a uniquely inspired one, who scraped together only enough technical expertise to realize the dramatic and scenic effects of his ultimately 'unmusical' *Gesamtkunstwerk*. The scores of even his earliest works – let alone those of *Tristan* or *Parsifal* – are sufficient to disprove this. Furthermore, the correspondence of this early period and numerous later reminiscences underscore the profoundly respectful debt Wagner acknowledged toward the Kanter of the Leipzig Thomaskirche, (Christian) Theodor Weinlig, from whom he received about half-a-year's formal training in harmony and counterpoint in the 'strict style' subsequent to the lessons from Müller. Otto Daube (1960) suggests that the composition of Walther's Prize Song under Sachs's guidance in Act III of *Die Meistersinger* can be seen as an affectionate homage to the teaching methods of old Weinlig.

Along with this dose of theoretical study Wagner had, by 1831, absorbed a fair sampling of the Viennese instrumental classics, just now in the first stages of 'canonization' as such. Besides the (still controversial) Ninth Symphony of Beethoven, he copied or arranged the scores of the Fifth Symphony, the *Egmont* Overture, Haydn's Symphonies nos. 103 and 104, and possibly other works as well. In return for his arrangement of the Ninth, although never published, Wagner received from B. Schott's Söhne in Mainz printed scores of that work, the *Missa Solemnis*, the string quartets op. 127 and op. 131, and Hummel's arrangements of other Beethoven symphonies. This early immersion in the music of Haydn, Mozart and especially Beethoven resulted in a variety of sonatas, overtures and most significantly the C major Symphony (WWV 29) of 1832. This last work reminded some of its early listeners of Beethoven's Seventh Symphony, particularly the propulsive rhythms of the first movement, with its broadly scaled slow introduction, and the intertwining of graceful melodic figuration and a steady, tread-like rhythmic foundation in the A minor Andante. The piece as a whole might remind modern listeners of Schubert, whose music seems to have been unknown to Wagner at this time, however. The grand proportions of this early symphony already signal the ambitious, monumental tendencies which would characterize his works at every stage.

A passion for the theatre had by no means been eclipsed, however, and upon assuming his first professional post as chorus master and assistant to his brother Albert at the Würzburg theatre, in early 1833, Wagner was hard at work on the 'grand Romantic opera' in three acts, *Die Feen*. As in the symphony and in the subsequent two operas – *Das Liebesverbot* (1835) and *Rienzi* (1838–40) – Wagner's ambition to outdo all of his models is unmistakably apparent in his first completed opera. The immediate models here are Weber's *Euryanthe* (likewise styled a *grosse romantische Oper*, without spoken dialogue) and *Oberon*. The supernatural, fairytale subject matter recalls something of the atmosphere of *Oberon* and the French *opéra féerie* cultivated in the early 19th century. This lighter style of dialogue opera, in both the German and French traditions, is here fused with the heroic-chivalric idiom of *Euryanthe*, with added emphasis given to the through-composed scene complex and the large-scale finale, found here in all three acts. Arindal's first scene and aria ('Wo find' ich dich, wo wird mir Trost?') follows closely the example of Lysiart's scene at the beginning of Act II of *Euryanthe* ('Wo berg' ich mich, wo find' ich Fassung wieder?') in its various phases of recitative, cantabile (arioso) and agitated aria (with stretta). The analogous solo scene for the fairy Ada in Act II suggests the influence of Leonore's great scene in Act I of *Fidelio*, and the text of Wagner's closing chorus ('Ein hohes Los hat er errungen . . ./ Drum sei's in Ewigkeit besungen') borrows directly from the second finale of Beethoven's opera in its diction and rhyme. Finally, the style of dramatic (accompanied) recitative and general melodic idiom are much indebted to Heinrich Marschner, whose *Der Vampyr* and recently created *Hans Heiling* Wagner helped stage in Würzburg. In a letter to Rosalie (11 Dec 1833) he describes the individual numbers of *Heiling* as 'very pretty' but criticizes the larger design – or lack of one – and what he feels are exceedingly weak endings to each of the acts. It is precisely this lack of larger, compelling dramatic and musical shape that continued to dissatisfy Wagner in the bulk of contemporary German opera, and which he sought to remedy: 'this might almost encourage me to entertain vain hopes about my own opera!', he adds optimistically.

Heiling shares with *Die Feen* and Wagner's later 'Romantic' operas of the 1840s the then popular motif of a supernatural being who longs for mortal union, but at the risk of tragic betrayal by the moral weakness of human nature. Interest in this theme of the Undine and Melusine stories was ripe just at this time and had recently received operatic treatment from E.T.A. Hoffmann and Conradin Kreutzer, among others (Lortzing's *Undine* followed in 1845). The inclusion of the comic servant pair, Gernot and Drolla, within a context of the supernatural and fantastic, recalls the tradition of the Viennese *Zauberposse* or semi-farcical magic play, still current in the plays of Ferdinand Raimund. Wagner had been favourably impressed by the vitality of the genre during his Viennese sojourn the previous summer (1832). The supernatural trials undergone by Wagner's hero, Arindal, in the Act II finale naturally remind one of the pre-eminent example of this tradition, Mozart's *Die Zauberflöte*, and the reunification duet of Gernot and Drolla evokes the world of Papageno and Papagena. This number, especially its closing 6/8 section, is Wagner's only essay in the style of the popular Singspiel, apart from an insertion aria for Carl Blum's comic opera *Mary, Max and Michel* (WWV 43, 1837).

Early career and Paris years (1833–42)

Wagner referred to the middle of the 1830s, in retrospect, as his artistic *Flegeljahre*, a period of sowing aesthetic 'wild oats'. This temporary degeneration of artistic goals and standards, as he later styled it, was to culminate in his attempt to outbid Meyerbeer and Halévy as master of grand opera spectacular in *Rienzi*. Whether or not one feels compelled to excuse this 'lapse' in the career of the future composer of world-redeeming music dramas, its significance in Wagner's development should not be underestimated. The writings from this period express a strong dissatisfaction with the state of contemporary German opera and a sense that what it especially lacked – effective dramatic construction and a proper appreciation of expressive vocal melody – might profitably be studied in French comic and grand opera as well as in the Italian bel canto repertory. The seeds of this rebellious phase (closely allied to Wagner's contemporaneous involvement with the intellectual-revolutionary Young German movement) might possibly be traced back to a visit to Vienna in 1832 when Wagner witnessed the unbounded local enthusiasm generated by Hérold's *Zampa*. A still more crucial experience was the performance of Wilhelmine Schröder-Devrient in Bellini's *I Capuleti e i Montecchi* at Leipzig in March 1834. Whatever the truth of Wagner's later claim that this singer's dramatically charged assumption of Beethoven's Leonore had already determined the future course of his entire career as early as 1829 (see 'Myths and Legends', p. 133), her Romeo unquestionably fired his enthusiasm for Bellini's art, as well as for the compelling theatricality of this unique dramatic soprano. Later references to the 1834 experience tend to diminish the role of Bellini's contribution while emphasizing Schröder-Devrient's magnetic musical stage presence. Acknowledging the strongly formulaic, conventionalized aspects of the Italian bel canto genre, he nonetheless saw it at this time as an antidote to the 'boundless disorder, confusion of forms and of periodic and harmonic structure in the works of so many recent German opera composers'. 'And indeed', he continues, 'our immediate perception of a single, entire dramatic passion on stage could be vastly facilitated by means of a *single* clear, well-formed melody rather than by hundreds of fragmented commentaries in the form of harmonic nuances or the disruptive interjections of this or that instrument.' (SS XII, 20) These opinions were no mere momentary aberration in the thought of this otherwise staunch cultural nationalist (not to say chauvinist): a number of passages in the later writings – e.g. *Über das Dirigieren* (*On Conducting*, 1869) – confirm his abiding belief in the importance of sustained linear projection in dramatic composition and in performance, and Wagner maintained (to Wolzogen) that he had learned from Bellini that which 'Herr Brahms and Co.' never had. On the other hand, the deprecation of the awkward, faltering expressive means of German opera, and the suddenly scathing attitude adopted toward *Euryanthe* at this time can surely be read also as a self-critique by the composer of *Die Feen*, now under the spell of Young German sensualism and wishing to shuck off his provincial roots. However different in style and character, *Das Liebesverbot* and *Rienzi* are both the products of a newly awakened cosmopolitan ideal which aimed to fuse the sensuous appeal of Bellinian melody with the vitality and grandeur of French genres and the native 'seriousness' of the German tradition.

The urge to synthesize what he found most effective in contemporary national styles was something Wagner, like others before him, characterized as a typically German impulse. In 1840 he was still willing to praise Meyerbeer along these lines, placing him in the tradition of such operatic masters as Handel, Gluck and Mozart. A repertory of mixed national products (normally sung in translation) was also characteristic of German theatres from the beginning of the century. It is reasonable to assume that the young musician's synthetic urge was due in part to his exposure to such varied operatic fare in the posts he occupied as theatrical music director up to 1839. The accompanying table (fig. 1) lists the repertory Wagner is known to have conducted or otherwise observed during his time in Würzburg, Magdeburg, Königsberg and Riga, and on other travels.

Fig. 1: *Wagner's operatic repertory in the 1830s*

Year	Location	Composer	Work
(rehearsed/conducted by Wagner)			
1833	Würzburg	Auber	*Le Maçon*
			La Muette de Portici
			Fra Diavolo
		Beethoven	*Fidelio*
		Boieldieu	*Jean de Paris*
			La Dame blanche
		Cherubini	*Les Deux Journées*
		Hérold	*Zampa*
		Marschner	*Der Vampyr*
			Hans Heiling
		Meyerbeer	*Robert le diable*
		Paer	*Camilla*
		Rossini	*Tancredi*
			Otello
		Weber	*Der Freischütz*
			Oberon
(attended by Wagner)			
1834–5	Leipzig	Auber	*Gustave III, ou Le Bal masqué*
			Le Philtre
		Bellini	*I Capuleti e i Montecchi*
1835	Nuremberg	Weigl	*Die Schweizerfamilie*
(rehearsed/conducted by Wagner)			
1834–6	Magdeburg	Auber	*Le Maçon*
			Fra Diavolo
			La Muette de Portici
			Lestocq
		Bellini	*La straniera*
			I Capuleti e i Montecchi
			Norma
			I puritani
		Beethoven	*Fidelio*
		Boieldieu	*La Dame blanche*
		Cherubini	*Les Deux Journées*
		Gläser	*Des Adlers Horst*
		Halévy	*La Juive*
		Hérold	*Zampa*
		Marschner	*Der Templer und die Jüdin*
		Mozart	*Don Giovanni*
		Paisiello	*La molinara*
		Rossini	*Tancredi*
			Il barbiere di Siviglia
			Otello
		Schenk	*Der Dorfbarbier*
		Spohr	*Jessonda*
		Weber	*Der Freischütz*
			Euryanthe
		Weigl	*Die Schweizerfamilie*

Year	Location	Composer	Work
(attended by Wagner)			
1836	Berlin	Spontini	*Fernand Cortez*
1836–7	Königsberg	Bellini	*Norma*
			I puritani
		Halévy	*La Juive*
1837	Dresden	Halévy	*La Juive*
		Spohr	*Jessonda*

(rehearsed/conducted by Wagner)			
1837–9	Riga	Adam	*Le Fidèle Berger*
			Le Postillon de Lonjumeau
		Auber	*Le Maçon*
			La Muette de Portici
			Fra Diavolo
		Beethoven	*Fidelio*
		Bellini	*I Capuleti e i Montecchi*
			Norma
		Boieldieu	*La Dame blanche*
		Cherubini	*Les Deux Journées*
		Dorn	*Der Schöffe von Paris*
		Hérold	*Zampa*
		Méhul	*Joseph*
		Meyerbeer	*Robert le diable*
		Mozart	*Die Entführung aus dem Serail*
			Le nozze di Figaro
			Don Giovanni
			Die Zauberflöte
		Rossini	*Il barbiere di Siviglia*
			Otello
		Spohr	*Jessonda*
		Weber	*Preciosa*
			Der Freischütz
			Oberon
		Weigl	*Die Schweizerfamilie*
		Winter	*Das unterbrochene Opferfest*

Italian and French influences

Das Liebesverbot is in many ways the logical outcome of these diverse impressions filtered through the ears and mind of an ambitious young Kapellmeister. In *A Communication to my Friends* Wagner describes the 'childish glee' he at first derived from conducting the fashionable Italian and especially French repertory of the time, with its flashy and beguiling orchestral effects (GS IV, 256). Such gleeful impressions are immediately reflected in the opening pages of the *Liebesverbot* Overture, with its battery of castanets, tambourine and triangle, along with the liberal application of woodwinds (including piccolo), brass and percussion throughout the score.

The portentous trombone tones of the Ban on Love motif itself are already a Wagnerian characteristic, however; this sound, like that of the brassy coda to the piece, is also to be found in several of the early concert overtures. It was to cost Wagner a considerable effort over the years to curb this tendency to over-orchestrate, as demonstrated in his repeated attempts to revise the score of *Der fliegende Holländer*.

Attempting to identify what is specifically Italianate in *Das Liebesverbot*, Friedrich Lippmann concludes: 'a great deal, yet nothing quite precisely'. Some coloratura writing still recalls that of Rossini, while exaggerating Rossini's use of chromatic auxiliary notes. Other lyrical profiles are modelled on Bellini (a tendency to linger on the third degree, approached from the lower fifth or from above by appoggiatura), while harmonic activity, orchestral texture and formal proportions are all greatly amplified. Melodic traits typical of the contemporary German 'lyrical' style are the use of an ornamental turn-figure and the ubiquitous melodic appoggiatura from the sixth to fifth degrees (both may conveniently be observed in the principal melody of Rienzi's famous Prayer).

More pronounced is the French influence, not only the *opéra comique* idiom of Auber's *Fra Diavolo* or Hérold's *Zampa* but also that of such early grand operas as Auber's *La Muette de Portici* (*Masaniello*) and Meyerbeer's *Robert le diable*. The ardent enthusiasm kindled in the young Wagner by *La Muette* was later recounted in his *Erinnerungen an Auber* (*Reminiscences of Auber*, 1871): '[. . .] the recitatives seemed to strike like lightning, the choral ensembles raged by like storm-clouds, and in the midst of this raging chaos a sudden admonition to calm contemplation would alternate with renewed calls-to-arms [. . .]. Just as the subject lacked for neither the most terrible nor the most tender details, Auber executed in his score every sort of contrast and mixture of formal outlines, imbuing it all with the most drastic and explicit coloration' (GS IX, 45). The theme of popular uprising against corrupt authorities in *Das Liebesverbot* and the transferral of Shakespeare's action to Sicily reflect the example of Scribe's libretto for *La Muette*, and perhaps of *Zampa* with its Sicilian pirates.

Auber's score also left its mark on that of *Das Liebesverbot*. The D major carnival scene and chorus beginning Wagner's Act II finale is nearly a *contrafactum* of Auber's lively Market Chorus in Act III (also in D), and the animated chorus of insurrection at the end of that act ('Courons à la vengeance') could be the model for a number of Wagner's crowd scenes. Indeed, despite the hedonistic carnival backdrop of *Das Liebesverbot* it often seems to aspire to the scope and pathos of grand opera, in the ostentatious breadth of its choral-ensemble scenes and in such extended lyric numbers as Friedrich's scene–cavatina–cabaletta complex in Act II or the Isabella–Luzio duet in Act I, with its *Rienzi*-like march rhythms and large-scale repetitions.

Among the *opéra comique* repertory Hérold's *Zampa* is much in evidence. A characteristic harmonic progression (I–I$_3^{5\sharp}$–IV$_4^6$ resolving to I, over a tonic pedal) – first heard in the main theme of the Overture and later in the Claudio–Isabella duet of Act II and Luzio's carnival song – occurs repeatedly in Hérold's opera as well (see Alphonse's aria 'Mes bons amis' in Act I, the sailors' chorus preceding it, or the ritornello to Zampa's aria 'Il faut céder à mes lois' in Act II). The ever-popular overture to *Zampa* is surely the prototype for Wagner's overture, both interrupting their rollicking main themes with abrupt gestures of warning. In such purely comic numbers as those of the stock figures of Brighella and Dorella we find Wagner adopting the idiom of Hérold or Auber at their most frivolous. Yet even here he attempts to expand their limited harmonic range while capitalizing on Auber's manner of conversational declamation over continuous motivic accompaniment to create larger, more fluid forms.

Rienzi, Paris and French grand opera

Parisian grand opera was unquestionably the dominant new musical genre of the 1830s. The productions of Eugène Scribe and his principal collaborators (Auber, Halévy, Meyerbeer) travelled worldwide and profoundly influenced more than one generation of opera composers. The impact on Wagner is most obvious in his own essay in the genre – *Rienzi* – but its dramaturgical and even musical repercussions are evident to some degree in every work up to *Parsifal* (Gutman, 1968). The vehemence of Wagner's attack on the genre, as personified by Meyerbeer, in *Oper und Drama* (*Opera and Drama*) seems to betray a characteristic fear and loathing of his own origins (like the earlier critique of *Euryanthe*), while at the same time underscoring the immense transformation the genre had truly undergone in Wagner's hands in the meantime.

Rienzi (1838–40) stands in the same relation to Halévy and Meyerbeer as *Das Liebesverbot* did to the models of Bellini and Auber in its unbridled ambition to outstrip them. In *Mein Leben* Wagner mentions the eye- and ear-opening experience of an 1836 Berlin production of Spontini's *Fernand Cortez* under the exacting direction of its composer. Another decisive influence was probably Halévy's *La Juive*, which he heard first in Königsberg and soon afterwards, in what must have been a considerably more adequate production, in Dresden. *Rienzi*, with its latter-day Roman heroics, attempts to synthesize the classicizing, neo-Gluckian pomp and rhetoric of Spontini's *premier empire* operas with the more up-to-date idioms of Halévy and Meyerbeer.

Despite Hans von Bülow's *bon mot* that *Rienzi* is 'Meyerbeer's best opera', there is little in the score that can be identified as specifically Meyerbeerian. At the notion that anything at all could be called 'Meyerbeerian' Wagner vehemently protested in a letter to Schumann of 1843 (echoing Schumann's own sentiments, in fact, as expressed in his well-known review of *Les Huguenots*). But the ideal of cosmopolitan eclecticism was not yet anathema to Wagner in 1839. Several essays from this period – including a posthumously published panegyric on *Les Huguenots* (SS XII) – prove quite the opposite; whatever doubts Wagner later came to have about the value of *Rienzi*, it was not composed in a spirit of cynicism. Its stylistic ingredients are the Spontini heroic march type (used in instrumental, solo and choral contexts); a cantabile style related to that of Weber, Marschner and Spohr, featuring liberal use of the turn-figure mentioned above; energetic cabaletta movements in the modern Franco-Italian style; and grandiose finale tableaux built up along the lines of those in *La Juive*. On top of these is the tendency for increased harmonic activity as a means of expressive intensification, already encountered in *Liebesverbot*, often entailing Wagner's besetting abuse of diminished-seventh harmonies and string tremolo. The orchestration is consistently fuller and more homogeneous than that of Meyerbeer, and closer, again, to Halévy. (Meyerbeer approached the orchestra more in the spirit of Berlioz, continually experimenting with contrasting sonorities and textures.) While Wagner was deeply impressed by the performances of Berlioz's music he heard in Paris (and had the opportunity to read in the *Revue et Gazette Musicale* excerpts from what was to become the famous treatise on orchestration), it would take at least another decade or more for the lesson to sink in (Voss, 1970). Wagner seems to have felt a genuine distaste for one feature of Meyerbeer's style (or Berlioz's, for that matter): the frequent alternation of triple and compound metres with common duple time. While *Rienzi*, like *Lohengrin*, maintains a stolid 4/4 for nearly the entire duration of its five acts, Act I alone of *Les Huguenots* includes sections in 12/8, 4/4, 3/4, 2/4, 3/8, and 9/8. Here again it would take Wagner some time to break loose of the metrical straitjacket of his earlier style. Only with the *Ring* does he begin to allow a wider variety of metres to permeate his music, now mediating subtly between them, avoiding the sense of a merely 'calculated' variety of which he would no doubt have accused Meyerbeer.

Several critics, beginning with Paul Bekker (1924), have commented on the greater psychological depth and musical finesse of the latter three acts of *Rienzi*, those composed after arriving in Paris. Something of this could be attributed to new musical experiences in the French metropolis; it is possible that he was not familiar with the music of *Les Huguenots*, for instance, until this time. But his protracted work on assorted arrangements of Donizetti's *La Favorite* and Halévy's *La Reine de Chypre* came too late to have any influence on his own opera, and the former work had little appeal for him, in any case. In fact, if we are to believe Wagner's own testimony, the crucial experiences of this period were of a quite different nature: performances of Beethoven's symphonies by the Conservatoire orchestra under François Habeneck (in particular the first three movements of the Ninth) and his first exposure to the music of Berlioz – the *Symphonie fantastique*, *Roméo et Juliette*, and the recently composed *Symphonie funèbre et triomphale* (1840). In his letters to the Dresden *Abend-Zeitung* it is this last work, strangely enough, which Wagner singles out for the greatest praise, while he remained ambivalent about the 'extravagant' style of this composer in general. In any case, the level of performance Wagner encountered in Paris – at the Opéra or the Conservatoire concerts – came as a revelation. The standards here were far beyond anything he had experienced, including the Leipzig Gewandhaus concerts of a decade earlier (before the advent of Mendelssohn). In *Mein Leben* he admits that Berlioz's concerts literally 'overwhelmed' him: the 'boldness and precision' of the orchestral playing elicited by the composer left him numb. Wagner's plans for a symphony on the subject of *Faust* – eventually scaled down to the one-movement *Faust* Overture – would seem to have been the product of joint impressions of Beethoven's Ninth and Berlioz's 'dramatic symphony' after Shakespeare.

The 'Romantic operas' as generic and stylistic synthesis (Dresden 1842–9)

Alluding to his short story of early 1841, *Ein Ende in Paris* (*An End in Paris*), Wagner later maintained that the young composer who had come to conquer the Parisian stage with his grand historical opera had indeed died, in spirit (GS IV, 263). In many respects *Der fliegende Holländer* would seem to confirm this demise of the would-be rival of Meyerbeer. But several points are worth considering with regard to the background of the three 'Romantic operas' of the 1840s: *Holländer*, *Tannhäuser* and *Lohengrin*. The designation 'Romantic' implies that they belong to a German rather than French tradition. But the *Holländer* was originally conceived for the Paris Opéra, albeit as a curtain-raiser in one act rather than as a full five-act spectacle. Wagner may have thought to turn this limited format to advantage as an experiment in dramatic concision and musical unity; but he clearly would have taken full advantage of French orchestral skills, while the stormy atmosphere and the 'phantom vessel' of the story would also offer choice opportunities for the celebrated stage machinery of the establishment on the rue Le Peletier. Wagner had been mightily impressed, along with all the bourgeois Parisian philistines, by the thrilling *mises-en-scène* devised by Duponchel, Monnais, Pillet and their staff. His next two operas were not composed until after *Rienzi* had been vindicated by its tremendous success at the Dresden Court Opera; by that time Wagner had reason for thinking twice about the wisdom of rejecting out of hand anything and everything pertaining to French grand opera.

In the letter to Schumann mentioned above (25 February 1843) Wagner protested vehemently against the notion that *Der fliegende Holländer* contained elements of Meyerbeer. This is the first in a series of such protestations that would culminate in the scurrilous attacks on that composer in *Das Judentum in der Musik* (*Jewishness in Music*, 1850) and *Opera and Drama* (1851). A letter to Eduard Hanslick of 1 January 1847 (prior to the onset of *that* much publicized mutual antipathy) represents a mid-point in this escalation of hostility: here the composer of *Tannhäuser* explains to the young critic the 'world of difference' between his art and Meyerbeer's commercial productions. Did the man protest too much? The subsequent development of Wagner's style explains something of the motivation behind these attacks, if not everything. Wagner had indeed been trying to revise the aesthetic foundations of his grand opera models during the 1840s, and the protracted, even psychologically painful gestation of a radical new approach in the *Ring* led the frustrated, compositionally inactive exile to lash out at a style he was determined to leave far behind. But such ranting polemics might well have puzzled an observer of around 1850.

Der fliegende Holländer is traditionally identified as a return to Wagner's 'roots' in the German Romantic tradition of Weber, Spohr and Marschner. The 'Romantic' opera fostered by these composers and such lesser colleagues as Kreutzer, Lindpaintner, Gläser, Dorn, *et al.* in the 1820s and 30s was as much indebted to the Revolutionary and post-Revolutionary *opéra comique* – particularly the works of Cherubini, Méhul, Nicolò Isouard and Boieldieu – as to any continuous vernacular Singspiel tradition. The origins of the *Holländer* in such isolated 'character' numbers as Senta's Ballad, the Norwegian Sailors' Chorus and that of the Dutchman's spectral crew betray its debt to this older Franco-German tradition. Wagner had criticized the more ambitious works of his German predecessors, such as *Euryanthe*, *Jessonda*, or Marschner's operas, for their musical shortwindedness, fussy attempts at harmonic expressivity, and a lack of broad dramatic-musical pacing, even where they aimed at increased continuity between numbers. In Auber's *Muette de Portici*, on the other hand, or the fourth act of *Les Huguenots* (with the 'Benediction of the Daggers' and the climactic Valentine–Raoul duet), he admired the vivid integration of chorus in the action, the evocation of historical and local colour, and the 'large bold strokes' with which these composers, like Halévy, executed their large-scale dramatic tableaux. If from the 1840s on Wagner's rhetoric became increasingly nationalistic and anti-French, it would be a mistake to believe that he had purged himself of all 'foreign' influences. Rather, they had been fully absorbed into his system.

Senta's Ballad – the thematic 'kernel' of *Der fliegende Holländer*, Wagner later claimed – has numerous precedents in both French and German works of the previous generation. Most prominent would be Jenny's Ballad, 'D'ici voyez ce beau domaine', from Boieldieu's immensely popular *La Dame blanche*, and Emmy's *Romanze*, 'Sieh, Mutter, dort den bleichen Mann', from Marschner's *Der Vampyr*. Like Wagner's number, both are quasi-folk ballads of eerie Romantic colouring, and both include a choral refrain. Also like Senta's Ballad, their narrative content has a direct bearing on the action, describing a mysterious otherworldly figure who will soon appear. Another prototype could be Raimbaud's

Ballad in Act I of *Robert le diable* ('Jadis régnait en Normandie'). Again, the tale of a sinister, demonic figure is recounted, and here to folklike 6/8 rhythms not unlike those of Senta's song. As in Marschner and Wagner, this figure reveals himself upon the conclusion of the ballad. Raimbaud's Ballad reverses the musical character of verse and refrain, beginning innocently in C major followed by a shuddering C minor refrain, perhaps not without a touch of irony. But the second and third verses are sung to an increasingly active and chromaticized accompaniment, the third verse ('De cet hymen épouvantable') also subsuming the shuddering rhythmic figure of the refrain. The process presumably reflects the mounting tension of the situation, in which the diabolical duke Robert stands by while hearing his character defamed. It presents a striking analogy with Wagner's treatment of the jejune C major Sailors' Chorus in Act III, since it likewise entails the provocation of a sinister element which finally responds in violent eruption. An earlier precedent might be the bridal-wreath chorus in *Der Freischütz*. Another C major refrain is harmonically destabilized, here diverted to a sombre A minor close after an ill-omened funeral wreath is brought to the scene by accident. However, Meyerbeer anticipates Wagner in a way that Weber does not: Raimbaud's Ballad is used as a reminiscence motif throughout Act I and again near the end of the opera.

Of the two most widely admired qualities of *Der fliegende Holländer* – its dramatic concision and musical continuity – the first may be attributed to Wagner's own innovative conception, but the second still owes much to the example of French grand opera. The choral-ensemble 'Introduction' encompassing smaller solo forms (here the Steersman's Song) had long been a feature of French and Italian opera, as in the opening scene of *Robert le diable* with its Ballad, just discussed. And the tendency to link nominally independent numbers into musically continuous complexes – as in the 'scene, duet and chorus' ending Act I of the *Holländer*, the 'aria, duet and trio' (Daland, Senta and the Dutchman) comprising the Act II finale, or the duet, cavatina and ensemble scene with which the opera closes – derives principally from the example of Halévy and Meyerbeer. Typically, the later acts of their operas (and many modelled after them, including *Rienzi*) will contain only two or three musical divisions, with little or no break between them. Act IV of *Les Huguenots* was one such model particularly admired by Wagner, as mentioned, for the controlled dramatic intensification of the long 'Benediction of the Daggers' ensemble leading into the highly charged *Grand duo*, 'Tu l'as dit'.

Tannhäuser and *Lohengrin* are even more clearly the product of this synthesis of German and French generic and formal models. Apart from the Tristanesque revisions of the Bacchanal and of Venus's role, there is little in the *Tannhäuser* score that should have disturbed the sensibilities of Parisian audiences in 1861. The elimination of officially designated numbers in favour of dramatic scenes was a significant gesture, historically, but hardly obscures

the identity of Elisabeth's Hall of Song Aria in Act II ('Dich teure
Halle'), or of her *preghiera* ('Allmächt'ge Jungfrau!') or Wolfram's
Romanze ('O Du mein holder Abendstern') in Act III. Tannhäuser's reunion with his fellow *Minnesänger* in Act I scene 4 and the
song-contest in Act II are easily recognized as conventional finale
structures. The entry of the guests to a multi-sectional 'grand
march' and Tannhäuser's catastrophic interruption of the decorous ceremonial proceedings (the song-contest) followed by a
turbulent ensemble, an expiatory prayer (Elisabeth's intercession)
and a chain of elaborately textured choral-ensemble units, all have
precedents in the grand opera repertory, and continued to be
imitated almost to the end of the century. Two earlier examples of
the interrupted ceremonial scene well known to Wagner were the
Act I finale of Spontini's *Olympie* (1819, rev. Berlin 1821 and Paris
1826) and that of Auber's *La Muette de Portici*, where Fenella
suddenly recognizes the identity of her noble seducer. In the Act
III finale of *La Juive* (1835) Rachel similarly recognizes and
denounces Prince Léopold in the midst of public festivities,
initiating a particularly elaborate series of ensemble sections. (The
locus classicus of this finale type – the coronation scene of Scribe's
and Meyerbeer's *Le Prophète* – had not yet reached the stage.) This
familiar situation, and its concomitant musical types of religious
processional, agitated ensemble *scena* and massed choral response,
is encountered again in Act II scene 4 of *Lohengrin*, where Elsa's
stately procession to the minster is interrupted by the treacherous
Ortrud. The analogous scene in *Götterdämmerung* (Act II scene 4) is
based on the same elements, here a double wedding scene,
interrupted by the outraged Brünnhilde upon recognizing the ring
on Siegfried's hand. Such a piece of grand-operatic dramaturgy is
less surprising when we recall that it had originally been drafted in
1848.

There is little evidence that Wagner was much influenced by the
newer repertory introduced at the Dresden theatre during the time
of his employment there. The operas of Ferdinand Hiller premiered at Dresden (*Der Traum in der Christnacht*, 1845, *Konradin, der
letzte Hohenstaufen*, 1847) failed to fire the enthusiasm of the public
at large, let alone of Wagner (although the latter opera did
coincide with his continuing preoccupation with the Hohenstaufen
dynasty, manifested in the plans for *Die Sarazenin* and *Friedrich I.*
and in the *Wibelungen* essay of 1849). He felt compelled to decline,
as tactfully as he could, Spohr's latest opera, *Die Kreuzfahrer* (1845),
which the composer had submitted to the Dresden theatre: despite
the fact that the work had evidently been influenced by Spohr's
own experiences of Wagner's music, it did not impress the younger
composer favourably. Marschner's *Kaiser Adolph von Nassau*, given
its first performance by Wagner in 1845, elicited no more than a
faintly disguised contempt for its reliance on a feeble *Männerchor* or
glee-club idiom mixed with cheap Italianisms – especially a
'revenge' ensemble and stretta whose 'amateurishness and vulgar-
ity' would have shamed even the 'humblest pupil of Donizetti'

(*Mein Leben*). The operas of his colleague Karl Gottlieb Reissiger (1798–1859) were of no greater interest to him.

On the other hand, a newly-awakened interest in the Classical tradition of Gluck and Spontini seems to have had an impact on *Lohengrin*, perhaps corresponding also to Wagner's growing fascination with classical Greek drama during the 1840s. The first stimulus in this direction was partly fortuitous. He was entrusted with a revival of Gluck's *Armide* as his first assignment in Dresden, and the next year he invited the aging Spontini to guest-conduct *La Vestale*. His success with *Armide* led to more Gluck productions, most significantly a comprehensive revision of *Iphigénie en Aulide*. The characterization of Iphigénie's noble, affecting dignity by means of blended woodwind-choir accompaniments in Act III (somewhat retouched by Wagner) seems to have left its mark on the role of Elsa in *Lohengrin*, although it is evident already in parts of Elisabeth's music, too. Spontini's influence may be detected on a more general level in the atmosphere of 'restrained' grandeur which noticeably departs from the more hectic, pointed contrasts of later grand opera prototypes, or from Wagner's earlier works, for that matter. Berlioz had already noted the generic resemblance of the 'Marche triomphale et choeur' of Spontini's *Olympie* to the music of *Rienzi* upon hearing the latter opera in 1843. The lengthy orchestral lead-in of Spontini's march couples a sustained crescendo with a gradual amplification of instrumental texture, based on a continual reiteration of tonic harmonies, the chorus entering at first *piano*, but then bursting forth in triple *forte* at its second entrance ('O triomphe, gloire immortelle'). A strikingly similar effect is achieved at the opening of Act II scene 3 of *Lohengrin*, where it also serves as atmospheric transition from the brooding nocturnal atmosphere of the previous scenes to the festive atmosphere of the new day. Wagner's effect is based on a long series of D major fanfares, first offstage and later in the orchestra, over a sustained tonic pedal. The climactic 'breakthrough' here occurs with a stepwise modulation out to C major (♭VII), accompanied not by chorus (as in Spontini) but by the heraldic trumpet calls already familiar from Act I. (This experiment with timbral, spatial and rhythmic elements within a static harmonic field anticipates the even bolder experiment of the Prelude to *Das Rheingold*.) Wagner also commented later in life that the jubilant finale to Act I of *Lohengrin*, with its forward-driving momentum, owed much more to the example of Spontini than to Weber.

The formulation of this comment (recorded by both Hans von Wolzogen and Cosima) betrays his sensitivity to the palpable presence of Weber's *Euryanthe* elsewhere in *Lohengrin*. These correspondences have long been noted (see Tusa, 1985–6, for the most recent and extensive comparison). In many respects Wagner strengthened the dramatic relationships and situations he borrowed from Helmine von Chezy's notorious libretto. Most prominent among these parallels is that between the pure, candid heroine (Euryanthe, Elsa) and her insidious, scheming rival

(Eglantine, Ortrud). The second act of each opera opens with a scene between the dark-hued soprano villainess and the low-voice male accomplice she has ensnared (Lysiart, Telramund), who bemoans his disgraced position in a vehement 'rage' aria. The two conspire, in each case, in a recitative *scena* followed by a vengeance-swearing duet, each to similar accompaniments on low brass and with tremolo or repeated-note string figures. The motivic material associated with the 'parallel' characters, Eglantine and Ortrud, is that most extensively recalled and transformed in each opera (see below).

To a limited extent, the accompanied recitative and arioso styles of Weber's opera inform Wagner's much freer application of these styles in all of his 'Romantic' operas. But much else derives from the example of French grand opera. One might say that the contrast between *Euryanthe* and these later French models, and the attempt to synthesize elements from both, taught Wagner the crucial lesson he would soon attempt to verbalize in his theoretical writings – that large, coherent and 'dramatic' musical forms might be written into the libretto itself, and that the best dramatic poet, from the composer's point of view, is one who is at the same time a 'musician'.

The music drama and its antecedents

Reminiscence motif and leitmotif

THE ORIGINS OF Wagner's most celebrated and controversial innovation, the so-called 'leitmotif', have been much discussed over the years. Generally accepted now is a distinction between the 'true' leitmotif technique of Wagner's mature works and the older tradition of 'reminiscence' motifs of various types which can be traced back to the later 18th century. Wagner's real innovation, beginning with *Das Rheingold*, was the creation of a continuous musical 'fabric' woven more or less consistently from motivic ideas introduced – either in the orchestra or in the vocal part – in such a way as to establish certain dramatic, emotional, visual or conceptual associations. In the 'music dramas' of the mature period musical form is determined above all by motivic incidence, transformation and development, in conjunction with such other factors as tonality, tempo and even instrumentation. All of these, in turn, are determined to some extent by the dramatic structure itself. The reminiscence motif, on the other hand, exists largely outside the structure of closed musical numbers, or involves the repetition of some discrete portion (from a phrase to a whole strophe or other section) of a set number elsewhere in the opera – often in the context of recitative, arioso or melodrama. (The status of Wagner's own motivic procedures in the works of the 1840s falls somewhere in between.)

Among the earliest examples of reminiscence motif usually cited are those from the *opéra comique* tradition. Grétry's *Richard Coeur-de-lion* (1784) is well known for the way in which Blondel's *romance*,

'Une fièvre brûlante', is brought back no fewer than eight times in varying guises, and integrated into the progress of the action. Cherubini made similar use of the ballad 'Un pauvre petit Savoyard' in *Les Deux Journées* (1800). Winton Dean (1982) discusses earlier examples of recurring associative figures in works by J.B. Lemoyne (*Electre*, 1782) and Méhul (*Euphrosine*, 1790, *Mélidore et Phrosine*, 1794, and *Ariodant*, 1799). Aside from *Les Deux Journées*, most of these works were probably not familiar to Wagner, although he was quite fond of Méhul's *Joseph*, which remained in the repertory of smaller German theatres well into the 19th century.

In Germany the reminiscence motif can be traced back to the *Melodram* ('melodrama', i.e. spoken drama or pantomime with a musical score) of the later 1770s (Abbé Vogler's *Lampedo* and Reichardt's *Ino*, both 1779), as well as Singspiels by Georg Benda, C.G. Neefe, Wenzel Müller and Peter von Winter (Wörner, 1931–2). In some cases the scope of the musical reminiscence was very limited, as with the three 'Masonic' chords in Mozart's *Zauberflöte* or similar 'quotations' within *Idomeneo*, *Figaro* and *Così fan tutte*. Melodrama, pantomime and accompanied recitative are significant in the development of musical reminiscence and leitmotif on a more general level in that they emphasize the role of short, plastic, expressive orchestral gestures to accompany stage action and to convey the expression of 'mute' feelings as direct musical discourse.

Again, with the exception of Mozart, few if any of these works would have had any direct impact on Wagner. More significant by far is the varied use of reminiscence motif by Weber. Weber had no doubt absorbed some ideas here not only from the German Singspiel and melodrama – he was familiar with Hoffmann's experiments in this direction in *Undine* – but also from the contemporary *opéra comique* repertory, which he knew well. In Louis Spohr's *Faust*, first conducted by Weber in Prague in 1816, he admired the 'felicitous and well-wrought' application of 'certain melodies running through the whole [score] like delicate threads and lending it a sense of artistic unity.' In these words Weber strikingly anticipates the language of Wagner's own theoretical writings with regard to the role of musical motifs or *Grundthemen* in the music drama.

Weber himself codified the practice of constructing the overture from thematic material prominent in the opera. The implications of Weber's procedures are clearly reflected in melodic, stylistic and structural details of Wagner's overtures from *Die Feen* to *Tannhäuser* (the curtailment of the recapitulation in favour of a triumphant transformation of second-theme material in the coda, for instance). The use of a specific harmonic configuration as 'motif' in *Freischütz* – the incomplete diminished-seventh chord, filled in by offbeat strokes on the timpani and bass, associated with Samiel – has important consequences for Wagner's motivic technique, most obviously in the leitmotivic status of the '*Tristan* chord', but also in such primarily harmonic motifs as that of the Tarnhelm and its variant associated with Gutrune's 'brainwashing' potion in the *Ring*.

Associative instrumental timbres such as those of Samiel's chord (tremolo strings, timpani) or the shrill, mocking piccolo figure in Caspar's Lied (imitated by Marschner in a recurrent gesture of 'infernal laughter' in *Der Vampyr*) also had an impact on Wagner's procedures, which frequently involve the association of characteristic timbres (and often concomitant keys) with individuals or broader dramatic levels. The high, soft woodwind accompaniments of Senta, Elisabeth and Elsa have been mentioned. Similar timbral groupings – also featuring clarinet, bassoon and high-register cello – associated with Weber's heroines Agathe and Euryanthe, are characteristic of Brünnhilde's music in *Siegfried* Act III and in parts of *Götterdämmerung* (see especially the transition to the Brünnhilde–Waltraute scene in Act I). Brass fanfares and horn calls naturally connote aspects of the outer, 'public' world so often played off against private conflicts in opera. The popular hunting choruses in both of Weber's best-known operas serve this function, as do similar hunting choruses and regal fanfares in many French operas. Prominent instances in Wagner's works include the various public assemblies in *Lohengrin*, with the abundant use of stage trumpets, the traumatic moment of arrival in Cornwall closing Act I of *Tristan und Isolde*, and the offstage hunting party in Act II, where the typical horn-call figures are manipulated with great sophistication. The use of brass and especially trombone choir in sacred, chorale-style contexts in *Tannhäuser* and *Parsifal* has numerous operatic precedents, in addition to German church music practice since the 17th and 18th centuries.

Various types of reminiscence motif had been sporadically, but increasingly, employed by French and German composers from 1800, and also in Italian opera from Rossini onwards, typically involving the repetition of a lyrical phrase from a set number (romanza, cavatina, etc.) in the context of a recitative or *scena*. By the 1840s the technique was widespread. It is applied, more or less extensively, in works by Lindpaintner (*Die Genueserin*, 1838), Reissiger (*Adèle de Foix*, 1841), Lortzing (*Hans Sachs*, 1840, *Casanova*, 1841, and especially *Undine*, 1845, and *Rolands Knappen*, 1849), Franz Lachner (*Catarina Cornaro*, 1841), Flotow (*Alessandro Stradella*, 1844, and *Martha*, 1847), and the later works of Spohr and Marschner, to mention only instances from the German repertory. Thus Wagner's development of the technique of associative motifs should be seen as an extension, if uniquely ambitious in scope, of contemporary practices. There is little evidence of his own influence on other composers before the 1850s, with the exception of the few who had direct contact with his Dresden operas: Reissiger, Spohr and Schumann, whose *Genoveva* (composed 1848) comes perhaps closest to Wagner's mature leitmotif technique of any work up to that time.

What distinguishes Schumann's and Wagner's technique from most others is not merely the higher incidence of motivic recurrence, but also the extent of motivic transformation and development in accordance with dramatic or psychological context and, consequently, overall integration. Aside from the new form-defining role of leitmotif in Wagner's mature works, this reflection of mutable, dynamic emotional and psychological processes in motivic transformation is his most crucial innovation. Again, Weber seems to have shown the way. The serpentine semiquaver string figure suggesting Eglantine's duplicitous character upon her first appearance in *Euryanthe* (Recitative: 'So einsam bangend find' ich dich?') is variously developed throughout the opera: as the accompaniment to the subsequent aria (no. 6), again in the recitative and aria sections of her solo scene, 'Betörte! die an meine Liebe glaubt' (no. 8), and briefly in Act III (no. 19). Another principal reminiscence motif of the opera – the striking passage for divided upper strings associated with the apparition of Emma's ghost – returns one last time at the joyful conclusion of the opera, transposed to C major with its originally bold chromatic part-writing now diatonically transformed. It is open to question, however, whether all the variants of Oberon's horn call cited by John Warrack (1968) can be traced to the original rising major third, as first heard in the overture.

Finally, a few French precedents familiar to Wagner might also be mentioned. Best known, of course, is the *idée fixe* of Berlioz's *Symphonie fantastique*, transformed as waltz-trio, lyrical interlude, psychological 'flashback' and grotesque parody. Wagner may also have been aware of *Harold en Italie*, with its pensive viola theme woven into the predominantly orchestral texture of each movement. Besides Raimbaud's Ballad in *Robert le diable*, mentioned earlier, Meyerbeer used the famous chorale, *Ein' feste Burg* in a variety of transformations in *Les Huguenots*. The pseudo-Catholic chant *Ad nos, ad salutarem undam* is treated similarly in *Le Prophète*. Among other composers, Halévy made effective use of transformed reminiscences of a *romance* in *Guido et Ginevra* (1838), his most recent success at the time Wagner first arrived in Paris. The D♭ tune to which Guido sings of his first encounter with the unknown beauty (Ginevra) is transposed and rhythmically transformed in a later scene (Recitative, no. 16) where he believes he finds her dead in the Medici crypt. The theme is more extensively developed (through E, B♭ and G) in the Scene and Duet (no. 22) in which Ginevra is eventually revived. (The situation recalls another Berliozian transformation, the delirious return of the principal thematic group of the 'Scène d'amour' in *Roméo et Juliette* during the orchestral 'pantomime' of Roméo in the Capulets' crypt.)

The role of Beethoven

Without a doubt, the figure looming largest in Wagner's musical background is Beethoven (see also 'The Beethoven legacy', pp. 151–3). The same is true for other composers of the period, of course (notably Brahms), but a crucial distinction is the fact that Wagner was exclusively a composer of opera – the instrumental juvenilia and unrealized symphonic plans of his last years notwithstanding. Already in the Parisian novella *Eine Pilgerfahrt zu Beethoven* (*A Pilgrimage to Beethoven*, 1840) Wagner had anticipated a *Grundmotiv* of his later theoretical writings – the reconciliation of opera with the principles of the Beethovenian symphony – in a visionary synthesis, an ideal 'combined' or 'total artwork', as he later dubbed it. In a later context (1860), reflecting on the 'aesthetic conversion' of his Parisian period, Wagner spoke of his growing conviction at that time that 'the mighty current to which Beethoven had swelled the course of German music might be channelled into the bed of the musical drama' (GS VII, 87).

Already in 1840 the theoretical model for this diversion of the musical *Weltgeist* from instrumental to vocal genres was Beethoven's Ninth Symphony. The Ninth was the one work, aside from his own, with which Wagner was most deeply involved over the course of his lifetime. It had preoccupied him as a child in the 1820s and it 'brought him to his senses' as a wayward youth in Paris around 1840. The performances he conducted in Dresden between 1846 and 1849 represented a high-point in his career there, as well as fanning the flames of revolutionary ardour, some believed. Less successful was his performance of the piece at a concert of the Philharmonic Society in London in March 1855. But his last performance of the Ninth, a symbolic gesture to celebrate the laying of the cornerstone of the Bayreuth Festspielhaus in 1872, was a crowning achievement. A consequence of this latter occasion was the detailed essay *Zum Vortrag der neunten Symphonie Beethovens* (*On Performing Beethoven's Ninth Symphony*, 1873). He had discussed the work from a practical perspective in *On Conducting* (1869) and from a theoretical perspective in the Zurich writings of 1849–51, where it figures as a kind of scriptural prophecy of the musical-dramatic 'artwork of the future'. Wagner conducted other Beethoven symphonies (the Third to the Eighth) repeatedly from the Dresden period until the 1870s. And Cosima's Diaries offer ample evidence of the frequency with which all the major instrumental works were played and discussed in the Wagner household circle at Tribschen and Bayreuth.

Despite this intimate and prolonged involvement with the music of Beethoven, its direct impact on Wagner's music is not easily ascertained. Beethoven's influence on the 'style' or structure of the operas at all remains a moot point; in any case, it is not primarily manifested in surface resemblances. Among the examples adduced by Kropfinger in his study of the subject (1975), thematic 'echoes' of Beethoven are limited almost entirely to the early works: the piano pieces, overtures and C major Symphony. When Wagner returned to the Beethovenian 'source' later in life, his musical style had since been shaped by forces closer to hand (the many operatic models we have noted). Whatever inspiration he drew from this renewed contact with Beethoven had to be sublimated in accordance with the demands of the dramatic genre. Correspondences between Beethoven's music and Wagner's later operas exist therefore not so much on either the thematic or the structural level, but more abstractly. Those cited by Kropfinger between the String Quartet op. 132 and passages from *Tristan* and *Die Meistersinger*, for instance, involve similar rhythmic stratification of accompaniment textures and aspects of their metrical placement. One more immediate textural and rhythmic correspondence may be heard between the opening bars of the Adagio of the String Quartet op. 127 (one of Wagner's favourite works) and those of the love scene in Act II of *Tristan*, 'O sink' hernieder, Nacht der Liebe', with their gently pulsating background harmonies gradually emerging from a sustained E♭ in cello and viola parts. Wagner considered rhythm to be the most characteristic field of Beethoven's innovations, and the halting, stifled rhythms that accompany Alberich's curse in *Das Rheingold* or Hagen's 'dream' in *Götterdämmerung*, Act II scene 1, might owe something to Beethoven's love of displaced accent and metre (see for example the first movement of the A major Sonata, op. 101).

The closest point of identification with Beethoven in Wagner's own mind, however, was 'melody' – again on an abstract level, encompassing principles of motivic organization and development. By breaking down the schematic framework of Classical periodicity Beethoven, he claimed, was able to leave behind all the empty, polite formulas of the traditional language and invest 'every note, and even the pauses' with expressive significance. By exploring all the implications and consequences of his motivic ideas in manifold combinations, transpositions, and so forth, Beethoven succeeded in 'extending his melody, through the evolution of its constituent motifs, into a great, continuous composition which was nothing less than a single, perfectly coherent melody' (GS VII, 127). Wagner demonstrated this point to a young disciple, Felix Draeseke, one day at the time he was completing the *Tristan* score, singing to him the entire exposition of the first movement of the *Eroica* as a single melodic line. In the musical drama, the extension of an evolving 'web' of leitmotifs across the entire work is meant to achieve this same end, at least in theory. Equally important is the participation of all or many strands of the orchestral texture (*Orchestermelodie*), together with the vocal line, in the constitution of this ideal of 'infinite melody'. The late quartets of Beethoven inspired the formulation of this ideal: Wagner claimed that he had first understood the C♯ minor Quartet, op. 131, only after hearing a performance by the Maurin–Chevillard Quartet in Paris (1853) which disclosed to him the underlying 'melody' or *melos* of the piece (*Mein Leben*). The manipulation of paired semitone motifs in the opening movements of opp. 130, 131 and 132 has been compared to Wagner's procedures in *Tristan* and the permutations of the initial motivic complex in the Prelude and throughout the opera. While working on the piano arrangement of the score, Hans von Bülow wrote enthusiastically to Franz Brendel that this music 'links up directly with late Beethoven – it has nothing more to do with Weber or Gluck'.

Wagner and the 'moderns' (Berlioz and Liszt)

After his Kapellmeister years, as Carl Dahlhaus (1986) has remarked, Wagner seems to have taken next to no notice of the music of his contemporaries. As far as any influence on his own musical style is concerned, this seems to be true; the scattered references to recent composers and their works in his later correspondence or in Cosima's Diaries are, with few exceptions, arrogantly dismissive. The new or newly awakened enthusiasms documented there are instead mostly for older music, such as the belated 'rediscovery' of Bach, something of which may be reflected in the modernized chorale style and contrapuntal idioms of *Die Meistersinger* and *Parsifal*. But among contemporaries, the two composers whose music did occupy Wagner's attention to a considerable extent were Berlioz and Liszt – the two (non-German) composers with whom Wagner's name was joined under the banner of a 'New German School' around 1860.

Berlioz

His attitude towards Berlioz and his music was ambivalent from the beginning – that is, from the first unnerving encounter with the phenomenon in 1839–40 (see pp. 73–4). When, by the 1850s, Wagner was better able to appreciate this music, he was put off by the cool, unapproachable manner Berlioz seemed to adopt with him. Unlike the case of Beethoven, Berlioz's influence is to be detected closer to the surface. It is not difficult to imagine that the great musical 'contest' between the crews of Daland and the Dutchman in Act III of the *Holländer*, with its drastic superimposition of heterogeneous material, was inspired by the French master, with his penchant for this brand of 'dramatic' counterpoint between independent melodies (Wagner raises this technique to new heights in the closing scenes of Acts I and II of *Die Meistersinger*, or more decorously in the coda of the Prelude). The wild, shrill orchestration of the *Holländer* scene further suggest the brash extroversion of French Romanticism as manifested in the 'Dream of a Witches' Sabbath' from the *Symphonie fantastique* or the brigands' orgy in *Harold en Italie*. The combination of Pilgrims' Chorus and shepherd's piping in *Tannhäuser* is another piece of such counterpoint *à la* Berlioz, closely akin to the intertwining of Harold's viola theme with the orchestral chorale of Berlioz's pilgrims in the second movement of *Harold* (cf. CT, 14 Jan 1882).

The later Wagner draws more on this quieter side of Berlioz. The melancholy cor anglais passages in the 'Scène aux champs' of the *Fantastique* have often been compared to the long solo beginning Act III of *Tristan*. And the strange, almost hallucinatory quality of that chromatically meandering line has much in common with the monophonic meditations of 'Roméo seul' (violin I) beginning Part

Two of *Roméo et Juliette*. Wagner was fascinated and frustrated at once by the *adagio* 'love scene' in that work, which he described in the course of his open letter *Über Franz Liszts Symphonische Dichtungen (On Franz Liszt's Symphonic Poems*, 1857). Quite possibly he heard something of his ideal of 'infinite melody' here, too. Yet Berlioz's departures from conventional melodic and structural schemata puzzled Wagner, for whom they seemed to lack either 'inner musical' or explicitly dramatic justification. Juliet's *convoi funèbre* from the same work, however, contains the seeds of one of the most powerful passages in all of Wagner, the 'retrograde' scene-transition to the Grail temple in the final act of *Parsifal*, leading into Titurel's funeral cortège. Wagner uses as a kind of tonal axis the same note (E, the lowest note of the four offstage bells) that serves as the basis of Berlioz's alternating choral–orchestral litany. With his freely migrating ostinati, Wagner traverses a much vaster tonal terrain than Berlioz, building to an anguished climax of astonishing intensity. But in overall design and procedure – the superimposition of a freely developing, chromatic-contrapuntal texture over a steady, funereal tread – the passage finds a closer precedent in Berlioz than in any of Wagner's own works.

Liszt

For a relatively brief but concentrated period in the mid-1850s, Wagner maintained close contact with Franz Liszt. Although they began to drift apart by about 1860, this remained his most sustained and intimate association with another composer. Consequently, Liszt represents the last significant influence on the formation of Wagner's musical personality. Due to Wagner's exiled state the relationship was confined largely to written correspondence. But Liszt's visits to Zurich in July 1853 and October–November 1856 were all the more meaningful to the isolated Wagner, just then entering the decisive phase of his stylistic development. During the first visit Wagner claims to have heard parts of the *Faust* Symphony (presumably in an early sketch stage) and 'several of his latest symphonic poems' (*Mein Leben*), which at this date included *Ce qu'on entend sur la montagne, Héroïde funèbre, Tasso, Prometheus, Mazeppa* and *Festklänge*. He received the first published edition of the latter four works, along with *Les Préludes* and *Orpheus*, in the summer of 1856. Later that year, during Liszt's second visit, he heard the recently completed *Dante* Symphony, dedicated to Wagner and the subject of much discussion in their correspondence. The year before, while in London, Karl Klindworth had played Liszt's B minor Sonata for Wagner. The first of Liszt's visits to Zurich preceded the composition of *Das Rheingold* by half a year. The eagerly awaited printed scores were received just before the beginning of work on *Siegfried*. The first complete draft of Act I was completed soon after Liszt's second visit in 1856, and Wagner continued immediately with Act II until the impulse to devote himself to *Tristan* finally triumphed.

A detailed investigation of the influence of Liszt and Wagner on each other during this period remains to be written. Wagner recalled in *Mein Leben* that the meeting of 1853 played a decisive role in his resolve to begin the long-delayed composition of his monumental Nibelung project. And a frequently cited letter to Hans von Bülow written two months after the completion of *Tristan und Isolde* (7 October 1859) contains the admission that he has 'become quite another fellow, harmonically' since his acquaintance with Liszt's recent music. Indeed, by general consensus, the incipient 'dissolution of tonality' in the works from *Tristan* to *Parsifal* owes much to the experimental tendencies of Liszt's music of the Weimar period. Among Liszt's most prominent innovations are those resulting from symmetrical or other non-conventional divisions of the scale or of vertical chord structures: whole-tone and octatonic scales, the 'Gypsy' scale (with two augmented seconds), the diminished seventh (comprising three minor thirds) and the augmented triad (two major thirds). The vibrant, unstable sonority of the augmented fifth is the most immediately audible of these devices in Wagner's music of the 1850s and 60s, readily identified in Brünnhilde's *Walkürenruf* ('Hojotoho!') and Sachs's cobbling motif in *Die Meistersinger* (see, for example, the refrain to his song in Act II, 'Jerum! Jerum! Hallahallohe!') Act I of *Siegfried* – composed at the height of Wagner's exposure to Liszt's music – is saturated with the augmented triad, where it often forms the basis of sequential chain progressions (Mime's 'hallucination' at the beginning of Act I scene 3 and the beginning of the Forging Scene that follows). More audacious still is the Prelude to Act II, based on tritone and diminished-seventh chord structures to the near-exclusion of any controlling tonic, although nominally in F minor. Liszt had experimented with the similar procedure of using the diminished seventh and/or tritone as a controlling sonority and 'substitute' tonic in the first movement of the *Dante* Symphony and parts of *Prometheus*. Liszt's more systematic experiments, such as the famous 'twelve-tone' motto of the *Faust* Symphony (generated by a sequence of augmented triads), seem not to have interested Wagner as much. But the more freely structured 'transfiguring' effect of third-related chord sequences at the end of the *Faust* Symphony (III, bars 651ff.) and *Orpheus* (bars 209ff.) did catch his attention. The effect is paraphrased in the 'magic sleep' chords in *Die Walküre* and the motif of Wotan as 'Wanderer' in *Siegfried* (the upper line of the 'magic sleep' chords does happen to outline a complete chromatic scale, but without any obvious 'structural' implications). Hunting for precedents of the '*Tristan* chord' and its attendant 'Longing' (*Sehnsucht*) motif of four rising semitones has long been a favourite sport. But more relevant to the *Tristan* score than the melodic chromaticisms of Mozart, Spohr, Gottschalk or others is the manner of developing such fragmentary chromatic motifs in flexible, open-ended, often sequential units which Wagner seems to have learned primarily from Liszt.

Premonitions of the *Tristan* idiom have also been observed in an early orchestral fantasy by Liszt's pupil Hans von Bülow, later published under the title *Nirwana* (Spencer and Millington, 1987). Wagner corresponded with Bülow about this and other works, and in one letter (26 October) he remonstrates with the zealous young 'progressive' for the harmonic liberties in this 'suicidal' fantasy, evidently because the effort behind them is too apparent. In the same letter he advises Bülow of his conviction that true art 'consists precisely in communicating the strongest and most unusual feelings to a listener in such a way that his attention is not distracted by the material [. . .] but that he yields unresistingly, as it were, to an ingratiating allurement and thus involuntarily assimilates even what is most alien to his nature'. In outlining here his notorious tactic of aesthetic 'seduction', so often remarked upon by later generations of critics, Wagner has perhaps characterized something of the process of his own development – the process whereby he himself yielded to the 'allurements' of diverse and 'alien' impressions ranging from Bellini to late Beethoven, Gluckian Classicism to Marschner's *Schauerromantik*, Bach's counterpoint to Lisztian harmony, and assimilated these ingredients into a personal style as influential, in turn, as any in the history of music.

Patronage

IT IS ONE OF THE MANY paradoxes attending Wagner's career that, at a time when the economic support of composers and musical institutions had become almost entirely transferred to an urban bourgeois 'open market', he should suddenly find himself basking in the uniquely generous royal patronage of the young King Ludwig II of Bavaria. Of course, the beautiful dream of unconditional patronage, as it appeared in 1864, was not to last. But even though Ludwig's support was somewhat curtailed after his first years on the throne, the eventual success of the Bayreuth enterprise could never have been realized if Ludwig had not intervened at several crucial junctures. On the other hand, the Bayreuth Festival was essentially conducted as a modern commercial undertaking which would also not have been possible without the participation of numerous financial assistants and advisors (Emil Heckel in Mannheim, Voltz and Batz in Mainz, Feustel in Bayreuth). Even if Bayreuth was conceived as something quite apart from the everyday theatrical fray of the European capitals, it depended essentially on the same range of patrons, from an illustrious assortment of crowned heads (whose presence was undoubtedly an asset in generating publicity and prestige for the event) to wealthy curiosity-seekers and a wide spectrum of middle-class musicians and enthusiastic laymen that made up the ranks of the early 'Wagnerians'.

Wagner's career as a whole reflects something of the diverse systems of patronage opened up in the 19th century, and also the difficulty of functioning as an independent artist even in the

Patronage, commissions and royalties in Wagner's day

supposedly propitious milieu of this new, post-feudal era. The two central locales of his youth – Leipzig and Dresden – can be taken to represent two basic systems of musical patronage that continued to co-exist throughout much of the century. Leipzig was a paradigm, in many ways, of the new bourgeois musical culture, with its subscription concerts (the famous Gewandhaus concerts) and its municipal theatre, operated as a private business with occasional extra funds supplied by the city council or some independent consortium of merchants. As a major centre of music publishing, Leipzig also symbolized another important source of livelihood for the new, 'independent' composer. It was in such an environment that the young, utterly inexperienced Wagner was able to hear some of his first larger works performed (the C major Symphony and several overtures – with mixed success), and even have some smaller works published, such as the B♭ Sonata, WWV 21. Dresden, on the other hand, continued the tradition of official court patronage of the theatre and its various appendages, including the long-standing court orchestra (*Hofkapelle*). The co-existence of German and Italian operatic theatres or seasons in conservative centres like Dresden, Munich or Vienna was a relic of dynastic traditions, in part. But by Wagner's time the court theatres also depended very much on public ticket sales to supplement their royal (state) subsidies. A mid-19th-century source (F.C. Paldamus, 1857) lists twelve court theatres operating within the German states, in addition to several more that had been leased to private management (a further half-dozen or so did not include opera or ballet in their repertory). The number of municipal theatres was considerably greater, and there also still existed throughout the earlier part of the century a number of itinerant troupes offering a mixture of plays, Singspiel and opera (Goslich, 1975).

The smaller municipal theatres (*Stadttheater*), such as employed Wagner in Magdeburg or Riga, often found themselves in financial straits. Programming, casting and schedules were often a very *ad hoc* affair (the disastrous quasi-premiere of *Das Liebesverbot* in Magdeburg offers an extreme example). Similarly, the Théâtre de la Renaissance in Paris – lacking the official licence and subsidy enjoyed by the principal theatres – went bankrupt just as Wagner was pinning his hopes on it as a venue for his Parisian break-through. The official operatic institutions of the larger cities like Paris, London or Vienna had all been privatized in the 19th century. The Paris Opéra (Académie Royale de Musique) still operated under a royal licence and benefited from state subven-tion. In the years after 1831, when the management was offered to Louis Véron, as part of an administrative experiment, the subvention ranged from 710,000 to 800,000 francs. Italian opera houses had been run on a similar entrepreneurial basis since the 18th century, despite the continued aristocratic affiliation of some theatres (Naples or Parma, for instance). Other theatres, especially in smaller centres, were jointly managed by a group of shareholders that might consist of both nobility and middle-class members; occasionally a collective of singers, performers and even stage-hands might take control (a situation visualized by Wagner in various proposals for theatrical reform), but these artists' 'collectives' were normally just a temporary solution in the absence – or in the event of bankruptcy – of the impresario (Rosselli, 1984).

Commissions and royalties

Throughout the earlier part of the 19th century, most composers working for Italian or French theatres continued to work on the basis of specific seasonal commissions. In Italy, this commission or *scrittura* meant providing a score in time for the forthcoming season and tailored to the needs of a specific cast. Performance rights, and often the autograph itself, would devolve to the impresario (Cagli, 1979).

For Germans, however, the business of operatic composition was less codified. Opera scores might be written purely 'on speculation', without any distinct performance situation in mind (no differently from songs or chamber music). The finished score might be submitted for review by one or more theatres, as with Wagner's successful submission of *Rienzi* to the Dresden Court Theatre. Numerous completed scores never saw the light of day (or rather, the footlights), as was the case with several of Schubert's operas and many works by lesser composers. The composers who stood the best chance of achieving a performance were those who held the post of Kapellmeister at a leading theatre. This accounts for the premieres of *Der fliegende Holländer* and *Tannhäuser*, for instance, as for those of some of Spohr's operas in Cassel, Marschner's in Hanover, and of many minor figures besides (Franz Lachner in Munich, Heinrich Dorn and Wilhelm Taubert in Berlin, Chelard in Weimar, etc.) Wagner continually railed against the domination of the German opera houses by 'second-rate' French and Italian fare in 'wretched' translations. But there were also directors who made a point of fostering new and ambitious works. Spohr, for instance, became an early exponent of Wagner's operas, as did, of course, Liszt in Weimar, where he also premiered (with minimal success) operas by such younger composers as Raff, Rubinstein and Cornelius.

The protection of a composer's rights and the payment of suitable royalties remained a troublesome issue well into the 19th century. Rules for domestic copyright of dramatic and musical works were worked out in the earlier decades of the 19th century in some countries (in 1833 and 1842 in England, for instance, for dramatic works and musical compositions, respectively). Copyright and royalty issues were especially problematic in the fragmented Italian and German states, prior to unification; German copyright laws were not regularized until 1870. And at mid-century there was still no adequate understanding on matters of international copyright: Verdi, for example, lost a lawsuit in 1856 against the manager of the Théâtre-Italian over an unauthorized production of *Il trovatore*. Wagner ran into trouble in transferring the publishing rights for *Tannhäuser* – which were nominally still under the control of Meser/Müller in Dresden – to Flaxland in Paris.

Meyerbeer, as music director of the Berlin theatre in 1843, had been among the first to demand royalty payments at a fixed percentage (10 per cent) in place of a single, flat fee. But the co-existence of both alternatives is demonstrated by Wagner's dealings with Flaxland around 1860. His first agreement entails a combination of fixed fee (1000 francs for each of the Dresden operas) and a decreasing series of royalty payments. A subsequent agreement stipulates 250 francs for each performance of *Tannhäuser* (amounting to only three, in the event). Another proposal suggests a flat fee of 10,000 francs for the French rights in perpetuity for the four operas from *Rienzi* to *Lohengrin*. Verdi, by comparison, had been paid up to 60,000 francs by Ricordi for each of his works during the period 1847–57. By the 1860s a successful opera at the Théâtre Lyrique in Paris might bring in 4000–8000 francs per performance in gross receipts (thus generating an average royalty payment of 600 francs per performance for the composer, calculated at 10 per cent).

Wagner's own financial situation was never regular, of course, and his perennial requests for advances against future income make it difficult to calculate precisely what he was actually paid for a given work. (The firm of Schott in Mainz, publishers of the *Meistersinger* and *Ring* scores, was constantly beset with such requests throughout the 1860s and 70s, and frequently complied.) And Wagner was perhaps less than forthright in selling the ownership of the *Ring* scores to the most promising patron to hand – first to Otto Wesendonck in Zurich, and then to Ludwig II for 30,000 gulden in the 1860s. In a previous effort to pay off debts back in Dresden, Wagner had assigned the income from publication of his earlier operas to Anton Pusinelli and two others, while retaining for himself fees from theatrical performances.

Performance fees remained a fairly steady source of income for Wagner, especially from the more popular Dresden operas. Before the German copyright law of 1870, stipulating percentage-based royalties for performances of copyrighted material, Wagner usually received a single, flat fee for performance rights. Performances of *Tannhäuser* in Frankfurt in 1853 secured him 25 louis d'or (100 francs), for instance. A request for 30 louis d'or for *Der fliegende Holländer* at Hamburg some years later was not met, much to Wagner's indignation, but he was paid 40 louis d'or (160 francs) for the performance rights of *Die Meistersinger* in 1869. At about the same time the Berlin theatre offered Wagner a 7 per cent royalty fee for each performance of his works there, including advances of 50 to 100 Friedrichsdor (about 1000–2000 francs). Later Wagner stipulated a 10 per cent royalty fee on the receipts from Angelo Neumann's touring *Ring* production. He had initially resisted selling the performance rights to the *Ring* operas, but had to give in to the demand for them in the financial aftermath of the 1876 Bayreuth Festival. The festival project itself, with its painstakingly canvassed 'society of patrons' and private investors (the *Patronatsscheine* or 'certificates of patronage') represents a unique financial and administrative achievement in the history of music up to that time. Both that achievement and the devotional commitment of the royal patron Ludwig II stand out as emblems of Wagner's singular position in 19th-century music and culture altogether.

THOMAS S. GREY

Section 6

WAGNER AS AN INDIVIDUAL

Paternity	94
Family	95
Appearance and character	97
Wagner as a conductor	99
Wagner's working routine	102
THE PORTRAITS (plates 1–20)	104
Wagner as polemicist	114
Finances and attitude to money	116
Wagner and women	118
Relationship with King Ludwig II	121
Dealings with publishers	124
Dealings with critics	126
Wagner as scapegoat	128

WAGNER AS AN INDIVIDUAL

IT WILL PROBABLY NEVER be conclusively established whether Wagner's true father was the police actuary Carl Friedrich Wagner, to whom his mother Johanna was married, or the actor and painter Ludwig Geyer. Geyer was a close friend of the family, and after Friedrich's death on 23 November 1813 (just six months after the baby Richard was born), he attended to the financial needs of the widow and her family. Johanna visited Geyer in Dresden in February 1814 and they became engaged; they were married on 28 August 1814 and a child, Cäcilie, was born to them six months later. Until he died in 1821, Geyer was thus Richard's actual father; the boy bore the surname Geyer until he reached the age of fourteen (1827), when he reverted to Wagner.

Paternity

A possible piece of evidence concerns Johanna's curious trek to Teplitz, Bohemia, shortly after Wagner's birth. The Napoleonic wars were raging around Leipzig, where the Wagners lived – the decisive Battle of the Nations was fought there in October 1813 – and Geyer invited Friedrich and Johanna to take refuge with him in Teplitz. Friedrich was required to stay in Leipzig on duty, but Johanna, and presumably the two-month-old Richard, undertook the extremely hazardous journey of well over 100 miles from Leipzig to Teplitz through enemy-occupied territory. Whether or not Teplitz was actually any safer than Leipzig in July 1813 is a matter of dispute, but one explanation offered for this unusually adventurous summer holiday is that Johanna was anxious to see Geyer again and show the baby to its father. The visit lasted only three weeks, because on 11 August 1813 Austria declared war on Napoleon and all aliens had to leave Bohemia within forty-eight hours.

On its own, the Teplitz episode, which came to light only in the present century, provides no firm evidence. Nor does the fact that the baptism of the baby took place as late as three months after his birth – odd though that is. Studies of the letters written by Geyer to Johanna in the aftermath of Friedrich's death, and of portraits of the Wagner family, have all proved similarly inconclusive.

Much of the confusion that surrounds the issue dates back to Nietzsche's assertion in *Der Fall Wagner* (*The Case of Wagner*, 1888) that the composer's father 'was an actor named Geyer'. Since Nietzsche had read the proofs of *Mein Leben*, then only privately circulated, it was assumed that he was drawing on the authority of that document. In fact, both the first printing of 1870 and the original manuscript of the autobiography made reference to 'my father, Friedrich Wagner', but that was not generally known until after Hurn and Root, in their mistitled book *The Truth about Wagner* (1930), had fanned the flames of speculation with their statement that Wagner had, in the first edition of *Mein Leben*, named Geyer as his true father.

The most interesting aspect of the paternity issue is the fact that Wagner himself was never sure of the identity of his father; worse still, there was a suggestion that Geyer had Jewish blood. Much as Wagner treasured the memory of Geyer, the possibility that he might himself be of Jewish descent almost certainly – given the historical and cultural context of 19th-century Germany – intensified his inferiority complex and in turn his anti-Semitic tendencies. It has subsequently been demonstrated beyond all doubt, however, that whether or not Geyer was Wagner's real father, he was of thoroughly Protestant stock.

BARRY MILLINGTON

Family

AS IF WAGNER'S PATERNITY were not sufficiently intriguing (see preceding section), an air of mystery also hangs over his mother: not over her identity but over her parentage. Until recently it was thought that Johanna Rosine Wagner, *née* Pätz, might have been the illegitimate daughter of Prince Constantin of Saxe-Weimar-Eisenach (the brother of the Grand Duke) and a tanner's daughter from Weissenfels. Research has now shown, however, that Johanna was not the prince's daughter, but his mistress (Gregor-Dellin, 1985).

Born on 19 September 1774 (date from Gregor-Dellin, who also gives baptism date of 21 September), Johanna was the sixth child of Johann Gottlob Pätz, a baker in Weissenfels, and his first wife, Dorothea Erdmuthe, *née* Iglisch. Her mother died when Johanna was fourteen and her father married again. She left school in 1789 and it appears to have been in the following year, when the prince spent two lengthy periods in Weissenfels, that he seduced the baker's daughter, then aged fifteen or sixteen. 'Did she deliver his breakfast rolls?', speculates Gregor-Dellin, with the novelist's eye for romantic detail that characterizes his Wagner scholarship. And indeed she may have done, though the prince then took her off to Leipzig, where he lodged her at the house of one Frau Sophie Friederice Hesse. He gave Johanna an allowance for clothes and finery, and had her educated in elocution, writing and millinery. When the prince went off to war and to his death (in 1793), Johanna, whose surname had been adjusted to Bezin (though it was rendered in a variety of other ways too), received her final allowance and was abandoned to her fate. She married Carl Friedrich Wagner in 1798. It is this chain of events that explains why Johanna was so enigmatic, as Wagner noted in his autobiography, regarding her name, age and origins.

Friedrich died when Wagner was only six months old and the boy grew up to regard Ludwig Geyer as his father until he too died in 1821. Geyer was particularly fond of Richard and called him 'the Cossack'; he was later recalled by Wagner with great affection. But Wagner's uncertainty as to the identity of his real father evidently had a profound effect on his psyche, as is betrayed by the obsession with fatherless children (Siegmund, Siegfried, Tristan and Parsifal) in his operas.

The psychological ramifications of his relationship with his mother are no less complicated. She is described in *Mein Leben* as a 'remarkable woman', who 'represented a strange mixture of practical domestic efficiency and great spiritual sensitivity [. . .]. Her chief character trait appeared to be a wry sense of humour and a good temper'. Wagner goes on to note that he hardly remembered ever being caressed by her: displays of affection did not take place in his family at all. 'On the contrary, a certain impetuous, almost vehement, boisterous manner naturally manifested itself.' His mother spoke 'in almost histrionic tones' of the great and beautiful in art, though she was not favourably inclined towards the theatre, against which she warned him earnestly, threatening him with her curse if ever he thought of entering it as a profession.

There is evidence here, then, both of tender feelings towards his mother and of emotional deprivation – a dichotomy that can also be discerned in his letters. Typical of his letters to her, infrequent though they were, is the effusively fond tone of that of 25 July 1835: 'Only you, dearest mother, do I still recall with feelings of the most heartfelt love and deepest emotion [. . .]. I am overcome by feelings of gratitude for the glorious love of which you recently gave your son such heartfelt and earnest proofs, so much so that I might well be tempted to write and speak of them in the most tender tones of a lover addressing his beloved.' Against this has to be set the harshly critical tone of Wagner's letter of 11 September 1842 to his half-sister Cäcilie and her husband: 'she creates nothing but trouble because of her remarkable penchant for misrepresenting & distorting everying, & for indulging in endless gossip [. . .]; what most annoyed Minna was our mother's really offensive avarice & egoism which we were exposed to *ad nauseam* in various trivial ways, but especially in her treatment of the servants'. Gregor-Dellin (1980 and 1985) suggests that the contradictions in Wagner's attitude towards his mother are consistent with the psychology of the mother-fixated son who feels betrayed by his mother. Wagner could scarcely have been unaware of his mother's dark secret, he continues, and his feelings of betrayal, weighing all the more heavily in the absence of a father, may have led him subconsciously to create a block in his relationship with other women; certainly he appears to have been attracted to 'unavailable' women.

Such a mother-fixation may well also be responsible for the confusion of the maternal and the erotic in many of Wagner's characters. Kundry deliberately rekindles maternal longings in Parsifal before delivering her traumatic kiss, while Siegfried momentarily mistakes the reawakened Brünnhilde for his mother.

Shortly before this, when Siegfried discovers that the still sleeping Brünnhilde is not after all a man, he calls on his mother for help – a moment which Thomas Mann described as 'a blend of mythical unsophistication and psychological, indeed, psychoanalytical modernity'.

Richard was the ninth child to be born into the family of Friedrich and Johanna. Two (Carl Gustav and Maria Theresia) died in infancy. The oldest child was Albert, who became a singer and stage manager, and whose three daughters included the adopted Johanna, who achieved celebrity as a soprano under the name Johanna Jachmann-Wagner. The only other surviving brother was Carl Julius, who became a goldsmith. Of Wagner's sisters, Rosalie, Luise, Clara and Ottilie, the first three all took to the stage (Rosalie and Luise as actresses, Clara as a singer, though she lost her voice at an early age). (See also 'Who's Who', pp.32–3.) The stage careers of his sisters naturally stimulated the young Richard's imagination, though it was his half-sister Cäcilie (born to Johanna and Geyer in 1815) to whom he was closest both in years and in temperament.

Mention should also be made of Friedrich's brother Gottlob Heinrich Adolf, the 'Uncle Adolf' about whom Wagner speaks with such warmth in *Mein Leben*. Adolf was a renowned and respected scholar in the fields of literature, history, philosophy and philology. He made the acquaintance of Schiller, Fichte, Tieck and others, and achieved a considerable reputation with his translations from and into various languages. Wagner's autobiography tells how Adolf introduced him to, and fired him with enthusiasm for, the Greeks, Shakespeare, Dante and much more besides.

BARRY MILLINGTON

Appearance and character

The infant Wagner was a sickly child, so much so that it was feared he would not survive. He remained pale and slim, with a rather too large head for the size of his frame. The result was a certain gawkiness, which did not prevent him from acquiring a considerable acrobatic agility in his youth. As a man he was not tall, but neither was he the dwarf he is sometimes made out to be: his Swiss passport of 1849 records his height as 5ft 6½in. (1m. 69.16cm).

His physical appearance in 1839 was described by the painter Friedrich Pecht:

> strikingly elegant, indeed aristocratic in his appearance, despite his somewhat short legs, and with such a strikingly beautiful woman on his arm [his wife Minna] that she alone would have sufficed to make the couple interesting, if Wagner himself had not had such an arresting head that one's attention was involuntarily fixed upon him. (Barth, Mack and Voss, 1975)

Meeting him a few years later (1843), the author Eliza Wille described him thus:

It had remained a fleeting encounter [. . .]. But Wagner's features had impressed themselves on my mind: his elegant, supple figure, the head with the mighty brow, the acute eye and the energetic lines around his small and tightly closed mouth. A painter who was sitting next to me drew my attention to his straight, protruding chin, which seemed to be carved out of stone, giving the face a special character. (Barth, Mack and Voss, 1975)

The almost universal image of Wagner, in terms of his character and behaviour, is that of an arrogant, self-centred, manipulative opportunist and sybarite, who relieved other men of their wives as readily as he relieved the wealthy of their cash. There is more than a grain of truth in all this, but the conventional image, which relies unduly on cliché and mindless repetition, needs to be brought into sharper focus.

Wagner did not, it is true, suffer fools gladly. Nor did he pretend to admire the work of those contemporaries with whom he was not in artistic sympathy (see 'Contemporary composers', pp.170–73). But nor did he withhold praise where he thought it was due. And, contrary to received opinion, Wagner cannot justly be accused of ingratitude. His letters overflow with expressions of effusive thanks: sometimes for money received, but even more often for love and understanding shown. He expected much of his friends, but he gave generously in return, not only gifts, but also in terms of aid, affection and moral support. The financial arrangements he made for his first wife Minna after their separation, and for Minna's daughter Natalie, went far beyond the bounds of obligation. His impassioned letters to such stalwart friends as Liszt, Anton Pusinelli and Eliza Wille give the lie to the notion that he was indifferent to the feelings of others, while cynics who invariably interpret such documents as opportunistically motivated reveal more about themselves than about Wagner.

One's view of Wagner's character is inevitably coloured by one's attitude to the 19th-century notion of a genius and the social expectations such a category engendered. The classic formulation was made by Malwida von Meysenbug in 1860:

A man so dominated by his elemental spirit should from the beginning have had a high-minded and understanding woman at his side – a woman who understood how to mediate between the genius and the world by realizing that the two were bound to be eternally poles apart. Frau Wagner [Minna] never realized this. She tried to mediate by demanding concessions towards the world from the genius, which the latter could not and must not make. (Barth, Mack and Voss, 1975)

Minna was not willing to gratify such self-centredness, but dozens were, doubtless realizing that those were the conditions on which any relationship with the composer rested. There is no lack of testimony to his arrogant, domineering nature and to his incorrigible egoism. Wagner himself made no bones about his conviction that through his earlier suffering as a penniless artist, he had, with the recognition of King Ludwig in 1864, *'acquired a superior right*, an entitlement which, even if it had not been acknowledged by the world, would have raised me far, far above the world and thus, even in the depths of my misery, would have made me *inwardly a hallowed and blessed human being*.' (letter to Eliza Wille, 26 May 1864)

Wagner's charisma was evidently extraordinary: his personality attracted and repulsed with much the same intensity as did his music. One admirer who remained sceptical of the advantages of close contact with such egoism was the composer Peter Cornelius:

> Our great friend has to talk about *himself*, he has to sing and read from his *own* works, or he is unhappy. That's why he always wants to be surrounded by a small, intimate circle, because he can't have what he wants with other people. (Barth, Mack and Voss, 1975)

Cornelius feared for his own independence as a composer, in spite of, or perhaps because of, Wagner's protestations of his great interest in Cornelius's work. Wagner exerted pressure amounting to moral blackmail on Cornelius to persuade him to take up lodgings with him in 1864, and he made a similar attempt with Heinrich Porges – in the latter case to no avail.

The early days in Munich were a time of oppressive loneliness for Wagner and he sought desperately for companions both male and female – the former for platonic relationships, the latter usually for something more (see 'Wagner and women', pp.118–21). It was simultaneously, however, a time of unprecedented physical comfort for him. King Ludwig's patronage freed him from financial worries for the first time in his career (though even before his saviour's advent Wagner had been luxuriously furnishing his apartment in Penzing in blithe disregard for the consequences). Now, once again with the help of the Viennese milliner and seamstress Bertha Goldwag, he decked out his Munich house with satins, velvet drapes and portières, at the same time equipping himself with a wardrobe of dressing gowns and suits in silk lined with fur (in various colours with matching slippers and neckties), shirts and underclothes in silk and satin, and delicate scents with which to perfume the atmosphere.

Such hedonistic indulgence has attracted much critical sniping, less tolerable when directed against supposed 'effeminacy' than against the perceived inconsistency with a creed of Schopenhauerian renunciation. But it is a fruitless sport to set the theories of a philosopher or his adherents against their practical realization in everyday life: such ideas are generally grounded in ideal, utopian conditions, not those dictated and distorted by social reality.

BARRY MILLINGTON

Wagner as a conductor

UNTIL HE WAS THIRTY-FIVE Wagner was obliged to conduct in fulfilling his duties as a music director/Kapellmeister in Magdeburg (1834–6), Königsberg (1837), Riga (1837–9) and Dresden (1843–9); in addition, during the early years of his Swiss exile he conducted frequently in Zurich. Much of this activity involved conducting operas which made up the standard repertory in the Germany of the 1830s and 40s – which meant not only important works by Mozart, Beethoven, Weber, Bellini and Marschner, but also a considerable number of now-forgotten works. Wagner's enthusiasm for conducting opera was variable: at times disgusted at having to preside over works which he considered artistically threadbare, he nevertheless worked tirelessly to present operas he admired responsibly and convincingly, and in fact went so far as to produce his own performing versions for new productions of Gluck's *Iphigénie en Aulide* (Dresden 1847) and Mozart's *Don Giovanni* (Zurich 1850). In addition, he found or created opportunities for conducting in concert as well: premieres of some of his early occasional pieces appeared in concerts he conducted in Magdeburg and Königsberg, and during his tenure in Riga he established a concert series with the opera orchestra (consisting of a mere twenty-four members) at which he had his first opportunity to conduct most of Beethoven's symphonies as well as other works. In Dresden he conducted *Rienzi* and the premieres of *Der fliegende Holländer* and *Tannhäuser*, and his activities there culminated in four memorable Palm Sunday concerts (the first in 1846), three of them featuring Beethoven's Ninth Symphony.

Wagner took his growing reputation as a composer and celebrity in the early 1850s as confirmation of his belief that conducting was on the periphery of his life's work, and consequently never again took on a permanent post. Indeed, in the second phase of his conducting career the vast majority of the works Wagner conducted were his own, performed at specially arranged concerts. One of his only important engagements for his conducting alone took him to London: lured by unkept promises of ample rehearsal time and a deputy to conduct minor works, he directed eight concerts for the (Old) Philharmonic Society in March–June 1855. But already in Zurich in May 1853 a precedent had been set for his future conducting appearances. There, with an invited orchestra of seventy players and a chorus of 110, Wagner conducted excerpts from *Rienzi*, *Der fliegende Holländer*, *Tannhäuser* and *Lohengrin*. During preparations for the production of *Tannhäuser* in Paris in 1861, Wagner conducted three concerts of his own works (including the *Tristan* Prelude) in January and February 1860 at the Théâtre-Italien. Beginning in November 1862 he spent over a year on a concert tour, conducting orchestras in his own works (including portions of the *Ring* and *Die Meistersinger*, both unfinished) in Leipzig, Vienna, Prague, St Petersburg, Moscow, Budapest, Karlsruhe, Löwenberg and Breslau. These concerts served to fan public enthusiasm for works which were yet to be performed in their entirety and also to enhance Wagner's reputation as a conductor. Later still, when being a Wagnerian was fashionable after King Ludwig II had become his benefactor, Wagner gave memorable concerts for his admirers and members of the numerous Richard Wagner Societies in Mannheim (1871),

Vienna (1872), and Hamburg, Berlin and Cologne (1873). After completing *Götterdämmerung* in 1874, Wagner undertook to conduct numerous concerts intended to raise funds for the first Bayreuth Festival (1876), and in March 1876 he conducted *Lohengrin* in Vienna. After the Festival, in order to help defray the enormous deficit which was its immediate legacy, he and Hans Richter shared conducting duties in a series of concerts featuring Bayreuth singers at the Royal Albert Hall in London (1877). The only sizeable programme not devoted to his own music that Wagner conducted after 1870 was the performance of Beethoven's Ninth on his fifty-ninth birthday, the day on which the cornerstone of the Bayreuth Festspielhaus was laid (22 May 1872). In his final years Wagner conducted a number of private premieres and revivals for Cosima's birthday – the *Siegfried Idyll* in 1870, the *Parsifal* Prelude in 1878, and his early Symphony in C in 1882. An anomaly of Wagner's conducting career is that, except for the well-known occasion on which he directed the final scene of *Parsifal* at the last performance of the work at Bayreuth in 1882, he never had occasion to conduct a stage performance of any of his post-*Lohengrin* works.

Wagner's influence as a conductor was immense. Until his advent, the role of the conductor was generally understood to be that of a genial, neutral convener of the orchestra. Wagner, on the other hand, believed that a performance which adequately portrayed the conception of a profoundly expressive work – which included all the music about which he cared deeply – was by necessity heavily inflected in a variety of parameters, notably those of dynamics and tempo, and that it was the responsibility of the conductor to develop an interpretation of the music which could be conveyed to and realized by the orchestra. Consequently Wagner's performances occupied a vastly expanded dynamic range which often juxtaposed dynamic extremes; further, he advocated a flexibility of tempo resulting from a belief that the specific character of each theme implies its own tempo. In accordance with this principle, Wagner endowed lyrical themes with a weighty earnestness which stood in stark contrast to the fleet energy of figuration or principal themes in fast movements. Unsympathetic listeners noted ragged ensemble as a by-product of these tempo modifications (especially when the orchestra in question was insufficiently familiar with Wagner's style), but many others found the 'inner meaning' of important music clarified through his expressively explicit performances. Wagner seems generally to have inspired enthusiasm and loyalty from the players he directed, and his preferred practice (which he himself did not achieve consistently) of passionate, painstaking rehearsal – often accompanied by poetical imagery to convey the meaning of certain pieces to his players – followed by a performance in which his gestures and leadership were comparatively precise and restrained has ever since been held as a model. It is symptomatic of the force of Wagner's musical personality – and of his centrality to his times –

that his understanding of the music which inspired him launched a large-scale shift in performance style.

DAVID BRECKBILL

FOR ALL THE SEEMINGLY terminal disarray of his personal and financial affairs, Wagner was usually able to maintain a meticulous, orderly routine in the process of sketching, drafting and orchestrating his operas. Like any composer, he made use of ideas sketched out or hastily jotted in the odd moment of inspiration. But for the most part, Wagner's working habits were far from those of the frenzied Romantic genius of the Beethovenian prototype. A great deal of 'pre-compositional' activity must have taken place in his mind rather than on sketch paper; for when he sat down to the first stage of composition (the so-called *Gesamtentwurf*, the 'preliminary' or 'first complete draft') the work seems most often to have proceeded smoothly and with few false starts or major interruptions. (For more on Wagner's sketching procedures, see 'Autograph manuscripts', pp.203–19.)

In the case of the earlier operas, up to *Lohengrin*, Wagner tended to devote the summer months to composition. This is partially due, of course, to the exigencies of his post of Kapellmeister in Dresden in the 1840s. In those years, orchestration would occupy whatever spare time could be devoted to it during the autumn, winter or spring months. From the Zurich period onwards, however, no such pattern is evident. Without a fixed schedule of duties, composition was dictated by the availability of sufficient blocks of uninterrupted free time and of suitably calm and stable external conditions.

The search for such external and internal conditions propitious to musical composition was an ongoing one. In his earlier Zurich residences Wagner was plagued variously by a nearby blacksmith, pianistic neighbours and other sonic distractions. When he was finally blessed with an ideal setting for creative work in the form of the Wesendoncks' guest cottage (the 'Asyl') – complete with resident muse in the person of Mathilde – the idyll was quickly shattered by the famous domestic altercations of 1858. The large, silent rooms of the Palazzo Giustiniani, in Venice, suitably hung with heavy fabrics, provided a congenial ambience for the composition of the second act of *Tristan und Isolde*. The repeated disruptions of the following years presented numerous obstacles to the establishment of a proper creative environment. But Wagner's later domiciles at Tribschen and Bayreuth finally afforded him the orderly physical space and auditory repose he was always seeking.

Wagner preferred to have a keyboard at his disposal while working out the early and middle stages of his scores. It is usually maintained that he did not compose 'at' the piano, but needed the opportunity to hear his initial ideas once he had set them down.

Wagner's working routine

Plates 1–20

THE PORTRAITS

No AUTHENTICATED PORTRAITS of Wagner survive from the years of his youth, and very few from his early manhood. The earliest surviving portrait is an anonymous silhouette made of him in Magdeburg in 1835, when he was 22 years old (plate 2). After that, there are all too few portraits of him from the Paris, Dresden and Zurich years (1840s and 50s). Included here are a drawing by his friend Ernst Benedikt Kietz (plate 3), dating from the period when they were both struggling to survive in Paris (1840–42), and a watercolour from 1853 (plate 4) by Clementine Stockar-Escher, a talented amateur painter from a wealthy family of some standing in the Swiss representative assembly. Both the latter portraits, depicting handsome, gentle and kindly physiognomic features, are clearly idealized to some degree.

The photograph in plate 5 tells a different story. Taken by the Parisian firm of Pierre Petit & Trinquart in February or March 1860, it dates from the composer's second extended stay in the French capital, a visit which resulted in three financially disastrous concerts and the débâcle of the *Tannhäuser* production. The photograph of the 47-year-old Wagner shows a ravaged, but determined, half-profile, commanding eyes and a broad brow exaggerated by a rapidly receding hairline.

The oil painting of December 1864/January 1865 by the composer's old friend Friedrich Pecht (plate 6), at that time practising as a painter and art authority in Munich, resulted from King Ludwig's desire to have a portrait of the composer. Joseph Bernhardt was the artist suggested by the king, but Wagner preferred to sit to someone who knew him, since other artists had experienced difficulties with the volatility of his facial expression. The bust in the background is of the youthful monarch.

Wagner was photographed on several occasions in the 1860s and 70s. Plate 1 is from a group of half-a-dozen pictures taken in Munich, probably on 11 November 1864, by Joseph Albert. Plate 7 is one of a group taken, also in Munich, in the second half of 1865, by the court photographer Franz Hanfstaengl; the subject's dress and the backdrop of drape and carved furniture reflect his new-found material security under the king's patronage. Plate 8 is from another series by Hanfstaengl, this time dating from December 1871. Both Wagner and Cosima were delighted with the result; when a copper engraving was made eight years later, Wagner told the engraver, Alfred Krausse, that he considered the portrait the best likeness of him yet produced.

Plate 9, the oil portrait by Franz von Lenbach, is probably the most famous of them all. Lenbach was the leading German portraitist of his era, and many prominent statesmen (including Bismarck, Ludwig I and Gladstone) and other celebrities sat for him.

He painted more than a dozen portraits of Wagner, though not generally from life: plate 9, for example, was done from a photograph by Hanfstaengl. It captures all Wagner's most distinctive features: the broad brow, the prominent, Roman nose, the determinedly jutting chin.

Three of the portraits in this book (plates 10, 16 and 17) will be unfamiliar to most readers, since they have very rarely been reproduced before. Three weeks after the laying of the foundation stone of the Bayreuth Festspielhaus, Wagner sat for the Viennese medal maker Anton Scharff on 12 June 1872. Plate 10 is the bronze cast subsequently made by Scharff from his original model. The cast is owned by Martin Geck, the author of the definitive study of Wagner portraits. Plate 16 illustrates the marble relief made by Gustav Adolph Kietz (the younger brother of Wagner's old friend) two years before the composer's death. Kietz lived in Dresden, and when Wagner revisited the city in September 1881 to see his dentist, Kietz took the opportunity to make a second model of his head from life (he had already produced a marble bust of Wagner in 1873). Plate 17 (see also frontispiece) is the bronze cast made in 1880–83 by Lorenz Gedon, described by Lenbach as 'the greatest living sculptor'. It is a magnificent piece, catching the physiognomic characteristics of Wagner – especially the eyes – to perfection.

Plate 11, one of a series of three photographs taken by the Viennese court photographer, Fritz Luckhardt, on 9 May 1872, shows the profile of Wagner's wife Cosima, no less striking than that of the composer himself. Wagner's affection for his son Siegfried is evident in the photograph taken in Naples on 1 June 1880 (plate 13), five days before the boy's eleventh birthday. Also reproduced here are four of the innumerable contemporary caricatures of Wagner (plates 12, 14, 15, and 19): at once a tribute to his celebrity and a valuable index of how he was regarded in his lifetime.

The last known photographs of Wagner were taken by Joseph Albert on 1 May 1882, nine months before the composer's death. Plate 18 is one of the pair of photographs taken on that occasion. By an extraordinary stroke of fate, however, a portrait of Wagner was sketched on the very eve of his death. In the September of 1882 Wagner had moved with his family to Venice, where he was to live out the last few months of his life. No one could have known how close the end was when, on the evening of 12 February the following year, Paul von Joukowsky made his drawing of Wagner (plate 20). Inscribed by Cosima 'R. reading', it shows the eyes apparently closed, the brow furrowed, but the expression peaceful. Wagner suffered his final heart attack the following day.

BARRY MILLINGTON

1 Photograph by Joseph Albert, 1864

2 Anonymous, silhouette, 1835

3 Ernst Benedikt Kietz,
   drawing, 1840–42

4 Clementine Stockar-Escher,
   watercolour, 1853

5 Photograph by Pierre Petit & Trinquart,
Paris, 1860

6 Friedrich Pecht, oil painting, 1864–5

7 Photograph by Franz Hanfstaengl, 1865

8 Photograph by Franz Hanfstaengl, 1871

9 Franz von Lenbach, oil painting, 1871

10 Anton Scharff, bronze cast, 1872

11 Photograph of Richard and Cosima Wagner
by Fritz Luckhardt, 1872

12 Viennese caricature of 1873
by Karl Klic, turning the
tables on Wagner and his
anti-Semitism

13 Photograph of Wagner with
his son Siegfried, 1880

14 Aeschylus and Shakespeare, two dramatists unequivocally
admired by Wagner, pay their respects; *Berliner Ulk*, 1876

15 With a Prussian helmet as
a podium, Wagner annihilates
the opposition conducting his
'music of the future'; *Figaro*,
London, 1876

17 Lorenz Gedon, bronze cast, 1880–83

16 Gustav Adolph Kietz, plaster cast
of marble relief, 1881

18 Photograph by
Joseph Albert, 1882

19 Wagner dispenses with the services of St Peter at
the gate of Heaven; *Der junge Kikeriki*, Vienna, 1883

20 Paul von Joukowsky, drawing of Wagner on the eve of his
death, 1883

Understandably, perhaps, his need for the piano seems to have increased with the more complex idiom of the mature music dramas. In the 1860s he had a special kind of 'piano-desk' constructed, described by one observer as 'a piano of special design (almost an altar), furnished with drawers and a plane like a table'. The elegant piano he had received from the Paris firm Erard in the 1850s soon became 'indispensable' in the process of composing, by his own admission (Newman, 1933–47). This instrument followed him throughout the peregrinations of the *Tristan* and *Meistersinger* years.

A less conventional prerequisite to compositional activity was the habit for extravagant dressing gowns, perfumes and other physical indulgences on which he seems to have become increasingly dependent. The desire to be caressed by silks, satins and furs has been explained, on one hand, by the chronically sensitive condition of his skin. On the other hand, the impulse toward 'dressing up' in quasi-historical outfits *à la* Rembrandt or Dürer seems intimately related to the essentially theatrical nature of his creative being. What began as the need to guarantee physical well-being as a condition of intellectual activity eventually reached the level of a 'fetishistic' obsession, in the view of Robert Gutman (who imagines the composer of *Parsifal* as a decadent voluptuary out of Huysmans, seated at his work table in Wahnfried and inhaling the aromas of exotic bath oils from the room below while recalling the fleshly charms of Judith Gautier, she who also kept him supplied with the finest Parisian luxuries – Gutman, 1968). Wagner himself explained this side of his character in a letter to Liszt: 'mine is an intensely irritable, acute and hugely voracious, yet uncommonly tender and delicate sensuality which [. . .] must be flattered if I am to accomplish the cruelly difficult task of creating in my mind a non-existent world.' (15 Jan 1854).

For the most part, however, Wagner's external requirements were not out of the ordinary. Above all, he needed sufficient peace and quiet, and he preferred to break up periods of mental concentration with an occasional outdoor excursion. 'My work-room has been laid out with all my well-known pedantry and need for elegant comfort', he writes of his new quarters in the Zurich 'Asyl'; 'the desk is next to the large window with a splendid view over the lake and Alps; peace and tranquillity surround me. A pretty and already well-kept garden offers me space for short walks and little resting-places' (letter to Liszt, 8 May 1857). A lengthy communication to King Ludwig of 23/24 February 1869 contains a description of Wagner's daily routine at Tribschen while working on the third act of *Siegfried*. 'Nulla dies sine linea' is his motto these days, he declares – at least a few lines of music every day. After a therapeutic douse of cold water, a 'modest breakfast' and a glance at the papers, Wagner settles down to his score at about 10 o'clock. 'This always gives me three beautiful, uniquely enjoyable and substantial hours each morning. At 1 o'clock Jacob [the man-servant] calls me to table.' After lunch Wagner is joined by his 'canine masters', withdraws into the salon for coffee, newspapers, letters and a short nap or a session at the piano. Then at 3 o'clock he dons his 'fearsomely large Wotan hat' and sets off for Lucerne accompanied by the dogs, Russ and Koss, to visit the post office, bookshops, etc. Upon returning to Tribschen about 5 o'clock, a brief rest precedes another several hours' work until an 8 o'clock supper and his habitual and wide-ranging post-prandial readings. The well-ordered routine described here resembles, in most particulars, descriptions of his working habits from other periods as well. Sometimes, as when working on the score of *Tristan* in Venice, Wagner found himself unable to compose for more than a brief time each day; the 'fresh lively, and fiery sections go incomparably faster' than those concerned with Tristan's pain and mental anguish (Act III), he informs Mathilde Wesendonck some time later, from Lucerne (30 May 1859). In a few cases the flood of inspiration would sweep away all routine. The first draft of *Der fliegende Holländer* was composed at an especially fast clip, for instance, in a matter of weeks. And in the early stages of *Die Meistersinger*, Wagner found himself unable to leave off work on Act I scene 2 until 6.30 pm one day, writing without pause since the morning. During the later years, in Bayreuth, it became increasingly difficult to isolate himself from the onslaught of correspondence, business affairs, visitors and various (often quite bizarre) solicitations of a kind which, as a world-renowned figure, he now attracted in quantity. It was Cosima's responsibility to intervene in these matters, and she served as a kind of informal secretary. Mounting distractions aside, the various phases of composition still required more time and effort from the older composer than in the past. The 'preliminary' and 'orchestral' drafts of each act of *Parsifal* took about six months to complete, for instance, while the analogous stages had been accomplished in three months or less with *Siegfried* or *Tristan*. Otherwise, Wagner did his best to maintain his regular habits, a peculiar synthesis of bourgeois sobriety and the indulgences of the 'decadent' aesthete. The purposeful discipline of his daily routine seems to be mirrored, in some sense, in the larger picture of his career – a career whose principal productions had nearly all been conceived by the middle of Wagner's lifetime and had merely to await the appropriate moment for their eventual execution.

THOMAS S. GREY

Wagner as polemicist

WAGNER BECAME WIDELY KNOWN during the 1850s chiefly as a polemicist. For most of his life more people read his writings or read others promoting them or attacking them, than heard substantial amounts of his music or, even less, saw his operas on stage. A polemical style was essential to his prose and was largely responsible for the breadth of his public. While many of his essays delve deep in aesthetic and philosophical aspects of music, his biting critique of the musical world and society as a whole was the key to the extraordinary impact of his ideas upon musical and artistic life.

Wagner's writing essentially set the framework of the most important issues in musical life from about 1850 to the turn of the 20th century. As such he stood among the most significant musical polemicists in the modern age, comparable with Jean-Jacques Rousseau in the 1750s and John Cage since the 1950s. Wagner was quite self-conscious in this role. In an essay published in volume VIII of his *Gesammelte Schriften* (*Collected Writings*), for example, he proudly defined a set of pieces as 'cheerlessly polemical' and admitted further that:

> one remarkable result of the enormous and, in itself, vexatious notice which the latter publication [*Das Judentum in der Musik*] aroused was that my writings on art were from that time eagerly read, or at all events bought; something that in Germany, unless an author has been admitted into one of the closely guarded literary circles, seems to be possible only through a scandal – as the present case shows – however unintended. (GS VIII, 204)

Wagner's purpose in writing can nevertheless be traced back to the needs of his musical works. Even though he became deeply engaged in a wide range of intellectual subjects he ultimately wrote in the hope of achieving as sympathetic a context as possible for the performance of his works. That gave his writings a unity of meaning and thrust, despite the diverse circumstances and sets of ideas with which each was associated.

His polemics were, if anything, moral, indeed moralistic in nature. His writings grew out of a century-old critical tradition within musical life that questioned the seriousness with which performing institutions and the publishing business treated music (see Weber's essay in Large and Weber, 1984). Wagner began writing this kind of prose during his stay in Paris between 1839 and 1841. Looking chiefly to the stylistic model of Hector Berlioz, he wrote *feuilletons* for the *Revue et Gazette Musicale*, some of which were translated and reprinted in Dresden. He launched a bitter attack on the public, on popular performers, and on the opera, calling listeners philistines and musicians aesthetic reprobates interested only in profit. In *Der Virtuoso und der Künstler* (*The Virtuoso and the Artist*) he stated that '[the public's] attention and curiosity is aroused primarily by displays of skill; pleasure in that generates interest in the work itself. Who can blame the public for that? Is the public not the very tyrant whom we wish to win?' (GS I, 170). Note in the penultimate sentence the half-deference to the public. The trick to such a polemic, in which Wagner excelled, was to make it entertaining to a wide readership despite its iconoclasm. One suspects that many people who had only limited sympathy with his ideas enjoyed seeing him vent his spleen.

The most important period of his writing – the point at which his name became widely known – came with the publication of a series of independent essays between 1849 and 1851. He wrote them under the influence of revolutionary rhetoric, but his main concerns were artistic rather than political as such. In *Die Kunst und die Revolution* (*Art and Revolution*, 1849) he deplored the loss of a unique opportunity by which artists could have, let us say, seized control of the means of artistic production:

> The former foundations of industry, of commerce and of wealth, are now threatened; and though tranquillity has been outwardly restored, and the general physiognomy of social life completely reestablished, yet a ravaging anxiety, a tormenting fear still gnaws at the entrails of this life [. . .]. He who wishes to preserve what he has, declines the prospect of uncertain gain; industry is at a standstill, and Art no longer has the means to live. (GS III, 8)

In this series of essays Wagner always prefaced his philosophical disquisitions on the nature of art with polemics against the conventions of the opera world. In *Das Kunstwerk der Zukunft* (*The Artwork of the Future*) he inveighed against 'this fiend, this crazy need-without-a-need, this need of need – this *need of Luxury*, which is in fact *Luxury itself* – that governs the world.' (GS III, 49) In *Ein Theater in Zürich* (*A Theatre in Zurich*, 1851), before spelling out a programme for transforming the city's theatre, he first denounced it, saying that 'until now the theatre has served for a kind of entertainment that one sought from purely accidental personal inclination, failing to connect it with any object to which one might suppose oneself pledged by considerations of a common inner need.' (GS V, 36–7) Nor did Wagner lose his polemical tendency in the late 1860s and 70s, even when he wrote to flatter Ludwig II. He showed how he could still rise to the occasion when in 1865 he appealed to the king to build a music school, declaring that 'the strangely flaccid, shapeless, superficial mannerism of the orchestral works of the post-Beethovenian school, woven from heterogeneous strands of style, betrays no trace of influence from Beethoven's astonishing quasi-architectural structures.' (GS VIII, 167)

Wagnerian polemics indeed became established as the language of a musical party. In 1852 the editor of the *Neue Zeitschrift für Musik* announced that propagation of Wagner's ideas would be his journal's leading goal, and in so doing he recalled the composer's own words: 'Determined adherence to party is therefore the new principle for which I call, determined struggle against that which is not vital, opposition to thoughtless routine which frustrates striving for the better.' (1 Jan 1852, p. 37)

WILLIAM WEBER

MORE NONSENSE HAS BEEN uttered on this topic than on almost any other connected with Wagner. The conventional image, wearisomely peddled, is that of an unscrupulous, exploitative scrounger, constantly touching friends, patrons and publishers for loans with which to subsidize a life of luxury. Such a view betrays an

Finances and attitude to money

extraordinary failure of imagination, as well as a lack of under-standing of the historical situation.

Until the German copyright law of 1870, passed almost at the end of Wagner's career, composers in that country could expect no percentage royalty on performances of their works, as of right; a single, flat fee was normally payable, any profits accruing to the publisher and the theatre (see 'Patronage, commissions and royalties in Wagner's day', pp.88–92). Even when he succeeded in getting his operas on to the stage, therefore, Wagner could scarcely expect a fair return for his labours. But the nature of his works – avant-garde, lengthy and 'difficult' – exacerbated the situation since publishers and theatre managements often proved as timid as Wagner was uncompromising in his demands for the highest artistic standards. If he had been driven primarily by love of money, or the rewards it can bring, he could have thrown off popular successes like Offenbach or Meyerbeer, or even continued to write in the vein of *Rienzi* and *Tannhäuser*, which would have assured him a steady income at the very least. Instead he chose to alter the path of operatic history, and in the process suffered constant financial hardship until his 'rescue' by King Ludwig II in 1864.

The uniqueness of the Bayreuth project, the enormous scope of its progenitor's ambition, and the near-impossibility of its realiza-tion in existing 19th-century conditions, might reasonably have provoked a more sympathetic response than the moral cavilling it usually elicits. In our own time, artists and administrators are driven to extend the begging-bowl to patrons, sponsors and funding bodies of all kinds – yet no moral censure seems to attach itself to such behaviour.

In the 19th century, as now, publishers and impresarios were in business to make a profit, and composers and artists could perhaps be forgiven for imitating some of the ruthlessness with which they themselves were treated. Moreover, the failure of successive publishers to match Wagner's own confidence in his 'artwork of the future' necessarily condemned him to the role of the perpetual mendicant.

Seen against this background, Wagner's negotiations with his publisher Schott and his patron Otto Wesendonck over the *Ring* scores take on a different aspect. In August 1859 Wesendonck made Wagner an unsolicited offer of financial help to finish the *Ring*. Wagner felt unable to accept either a loan or a gift, but instead he proposed a business deal (this was the usual arrange-ment with Wesendonck, incidentally, whose beneficence was always balanced by his business acumen: even the little house, the Asyl, he so 'generously' put at Wagner's disposal was leased to him at a commercial rate). The deal stipulated that Wesendonck would buy the copyright in the four scores for 6000 francs each and enjoy the proceeds, while Wagner would receive the revenues from public performances. When Wagner later the same year responded to Schott's approach to publish a score of his by offering him *Das*

Rheingold for 10,000 francs, it was on the understanding that Wesendonck would be reimbursed by Schott. At this point, too, Wagner hit on the ingenious idea of asking Wesendonck to regard his 6000 francs as an advance payment for the fourth work in the tetralogy, as yet unwritten. Such resourcefulness, worthy of the business world from which Wesendonck had recently retired, gained his agreement, willing or otherwise, and scarcely deserves the degree of opprobrium it usually attracts.

There is a further aspect of Wesendonck's patronage which is often overlooked. Quite apart from the fact that he regarded his subventions to Wagner as investments, albeit somewhat risky ones, he was a member of the class of *nouveaux riches* who dispense patronage not out of mere altruism, but because their very identity depends on such gestures. Craving the social respectability that money alone cannot bring, they latch on to great art and artists in order to revel vicariously in their status. Wagner was as valuable to the Wesendoncks as they were to him: Otto the silk importer and Mathilde the dilettante poet would scarcely be remembered now had they not been immortalized by their contact with Wagner.

A final point needs to be made in this context. Wagner had a deep-seated loathing for accumulated wealth and all its trappings which he retained, in spite of his latterly acquired comfortable status, throughout his life. His ideological position is as clear in allegorical form in the *Ring* as it is in polemical form in the theoretical writings (especially those of the Zurich period). Love of money undermined the fabric of society, he believed, and was at the root of all the lovelessness he saw around him. After a temporary rift in the long friendship with his Dresden doctor Anton Pusinelli – caused by Wagner's failure to meet his financial obligations – Wagner wrote to his friend: 'The whole monstrous curse of "money" now became clear to me: the quite natural position of the needy in relation to the wealthy had, in consequence, separated friend from friend.' (Lenrow, 1932) Money was not, therefore, a commodity to be treated with circumspection, as far as Wagner was concerned. In as far as it became available, its only purpose was to enhance the value of life: to provide material comforts for oneself and others, and above all to make possible the production of art.

BARRY MILLINGTON

Wagner and women

IF THE POPULAR CONCEPTION of Wagner as Don Juan is to be believed, his libidinous activities, generally involving other men's wives, would scarcely have left him enough time to compose. Clearly the notion requires some reappraisal. To begin with, his serious and casual affairs taken together hardly exceed a dozen, which is some way short of Don Juan's reputed 1003 in Spain alone. It is nevertheless significant that that dozen includes a high proportion of 'attached' women. The obvious psychological explanation, that Wagner's emotional life was profoundly and traumatically affected by his parentage and consequent mother-fixation (see 'Paternity', pp.94–5, and 'Family', pp.95–7) cannot easily be dismissed. A deep-seated fear of emotional commitment to women may well have induced Wagner to engage in a series of 'pursuits of the unattainable', according to which mechanism the subject attempts conquest, part desiring victory, part dreading it; he (i.e. Wagner) is on one level seeking satisfaction, but on a deeper, subconscious level, inviting frustration and rejection.

There is also, however, a social dimension to Wagner's behaviour which cannot be ignored. For the best part of his life – until the final years with Cosima – he loathed the institution of marriage, based as he perceived it to be on lovelessness and property rights. The 1849 outline for a drama or opera, *Jesus von Nazareth*, deals explicitly with the conflict between bourgeois propriety and love freely given and received. Nor is it a coincidence that all the marriages in the *Ring* are portrayed as joyless and destructive, while true love flourishes in less conventional couplings (brother/sister, aunt/nephew). That Wagner saw his affair with Jessie Laussot in 1850 as a deliberate assault on the institution of marriage is clear from his letter of 26/27 June 1850 to Julie Ritter: 'How delighted I was to discover in her letters not a single trace of that barbarous and unworthy bourgeois hypocrisy! She was nothing but *love*: we dedicated ourselves to the *God of love*, and scorned all the idols of this miserable world'. (The same letter makes astonishing reference to what Wagner believes to be his inability to win a lover 'whom I should not have had to woo from anyone' – a recognition, in other words, that he subconsciously shrinks from embracing the 'attainable'.)

The reason given by Wagner in later years (CT, 1 Apr 1874) for marrying his first wife Minna in 1836 nevertheless involved bourgeois respectability. He had initially 'approached her very thoughtlessly and had then perceived that she was a respectable person'. Propriety was a sensitive issue with Minna: as an actress her morals were always liable to be impugned, and she was obliged, throughout her life, to conceal the illegitimacy of her daughter Natalie – the consequence of Minna's seduction at the age of fifteen by a guards captain – by passing her off as a younger sister. Wagner's later comment to Cosima is consistent with what he confided to his friend Theodor Apel at the time (letter of 2 October 1835) about his relationship with Minna: 'You know my modern attitude towards love, which is what first brought me together with Minna; my wretched bourgeois outlook soon usurped my modern views, & all that was left was love' – in other words, the liaison began as purely sensual gratification, but subsequently the bourgeois desire for a secure, respectable relationship converted his feelings into love. Physical attraction was clearly the motivating factor, and contemporary accounts confirm that Minna was indeed strikingly beautiful. She had not the aptitude, however, to act as an intellectual sounding-board, nor the inclination to serve as muse; further, she was quite unsympathetic to Wagner's more progressive ideas, whether in the political or artistic spheres. By 1850 the marriage was effectively dead, though Wagner, who felt 'bound to her by a thousand chains of old and mutual suffering' (letter of 26/27 June 1850 to Julie Ritter), and who later feared that a divorce would prove too much for her weak heart, continued to support her financially until her death in 1866, even though they spent a good deal of the final decade living apart.

Up to the point at which it was acknowledged that their marriage had irretrievably broken down (letter of 16 April 1850 to Minna), Wagner was, as far as is known, faithful to his wife. In 1850, however, he encountered the twenty-one-year-old English-woman Jessie Laussot (*née* Taylor), fluent in German, a passionate admirer of his music and able to discuss it with him on his own terms. Her marriage was a troubled one and the pair conceived the idea of 'eloping' to Greece or Asia Minor – an adventure that was aborted by Jessie's husband and mother when they were apprised of the relationship.

Wagner's affair with Mathilde Wesendonck was not a great deal longer-lived. They first met in 1852, but the affection they felt for each other fully blossomed only in 1857, when Wagner and Minna were inhabiting the Asyl, adjacent to the Zurich villa of the Wesendoncks. Even then it is doubtful whether the relationship was consummated. Wagner always insisted, to Minna, his sister Clara and others, on the 'purity of these relations' that 'never offended against morality' (letters to Minna Wagner of 23 April 1858 and to Clara Wolfram of 20 August 1858) and it certainly seems implausible that *Tristan und Isolde*, that definitive expression of yearning and unsatisfiable desire, could have been composed at a time of emotional fulfilment.

Mathilde was nevertheless an efficacious muse, as was Judith Gautier – albeit of a greater intellectual calibre – two decades later (see 'Who's Who', p.25, for details of her 'affair' with Wagner). The liaison, if such it may be called, was the only serious disruption (discounting the Carrie Pringle Affair, see below) of the marital bliss enjoyed by Wagner and Cosima from 1870 (though Cosima's husband, Hans von Bülow, had had good reason to be jealous since at least July 1864) to Wagner's death in 1883. The couple revered each other, and their relationship was founded as much on intellectual sympathy as emotional commitment. Yet it cannot be described as a marriage of equals – Wagner's incorrigible egoism was if anything reinforced by Cosima's endemic subservience and idolatry. In spite of the strength of character she demonstrated, especially after Wagner's death, Cosima was less than sympathetic to the emerging movement for the emancipation of women (see, for example, CT, 19 Dec 1873). Wagner, on the other hand, though able to live with the conventional sexual roles which required him to be waited upon hand and foot for most of his life, nevertheless had an unconventionally progressive attitude towards women. Women were 'alone capable of educating us' men, he told Theodor

Uhlig (letter of 27 December 1849), while 'we shall not become what we can and must be until such time as – womankind has been awakened' was how he put it to August Röckel (letter of 24 August 1851), making reference to the reanimation of Brünnhilde in Act III of *Siegfried*. Brünnhilde it is too whose feminine wisdom ultimately restores sanity and hope to a strife-ridden world, ruined by naked male ambition.

Carrie Pringle was the young English soprano who took the part of a Flowermaiden in the Bayreuth performances of *Parsifal* in 1882. It is possible, but unproven, that she and Wagner had a sexual relationship at that time. In any case, the announcement of a visit from her appears to have provoked the furious row between Wagner and Cosima that led to his fatal heart attack.

These are the only 'affairs' of any consequence. It remains to mention the handful of harmless pre-marital diversions in Wagner's youth (reported in *Mein Leben*), the friendships with Mathilde Maier, Friederike Meyer and Blandine Ollivier in the early 1860s, none of which appears to have developed into undue intimacy, the brief fling with Seraphine Mauro (niece of Joseph Standhartner and lover of Peter Cornelius), and the Völkl sisters. Lisbeth Völkl was the 'sweet-tempered, obliging' seventeen-year-old mentioned in Wagner's letter to Mathilde Wesendonck of 3 August 1863; for a short time in Penzing, she entered Wagner's service – though precisely in what capacity remains unclear. Lisbeth's elder sister, Marie, was the recipient of the intriguing letter of 6 December 1863, in which Wagner urges the girl to have his room warm in readiness for his return from Breslau: 'Heavens! how I'm looking forward to relaxing with you again at last. *(I hope the pink drawers are ready, too???)*' To whom the pink drawers belonged, and to what purpose they were to be put are problems that Wagner scholarship has hitherto failed to solve. More research needs to be done in this area.

BARRY MILLINGTON

Relationship with King Ludwig II

THE IDEA OF A PENURIOUS artist rescued by a monarch, who cancels his debts, establishes him in luxury, and immerses himself in the composer's works with the enthusiasm of a fanatic, is the stuff of fairytale. But it became reality when King Ludwig II ascended the throne of Bavaria in March 1864. Already an avid Wagnerian, he wasted no time in summoning the composer to the royal castle Schloss Berg (just outside Munich), installing him in the Villa Pellet, overlooking the adjacent Lake Starnberg, and presenting him with 4000 gulden – the first of many subventions to ease Wagner's financial burdens.

'He sends for me once or twice a day', Wagner told Eliza Wille, reporting on the early stages of the relationship. 'I then fly to him as to a lover [. . .]. Thus we sit for hours on end, lost in each other's gaze.' (letter of 26 May 1864) For Wagner, the eager attention of one so exalted was unprecedented. For Ludwig, temperamentally inclined to extravagant Germanic fantasies featuring castles, forests and swans, the operas of Wagner were a treasure-trove. Doubtless his troubled emotional life – his homosexual tendencies could not easily be reconciled with the public demands of kingship – caused him to seek vicarious satisfaction in the heightened passions of the operas.

In the same letter to Eliza Wille, Wagner optimistically suggested that 'Everyone will come to love me in time; even now the young king's immediate entourage is happy to discover and know the sort of man I am, for they can all see that my immense influence upon the prince's mind can lead only to the common good'. Wagner was to pay for his hubris. By the beginning of 1865 he had already suffered his first, temporary, fall from royal favour. His indiscreet reference to the king (in his absence) as '*Mein Junge*' ('My boy') was faithfully retailed to Ludwig by his scheming cabinet secretary Franz von Pfistermeister, who along with the prime minister Ludwig von der Pfordten ('Pfi' and 'Pfo' Wagner dubbed the pair), was to lead the opposition to the king's favourite when it got under way later that year.

The campaign against Wagner was motivated both by anger at the large sums being distributed from the public purse – Wagner had been granted an annual stipend of 8000 gulden and an additional payment of 40,000 gulden to discharge pressing debts – and by resentment that Ludwig's domestic and foreign policies were apparently being increasingly dictated from across the lake. Both charges were partially justified, though Wagner's supposed abuse of the royal exchequer needs to be seen in perspective. The total amount received by him over the nineteen years of his acquaintance with the king – including stipend, rent and the cash value of presents – was 562,914 marks. This amount, which is less than one-seventh of the yearly Civil List (4.2 million marks), may be compared with the 652,000 marks spent on the bed-chamber alone of Herrenchiemsee, or with the 1.7 million marks spent on the bridal carriage for the royal wedding that never took place. A further statistic of relevance, in view of the comparative unpopularity of the kind of works Wagner was attempting to produce (see also 'Finances and attitude to money', pp.116–18), is that Meyerbeer received 750,000 marks for a hundred performances of *Le Prophète* in Berlin (Eger, 1986).

Nevertheless, the mounting hostility of both courtiers and commoners eventually compelled Ludwig, with great reluctance, to banish Wagner from Munich; he left discreetly at first light on 10 December (1865). By the following spring, Wagner had taken up residence at Tribschen, on Lake Lucerne, and on the composer's birthday (22 May) the king turned up on his doorstep, announcing himself as Walther von Stolzing. An even more startling announcement was that of his intention to abdicate, in order to be able to live at the revered one's side. This was hardly convenient for Wagner, since Cosima had all but taken up residence with him – she was there when Ludwig made his birthday visit – and the king seems to have been the last person in Munich to find out about the affair. Wagner was not slow to realize the strategic and financial implications of such an abdication, and successfully urged him to continue. An attack in the Munich *Volksbote* on 31 May (there had also been one the previous November) made reference to '"Madame Hans de Bülow" . . . with her "friend" (or what?) in Lucerne' – a thinly veiled allusion to Wagner's liaison with Cosima. A mendacious refutation (in which Wagner, Cosima and Bülow were all implicated) was issued, but soon the truth was obvious even to Ludwig.

The strain this deception put on Wagner's royal relationship was exacerbated by their differences over performances of Wagner's works. Ludwig's insistence on a staging in Munich of *Lohengrin* (it finally took place on 16 June 1867) resulted in clashes over casting (Ludwig complained that the sixty-year-old Tichatschek was a travesty of the youthful knight), costuming (nor had he worn the blue cloak specifically requested by the king) and scheduling. The subsequent premieres of *Das Rheingold* and *Die Walküre* in 1869 and 1870 respectively engendered further hostility: when it became evident that justice was not going to be done to the works, Wagner tried to prevent them from taking place, but Ludwig was adamant.

By 1871 plans were firmly in hand to establish the long-desired *Ring* festival in the Bavarian town of Bayreuth. Ludwig accepted reluctantly, but apparently with good grace, the idea of the festival being inaugurated outside Munich. However, a surprisingly frank passage in a letter to Friedrich Feustel and Theodor Muncker (respectively the chair of Bayreuth's town council and its mayor) indicates Wagner's impatience and annoyance with what he regarded as Ludwig's obstructive behaviour. This passage was deleted from the printed edition and published recently for the first time (Spencer and Millington, 1987).

Early in 1874, Ludwig failed to provide the necessary guarantees for the completion of the theatre, but just as Wagner was reconciling himself to further postponement of the project, the king had a change of heart: 'No, no and *no* again! it shall not end like this! Help must be forthcoming! Our plan must not fail.' (letter from Ludwig to Wagner of 25 January 1874) When the festival eventually took place in 1876, Ludwig attended the dress rehearsals and returned for the third cycle only on Wagner's assurance that he would be protected from the public gaze. Ludwig initially offered no help in discharging the crippling financial deficit of the festival. But by an agreement finally concluded in March 1878, the king was given the right to produce all Wagner's works in Munich without payment, in return for which he voluntarily offered to set aside 10 per cent of all such receipts until the deficit was cleared.

Wagner's last meeting with King Ludwig was on 12 November 1880, when the *Parsifal* and *Lohengrin* Preludes were performed for him privately in Munich. Ludwig failed to attend the premiere of *Parsifal* at Bayreuth in 1882, pleading ill health, but private performances were given in Munich in 1884, the year after Wagner's death, and three more in April 1885. In 1886, he was officially declared insane and deposed on 10 June; five days later he was found drowned in Lake Starnberg with his doctor.

BARRY MILLINGTON

Dealings with publishers

GIVEN THAT THE RELATIONSHIP between a writer or composer and his publisher is on the one hand a commercial arrangement, on the other an embodiment of shared objectives and the expression of mutual support to achieve them, the dealings of the 'difficult' Wagner with his publishers were bound to be fraught with controversy and recrimination. In Wagner's eyes it was a publisher's prime duty to guarantee for him the material circumstances that would allow him to carry out his projects assured of unstinting support, above all financial, in perpetuity. Without this assurance, he argued, he would not be able to give the world the works it was in him to give; and since it was to these works that the publisher too was looking for his own reputation and profit, it was in the publisher's long-term interests to view the matter in the same light. Wagner thus cast his publishers in the role of patrons or sponsors rather than of business partners.

Until Wagner's fame was certain, and with it their financial rewards, publishers saw things differently. His propensity for running up huge debts in order to finance his chosen life-style meant that he was continually approaching them for advances and loans against works he promised to deliver by unrealistic deadlines. If they declined, he made them responsible for any delay. Thus having contracted with Schott's in 1862 for *Die Meistersinger von Nürnberg*, he came back time and again for advances until finally delivering the completed score in 1867 with the cool observation that they could have had it three years earlier if they had been more generous towards him. 'It was unfortunate, God knows', he wrote to Franz Schott, 'that you did not do the right thing.' Small wonder that Schott was aggrieved. 'Let me assure you', he told Wagner, 'that there is not a music publisher in the world who can satisfy your demands. Only an immensely rich banker, or a prince with millions of marks at his disposal, can do so.'

There is, however, another side to the coin. Like most artists Wagner was ill-equipped to deal with the sophistications and sharp practices of the business world, where in matters such as author's copyright they often received a raw deal. Contracts made little effort to protect the artist against misuse of his work, even if it were possible to agree a definition of the term 'misuse'. Particularly blatant exploitation occurred in international dealings, where disputes arose over what rights were covered and what were not. The success of *Rienzi* in Dresden in October 1842, for example, followed by that of *Der fliegende Holländer* ten weeks later, had launched Wagner's career on a triumphant path, and Schott's joined the bandwagon by issuing for the German market a pirated edition of his Heine song *Les Deux Grenadiers*, which had been published in Paris two years earlier. Wagner had no copyright protection outside France, and although he publicly protested in the pages of the *Neue Zeitschrift für Musik*, he gained no redress and could only watch the profits of his labours disappear into other people's pockets. Subject to treatment of this kind, he retained a not unnatural suspicion of publishers to the end of his life.

Schott's of Mainz were in fact both the first and the last publishers with whom Wagner dealt. In 1830, as a boy of seventeen, he sent them a piano arrangement of Beethoven's Ninth Symphony; they did not publish it but at least acknowledged his skill and enterprise by presenting him in return with a copy of the score of the symphony, as well as of the *Missa Solemnis* and other works. His first work to be published was a Piano Sonata in B♭, which Breitkopf & Härtel accepted in 1832 for a fee of 20 thalers and 'tactlessly' reissued thirty years later, as Wagner put it in *Mein Leben*, when he had become famous but without a penny of the proceeds coming his way.

In 1843 he offered *Der fliegende Holländer* to Breitkopf for a suggested fee of 1000 thalers. Breitkopf agreed to publish it, while declining to pay any fee. Wagner's reaction was predictable, and instead he had it printed at his own expense (more accurately, by extended credit), together with *Rienzi* and *Tannhäuser*, by the Dresden court music dealer C.F. Meser. In 1848 he proposed that Breitkopf buy the rights of these three operas, so that he could pay off his debts to Meser. They turned him down in what must have been one of the costliest miscalculations in the history of music publishing. In 1852, however, realizing his growing importance, they accepted *Lohengrin* and *Eine Mitteilung an meine Freunde (A Communication to my Friends)*, but when offered the as yet unwritten four-part *Ring des Nibelungen*, they took fright at the magnitude of the commitment, and it was left to Schott's to take it over. The last of Wagner's works to be published by Breitkopf & Härtel was *Tristan und Isolde* in 1859. In that year Franz Schott acquired from Wagner the publishing rights for *Rheingold* for the substantial sum of 10,000 francs, and from then on – *Die Meistersinger von Nürnberg*, the *Ring* cycle, *Parsifal* – his music dramas bore the Schott imprint.

Not – Wagner being Wagner – that everything was plain sailing from then on. Against the terms of his contract, he took his *Kaisermarsch* (1871) to the Leipzig house of C.F. Peters and threatened to transfer all his future works there if a further substantial advance were not forthcoming from Schott's. Franz Schott gave way and drew up a new contract in 1874, providing for a fresh payment of 10,000 gulden against future works. It was a bottomless pit. But Wagner was used to getting his own way.

Wagner's correspondence with his two principal publishers is contained in *Richard Wagners Briefwechsel mit seinen Verlegern*, 2 vols, ed. Wilhelm Altmann, Leipzig/Mainz, 1911. Volume 1 contains his dealings with Breitkopf & Härtel, Volume 2 with Schott's.

RONALD TAYLOR

THE STORY OF WAGNER's relationship with professional critics is the story of a running battle. The battle started during his years as Kapellmeister to the Saxon court in Dresden in the mid-1840s – 'one of the happier periods in my life', he later ironically called it, 'in that I avoided looking at any musical journals'. Two things, he went on in his epistle *Über musikalische Kritik* (*On Music Criticism*), addressed to the editor of the *Neue Zeitschrift für Musik*, had prevented him from achieving his aims in Dresden. One was 'the totally perverted state of public taste', for which the public itself could in the last analysis hardly be held responsible; the other was 'the stupidity and dishonesty of the critics [. . .] who were guided neither by emotion nor by reason but based their activity on debauching the masses, and lived off this debauchery'.

Dealings with critics

It is a two-pronged attack that Wagner launches. The one thrust comes from a determination to refute what he sees as ignorant prejudice, masked as critical comment, against himself, both his compositions and his conducting. He could not refrain from remonstrating in public with the perpetrators of misconceived judgments. Accused of taking the Overture to *Figaro* too fast, he produced an eye-witness who remembered that at the rehearsals for the first performance in Vienna Mozart had constantly urged the orchestra to play faster and faster. In Berlin for a performance of *Der fliegende Holländer* in 1844, he was pained to read the reviews the following day, with their 'despicable tone and the brazen impertinence with which they displayed their rabid ignorance in this, their first account of me and my work'.

He was especially incensed by those critics who waited for one of the 'big names', such as Rellstab, to deliver his verdict on a work, then fell meekly into line behind him without making any attempt to study or assess the work on their own account. This resulted in the spread of the most bizarre accusations, cooked up, he was convinced, with the intention of causing him the greatest possible offence and misleading the public to the greatest possible extent about the true nature of his works. Even contemporary political issues were dragged in to bolster the case against him. 'They made out', he said, 'that I had provocatively given *Tannhäuser* a reactionary slant, since it was clear that, as Meyerbeer's *Huguenots* was a glorification of Protestantism, so *Tannhäuser* was a glorification of Catholicism, and for a long while the rumour persisted that the Catholic Church had bribed me to compose *Tannhäuser*.'

At times Wagner became almost paranoid about the criticism directed at him. The hostility, for example, with which the London press greeted his concerts for the Philharmonic Society in 1855 he ascribed to the critics' being in the pay of Meyerbeer. His reputation as a stormy petrel had, of course, preceded him, and the knowledge that he was closely associated with Liszt did not help, but in reality it was as much the challenge of his personality and his music *per se* that unbalanced the critical judgment of men not accustomed to such total, overwhelming demands as those Wagner made. Critics who sensed that Wagner represented something powerfully new which had to be confronted head-on, and who stated their views accordingly, themselves ran the risk of being taken to task by the conservative establishment, as happened to Hermann Franck over his early essay (1845) on *Tannhäuser* – a brave supportive effort for which Wagner remained eternally grateful.

In terms of personalities the most famous critic with whom Wagner skirmished, on a series of occasions, was the much-respected, much-feared Eduard Hanslick of Vienna, author of an influential treatise on aesthetics *Vom Musikalisch-Schönen* (*On the Beautiful in Music*, 1854). Hanslick had written enthusiastically about *Tannhäuser* in 1845 but, as a musical purist, he had grown increasingly disapproving of the direction in which Wagner was moving, and by the 1860s had become for Wagner the figurehead of the critical movement against him. 'When art enters a period of luxury', said Hanslick, 'it is already on the decline. Wagner's operatic style recognizes only superlatives, and a superlative has no future. It is an end, not a beginning [...]. One could say of this tone poetry: there is music in it – but it is not music.' In *Die Meistersinger von Nürnberg* Wagner then cast Hanslick as the pedant Beckmesser, soulless, small-minded symbol of anti-art. Invited to a reading of the libretto of the opera which Wagner gave to a group of friends in Vienna in 1862, Hanslick (as Wagner relates in *Mein Leben*) became increasingly incensed, until finally he stormed out of the room, unable to blind himself to the lampoon and convinced that the whole occasion had been engineered merely in order to humiliate him. After this the animosity between the two men became absolute, with Hanslick left espousing the cause of Brahms in an artificially generated feud between Brahmsians and Wagnerians, while Wagner marched singlemindedly on toward Bayreuth. Hanslick was a formalist, spokesman for an aesthetic of 'pure', i.e. abstract music, who saw in the theory of the *Gesamtkunstwerk* a total negation of the true inner values of music and who censured Wagner for what he described as 'the violation of music by words' and 'the unnaturalness and exaggeration of the expression'.

Petty-minded as it sometimes became, the Wagner–Hanslick dispute nevertheless rested on a solid foundation – the philosophical foundation of the moral responsibility of art, the eternal antithesis of Classic and Romantic which Goethe equated with that of the healthy and the morbid, the presence of that demand for total emotional submission which has made Wagnerians of some and anti-Wagnerians of others.

The other thrust of Wagner's antipathy towards critics in general goes beyond his personal antagonisms. It derives from his basic contempt for their failure to carry out in a responsible way their duty to the public. The taste of the public may be low and untutored but it is at least naively, 'naturally' so, whereas the depravity of the critics, as Wagner calls it, proceeds from an 'arbitrary set of principles' which they have chosen to apply, making no honest effort to confront the objects of their criticism openly and in the terms that those objects themselves require. This, in Wagner's eyes, means the forfeiture of all respect and the invalidation of their activities. He never saw any reason to revise his views.

RONALD TAYLOR

SOMETHING OF WAGNER'S SOCIAL and family background, his personality and character traits, has been outlined in the foregoing sections. It is hoped that certain misapprehensions may have been rectified and perspectives clarified, but it remains to propose a more radical and wide-ranging reappraisal of the conventional image of Wagner the man.

Wagner as scapegoat

Wagner stands accused of egoism, overweening ambition, opportunism, deceit, spite, jealousy, arrogance, philandering, profligacy and racism. A formidable catalogue, and there is truth in every item. A casual reading of either Cosima Wagner's Diaries or of Wagner's own letters will abundantly confirm such flaws in his character. But it will also reveal a set of more admirable traits, which in any other case would have gone considerably further to redeem the flaws. There are countless examples, too, of Wagner's generosity, kindness, gentleness and sensitivity, while the tired clichés about his supposed profligacy and philandering, for example, bear all too little relation to either the facts or the historical context.

What appears to have happened is that all the negative traits associated with Romantic artists in general have been projected on to Wagner and, moreover, been magnified out of all proportion. Just as Wagner himself inflated everything he touched – grand opera, the orchestra, nationalism – so he attracts, in turn, a degree of opprobrium scarcely justified by his faults. A classic case of the scapegoat phenomenon.

There is no question of trying to cover over the flaws in the way that the Bayreuth Circle and its associated hagiographers did in the past. Rather it is a matter of recognizing the unwisdom of expecting moral stature to be commensurate with creative genius. Indeed, one can go further and say that exceptional creative ability almost inevitably entails a degree of self-centredness, of naked ambition, of intolerance. In the 20th century such qualities are not generally admired, and artists not encouraged to flaunt them. In the 19th century, however, the aura of the heroic figure of the genius-artist encompassed precisely such characteristics as these: personal peccadilloes could be condoned, even accepted as part of the package.

There is also a more pointed aspect of the scapegoat phenomenon. Many of the character flaws with which the negative image of Wagner is invested – deceit, greed, opportunism, spite – are so common as to be universal. When we criticize Wagner for giving alternative versions of the same event to different people – even perhaps in a pair of letters bearing the same date – we would do well to be more aware of our own propensity for such behaviour. When we accuse Wagner of sharp practice in his financial dealings or of insensitivity in his sexual conduct, we might first stop to consider whether our own track record in these spheres entitles us to cast the first stone.

It is, of course, the ultimate irony that Wagner, who endowed a whole race, the Jews, with a negative image of unmitigated trenchancy, should himself be cast in the role of scapegoat. There may even be thought to be some justice in the fact. Nevertheless, historical truth is ill served by the desire for revenge.

BARRY MILLINGTON

Section 7
MYTHS AND LEGENDS

MYTHS AND LEGENDS

MORE HAS BEEN WRITTEN about Wagner than about any other human being except Jesus Christ and Napoleon. There is no truth in the statement whatsoever, but no book about Wagner would be complete without it. That more myths and legends have been propagated about Wagner than about any other composer in the history of music might be an easier proposition to sustain, and certainly the canard about Wagner literature is as good a place as any to start.

The myth has come down to us in various forms. Jesus Christ and Napoleon are favourite contenders for the bibliographic yardstick, but Jesus Christ and Shakespeare are another popular coupling, while Karl Marx also makes regular appearances, and an American variant offers Jesus Christ and Abraham Lincoln.

As for the origins of the myth, some scholars believe that they are forever lost in the mists of antiquity. Others trace them to Bryan Magee's brilliantly perceptive and influential *Aspects of Wagner*, first published in 1968. What Magee actually said, however – 'The number of books and articles written about [Wagner], which had reached the ten thousand mark before his death, overtook those about any other human being except Jesus and Napoleon' – referred to the situation obtaining shortly after Wagner's death. Even at that point, it is unlikely that the claim was literally true – Shakespeare alone has been responsible for the destruction of several rain-forests – but the *British Museum General Catalogue of Printed Books* to 1955 does indeed suggest that up to that point, more books had been written about Wagner than about Bach, Beethoven, Mozart, Marx, Schiller or Dickens. Wagner trails Goethe by a short margin, however, and Shakespeare by a considerably larger one.

In recent decades the position has changed drastically, especially if one looks at the general bibliographic situation (including scholarly articles as well as books). A glance at Schott's *Bibliographie des Musikschrifttums* shows that in typical years in the 1970s and 80s, Wagner literature was consistently outstripped by that on Bach, Beethoven and Mozart. Even in the Bayreuth centenary year of 1976, when the subjective impression was of an unstoppable torrent of Wagneriana, less was written about him than about either Mozart or Bach.

Having, one trusts, shot down the most persistent canard of all about Wagner, we may now turn to some of the other popular myths that have entered the tradition. They fall into two main categories: those originated by Wagner himself, either for ideological reasons or out of blithe disregard for the proprieties of positivistic music history, and those which have taken root at some point during the previous century and continued to blossom perennially.

In the first category, there are five favourite myths that have all been challenged by musicologists over the last couple of decades, but whose tenacity still allows them an occasional airing. The earliest, in biographical terms, concerns the supposedly formative theatrical experience, recounted in *Mein Leben*, in which the dramatic soprano Wilhelmine Schröder-Devrient made a momentous impression on the sixteen-year-old Wagner with her vibrant, ecstatic portrayal of Leonore in Beethoven's *Fidelio* at a guest performance in Leipzig. The lack of documentary evidence of any such performance of *Fidelio* in Leipzig in 1829, coupled with the knowledge that Schröder-Devrient's performance as Romeo in Bellini's *I Capuleti e i Montecchi* shortly after did indeed impress itself on Wagner's imagination, inevitably suggests that the recollection has been tailored to the image of himself that Wagner wished to project: that of Beethoven's natural successor. The conviction of the young Wagner – and it grew scarcely less dim as he got older – that it was his shoulders onto which the Beethovenian mantle had been destined to fall – is embodied most clearly in the novella of the Paris years *Eine Pilgerfahrt zu Beethoven* (*A Pilgrimage to Beethoven*, 1840). There the revenant Beethoven obligingly outlines the future Wagnerian music drama as the continuation of his own work: poetry and music to be united in a new synthesis; arias, duets and other divisions to be replaced by the continuous fabric of a drama. Later theoretical works, culminating in the bicentenary essay *Beethoven* (1870), further explore the fundamental relationship of poetry and music against the background of the Beethovenian symphonic legacy.

Whether one takes the censorious view that Wagner deliberately falsified his recollection of Schröder-Devrient, or the more charitable one that two memorable theatrical events were here fused into one in an act of poetic re-creation, is ultimately a matter of taste. Much the same is true of Wagner's autobiographical account of the genesis of the *Faust* Overture. The work is described in *Mein Leben* as the direct result of the experience of hearing Beethoven's Ninth Symphony in Paris. But the rehearsals of the Ninth which Wagner attended in Paris almost certainly took place in the early months of 1840 rather than in October or November 1839, and since the *Faust* Overture was sketched in December 1839 and completed on 12 January 1840, the pedigree of the work must surely be open to question. A far more likely inspiration is the *Roméo et Juliette* Symphony of Berlioz, which revealed to Wagner, as it did to a whole generation of composers, the possibilities for a new kind of choral symphony, one that was based on a literary classic and that contrived to reconcile a programmatic subject with the traditional abstract symphonic form. *Roméo et Juliette* received its premiere in Paris on 24 November 1839, and Wagner is known to have attended either that performance or the one on 1 December. He is also known to have been deeply impressed by the work – though later in his career he was much cooler in his enthusiasm for Berlioz's music.

A further brace of canards date from this period. The stormy sea-crossing from Pillau to London (*en route* for Paris) in July 1839 forced Wagner, his wife Minna and the crew of the vessel *Thetis* to take refuge in a Norwegian fjord – they went ashore at a small fishing village called Sandviken, on the island of Boröya. According to the ever-inventive *Mein Leben*, written a quarter of a century later, it was the experience of this calm after the storm, and of the crew's shouts echoing round the granite walls, that provided the creative inspiration for *Der fliegende Holländer*. The sharp rhythm of those shouts immediately began to shape them into the chorus of the Norwegian sailors, we are told, and the opera even began to take on 'a definite poetic and musical colour'. The prosaic truth is that the opera was originally set not in Norway at all, but in Scotland, and there is no tangible evidence of any musical composition from as early as 1839 (see 'The Music: *Der fliegende Holländer*', p.278).

The legend attached to a French version of the Flying Dutchman story, Pierre-Louis Dietsch's *Le Vaisseau fantôme*, was initiated by Wagner in all innocence, but has proved no less durable. Having sent a copy of his prose draft for the *Holländer* to the librettist Eugène Scribe in May 1840, Wagner the following month tried to interest Meyerbeer in it too, in the hope that the latter might use his influence to have it accepted by the Paris Opéra. As a result, Wagner was introduced to Léon Pillet, the new director of the Opéra, who finally bought the story from him. Pillet then gave the draft to two French librettists, Paul Foucher and Bénédict-Henry Révoil, who subsequently produced a text based on the Flying Dutchman legend, which was set by Dietsch and staged at the Opéra in November 1842, the very month in which Wagner's work went into rehearsal in Dresden. Wagner, who did not see the French production, not unreasonably assumed that Foucher and Révoil had based their story on his *Holländer* draft. In fact, as an examination of the libretto reveals, the French duo drew hardly at all on Wagner's draft, but on various other versions, primarily Captain Marryat's novel *The Phantom Ship* and to a lesser extent on Heine, Sir Walter Scott (from whose novel *The Pirate* they took several names and other details), as well as probably Fenimore Cooper (*The Red Rover*), the tales of Wilhelm Hauff and several poems. All in all, the melodramatic, but none-too-weighty tone of *Le Vaisseau fantôme* – which conformed to Pillet's demand for a piece 'selon le goût français' – bore little resemblance to that of the sombre *Fliegender Holländer* (see Millington, 1983 and 1986).

Still in Paris, we come to another legend for which Wagner was responsible, this time knowingly. The period he and Minna spent in Paris between 1839 and 1842 was a time of extreme hardship. Appeals to the well-heeled friend of his youth, Theodor Apel, went unheeded for over a month, and faced with the real threat of imprisonment for debt, it seems that Wagner resorted to a desperate ruse to persuade Apel to part with some cash. A letter dated 25 October 1840, the first of a pair sent by Minna but drafted by Wagner, states that he had had to leave her that very morning for the debtors' prison. The notion that Wagner did a stint behind bars, possibly even composing a part of *Rienzi* there, has taken a firm hold on the Wagner literature, but is almost certainly false. Among a number of items of evidence, the most compelling are the letter from Wagner to Heinrich Laube of 3 December 1840, which refers to those days of early December as terrible beyond imagination, and to the imminent 'loss of personal liberty' – which hardly tallies with incarceration earlier in October – and that to Friedrich Brockhaus of the following spring, in which Wagner appears to be justifying to his brother-in-law the ruse of the Apel letters, the truth of which Brockhaus had discovered (see *Sämtliche Briefe*, i, and Millington, 1984).

If the conception of *Der fliegende Holländer* is open to some question, the genesis of the later works is no freer from mystification. The traditional version of the initiation of the composition of the *Ring* follows the one in *Mein Leben*. According to that picturesque account, Wagner had to cut short his trip to Italy when the inspiration for *Das Rheingold* came to him as he lay half asleep in a hotel room in La Spezia – the sound of rushing water supposedly resolving itself into a chord of E♮ major, repeated incessantly in arpeggio figurations. Doubt has been cast on the plausibility of the account on musicological grounds (see Deathridge, 1977) and it is curious, to say the least, that such an auspicious sign as a 'vision' heralding the origination of the *Ring* should have been mentioned by Wagner in none of his letters of the period; indeed, the fact that such a 'vision' was first mentioned in a letter to Emilie Ritter of 19 December 1854, shortly after Wagner had read Schopenhauer's *Parerga und Paralipomena*, in which the connection of dreams and creativity is discussed, seemed to clinch the case against it. However, Warren Darcy (1989–90; see also 'Autograph manuscripts', p.217) has argued that while a degree of scepticism is called for, it is not possible to determine, on the basis of the surviving evidence, the precise sequence of events and thus the authenticity or otherwise of Wagner's hydrokinetic account.

The conception of *Parsifal* is similarly shrouded in mythopoeic fantasy, but in this case it is possible to dispel the mists of obscurantism. Wagner describes in *Mein Leben* how he and Minna moved into their new house, the Asyl, at the end of April 1857, and how he woke one morning to find the sunshine flooding in; buds were opening in the little garden, and the birds were singing. It was Good Friday and, recalling how the significance of that holy day had struck him when reading Wolfram's *Parzivâl* in Marienbad (in 1845), he immediately made a sketch for an opera on the subject.

Whatever the mystic significance of Good Friday to the *Parsifal* project, it could not have been that day on which the above took place, since Good Friday in 1857 fell on 10 April, at which time the Wagners were still living in the Zeltweg in Zurich. Curt von Westernhagen (1968) tried to salvage the poetry of the account by suggesting that Wagner may have walked out to the Asyl on Good Friday while it was still in the builders' hands. But this theory is contradicted by Wagner's mention of waking up in the Asyl.

Many years later, Wagner actually admitted that he had been 'mistaken' about the date. The entry for 22 April 1879 in Cosima Wagner's Diaries reads: 'R. today recalled the impression which inspired his "Good Friday Music"; he laughs, saying he had thought to himself, "In fact it is all as far-fetched as my love affairs, for it was not a Good Friday at all – just a pleasant mood in Nature which made me think, 'This is how a Good Friday ought to be.'"' (See also CT, 13 Jan 1878.)

Rather than accusing Wagner of outright mendacity, there is much to be said for entering into the spirit of such a confession and regarding his accounts of the genesis of his works and of formative experiences in his life as the poetic, if not the historical, truth. He would doubtless have endorsed the sentiments of another rewriter of history, Oscar Wilde: 'What is true in a man's life is not what he does, but the legend which grows up around him. You must never destroy legends. Through them we are given an inkling of the true physiognomy of a man.' Anti-historical this might be, but it is worth remembering that the myths and legends of an artist like Wagner do contain a reality of sorts, perhaps even a deeper reality than that signified by mere historical events.

It remains to mention a handful of legends that are still frequently perpetuated in the Wagner literature:

Wotan's eye

It is often said that conflicting reasons are given for the absence of one of Wotan's eyes in the *Ring*. He is stated, by the First Norn in *Götterdämmerung*, to have sacrificed his eye at the Well of Wisdom, while he also appears to tell Fricka, in Scene 2 of *Das Rheingold*, that he sacrificed it to gain her as wife. There are many contradictions in the *Ring*, but this is not one of them. When Wotan staked a pledge for Fricka it was not *one of his eyes* but *his one eye* ('mein eines Auge setzt' ich werbend daran'); in other words, having already sacrificed one eye at the Well of Wisdom, he pledged the remaining one for Fricka but was not, in the event, called upon to forfeit it. A careful reading of the libretto (*Das Rheingold*, Scene 2), in conjunction with the prose scenario of March 1852, places the matter beyond any doubt, though some of the world's leading Wotans continue to point to the wrong eye at the relevant passage.

The Valkyries as daughters of Erda

It is generally assumed that Brünnhilde's eight Valkyrie sisters are, like her, daughters of Erda. But as Andrew Porter (1977) has pointed out, there is no evidence that they are, and some to suggest that they are not. Wotan, in his narration in Act II of *Die Walküre*, mentions only that Erda bore him Brünnhilde, and in Act III of *Siegfried*, Erda recalls: 'I myself, with all my knowledge, was once mastered by a ruler. A wishmaiden I bore to Wotan.' There is no indication here that the congress of Wotan and Erda was anything other than a one-night stand.

For the true parenthood of the other eight Valkyries we must look to Act II of *Die Walküre*, where Fricka reproaches Wotan for his roving eye. Both in the depths and on the heights he has betrayed her, she says, sating his lust with what were evidently supernatural beings resident in those habitats; the 'brazen maidens' ('schlimme Mädchen') who resulted from those unions, he has since led into battle (a clear reference to the Valkyries).

The 'Porazzi Theme'

The plangent theme in A♭ known as the 'Porazzi Theme' and sentimentally described as Wagner's 'last musical thought', is neither of those things. The true 'Porazzi Theme' is one in E♭, with falling fifths, and inscribed by Cosima Wagner as 'Melodie der Porazzi!' (see 'The Music: Themes and melodies', p.313); it was evidently noted down while the Wagners were staying at the Piazza dei Porazzi in Palermo (2 February – 19 March 1882). The A♭ theme, on the other hand, almost certainly dates from 1858, the period of *Tristan* (see 'The Music: Theme in A♭ major', p.320).

The 'Starnberg Quartet'

The myth of the 'Starnberg Quartet', though traceable back to Wagner himself, was unknowingly propagated by Ernest Newman (1933–47). Cosima Wagner's Diaries recount how Wagner referred to the theme sung in *Siegfried* Act III to the words 'Ewig war ich, ewig bin ich' (also the main theme of the *Siegfried Idyll*) as dating from the 'Starnberg days' (i.e. the summer of 1864 when they were together at the Villa Pellet, overlooking Lake Starnberg, and during which they consummated their relationship – their first child Isolde was born the following April). In another diary entry, Wagner referred to the theme as the one 'which had come to him in Starnberg (when we were living there together), and which he had promised me as a quartet' (CT, 19 May 1869 and 30 Jan 1871). Newman, not unreasonably, concluded that Wagner had indeed planned to write a string quartet for Cosima based on that theme, and the scholar Gerald Abraham even managed a reconstruction of the supposed movement (published by Oxford University Press in 1947).

More recent research, however (Voss, 1977), has shown that whatever else may have been conceived that summer, it was not the 'Ewig war ich' theme: the latter dates from 14 November 1864, by which time Wagner was living alone in Munich. Furthermore, the theme was worked out sometimes in five or six parts, suggesting that it was from the start intended not as a quartet, but for *Siegfried*. Wagner may indeed have intended to honour Cosima with a quartet, and he certainly did so with the *Siegfried Idyll* of 1870, but the two projects can only be linked by the kind of Romantic mystification in which he was a past master.

BARRY MILLINGTON

Section 8

OPINIONS AND OUTLOOK

Social and political attitudes	140
Philosophical outlook	143
Religious beliefs	146
Literary tastes	149
The Beethoven legacy	151
Opera and social reform	153
Wagner and the Greeks	158
Wagner and the Jews	161
Wagner's Middle Ages	164
Bayreuth and the idea of a festival theatre	167
Contemporary composers	170
Wagner, animals and modern scientific medicine	174
Wagner's critique of science and technology	177

WAGNER WAS BORN DURING the Wars of Liberation, shortly before the Battle of the Nations which ended the Napoleonic Empire in Germany. Political ferment was in the air during his student years in Leipzig, where Louis-Philippe's *coup d'état* in Paris of 29 July 1830 led to violent clashes between the police and the local German students' associations. 'With one stroke', he wrote in his *Autobiographische Skizze (Autobiographical Sketch)*, 'I became a revolutionary, and reached the conviction that every aspiring human being should concern himself exclusively with politics.'

Wagner's campaign of political self-aggrandizement was fuelled by his sense of frustration as a creative artist compelled to endure the petty bureaucracy of the Biedermeier era in a succession of provincial German opera houses, and to submit to the humiliation of some four years of near-destitution in London and Paris. Almost immediately on his appointment to the Saxon court in 1843, a crisis of allegiance arose between the need to curry favour with his patron, Friedrich August II – whom he petitioned in two extended pamphlets and praised in a few minor musical compositions – and the conviction that progress would be possible only under a political system that made drastic concessions to the mounting republican sentiment of the *Vormärz* (the period from 1815 to the outbreak of revolution in 1848). An agonizing ambiguity of commitment was implicit in many of the unfulfilled creative projects of the last Dresden years. It became explicit in the notorious Vaterlandsverein speech of 14 June 1848, where the demand for an egalitarian society untrammelled by class, property, religion and law was linked incongruously to a no less urgent appeal for the recognition of the hereditary status of the Royal House of Wettin (here there are interesting parallels in the plot of the immensely successful *Rienzi*, and also in the contemporary *Der Nibelungen-Mythus* (*The Nibelungen Myth*) and the first version of *Siegfrieds Tod*).

In 1849, under Mikhail Bakunin (Dr Schwarz), colossal, leonine, loquacious and charismatic, Wagner appears to have been subjected to a process of relentless indoctrination which had issue in the effusive political poem, *Die Not* (*Need*), contributed to August Röckel's short-lived democratic *Volksblätter* in March (for a brief period, Wagner himself acted as editor of this subversive journal). At this time, Wagner probably discussed Proudhon's *Qu'est-ce que la propriété?*, with its call for 'the destruction of everything that curbed the uninhibited expression of the social instinct' (as the Countess d'Agoult put it in her definitive *Histoire de la révolution de 1848*). Some

Social and political attitudes

three decades later, the names of Bakunin and Proudhon were still connected in Wagner's mind (CT, 7 Sep 1878). During his exile in Switzerland, Wagner's republican sympathies were intensified by his friendship with the laureate of German socialism, Georg Herwegh – like Bakunin, one of Karl Marx's closer associates and a lifelong friend of the philosopher Ludwig Feuerbach under whose reluctant banner the revolutions of the 40s had been unsuccessfully fought.

It is notable that the hopes expressed in Wagner's politically orientated aesthetic tracts of this period transcended purely nationalist aspirations. 'The art of the future', he wrote in *Die Kunst und die Revolution* (*Art and Revolution*), 'must embrace the spirit of a free mankind, delivered from every shackle of a hampering nationalism; its racial imprint must be no more than an embellishment [. . .], not a cramping limitation.' His involvement, closely monitored by police agents, with a circle of exiled radicals in Zurich helped to sustain his faith in the republican cause long after the failure of the revolutions had become patently obvious and, with Louis-Napoléon's *coup d'état* of 2 December 1851, Europe had entered the era of *Realpolitik*.

Wagner's rescue on 4 May 1864, two years after the granting of his amnesty, by Ludwig II of Bavaria spoke eloquently for the king's artistic idealism and political insouciance. At the time of the *Huldigungsmarsch*, which marked Ludwig's nineteenth birthday, Bavaria stood on the brink of a constitutional crisis provoked by Bismarck's expansionist policies in Prussia. Wagner's sybaritic life-style in his villa in the Briennerstrasse in Munich, his plundering of the Bavarian exchequer and his machinations at the Hoftheater posed a serious threat to Ludwig's credibility in the first years of a difficult reign (but see also 'Relationship with King Ludwig II', pp.121–4). Nor were the king's interests advanced by Wagner's sudden enthusiasm during the composition of *Die Meistersinger* for the cause of German cultural and political unity. 'My own artistic ideal stands or falls with the salvation of Germany: without Germany's greatness, my art was only a dream', he told the political theorist Constantin Frantz on 19 March 1866 on the eve of the outbreak of the Austro-Prussian War.

The discussion was carried over into the essays *Über Staat und Religion* (*On State and Religion*) and the anti-Semitic *Was ist deutsch?* (*What is German?*), written in 1864 and 1865 respectively for the edification of Ludwig II who, however, warily distanced himself from their contents. Similar views were expressed in the articles *Deutsche Kunst und deutsche Politik* (*German Art and German Politics*) serialized in the *Süddeutsche Presse* in 1867 until suppressed by the authorities in deference to public opinion. 'Plainly they feared lest I should talk my head off', Wagner recalled sarcastically in *Wollen wir hoffen?* (*Shall we hope?*) in May 1879. Nonetheless, it was largely due to Wagner's diplomacy that the king was weaned away from an impending abdication (telegram to Wagner of 15 May 1866), and the House of Wittelsbach survived the collapse of the Austro-

Bavarian coalition, the Austrian defeat at Königgrätz and the Peace of Prague of 23 August 1866 with the proclamation of Bismarck's North German Confederation on 16 April 1867. If Wagner's conduct was often shamelessly manipulative, it would be mistaken to claim that it worked invariably to Ludwig's disadvantage.

With the marked cooling in the friendship after 1868, Wagner seized the opportunity to reassess his political affiliations. Early in 1870, his choice of Bayreuth in the centre of the new Germany-to-be as the site for his projected festival theatre showed an acute perception of the turn of the political tide.

No lover of France – as early as 22 October 1850, he had recommended to Uhlig that Paris, the hub of the capitalist conspiracy, be burned to the ground – Wagner greeted the outbreak of the Franco-Prussian War with an almost morbid satisfaction, mocking his brother-in-law Emile Ollivier's impending surrender in his scurrilous Offenbach–Aristophanes satire, *Eine Kapitulation*, and commemorating the crowning of Wilhelm I in the Galerie des Glaces at Versailles on 18 January 1871 in the jingoistic doggerel of *An das deutsche Heer vor Paris* (*To the German Army Before Paris*), acknowledged by Bismarck on 21 February:

> Die uns geraubt,
> die würdevollste aller Erdenkronen,
> auf seinem Haupt
> soll sie der Treue heil'ge Taten lohnen.

> (The proudest of all earthly crowns, once stolen from us,
> upon his head shall reward his holy deeds of devotion.)

The acclaim that on 25 April 1871 greeted Wagner's triumphal entry into Berlin, where he was received by Bismarck and a few days later conducted a performance of the *Kaisermarsch* in the presence of the newly crowned emperor and empress, set the seal on his brief period of identification with the *arriviste* politics of the Second Reich.

Any hopes that Wagner may have entertained of floating the Bayreuth Festival on the economic miracle of the *Gründerzeit* were to be cruelly disappointed. His appeal of 24 June 1873 to Bismarck as 'the only truly supportive and ennobling authority' remained unanswered. Then, in December 1875, a loan of 30,000 thalers authorized by Wilhelm I was unceremoniously cancelled. For Wagner, the boorish indifference in governmental circles continued to rankle, furiously, until further mention of the name of 'this beastly agitator' (CT, 18 Mar 1880), the Federal Chancellor, was proscribed in the Bayreuth household.

In the event, the Kaiser put in a token appearance at the first performance of the *Ring*, tactlessly leaving before the cycle was complete. After this, even in public, Wagner was set against compromise. In 1878, the publication in the *Bayreuther Blätter* of an attack on Bismarck by Constantin Frantz alienated a section of the Berlin Wagner-Verein; while Wagner's abrupt departure from the stage during the ovation at Neumann's Berlin production of *Götterdämmerung* on 29 May 1881 was widely interpreted as a direct affront.

It can therefore be said that for all his continuing concern with the German national identity and the identity of German art, Wagner did not fall in with the 'Deutschtümler' and their popular cult of national supremacy; nor, *pace* Nietzsche, usually well informed in his assessments, did he 'condescend' to Bismarck in the final phase. On the contrary, as a veteran revolutionary, turning increasingly towards America and Russia, he defied the Reich as openly as it by withholding support for Bayreuth had defied him. Inevitably, the second Bayreuth Festival was ostracized by the Prussian hierarchy (and by Ludwig II). As Wagner was well aware, his reputation as an artist was too impregnable for this to have seriously damaging consequences.

ROGER HOLLINRAKE

Philosophical outlook

WAGNER WAS NOT A STUDENT of contemporary philosophy in an academic sense. The names of Kant and Fichte, the founders of Idealism, are seldom encountered in his writings. At Leipzig, his study of Schelling's *System des transzendentalen Idealismus* (*System of Transcendental Idealism*) proved wholly unrewarding and was never resumed; at Dresden, a more determined assault on Hegel's lectures on the philosophy of history foundered with the outbreak of the revolution. The pervasiveness of Hegel's influence on 19th-century thought, however, should not be underestimated. It is probable that, directly or indirectly, Wagner's debt to the philosopher was far greater than his own subsequent testimony – and the contents of his libraries at Dresden and Bayreuth – would lead us to believe (see also under entry for *Der Ring des Nibelungen*, p.286).

Well before his arrival in Dresden in 1842, Wagner had fallen under the spell of the progressive politics and liberal ideas of the Young Germans. He had begun to maintain intermittent but lifelong contact – not always cordial – with Heinrich Laube; and at Laube's house had been introduced, in 1839 or 1840, to Heinrich Heine. This prepared for a ready identification with the aims of the writers of the pre-revolutionary period, although the dates of systematic study are obscure. Certainly, Pierre-Joseph Proudhon, whose seminal *Qu'est-ce que la propriété?* was published in 1840 during Wagner's residence in Paris, appears to have influenced the synopsis for the *Ring* cycle, although Wagner claimed to have investigated Proudhon's critique of capitalism only after his flight to La Ferté-sous-Jouarre in 1849. It is also difficult to say precisely when Wagner encountered the writings of the briefly celebrated Young Hegelians: Ludwig Feuerbach (recommended by the

German Catholic priest in the Calabrian hat, Metzdorf), David Strauss, Bruno Bauer and the Bayreuthian, Max Stirner. The inventories of his Dresden and Bayreuth libraries are again singularly unhelpful. In the prose outline *Der Nibelungen-Mythus* (*The Nibelungen Myth*), Siegfried, not yet fearless, is already the representative of a free, emancipated humanity. 'In man, the Gods seek to implant their own divinity', Wagner wrote, 'and their aim would be attained even if in this human creation they should annul themselves.' The iconoclastic note is again struck in the plans for *Jesus von Nazareth* and *Achilleus*, drafted at the time of discussions with the anarchist Mikhail Bakunin, in 1849. The name of Karl Marx is conspicuously absent from Wagner's writings; but it is to be remembered that Bakunin and, later, Herwegh, Wagner's companion in Zurich, were close personal associates of Marx. 'I call revolution the conversion of all hearts and the raising of all hands in honour of the free man', Ruge announced in the preface to Marx's *Deutsch-Französische Jahrbücher* in 1844. 'The criticism of religion ends in the teaching that man is the highest being for man', Marx wrote in the same year. In the background to all these statements is the anti-philosophy of Feuerbach's *Das Wesen des Christentums* (*The Essence of Christianity*) of 1841: 'The question of the existence of God is for me nothing but the question of the existence of man.'

Feuerbach, indeed, was to colour all the theoretical tracts of Wagner's Zurich period, including, notably, *Das Kunstwerk der Zukunft* (*The Artwork of the Future*), addressed to the philosopher and acknowledged by him in September 1850 (the deletion of this address in Wagner's collected writings may have been due to the inclusion of a more measured tribute in the preface to the third and fourth volumes). The label 'Zukunftsmusik' (Music of the Future) continued to be applied to the music of the progressive German school long after its origins in Feuerbach's *Grundsätze der Philosophie der Zukunft* (*Principles of the Philosophy of the Future*) had been forgotten. Feuerbach's influence, too, infuses the poetic text of the *Ring*, completed with encouragement from Herwegh who, in December 1851, soon after his first meeting with Wagner, combined in an unsuccessful attempt to entice the now beleaguered philosopher to join the Zurich circle of expatriate revolutionaries.

Within a year of the letter to Röckel of 25/26 January 1854 in which the *Ring* poem was construed retrospectively – without acknowledgment – in terms of the 'I' and 'You' of *The Essence of Christianity*, Wagner alighted on the discussion of tragedy in Book III, § 51, of Schopenhauer's *Die Welt als Wille und Vorstellung* (*The World as Will and Representation*). The contrast between Feuerbach's deification of man and Schopenhauer's despair at the human condition could hardly have been greater. Wagner recalled in *Mein Leben*: 'For those seeking in philosophy their justification for political and social agitation on behalf of the so-called "free individual", there was no sustenance whatever here.'

After a period of adjustment, Wagner's obsession with Schopenhauer, and with Schopenhauer's sources in Buddhism and

Brahmanism, previously neglected, in effect precluded further philosophical attachments.

The following Wagnerian traits are listed by Nietzsche in *Die fröhliche Wissenschaft* (*The Gay Science*), § 99, as derived specifically from Schopenhauer: Wagner's use of categories such as 'will', 'genius' and 'pity' ('Mitleid', 'Mitleiden'); his exasperation at the corruption of the German language (Schopenhauer, who wrote an untypically lucid German prose, had denounced Kant's successors, especially Hegel, as a cult of ponderous incomprehensibility); his anti-Semitism (an over-simplification); his attempt to construe Christianity as a sect of Buddhism (rather than of Judaism); and his reverence for animals. Schopenhauer's aesthetics, too, were important for Wagner, who found here a way of explaining the dominance of music among the elements of his new synthetic art form (despite the fact that Schopenhauer had dismissed opera as a debased genre precisely because it involved a fusion of media).

For all that, Wagner's attitude to Schopenhauer, like his attitude to Young Germany, Hegel and the Young Hegelians, was one of imaginative, retrospective identification rather than of literal dependence. If the parities are notable so are the disparities. Nietzsche, when discussing the hedonistic Siegfried as Wagner's most characteristic creation, rightly remarked that 'nothing could be more contrary to the spirit of Schopenhauer'; and the glorification of erotic passion in *Tristan und Isolde* can be brought into line with Schopenhauer only if it is accepted that the abhorrence which the philosopher expressed in his *Metaphysik der Geschlechtsliebe* (*Metaphysics of Sexual Love*), and in his vitriolic essay *Über die Weiber* (*On Women*), was not meant to be taken at its face-value (fortunately, perhaps, the formal rejoinder which Wagner outlined to Mathilde Wesendonck in 1858 was never completed). It argues some temerity on Wagner's part that in December 1854 he should have sent a copy of the *Ring* poem to Frankfurt (Schopenhauer's marginal notes, transcribed in Ellis, 1900–08 (IV, 440–46), are of some interest); that in the same month he should have prevailed on Franz Bizonfy, as spokesman, to invite Schopenhauer to Zurich; and that in March 1856 he should have participated in a scheme to create a chair in Schopenhauerian philosophy at Zurich University. Schopenhauer's rejection of these overtures – above all his aversion to the 'infamous' *Ring*, of which Wagner may have been apprised by an article on Schopenhauer's annotations to the text by Max Goldstein in the *Deutsches Montagsblatt* in 1882 (CT, 6 Dec 1882) – was registered twenty years after the philosopher's death with a sense of disappointment amounting to personal grievance.

Parsifal, regarded as a homily on the virtue of compassion – the erotic element here demoted to a source of temptation and sin – was to achieve a more spontaneous accord with Schopenhauer's misogynistic asceticism (but not with his atheism). In the late writings in the *Bayreuther Blätter*, however – notably in *Religion und Kunst* (*Religion and Art*), and its sequels written after study of

Gobineau's *Essai sur l'inégalité des races humaines* with its disturbing theory of racial degeneration – Wagner invested the text with a dense accretion of esoteric thought.

ROGER HOLLINRAKE

WAGNER WAS BROUGHT UP in a conventional Protestant household. *Religious beliefs*
His mother, Johanna, who was in the habit of regaling the family with 'pathos-filled, sermon-like discourses on God and the divine in human beings' (*Mein Leben*), played a part in his early religious education. At the time of his confirmation in 1827, however, there was little evidence of any precocious interest in theological issues, which in later life Wagner approached with a marked independence of mind. The characteristic themes of guilt, atonement and redemption as they appear in the early operas carry largely secular connotations; considering Wagner's attraction to the anti-clericalism and anti-Catholicism of the 1830s, the incidental references to religion in *Tannhäuser* and *Lohengrin* appear more as concessions to 19th-century taste than as expressions of deeply-held religious convictions.

There is, however, a sense in which Wagner's life may be seen as a tortuous progress towards the formulation of a personal creed: a creed conveyed through the mythic symbols of his art, which at least by the time of *Das Kunstwerk der Zukunft* (*The Artwork of the Future*) of 1849 had been invested with a quasi-religious function and significance.

Insight into the evolutionary process is afforded by the sketches for a five-act drama or music drama, *Jesus von Nazareth*, of early 1849: one of the more notable consequences of Wagner's exposure to the progressive thought of the 1840s. Here a selection of incidents from the New Testament is expounded in terms of the materialism of Proudhon which had already contributed to the scenario *Der Nibelungen-Mythus* (*The Nibelungen Myth*) of 1848, and the secular humanism of Feuerbach's topical *Das Wesen des Christentums* (*The Essence of Christianity*). The feverish interest aroused by Feuerbach's anthropocentric – or anthropotheistic – philosophy among the young radicals of Germany is, of course, a matter of historical record. As Engels remarked in his seminal early study: 'Enthusiasm was general. We all became Feuerbachians', adding that Feuerbach's 'extravagant deification of love was excusable if not justified after the intolerable sovereign rule of "pure reason" [i.e., Kantian philosophy].' Here, too, Wagner encountered the conception of theology as a divisive force inspired by resentment, egoism and national pride, inimical to art and totally opposed to the universality of the Christian message. Jesus, he contended, echoing Feuerbach in the notes for *Jesus von Nazareth*, owned no specific national allegiance: 'Through Adam, he had sprung from God, and therefore all men were his brothers.' It follows that soon after drafting *The Nibelungen Myth*, probably with encouragement from

Bakunin, Wagner read – or re-read – *The Essence of Christianity* and, fired by the eudemonistic philosophy of love which Feuerbach had developed in part from the *bien-être* of Holbach's *Système de la nature*, set about to translate it into terms of the 'ideal theatre of the future' (the Feuerbachian phrase he uses when discussing *Jesus von Nazareth* in *Mein Leben*).

From the conflation of material from the discarded *Jesus von Nazareth* arose the symmetrical ordering of concepts – fearlessness, freedom and love *versus* fearfulness, lack of freedom and lovelessness – that is one of the most conspicuous features of the text of the *Ring* poems as they stood after their 1852 revisions. 'No law can bring about the rich and prospering deeds of love', we read in *Jesus von Nazareth*, 'for the law is the restraint of freedom, and love is creative only when it is free.' When in the closing scene of the revised text Brünnhilde, the emancipated woman of the future, abjures private property – 'Nicht Gut, nicht Gold, noch göttliche Pracht. . . .' ('Not possessions, nor wealth, nor divine splendour. . . .') – and freely and fearlessly proclaims the redeeming power of love, the eschatology of the well-known Chapter 26 of *The Essence of Christianity* finds its representative dramatic embodiment.

Wagner's humanist stance, intensified by the experiences of his first years of exile, did not pass without remark. 'Your greatness also makes for your misery', Liszt wrote censoriously on 8 April 1853 soon after receiving a copy of the poetic text of the *Ring*, 'until you sink down in *belief* and allow both to rise up.' Wagner flared up in his reply of 13 April: 'I too am bitterly scorned for my faith [. . .], for I believe in the future of humanity, and I derive this belief simply from my innermost need.'

A new phase, however, began in 1857 with the decision to develop the subject of Parsifal. This is not to say that Wagner had opted for 'belief' (i.e., the faith of Rome) in Liszt's sense. Rather, he had come under the influence of the neo-Buddhism of Schopenhauer's *Die Welt als Wille und Vorstellung* (*The World as Will and Representation*), and had departed further from the orthodox Christian position.

The initial result of Wagner's conversion (if such it may be called) to Schopenhauer's philosophy was a sketch for a music drama, *Die Sieger*, based on an incident in the legendary life of the Buddha recounted in Burnouf's *Introduction à l'histoire du bouddhisme indien*. Linked to this in May 1856 was an amendment to the peroration of the *Ring* in which the Feuerbachian affirmation of love was replaced with verses affirming the Buddhist doctrine of metempsychosis and the bliss of extinction. The two endings, despite their conflicting religious affiliations, were not mutually exclusive. 'The life of man', Wagner had written in *Jesus von Nazareth*, 'is a continual slaying of the self [. . .]. Death accordingly is the most perfect deed of love: it becomes such through our consciousness of a life consumed by love.' Nor in point of fact was Wagner's new interest in Buddhism and Brahmanism totally incompatible with his former interest in Christianity. In Schopenhauer's words: 'I cannot give up the belief that the doctrines of Christianity can in some way be derived from these primitive religions.' Wagner had already hinted at this theory independently in his early study, *Die Wibelungen* (*The Wibelungs*), in tracing the evolution of the story of the sacred quest. He enlarged on the subject in a letter of 7 June 1855 to Liszt, citing modern research as having established conclusively that Christianity 'is no more and no less than a branch of that venerable Buddhist religion which, following Alexander's Indian campaign, found its way, among other places, to the shores of the Mediterranean.' (See also, especially, the letter to Röckel of April 1855.)

On this showing, it would appear that for Wagner the humanist Siegfried, 'a *fearless* human being, one who never ceases to *love*', and the Christian (or Buddhist) Parsifal were not totally distinct and incompatible personalities, but complementary aspects of a single mythic prototype.

Certainly, when in 1865 Wagner presented Ludwig II with the synopsis of *Parsifal*, the intention was clear: to establish the universality of the Gospels by breaking the confining barriers of a mendacious tribal theology (the spectre of the anti-clerical Feuerbach was never completely exorcized) and by affirming the doctrinal content of the ancient sources of oriental religious enlightenment in which, according to Schopenhauer, Christianity had originated. The problem with primitive Buddhism, he was to declare in the last pages of *Heldentum und Christentum* (*Heroism and Christianity*) in 1881, was its tribal exclusiveness. Charges of parochialism and élitism, however, could as well be levelled at the ecclesiastical establishment which, by accepting Christ's limited Messianic office, had transformed a potentially world-encompassing religion into a narrowly introverted, racialist (i.e., pro-Semitic) sect. 'The Christian religion', he reiterated in *Was ist deutsch?* (*What is German?*), first printed in the *Bayreuther Blätter* in 1878, 'belongs to no specific national stock: Christian dogma addresses purely human nature' ('die reinmenschliche Natur').

From the orthodox Christian standpoint, the syncretism of *Parsifal*, which transposes the principal doctrines of Buddhism along with material from the Gospels and the liturgy of the Eucharist into the context of a Christianized redaction of the legend of the Grail – a mystical emblem unrecognized by any ecclesiastical authority – is bound to remain problematical; not that Wagner when he restricted performances of the music drama to Bayreuth was oblivious to the fact. From the time of its inception, the Festspielhaus, 'a Castle of the Grail devoted to art' ('eine Gralsburg der Kunst'), as he described it on 11 August 1873 to Ludwig II, had existed to enshrine 'the world's profoundest secret': a sacerdotal rite of purification and regeneration protected from the profane and accessible only to those initiated into its mysteries ('die Eingeweihten').

It may be replied that Wagner only compromised his high standing as an artist by his attempt to inaugurate a surrogate super-religion in an age of unbelief. No doubt it can be argued, that, like many reformers, he was in the end impelled by the force of his anti-élitist zeal into a new élitism of his own. Parsifal's benediction, the outcome of some twenty-five years of constant reflection, however, stands as the long-premeditated culmination of his life's work, resting on a substratum of thought, penetrated with difficulty, that both reflects and illuminates the tensions of an age of profound spiritual disquiet.

ROGER HOLLINRAKE

Literary tastes

THE EARLIEST LITERARY INFLUENCE on Wagner seems to have been Greek literature, to which he was introduced at school. Shortly afterwards came the writings of the German Romantics and, in particular, the novels and short stories of E.T.A. Hoffmann, Ludwig Tieck and Friedrich Schlegel, his knowledge of which he owed, at least in part, to his uncle, Adolf Wagner. Although the composer later displayed a typically ungenerous attitude to Hoffmann, Tieck and other Romantic writers, there is no denying their seminal importance for the whole of his later oeuvre in terms of subject-matter and themes, from fairytale motifs to the supernatural and the world of dreams, from the mood of world-weariness to the artist's role in society.

By the 1830s Romanticism was a spent force in German literature and was replaced by the Young German movement. Writers such as Karl Gutzkow and Heinrich Laube (works by both of whom Wagner is known to have read) spoke out against existing social and political conditions, against out-dated moral precepts, philistinism and the mysticization of religion; both men served terms of imprisonment as a result. The most immediate result of Wagner's espousal of Young German ideals was the comic opera *Das Liebesverbot*, in which he pilloried German puritanism and lauded southern hedonism; but an interest in politics and socialist ideas, together with a loathing of philistinism, coloured his outlook for the rest of his life, so much so that it is often difficult to disentangle the strands of literary, political and philosophical influence. It was probably also at this time – in other words, during the mid-1830s – that Wagner was introduced to the writings of Heinrich Heine and Edward Bulwer-Lytton, both of whom were to be of influence on the works of the following decade.

No one could claim, however, that Wagner was anything other than a fitful reader at this stage in his career. An initial turning-point seems to have come in Paris in the winter of 1841/2, when his conversations with the classical and medieval scholar Samuel Lehrs not only revived his love of Greek literature but awakened an interest in the German Middle Ages. Following his appointment as Kapellmeister to the Royal Court of Saxony Wagner began building up a library of around two hundred volumes, consisting, for the most part, of medieval and classical texts. Among the other authors represented were Byron, Calderón, Gibbon, Goethe, Hegel, Herder, Kleist, Lessing, Molière, Rousseau, Hans Sachs, Schiller, Shakespeare and Tieck. It should be emphasized, however, that the presence of a book in Wagner's library does not mean that he read it (in some cases, the pages of the volume are still uncut), while we know that he had access to other libraries, both public and private, so that the absence of a work is no proof that Wagner cannot have read it.

Wagner forfeited his Dresden library when he fled the city in May 1849. We are less well informed about his bibliophilic habits during the next two decades, though at least some of the volumes acquired during these years must have found their way into his library at Tribschen and Wahnfried. Among the entries in the Annals, only a handful of literary names stand out: in London in 1855 Wagner read Dante's *Divine Comedy* and Adolf Holtzmann's collection of Indian tales; in 1856 he read Scott and Byron and the following year added Calderón to his collection. In 1864 we find him dipping into Chateaubriand, George Sand, Gustav Freytag and more Scott, and, in 1865, we know that he read the *Ramayana* and Hugo's *Les Misérables* in quick succession. On the whole, however, it was philosophy and history which occupied Wagner's attention during these years.

Not until the late 1860s, when he settled down to a life of connubial domesticity with the cultured and well-read Cosima, does Wagner appear to have begun to read more widely and deeply. Scarcely an evening went by without the two of them reading aloud to each other from at least one of the 2500 volumes which ultimately came to rest on the shelves of the Wahnfried salon. All the leading Greek and Roman authors were represented here (although Wagner always had a low opinion of Latin literature), as were the most important works of Indian, Arabian, Spanish, English, French and German literature. (Books on philosophy, history, theology, music, law, art and natural science made up the remainder of the collection.) Time and again, however, Wagner and Cosima returned to the same canonical works of world literature which they considered absolutely 'indispensable' (CT, 4 Jun 1871): the list included Homer, Aeschylus, Sophocles, Plato's *Symposium*, the whole of Shakespeare, Cervantes' *Don Quixote* and Goethe's *Faust*. (As Dieter Borchmeyer has pointed out, the omission of Dante's *Divine Comedy* is probably no more than an oversight.) Not only is *Faust* the sole work of German literature to figure in the list, it is also the most recent one: Wagner, significantly, had little time for 19th-century art, which he regarded as ripe for supersession by the artwork of the future. Only Balzac seems to have enjoyed his unqualified approval, a realist who had exposed the evils of modern society, while acknowledging the utter hopelessness of the *comédie humaine*. At the same time, Wagner's increasing interest in the populist, 'improvisational' element in art, and in 'open' as opposed to 'closed' form, now made him prefer Lope de Vega to Calderón, Gozzi to Goldoni, Molière to Corneille and Racine, and to rank Shakespeare above them all. If Wagner's literary judgments sometimes seem unsophisticated, it is because they were formed against the foregoing background, not because there is any truth in Marianne Wynn's claim that 'Wagner was an appalling judge of literature' (Wynn, 1980).

STEWART SPENCER

The Beethoven legacy

WAGNER WAS BY NO MEANS alone in his desire to be seen as the legitimate musical offspring of Beethoven, although he was probably the most vocal in staking his claims to spiritual and aesthetic primogeniture. Nearly every major composer up to Schoenberg – from the early Romantic radical, Berlioz, to the late Romantic conservative, Brahms – recognized in Beethoven an imposing ancestral figure whose achievements defined the main avenues of musical development in the 19th century. As an opera composer who had publicly announced the demise of Classical instrumental forms in his own time, Wagner was perhaps obliged to argue his case more forcefully than other composers, like Brahms, who continued to cultivate the central Beethovenian genres of sonata, chamber music and symphony.

Wagner's concern with Beethoven was certainly more than mere show, or simply a 'public relations' scheme to convince the public of his seriousness of purpose – yet such motives cannot be entirely dismissed. It is difficult, for instance, to distinguish the 'authentic' components of his earliest Beethoven experiences, as recounted in *Mein Leben* and elsewhere, from the undeniable element of retrospective idealization. At an early age he was already entranced, he claims, by the mysteries of the Ninth Symphony (especially the 'spectral' sonority of its opening); the Seventh Symphony had an 'indescribable effect' on the young Wagner when he heard it for the first time in a Leipzig Gewandhaus concert; and the very image of the composer, the knowledge of his deafness, and the news of his recent death all penetrated his youthful consciousness profoundly, according to his later recollections. The conjunction of Beethoven and Shakespeare – Wagner maintained that he encountered images of both artists in 'ecstatic' dream-like visions as a boy – is clearly imbued with symbolic and prophetic import, even while it is entirely plausible that the ardent young musician and theatromane was genuinely fascinated by these figures. (Wagner's early piano arrangement of the Ninth Symphony, as well as manuscript copies of the full scores to the Fifth and Ninth, offer concrete evidence of his early enthusiasm for the composer: see also 'Musical Background and Influences', p.65–6 and 82–5). Similarly problematic are the famous account of Wilhelmine Schröder-Devrient's (undocumented) 1829 guest performance in Beethoven's *Fidelio* at Leipzig (see 'Myths and

Legends', p.133) and the revelatory – but also imprecisely documented – experience of the Ninth Symphony under Habeneck in Paris around 1840 that brought him back to the cause of 'true German music' (see 'Musical Background and Influences', pp.73–4 and 83). Whether these recollections are strictly accurate or the result of an imaginative conflation of circumstances, their symbolic significance is, again, readily apparent. Wagner's activity as a conductor of Beethoven's music, on the other hand, is a matter of verifiable record, culminating in the 1872 performance of the Ninth Symphony at the foundation-laying ceremony for the Bayreuth theatre and in the extensive commentary on performance issues in this work written the following year (*Zum Vortrag der neunten Symphonie Beethovens* – *On the Performance of Beethoven's Ninth Symphony*, 1873).

The Ninth Symphony also plays a pivotal role in Wagner's theoretical writings. Already in the novella from the Parisian years, *Eine Pilgerfahrt zu Beethoven* (*A Pilgrimage to Beethoven*, 1840), the Ninth is represented as Beethoven's attempt at an ideal fusion of poetic and musical expression, transcending the limits of operatic convention that had hampered the great composer in *Fidelio*. There are direct biographical links between Wagner's performances of the Ninth in Dresden between 1846 and 1849 and the revolutionary fervour of that period, and soon afterwards the work became a keystone in his doctrine of artistic 'revolution', with the 'total artwork of the future' as its goal. In both *Das Kunstwerk der Zukunft* (*The Artwork of the Future*, 1849) and *Oper und Drama* (*Opera and Drama*, 1851) the Ninth Symphony is interpreted as Beethoven's artistic testament, an aesthetic confession to the effect that 'absolute music' had reached the limits of its expressive capacities and that the way of the future must lie in the union of music and poetry (or more specifically, of symphony and drama, as the 'highest' genres within those arts):

> Beethoven's last symphony represents the redemption of music from out of its own, particular element into the domain of communal art. It is the human gospel of the art of the future. No further progress is possible beyond this work [i.e. in the realm of instrumental music], for its immediate and necessary consequence is none other than the perfected artwork of the future, the communal drama, to which Beethoven has forged the artistic key. (GS III, 96)

After establishing his claim to Beethoven's legacy in theory, it remained for Wagner to carry out his mission in practice in the mature 'music dramas', beginning with the grandiose project of the Nibelung cycle. Klaus Kropfinger (1975) suggests that this compositional 'mission' also came to supplant Wagner's activity as an interpreter of Beethoven's works, which tapered off after the mid-1850s (this only reflects the course of Wagner's conducting activities as a whole, however – see 'Wagner as a conductor, pp.99–102). In any case, the figure of Beethoven did not disappear from his critical and theoretical writings. In '*Zukunftsmusik*' ('*Music of the*

Future', 1860) Beethoven is identified as the progenitor of Wagner's motivic-melodic technique and thus a model for the concept of 'infinite melody'. The commemorative essay *Beethoven* (1870) offers a re-evaluation of Schopenhauer's philosophy of music (and aesthetic theory in general), supplementing the philosopher's tentative insights with Wagner's own understanding of the only composer – besides himself – suited to a fuller demonstration of these insights. Here, as in later writings (*Über die Anwendung der Musik auf das Drama – On the Application of Music to the Drama*, 1879), Wagner continues his ongoing attempt to reconcile the symphonic heritage of Beethoven with the principles of the musical drama. The impulse behind musical and dramatic expression is fundamentally the same, Wagner argues (in *Beethoven*); but what he regards as Beethoven's attempt to dramatize the process of thematic exposition and development from within the framework of received, abstract, dance-derived musical forms can more fittingly be realized within the musically conceived drama, where music is given a broader and more flexible arena for the unfolding of its structural and expressive potential.

In the later writings of the Bayreuth period Wagner reacts somewhat peevishly to the fact that contemporary composers (such as Brahms) have blithely disregarded his dictum about the historical obsolescence of the symphonic genre. More 'progressive' composers (those inclining towards programme music) are censured for the unauthorized dramatic gesturings of their music, while Brahms, on the other hand, is faulted for transplanting the detailed, nuanced motivic workings of a chamber music style into the inappropriate 'public' sphere of the symphony. Realizing, perhaps, that one way or another his pronouncements about the end of the symphony had been definitively overridden, Wagner himself planned to close his career with a series of single-movement symphonies which, unfortunately, were not realized before his death. Possibly he sensed that only in this way – by issuing his own original examples of the post-Beethovenian symphony – could he be sure of consolidating his claim to the Beethoven legacy, in the event that posterity might not accept his music dramas as sufficient proof of his hereditary rights.

THOMAS S. GREY

Opera and social reform

THE OVERRIDING GOAL of Wagner's career was to gain full control over the production of his works so that they might be performed in the manner he believed necessary to them. But to accomplish that he had to challenge some of the most basic principles of opera life and demand a wholesale reform of both its musical and its social practices. We will here discuss the nature of his reforming ideas, the role of nationalism within them, and the concept of regeneration as their intellectual keystone.

In posing these ideas, Wagner played a David to the Goliath-like world of opera that was the most important place of entertainment among the European upper classes. Let us remember that upper-class society in the 18th and early 19th centuries was much more unified and public in the major cities than is true today. One went to the opera not just to 'be seen', but because a great deal of personal and political business was done there; the power of the élite was articulated in ritual fashion. Opera served these social needs and was therefore defined by it. This is not to say that people did not listen to the music; they came to know the key arias by heart and understood them in sophisticated ways. But a night at the opera was long and discontinuous, and focused upon the individual singer much more than upon the work itself. Librettists and composers had to accept these conventions if they were to survive in a cut-throat professional world.

Wagner challenged the social and musical traditions of opera in an extraordinarily comprehensive way. Opera had had many critics throughout its history, from the attacks on castrati in England during the 1720s to the vision of a reformed, popular opera articulated by the Italian nationalist Giuseppe Mazzini in the 1830s (see Marion Miller's chapter in Large and Weber, 1984). But none mounted as sweeping a campaign against the tradition as Wagner, and none approached the problem from both a theoretical and a practical standpoint. He approached the problem in part as an over-ambitious Kapellmeister, intending to obtain greater authority over the performance of his operas. To accomplish this goal, however, he mounted a large-scale social and intellectual redefinition of opera that was at once vicious in its musical politics and lofty in its philosophical statement. The end product was an alternative world of opera based on a new set of social principles and musical practices – what evolved as the Bayreuth Festival.

From 1849 on, Wagner sketched out in his writings a programmatic design for the reform of opera. His prose tended to fall into three genres, sometimes in the same work: a social critique of the opera world, practical guidelines for reform, and theoretical frameworks for the philosophical basis of musical theatre. That he wrote in all three categories during the critical first stage of his publications, 1849–51, suggests the remarkable breadth of his thinking and of his professional plans.

Wagner's critique of the opera world was polemical in style (see 'Wagner as polemicist', pp.114–16) and moral in thrust. His thinking focused upon key words or concepts that were the object of his attack: the philistine public and its worship of luxury and fashion. He attacked the public for being concerned with opera only for its social glamour, and not for its artistic meaning. In *Oper und Drama* (*Opera and Drama*, 1850–51) – his main early theoretical treatise – he stated that 'our theatre-going public has no *need* for works of art; it wants to be *diverted*, when it takes its seat before the stage, not to *collect* itself; and the need of the person addicted to diversion is merely for artificial *details*, not for an artistic *unity*.' (GS

IV, 225) 'This ruler and this giver of orders', he concluded, 'is – *the philistine.*' (GS IV, 226) He disparaged the public on ethical grounds: 'When today we talk of opera music, in any strict sense, we no longer speak of an art, but of a mere article of fashion.' (GS IV, 308)

It is important that, for all Wagner's philosophizing, he was sometimes quite specific in mounting a programme for reform of the opera. A typical statement (recapitulating proposals made in Dresden) came in *Ein Theater in Zürich* (*A Theatre in Zurich*, 1851), where he called for the town fathers to reshape their theatre from top to bottom. He insisted that they should hire singers who were also trained as actors; train them on a year-round basis; actively recruit German poets and composers to develop works; limit performances to no more than three per week; and found a Commission for Theatrical Affairs to govern the institution. He laid down a similar educational programme in a report he made to Ludwig II in 1865, calling for a school by which singers would be much more fully trained in the theory and practice of music than was conventional at the time. Later in Bayreuth he continued his programme of reform – forbidding the conventional boxes in the theatre, discouraging applause during acts, and turning down lights at the start of performances.

Wagner always set such details within a larger framework, conceiving a reformed world of opera defined in terms quite foreign to those of operatic tradition. In the Zurich essay, for example, he drew parallels between what he wanted the theatre to become and *Volk*-like activities such as village festivals and the singing societies in German towns. In *Das Kunstwerk der Zukunft* (*The Artwork of the Future*) he presented the idea of opera as the product of a 'free artistic fellowship' of the *Volk* under the leadership of the Hero and of the Poet, who emerges from and is reabsorbed into the fellowship (GS III, 166).

A major thrust of the post-revolutionary essays was his antagonism to conventional posts such as that of Kapellmeister. In *Eine Mitteilung an meine Freunde* (*A Communication to my Friends*, 1851), he surveyed the ideas he had been publishing over the previous two years and stated that 'now I had to speak out against the entire artistic system, *in terms of its relation to the whole socio-political situation of the modern world.*' (GS IV, 335) He rejected such a post not only because it provided limited authority over productions, but also because what was expected of the musician in his eyes was 'to cater for a nightly entertainment, never energetically demanded, but forced down people's throats by the spirit of speculation, and lazily swallowed by the social ennui of the dwellers in our larger cities.' (GS IV, 305)

Nationalism occupies a special place in Wagner's theoretical scheme. He never became a proponent of a politically unified Germany, especially under Prussian auspices ('the idea of the Prussian state has refused to work', he asserted in 1867 (GS VIII, 104). While he made overtures, unsuccessfully, to the newly born

German Empire after its founding in 1871, he maintained an allegiance to Bavaria, writing passages about King Ludwig that are reminiscent of 17th-century royal eulogies. But such opportunism apart, nationalism played a crucial role in his idealistic vision of a reformed opera. The idea of the *Volk* was the most important such influence upon his thinking, for through its rebirth he saw the end of the philistine public and the regeneration of society as a whole.

Wagner's nationalism fit the pattern found among Russian and Czech composers by which the idea served as a means of helping a national musical culture compete better with powerful cosmopolitan idioms. Just as Wagner wished to overcome the international predominance of Franco-Italian opera over German at mid-century, so Tchaikovsky strove to keep his works from being overshadowed by the German-Austrian classics after they became the core of most orchestral repertories by the 1860s. Wagner criticized Germans for accepting the French language and French opera as the focus of their culture; in *Deutsche Kunst und deutsche Politik* (*German Art and German Politics*, 1867), he spoke of a 'betrayal of the German spirit' (GS VIII, 41) that occurred when, after the War of Liberation from Napoleon had kindled a national feeling, his compatriots went straight back to their old Francophile habits. He steadfastly refused to recognize the French origins of much of his musical and dramatic style (see Laudon, 1979).

Wagner's nationalism was closely bound also to his critique of musical culture. He identified French culture, and specifically Paris, as the source of musical philistinism: 'Let us therefore turn from the French,' he said, 'from whom we have nothing to gain but the ordinary theatre and theatrical virtuosity' (GS, VIII, 75). The German Spirit he identified as musically more serious than the French and far truer to the highest principles of art. But nationalism was not enough to undergird so sweeping and ambitious a plan for operatic reform as that he conceived. He also called upon the authority of the ancient Greeks as an origin of the German Spirit and of the music drama, where the *Volk* would come the most fully to consciousness. In *Was ist deutsch?* (*What is German?*, 1865) he stated that 'through its most intimate understanding of the Antique, the German Spirit became capable of restoring the purely human itself to its pristine freedom' (GS X, 41).

Wagner's anti-Semitism – found most prominently in *Das Judentum in der Musik* (*Jewishness in Music*, 1850) – was closely related to his nationalism and to his reform of opera. In *What is German?* he declared that 'in this singular phenomenon, this invasion of the German nature by an utterly alien element, there is more than meets the eye' (GS X, 43). By that he meant the superimposition of French upon German culture, as had long been done both by Jews and by misguided rulers such as Friedrich the Great through 'a mind which misunderstood the very essence of the German nature.' (GS X, 43) According to his paranoid mental outlook, Jews stood in the way of the reshaping of opera by the *Volk*.

Wagner was, if anything, exceptional in the intensity of his anti-

Semitism during the middle years of the century. The most important recent study on the subject, by Jacob Katz, a historian of anti-Semitism, argues that while there was a long tradition of deprecating Jews, the predominant tendency during the liberal 1850s and 60s was their assimilation into German society and politics. In that context, argues Katz, Wagner's vindictive anti-Semitism appeared 'bizarre, capricious, and untimely' (Katz, 1985); only in the 1870s did an anti-Semitic movement develop that proposed the expulsion of Jews from German culture. Katz thinks that his unusual tendency in this regard emanated specifically from his early antagonism towards Meyerbeer and that it remained distinct from the more vulgar kind of anti-Semitism that developed in his later years. Wagner's extreme ambitions for the reform of opera were thus a major contributory factor in the genesis of his anti-Semitism, since in Meyerbeer's works he saw the most comprehensive example of what he thought was corrupt about opera.

The keystone of his ideas of a reformed opera was social regeneration. In the most basic terms, this meant the return of society to its pure, original spirit through the ritual of the music drama; by purging opera of its corrupted tradition, society would be regenerated. Wagner applied the term 'regeneration' in different ways as his intellectual interests progressed. In *German Art and German Politics* he defined it in Romantic and nationalistic terms; condemning Friedrich the Great for his contempt for things German, he called for 'a total regeneration of the European folk-blood' and 'a rebirth of the folk-spirit' within the German theatre (GS VIII, 33). In 1872 he spoke of a regeneration of the artistic profession and public taste, something that could be accomplished only by 'taking our singers back to the starting-point of their so degenerated art, to where we find them acting still as players' (GS IX, 202). But in *Über die Bestimmung der Oper* (*On the Destiny of Opera*, 1871) he was much less hopeful that such a thing could happen, expressing his doubt that it could be effected by 'the circuitous route of a regeneration of our public spirit' (GS IX, 134).

The idea was a unifying force in his writings of the late 1870s and early 1880s, blending variously Christian thought, social Darwinism, vegetarianism and racism. In *Heldentum und Christentum* (*Heroism and Christianity*, 1881) he argued that the human race had become degenerated by the substitution of animal for vegetable food, leading to 'the assumption of a change in the fundamental substance of our body, and to a corrupted blood' (GS X, 275). Regeneration could be effected, he argued, by the adoption of a vegetable diet and through the agency of Christ's pure blood. He spoke of new 'radical persuasion' that 'the great regeneration' would 'spring from nothing save the deep soil of a true religion' (GS X, 243). By means of the universal spiritual truths and mythic symbols of religion, society could once more become whole. Seen in the context of such essays as *Heroism and Christianity*, with which it is contemporary, Wagner's last opera, *Parsifal*, acquires an ideological significance that has not always been acknowledged.

WILLIAM WEBER

Wagner and the Greeks

AT THE KREUZSCHULE in Dresden, which he attended between 1822 and 1827, Wagner made a promising start in Greek. But when the family moved back to Leipzig, he fell behind in his studies, and was even moved down a class, because his music was leaving too little time for other things. In 1830 a private tutor was engaged to teach him Greek, but the experiment was a failure, for which Wagner characteristically blamed the proximity of a tanner's yard, whose smell affected his delicate nostrils. During his stay in Paris between 1839 and 1842 his interest in Greek studies was revived, partly through his friendship with Samuel Lehrs, a philologist well versed in the classics. But he was dissuaded from his attempt to study the literature in the original language by Lehrs, who advised him that it would be a major commitment, that he could manage with the help of translations, and that he should concentrate on his music. Lehrs was right: Wagner was no scholar, but he was uncommonly skilful at making use of vernacular editions.

After 1843, when he was appointed Hofkapellmeister at the Saxon court at Dresden, Wagner was able to advance his literary education. During the glorious summer of 1847, when he was finishing *Lohengrin*, he experienced a kind of revelation regarding Greek literature. He read Aristophanes in J.G. Droysen's translation, then several dialogues of Plato, and later the *Odyssey*; but the author who impressed him most was Aeschylus, again read in Droysen's version. In his autobiography he tells us that after this experience he was never again able to reconcile himself to modern literature; and indeed he never lost his enthusiasm for Greek poetry. The eagerness with which he took up the twenty-four-year-old Nietzsche after their first meeting in 1868 shows how pleased he was to meet a professional classical scholar who admired his work. After reading the manuscript of his *Die Geburt der Tragödie* (*The Birth of Tragedy*) to Wagner and Cosima, Nietzsche added a section, not to the advantage of the book, arguing that Wagnerian music drama represented the rebirth of classical tragedy. Wagner was naturally delighted with the result and during the controversy after the work's publication, he defended it in an open letter to the author. As late as 1880, while he was staying near Naples, Wagner read aloud from the *Oresteia*, and Cosima wrote in her Diaries (23 Jun 1880) that she had never seen her husband so transfigured.

Greek influence on the early operas is minimal. Wagner liked to think that *Der fliegende Holländer* and *Tannhäuser* were influenced by the *Odyssey*, and *Lohengrin* by the legend of Semele, but such parallels, if they exist at all, amount to very little. *Die Meistersinger* resembles *The Frogs* of Aristophanes, an author much admired by Wagner, in that both deal with poetic rivalries and disputes over artistic principles, but the resemblance is very slight. Nor, if Wagner himself had not written that the address of Hans Sachs at the end of the opera was influenced by the reconciliation at the end of Aeschylus' *Eumenides*, would anyone have guessed it. The superficial resemblance between the plot of *Tristan* and that of Euripides' *Hippolytus* has very little significance; and how different is the treatment! It seems that the idea, found in *Parsifal*, of the wound which could be cured only by the spear which had inflicted it, was suggested to Wagner by the legend of Telephus, which was the subject of a lost play by Euripides and is mentioned by Goethe in his *Tasso*. But Wagner has invested it with a symbolic significance, expressive of his own conception of the redeeming power of love, which is foreign to Greek ways of thinking.

In the construction of the libretto of the *Ring*, however, which Wagner began in 1848, the part played by Aeschylus is of great importance; in Aristotelian terminology Wagner may be said to have imposed a Greek form upon matter supplied by the Nordic legends.

The idea of a tetralogy is Greek; at the dramatic festivals each of three tragedians produced three tragedies, together with a lighter entertainment called a satyr-play, which had a chorus of satyrs. Aeschylus often composed a trilogy on a continuous theme, the satyr-play also having a loose connection with the subject of the tragedies. One tragic trilogy, the *Oresteia*, survives entire, consisting of the three tragedies *Agamemnon*, *The Choephori* (*The Libation-Bearers*) and *The Eumenides* (*The Kindly Ones*); the accompanying satyr-play is lost. The manner in which Aeschylus contrives to invest the story of the vendetta in the House of Atreus with a cosmic significance seems to have inspired Wagner in his treatment of the saga material. Further, Aeschylus, especially in his choral lyrics, makes use of certain themes which pervade the entire *Oresteia*, often associating a particular theme with a particular image. There is an obvious affinity between this practice and Wagner's use of the leitmotif to mark a recurrence of the principal themes of his tetralogy – the ring, the curse, the giants, love, and so on. Even if Wagner was not the inventor of the leitmotif (see 'A Wagnerian Glossary', pp.234–5), he was surely the first to use it in such a subtle and pervasive fashion, and it seems probable that it was suggested to him by his study of this favourite author.

In a general way, therefore, the influence of the *Oresteia* on the construction of the *Ring* is considerable. But a recent attempt (Ewans, 1982) to show that it had also an important influence on the details of the plot is mistaken (see Lloyd-Jones, 1982); in this respect, the work of Aeschylus that had most influence on the *Ring* is *Prometheus Bound*.

This play was a favourite work in the Romantic period. It is the sole survivor of its trilogy, though we have considerable fragments of *Prometheus Unbound*, which must have followed it directly. The nature of the third play is a mystery, and we cannot even be certain of its name. *Prometheus* differs in many ways in style, language and metre from the other surviving works of Aeschylus, and many scholars believe that it is not by him at all; still, we must reckon with the possibility that Aeschylus, like other great poets, was capable of varying his way of writing very considerably. What matters to us, however, is not the best reconstruction of the trilogy, but the reconstruction that Wagner found in Droysen's translation.

Droysen believed that *Prometheus Bound* was the second play of the trilogy, the first having dealt with the theft of the fire from Zeus by Prometheus and his gift of it to mortals. At the start of the extant play, the fire god Hephaestus, on Zeus' orders, fastens Prometheus to a remote rock in the Caucasus for an indefinite period of time. Prometheus consoles himself with the knowledge that he possesses a secret – told him by his mother the earth goddess, who has the gift of prophecy – that will in due course place Zeus in his power. One day Zeus will desire a female who is destined to bear a son mightier than his father. On the surface, the character in Greek myth most like Brünnhilde is Athena; both are warrior maidens, the favourites of their fathers. On the surface, the character in Norse myth most like Prometheus is Loge; both are craftsmen, connected with fire, and both are alienated from the other gods. But Brünnhilde and Prometheus also have several things in common. Each is the offspring of an earth goddess who has the gift of prophecy. In Norse mythology there is no such goddess; Erda is a direct importation from Greek religion. In *Das Rheingold*, when she appears, to warn Wotan not to keep the ring, only the top half of her is visible above the ground; that is a habit of Greek earth goddesses, which Wagner may well have observed upon Greek vases. Both Brünnhilde and Prometheus defy the ruler of the gods, and in consequence a fire god is ordered to secure each of them for an indefinite period of time. Each befriends and comforts a female person, pregnant, distraught, and pursued by the great god; Brünnhilde is to be released by Sieglinde's son, Prometheus by the descendant of Io, a mortal princess.

The use Wagner has made of Prometheus in creating the figure of Brünnhilde is of prime importance, for it is through Brünnhilde, together with the innovation of making Wotan propagate the Volsungs in order that the ring may be recovered, that the fate of Siegfried is linked with that of Wotan. In the *Volsunga Saga* the gods who correspond to Wotan and Loge are taken prisoner by enemies, one of whose brothers the Loge figure has killed. To pay their ransom they need gold, which they steal from the figure that corresponds to Alberich. In Wagner, the gold is needed to pay for the building of Valhalla.

That last change is vital, for it enables Wagner to make out of the Nordic myth a story of crime and punishment, like that of the *Oresteia*. In the latter work, too, the curse of Thyestes on the House of Atreus, and in the Theban trilogy of Aeschylus the curse of Pelops on the House of Laius, play an important part; so in the *Ring* does the curse of Alberich. Just at the time when he was working on the libretto of the *Ring*, Wagner was engaged in writing his theoretical works, in which Greek art plays an important part. The history of art, Wagner argued, consists of a chain of independent links, and since Greek art supplied the first link in the chain, progress in modern art is impossible unless we consider where we stand in relation to the Greeks. Unlike most contemporary art, Greek tragedy was not simply an entertainment, but a religious ritual; its subject-matter was saga, which was the product of the people, and which enshrined the people's ancestral wisdom. Tragedy was a combined work of art (*Gesamtkunstwerk*), in which words, music and dance all played a part, all being supplied by a single person, who not only wrote the words and music and choreographed the dances, but trained the performers and directed the performance. (For Wagner's comparable schema, see 'A Wagnerian Glossary: *Gesamtkunstwerk*', p.232–3.)

Greek tragedy was indeed part of a religious festival, but its religion was very different from Christianity, and entertainment was certainly part of its purpose. How much did Greek religion and Greek ways of thinking influence Wagner? Surely very little. The *Oresteia* and even the Prometheus trilogy ended with Zeus firmly in control; the idea that the ruler of the universe, whose main attribute was not goodness but power, might be replaced by a kinder, gentler ruler was foreign to Greek thought, at least during the archaic and classical ages.

The kind of world order of which Wagner – influenced first by Young Hegelians and later by socialists and anarchists – approved was very unlike that of Greek tragedy. Moreover, his idiosyncratic Christian beliefs were deeply conditioned by two special factors: first by his Rousseauite conviction that man's natural impulses must be good, and secondly by his Romantic belief in the redemption of man by the love of woman. The former undermines the belief in guilt and responsibility, without which tragedy is scarcely possible, and the latter imports a sentimental element wholly remote from Greek ways of thinking.

HUGH LLOYD-JONES

Wagner and the Jews

VITRIOLIC AND INDIVIDUALLY characterized as it was, Wagner's anti-Semitism was no isolated phenomenon. Rather, it should be seen as an extraordinarily concentrated manifestation of an historical tradition, which erupted in a specific form in the context of 19th-century German nationalism. Anti-Semitism was rife in the medieval era, in Lutheran times (the great reformer called for the burning of synagogues) and during the Enlightenment. Indeed, the emancipating reforms of the late 18th century even contributed to the rise of anti-Semitic sentiment in the decades to come. But the surge of German nationalism in the 19th century, and the concomitant search for a national identity, caused the German people to celebrate what they had in common and anathematize elements perceived as alien.

According to the *völkisch* ideology (*Volk* = 'the people'), which had evolved with the first stirrings of national consciousness in the 18th century, Jews were intrinsically un-German. Given that the *völkisch* outlook urged a return to a mythical primordial world inhabited by peasants of pure Germanic blood, the Jews, regarded as a race of wanderers and settlers, were inevitably cast as rootless outsiders. Nor was it merely a reactionary fringe that expressed such anti-Semitic sentiments: even among liberals and other progressives it was part of the common currency of thought and discourse. Such middle-class liberals, anxious about their social standing and possible proletarianization in the newly industrialized Germany, were no less prone than other classes to harbour resentment against a group of outsiders and cast them in the role of scapegoats.

This was the ideological background against which Wagner entered the debate with his notorious essay *Das Judentum in der Musik* (*Jewishness in Music*, 1850). With barely restrained racially abusive stridency, he inveighed against Jewish artists who, motivated solely by commercial instincts and lacking a culture of their own, could only imitate the art produced by the host culture. Meyerbeer was singled out (though not by name) as the paradigmatic Jewish composer of trivial diversions, put on solely to entertain a bored public. True Germans, claimed Wagner, could only be repelled by the displeasing physical appearance of Jews, by the shrill, sibilant buzzing of their voices, and by the grotesque gurgling one heard in their synagogues. Only by renouncing their Jewishness could Jews be redeemed.

Along with the racial abuse, which conformed to the traditional anti-Semitic stereotypes, Wagner advanced a thesis of some originality. What he suggested was that it was the very rootlessness of Jewish artists that prevented them from speaking in a natural, instinctive voice and thus articulating the inner feelings and emotions of the German people. Their art could not therefore penetrate the depths of the soul in the way Wagner believed true art should; instead it dealt merely in surface appearances.

Were it not for the insidious racialist invective, one might be more inclined to acknowledge the at least partial truth of Wagner's observations. As Bryan Magee (1968) has pointed out, there is some truth in Wagner's argument, to the extent that it relates to a transitional period – the period of Wagner's time in which Jewish artists were among the first to be emancipated from the ghettoes and take their place in what had been previously a society closed to them. Wagner, to his credit, was 'offer[ing] explanations for what other people had not even noticed'.

There is also an element of personal animus in Wagner's anti-Semitic diatribe, though this needs to be kept in perspective. As he admitted in a letter to Liszt of 18 April 1851, he had been goaded beyond endurance by 'this Jewish business', and by 'their damned scribblings'. In particular, Meyerbeer, though a 'perpetually kind and obliging man' reminded him of 'the darkest – I might almost say the most wicked – period of my life, when he still made a show of protecting me; it was a period of connections and back-staircases'. With this reference to the infinitely frustrating and degrading experiences of the Paris years (1839–42), when he had failed to make any significant impression on the musical capital of the world, Wagner candidly·exposes a gaping wound, into which salt has been rubbed by those who propound 'the mistaken view that I have something in common with Meyerbeer'.

Jewishness in Music, then, was at once an act of exorcism and an attempt to set the record straight. But it would never have been written, nor taken the form it did, had it not been for the particular historical juncture at which Wagner's personal experiences occurred. That, too, is the reason that Wagner's anti-Semitism, sustained over the course of the following three decades, made such a momentous impression on his, and subsequent, eras. Wagner's own insecurities and frustrations were reflected in those of German society at large, and the sentiments to which he gave voice touched a chord with his fellow-Germans. In later years, moreover, his status and charisma reinforced the power of the message, endowing it with a gravity and a respectability that it often lacked in other manifestations.

Wagner's decision to republish *Jewishness in Music* in 1869 was questioned by those close to the composer, including Cosima, herself no philo-Semite. Their fears proved to be justified: anti-Semitic sentiment, evident in the unending discussion of the 'Jewish Question' throughout the 19th century, had receded somewhat by the late 1860s largely as a result of the rapid expansion of the German economy between 1848 and 1873. The collapse of the stock market in 1873, however, and the ensuing two-decade-long depression, provided a fertile breeding-ground for prejudice against national and religious minorities. Nor did the removal of outstanding civic and legal disabilities against the Jews, which came in 1874 in the aftermath of the unification of Germany, diminish the hostility towards them: if anything, it exacerbated it.

Not that Wagner was oblivious to the practical consequences of alienating the sizeable and influential Jewish contingent in the musical community. His refusal in 1880 to sign Bernhard Förster's 'Mass Petition against the Rampancy of Judaism' was doubtless motivated in part by personal interest: as Hans von Bülow wryly put it: 'The master did indeed poke the fire, but he let others burn their fingers in it.' But it is also the case that Wagner found such public campaigns vulgar, preferring to operate on a more elevated level, through theoretical argument and even aesthetic representation.

With regard to the latter category, the consensus view has long been that the works themselves are 'untainted' by the racist ideology of Wagner the man. However, this notion has been increasingly challenged in recent years. Gutman (1968) and Zelinsky (1978) both alluded to the darker undercurrents of racial supremacy and anti-Semitism in *Parsifal*, while the present author

(Millington, 1984, 1988 and 1991; see also 'The Music: *Die Meistersinger* and *Parsifal*, pp.304 and 308) has demonstrated how the concepts of racial purity and regeneration formulated by Wagner in his last years were woven into the ideological fabric of his works, and Paul Lawrence Rose, in a masterly study of the subject (1992), has shown how even *Tristan und Isolde* is steeped in the same ideology.

Wagner's anti-Semitism underwent a shift in the final years of his life, partly under the influence of Count Gobineau (see 'Who's Who', p.25), taking on aspects of the fashionable theory of the races that was to be developed further, with catastrophic consequences, in the Wilhelminian and Nazi eras. But even these newly formulated anti-Semitic obsessions, faithfully recorded as they are on virtually every page of Cosima Wagner's Diaries, could not deter the band of Jewish admirers – Joseph Rubinstein, Hermann Levi and Heinrich Porges among them (see 'Who's Who', pp.30, 27 and 30) – who continued to surround Wagner as other Jews had done in earlier times. Indeed, the 'scientific' nature of his latter-day anti-Semitism tended to depersonalize Wagner's hostility towards the Jews. Where previously a Meyerbeer or a Mendelssohn would have been the prime target of an attack, now it was merely as representatives of 'Jewishness' that his Semitic colleagues were branded as second-class citizens. This relative objectivity, taken with the phenomenon of 'Jewish self-hatred' (see Gay, 1978), as a result of which guilt-obsessed Jews came to Wagner for something resembling redemption – as the anti-Semite Eugen Dühring put it, they were receiving indulgence for the cardinal sin of their Jewishness – goes a long way to explaining the oft-remarked paradox of Wagner's many Jewish friends. What attracted such people to Wagner penetrates to the heart of the matter. The sense of not belonging, of alienation, induced by their historical and cultural situation, caused them to embrace the sort of common folk culture, based on mythology and on a revival of the German spirit, that was symbolized by Wagner. It was the very richness of the cultural experience offered by Wagner, seasoned as it was with more than a hint of 'blood and soil', that drew to him precisely the kind of people he most despised.

BARRY MILLINGTON

MEDIEVAL LITERATURE is essentially aristocratic in nature: the problems of contemporary knighthood are discussed with an immediacy and ethical awareness intimately bound up with the Age of Chivalry. Once that age had passed, the chivalric ideal was bound to degenerate into a mere retelling of increasingly quixotic adventures. Poets such as Hartmann von Aue and Wolfram von Eschenbach inevitably suffered more than Gottfried von Strassburg: illicit love, after all, has never long been out of fashion. The majority of medieval manuscripts suffered the neglect of gen-

Wagner's Middle Ages

erations until their rediscovery during the second half of the 18th century. Initial interest in them was purely philological, and it was left to the German Romantics of the early 19th century to put these texts to literary use.

The Romantic movement had emerged in Germany as a reaction against the sceptical and utilitarian spirit of the Enlightenment, with its dogmatic and rigid rationalism. A new sense of nationalism came into being, fired not least by the Wars of Liberation of 1813–15 and by the political reaction that followed. A longing for a united Germany made itself felt, a Germany as powerful and respected as under the Hohenstaufen Empire of the 12th and 13th centuries. The dominant mood was one of inadequacy in the present and of nostalgia for the past and specifically (though not exclusively) for the medieval past. Many of the early Romantic poets, including Tieck, Immermann and Hoffmann, borrowed freely from medieval narrative and lyric poems in their evocations of a lost world of religious mysticization and decorous passion. Not only poets but opera librettists, too, drew on these and related themes, much to the despair of Heinrich Heine, who complained, with some justification, in 1836 of 'this constant obsession with coats of mail, jousting stallions, châtelaines, respectable guild-masters, dwarfs, squires, castle chapels, love and religion, and all the rest of your medieval rubbish [...]; the German Middle Ages have entered into our midst in broad daylight and are sucking the lifeblood from our breast'.

Wagner's interest went deeper than the superficialities of medieval local colour. It is an interest which he owed to the philologist Samuel Lehrs who, not untypical of scholars of the time, was versed in both classical and medieval studies and who introduced Wagner to his first specifically medieval subject, *Tannhäuser*, probably during the winter of 1841/2 in Paris. The composer spent the 1840s assiduously assimilating medieval ideas through the translations and scholarly writings of such figures as Christoph Theodor Leopold Lucas, Jacob and Wilhelm Grimm, Georg Gottfried Gervinus, Karl Lachmann, Karl Simrock, Friedrich Heinrich von der Hagen, Ludwig Ettmüller, Carl Wilhelm Göttling and Franz Joseph Mone, scholars who, largely forgotten today, were generally highly regarded in their day. It was here that Wagner found the subject-matter not only for *Tannhäuser* but also for *Lohengrin*, the *Ring*, *Tristan und Isolde*, *Die Meistersinger von Nürnberg* and *Parsifal*; in other words, his life's work was already planned out in Dresden during the 1840s.

Among the important themes which Wagner derived from his reading of medieval texts are the ineluctibility of fate, the perversity of women and the destructive nature of love. 'No one can deny his fate' are Sigurd's dying words in the *Saga of the Volsungs*, a fatalistic message which runs through the remainder of Wagner's mature music dramas and, at least in the case of *Parsifal*, raises disturbing ethical questions concerning the nature of the hero's election as predestined ruler over the Grail community.

Medieval writers were never able to forgive Eve for flouting God's command in the Garden of Eden: women, they concluded, were incorrigibly perverse and always did precisely what they were told not to do. This medieval conviction finds an echo in a number of Wagner's female characters: in Elsa, who insists on asking the forbidden question in spite of the threat of fearful consequences; in Brünnhilde, who refuses to hand back the ring, although she knows that by doing so she will save the gods and the world from destruction; in Isolde, who extinguishes the torch in King Mark's garden in spite of Brangäne's warnings that it is not yet safe to do so; and in Kundry, who perversely returns to Klingsor's domain in order to seduce the Knights of the Grail, in spite of the suffering which ensues. In each case, moreover, it is love which blinds the individual to the folly of her actions – a destructive and demonic love which Wagner has taken over from his medieval source material. Love, for Gottfried von Strassburg, was 'that pleasing malady that works such miracles as changing honey to gall, turning sweetness sour, setting fire to moisture, converting balm to pain'; for Wagner, too, the theme of *Tristan und Isolde* was 'love as fearful torment', as he told August Röckel in a letter of 23 August 1856.

This view of the destructive nature of love was not the only one to prevail in late 12th- and early 13th-century Germany but was countered by a contrasting belief in its educative, inspirational qualities. Whereas the former view derives from classical antiquity, and from Ovid in particular, the latter can be traced back, at least in part, to Provençal models of the 12th century. The result was a genre of love poetry (*Minnesang*), which took as its starting-point the extra-marital, but chaste, relationship between the poet-knight and his lady, whom he generally affected to regard as his social superior. The poet's love for her was intended to inspire in him an awareness of ideal courtly qualities such as honour, loyalty and clemency, but the onesidedness of the affair clearly made it unsatisfactory and, in Germany at least, the affectation quickly passed. By the early years of the 13th century, a further genre of erotic poetry (*nidere minne* in contrast to the earlier *hôhe minne*) had gained the upper hand, in which the lover became the poet's social inferior, a village girl whom he met in the formalized setting of an awakening spring. Meanwhile, the earlier view of love as a dark, demonic force continued, as before, to enthral the imagination of medieval German poets, with the result that both views – the destructive and the educative – frequently sit side by side within the same poetic oeuvre. What invariably strikes the 20th-century reader as inconsistent evidently did not offend the aesthetic sensibilities of contemporaries of Wolfram or Gottfried; what is involved here, after all, is not personal commitment but rhetorical attitudinizing.

It must be said that, in the libretto to *Tannhäuser*, Wagner *has* assumed that the contestants in the Wartburg Tournament of Song are not only deeply committed to their individual views but that they are prepared to defend those views with the sword. None the less, one can only be impressed by Wagner's understanding of the different types of medieval lyric and by the way in which he has attributed them to the various poets assembled at the Thuringian Court in the early years of the 13th century: Reinmar and Walther von der Vogelweide certainly wrote love lyrics in the contemplative vein of *hôhe minne* and their contributions to the song-contest in Act II are accordingly confined to extolling a love which is seen as the source of all virtue.

The historical Tannhäuser, on the other hand, did not enter the scene until thirty years after the events depicted in the medieval *Wartburgkrieg* had allegedly taken place. (Dating from the second half of the 13th century, the poem depicts events said to have occurred in 1206/7, although the historical authenticity of the poem has often been called into question.) By now *hôhe minne* had long since ceased to be a box-office draw; *nidere minne* was back in fashion, as Wagner's minstrel makes clear in his advocacy of consummated love. Only in the case of Wolfram von Eschenbach could Wagner's characterization be cause for any dissent, although the composer's 19th-century contemporaries are rather more to blame than he is for seeing in Wolfram the representative of a chaste and devotional piety in matters of love. If, in *Tannhäuser*, it is this German Romantic view of love which triumphs, love's victory was to be short-lived; for it is love's potentially annihilating force which dominates Wagner's remaining oeuvre, a theme which is perhaps the most important thematic link between him and his medieval sources and which certainly sets him apart from his Romantic predecessors. Even *Die Meistersinger von Nürnberg*, which is based on Renaissance rather than medieval material, shares that theme, in Sachs's abjuration of his love for Eva and his refuge in art. Love, according to Kurwenal, is 'der Welt holdester Wahn' ('the world's fondest illusion'), that same *Wahn* which Sachs accuses of bringing suffering into the world and which the Knights of the Grail forswear in their search for the peace that passeth all understanding.

STEWART SPENCER

Bayreuth and the idea of a festival theatre

WITH THE INAUGURATION of the first Bayreuth Festival in 1876, Wagner witnessed the realization of an ideal dating back almost thirty years. It was his disaffection with conditions at the Royal Court Theatre in Dresden which encouraged him to think in terms of reform and to draft his *Entwurf zur Organisation eines deutschen Nationaltheaters für das Königreich Sachsen (Plan for the Organization of a German National Theatre for the Kingdom of Saxony)* in 1848. The rejection of his scheme to transform Saxony's theatres from places of nightly entertainment to state-subsidized shrines of High Art helped to foment and focus his revolutionary fervour. Following his flight from Dresden in May 1849, his rekindled interest in Greek literature and, in particular, Aeschylus's *Oresteia* and *Prometheia* (as reconstructed by Droysen, see 'Wagner and the Greeks', p.158) provided the starting-point for a utopian vision of an artwork of the future divorced from the cheap showmanship and empty virtuosity which, he argued, characterized contemporary opera productions in Germany.

From the Greek ideal transmitted by Droysen he appropriated the idea of myth as the *fons et origo* of tragedy and the notion of a national festival that united the country in a commonality of public interest. Wagner's Hegelian outlook prevented him from thinking that the Greek ideal could ever be revived, and so it was not a classical myth which he held out as the vehicle for his revolutionary art but a Germanic one embodied in the figure of Siegfried.

In the short term, Wagner was happy to think of *Siegfrieds Tod* (*Siegfried's Death*) being performed under Liszt's direction in Weimar, in other words, in an existing repertory theatre, albeit with performers specially trained as singing actors (see Wagner's letter to Liszt of 20 July 1850). News that the Weimar premiere of *Lohengrin* on 28 August 1850 had apparently fallen short of expectations convinced its composer of the need to mount his own festival staging of *Siegfrieds Tod*, and so we find him writing to Ernst Benedikt Kietz on 14 September 1850:

> I cannot reconcile myself with the idea of trusting to luck and of having the work performed by the very first theatre that comes along: on the contrary, I am toying with the boldest of plans, which it will require no less a sum than 10,000 thalers to bring about. According to this plan of mine, I would have a theatre, made of planks, erected here on the spot [i.e., in Zurich], invite the most suitable singers to join me here and arrange everything necessary for this one special occasion, so that I could be certain of an outstanding performance of the opera. I would then send out invitations far and wide to all who were interested in my works, ensure that the auditorium was decently filled and give three performances – free, of course – one after the other in the space of a week, after which the theatre would be demolished and the whole affair would be over and done with.

In a letter to Theodor Uhlig, written a week later, Wagner repeats the same ideas, adding that, in allocating tickets, preference should be given to young people, universities and choral societies, and that not only would the theatre be torn down after the performance, but the score of the work would be burned. Rarely has an artist shown such faith in the proselytizing potential of his art: a single performance of *Siegfrieds Tod* would be sufficient, he believed, to incite the masses to insurrection.

By the autumn of the following year, 1851, the Grand Heroic Opera had been expanded to the four-part *Ring*, but Wagner's revolutionary fervour remained as irrepressible as ever, as is clear from his letter to Uhlig of 12 November 1851:

> A *performance* is something I can conceive of only *after the Revolution*; only the Revolution can offer me the artists and listeners I need. [. . .] Out of the ruins I shall then summon together what I need: I shall *then* find what I require. I shall then run up a theatre on the Rhine and send out invitations to a great dramatic festival: after a year's preparations I

shall then perform my entire work within the space of *four days*: *with it* I shall then make clear to the men of the Revolution the *meaning* of that Revolution, in its noblest sense.

The change of locale is significant for, as Matthias Theodor Vogt has pointed out (Vogt, 1992), the Rhine at this time formed the frontier between Germany and France: a performance of the tetralogy in post-revolutionary Germany was clearly meant as a rallying-cry to the French, inviting them to rise up and throw off the oppressor's yoke.

With the passing years Wagner's revolutionary ardour cooled and by 1857 we find him once again thinking in terms of a performance of the cycle in Weimar (see his letter to Hans von Bülow of 9 February 1857). Liszt's resignation as Grand Ducal Director of Music Extraordinary at Weimar put paid to this particular plan, so that when Wagner published the poem of the *Ring* in the winter of 1862/3, he prefaced it with an appeal to *any* German prince willing to underwrite the venture. The *Ring*, he hoped, would be staged in a smallish town, in a 'temporary theatre, as simple as possible, perhaps built solely of wood' (GS VI, 273), with an amphitheatre-like auditorium and a sunken orchestra pit. (In its design, the interior of this theatre appears to have been influenced by that of the theatre in Riga, where Wagner had been musical director from 1837 to 1839.) A festival performance of the *Ring* on four consecutive evenings would not only have a salutary effect on German opera by inculcating in the performers an awareness of their higher mission, it would also find members of the audience in a more receptive, more reverential frame of mind: in turn, their 'taste' would be improved and the 'German spirit' restored to its former 'national' dignity (GS VI, 279–80). And so, when Ludwig II responded to Wagner's appeal for a nationally minded patron, these abstract musings began to take on concrete form as part of a programme of political reform and moral regeneration: Ludwig, in the guise of Siegfried, would awaken the sleeping Germany to a new and purer life (see Wagner's letters to Ludwig of 23 September 1865 and 25 April 1867).

Plans were taken in hand to build a festival theatre in Munich; the idea, it is true, came from Ludwig, but there is no reason to think that Wagner was not happy to fall in with them, not least because the architect, Gottfried Semper, worked in close collaboration with him. Here, already, are the amphitheatre-shaped auditorium, the hidden orchestra and the double proscenium that were to typify the Bayreuth Festspielhaus. In the event, political intrigue prevented the scheme from being realized and, at least for a time, Wagner seems to have been reconciled to a production of the *Ring* at the Court Theatre in Munich (see his letter to Lorenz von Düfflipp of 5 February 1868). The insufficiencies of the staging of *Das Rheingold* in September 1869 persuaded him to cast around for an alternative venue. Hans Richter reminded him of the existing opera house in Bayreuth – the entry in Brockhaus's Encyclopaedia which is normally thought to have prompted the choice merely served to confirm it (CT, 5 Mar 1870) – and, although the Rococo building proved unsuitable, the assistance offered by the local council encouraged Wagner to settle on Bayreuth as the site for his Festival Theatre.

The choice was also politically motivated: not only was Bayreuth under Bavarian rule, thereby allowing Wagner to continue to dip into Ludwig's exchequer, but its historical links with Prussia suggested a *démarche* in the direction of Bismarck, whose militaristic cause the composer now espoused. In 1874 Wagner even went so far as to offer to stage the *Ring* at Bayreuth as a quinquennial celebration of Germany's victory over France.

The scheme was funded by (undersubscribed) 'Patrons' Certificates', by contributions from Wagner Societies all round the world, by private donations (including Cosima's inheritance from her mother) and by a loan from Ludwig II. The theatre, designed by Otto Brückwald but incorporating features of Semper's Munich model, was completed just in time for the 1876 opening and, although the inaugural *Ring* disappointed Wagner in many ways, his achievement in having brought so gargantuan an enterprise to fruition is bound to command admiration.

From the outset, a production of the *Ring* in a festival theatre had been bound up in Wagner's thoughts with the idea of the 'German spirit'. He now felt let down by that spirit (see his letter to Ludwig of 29 December 1877). The *Ring*, which had once been a lesson in revolutionary thinking, was now consigned to a phase in world history that predated the degeneration of the species (CT, 2 Oct 1882), reflecting a pristine Germanic Paradise which could never be regained but which could only be offset by the ecumenical fellow suffering of the work to which the composer now turned his attention, consciously consecrating the Bayreuth stage with his 'farewell work to the world'.

STEWART SPENCER

THROUGHOUT HIS LIFE Wagner was more comfortable in extolling the merits of deceased composers than of those still living. One could speculate as to the reasons for this reticence on Wagner's part: perhaps the intense inner concentration necessary to his own development led him, after a certain point, to reject external stimuli, or perhaps, as with Berlioz, the embittered struggle for recognition drained whatever reserves of altruism he may once have possessed. Certainly Wagner's overweening arrogance must also be taken into account. His attitude toward most music of his own time is one of profound ambivalence, at best. Any expression of admiration was almost always qualified, and his opinions would shift radically over time, often to the point of complete reversal. Rossini's *Otello*, for instance, is praised in some contexts for its warmth of feeling, melodic flow, and other expressive virtues, while elsewhere dismissed as 'that absurdity' (cf. CT, 13 Nov 1870, 18 Apr 1876, and 1 Feb 1879). Wagner more than once drew

Contemporary composers

attention to the 'unmistakably dramatic' qualities of Spontini's operas, but repudiated them on other occasions for their tedious recitatives and endlessly repeated phrases, dismissing them as a childish 'clutter of trivialities' (CT, 1 Apr 1878, 5 and 6 Nov 1878).

Among the older generation of opera composers in Germany still active during Wagner's lifetime he acknowledged some debt to Spohr and Marschner, but had nothing good to say about their later operas (in this he only concurred with critical opinion at large). He appreciated a genuine lyrical vein in certain numbers and a general level of conscientious craftsmanship in their oeuvre as a whole, but continued to miss the 'self-assurance' he (sometimes!) admired in Spontini, for instance, or any real dramatic flair. Such 'honest German' qualities, as he likes to style them, are vitiated by 'coarseness', 'clumsiness and insipidity' and a 'drunken lack of culture' in Marschner's case, 'silliness', shallow sentimentality and an exasperating tendency to lapse into polite, violinistic melodies *à la polacca* in the case of Spohr. An 1852 letter to his friend Uhlig dismisses Marschner in similarly harsh terms, as 'nothing but Italian music, wrapped in leather, fitted out with thick German soles and rendered academic and impotent'. (The remark may well register some fear of Wagner's own musical 'impotence' at this difficult juncture in his career, as well as a lingering need to exorcise such awkward, 'provincial' influences from his own idiom, a need he had felt since the 1830s.) Of composers of lighter genres, such as Lortzing or Flotow, he left almost no recorded opinions at all, although he can hardly have been ignorant of their works, including Lortzing's 1840 comedy on the subject of Hans Sachs, after J.L. Deinhardstein.

Implicit in Wagner's usual tone of condescending approval of certain 'honest' and 'solid' aspects of earlier German opera (or the popular ballads of Carl Loewe) is, no doubt, a contrast with the slick and suspect 'professionalism' of Meyerbeer or Mendelssohn. Naturally it is difficult to disentangle Wagner's attitudes here from his notoriously unabashed anti-Semitism and Francophobia (in the case of Meyerbeer's grand operas). Yet he never retracted his initial admiration of the French-Jewish composer Halévy, nor his lasting affection for the works of Auber, at least those he had conducted as a youth (*La Muette de Portici, Lestocq*). The vehement polemic sustained against Meyerbeer around 1850 must be attributed to a combination of biographical-psychological motives and the accelerating pace of Wagner's radical alienation from operatic norms of the day, as embodied in Meyerbeer's successes. It might be argued that, from an objective aesthetic viewpoint, Meyerbeer's works really do present a greater affront to Wagnerian notions of musical-dramatic unity and integration than those of Auber or Halévy. Likewise, Wagner's disparagement of Mendelssohn can be attributed at least partially to a legitimate incongruence of aesthetic ideals, if not without an admixture of personal bias and professional envy. We may rightly take offence at the bogus sociology behind his assessment of the 'impersonal', 'superficial' or 'derivative' aspects of Mendelssohn's music, but at some level Wagner's comments do reflect a genuine divergence of aims. Even in *Das Judentum in der Musik* (*Jewishness in Music*, 1850) he did not actually dispute the high quality of Mendelssohn's works, and in later years Wagner professed a deep admiration for Mendelssohn's *Calm Sea and Prosperous Voyage* and particularly the *Hebrides* Overture, frequently played at Wahnfried and publicly praised in the essay *Über das Dichten und Komponieren* (*On Poetry and Composition*, 1879). (Granted, this selection served to marginalize Mendelssohn as a 'landscape' composer, unable to communicate vital 'human' feelings.)

Among other prominent figures of the early Romantic generation, Schumann was perhaps the least appreciated by Wagner. It is unclear how much he knew of the piano music, but like many others at the time he deplored the direction of Schumann's later works, which he (like some others) attributed to the dual encroaching influences of Mendelssohn and mental illness. (At different times disciples such as Theodor Uhlig and Joseph Rubinstein sought to defend Schumann's music to Wagner, but his disdain only increased with years.) He knew still less of Chopin's music – a fact which he regretted in later life but did little to remedy. (Cosima records the pleasure he took in some of the Preludes.) Wagner displayed perhaps the greatest ambivalence toward the music of Berlioz. The maverick French composer had fascinated him since his early Paris days, while fundamental cultural, linguistic and stylistic differences maintained a certain distance between the two. The 'lamenting, melancholy' side of the composer was his best feature, Wagner informed Cosima, while the raucous finale of the *Symphonie fantastique* – which had put him off as a young man in Paris – still seemed 'stiff and disagreeable' in 1875. 'What particularly strikes me', he added (echoing earlier criticisms), 'is Berlioz's inability to develop his themes, which are often very fine, something he shares with Schubert' (CT, 6 Oct 1875). He harboured similarly mixed feelings about Liszt, while his complicated relationship to the man (and subsequent marriage to the daughter) necessitated a good measure of tact. Wagner was favourably impressed by Liszt's experimental harmonic procedures (see 'Musical Background and Influences', p. 87) and perhaps by the technique of thematic transformation which Liszt was developing concurrently with Wagner's expansion of his own 'leitmotif' technique. But, as with Berlioz, Wagner preferred the quieter, more reflective side of Liszt's musical personality (*Orpheus*, the St Francis *Légendes*) to the brash extroversion of *Les Préludes* or *Mazeppa*. He also disapproved of the later sacred works, such as *Christus*, on both musical and ideological grounds (his reactions to the Weimar premiere covered 'all extremes from ravishment to immense indignation' – CT 29 May 1873).

On the subject of his most illustrious operatic contemporary, Verdi, Wagner was able to maintain an almost complete silence. To the extent that they are mentioned at all by Wagner (or

Cosima), Verdi and Donizetti are stigmatized as indices of a decadent tradition, of which Rossini and Bellini constituted the last healthy bloom. But after his enforced labour on the score of *La Favorite* in Paris, Wagner made no attempt to keep abreast of the Italian repertory.

The same can be said of most music by younger composers, of whatever nationality: by and large they were either ignored by Wagner altogether, or else summarily dismissed. During the concert tours of the early 1870s Wagner attended numerous operatic performances in search of potential talent for Bayreuth, and did hear some newer works, including Gounod's *Roméo et Juliette* ('nauseating', remarks Cosima), Goldmark's *Die Königin von Saba* ('no gold, no marks, but plenty of Mosenthal' – an allusion to the inept librettist), Rubinstein's *Die Maccabäer* ('one can nowadays only make an effect if one writes in a Wagnerian style'), Meyerbeer's *L'Africaine* (a 'profanation'), and Bizet's *Carmen* ('much tastelessness' – although it is unclear if Cosima's remark refers to the opera or to the artists' reception following). Even those figures identified with Wagner as members of the 'New German School', such as Joachim Raff or Peter Cornelius, were never taken very seriously by him as composers. One exception was Hans von Bülow, whose symphonic poem *Nirwana* (composed in the 1850s, revised and published in 1866) Wagner proclaimed as 'much more significant than any other modern composition'. And he did provide Bruckner with some slight encouragement by accepting the dedication of the Third – and henceforth 'Wagner' – Symphony in 1875, but his encouragement went no further than that. Bruckner's more powerful Viennese rival, Brahms, received more of Wagner's attention, most of it negative. Wagner was doubtless irritated by the factionalism engendered by the musical press. But his reactions to Brahms also betray a strain of mere ill-humoured petulance at the celebrity enjoyed by the younger 'anti-Wagnerian'. This is clearly evinced in reactions (as recorded by Cosima) to passages in Brahms' First and Second Symphonies, ranging from 'trivial' and 'vulgar' to 'utterly shocking' and 'downright disgusting', while pointed allusions to the composer in the essays *On Poetry and Composition* and *Über die Anwendung der Musik auf das Drama* (*On the Application of Music to the Drama*) convey an explicit annoyance with Brahms for presuming to wrest from Wagner the mantle of Beethoven and the *ars musicae severioris*. A subtler critique emerges in the second essay: the notion that Brahms has transferred a 'chamber music style' – i.e. a denser, more esoteric deployment of motivic and tonal structure – to an inappropriate context, the public symphony (GS X, 183). Wagner's reactions to Brahms, as to so many of his contemporaries, suggest again the commingling of personal animus with musical insight, filtered (like most of Wagner's insights) through the refracting lens of aesthetic speculation and stubborn bias.

THOMAS S. GREY

OPINIONS AND OUTLOOK

Wagner, animals and modern scientific medicine

IT IS DIFFICULT TO THINK of any opera composer or dramatist who has been more actively concerned in his artistic oeuvre with the question of man's relationship to nature and the animal world around him than Wagner. He had various pets as companions throughout his life, was strongly opposed to hunting as a sport, and espoused the cause of vegetarianism. The last was a theoretical rather than a practical issue for Wagner: his response to Nietzsche's abstention from meat was unsympathetic. But from an early period the concept of *Mitleiden* (compassion, literally 'suffering with') was a key one in Wagner's outlook, and for him it was directly related to the relationship between the human and animal worlds. A letter to Mathilde Wesendonck of 1 October 1858, for example, describes a brutal scene of slaughter at a poulterer's; the letter goes on to develop the theme of fellow-suffering, making clear that it is central to Wagner's art as much as to his philosophy of life.

The ethical and medical justification for animal experiments had become the subject of violent disagreement in Wagner's household at least as early as 11 October 1878, when Cosima mentioned the topic in the course of a conversation with Malwida von Meysenbug, a close friend of the family. According to Cosima's diary, Wagner had expressed 'his repugnance for such senseless crimes, which will never bring people any nearer to the nature of things' (CT, 11 Oct 1878). Nine months later he was sent a book which 'moved and incensed' him deeply (CT, 31 Jul 1879). It was *Die Folterkammern der Wissenschaft: Eine Sammlung von Thatsachen für das Laienpublikum* (*The Torture Chambers of Science: A Collection of Facts for the Lay Public*) (1879), a propagandist tract in which Ernst von Weber (1830–1902), a Saxon landowner, had denounced, in words and pictures, experiments on animals in medical laboratories and appealed to his readers to follow the example of the English and demand the legal abolition of such practices. He described all these experiments, whether or not they involved a surgical incision, under the general heading of 'vivisection', literally, the cutting open of living bodies. England was, in fact, the only country at this time where legal regulations existed, limiting the use of animals in medical research.

Appalled by the atrocities reported in Weber's profusely illustrated pamphlet, Wagner seized the initiative in a letter of 9 August 1879 in which he told Weber of his decision to devote himself and his whole family to the cause of the newly founded antivivisectionist movement in Germany and a week later asked Weber to regard him as a 'founder member of the International Society for the Prevention of the Scientific Torture of Animals' which Weber was planning to set up, underlining his commitment with a generous donation.

Encouraged by a visit from the militant Weber on 12 September 1879, Wagner saw himself obliged to speak out on the subject of animal experiments in an Open Letter, which occupied his attentions from 20 September to 9 October, distracting him, for the duration, from his work on the score of *Parsifal*.

174

The article was published in the *Bayreuther Blätter* at the end of October under the title 'Offenes Schreiben an Herrn Ernst von Weber, Verfasser der Schrift: "Die Folterkammern der Wissenschaft"' ('Open Letter to Herr Ernst von Weber, Author of the Essay: "The Torture Chambers of Science"'). Wagner sent Weber a copy of the article in proof form and, in an access of anti-scientific feeling, insisted that 'a mass petition' was 'quite indispensable'. At the same time he expressed the hope that 'their lordships, the vivisectors, may be put in very real fear of their lives: in other words, they should be made to believe they can see the common people advancing on them with cudgels and clubs'.

Wagner begins his Open Letter by emphasizing that he is speaking as an artist and that he is prompted to do so by a vague feeling of unease at the uncivilized behaviour of his 'despiritualized age', an age characterized by the 'spectre of science [. . .] which has worked its way up from the dissecting table to the firearms factory' (GS X, 194). On the one hand he sees a science which obeys only reason and the principle of that utilitarianism which alone is believed to encourage the state and, on the other, he advocates an investigation of oft-despised feeling as the path to true insight, without, however, regarding reason as having been rendered wholly redundant in this way. In consequence, experimental medicine makes no sense for Wagner: since it is unfeeling – a charge he supports by insisting that it allows experiments not only on animals but, in certain cases, on humans – it cannot grasp the true cause of illness-related suffering.

In making this assertion, Wagner repeats a claim already advanced by doctors and, above all, laymen with an interest in natural cures, namely, that the efforts of researchers in the field of natural science were concerned with diagnosis but never with therapy. That was why experiments on animals never alleviated a patient's suffering, still less provided a cure, so that, ultimately, they were of no real use to people. Ideas such as these are the product of a radical socio-cultural understanding of illness which Wagner had already expressed decades earlier in the dramatic fragment *Jesus von Nazareth* (1849), a work shot through with socialist and Hegelian ideas.

None the less, Wagner places a very high value on medical activity in his Open Letter. The doctor, he believed, could obtain an insight into his patients' illness by empathizing with them, thereby gaining an instinctive grasp of the true nature of the ailing individual, which, in turn, would inspire confidence. Rejection of this practice, he went on, would lead to the emergence of a 'speculative physiologist pursuing abstract findings intended to enhance his own reputation' (GS X, 199), a form of science which would lead to falsification and bungling incompetence and hence to a loss of confidence. Obsessed with purely rational concerns, the experimental researcher was interested first and foremost in those illnesses which were due to civilization itself and which the well-to-do brought down on themselves through overeating and their unnatural way of life. It was, therefore, morally just as irresponsible to study artificially induced diseases in animals as it was to use impoverished hospital patients as guinea pigs, since such patients 'allowed themselves to be exploited by the rich even as they lay dying' (GS X, 205).

In Wagner's opinion it would be a sign of progress if the pauper were allowed the rich man's dietary excesses which, harmful to the latter, would help the former recover his health. Instead of seeking to remove such excesses and ensure a fairer distribution of wealth, so-called science concerned itself chiefly with dealing with superficial symptoms. This idea, too, is already implicit in *Jesus von Nazareth* (SS XI, 296).

A new point in Wagner's Open Letter, however, is his assertion that the findings of natural science were now being used for military ends. Accordingly, the official state apostles of compassion were chiefly to be found among the army authorities, who cynically pointed out that more accurate bullets could curtail life's needless suffering 'wholesale and in summary fashion' (GS X, 198).

Wagner's Open Letter to Weber was part of a wider debate on the subject, a debate conducted, in emotive terms, in a series of pamphlets which examined the medical significance of, and moral justification for, experiments on animals. Supporters of such experiments paid little heed to Wagner's remarks or did not take them seriously, while his enemies in the newspaper world regarded the essay as a welcome excuse for complacent attacks.

On the other hand, many opponents of animal experiments wrote to Wagner privately to express their support, which gave him a great deal of satisfaction (see CT, 22 Dec 1879 and 9 May 1880). Publicly, the response was more muted, although the composer's name undoubtedly lent a certain respectability to the antivivisectionist cause. Only after his death, however, was *Parsifal* discovered to be 'an imperishable monument to the love which seeks to protect the animal kingdom from every form of cruelty'. As Cosima reports, Wagner had already predicted this interpretation, noting with wry amusement: 'I have always been fated to carry out in prose (in life) what I have put into my poetry – that scene with the swan, people will think it came from my view on vivisection.' (CT, 6 Feb 1881)

Wagner's committed condemnation of scientific experiments on animals sets out, therefore, from his specific interpretation of the relationship between humans and animals, a relationship typified by the concept of fellow-suffering. This latter has a pragmatic element to it which, Wagner argued, must also influence not only doctor–patient relationships but human relationships in general, including man's attitude to nature. We are entirely justified in speaking of a Wagnerian 'cosmology of compassion', in graphic contrast to which the composer saw the civilization of his day beset by an unfeeling, technologically orientated utilitarianism increasingly geared to a state that was addicted to militaristic expansionism.

Wagner's attitude to animal experiments, therefore, is concerned on a wider level with a contemporary problem which he himself found deeply unsettling: did the spread of knowledge necessarily mean the abandonment of ethical values? On the medical front, he introduced one aspect into the discussion which had largely been ignored in medical circles but which, taken up by individual antivivisectionists, now appears particularly modern. It is the view that illness is caused first and foremost by socio-cultural factors: in other words, by social living conditions and habits. Only by changing those conditions – by hygiene in the widest sense – could disease be wiped out. For the rest, Wagner based his arguments on those of the leading antivivisectionists of the day, adopting their belief that, in treating patients, the experimental method was barbarous, useless and utterly misguided.

As for the moral aspect of the relationship between animals and humans, Wagner refused to remain on the sentimental level of personal anecdote, a failing which was the besetting feature of the majority of those of his contemporaries who opposed experiments on animals. He did not become entrenched in personal polemics. His chance encounter in 1879 with Weber's 'enlightened' essay was merely the catalyst which triggered off a conscious public formulation of his cosmology of compassion, which he believed would not only counteract the prevailing utilitarian philosophy of the day but which, above and beyond art, would provide the means by which to change the world.

JOACHIM THIERY and ULRICH TRÖHLER
translated by Stewart Spencer

Wagner's critique of science and technology

'SCIENCE IS THE HUMAN intellect's ultimate power; but the enjoyment of that power is art', Wagner opined in 1849 (SS XII, 260). Thirty years later, on 31 March 1880, he wrote to tell King Ludwig II of his continuing scientific observations:

A problem which I have been unable to solve until now concerns the reason for the degeneration discernible in the human race: the fact that such degeneration has existed since the beginning of recorded history points to a prehistoric phase in which the human race had already reached its truest pitch of perfection. I am now engaged in investigating this question: an essay on animal cruelty has set me on the right track.

It was this essay, the 'Open Letter to Ernst von Weber', which prompted Wagner to write his 32-page treatise *Religion und Kunst* (*Religion and Art*), first published in the *Bayreuther Blätter* in March 1880. Here he adopts the optimistic view that the renewal of society which he believed was urgently needed, and which he described as 'regeneration', was already in prospect, its chief manifestations being vegetarianism, animal-protection societies (especially those directed against 'the shamefully discreditable excesses of speculative animal vivisection as practised in our physiological operating theatres'), the temperance societies that sought to combat alcohol abuse, the peace movement, workers' associations and true socialism. As a unifying link between all these movements – movements which had no doubt sprung from a common, if unconscious, religious root – Wagner saw the kind of compassion which constitutes humankind's essential nature. But organized socialism, banned in Bismarck's Empire as recently as 1878, would only have a chance, he believed, if it could form a close alliance with the foregoing groups, for on its own it was politically ineffectual.

According to Cosima's diary entry of 8 January 1880, Wagner himself attributed his changing attitude to vegetarianism to his recent reading of a monograph, *Thalysia, or the Salvation of the Human Race*, by the French vegetarian Jean Antoine Gleizès (1773–1843). Here Gleizès had maintained that 'the slaughter of animals was the principal source of man's errors and crimes, the habit of eating the flesh of animals the principal cause of his ugliness, diseases and the brevity of his life'. Later, Cosima noted: 'R. cites an instance from N. America, mentioned by Gleizès, in which prisoners have become quite docile as the result of a vegetarian diet.' (CT, 28 Feb 1881) In *Religion and Art*, these nutritional speculations culminate in the highly imaginative idea of moving whole populations from colder regions to warmer ones, since Wagner was convinced that only in colder climates was it necessary to eat meat.

His criticism of medicine, expressed in his 'Open Letter to Ernst von Weber', and the idea of an alternative lifestyle developed on a socio-cultural basis were now applied to the whole of contemporary society, a society characterized by its credulous faith in progress. Technological progress, in particular, was a thorn in Wagner's flesh. 'The sailboat,' he exclaimed in 1880, 'that was a true discovery, it speaks to me, whereas all these machines tell me nothing.' (CT, 2 Jul 1880) And, unlike his soulmate Schopenhauer, whose first consideration had always been the welfare of animals, the much-travelled Wagner even denied that the railways served any useful purpose, telling Cosima his reaction to the recently opened Gotthard rail link: 'Nothing worth mentioning comes from such works, he observes, for, as Proudhon says, "Le génie est sédentaire" [genius is sedentary].' (CT, 14 Mar 1880) The following year he spoke 'half in jest and half in earnest about the downfall of the human race, which one is always seeking to counter by erecting telegraph poles and building railroads.' (CT, 4 Dec 1881) And, during the same winter month, in private conversation with Cosima, he went on to insist that 'when people are buried in coal mines, I feel indignation at a community which obtains its heating by such means.' (CT, 16 Dec 1881) But in Sicily in 1882, when he heard that the coal industry was being replaced by electricity, he argued strongly against it. '"It is still a machine," he exclaims, and tells me [Cosima] what crippling conditions have been brought about by machines. No, no improvements of this sort, but moving to fine climates in which one can live naturally.' (CT, 25 Mar 1882) And Cosima recalled the composer's reaction to a new and epoch-making technological development: 'recently, when the phonograph was mentioned, he spoke of the foolishness of expecting anything from such inventions – people were turning themselves into machines.' (CT 7 Oct 1882) But what worried him most of all was the increasingly open use to which scientific knowledge was being put by a government arming itself for war. As he told his set-designer, Paul von Joukowsky (1845–1912):

> Moths fly into the lamp because Nature is imprudent, whereas for human beings the task is to extinguish this light – not the light of knowledge, but that of a false science, a science which the princes foster while at the same time they continue building up their armies. (CT, 8 May 1880)

Wagner's openly acknowledged fears for the future increased during the final years of his life, finding perhaps their clearest expression in the closing paragraphs of *Religion and Art*, where he issues a dire and prophetic warning, painting an apocalyptic picture of what will happen if science and technology continue unchecked:

> Even now the armoured monitors, against which the proud and glorious sailing ship cannot hold her own, offer a sight of spectral horror: mutely dedicated men, no longer with the looks of men, operate these monsters and will nevermore desert their posts, though they are in the terrible stokehole. [. . .] It is altogether conceivable that not only this, but art and science, bravery and points of honour, life and property could one day explode as the result of some incalculable error. (GS X, 252)

In his final essays on the issues of the day Wagner went beyond the superficial reasons for conducting experiments on animals and revealed himself to be both a sensitive observer of the radical changes brought about in 19th-century living conditions in the wake of the Industrial Revolution and an ethically orientated thinker who lamented his contemporaries' lack of sensitivity, regarding with some suspicion the first generally effective link between science and technology designed to dominate nature and dismissing it with dogmatic finality. At a time when similar topics are again a subject for lively debate, Wagner's disapproval of an age that was geared to technological progress and of the belief that nature, far from being teleologically determined, could be controlled by man appears as relevant as ever. Only in its axiomatic self-righteousness, however, does such a criticism – both in Wagner's day and our own – ignore the potential consequences that would follow not only for the individual but for society as a whole if we tried to do without technology.

JOACHIM THIERY and ULRICH TRÖHLER
translated by Stewart Spencer

Section 9

SOURCES

Autobiographical writings	182
Diaries	186
Letters	190
Collected writings	193
Autograph manuscripts:	
Sketches/drafts (text)	196
Sketches/drafts (music)	203
Scores	219
WAGNER'S HAND (plates 21–30)	208
Printed editions:	
Breitkopf edition	221
Sämtliche Werke (Schott)	223
Miscellaneous	225

SOURCES

WAGNER FIRST BEGAN making notes for a projected autobiography in August 1835. He was at a low ebb – penniless, artistically uncreative, unhappy in love and believing himself abandoned by his friends – and the decision to take stock of his life and keep a record of its outward events may well have answered a psychological need. As John Deathridge has noted (Deathridge/Dahlhaus, 1984), the opening entry resembles nothing so much as 'the start of an article in a dictionary of music'. This *Rote Brieftasche* (Red Pocketbook) was apparently kept up to date until the winter of 1865/6 and served as the basis for *Mein Leben* (*My Life*). Only the first four sides have survived, covering the period from 1813 until 17 September 1839, the date of Wagner's arrival in Paris. For the early period Wagner's memory occasionally played him false, but there is no evidence of any systematic falsification. The same cannot be said, however, for the so-called Annals, which represent a continuation of the Red Pocketbook. The entries from the latter, covering the period from Easter 1846 onwards, were transferred to *Das Braune Buch* (The Brown Book; see 'Diaries' below, pp.186–7) between February 1868 and early 1869 and it appears that Wagner took the opportunity to introduce a handful of editorial changes at this stage, weaving a web of mysticization around several allegedly seminal experiences. At the same time – as Otto Strobel points out in his exemplary edition of the text for the period from 30 April 1864 to the end of 1868 (Strobel, 1936–9) – Wagner's own errors in dating several of the entries suggest that the information contained in the Annals needs to be treated with caution.

Wagner's first published piece of autobiographical writing was his *Autobiographische Skizze* (*Autobiographical Sketch*), which appeared in Heinrich Laube's *Zeitung für die elegante Welt* on 1 and 8 February 1843. It covers the period from Wagner's birth in 1813 to his return to Germany in April 1842 and was intended to introduce local audiences to their new operatic star following the spectacularly successful first performance of *Rienzi* the previous October. Wagner adopts the persona of the 19th-century dandy, a dilettante for whom composing came naturally. At the same time, we find him attempting to forge a link between his life and art by suggesting, for example, that *Der fliegende Holländer* was inspired by his own experiences among the Norwegian fjords – conveniently forgetting that the opera, like its source, had been set in Scotland until only weeks before its Dresden premiere in January 1843 (see 'Myths and Legends', p.134). A number of small but significant changes were

Autobio-graphical writings

made to the text when Wagner republished it in volume 1 of his collected writings in 1871: Heinrich Heine's original contribution to the Dutchman legend, for instance, was now denied completely.

In July 1851 Wagner began work on *Eine Mitteilung an meine Freunde* (*A Communication to my Friends*), a 36,000-word introduction to the libretti of *Der fliegende Holländer*, *Tannhäuser* and *Lohengrin*, which were included in the original brochure. Completed in mid-August 1851 and published in December of the same year, the essay was subsequently revised and taken over into volume 4 of Wagner's collected writings. *A Communication to my Friends* was the last of the major essays that Wagner wrote in Zurich between 1849 and 1851 and was in part an attempt to set the earlier writings in their autobiographical context and thus to preempt the misunderstandings to which he felt they had been subjected (see, for example, his letters to Franz Liszt of 16 August 1850 and Theodor Uhlig of 6/7 May 1852). Accordingly, Wagner adopts what might be called a behaviourist stance, seeking to see his works as the product of an environment which he had now outgrown. One consequence of this approach is that an even tighter bond is forged between Wagner's life and works: in *Rienzi*, *Der fliegende Holländer*, *Tannhäuser* and *Lohengrin*, the artist is seen in conflict with society. But to regard *A Communication to my Friends* as a key to understanding Wagner's early operas – as several generations of writers on Wagner have tended to do – is to fail to appreciate the sea-change that had taken place in Wagner's thinking over the intervening period. The *völkisch* ideology which Wagner adopted in the late 1840s obliged him to deny the literary origins of his Romantic operas and to see them instead as products of the popular creative spirit. At the same time, he is guilty of attempting to turn these early works into proto-music dramas by applying the principles of *Oper und Drama* (*Opera and Drama*) to them: to claim that Senta's Ballad is the 'thematic seed' of the entire score of *Der fliegende Holländer* is not borne out by an examination of the sketches or finished work. Finally, Wagner's new-found interest in the ethnocentric materialism of the philosopher Ludwig Feuerbach has encouraged him to project Feuerbachian ideas on to a work like *Lohengrin*, notwithstanding the fact that such ideas sit distinctly uncomfortably with the underlying thrust of this last of Wagner's Romantic operas. The final section of *A Communication to my Friends* is given over to the turbulent genesis of the *Ring*: Wagner's decision to turn the scenario into a four-part work and stage it at a festival specially organized for that purpose was taken between the completion of the initial draft of the essay and his revision of the printed proofs. The published version of the text thus looks forward to the course that Wagner's life was to take during the decades that followed.

It is when we turn to *Mein Leben* that we find Wagner at his most tendentious. He began work on the first part of it on 17 July 1865, apparently in response to a request from King Ludwig II of Bavaria (see Ludwig's letter to Wagner of 28 May 1865: 'It would give me inexpressible joy to receive from you a detailed description of your intellectual development and also of the external events of your life'). *Mein Leben* covers the period from Wagner's birth to his summons to Munich in 1864. It falls into four parts and was dictated to Cosima Wagner (or Cosima von Bülow as she still was when the sessions began in 1865), before being corrected by Wagner himself. The dictation extended over many years, often with lengthy interruptions:

Part I (1813–42)   17 July 1865 – winter 1866/7
Part II (1842–50)   Winter 1866/7 – November/December 1868
Part III (1850–61)   November/December 1868 – 19 April 1873
Part IV (1861–64)   10 January 1876 – 25 July 1880

As work on the volume proceeded, it seems to have occurred to Wagner that a wider audience might be drawn into his confidence: as he wrote to Anton Pusinelli on 13 January 1870, it was important

> that my friends should know of the existence of a document which could emphatically refute all the distortions & calumnies which circulate about me, as they do about nobody else. To protect such a manuscript against loss, I am now in the process of having a very small number of copies of it printed at my own expense. These shall in part be left to my family; but even during my lifetime I should like to give a copy each to you and perhaps two other younger and entirely trustworthy friends, in return, of course, for the most faithful pledge never to let it out of their sight, nor to publish it after my death. Against this, it will be of use to these few people even now, since it will enable them to contradict false statements that may be made concerning my life (more especially these absurd biographical sketches that appear from time to time) by relying for whatever corrections may seem necessary upon the dictated material itself.

In the event, however, the implied imperative that *Mein Leben* should contain nothing but the 'unvarnished truth' was sacrificed to the conditions under which it was dictated. It was inevitable, of course, that Wagner should attempt to spare Cosima's feelings by drawing a veil over a number of his romantic attachments and underplaying the extent of his affair with Mathilde Wesendonck (whom, even as late as June 1863, he was still describing as 'my first and only love'). Equally, he no doubt thought he was flattering Cosima by advancing the date of his involvement with her to November 1863, although contemporary evidence suggests that it was not until the following summer that she herself took the initiative and threw herself into Wagner's arms and bed. By the same token, Wagner – self-appointed privy councillor to King Ludwig II – was at pains to play down his role in the Dresden Uprising of May 1849, believing, quite rightly, that his actions on the barricades would not have found favour in the eyes of a monarch whose grandfather had been forced to abdicate by just such revolutionary goings-on in Munich.

In a sense, however, these are venial distortions compared with the wider strategies involved in writing *Mein Leben*. In the first place, Wagner was anxious to see himself as Beethoven's natural successor, a German musician in whom the music drama achieved its natural, inevitable culmination. Hence his fictitious account of the ostensibly seminal experience of Schröder-Devrient's Leonore in Leipzig in 1829; hence, too, his claim that it was Beethoven's Ninth – rather than Berlioz's *Roméo et Juliette* – which persuaded him to embark on his *Faust* Overture (see 'Myths and Legends', pp.133–4). Second – and presumably under the influence of his reading of Schopenhauer in the autumn of 1854 – Wagner abandoned the behaviourist outlook of his Feuerbach phase and presented himself to the world as a natural genius, a picture which he was able to paint by mythologizing the act of creative inspiration: time and again in *Mein Leben*, blinding aesthetic experiences are described as crucial to the genesis of each of the music dramas of his maturity. Yet, even if *Mein Leben* remains factually unreliable, it is of value as a masterly account of Wagner's perception of himself as an artist, a defence, in Deathridge's words, of 'the cause of art itself which, at least as he saw it, was being increasingly threatened by the decline of Western civilization' (Deathridge, 1987).

It remains to say something about the publishing history of *Mein Leben*. Volumes 1–3 were published by the Basle printer, G.A. Bonfantini, in 1870, 1872 and 1875. (Basle was chosen to allow Nietzsche to superintend the printing process.) Volume 4 was published by Theodor Burger of Bayreuth in 1880. The original print-run of fifteen was increased to eighteen from volume 2 onwards. Copies of each volume were sent to a select band of 'true and trusted friends' on publication. Following Wagner's death, however, Cosima wrote to the various recipients, asking them to return their copies. Most of these copies appear to have fallen victim to her penchant for pyromania. However, Bonfantini had run off an extra copy of the first three volumes for himself and these were acquired in 1892 by the indefatigable Mary Burrell, who, appalled by what she read there, declared that 'Richard Wagner is not responsible for the book' (Burrell, 1898). (Nietzsche, it will be recalled, had earlier dismissed *Mein Leben* as 'fable convenue': Nietzsche, 1888.) It was in part to scotch the resultant rumours and speculations that Wahnfried sanctioned the first commercial edition of *Mein Leben* in 1911.

Printer's errors bedevilled the edition from the outset: Bonfantini's compositor evidently had difficulty deciphering Cosima's handwriting (he was not the last to suffer such problems), so that 'Sommer 1850' appeared as 'Januar 1850', Wagner's 'universales Schlafzimmer' in Paris became a 'miserables Schlafzimmer' and so on. In addition – and largely out of deference to characters in the drama of Wagner's life who were still alive – seventeen passages were suppressed or rewritten. Far from staunching the flow of speculation, the 1911 edition merely added to it, culminating in the publication of *The Truth about Wagner* (Hurn/Root, 1930), in which Philip Dutton Hurn and Waverley Lewis Root falsely claimed that on the very first page of the private edition of 1870 Wagner had identified Ludwig Geyer, not Friedrich Wagner, as his natural father (see 'Paternity', pp.94–5). This, in turn, led to the publication of the suppressed passages in *Die Musik*, xxii (1929/30), 725 (Eng. trans. in Newman, 1931).

The 'first authentic edition' of *Mein Leben*, edited by Martin Gregor-Dellin and published in 1963, was less than a startling revelation, therefore, since – with the exception of the printer's errors mentioned above – the contents had already been known. Moreover, the inadequacy of the annotation of the 1963 edition rules it out of court as anything other than a stopgap. A fully annotated, critical edition of the complete text, including changes made by Wagner during dictation, remains as pressing as before. (Plans for Martin Gregor-Dellin to superintend such an edition were abandoned on the author's death.) *Mein Leben* has twice been rendered into English – an anonymous but serviceable translation published contemporaneously with the German original in 1911, and Andrew Gray's 1983 translation, the relentless 20th-century colloquialisms of which are something of an acquired taste.

STEWART SPENCER

Diaries

ALTHOUGH THE WORD 'diaries' is normally associated in a Wagnerian context with the Diaries kept by Cosima Wagner between 1869 and 1883, there are at least four other texts to which the term can be applied.

During the summer of 1840 Wagner kept a brief record of his life in Paris and, in particular, of the difficulty of making ends meet. Only three entries appear to have survived, dated 23, 29 and 30 June (see SS XVI, 4–6). Between 21 August 1858 and 4 April 1859 Wagner kept a 'Diary since the Time of my Flight from the Asyl on 17 August 1858' (the 'Venice Diary') in which he attempted to reconcile himself with the termination of his relationship with Mathilde Wesendonck. The diary was sent off to Mathilde, in two parts, on 12 October 1858 and on its completion the following April. (The text was published by Wolfgang Golther in his edition of the Wesendonck correspondence; the original manuscript is believed to have been destroyed by Cosima.) Finally, between 14 and 27 September 1865 Wagner wrote out a series of diary entries for King Ludwig, prescribing the king's role in the cultural regeneration of Germany. Excerpts from this 'diary' were included in the *Bayreuther Blätter* in 1878; the complete text was published by Otto Strobel in his edition of the correspondence between Ludwig and Wagner. (For the Red Pocketbook see 'Autobiographical writings', p.182.)

Das Braune Buch (The Brown Book) was the name which Wagner gave to a leather-bound notebook presented to him by Cosima at some date between mid-1864 and August 1865. Her intention in giving it to him seems to have been that he should use it for writing messages to her during their absences; and until the two of them took up residence together at Tribschen in July 1868, this was the chief purpose which it served. Yet even here, under the ostensible pretext of writing to Cosima, Wagner's constant preoccupation was his *own* aesthetic. It is no coincidence that he addresses her as 'my soul'. The tone of the early entries is one of overwhelming gloom, of despair at life's suffering tempered only by the solace of refuge in his art. Later, the Schopenhauerian element acquires a more positive aspect, as emerges from his belief in the self-authenticating beauty of art and from his conviction that all human behaviour might be reduced to musical terms. But, in addition to serving as a form of private confessional, the Brown Book also did duty as a sketchbook for literary ideas: it was here, for example, that Wagner wrote out the 1865 prose draft of *Parzival* (as it was then called), together with a brief outline for a drama on the life of Martin Luther and the anti-French 'farce', *Die Capitulation* (later retitled *Eine Kapitulation*). Various poems, drafts of prose works, the Annals for the years 1846 to 1868 and a series of entries on the theme of cultural regeneration complete the contents of the diary, which Wagner kept with increasing infrequency during the final years of his life.

Following Wagner's death the volume was reappropriated by Cosima, who subsequently handed it on to her daughter Eva. In turn, Eva claimed to have been granted 'absolute right of disposal' over it, a right which she interpreted as a licence to remove and destroy seven pages (fourteen sides) of the volume, and to paste over a further five. In 1931 she transferred the Brown Book to the Richard-Wagner-Gedenkstätte der Stadt Bayreuth, with instructions that it be made available only to 'trustworthy persons'. Excerpts from the volume were published by Otto Strobel in his edition of the correspondence between Ludwig and Wagner and also in Bayreuth Festival programmes for 1934 and 1937. Although at least half the contents of the Brown Book had already been transcribed and published *before* it passed into Eva's hands, the first complete edition of it was none the less a valuable addition to the Wagner literature, covering, as it does, the final seventeen years of Wagner's life and allowing us a fascinating insight into the aesthetic concerns of that period. Joachim Bergfeld's diplomatic edition of the text (Bergfeld, 1975) is compromised by his uncritical attitude to his subject and by a failure to take account of the wider aesthetic issues. (To dismiss Wagner's ivory tower mentality as 'the imaginings of a fevered mind' is to ignore the wider background of the age.) An English translation by George Bird appeared in 1980.

On 21/2 July 1865 Wagner wrote to inform King Ludwig: 'We have decided to continue the dictation [of *Mein Leben*] up to the time of my association with you, my dear and glorious King: from then on Cosima shall continue the biography on her own and, I hope, will one day complete it.' In the event, the plan was not realized: Cosima was too busy sorting out her own private and emotional life during the 1860s to devote any time to an account of

Wagner's goings-on, and it was not until she moved in with him at Tribschen that she began to keep a systematic record of their life together in the form of a diary. Although this diary would no doubt have provided the raw material for such a biography, it is no substitute for one, as Wagner himself repeatedly insisted: three days before he died, he told Cosima that he still intended to 'finish the biography', a remark which – to quote John Deathridge – 'casts at least one shadow of doubt on the optimal "authenticity" Cosima's Diaries are generally thought to represent' (Deathridge, 1987).

The Diaries fill twenty-one identically bound volumes, although the number of pages in each ranges from 160 to 356, while each page contains between fourteen and thirty-six lines of text, so that the total number of words amounts to nearly one million. Apart from additions and amendments in Cosima's own hand, the text also includes corrections and entries in Wagner's handwriting, notably for the period 5–12 June 1869, during which Cosima gave birth to Siegfried. It appears that Cosima did not make regular entries in her diary but wrote them out in batches of several days at a time, relying on jottings from a smaller notebook. As her eyesight deteriorated, so her handwriting became increasingly indecipherable, leading to a number of conjectural readings. But even clearly decipherable passages have been mistranscribed, resulting in unfortunate misunderstandings of textually important passages (Spencer, 1983).

The Diaries break off on 12 February 1883, the eve of Wagner's death. They remained in Cosima's possession until 1908, when her daughter, Eva, married the English-born (but rabidly anti-English) historian, Houston Stewart Chamberlain. According to Eva's later sworn testimony she received the Diaries as her dowry. As with the Brown Book it appears to have been Eva who crossed out whole sentences in an attempt to render them illegible. Almost all of these passages – containing derogatory remarks about Liszt, Hans von Wolzogen and Bismarck – have been restored in the published edition.

At the time of the alleged deed of gift the Diaries were in fact in Riga, where they were being consulted by Carl Friedrich Glasenapp, Wagner's official biographer, for the final volume of his six-volume life of the composer. Glasenapp made extensive, if unacknowledged, use of the text. During the 1920s Richard Graf Du Moulin Eckart was granted access to the Diaries in compiling his biography of Cosima, first published in 1929–31. Shortly afterwards Eva prepared a series of extracts for Arturo Toscanini: running to 130 quarto pages, these excerpts were subsequently published – with incorrect dates and errors of transcription – in the *Bayreuther Blätter* between 1936 and 1938.

In 1935 Eva presented the Diaries to the Richard-Wagner-Gedenkstätte der Stadt Bayreuth, but on condition that Otto Strobel, the Wahnfried archivist, should never have access to them. Strobel had incurred Eva's indignation in 1934 when he discovered that the correspondence between Wagner and Cosima was missing from the Wahnfried archives and reported the loss to the police. It was Eva herself who turned out to be the culprit, although she swore on oath that she had burned the letters in 1930 at her late brother's specific request. In 1939 she returned to the offensive, repeating her demand that Strobel should never be allowed near the Diaries and insisting, for good measure, that they should be immured in the vaults of a Munich bank until thirty years after her death. Eva died on 26 May 1942. The Wagner family attempted to have the embargo overturned in 1954 and again in 1959 but on both occasions the case was dismissed. The embargo expired on 26 May 1972 but a further legal delay followed, arising over the terms on which the Diaries would be handed over to the town of Bayreuth. Accordingly, it was not until March 1974 that the twenty-one volumes returned to Bayreuth, under police super-vision, for the task of transcription and publication. A somewhat unseemly scramble then ensued as the German publishers attempted to see the Diaries into print in time for the Bayreuth centenary celebrations in 1976, with the result that the German edition suffers from occasional shortcomings in terms of transcrip-tion and annotation (Gregor-Dellin/Mack, 1976–7). From this point of view, Geoffrey Skelton's admirable English translation (1978–80) represents an advance on the German original, although, as he modestly points out in his introduction, only Cosima's stilted German can really lay claim to being regarded as a 'fully authentic document'.

Cosima's Diaries are undeniably valuable from both a biogra-phical and socio-historical point of view. With the possible exception of Goethe, we know more about Wagner's daily activities, at least during the final fourteen years of his life, than about any other major artist. At the same time, the Diaries provide a riveting portrait of the social mores of the late 19th-century German bourgeoisie. Yet the insights which they have to offer are incidental rather than revelatory, a state of affairs for which Cosima herself is largely to blame. Her self-mortifying attitude acts as a distorting mirror: she suffered untold agonies of conscience over her treatment of Hans von Bülow and used the Diaries as a form of exquisite penitence, pouring out her feelings of guilt and attempting to justify her behaviour in the eyes of her various children. Moreover, her blind infatuation with Wagner – taken to the point of hagiographical relic-worship when she preserves single hairs from his eyebrows and dotes on them daily – is scarcely calculated to provide an objective picture of Wagner, while the ageing voluptuary himself appears to have conducted affairs on the side – notably with Judith Gautier and perhaps also with Carrie Pringle – for which the Diaries inevitably provide less than detailed documentation.

None the less – and allowing for Cosima's refracting lens – the Diaries are not wholly unrewarding. It is interesting, and occasionally alarming, for example, to discover the extent to which

Wagner resented his dependence on King Ludwig and how the racist views which he had held since the late 1840s began to assume ever more irrational dimensions as he sank into crabbed old age: rumours of an armistice in the Franco-Prussian War of 1870 'bring us no joy; R. favours the bombardment [of Paris]' (CT, 4 Nov 1870); 'He makes a drastic joke to the effect that all Jews should be burned at a performance of *Nathan*' (CT, 18 Dec 1881); 'We come back to the subject of race, wondering which theory is right, Schop[enhauer]'s or Gobineau's. R. feels they can be reconciled: a human being who is born black, urged toward the heights, becomes white and at the same time a different creature.' (CT, 16 Oct 1882) Equally, and perhaps not unrelatedly, the Diaries afford evidence of Wagner's pathological fear and insecurity, an insecurity expressed in many of his dreams. In his professional life, too, he was plagued by self-doubts: 'I am no poet,' he told Cosima on 22 January 1871 and, five years later, 'R. persists in saying he himself is no musician!' (CT, 17 Feb 1876) On 22 July 1880 he added (less surprisingly), 'I am not a writer.' And yet, as Dieter Borchmeyer has pointed out in his detailed assessment of Cosima's Diaries (Borchmeyer, 1982), Wagner was all these things and more: only in their synthesis would the musician find his justification; only then would music become part of an integral process of education. While it is often difficult to distil this idealistic content from the trivial details that litter the pages of Cosima's Diaries – R.'s insomnia and illnesses, the minutiae of life at Tribschen and Wahnfried and the conversational banalities which turn the 20th-century reader into an involuntary voyeur – it is an effort which needs to be made by every reader who is more interested in the ideology that underlies the Bayreuth Festival than in the colour of Wagner's satin dressing-gowns.

STEWART SPENCER

WAGNER WAS AN INDEFATIGABLE correspondent. His need to *Letters* communicate with others, particularly during his years of exile, coupled with the organizational demands of performances of his works, obliged him to set aside long periods to keep his correspondence up to date. It is impossible to calculate how many letters he may have written in the course of his life, but the surviving corpus is reckoned to run to between ten and twelve thousand.

At what point Wagner started to write with an eye to posterity is difficult to say, although a reference in his letter to Minna Wagner of 21 May 1862 ('Anyone who finds letters from *you* in my possession will read there that my wife calls me and my behaviour towards her "heartless", "brutal" & "vulgar". So this will no doubt also find its way into my biography') suggests at least the possibility that future biographers might use his correspondence as a source of (dis)information. Confirmation that this was so came spectacularly in 1877, when Daniel Spitzer published sixteen letters from

Wagner to the Viennese seamstress, Bertha Goldwag, placing orders for prodigious quantities of silks and satins. Spitzer maliciously prefaced the collection with a line from *Die Walküre*: 'Wie gleicht er dem Weibe!' ('How like the woman he looks!') Wahnfried realized the damage this was likely to cause to the image of the Master which it was slowly beginning to assemble: it was clear, for example, that Wagner's incendiary correspondence with Theodor Uhlig ('I assure you that I no longer believe in any other revolution save that which begins with the burning down of Paris') was scarcely calculated to enhance that image, and so attempts were made to reclaim the originals of these and other letters. It was a process which, continued by Cosima after Wagner's death, involved a mixture of cajolery and threats of legal proceedings, but the stratagem succeeded and Cosima was able to set to work, with her team of in-house editors, to publish a suitably censored version of Wagner's letters to his various correspondents. (Wagner himself had kept copies of many of his letters, so that these, too, could often be used as the basis of later editions.) Between 1887 and 1911 some fifteen volumes issued from Wahnfried, containing around 2450 letters to Franz Liszt* (1887), Theodor Uhlig, Wilhelm Fischer and Ferdinand Heine* (1888), August Röckel* (1894), Ferdinand Praeger (1894), Eliza Wille (1894), Otto Wesendonck* (1898), Emil Heckel* (1899), Mathilde Wesendonck* (1904), Family Letters* (1907), Bayreuth Letters* (1907), Minna Wagner* (1908), Bayreuth artists (1908), friends and contemporaries (1909), Theodor Apel (1910) and the publishing houses of Breitkopf & Härtel and B. Schott's Söhne (1911). These years also witnessed the independent publication of letters to Ernst von Weber (1883), Johann Herbeck (1885), Josef Hoffmann (1896), Wendelin Weissheimer (1898) and Angelo Neumann* (1907), together with many smaller collections in journals and periodicals. The asterisked volumes were also translated into English.

Later collections of importance to be published during the inter-war years include the correspondence with Friedrich Nietzsche* (1915), Hans von Bülow (1916), Julie Ritter (1920), Hans Richter (1924), Albert Niemann (1924), Johanna and Franziska Wagner* (1927), Mathilde Maier (1930), Anton Pusinelli (1923, available only in an execrable English translation), Judith Gautier (1936; the French originals were not published until 1964) and King Ludwig II of Bavaria (1936–9). Mention should also be made here of Julien Tiersot's edition of the *Lettres françaises* (1935). These eleven volumes contained a further 1100 letters. Important post-war editions include the Burrell Collection (Eng. 1951, Ger. 1953), the letters to Wilhelm Baumgartner (1976) and Cosima Wagner (1979), and the holdings of the Wagner Museum at Tribschen (1961) and of the British Library, London (1982–4). Individual letters and smaller collections have continued to appear in often out-of-the-way periodicals and auction-house catalogues, so that a complete bibliography of Wagner's letters would run to around one hundred separate publications.

With the exception of Otto Strobel's edition of the Ludwig–Wagner correspondence, all these editions were compromised by omissions, inadequate annotation and uncertain editorial principles. (And even in the case of Strobel, as Egon Voss has pointed out, the aim was always 'to glorify Wagner as both man and artist': Voss, 1982b.) The most conspicuous example of such censorship is perhaps Wagner's letter to Princess Carolyne Sayn-Wittgenstein of 12 April 1858, the printed edition of which runs to barely a quarter of Wagner's original. Moreover, any volume which limits itself to a single correspondent, often with only one half of the correspondence, necessarily precludes an overview of Wagner's multifaceted personality.

Apart from catalogues by Kastner (1897) and Altmann (1905, R1971), the first attempt to collect and publish Wagner's letters was the one undertaken by Julius Kapp and Emerich Kastner in 1913; unfortunately, the First World War brought a premature end to the undertaking after only two volumes. A second attempt was made in the early 1960s, when the then Richard-Wagner-Familienarchiv in Bayreuth signed an agreement with the VEB Deutscher Verlag für Musik in Leipzig for an edition of all of Wagner's available letters in chronological order. The Leipzig firm was chosen *faute de mieux*, since no West German publisher had been willing to take on the project. The edition was originally planned to run to fifteen volumes and contain some 5000 letters. If this had been the only miscalculation, the undertaking might still have merited scholarly respect. But the harnessing together of two completely incompatible part-time editors (the excellent Marxist musicologist, Werner Wolf, and the right-wing Bayreuth archivist, Gertrud Strobel) and the state- or self-imposed censorship of the one as of the other (Wolf had only limited access to documents in the West, while Strobel seems to have been blind to the existence of any documents outside the family archives in Bayreuth) led to an edition notable only for its incompleteness and unreliability. As Egon Voss pointed out in a damning review of the edition (Voss, 1978), no fewer than one hundred letters were missing from the first three volumes alone, to say nothing of omissions from countless others. The first four volumes, covering the period up to September 1852, appeared between 1967 and 1979. Following the death of Gertrud Strobel in 1979 and the superannuation of Werner Wolf shortly afterwards, a new team of editors was pressed into service in the persons of Hans-Joachim Bauer and Johannes Forner. Volumes 6 and 7 appeared in 1986 and 1988, taking the reader through to March 1856. (Volume 5 has yet to appear at the time of writing.) Apart from adopting a confusingly different editorial style, the latest volumes are characterized by the same degree of carelessness and ignorance which marred the earlier ones and it is almost with relief that one hears that the whole project may have to be abandoned following the reunification of Germany and the withdrawal of state support from the original East German publisher. At least a fresh start might then be made, allowing a new scholarly edition to be taken in hand which would take account of the latest research and, ideally, include the letters *to* Wagner, since the unilateral approach adopted by the vast majority of the editions mentioned above inevitably gives, at best, a partial view of the subject. (It may be added that more and more Wagner letters keep coming to light, so that the complete edition was ultimately planned to run to forty volumes, which – at the existing rate of progress – would have taken another 150 years.)

Apart from the Burrell Collection and the individual volumes already mentioned, the major sources of Wagner's correspondence in English translation are the two volumes of *Selected Letters of Richard Wagner*, selected and edited by Wilhelm Altmann and translated by M.M. Bozman (London and Toronto, 1927), and the *Selected Letters of Richard Wagner*, translated and edited by Stewart Spencer and Barry Millington (a selection of 500 letters, including original texts of passages omitted from existing printed editions).

Wagner's letters are of value from a number of different points of view. In the first place, they provide us with a more objective picture of the composer than the idealized view which he and his followers were at pains to promulgate. (In particular, Wagner's gradual change of attitude towards Giacomo Meyerbeer, from servile gratitude to clinical paranoia, can be charted in detail in his letters of the 1830 and 1840s.) Second, they offer rare and repeated insights into Wagner's compositional procedures of a kind not found elsewhere in his voluminous oeuvre: they are especially useful, for example, in documenting progress on the early stages of the *Ring* and in disentangling reality from the myth of the so-called La Spezia vision (see 'Myths and Legends', p.135). Third, they present interpretations of his own operas and music dramas largely undistorted by the special pleading of his autobiographical writings. And, fourth, they allow us to build up a composite, demythologized image of Wagner in all his contradictions and trivial concerns, as he adopts a series of different personae depending on the recipient of the letter in question. Finally – and with the exception of the effusively overwritten letters to Ludwig II – they reveal a spontaneity of expression conspicuous by its absence from the majority of his prose writings.

STEWART SPENCER

Collected writings

ON 6 JANUARY 1865 WAGNER wrote to King Ludwig II of Bavaria: 'Many years ago I intended to collect and publish my writings in an edition which I later abandoned'. It is not clear at what date this plan was drawn up, although the latest text to be included dates from 1854, which suggests, at least, a *terminus ante quem*. Only four volumes were envisaged, comprising a series of essays on theatre reform (volume 1); *Über musikalische Kritik* (*On Music Criticism*), *Das Judentum in der Musik* (*Jewishness in Music*), *Über das Dirigieren* (*On Conducting*) ('not yet written up'), several programme notes and instructions for staging *Der fliegende Holländer* and *Tannhäuser* (volume 2); essays from Wagner's years in Paris (volume 3) and the prose drafts for *Die Sarazenin* (*The Saracen Woman*), *Jesus von Nazareth* and *Wieland der Schmied* (*Wieland the Smith*), together with the essay *Die Wibelungen* (*The Wibelungs*). Existing brochures and pamphlets, including the libretti of his operas, were not included in this edition on the grounds that they were already widely available.

By 26 April 1868 – the date of the relevant entry in the Brown Book – Wagner had expanded this scheme considerably. The planned edition now comprised ten volumes, including all the pamphlets previously omitted. The order was now chronological, beginning with the Paris essays. Only the final three volumes violated this sequence, containing, as they did, the libretti to all of Wagner's operas and music dramas starting with *Der fliegende Holländer*. The final volume was reserved for 'Reminiscences of my life. (From the biography.)'

Wagner himself superintended the subsequent publication of the first nine volumes of his *Gesammelte Schriften und Dichtungen* (*Collected Writings and Poems*), which appeared in 1871 (vols 1–2), 1872 (vols 3–6) and 1873 (vols 7–9). (Volume 10 followed, posthumously, in 1883.) The basic outline was chronological, with the various libretti now being inserted in their correct sequence. Wagner defended this approach in a foreword to volume 1: 'I avoided the temptation to assemble my scattered writings in such a way that they might have assumed the appearance of an actual scientific system, which our professional aestheticians might easily have treated as an impertinence; on the other hand, by keeping a kind of diary of my work, I was also able to include my poems in their proper biographical place, instead of putting them all together in a special volume, which would almost certainly have incurred the contemptuous anger of our professional poets' (GS I, iv). In this way, Wagner believed, the world would have a clearer idea of his intellectual development and, by being able to place his works in their biographical and historical context, be in a better position to understand them. (A chronological approach also helps us to trace the development of Wagner's prose style from the 'brilliant stylist' of the Paris period (Deathridge/Dahlhaus, 1984) to the rebarbative writings of the later years, in which content is all too often sacrificed to form.)

Unfortunately, the tendentious aim that underlies the collected writings could be sustained only by tampering with the evidence. In some cases, the dating of the individual essays is manifestly wrong: in volume 2, for example, the essay *The Wibelungs* should be dated 1849, not 1848, while the *Entwurf zur Organisation eines deutschen Nationaltheaters für das Königreich Sachsen* (*Plan for the Organization of a German National Theatre for the Kingdom of Saxony*) was completed in 1848, not 1849. In the former case Wagner seems to have been anxious to illustrate his thesis that, by the late 1840s, he had abandoned history in favour of myth; while the incorrect dating of the latter draft may be related to his wish to minimize his involvement in the revolutionary movement of the period by limiting it to a much briefer span of time. Elsewhere, Wagner certainly made changes to the texts of his earlier essays when preparing them for inclusion in his collected works, but, in the absence of an urgently needed historico-critical edition itemizing the changes, it is impossible for present-day readers to know where such alterations have been made and, by implication, to trust the text they find before them.

The first edition of 1871–83 was reset in 1887–8 and subsequently reprinted in 1897–8 and 1907. (For the sake of convenience most writers refer to the later editions, since the first edition is generally hard to come by.) The second edition of 1887–8 was reprinted in 1976. Between 1911 and 1916 Hans von Wolzogen and Richard Sternfeld added six further volumes to the ten-volume set to form the *Sämtliche Schriften und Dichtungen (Volks-Ausgabe)* (*Complete Writings and Poems – Popular Edition*), but their editorial principles reveal an almost perverse desire to be different. Not only have the editors modified Wagner's 19th-century orthography, they have partially – but inconsistently – abandoned the chronological arrangement of the earlier volumes, preferring, instead, to divide up the entries thematically. Finally, they have included a number of letters or excerpts from letters in their edition – a thoroughly arbitrary procedure which is bound to beg the question why these particular letters have been included, but not the ten or twelve thousand others that Wagner is believed to have written. (These letters continue to figure in all subsequent lists of Wagner's 'writings', although they have no valid claim to be considered as such.) Both the sixteen-volume *Complete Writings* and the 1976 reprint of the ten-volume *Collected Writings* have long been out of print, as have three other collected editions of Wagner's writings, namely, by Julius Kapp (14 vols, [1914]), Wolfgang Golther (10 vols, [1914]) and Dieter Borchmeyer (10 vols, 1983). Plans to embark on a new critical edition of Wagner's writings under the editorship of Carl Dahlhaus were abandoned on Dahlhaus's death. As Egon Voss has pointed out (Voss, 1987), the problems of establishing the scholarly basis for such an edition are formidable: in many cases no autograph survives; especially during his earlier career Wagner published many articles anonymously or pseudonymously; and the authenticity of essays which, in the past, have been attributed to Wagner has latterly been called into question – it is not at all clear, for example, that Wagner wrote *Die deutsche Oper* (*German Opera*) and *Pasticcio* (both published in 1834 in Laube's *Zeitung für die elegante Welt* and Schumann's *Neue Zeitschrift für Musik*), while there is circumstantial evidence to suggest that it was August Röckel, not Wagner, who wrote *Der Mensch und die bestehende Gesellschaft* (*Man and Existing Society*) and *Die Revolution* (published on 10 February and 8 April 1849, respectively, in Röckel's seditious *Volksblätter*).

Between 1891 and 1899 William Ashton Ellis undertook a serialized translation of Wagner's prose writings (PW) for the

London branch of the Wagner Society. (It was subsequently reissued in eight volumes between January 1893 and 1899.) Ellis adopted a largely thematic approach to the material ('In acting thus, I was governed by the desire to lose no time in bringing out the real substance of Wagner's art-theories', PW I, viii). Although he did at least have the advantage of understanding what Wagner was trying to say, he believed, unfortunately, that only by reproducing Wagner's sentence structures and word-formations could he convey the sense and tone of the original. As a result, Ellis's translations can really only be understood by readers already familiar with the German, as the following excerpt from *Das Kunstwerk der Zukunft* (*The Artwork of the Future*) may show:

> Then men shall start therefrom, forsooth upon their steamboats, to cross the open sea; the breath of all-enlivening breezes replaced by sickening fumes from the machine. Blow the winds of heaven eastward: what matters it? – the machine shall clatter westward, or wherever else men choose to go. Even as the dance-wright fetches from the continent of Poetry, across the steam-tamed ocean crests of Music, the programme for his novel ballet; while the play-concoctor imports from the far-off continent of Dance just so much leg-gymnastics as he deems expedient for filling up a halting situation. (PW I, 111–12)

Ellis's translation was reprinted in 1972 and, for all its waywardness, remains the standard English version of Wagner's writings in prose. No new translation of the complete writings is planned at the time of going to press.

STEWART SPENCER

SOME OF WAGNER's autograph manuscripts have disappeared, others were purchased by private collectors. The rest repose in libraries and archives throughout Europe and the United States. Fortunately, most of these documents are housed in the National-archiv der Richard-Wagner-Stiftung in Bayreuth, and are readily available to scholars. Of particular importance are the textual and musical manuscripts relating to the operatic compositions.

Autograph manuscripts

Sketches/drafts (text)

Wagner's usual procedure for constructing an operatic libretto involved four distinct steps: a brief prose sketch, a more elaborate prose draft, a verse draft, and a fair copy of the poem. The following discussion examines each of these stages in turn, with specific reference to the *Ring* manuscripts.

The prose sketches

The initial stage generally took the form of a succinct prose outline of the dramatic action. For example, the prose sketch to *Das Rheingold* (autumn 1851) is written on the recto (front) side of a single sheet of paper; it contains two brief paragraphs followed by a third and longer one, each prefaced by a Roman numeral. The first two paragraphs outline the events of Scenes 1 and 2 of the completed opera, while the third covers those of Scenes 3 and 4; apparently Wagner planned the work in three main divisions. The first paragraph originally read:

> I. The three Rhinedaughters. Wodan (bathing) – (Fricka is the Rhinedaughters' aunt.) Alberich from the depths. He woos all three women, one after another, and is rejected. – The gold glows. 'How to win it?' 'He who renounces love.' – Alberich steals the gold. – Night.

However, Wagner later inserted after 'Wodan (bathing)' the remark 'W. knows about the gold's properties'.

This sketch is interesting because it shows that Wagner originally planned to introduce Wotan (spelled 'Wodan' in all the *Ring* manuscripts) into the very first scene, presumably in order to witness the theft of the gold. He later decided to postpone the god's initial appearance until the opening of Scene 2, mercifully eliminating the 'bathing' episode. However, this necessitated some other mechanism by which Wotan could learn about Alberich and the ring.

In the case of *Das Rheingold* and *Die Walküre*, Wagner made supplementary prose sketches in a pocket notebook (winter 1851–2). One of these begins: 'Wodan as yet knows nothing about the power of the gold', and, after referring to the giants' demand for the Rhinegold as ransom for Freia, continues: 'Wodan and Loke go first to the Rhinedaughters; here they learn what has happened, and are solicited for help and restitution.' Thus Wagner decided to make Wotan hear about the events of Scene 1 from the Rhinedaughters instead of directly witnessing them himself.

However, another supplementary prose sketch reads: 'During the dispute over Freia, Loke finally arrives: in answer to Wodan's reproaches over his absence (since he promised to get rid of the giants) he informs them about the lament of the Rhinedaughters, who have complained to him about Alberich's theft.' Here Wagner hit upon his final solution: he made Loge (originally spelled 'Loke') the agent who informs Wotan about Alberich and the gold. This ultimately blossomed into Loge's magnificent Narration, the musical highlight of Scene 2.

The prose sketch for *Die Walküre* begins on the verso (back) side of the sheet whose recto contains the *Rheingold* sketch; it continues onto the recto side of another sheet, upon whose verso has been jotted the sentence which opens the final paragraph of *Oper und Drama* (*Opera and Drama*). This tells us that Wagner probably wrote out the *Rheingold* sketch first; if the latter had not already existed, he would doubtless have continued the *Walküre* sketch onto the reverse side of the same sheet, not a different one. Thus the physical layout of the manuscripts can sometimes help us decide matters of chronology even when, as here, the documents themselves are undated; in this case, we learn that the time-honoured notion of

Wagner writing the text of the *Ring* 'backwards' is not entirely true. The prose sketch for *Die Walküre* outlines only the events of the first two acts. No prose sketch for Act III is extant, although it may have been written upon a third sheet which has disappeared; perhaps the *Opera and Drama* sentence dissuaded Wagner from using the verso of the second sheet for this purpose. As with *Das Rheingold*, the pocket notebook contains supplementary prose sketches, although again these pertain only to Acts I and II.

Among other interesting points, the *Walküre* sketches reveal that once again Wagner intended to introduce Wotan into the action immediately – as a visitor to Hunding's hut in Act I. In fact, the god was to enter and thrust a sword into the ash tree, whereupon Siegmund would promptly withdraw the weapon; the act was to continue from there! One of the supplementary sketches informs us that Wotan is to spend the night in the hut, his bed placed so as to command a good view of the final scene between Siegmund and Sieglinde! Although we can only be eternally grateful to Wagner for once again removing Wotan from the early stages of the drama, it is interesting to note that at least one modern production (Seattle 1986) restored Wotan to his original place, making him a silent observer of the events of Act I.

Despite their brevity, the prose sketches sometimes anticipate dialogue, although this is usually cast in prose rather than verse. We have already seen one example from the *Rheingold* sketch: 'The gold glows. "How to win it?" "He who renounces love."' A somewhat more significant example occurs in the *Walküre* sketch. Towards the end of the single paragraph outlining Act I comes the line: 'Siegmund: "Weib und schwester, so glühe denn Welsungenblut!"' ('Siegmund: "Wife and sister, so may the blood of the Volsungs glow!"'). This was ultimately versified as: 'Braut und Schwester / bist du dem Bruder – / so blühe denn Wälsungen-Blut!' ('Bride and sister are you to the brother – so may the blood of the Volsungs bloom!') It is rather remarkable that Wagner hit upon his 'curtain line' so early in the game.

The prose sketches for *Das Rheingold* and *Die Walküre* demonstrate that Wagner sometimes changed and/or added to these terse outlines before proceeding to the next stage (the prose draft). This is also true of the brief, rather fragmentary prose sketches for *Der junge Siegfried* (the original version of *Siegfried*). That these sketches (spring 1851) have survived at all is a stroke of fate: Wagner used the large sheet of paper on which they were written as the wrapper for the verse draft! In the middle of this sheet are three brief entries, one for each act, as well as a note pertaining to the entry for Act II. At the top of the sheet are two further expansions of the Act II events; these were made at the time of the initial entries. At the bottom of the sheet are three more entries, the first relating to the game of riddles between Wotan and Mime, the second and third to Wotan's confrontations with Erda and Siegfried; these entries were made later than the others. The entries for Act II show that Wagner originally planned to introduce the Nibelungs *en masse*, not just Alberich and Mime. Those for Act III show the gradual emergence of the notion of the gods' self-destruction: the earlier entry reads 'Wodan and the Wala: end of the gods', while a later one runs: 'Wodan and the Wala. – Guilt of the gods, and their necessary downfall: Siegfried's destiny. – Self-destruction of the gods.'

Of the four *Ring* dramas, only *Siegfrieds Tod* (the original version of *Götterdämmerung*) did not require a prose sketch. This is because Wagner began the project by drawing up a lengthy prose 'scenario' (October 1848), in which he outlined his entire reconstruction of the Nibelung myth, beginning with Alberich's theft of the gold and concluding with Brünnhilde's self-immolation. Much of this scenario – originally entitled *Die Nibelungensage (Mythus)* (*The Nibelung Legend (Myth)*) – is devoted to the story of Siegfried's downfall, the only part of the story intended for operatic treatment; it therefore substituted for the usual prose sketch. The scenario also includes background information which was ultimately expanded into the first three dramas of the tetralogy; however, this material was so sketchy, and needed such elaborate reworking, that it necessitated the prose sketches described above.

The prose drafts

The second stage of textual composition fleshed out the succinct outline of the first. Here Wagner would elaborate his story down to the smallest detail, including much dialogue (still cast in prose). However, changes and additions – sometimes significant ones – often occurred during versification, so that the prose draft, despite its length and density, does not necessarily represent the final form of the story.

As an example, consider the ten-page prose draft for *Das Rheingold* (23–31 March 1852). Its title was originally simply *Der Raub: Vorspiel* (*The Rape: Prologue*), but this was later changed to *Der Raub des Rheingoldes: Vorspiel* (*The Rape of the Rhinegold: Prologue*), to which was appended still later the remark 'oder: *Das Rheingold?*' ('or: *The Rhinegold?*'). Throughout this draft, the Rhinedaughters are nameless, differentiated only as 'the first', 'the second', and 'the third'. However, the left margin of page 1 contains two groups of names: first Bronnlinde, Flosshilde, and Wellgunde, then Woghilde, Wellgunde, and Flosslinde. The second group of names was carried over into the verse draft, but altered in that manuscript to the familiar Woglinde, Wellgunde, and Flosshilde. The prose draft thus reveals Wagner wrestling with both the title of the opera itself and the names of three of its characters.

Far more remarkable than this, however, is what the manuscript does *not* contain. There is, amazingly, no mention of Wotan's spear! In the completed opera, Wotan uses this weapon to prevent Donner from braining the giants with his hammer, thus interposing the force of law. However, when Donner first threatens the giants

(Scene 2), the prose draft reads simply 'Wodan steps between them: nothing through force: he must protect the treaty.' Considering the symbolic and musical ramifications of the spear, its complete absence in the prose draft is truly astonishing.

Another thing which the prose draft lacks is any mention of Loge (Loke) as the god of fire. Wagner originally conceived of this character merely as a trickster and a teller of unwelcome truths, not as a fire god. This strongly suggests that when Wagner wrote out the prose draft of *Das Rheingold*, he had not yet decided to end the tetralogy by destroying the gods and the world by fire.

The prose draft for *Siegfrieds Tod* (October 1848) begins not with the Norns' Scene but with Act I proper – that is, with the scene for Gunther, Gutrune and Hagen. Only after completing this draft did Wagner decide to add a two-part Prologue, in order to fill the audience in on the drama's prehistory and introduce them to Siegfried and Brünnhilde. The Prologue required its own prose draft; however, this draft is almost entirely cast in dialogue, much of it coming very close to its ultimate versification. Again, the manuscripts tell us much about the genesis of the text. In this case, they explain why Wagner did not label the Norns' Scene plus the following duet as 'Act I scene 1': in his original conception, Act I opened upon Gibichung Hall, and because he drafted the Prologue later, he thought of it as 'preliminary' in nature.

The verse drafts

During the third stage of textual composition, Wagner turned his prose draft into poetic dialogue. As we have seen, the prose drafts already contain frequent passages of dialogue; although most of this is cast in prose, some lines do anticipate their final poetic form. However, the task of versification now began in earnest, whether it was the *Strabreim* (alliterative verse) of the *Ring*, the *Endreim* (end-rhyme) of the earlier operas, or the combination of these two techniques in the later works. Sometimes Wagner (whose skill as a poet is widely underrated and even, in some quarters, actively disparaged) would hit upon his definitive wording immediately; not infrequently, however, a verse required extensive revision before it satisfied him.

As an example of the latter process, let us consider a brief passage from *Siegfrieds Tod*. In Act III scene 1, the Rhinedaughters warn Siegfried of the curse. In the verse draft, their warning ultimately takes the following form:

Siegfried! Siegfried!	Siegfried! Siegfried!
Wir weisen dich wahr!	We tell thee true!
Weich' aus! Weich' aus dem Fluche!	Shun it! Shun the curse!
Ihn flochten webende Nornen	Weaving Norns braided it
In des Urgesetzes Seil!	into the rope of primal law.

But Siegfried replies:

| Eurem Fluche fliehe ich nicht! | I do not flee your curse! |
| noch weich' ich der Nornen Gewebe! | Nor do I yield to the Norns' weaving! |

Wagner began the sisters' warning by writing 'Siegfried! Siegfried! / wir reden wahr'; he then crossed out 'reden' and wrote 'weisen dich' in the left margin, indicating that it was to replace 'reden'. He next incorporated this substitute phrase ('weisen dich') into the main text by crossing out 'wahr' and continuing with 'weisen dich wahr!'; then he crossed out the marginal notation. The mermaids' last two lines originally ran: 'In des Urgesetzes Seil / Flochten Nornen die ein!'; Wagner wrote the final version in the left margin, but this time did *not* cross out the originals. He drafted Siegfried's response as: 'Eurem Fluch weiche ich nicht! / Noch flieh' – but then stopped, crossed out 'flieh' and continued with 'weich' ich der Nornen Gewebe!' He then returned to the preceding line and wrote 'fliehe' *over* 'weiche', eliminating a verbal repetition. The patterns of cross-outs, overwritings and marginal notes in Wagner's textual manuscripts allow us to reconstruct his revisions with reasonable accuracy; however, an uninterpreted reproduction of these patterns would serve little purpose. It should be noted that Otto Strobel's transcriptions of some of the textual manuscripts for the *Ring* (1930) eliminate all variants and provide only the final versions of revised passages.

In addition to versifying the dialogue, Wagner also expanded (and sometimes altered) the scenic instructions, which, of course, he still wrote in prose. Sometimes, after finishing a verse draft, he would go back and amplify these directions even further. These later additions can be very important. For instance, we have noted that the prose draft of *Das Rheingold* contains nothing about Loge's magic fire. Similarly, there was at first precious little in the verse draft to connect this character with fire either. However, after completing the versification, Wagner entered as a marginal addition Loge's last speech, wherein the trickster contemplates turning back into flame and consuming the gods. The passage towards the close of *Die Walküre* wherein Wotan commands Loge to blaze up around Brünnhilde's rock was also an afterthought, as the final page of the verse draft reveals, and was perhaps added at the same time as the *Rheingold* insert. We can thus pinpoint fairly precisely the moment when Wagner decided to destroy the gods by fire – after he had completed the verse draft of *Die Walküre* (1 July 1852) but before he revised the Norns' Scene of *Siegfrieds Tod* (November or December 1852). In order to prepare for this conflagration, he expanded Loge's attributes by making him a god of fire; he changed 'Loke' to 'Loge' while writing the verse draft of the revised Norns' Scene.

The fair copies

After completing the verse draft, Wagner would prepare a fair copy of his poem. Wagner's fair copies are beautifully written, and usually free of corrections or alterations (except in those cases where a particular copy was used as the basis of a later revision). Where a verse draft contains two or more versions of the same passage, the fair copy generally incorporates the final version. Occasionally, however, the fair copy differs in places from the verse draft. This is the case with the first fair copy of *Siegfrieds Tod* (presumably December 1848), which alters some of the scenic directions; inasmuch as the *Gesammelte Schriften* version of this text (GS II) is based upon the original wording of the first fair copy, it too differs slightly from the verse draft. Because the first fair copy of *Der junge Siegfried* (summer 1851) differed in places from the original, the latter was corrected by Theodor Uhlig to make the two manuscripts agree.

Sometimes, for one reason or another, Wagner would make more than one fair copy of a poem. For example, he made a second fair copy of *Der junge Siegfried* for Franz Liszt (August 1851). On the other hand, sometimes the later revision of a poem might necessitate another fair copy; this was the case with *Siegfrieds Tod*. Almost immediately after completing the fair copy of this drama, Wagner extensively revised it, entering revisions in both the verse draft and the fair copy. He then made a second fair copy of the poem, reflecting the changes of the first revision (one of which was the addition of the Hagen's Watch episode to Act I). In May 1850, the hope of publication prompted Wagner to make yet a third fair copy of the poem; this manuscript thus represents the second copy of the first revision. As we know, Wagner extensively revised *Siegfrieds Tod* a second time (November/December 1852) after he had versified *Die Walküre* and *Das Rheingold*. He entered these new revisions into the third fair copy, replacing some of its pages with new ones and discarding the old. Wagner then made new fair copies of *Das Rheingold*, *Die Walküre*, and *Siegfrieds Tod*; for some reason, he never made another fair copy of *Der junge Siegfried*, which had undergone an equally far-reaching revision. There thus exist three versions and no fewer than four fair copies of *Siegfrieds Tod*; of these copies, the first is in the Stadtbibliothek Winterthur, Switzerland, the second (like the verse draft) reposes in an inaccessible private collection, and the last two are in Bayreuth.

Wagner's fair copies sometimes served as the basis of the first printed editions of his libretti. For instance, in 1853 Wagner had fifty copies of the *Ring* poem printed at his own expense; these were based upon his fair copies, which contain instructions for the printer. However, this 1853 imprint does not represent the final version of the text. Wagner often altered his texts while setting them to music, and he entered the changes to the *Ring* poem into his personal copy of the 1853 printing. Some but *not all* of these alterations were incorporated into the 1863 public printing and the 1872 *Gesammelte Schriften* version (GS V–VI). The latter therefore inhabits a rather nebulous 'no man's land' somewhere between the 1853 printing and the version found in the musical score. It is unclear why Wagner did not take more pains to make the GS imprint conform more closely to the version of the text found in the score, but his carelessness in this regard has proven disastrous for translators, critics and stage directors alike. In any case, scholars who attempt to trace the genesis of the *Ring*, and who are interested in how word might have inspired tone, cannot work from the *Gesammelte Schriften* text; they must consult the 1853 imprint, of which a small number of copies survive, and of which a facsimile edition was published (? Berlin, 1920).

In addition to their value in helping us trace the genesis of Wagner's libretti, the textual manuscripts also contain some musical sketches. These are discussed in the next section.

Sketches/drafts (music)

Because Wagner changed his method of composition several times, his musical sketches and drafts tend to vary in format and degree of complexity from one work to another. This has led to terminological difficulties, for while it is misleading to apply a single method of nomenclature to the musical manuscripts as a whole, it would be terribly confusing to change this nomenclature for every work. Various terminological systems have been proposed by Otto Strobel, John Deathridge and Robert Bailey; the terms used here are English equivalents of those adopted by the editors of the *Wagner Werk-Verzeichnis* (WWV).

In general, the term 'sketch' (*Skizze*) refers to an isolated fragment, while 'draft' (*Entwurf*) refers to a more or less continuous manuscript. More specifically, 'individual sketches' (*Einzelskizzen*) are pencil or ink jottings of vocal lines, instrumental motifs, abstract harmonic progressions, or contrapuntal studies; they vary greatly in length and complexity. A 'complete draft' (*Gesamtentwurf*) is a continuous musical realization of an entire act or, in the case of *Das Rheingold*, a complete opera. Detailed information about these various sketches and drafts follows.

The individual sketches

Before beginning the first complete draft of an opera, Wagner customarily made some preliminary musical sketches. While working on the complete draft, he often made supplementary sketches. He also jotted down musical ideas as they occurred to him, regardless of whether they pertained to an opera currently in progress.

In theory, therefore, there are at least three kinds of individual musical sketches: those made before sustained work on an opera began, those made while composition was in progress, and those made at random intervals. In actual practice, it is often difficult to decide into which category a given sketch falls, for these fragments (unlike the complete drafts) are usually undated.

The single sketches turn up in a variety of places: textual manuscripts (and, in the case of the *Ring*, Wagner's copy of the printed libretto), scraps of letter paper, pocket notebooks, and sheets of music paper. Some are in pencil, others in ink, depending upon what Wagner had to hand at the time. Some can be dated with reasonable accuracy and assigned to specific works, while others are more problematic. A few are actually labelled, and bear such titles as 'Fafner' and 'Waldvogel' – the sort of motif-naming Wagner supposedly did not do.

The fact that some sketches appear in the textual manuscripts has often been advanced as evidence of the 'simultaneity' of Wagner's dramatic/musical conceptions. In other words, Wagner supposedly conceived text and music simultaneously, but obviously could not write out both at the same time; he therefore worked on the text first, entering some musical ideas as they occurred to him. The implication, of course, is that many more musical ideas – perhaps even extended sections – were seething in his brain as well, but that these inspirations had to wait until Wagner the textual scribe handed over the pen to Wagner the musical scribe. As we shall see, this view of Wagner is simply not supported by his sketches and drafts. In any case, the fact that a musical idea appears in a given textual manuscript does not necessarily imply that it occurred to Wagner while he was working on that document; it *could have*, of course, but that particular manuscript might simply have been close to hand when inspiration struck. Wagner might even have intended the musical idea for a completely different work, possibly a non-dramatic one.

As an example, the verse draft of *Siegfrieds Tod* contains (p. 35) a musical sketch which runs from top to bottom in the left margin. This sketch, whose purpose has not yet been ascertained, is a four-part harmonization in F major written in tenor and bass clefs. The style, range and format suggest that it was intended for trombone choir, and might have been made while orchestrating an existing but unidentified work. On the other hand, it could have occurred to Wagner as a musical idea in its own right, in connection with *Siegfrieds Tod* or some other composition. Wagner could have made it while drafting the poem, or at any time thereafter.

On the other hand, sometimes a musical sketch can be related with some confidence to the textual manuscript in which it appears. For example, in the third fair copy of *Siegfrieds Tod* (the one made in 1850; see 'Sketches/drafts (text)', p.202), Wagner has inked in a treble staff and a one-bar melody in B minor. This appears on page 5 opposite Brünnhilde's lines 'Ging sein Lauf mit mir / einst kühn durch die Lüfte' and, because its rhythm exactly matches that of the words, is probably a sketch of the vocal part for these lines. But when did Wagner make this sketch? Presumably in the summer of 1850, during which he began but abandoned musical work on the Prologue to *Siegfrieds Tod* (the extant drafts do not continue as far as the lines in question). Wagner could have sketched this vocal line either before beginning his first draft of the Prologue, or while working on it; in other words, the item could constitute either a preliminary or a supplementary sketch.

In general, Wagner's individual sketches are either vocal or instrumental in conception. Vocal sketches may be texted or, as is far more frequently the case, untexted. In the former case, however, the underlaid text may not be the one ultimately associated with the melody; it may not even belong to the same opera! Some vocal sketches consist only of a single melodic line; others are more elaborate harmonic/contrapuntal settings. Similarly, a sketch for an orchestral motif may represent an incipient form of this theme, or it may contain a more or less extended development of one or more motifs. It is tempting to use some terminology such as 'simple'/'complex', or perhaps 'incipient'/ 'developmental', to differentiate between the two types of vocal and instrumental sketches, but this classification is not yet in common use. The 'complex' or 'developmental' type of sketch reaches its most extreme form in some of the sketch sheets for *Götterdämmerung*, which contain quite lengthy contrapuntal studies.

The second *Siegfrieds Tod* sketch mentioned above is an example of an untexted 'simple' vocal sketch, albeit one which was not ultimately used. As an example of an untexted 'complex' vocal sketch which *was* used, consider the one for Wotan's opening lines in *Siegfried* Act III (his awakening of Erda). This four-part setting, notated on two staves in a pocket notebook, probably dates from the end of September 1864, around the time Wagner was making his fair copy of Acts I and II, but almost five years before he began the complete draft of Act III. The sketch is headed: 'Wotan. Siegfr. III', and contains an initial version of Wotan's first antecedent phrase ('Wache, Wala! / Wala, erwach'![. . .]') Although terminated by a perfect rather than an imperfect cadence, it contains all the harmonic essentials of the final version, including the early appearance of the Neapolitan sixth chord (bar 2), and the enharmonically reinterpreted German augmented sixth chord (chromatically expanded during bars 3–6) which influences so markedly the act's background tonal structure. However, the top line of this sketch displays only the general outline of the final vocal melody and does not match its textual prosody; unfamiliarity with its ultimate context would make it difficult to determine whether this was a 'vocal' or an 'instrumental' sketch.

As examples of the 'simple' or 'incipient' type of *instrumental* sketch, let us consider a group of notations which Wagner entered into his copy of the 1853 *Ring* imprint – into a portion of that document which is now in the possession of Schott's publishing company in Mainz. These four pencil sketches all pertain to *Das Rheingold* Scene 2; they have faded terribly, and are extremely difficult to decipher. Each was obviously notated after February 1853 (when the printed copies were available for distribution), and at the latest by the time Wagner reached the corresponding part of the complete draft; however, they could all have been written before the complete draft was begun (1 November 1853). Each represents an early version of a different motif.

Page 5 contains a sketch for the all-important Valhalla motif;

this runs from top to bottom in the lower left margin, then from left to right in the bottom left margin. Written in the tenor clef, it seems intended for trombones, the instruments specified in the complete draft (later changed to Wagner tubas); the D♭ key signature is given, and the unspecified metre is clearly 3/4. This is a good example of how motifs often occurred to Wagner at their 'definitive' pitch levels.

Page 9 contains a sketch of the Freia motif, running from bottom to top in the right margin. The first portion is indecipherable, but the second part begins with a treble clef and presents the Freia motif in its lyrical D major form, that in which it appears later in Scene 2 when love-struck Fasolt sings about the goddess. Wagner may have conceived this lyrical D major form before the agitated E minor version to which Freia enters; or he could have written it as a variant on the E minor version, after he had entered the latter into the complete draft.

Page 10 contains a sketch of the Giants motif, running from top to bottom in the left margin; it comprises two bars, with the first barline misplaced. Tempo indications suggest that Wagner sketched this motif when he reached the entrance of the giants in the complete draft.

Page 11 contains a sketch for the triplet bass figure which precedes Donner's 'Fasolt und Fafner, / fühltet ihr schon [. . .]', running from bottom to top in the right margin. This sketch is so light that it could easily be overlooked.

Let us now consider a 'complex' instrumental sketch, again one which appears in Wagner's copy of the 1853 *Ring* imprint (p. 116). This untexted passage, harmonized in up to five parts, clearly relates to the passage in *Siegfried* Act III scene 3 where Brünnhilde first notices Grane grazing ('Dort seh' ich Grane, / mein selig Ross'); its main motivic idea is treated in sequence form in rising minor thirds. Wagner elaborated this motivic idea in another sketch on a separate sheet, but now treated the motif as a sequence a whole tone higher, as in the final score. However, this second sketch is headed: 'III^r Act oder Tristan'; apparently Wagner was uncertain whether the material belonged to *Siegfried* or *Tristan und Isolde*! Opting for the former, he elaborated its first phrase yet again, terminating it with the Love motif from *Die Walküre*. These three sketches thus represent the genesis of an instrumental passage (which in the completed opera precedes Brünnhilde's words), but one whose ultimate destination was at first undecided; they probably date from 1856/7, around the time Wagner broke off work on the *Ring*, and twelve or thirteen years before he began composing the act in which this passage was eventually to appear.

Sometimes a texted vocal sketch displays a melody familiar to us from one opera, coupled with the text from a different one! For example, on a sheet of paper interleaved into Wagner's copy of the *Ring* poem (after p. 114) there appears a texted vocal sketch of the 'simple' variety: melody plus harmonic background on one staff.

Plates 21–30

WAGNER'S HAND

WAGNER'S YOUTHFUL ENTHUSIASM for Beethoven resulted in a conscientious transcription for piano of the Ninth Symphony (the *Choral*); plate 21 shows the entry of the bass soloist in the last movement. The neatness of Wagner's hand is already in evidence here in the seventeen-year-old's manuscript; later it was to become less studied, more characterful. The alterations, made in red ink, to the autograph score of the *Faust* Overture (plate 22), date from some time between the completion of the work in its first version (January 1840) and the first performance of it in Dresden in July 1844. The original French instrumental designations are replaced by Italian and the note values of the first four bars halved. Most interesting is the new title (again in red ink) 'Overture', with the words 'to Goethe's *Faust*, Part 1' added in black: the piece had originally been conceived as the first movement of a *Faust* Symphony, but Wagner doubtless hoped to improve the chances of performance by making it a self-contained work.

The opening of the autograph score of the *Trauermusik* on motifs from Weber's *Euryanthe* (plate 23) shows the large body of wind instruments required for this outdoor piece (it was first played in a Dresden cemetery, on the occasion of the reinterment of Weber's remains): 5 flutes, 7 oboes, 20 clarinets, 10 bassoons, 14 horns, 6 trumpets, 9 trombones, 4 bass tubas and 6 muffled drums.

The juxtaposition of the opening of Act I of *Lohengrin* from two different stages of composition graphically illustrates Wagner's process of composition. The first complete draft (plate 24) has only a vocal part and a bass line, though the entire text was set to music at this stage. In the second complete draft (plate 25), harmonies, dynamics and instrumentation begin to be sketched in. The orchestration proper was reserved for the full score.

Plate 26, a characteristic example of Wagner's script, is the opening page of the poem for *Siegfrieds Tod* (*Siegfried's Death*), the work which eventually became *Götterdämmerung*, the final opera of the *Ring* cycle. Under the double-underlined title in this first fair copy of the autograph is the heading 'Eine grosse Heldenoper in drei Akten' ('A grand heroic opera in three acts'), followed by the dramatis personae.

Plate 27 is a sketch for Walther's Prize Song in *Die Meistersinger von Nürnberg* dating from 1866. The essential features of the song are present in the sketch, at the bottom of which appears the note '28 Sept. afternoon while waiting for C[osima] (R.)'.

The jingoistic spirit of the *Kaisermarsch* (*Imperial March*) of 1871 (see p.312) is evident from its ample scoring and martial rhythms, both clear on the first page of the autograph score (plate 28). The march was written originally for miltary band; the example shows the version made subsequently by Wagner for full orchestra. In a sketch dated 9 February 1876 for the Flowermaidens' music in Act II of *Parsifal* (plate 29), the words 'Amerikanisch sein wollend!' ('Wanting to be American!'), on the right-hand side of the sheet, are a reminder that the composition of the *Centennial March* to celebrate the hundredth anniversary of the American Declaration of Independence (see p.313) was also in hand at this time.

The handwritten notice (plate 30) posted by Wagner at the Bayreuth Festspielhaus on the first day of the first festival (13 August 1876) offers his last advice to the performers before their undertaking of one of the most ambitious ventures in the history of art. 'Clarity' is the watchword, and the composer urges his singers to give special attention to the text and the small notes: the large ones, he says, will look after themselves.

BARRY MILLINGTON

21 Wagner's piano transcription of Beethoven's Ninth Symphony,
beginning of last movement, 1830–31

22 *Faust* Overture, first page of autograph score, 1839–40

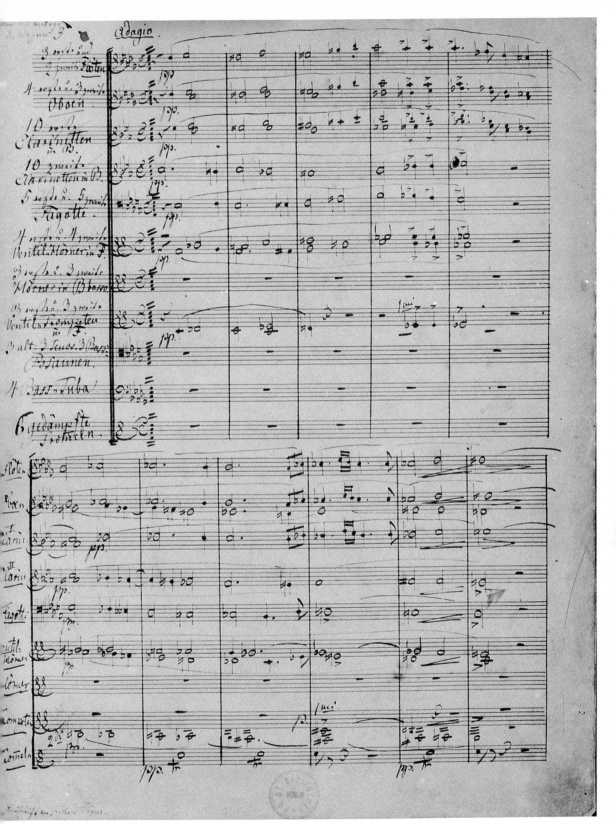

23 *Trauermusik*, on motifs from Weber's *Euryanthe*,
first page of autograph score, 1844

24 *Lohengrin*, opening of Act I, first complete draft, 1846

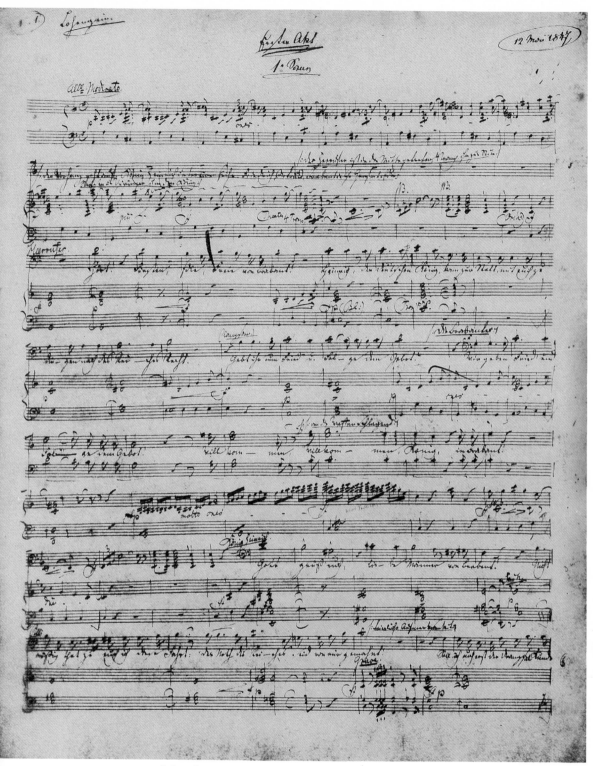

25 *Lohengrin*, opening of Act I, second complete draft, 1847

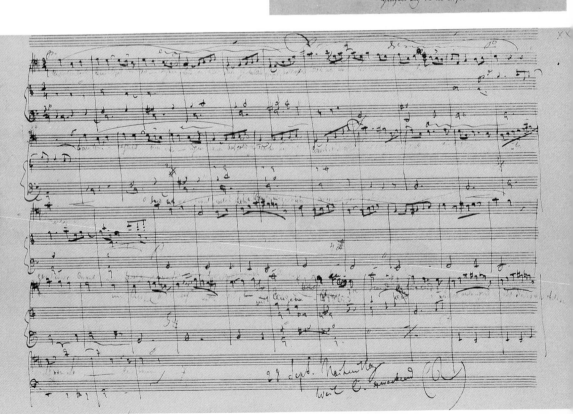

26 *Siegfrieds Tod*, first page of autograph of the poem, 1848

27 *Die Meistersinger von Nürnberg*, sketch for the Prize Song, 1866

28 *Kaisermarsch*, first page of autograph score, 1871

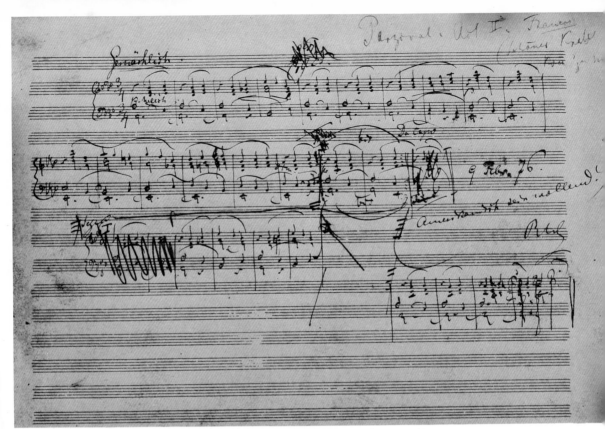

29 *Parsifal*, sketch for the Flowermaidens' music, Act II, 1876

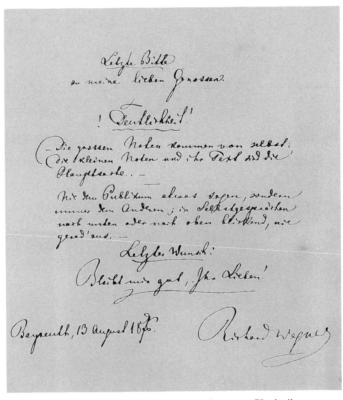

30 'Last request to my dear colleagues: Clarity!'
Wagner's handwritten notice posted at the Bayreuth Festspielhaus
on 13 August 1876, the first day of the first festival

The words come from *Siegfried* Act III scene 3 ('Süss erbebt mir / ihr blühender Mund') but the melody contains two motifs prominent in *Tristan und Isolde*: the rising chromatic line which dominates the Prelude and the encircling figure associated with King Mark. On the other hand, another sketch of the 'complex' variety is headed 'Im Asyl / erstes Motiv / 16 Mai'; untexted, it is worked out in several parts on two staves. On 21 May 1857, Wagner wrote to Mathilde Wesendonck that 'I found a melody which I didn't at all know what to do with, till of a sudden the words from the last scene of Siegfried came into my head.' Accordingly, on an interleaved page in his copy of the *Ring* poem (following p. 116), Wagner wrote out the 'Asyl' melody in tenor clef (transposed from B♭ to F), and underlaid it with Siegfried's words 'Sang'st du mir nicht, / dein Wissen sei / das Leuchten der Liebe zu mir?' from *Siegfried* Act III scene 3 (the sketch is dated '16 Mai (im Asyl)'). The problem here is that the melody in these sketches is the one that ultimately dominates Brangäne's Consolation in the first act of *Tristan*! The words from *Siegfried* were eventually set to the so-called 'World Inheritance' theme. This latter idea began life as a 'simple' *instrumental* sketch which probably dates from late 1864 or early 1865, while Wagner was working on *Die Meistersinger*; in fact, he entered a modified form of it into his second complete draft for that opera (bottom of page 82). He finally introduced the idea into his complete draft for *Siegfried* Act III scene 1 as part of the orchestral accompaniment to Wotan's words 'froh und freudig: / führe ich frei es nun aus.' Thus, although Siegfried does ultimately sing the melody, it was originally conceived as an orchestral theme.

The above examples certainly cast doubt upon the notion that Wagner simultaneously conceived both text and music. However, one must tread very cautiously in using these mostly undated sketches to reconstruct Wagner's compositional process. As a final example, consider the undated sketch sheet for *Das Rheingold*, which contains the Rhinedaughters' 'Weia-waga' melody (texted), an arpeggio sketch, and a threefold statement of the Nature horn theme. Much ink has been spilled over these jottings, especially by Curt von Westernhagen (1973) and John Deathridge (1977b), on the assumption that they are either preliminary sketches which preceded the complete draft or supplementary sketches made while that draft was in progress. However, it has been argued by the present author (Darcy, 1989–90) that they are neither, but were in fact made later, while Wagner was working upon the orchestration. The matter is not trivial, for upon it depends an accurate reconstruction of the genesis of the Prelude, one of the most original pieces of music ever penned. If only Wagner had dated his individual sketches!

The complete drafts

As mentioned earlier, Wagner changed his method of composition several times, with the result that his complete drafts differ considerably in format and complexity. A discussion of the various types of complete drafts is really inseparable from considerations of compositional process. This section therefore describes in detail only one complete draft, that for *Das Rheingold*. Information on Wagner's other complete drafts may be found in the section 'Compositional process' (pp.244–8).

The complete draft for *Das Rheingold* is a continuous pencil sketch of the entire opera. Wagner notated this draft on oblong half-sheets of staff paper, each created by tearing or cutting a larger sheet in half. Each half-sheet contains fourteen staves; thirty-eight sheets are written on both sides, while the thirty-ninth is written on one side only, resulting in seventy-seven written sides. The recto of each sheet has been numbered in the upper left corner. In the upper right corner of fol. 1^r is written '1 Nov:53'; on fol. 29^r, before the bar containing Loge's 'bist du befriedigt?' (Scene 4), the marking '1 Jan:54' appears; and the lower right side of fol. 39^r is marked '14 Januar 1854 / RW / Und weiter nichts?? / Weiter nichts??' Wagner's original pencil notation has been inked over, presumably by Mathilde Wesendonck. The paper has somewhat yellowed with age, but is still in remarkably good condition.

As Robert Bailey (1969) pointed out in connection with the *Tristan* manuscripts, Mathilde Wesendonck's inking over is often less than accurate. In addition, certain markings were not inked over at all, and the original pencil has faded, leaving only faint impressions in the paper. Furthermore, Wagner never erased his original thoughts; he either crossed them out (in the case of an immediate alteration) or wrote over them (in the case of a later alteration). Mathilde inked over everything, earlier and later versions alike, with results that are occasionally indecipherable. Also, there is no way of telling exactly *when* the inking over occurred. Bailey (1979) suggests that it was done before Wagner began the orchestration, on the premiss that he preferred to work from an ink draft. However, it seems unlikely the Wagner would have permitted Mathilde to tinker with such a valuable manuscript before he was finished with it; besides, he made his fair copy of the full score from the pencil 'instrumentation draft' (see next section) without having the latter inked over first. Probably Mathilde inked over the complete draft in order to preserve it for posterity, but only *after* Wagner had sketched the instrumentation. The matter is further complicated by the fact that Wagner made certain entries in the complete draft while scoring, a fact that Curt von Westernhagen, among others, conveniently ignores (1973). Thus, the mere appearance of an instrumentation marking alongside a theme in the complete draft does not necessarily imply that Wagner conceived theme and timbre simultaneously; ironically, only when an instrumental indication *differs* from the final scoring can one logically assume that it was made at the same time as the draft. In any case, preliminary sketches (now lost) could have preceded any given passage in the complete draft, making statements about the 'simultaneity' of Wagner's musical conceptions tenuous at best.

Throughout the complete draft, Wagner uses systems of either two or three staves, usually one staff for the vocal line(s) and one (sometimes two) for the instrumental part. Purely instrumental passages, such as the orchestral transitions between scenes, are elaborated on two (sometimes three) staves. The sparse texture of the instrumental staves allows us to see what Wagner considered most important about a given passage; it almost constitutes a sort of *a priori* musical reduction, and can often be used as a guide to analysis or as a check upon analytical results.

Scores

Wagner generally made only one full score (*Partitur*) of an opera. The composer prided himself on his calligraphic skill, and these documents are beautiful ink manuscripts. However, for some operas Wagner first made a pencil draft of the score (*Partiturerstschrift*), from which he then prepared a fair copy (*Reinschrift der Partitur*) in ink. Sometimes someone else – perhaps a professional copyist – would make a copy (*Partitur von fremder Hand*), using Wagner's score (or second score if two existed) as a model.

Wagner made only one score (in ink) of each of his early operas, including *Der fliegende Holländer*, *Tannhäuser* and *Lohengrin*. The autograph scores of *Holländer* and *Lohengrin* are extant, but that of *Tannhäuser* was inscribed directly onto lithograph masters, which were unfortunately destroyed during the reproduction process. The rather peculiar genesis of *Das Rheingold* (discussed at greater length in 'Compositional process'; pp.245–6) led Wagner for the first time to make two scores, a pencil draft and an ink copy.

The draft of the score for *Das Rheingold* is a unique affair, and warrants detailed description. Wagner notated a full ink score of the Prelude in brown ink on large bifolios of thirty-stave manuscript paper; the portion which has survived (bars 1–118) is written on two non-nested bifolios (eight written sides). In the upper right corner is written (in ink): 'Zürich, 1 Feb. 54 / RW'. Page 1 displays the heading 'Das Rheingold. / Vorspiel / und / erste Scene. / (auf dem Grunde des Rheines)'; however, it lacks the scenic indications found in both the 1853 text and the printed score. This document, then, began life as the usual full ink score.

When Wagner reached the opening of Scene 1, however, he found that he could not automatically score his complete draft. The manuscript at this point changes from a full ink score into a pencil sketch of the instrumentation, a document called by Wagner an '*Instrumentationsskizze*' (instrumentation sketch), by Strobel and the editors of WWV a '*Partiturerstschrift*' (draft of the full score), and by Bailey an 'instrumentation draft'. A missing portion of manuscript (bars 119–51) makes it impossible to ascertain exactly where Wagner switched to this reduced pencil format, but it probably happened at the entrance of the voices. Wagner also changed to a different paper size, a smaller twenty-stave sheet. He orchestrated bars 152–358 on these sheets; the sheet containing bars 240–50 is lost. He then again changed paper, creating a new format by tearing a bifolio of the large thirty-stave paper down the crease, then cutting or tearing each resultant sheet in half. He scored bars 359–420 on these 'half-sheets'; those containing bars 368–76 and 387–94 are missing. He worked out the instrumentation for bars 421–47 (the Rhinedaughters' first concerted song) directly in the complete draft, returning to the half-sheets at bar 448; thus, although WWV lists bars 421–47 of this manuscript as 'missing', they almost certainly never existed. Most of the remainder of this draft is notated on these half-sheets, except for several passages in Scene 4 whose complex instrumental texture required more staves; these sections are written on yet another type of paper, a thirty-stave sheet manufactured by Lard Esnault, 25 rue Feydeau, Paris.

Two weeks after beginning this document, Wagner began a fair copy. This was necessitated by the fact that his pencil 'score' is not set up like a regular score at all: the vocal line occupies the top staff of each page, the bass line the bottom one, while in between instruments and groups of instruments enter and exit in no fixed order or systematic arrangement. For a while, Wagner worked back and forth between the fair copy and the 'instrumentation draft' (as we shall call it), working out a passage in the latter, then entering it into the former. As he prepared to enter a passage into the fair copy, he calculated page and system divisions by means of various markings written in the margins of the instrumentation draft. The character of these markings changes as the instrumentation draft proceeds; together with the peculiar pagination of that draft, they allow us to surmise how Wagner switched back and forth between the two manuscripts. At one point Wagner hired a copyist, apparently hoping to spare himself the labour of completing his fair copy; however, the copyist's appalling errors soon disabused him of this notion, and Wagner dismissed him after he had completed the Prelude. The first portion of the instrumentation draft (excluding the missing portions) is in Bayreuth (except for one sheet which somehow found its way into the New York Public Library), the remainder (bars 448–end, plus supplementary harp parts) in the Scheide Collection at Princeton University (along with the anonymous copy of the Prelude). Unfortunately Wagner's fair copy of *Das Rheingold* has disappeared, but a beautiful copy by Friedrich Wölfel survives (in Bayreuth); judging by a comparison with facsimiles of two pages of Wagner's copy, it is extremely accurate.

The experience of scoring *Das Rheingold* thoroughly familiarized Wagner with his new *Ring* orchestra, making an instrumentation draft for *Die Walküre* unnecessary. He therefore made a regular full score in pencil, and later a fair copy in ink (now lost). Nevertheless, making the pencil score of *Die Walküre* did cause Wagner considerable difficulty (see 'Compositional process', pp.246–7).

With *Siegfried*, Wagner began his practice of finishing each act – including *two* complete drafts and a full score – before starting the next (again, see 'Compositional process'). For the first two acts of *Siegfried* and the Prelude to *Tristan* there exist full pencil scores as well as fair copies in ink. Beginning with Act I scene 1 of *Tristan*, Wagner reverted to his earlier practice of making only one full score (in ink). As each act of *Tristan* was completed, it was immediately sent to the printer for engraving, making the preparation of additional copies unnecessary.

To summarize: for the early operas up to and including *Lohengrin*, Wagner made only one full score, generally in ink. For *Das Rheingold*, *Die Walküre*, the first two acts of *Siegfried*, and the Prelude to *Tristan* there are *two* full scores, the first (draft) in pencil, the second (fair copy) in ink (although the draft of the *Rheingold* score is a special case, as described above). For the rest of *Tristan*, Act III of *Siegfried*, and all of *Die Meistersinger*, *Götterdämmerung* and *Parsifal*, there is only one full autograph score (in ink). However, copies by others do exist, made in preparation for the first engraving (*Stichvorlagen*). Those for *Siegfried* and *Die Meistersinger* were made by Hans Richter, that for *Götterdämmerung* by Joseph Rubinstein and Anton Seidl, and that for *Parsifal* by Engelbert Humperdinck.

Unfortunately, not all of these manuscripts are extant. The autograph scores of *Die Feen*, *Das Liebesverbot* and *Rienzi*, as well as Wagner's fair copies of *Das Rheingold* and *Die Walküre*, were presented by the composer on various occasions to King Ludwig II of Bavaria, and ended up in the Wittelsbacher Ausgleichsfond (the King Ludwig family archives). They were purchased from the Ausgleichsfond by the German Chamber of Industry and Commerce, which presented them in 1939 to Adolf Hitler as a gift on his fiftieth birthday. Hitler probably kept them in his bunker beneath the Berlin Chancellery, where they were presumably destroyed in April 1945. Although rumours of their survival continue to circulate, the whole incident must be judged as Hitler's final contribution to the cause of Wagner scholarship.

WARREN DARCY

Printed editions Breitkopf edition

ALTHOUGH TWO COMPLETE EDITIONS (*Gesamtausgaben*) of Wagner's works exist, neither, unfortunately, is complete. The more important of the two, the ongoing project published by B. Schott's Söhne (Mainz) under the title *Richard Wagner: Sämtliche Werke* (*Richard Wagner: Collected Works*), is described in the next section. The other, entitled *Richard Wagners Werke: Musikdramen – Jugendopern – Musikalische Werke* (*Richard Wagner's Works: Music Dramas – Youthful Operas – Musical Works*) was published by Breitkopf &

Härtel between 1912 and 1929. Edited by Michael Balling, only ten of the projected twenty or more volumes ever appeared. In 1971, Da Capo Press reprinted the series in seven volumes.

The gaps in the Breitkopf edition are hardly trivial: among the volumes which never appeared are those containing the scores of *Rienzi*, *Der fliegende Holländer*, *Die Meistersinger von Nürnberg*, *Parsifal*, and all four of the *Ring* operas. In addition, none of the ten existing volumes meets contemporary standards for a critical edition. Yet the series is certainly not without value.

For one thing, it does contain the scores of Wagner's earliest operatic endeavours: *Die Hochzeit* (of which only an introduction, chorus and septet were composed), *Die Feen* and *Das Liebesverbot*. Until the *Sämtliche Werke* editions appear, the Breitkopf edition affords us our only opportunity to study these little-known but formative works. In fact, the volumes containing *Die Hochzeit* (XII: 1912) and *Das Liebesverbot* (XIV: 1923) represent first printed editions; in the case of the latter, we must be grateful to Balling for undertaking its publication while the autograph score was still extant. In addition, the *Lohengrin* volume (IV: 1914) includes a six-page supplement containing the second portion of the Grail Narration, a passage Wagner excised before the Weimar premiere (28 August 1850). The first printed edition (1852) omitted this passage, as did all subsequent printings, so that only the Breitkopf edition allows us to study the Narration in its original form.

The volumes containing the non-operatic works are also noteworthy. Volume XV, entitled *Lieder und Gesänge* (1914) contains Wagner's songs for voice and piano, and in this respect has been superseded by the *Sämtliche Werke* version (SW XVII). However, it also includes three of Wagner's operatic inserts (for works of Marschner, Blum and Bellini), which are *not* yet available in the *Sämtliche Werke* edition (they are scheduled for SW XV, as is the *Hochzeit* fragment). Volume XVI (1914) contains works for *a cappella* male chorus, male chorus with orchestra (including the important *Das Liebesmahl der Apostel*) and mixed chorus with orchestra, all scheduled for SW XVI. Volumes XVIII (1917) and XX (1926) contain orchestral works, including the *Faust* Overture, the *Siegfried Idyll*, and the *Kaisermarsch*; again, many of these pieces have not yet appeared in the *Sämtliche Werke*.

Today's rigorous standards for a critical edition make it easy to criticize the Breitkopf enterprise. Certainly Balling's edition of *Tannhäuser* (III: 1929) pales by comparison with Reinhard Strohm's (SW V–VI), which when complete, will present two performing scores showing all variants. Yet Balling worked at a time when Wagner's manuscripts were not generally available; even so, he did attempt to collate several different sources, and his edition does represent to some extent each of the four 'versions' of the opera (it uses the fourth 'version' as a main text and includes selected earlier variants in an appendix). Before the publication of Strohm's edition, Balling's was certainly the closest thing available to a 'critical edition', and is no mean achievement for its time.

Sämtliche Werke (Schott)

The second complete edition is an ongoing project published by B. Schott's Söhne (Mainz) under the title *Richard Wagner: Sämtliche Werke* (*Richard Wagner: Collected Works*). Begun in 1970 in cooperation with the Bavarian Academy of Fine Arts, under the editorial leadership of Egon Voss and the late Carl Dahlhaus, this series maintains the very highest standards in its efforts to produce a critical edition of the complete Wagnerian oeuvre. The individual editors have consulted all relevant printed editions, performance parts and manuscripts in an effort to make each volume as 'definitive' as possible.

Unfortunately, such painstaking care has resulted in publication proceeding at a snail's pace: over the course of two decades, only about fourteen volumes have seen the light of day (less than one per year), and several of these are incomplete. However, those which have appeared are models of positivistic scholarship.

The general plan of this edition is as follows: Volumes I–XXI will contain the musical scores, Volumes XXII–XXXI the texts and documents associated with the stage works. In the first group, Volumes I–XIV are devoted to the completed operas (from *Die Feen* to *Parsifal*), while Volume XV will contain the *Hochzeit* fragment and the operatic inserts; Volumes XVI and XVII will feature the choral works and songs, Volume XVIII the orchestral pieces, XIX the piano works, and XX the arrangements; Volume XXI will contain miscellaneous items such as the *Kinder-Katechismus*. In the second group, Volumes XXII–XXX will present texts and documents for *Die Feen* to *Parsifal*, while Volume XXXI is devoted to stage projects which never reached the point of musical realization (including the infamous five-act tragedy *Leubald*). Most of these volumes comprise from two to five separate books. Many of the volumes which have appeared are incomplete, including (as of this writing) *Tannhäuser*, *Tristan*, the orchestral works and the arrangements. Among those volumes whose publication lies in the future are those containing *Die Feen* and *Das Liebesverbot*, *Lohengrin*, the operatic inserts, the choral works, the miscellaneous works, all the texts except those of *Rienzi* and *Parsifal*, and the second of the promised two volumes of *Ring* documents. On the bright side, the scores of *Rienzi*, *Der fliegende Holländer*, *Die Meistersinger*, *Das Rheingold*, *Götterdämmerung* and *Parsifal* are complete, as are the piano works and the songs with piano accompaniment.

As an example of the care which has gone into this project, consider Reinhard Strohm and Egon Voss's edition of *Rienzi* (SW III). One of Wagner's most popular operas during his lifetime, and the work which really established his reputation as a promising young composer, it has never been published in its original, complete version. Beginning with the Dresden premiere (1842), Wagner made numerous cuts to reduce the performing time of this sprawling work; these cuts were incorporated into the two extant hand copies (1842 and 1843) and the first printing (lithograph:

1844). The problem here is that Wagner's autograph score, containing the complete version, has disappeared; it was one of those manuscripts which found its way into Hitler's possession, and presumably (like Rienzi himself) went up in flames. The first copy of the autograph, that used for the Dresden premiere, was apparently complete, but also disappeared during the war. As a result, it is now impossible to reconstruct the original score. However, Strohm and Voss have also consulted Wagner's complete draft, which does contain the excised portions (although obviously not in orchestral form), as well as an 1844 piano reduction by Gustav Klink, who worked from Wagner's autograph and apparently ignored most of the composer's cuts. The editors reproduce portions of these latter two documents in SW III/5.

Isolde Vetter's edition of *Der fliegende Holländer* (SW IV) represents the very first publication of the opera's original version. As is now fairly well known, Wagner originally cast the opera in a single act and set it in Scotland; thus it appears in his autograph score. However, shortly after completing the work, Wagner decided to recast it in three acts and move the action to Norway; he also transposed Senta's Ballad down a whole step from A minor to G minor. These changes were incorporated into the first printing (lithograph: 1845), of which only thirty copies were struck. Wagner undertook further revisions in 1846 and 1852, and in 1860 he altered the ending of the Overture and the third act; these changes were incorporated into the edition of C.F. Meser (Adolph Fürstner) which appeared sometime between 1872 and 1877, as well as Felix Weingartner's 1897 edition of Fürstner's printing. Because the latter is the basis of the full-size and study scores currently available (see next section), Vetter's edition of the opera is truly invaluable. Fortunately the autograph score of *Holländer* escaped Hitler's grasp, although the complete draft was not so fortunate.

From Reinhard Strohm's edition of *Tannhäuser* (SW V–VI), we learn that, contrary to popular opinion, there exist four (not two) 'versions' of this opera: Wagner's autograph score (used for the 1845 Dresden premiere); an 1860 edition by C.F. Meser (Hermann Müller) incorporating the altered ending (the so-called 'Dresden version'); an 1861 version (not published), as performed in Paris; and an 1875 edition, as performed in Vienna, published by Fürstner (the so-called 'Paris version'). Wagner himself referred not to 'versions' but to 'new scenes' or 'alterations'. Strohm's edition, when complete, will contain two full performing scores: the first (SW V) uses the autograph as its main text, the second (SW VI) is based upon the form the opera had reached by 1875. Each volume will comprise three parts, the third containing all variants. To date, only the first two acts of the autograph version have appeared.

Because the autograph score of *Das Rheingold* is lost, Egon Voss's edition (SW X) is based upon Friedrich Wölfel's copy, as well as the first printing (1873) and a portion of its proofs. In questionable places, Wagner's complete draft and 'instrumentation draft' were also consulted. Voss's edition also includes, in brackets, remarks by people who were involved in the 1876 rehearsals and performances, such as Hermann Levi, Felix Mottl and Heinrich Porges; these comments relate to dynamics, articulation, expression, and – above all – tempo. The uniformity of agreement among the sources suggests that these remarks might well be authentic; if so, they accurately represent Wagner's intentions.

The results of this project more than justify its slow pace. Although many Wagner scholars now living will never witness the completion of the *Sämtliche Werke*, future generations will finally be able to base their work upon this marvellous authoritative edition.

Miscellaneous

Full-size scores (Dover edition)

Until fairly recently, the only Wagner scores on the market were of the so-called 'pocket' variety; the early full-size scores had long been out of print and were available only in large music libraries. This situation changed during the 1970s, when Dover Publications Inc. (New York) began issuing inexpensive reprints of selected early editions. These full-size, easy-to-read scores can now be purchased at lower prices than their miniature counterparts. The only disadvantage for the non-German-speaking student lies in the fact that, except for *Der fliegende Holländer*, none contains an English translation. The prefatory material, on the other hand, appears predominantly in English, sometimes with only the title-page and dedication in the original as well.

The *Holländer* score is Felix Weingartner's 1897 edition of Adolph Fürstner's printing. This contains the 1846/52 revisions as well as the 1860 version of the Overture and the end of Act III; it also includes a six-page appendix containing the original version of the Dutchman's Act III speech (from 'Erfahre das Geschick [. . .]' to 'Fahr hin, mein Heil, in Ewigkeit!') The English translation is by Paul England (author of that marvellously entertaining book *Fifty Favorite Operas*), the Italian by Alberto Giovannini. This 1897 edition was used as the basis of the pocket score described below.

The *Tannhäuser* score is the 1924 Peters edition. This incorporates the 1847 alterations into the original 1845 score (producing the so-called 'Dresden version'), and includes the 'Paris variants' in a supplement. The score also contains annotations by the conductor Felix Mottl based upon comments made by Wagner during a Vienna performance.

The score of *Lohengrin* is the so-called 'Neue Ausgabe' published by Breitkopf & Härtel in 1887; inasmuch as the first edition (1852) was lithographed from a copyist's autograph, this was the first engraved edition of the opera.

Three of the *Ring* operas are first editions published by Schott's: *Das Rheingold* (1873); *Siegfried* (1876) and *Götterdämmerung* (1876).

The *Walküre* score was published in 1921 by Peters, and contains annotations by Felix Mottl. Mottl's comments are also a feature of the *Tristan* (1914) and *Parsifal* (1921) scores, both put out by Peters; in the former case, Mottl's remarks relate not only to the music but to the dramatic shaping of the Isolde role, and include many stage directions. Finally, the *Meistersinger* score is that published by Peters in 1914.

All Wagner enthusiasts owe a special debt of gratitude to Dover for making these scores readily available.

Pocket scores (Eulenburg edition)

A pocket score (*Taschenpartitur*) is, of course, a miniature study score which can be easily carried about by students (although perhaps not in their pocket!) As regards the Wagner operas, there is only one edition currently available, that published by Ernst Eulenburg. In the case of *Tannhäuser*, Eulenburg put out the original pocket score; in all other cases, it took over plates from the first publisher.

The *Tannhäuser* score (1929) includes both the 'second Dresden version' of the opera, as well as new scenes and alterations made for the Paris performance (in an appendix). The French translation is by Charles Nuitter; naturally, the original version of each segment recomposed for Paris bears only the German text. The score contains no English translation, a fact which may limit its usefulness for American and British students.

The study score for *Der fliegende Holländer* was originally published by Adolph Fürstner in Berlin. This was based upon Felix Weingartner's 1897 edition of Fürstner's full score. It contains the 1846/52 revision, as well as the 1860 revision of the Overture and the ending of Act III. This pocket score is essentially identical to the full-size Dover reprint described above.

The study scores for *Lohengrin* (1906) and *Tristan* (1911) were originally published by Breitkopf & Härtel in Leipzig. In both cases, the English translation is by H. and F. Corder; the French translation for *Lohengrin* was done by Charles Nuitter, that of *Tristan* by Alfred Ernst.

All the other operas, including the *Ring*, were first published by B. Schott's Söhne (Mainz). In all cases the French translation is by Alfred Ernst, the English translation by Frederick Jameson (except that of *Parsifal*, which is by Margaret H. Glyn). All were originally published in multiple volumes (generally one per act), but the Eulenburg edition consolidated these. For example, Schott's issued *Das Rheingold* in two volumes (two scenes apiece), but the opera occupies only one volume in the Eulenburg edition. *Die Walküre* and *Siegfried* each fill three volumes in the Schott edition, one in the Eulenburg, while *Götterdämmerung* occupies three in the Schott edition and two in the Eulenburg (Volume I contains the Prologue plus Act I, Volume II the last two acts). In general, each volume of the Schott edition is paginated individually, while the numbering of the Eulenburg pages runs consecutively throughout an opera.

These study scores are obviously very useful, but their almost microscopic notation is guaranteed to enrich the local optician. In addition, more complex passages of score necessarily span two facing pages, requiring the reader periodically to rotate the book through ninety degrees. At one time, the greatest point in their favour was price: although hardly cheap, they allowed students to acquire complete Wagner scores without mortgaging their futures. However, they have recently been supplanted in this regard by the Dover reprints.

WARREN DARCY

Section 10
A WAGNERIAN GLOSSARY

A WAGNERIAN GLOSSARY

Abgesang. The third and closing unit in the poetic and musical '*Bar* form'* employed by Wagner in *Die Meistersinger*.

Absolute melody. Independently conceived, self-sufficient melody, by analogy with 'Absolute music'*. In Part I of *Opera and Drama* Wagner points to the style of Rossini's operas as the epitome of 'absolute melody'. The concept is emphatically restated, still with reference to Rossini, who is said to have taken his cue from the melodic idiom of the 'man in the street': '*naked, ear-pleasing, absolute melodic melody*, melody that is melody and nothing more, that creeps into our ears, we know not why, that we sing to ourselves, we know not why, that we exchange for another from one day to the next [. . .], that sounds depressing when we are happy and happy when we are out of sorts, and yet we continue to whistle, still without knowing why' (GS III, 251–2). The concept does not differ in essence from such related terms in Wagner's critical lexicon as 'instrumental melody', 'dance melody', or 'operatic melody' – indeed, it can be considered synonymous with the latter. But whereas 'dance' or 'instrumental' melody are justified in preserving an essentially formulaic, regular and symmetrical periodic structure, such stereotyped 'absolute' melody in opera represents, for Wagner, a shameless concession to facile, lazy habits of listening (on the part of the public) and to a wilfully 'egoistic' refusal (on the part of the composer) to mould musical thought to the needs of poetry and a 'Poetic [dramatic] intent'*. Wagner does implicitly concede that in some cases – as with Mozart or Gluck – 'absolute melody' can be expressively apposite to a text while also respecting its prosodic integrity. But such felicitous accommodation is no substitute, finally, for melody properly 'fertilized' or conditioned by the poetry and drama in the fullest sense.

Absolute music. The phrase that has come to denote the idea of 'pure', aesthetically autonomous (instrumental) music seems to have been coined by Wagner casually, but significantly, in the course of his 1846 'programme' for Beethoven's Ninth Symphony. Wagner draws attention to the striking manner in which Beethoven prepares the entrance of the human voice through 'that shattering recitative of the double basses which, answering the rest of the orchestra with a powerful and deeply felt discourse [. . .] nearly exceeds the boundaries of absolute music' (GS II, 61). Presumably the expression derives from the example of Ludwig Feuerbach, whose influence is so palpable in the 'Zurich writings' of a few years later (1849–51). Feuerbach had decried the baleful influence on recent German thought of what he called the 'absolute philosophy' propounded by Hegel – that is, a thoroughly abstract philosophy which seemed to function independently of the empirical realities of human existence (like many of this 'Young German' generation, Feuerbach disapproved of Hegel's apparent devaluation of the senses). The term 'absolute music' becomes much more prominent in *The Artwork of the Future* (1849) and especially in *Opera and Drama* (1850–51). In the context of Wagner's theories about the reunion of the separate arts in a *Gesamtkunstwerk** of the future, 'absolute music' acquires a distinctly pejorative connotation – music divorced from its origins and life-giving principles in dance, gesture, poetry and, above all, drama.

'Absolute music' has since become even more closely associated with Eduard Hanslick's pamphlet, *Vom Musikalisch-Schönen* (*The Beautiful in Music*, 1854), which upholds the autonomy of music as an essentially formal art, although Hanslick only once refers to 'pure absolute music' ('die reine, absolute Tonkunst'). Wagner, on the other hand, seizes on the adjective 'absolute' with a vengeance. He applies it in literally dozens of combinations throughout his writings: 'absolute melody', 'absolute artwork', 'absolute opera singer', 'absolute poetry' and so on, extending to such unlikely combinations as 'absolute rational language' (*Verstandessprache*), 'absolute effect', 'absolute recitative' and 'absolute aria'. The retrospective application of the term 'absolute music' to the aesthetic doctrines of the early Romantics thus involves an adjustment of emphasis (via Hanslick) from Wagner's essentially pejorative notion of a 'separate, egoistic' state to notions of transcendence, purity and ideality – aspects that had also adhered to the Hegelian sense

* An asterisk (*) indicates a word or phrase also included as a separate entry elsewhere in the glossary.

Note: The following Wagner titles are given throughout in English translation only: *Die Kunst und die Revolution* [*Art and Revolution*], *Das Kunstwerk der Zukunft* [*The Artwork of the Future*], *Oper und Drama* [*Opera and Drama*], *Eine Mitteilung an meine Freunde* [*A Communication to my Friends*] and '*Zukunftsmusik*' ['*Music of the Future*'].

of the 'absolute' and to which Feuerbach himself seems to have been sensitive.

Ahnung. See 'Anticipation, motifs of' and 'Leitmotif'.

Anticipation, motifs of. In the embryonic theory of 'Leitmotif'* sketched in *Opera and Drama* (Part III) Wagner described a motivic network of orchestral 'melody'* related to the dramatic vocal line ('verse melody'*) in a system of narrative 'tenses', as it were: past, present and future. The 'present tense' of a dramatic-musical motif would correspond to the moment of semantic definition, the presentation of a musical idea in immediate connection with a certain name, phrase, gesture or idea. Besides this single, 'definitive' occurrence, the motif may occur in advance, as an orchestral 'anticipation' (*Ahnung*), or else subsequently as reminiscence or recollection (*Erinnerung**) – that is, in 'future' and 'past tenses'. In speaking of the preparatory 'absolute orchestral melody'* as anticipation of a semantically determinate dramatic moment, when the musical idea will acquire associative meaning through word or gesture, Wagner seems to evoke (perhaps unconsciously) Romantic notions of 'absolute' or purely instrumental music as anticipation, intimation or foreboding of some ineffable feeling or experience (as in E.T.A. Hoffmann's notion of the '*Ahnung des Unendlichen*', 'intimation of the infinite'). In practice, of course, Wagner's 'leitmotifs' are not necessarily 'defined' in conjunction with text and vocal line, but often by a more general dramatic context, gesture, or some other visual sign. The motif of the Rhinegold, for example, is first presented as an 'anticipation', played by French horns beneath a gently undulating string figure. It remains an exclusively instrumental motif throughout the cycle, however: only an auxiliary motif, the so-called 'Rhinegold call' of the three Rhinemaidens, serves to fix that object (the Rhinegold) in a clear verbal-musical association, i.e. as 'verse melody'.

Art of transition. See 'Transition, art of'.

Artwork of the Future (*Kunstwerk der Zukunft*). The title of the second of Wagner's major aesthetic tracts from the post-revolutionary period (1849) derives from the social philosopher Ludwig Feuerbach, whose writings (e.g. *Grundsätze der Philosophie der Zukunft*, or *Principles of the Philosophy of the Future*, 1843) exerted great influence on Wagner at this time, and on the initial conception of *Siegfrieds Tod*. His enthusiastic adoption of such popular, reform-minded rhetoric with its apodictic pronouncements about the necessity of certain cultural and artistic developments 'of the future' was to haunt Wagner for a long time, providing ammunition for more than one generation of satirists. Wagner had already referred to 'the artwork of the future' in his previous essay, *Art and Revolution*. This artwork is, of course, the new, reformed musical drama which, after the requisite modifications of the existing social order, will constitute the modern and more powerful counterpart to the sacred dramas of the ancient Greeks. (Wagner is at pains to distinguish this new, revolutionary ideal from current attempts to revive Greek tragedy on the modern stage, in particular the 'model' revivals of Sophocles at the Berlin Court Theatre sponsored by Friedrich Wilhelm IV with the collaboration of Mendelssohn and Ludwig Tieck.) Wagner's concept is thus as much ideological as aesthetic. In the course of the eponymous essay he does admit that the separate arts may well owe their present attainments to their development as individual ('absolute') media – especially true of music – but he insists that any further progress will only be possible in the sphere of communal enterprise in the service of drama. The phrase 'artwork of the future' soon gave rise to the catchword 'music of the future'*, among other critical tropes.

Bar, Bar form (see also '*Abgesang*'*, '*Stollen*'*). A traditional poetic song form (AAB) consisting of two similar stanzas, or *Stollen*, followed by a third, contrasting unit by way of peroration (*Abgesang*); the resulting three-part form may then be strophically repeated, with new text. Wagner incorporated a number of *Bar* forms into *Die Meistersinger*, reflecting, on one level, the practices of the central and south German singers' guilds of the 15th and 16th centuries, while on another level his sophisticated adaptations of the form throughout the opera serve to exemplify aspects of his broader theme, the tension between tradition and innovation in the 'art of song'. Walther von Stolzing informs the mastersingers of his background in a well-made *Bar* ('Am stillen Herd'), a sign of his sound aesthetic instinct. In his Trial Song in Act I ('So rief der Lenz in den Wald') Walther – again instinctively – creates a more complex variant of the form in which contrasting sections are incorporated into each *Stollen* ('In einer Dornenhecken', 'Aus finst'rer Dornenhecken'), confusing the aesthetically myopic judge, Beckmesser. (It is of course symptomatic that Beckmesser and his colleagues fail to perceive the larger *Bar* form of the Trial Song because they refuse to hear it out: it concludes only amidst the ensemble pandemonium ending Act I.) Walther's Prize Song ('Morgenlich leuchtend im rosigen Schein') ultimately wins the approbation of public and masters alike. In both its original form in Act III scene 2 and in the closing scene of the opera it is significantly imbued with innovatory traits: on its first appearance its second *Stollen* modulates away from the initial key, and in the final scene Walther extemporizes impassioned amplifications of both *Stollen* before bringing the first *Bar* as a whole to a decorous close. Sachs describes the principle of the form to Walther in Act III through the metaphor of reproductive biology so favoured by Wagner himself: the two *Stollen* are like man and wife, the *Abgesang* representing their offspring. It should resemble them up to a point, but also develop in new, independent ways.

The concept of *Bar* form was applied extensively and at many levels by Alfred Lorenz in his analyses of the 'secret of musical form' in Wagner, not only in *Die Meistersinger* but in the other music dramas as well. Lorenz also suggested that *Die Meistersinger* reflects the *Bar* form on the largest possible scale in its disposition of two shorter acts – exposing and developing the dramatic conflicts – followed by a third, much longer act in which these culminate and find resolution.

Bühnenfestspiel ('stage festival play'). The official generic designation of *Der Ring des Nibelungen* ('A stage festival play for three days and a preliminary evening'). The idea clearly derives from the model of ancient Greek tragedy which had so deeply influenced Wagner at the time he conceived the work in the late 1840s, and which figures so prominently in the essays *Art and Revolution* and *The Artwork of the Future*. The conception of an idealized revival of the Greek theatre in modern European terms, as a means of moral, spiritual and aesthetic regeneration of society, remained a constant feature of Wagnerian ideology. See 'Bayreuth and the idea of a festival theatre', pp. 167–70.

Bühnenweihfestspiel ('stage festival consecration play'). This designation for *Parsifal* is an embellishment of that for the *Ring* cycle, underscoring the intended exclusivity of its association with the Bayreuth 'festival theatre', on one hand, and the expressly sacred, quasi-liturgical nature of its content, on the other. As with the *Ring*, Wagner set great store by the regenerative, even 'redemptive' function of this sacred festival-play, feeling compelled to distinguish it from the average operatic fare of the day and to preserve it from traffic with the unworthy repertory of the modern urban opera house.

'Deeds of music made visible' (*ersichtlich gewordene Taten der Musik*). See 'Music drama'.

Effect, 'effects without causes' (*Wirkungen ohne Ursache*). Central to Wagner's anti-Meyerbeer polemic in Part I of *Opera and Drama* is the quality of calculated, superficial 'effect', identified as the sole governing principle of modern French grand opera. The critique revolves around an untranslatable distinction between *Wirkung* and *Effekt* (the latter evidently suspect due to its Latin rather than Germanic etymology). The *Effekt* of Meyerbeerian opera is defined as '*Wirkungen ohne Ursache*' ('effects without causes'), that is, dramatic situations, vocal display, scenic spectacle, chorus and ballet are motivated only by the aim of creating striking

musical and visual effects, and are not the legitimate consequence of any poetic or dramatic 'cause' (GS III, 301–2). Wagner specifically alludes to the 'sunrise' closing Act II of *Le Prophète* (the inauguration of electric light on the operatic stage, acclaimed during the opera's triumphant first run in Paris in 1849). The whole situation, like the hymn sung by John of Leyden with the amassed chorus, is said to be merely trumped up by the composer in collusion with his 'private secretary', Eugène Scribe, in order to provide the opportunity for a stirring finale. Wagner seems unable to appreciate the fact that this 'artificial' situation is pointedly ambivalent: Jean, the leader of the 'proto-socialist' popular uprising in this scene, has previously been represented as a weak-willed pawn of the blatantly hypocritical Anabaptists; clearly the anti-heroic, politically cynical 'realism' of Scribe's libretto is entirely at odds with Wagner's own revolutionary ideals at this time. This misapprehension does not necessarily diminish the force of Wagner's critique regarding the general lack of psychological and dramatic integrity in the Scribe–Meyerbeer collaboration.

Endless melody. See 'Infinite melody'.

Erinnerung. See 'Reminiscence, motifs of'.

Gesamtkunstwerk ('combined' or 'total artwork'). Like many of the most widely disseminated Wagnerian terms, this one also derives from the so-called 'Zurich writings' of 1849–51. In *Art and Revolution* (1849) Wagner draws a traditionally idealized picture of the 'combined artwork' of ancient Greek tragedy, stressing not only the union of the 'separate arts' of poetry, dance and music in the service of drama, but equally the 'communal' aspect of the event itself – its social, ethical and religious function of uniting the Athenian people and fostering a spiritual bond among them through art. In this sense, the term might be rendered as 'communal' or 'collective artwork' (and indeed, Wagner also speaks of a 'communal [*gemeinsame*] artwork of the future' – GS III, 50). The original conception of the *Ring* cycle, as *Siegfrieds Tod*, was imbued with this version of the Greek ideal, which also gave rise to his vision of a 'stage festival play' culminating in the project of Bayreuth (see 'Bayreuth and the idea of a festival theatre', pp. 167–70). What distinguishes Wagner's version of the Greek ideal from the long tradition of classically oriented aesthetics since the Renaissance is the strong component of revolutionary social theory, loosely synthesizing ideas from Proudhon, Feuerbach and other 'Young Hegelian' forerunners of Marx. In the 'Zurich writings', however, emphasis shifts from social theory to history, criticism and aesthetic speculation (*Opera and Drama*). The notion that the 'separate arts' would gain in potency through such a union and that, in fact, they would otherwise be doomed to inevitable sterility and obsolescence was, of course, much criticized from the start. And while Wagner never relinquished his conviction of the aesthetic potential of the music drama, as he conceived it, the term *Gesamtkunstwerk* was abandoned (along with much else of Wagner's 'revolutionary' rhetoric) in later writings.

Gesture (see also 'Orchestral melody'*). The crucial importance of theatrical gesture in both spoken drama and opera is a recurring theme in Wagner's writings. In *Opera and Drama* he developed an elaborate, if somewhat contrived, theory of the correlation between orchestral accompaniment ('orchestral melody') and dramatic gesture (*Gebärde*). The basis of this theory is evident in many motifs in the *Ring* cycle, as well as in earlier works. The motifs of Wotan's spear and Siegmund's (later Siegfried's) sword are, as Carl Dahlhaus has pointed out, suggested by gestures associated with these objects: the portentous, gravitational impulse of the spear, planted firmly and decisively on the ground as a symbol of law and authority, or the bold, upward swing of the sword Nothung, triumphantly unsheathed by Siegmund. In later writings (e.g. *Über Schauspieler und Sänger – On Actors and Singers*, 1872) Wagner elaborated his ideas on the fundamental importance of gesture, mime and improvisation of all kinds in drama. He laments the disappearance from the modern theatre (spoken or operatic) of a true improvisatory art, which only survives, he maintains, in elements of popular culture: the Hanswurst and Kasperl plays of the traditional puppet theatre in which Goethe's *Faust* also had its roots. Wagner reflects here on the impressions received from performances by Wilhelmine Schröder-Devrient, whose inimitable combination of physical and vocal stage presence transformed works of such diverse quality as Beethoven's *Fidelio*, Bellini's *I Capuleti e i Montecchi* and Weigl's *Die Schweizerfamilie*. The 'salvation of dramatic art', Wagner concludes, lies precisely in the selfless collaboration of the dramatist (-composer) and the mimetic artist. In another essay from the same period (*Über die Bestimmung der Oper – On the Destiny of Opera*, 1871) Wagner attempted to convey the kinship of Shakespeare's plays with popular, improvisatory traditions by characterizing them as 'fixed mimetic improvisations of the highest poetic value' (GS IX, 143).

Grundmotiv ('fundamental motif'). Wagner occasionally referred to 'fundamental motifs' (*Grundmotive*) of his operas – without distinguishing clearly between dramatic 'motifs' and their musical-motivic embodiment – as 'leitmotifs'*. In *Opera and Drama* he speaks of the 'concentrated and fortified fundamental motifs of the similarly concentrated and fortified action, which will serve as pillars of the overall dramatic structure.' These motifs are described as 'malleable emotional elements' (*plastische Gefühlsmomente*) for which the musician will devise appropriately corresponding musical ideas (*melodische Momente*). These musical ideas will also serve as motifs of 'Anticipation'* and 'Reminiscence'* (GS IV, 201). The 'perfectly unified form' of the musical drama will result from the collaboration of poet and musician in arranging the structural occurrences of these dramatic and musical *Grundmotive* in carefully designed patterns of alternation and return. In *A Communication to my Friends* Wagner spoke of the characteristic fabric or network of principal themes (*Gewebe der Hauptthemen*) that was to spread across the whole expanse of the drama 'in the most intimate relation to the poetic intent'* of the drama (GS IV, 322). In a later context (1879) he speaks of a 'fabric of fundamental themes' (*Gewebe der Hauptthemen*) analogous to the presentation and development of themes and motifs in a symphonic movement, and now explicitly identified with what Hans von Wolzogen had recently catalogued as *Leitmotive* (GS X, 185). The terms *Grundmotiv* and *Grundthema* – unlike the now habitual 'leitmotif' – underscore an important distinction between the original, basic form of a motif and the multifarious modifications it may undergo in subsequent contexts.

Infinite melody (*unendliche Melodie*). Also translated as 'endless' or 'unending melody', *unendliche Melodie* is one of those Wagnerian coinages (like the 'total artwork of the future') that provided an easy target for the composer's detractors, who equated it with the seemingly amorphous, 'unmelodic' character of his vocal and instrumental lines and with the 'endless' proportions of the operas as a whole. Since then the phrase has stuck as an evocation of Wagner's open-ended musical syntax, above all the ubiquitous tendency in the later operas to elide cadential junctures by means of deceptive resolution or interruptive techniques. While Wagner used the phrase only once, towards the end of '*Music of the Future*' (GS VII, 130), the idea is adumbrated earlier in the essay and elsewhere. 'Infinite melody' is presented as the musical counterpart to Wagner's new conception of poetic-dramatic structure, although one could cite the instrumental Prelude to *Tristan und Isolde* as a paradigm of the kind of seamless, linear-evolutionary process connoted by the term. The general tendency towards cadential elision and free, irregular phrase structure of vocal lines is already characteristic of *Das Rheingold*, where its origins in traditional recitative idioms are still quite evident.

Wagner himself did not equate the term with these or any technical characteristics, however. Instead, he emphasized the aesthetic implications of a melody that never sacrifices dramatic, gestural expressivity or musical 'meaning' to easily apprehended but formulaic, hence 'meaningless' melodic patterns. In '*Music of the Future*' Wagner emphasized the correlation of 'infinite melody' with the emancipation of the libretto from the constraints of rhyming, metrical verse (although he was able to effect a compromise between them in *Die Meistersinger*). The consequent 'emancipation' of melody allowed the composer to forgo textual repetition for the sake of filling out the musical phrase. The 'form' of *Tristan und Isolde* – its infinitely evolving melodic-motivic substance – is said to be entirely prepared or prefigured in the 'weave of words and verses' (GS VII, 123).

Invisible orchestra (Bayreuth). As early as 1863 Wagner had conceived a plan for the situation of an orchestra pit well below the stage and covered by some form of moderating screen that would serve the dual purpose of enhancing the illusion of the stage picture (by hiding the orchestral sound source) and facilitating audibility of the singers and their declamation, further focusing the audience's attention on their utterance and gesture. In the foreword to the first publication of the *Ring* libretto (1863), a year before discussing plans for a festival theatre in Munich with Gottfried Semper, Wagner outlined the basic features of such a theatre. The lowered orchestra with its 'acoustic sound wall' would necessitate an amphitheatrical seating arrangement without balcony or side-loges, in order to ensure the orchestra's concealment from the audience (at the same time eliminating the tradition 'hierarchical' seating plan, which did not conform to Wagner's idealistic vision of the theatre). This 'sound wall' would also serve to filter out any 'extraneous' sounds produced by the operation of orchestral instruments, promoting a clean, balanced mixture of orchestral tone. 'Should not these mechanics of sound production, as well as the exertions of the conductor, be hidden from view with the same care one takes to conceal all the lines, wires, boards and scaffolding of the stage decorations in attempting to achieve the greatest degree of theatrical illusion?' (GS VI, 275) This same point is made with regard to the 'ideality' of pure instrumental music by the musical enthusiasts of Wagner's 1841 novelistic vignette *Ein glücklicher Abend* (*A Happy Evening*): the music is far better appreciated, they agree, without the distracting sight of the timpanist anxiously counting the beats before his next entrance, the 'distorted physiognomies of the wind players, the desperate exertions of the double basses and cellos, or the weary back-and-forth motion of the violin bows' (GS I, 137). In an essay written at the time of the construction of the Bayreuth theatre, Wagner recalls the epithet he and Semper had earlier coined for the space between the proscenium and the audience – the 'mystical abyss' (*mystischer Abgrund*), from whence would emanate the transfigured sounds of the orchestra, 'like the steams rising from Gaia's primeval womb, beneath the seat of the Pythia [the Delphic oracle]' (GS IX, 338).

Kunstreligion ('art-religion', 'religion of art'). The notion of a 'religion of art' or 'art as religion' has many ramifications for cultural tendencies of the 19th century as a whole, but finds in Wagner perhaps its most representative figure. The composer himself expressed the essence of this phenomenon at the close of his essay *Über Staat und Religion* (*On State and Religion*, 1864), written at the behest of Ludwig II. Wagner attempts to explain here how Ludwig will find at once spiritual guidance and personal 'redemption' through supporting and experiencing Wagnerian musical drama; furthermore, the present-day sectarian confusion of religion will be altogether subsumed into this artwork of the future (GS VIII, 29). An equally quintessential manifestation of the idea is to be found in the late essay *Religion und Kunst* (*Religion and Art*, 1880), whose very title is indicative: 'One could say that just where religion starts to become artificial, the responsibility for its preservation devolves upon art itself; for art takes those same mythic symbols that religion has posited as veritable truths and uses them for their metaphorical value, revealing by means of their idealized presentation the deep levels of truth contained in them' (GS X, 211). *Kunstreligion* in this sense is a reversal of the Hegelian postulate that art and religion would both be replaced (*aufgehoben*) by pure thought – i.e. philosophy – in the modern era. But many aspects of the doctrine of *Kunstreligion* can be traced back to Hegel's generation, when a revival of religious faith tended to merge with the new critical-aesthetic preoccupations of such figures as Schelling, Schleiermacher, Wackenroder, Hoffmann, Chateaubriand and Lamartine. Franz Liszt had promoted a merging of art and religion in an early essay on the synthesis of church and theatre (1835), influenced by the Saint-Simonian movement in France, while his later career embodies a more orthodox response to the ideal of *Kunstreligion*. In Wagner's works the explicitly Christian themes (and musical 'imagery') of *Tannhäuser* and *Lohengrin* reach their apogee in the 'stage festival consecration play' *Parsifal*, while the conception of the *Ring* tetralogy and the Bayreuth Festival itself grew from his desire to resuscitate the spirit of ancient Greek tragedy, as communal religious rite, in modern German-European form.

Leitmotif (*Leitmotiv*; see also 'Anticipation, motifs of', 'Reminiscence, motifs of', '*Grundmotiv*'). This most famous of all Wagnerian terms did not originate with the composer himself. However, the underlying concept of the 'leading motif' can be traced to Part III of *Opera and Drama*, where Wagner spoke of motifs of 'anticipation' and 'recollection' or 'reminiscence', musical ideas that would obtain a distinct associative meaning (relating to character, object, idea or emotion) in conjunction with a significant dramatic moment and concomitant text (see also 'Verse melody'*). In *Opera and Drama* and the subsequent *Communication to my Friends* Wagner spoke variously of principal 'melodic elements' or ideas (*melodische Momente*) and 'fundamental motifs' (*Grundmotive*), signifying here *dramatic* motifs to which certain musical ideas would correspond. These musical ideas would accumulate additional layers of significance through their modified reappearance in appropriate dramatic contexts throughout the drama, at the same time endowing the drama with a compelling sense of larger structural unity. Wagner's 'system' began as an amplification of practices of dramatic-musical recall that had found increasing favour since the later 18th century.

The actual term 'leitmotif' has often been attributed to F.W. Jähns, who used it in his study of the life and works of Weber (Berlin, 1871), although it clearly acquired currency only through Hans von Wolzogen, who published the first thematic guides to Wagner's works: those to the *Ring* (1876), *Tristan* (1880) and *Parsifal* (1882). A.W. Ambros used the word '*Leitmotiv*' as early as 1860, with reference to motif and transformation techniques in Wagner's operas up to *Lohengrin* and in the orchestral works of Liszt (*Culturhistorische Bilder*, [Leipzig 1860]). Wagner's use of 'leitmotifs' had also been analysed before Wolzogen by Heinrich Porges and Gottlieb Federlein, although without use of the specific term.

In his essay *Über die Anwendung der Musik auf das Drama* (*On the Application of Music to the Drama*, 1879) Wagner referred to Wolzogen's analysis of his 'leitmotifs', pointing out that Wolzogen had limited himself to a taxonomy of these motifs 'according to their dramatic significance and effect, but not [. . .] their role in the musical structure' (GS X, 185–6). The disposition, variation and development of such motifs through the course of the drama, Wagner suggests, would merit closer attention. In the preceding paragraph of the essay he had spoken of a 'network of fundamental themes' (*Grundthemen*), analogous to the presentation and development of thematic ideas in a symphonic movement, but corresponding here to the processes of dramatic action (that is to say, Wagner here acknowledges the concept of 'leitmotif' without explicitly sanctioning the term).

Melody (*Melodie, Melos*). Wagner was continually plagued by the charge that his music was 'without melody', an artificial patchwork of (leit-)motivic fragments arbitrarily summoned to accompany the appearance of some character, word or idea. The situation was exacerbated, as his critics heard it, by the tortuous, restlessly modulating, 'effect-seeking' progressions underlying the rapid comings and goings of these fragmentary motifs. Thus it may seem surprising that 'melody' should figure so centrally in the composer's own theoretical reflec-

tions – although less surprising if we recognize this as, in part, a strategy of self-defence.

Throughout his later writings, from *Opera and Drama* on, he returns again and again to the subject of melody. And Wagner is indefatigable in his aesthetic classifications of it: 'Absolute melody'*, 'operatic melody', 'Patriarchal melody'*, 'instrumental' and 'dance melody', 'folk melody', '*Urmelodie*', 'dramatic melody', and the infamous 'endless' or 'Infinite melody'*, to name only a few. Behind this taxonomic mania – which begins to recall David's pedantic recitation of the mastersingers' *Töne* and *Weisen* – is the apologetic aim of redefining 'melody' according to Wagner's own aesthetic doctrines. In particular he seeks to undermine the automatic equation of melody *per se* with the periodicity of 'dance-derived' instrumental melody, in which phrase structure, rhythm and harmonic progression are dictated by a sense for abstract symmetries. Wagner preferred to emphasize the motivic constituents of melody on the one hand – whether the 'absolute' motivic material of Beethoven's symphonies or the poetically engendered motifs of his own operas – and the large-scale thread (or fabric) spun (or woven) from these motivic elements, on the other; that is, he avoided speaking of the middle level that would correspond to the conventional period or phrase-group.

On different occasions he claimed to have discovered the key to understanding such pieces as Beethoven's C♯ minor Quartet, op. 131, or the first movement of the Ninth Symphony by grasping their underlying melody or 'melos' in this larger sense, which embraces all aspects of musical structure as a projection of melodic or motivic impulse. In a similar vein he spoke of the 'form' of *Tristan und Isolde* as a function of its melody, in this case, the conjunction of poetry, 'Verse melody'*, and a continuous orchestral fabric ('Orchestral melody'*) of expressive motivic ideas. Anticipating Schoenberg's notion of 'Musical prose'*, one could say that Wagner understood 'melody' as the meaningful or eloquent development of musical ideas, distributed throughout the texture, over the course of a composition.

Mime, pantomime. See 'Gesture'.

Modulation. In outlining a provisional theory of musical drama (*Opera and Drama*, Part III) Wagner proposed a correlation between musical modulation, *Stabreim** and poetic expression. Specifically, the musical setting of a given series of lines (a rhetorical or poetic 'period') should reflect their shifting course of emotional expression by means of 'modulation' or harmonic progression, ultimately establishing an overall sense of unity by returning to the original tonal point of departure at the end of the series. Such tonal unification of the 'poetic-musical period'* complements the poetic-verbal unity established at a lower level by alliteration (*Stabreim*) and assonance. The detailed correlation of *Stabreim* and modulation proposed here was clearly too restrictive for practical implementation. Yet the passage in *Opera and Drama* does convey a characteristic of Wagner's later harmonic practice, the technique later dubbed by Arnold Schoenberg 'wandering tonality' – a thoroughly flexible harmonic syntax free to move in any direction by means of enharmonically and chromatically determined part-writing. (Wagner's use of the term 'modulation' should be interpreted to encompass such local progressions as well as 'true' modulation across larger musical expanses.)

Later statements reinforce a fundamental conviction that such 'emancipated' harmonic syntax requires the justification of some dramatic motive, a 'poetic intent'*. A posthumously published fragment, evidently coeval with the composition of *Tristan*, reads: 'On modulation in pure instrumental music and in the drama. Fundamental difference. Rapid and distant transitions are often as necessary in the latter context [drama] as they are impermissible in the former, due to lack of motivation' (SS XII, 280; see also Abbate, 1989). The same idea resurfaces in the 1879 essays *Über das Opern-Dichten und Komponieren im Besonderen* (*On Opera Libretti and Composition in Particular*) and *Über die Anwendung der Musik auf das Drama* (*On the Application of Music to the Drama*). In the latter essay Wagner explains that the enharmonic modulations contained in the thematic material of Elsa's arioso near the beginning of *Lohengrin* present a perfectly comprehensible analogue to the details of the situation – she momentarily raises her modest gaze in a gesture of exaltation and growing confidence as she recalls the vision of her unknown protector – while the same phrases would appear contrived and unmotivated as the theme of a symphonic andante, for instance (GS X, 191–2).

Motif. See 'Anticipation, motifs of', '*Grundmotiv*', Leitmotif, 'Nature motif', 'Reminiscence, motifs of'.

Musical prose. Arnold Schoenberg considered 'musical prose' as an ideal common to the musical language of Wagner and Brahms alike – a tendency to break down the constraints of musical 'rhyme', so to speak, in favour of a 'direct and straightforward presentation of ideas, without any patchwork, without mere padding and empty repetitions' (Schoenberg 1975). Although the phrase owes its modern currency to Schoenberg, it appears that Wagner coined it himself. If the musician were to observe only the 'natural speech accents' of the verse he sets, Wagner maintained (*Opera and Drama*), he would treat the verse essentially as prose, as it should in any case be declaimed; at the same time, the regular metrical patterns of 'absolute melody'* would tend to be dissolved into a kind of 'musical

prose' (GS IV, 113–14). Paradoxically, the concept of musical prose is presented by Wagner not as a liberating ideal, but as the crux of a dilemma facing the composer who seeks to do justice to proper dramatic declamation on the one hand, and to the demands of melodic intelligibility on the other. (The passage, like many in the Zurich writings, probably echoes something of the frustrations Wagner faced in *Lohengrin*, in attempting to mediate between operatic tradition and an as yet unrealized ideal of 'musical drama'.) Schoenberg's definition of 'musical prose' comes very close, at any rate, to the distinctly affirmative characterization of 'infinite melody'* in '*Music of the Future*', a characterization meant to establish the aesthetic kinship between *Tristan und Isolde* and the technique of Beethoven's symphonic idiom (the *Eroica*). In Beethoven, as in *Tristan*, the melodic ideas (motifs) are arranged in a musical discourse of continuous eloquence, uniting structural and expressive purpose while eschewing the 'padding' of conventional melodic phraseology: the result is a large-scale 'form' consisting of 'a single, perfectly coherent [continuous or 'endless'] melody' (GS VII, 127).

Music drama. Paradoxically, the term that has come to be applied to Wagner's mature operas and to other works in a broadly construed Wagnerian tradition was not coined by Wagner, nor ever officially sanctioned by him. Nonetheless it has come to be accepted as a convenient means of distinguishing between the 'Romantic operas' up to *Lohengrin* and the thoroughly 'leitmotivic' dramas from *Das Rheingold* on, subsequent to Wagner's attempt to formulate a 'theory' of the musical drama. Since Wagner himself provided no uniform generic designation for the later works, recourse to this term seems justifiable. He certainly did take pains to distinguish his later works from the debased category of 'opera' – a central impulse behind much of his writing. But at the time of *Opera and Drama* Wagner tends to speak simply of 'drama' in the abstract – the 'drama of the future', or more generally the ideal or 'perfect artwork', and finally, of course, the '*Gesamtkunstwerk** of the future'. In a footnote towards the end of the *Communication to my Friends* (1851) he stated: 'I shall write no more operas: but as I do not care to invent any arbitrary name for these works, I will simply call them dramas, since that at least indicates the standpoint from which they are to be understood.' (GS IV, 343) Elsewhere in his writings Wagner tended to employ the phrase 'musical drama'. In a brief essay of 1872, *Über die Benennung 'Musikdrama'* (*On the Designation 'Music Drama'*), he speculates that it is from the expression 'musical drama' that the fashionable contraction 'music drama' has evolved. In this same context he proposes (although qualified by a characteristically sardonic tone) the grandiose designation 'deeds of music made visible' (GS IX, 306), based on his interpretation of drama as essentially an artistic 'deed' or 'action'. This latter phrase has been much cited for its implication that music is now accorded the priority earlier reserved for poetry or drama.

Music of the future (*Zukunftsmusik*). This famous epithet had become a favourite lance in the critical arsenal of the anti-Wagnerian press by 1860. It provided the title for the German publication of an essay from that year, first published in French simply as the 'foreword' to prose translations of the libretti of Wagner's operas *Der fliegende Holländer*, *Tannhäuser*, *Lohengrin* and *Tristan*. Addressed to the French public at the time of the Parisian *Tannhäuser* production, the essay attempts to clarify aspects of Wagner's musical development, his notorious 'theories', and current insights stemming from the experience of his latest work, *Tristan*. It does not, however, have much to say about the phrase 'music of the future', which Wagner had already sought to discredit in an open letter to Berlioz (*Journal des Débats*, February 1860), exposing it as a senseless perversion of his earlier title, *The Artwork of the Future* (1849). (Berlioz's somewhat irascible review of Wagner's concerts at the Théâtre-Italien that month had closed with a polemical 'non credo' pertaining to what he understood as the latest direction of the Wagner–Liszt 'school'; while admiring the excerpts performed from *Tannhäuser* and *Lohengrin*, he admitted to being thoroughly baffled by the *Tristan* Prelude.)

Wagner himself identified Ludwig Bischoff as the source of the epithet, editor of the *Niederrheinische Musik-Zeitung* and an associate of the Cologne-based composer Ferdinand Hiller, whom Wagner counted among his official enemies. Bischoff is said to have coined the phrase in 1859, according to some commentators: while a brief editorial entitled '*Zukunftsmusik*' (signed 'Lp.') does appear in that volume, and a lengthier, anonymous piece the following year, the term can be found in Bischoff's journal at least as early as 1857. An 1854 concert review by the Viennese music critic L.A. Zellner applied the term 'Zukunftsmusik' to the music of Schumann and Wagner alike, and the term also occurs in a letter of Louis Spohr from the same year. In any case, it had clearly achieved wide currency by the end of the decade, by which time it was equally associated with the recent orchestral works of Franz Liszt (the symphonic poems, and the *Faust* and *Dante* Symphonies).

Nature motif (*Naturmotiv*). Reflecting on the genesis of the nearly completed *Ring* cycle in 1871, Wagner referred to the 'new path' he had embarked upon with *Das Rheingold*. Here the composer began with the invention of 'plastic [malleable] nature motifs' (*plastische Natur-Motive*) which would continually evolve in individual, characteristic, expressive transformations over the course of the drama

(GS VI, 266). The word *Naturmotiv* corresponds closely to several formulations in other writings (*Grundmotiv*, *Grundthema*, *Hauptthema*), suggesting the all-important transformational capacities of Wagner's musical motifs in their basic, original forms. The particular term 'nature motif' and its association with *Das Rheingold* also connotes the elemental, largely triadic motifs characteristic of that work and generally associated with natural phenomena: the original 'nature motif' of the Prelude itself, swelling up from the depths of the Rhine (yielding the motifs of 'Erda' and the 'Twilight of the Gods' by modal alteration and inversion, respectively), the simple G major horn call heralding the Rhinegold, the winding triadic outline plus neighbouring sixth degree introducing Loge's Narration ('So weit Leben und Weben') – akin to the woodbird of *Siegfried* – Donner's majestic invocation of the storm clouds, and the 'anticipatory' statement of the Sword motif near the end of the opera. The bright, major-mode triadic profile of many of these ideas is also conditioned by the associative timbres of horns or trumpets. In a later essay (1879) Wagner explicitly designated the opening figure of *Das Rheingold* as a 'nature motif'. In this same context he also points to the manifold 'figurational, rhythmic and harmonic variation' undergone by a similarly elemental, diatonic motif, the so-called 'Rhinegold call', with which the Rhinemaidens first greet the illuminated gold (GS X, 188–9).

Operatic melody. See 'Melody', 'Absolute melody', 'Quadratic melody'.

Orchestral melody (see also 'Verse melody'* and 'Leitmotif'*). On a general level, this term from *Opera and Drama* (Part III) means just what it suggests: the instrumental 'accompaniment' to the opera or 'musical drama', or more specifically, the orchestral complement to 'verse melody'. In later writings Wagner tended to lay greater emphasis on the polyphonic strands making up this orchestral 'melody' or 'fabric' (*Gewebe*). That is, the primarily vertical conception of accompaniment (as chordal progression) in *Opera and Drama* yields later to a more horizontal or linear conception.

The expressive 'speech capacity' of the orchestra is explained as an analogue to the visible 'language' of dramatic gesture. Hence the semantic relation of 'orchestral melody' to gesture and movement is roughly analogous to that of 'verse melody' to the poetic text. Harmony, rhythm, motif and instrumental timbre combine to form a musical discourse that interprets for the ear, as it were, that which dramatic gesture conveys to the eye. Of course, it is bound at all times to the 'verse melody' as harmonic support, so that both elements form a unified nexus. Another primary function of 'orchestral melody' described in *Opera and Drama* is the deployment of motifs of 'anticipation'* and recollection or 'reminiscence'*, i.e. the 'Leitmotif'*. It is evident that Wagner is already trying to imagine here an orchestral texture constituted primarily of such associative motivic material, as he intended to implement in the composition of his Nibelung cycle.

Patriarchal melody. The term applied to the simple, hymn-like setting of the first verse of Schiller's ode *To Joy* ('Freude, schöner Götterfunken') in Beethoven's Ninth Symphony, deriving from Wagner's sociological metaphors of tonality and key relations in *Opera and Drama*, Part III. The notes of any single diatonic scale are compared to the members of an extended 'patriarchal' tribe, of which the tonic note functions as ruling patriarch. Beethoven's melody, like most traditional folk tunes and hymns, is 'patriarchal' because it remains entirely within the ambitus of a single scale (D). The tribal-family metaphor is further developed to explain the principles of musical modulation ('marriage' between families or tribes).

Poetic intent (*dichterische Absicht*). A concept loosely developed by Wagner over the course of *Opera and Drama*, understood to embody the essential conceptual 'truths' that the poet-dramatist seeks to convey. This poetic 'intent' also serves as the motivating – or here, 'fertilizing' – agent of the musical drama. Although the term occurs several times in passing in Part I, it is only consciously developed in the later sections of Part II, and then more fully in Part III ('Poetry and Music in the Drama of the Future'). At the end of Part II, in particular, Wagner develops this concept according to the metaphor of sexual reproduction: the poetic intent is the 'fertilizing seed' with which poetry (as the 'male' principle) inseminates music (the 'female' principle). From this union the musical drama is born. The burden of Wagner's sexual metaphor is twofold: (1) music, as a medium of pure expression, can only take on definite shape ('give birth') under some verbal, conceptual influence, and (2) the rational, reflective component of poetry (language) is incapable of reaching the genuine emotional sympathies of an audience until it enters into such a procreative union with music, the medium of pure and immediate expression. Throughout Part III Wagner speaks repeatedly of the 'realization' (*Verwirklichung*) of the poetic intent in the musical drama, stressing the need for this verbal, rational element to disappear or 'dissolve' in music. One might say that it must be sublated into music ('*aufgehoben*', in Hegelian terms) in order to be received on a purely emotional level by its audience, with no need of reflection or conceptual mediation. To the modern observer Wagner's doctrine of aesthetic immediacy may appear somewhat at odds with the complexities of his musical idiom, the frequent obscurity of his dramatic texts, and most of all with the problematics of the leitmotif.

Poetic-musical period. In *Opera and Drama* (Part III, section 3) Wagner describes a 'poetic-musical period' (*dichterisch-musikalische Periode*) as the basic structural unit of his ideal musical drama or 'artwork of the future'. Such a unit is to be understood as the necessary, appropriate alternative to the 'absolute-musical' period governing the melodic structure of conventional instrumental music and formal operatic 'numbers' alike. The reputation, or notoriety, of this term is largely due to its appropriation by Alfred Lorenz as the theoretical justification – deriving from the composer's own 'scriptural' authority – of his exhaustive formal analyses of the complete mature Wagnerian oeuvre. The *Opera and Drama* passage does represent one of Wagner's few relatively concrete pronouncements on matters of tonality and form. Like so much in his writings, however, the passage still remains frustratingly vague, even where it appears to offer technical insight into musical procedure. (The situation is perhaps only to be expected, considering that Wagner was struggling to formulate aesthetic and compositional principles for a radical musical undertaking he was still far from beginning, aside from a few abortive sketches). The concept of a 'poetic-musical period' essentially aims to express the fundamental difference between melodic structure and harmonic progression as determined by a 'poetic intent' (i.e. dramatic text) and the formulaic periodicity of the conventional operatic aria, ensemble or choral number. It is, again, typical of *Opera and Drama* that the theoretical formulation is far too dogmatically prescriptive for practical implementation.

Specifically, Wagner proposes that the 'Verse melody'* will remain within the ambitus of a single diatonic (major or minor) scale so long as the poetic affect informing it remains constant. As the expressive sense of the verse changes, the melodic line will 'modulate' freely to other key areas, closely related or further removed according to the scope of the 'emotional modulation' (so to speak) occurring in the text. Both congruent and contrasting affects may be unified, on a local level, by means of alliteration or *Stabreim**: for instance, the series *Liebe*, *Lust* and *Leid* ('love', 'pleasure' and 'sorrow'), or *Weh*, *webt* and *Wonnen* ('woe', 'weaves' and 'delight'). But it is left to the greater expressive-structural potential of musical modulation to embody a larger progression away from and back to a given point, i.e. from *Liebe* to *Wonnen* across the two series cited here (GS IV, 152–3). It was this suggestion of tonal closure that Lorenz cited in support of his analyses of tonally defined segments throughout the *Ring* and other operas, in conjunction with patterns of motivic exposition, development (variation) and reprise. Wagner does indeed speak of a controlling 'principal key' (*Haupttonart*) in this context, but Lorenz's zealous search for consistent tonal closure at all levels has been much criticized as a misrepresentation of the fluid, open-ended and evolutionary character of the musical-dramatic forms actually created by Wagner, and which are generally emphasized in other of his writings.

Quadratic melody. In the 1871 essay *Über die Bestimmung der Oper* (*On the Destiny of Opera*) Wagner speaks of the 'conventional quadratic structure of the musical phrase' ('Quadratur einer konventionellen Tonsatzkonstruktion'), which Beethoven's melody 'overgrew' in amazingly vital profusion yet without quite obscuring its own roots there. The state of 'sublime irregularity' exemplified by the Shakespearian drama – a goal towards which Beethoven's melody seemed to aspire – is only possible, we are told, when music is freed from its foundations in the symmetrical periodicity of song and dance forms by means of the drama (GS IX, 149). This critique of melodic *Quadratur* – the foundation of Classic-Romantic phrase structure on metrical units of 2, 4, 8 or 16 bars – recurs throughout Wagner's writings and is fundamental to his belief in the aesthetic imperative of drama as the means of emancipating music's fullest expressive potential.

Related formulations crop up at the end of *Über das Opern-Dichten und Komponieren im Besonderen* (*On Opera Libretti and Composition in Particular*, 1871), where Wagner speaks of the 'rhythmic and harmonic *Quadratur*' ('der Quadratur des Rhythmus und der Modulation') that forms the musical analogue of stereotyped, conventional operatic figures, theatrical 'masks' or 'figurines', invoking the heritage of Rossini (GS X, 174).

Reminiscence (recollection, *Erinnerung*), **motifs of.** See also 'Anticipation, motifs of'*, 'Leitmotif'*. The term now applied to a fairly widespread operatic practice since the later 18th century may originate with Wagner, who envisioned in *Opera and Drama* a consistently deployed network of motivic forecasts and flashbacks. The technique of thematic reminiscence had been frequently applied, with varying degrees of sophistication, by previous generations. Such a reminiscence could take the form of the reprise of an entire strophe or song (with text) to the subtle recollection of an individual melody, motif, or even chord or timbre at some dramatically apposite moment. The 'proto-leitmotivic' procedures of Wagner's earliest operas grow directly out of this recent French-German tradition.

In *Opera and Drama* Wagner develops the idea within the speculative framework of his ideal dramatic 'artwork of the future'. The 'system' proposed here is founded on the relation of all motivic occurrences – either as 'anticipation' or as 'reminiscence' – to a definitive congruence of motif and text, as 'Verse melody'*, the moment at which the principal textual or dramatic association of the musical motif is 'officially' established. The disposi-

tion of such motivic reminiscences across the drama will serve as 'emotional guide-posts through the entire, elaborately plotted structure of the drama' (GS IV, 200). In practice, naturally, the reminiscence motif assumed far greater prominence than the motif of anticipation, since Wagner's conception of the drama depended on a strictly limited number of dramatic motifs or situations, as well as a limited number of recognizable musical motifs. Furthermore, much of the power of Wagner's motivic procedure derives from the expressively significant modification of musical ideas (rhythm, harmony, orchestration, etc.), which are logically limited to 'reminiscence' contexts.

Romantic opera. The designation 'Romantic opera' has been applied to a wide variety of works ranging from late 18th-century *opéra comique* (works such as Grétry's *Zémire et Azor* and *Richard Coeur-de-lion*, Méhul's *Ariodant* or the operas of Cherubini), German Singspiel and Viennese magic opera (Reichardt's *Die Geisterinsel*, Wranitzky's *Oberon*) to French grand opera and the Italian *melodramma* of the earlier 19th century. It is predominantly associated, however, with German opera from Weber up to the middle-period works of Wagner: *Der fliegende Holländer* (1840–41), *Tannhäuser* (1843–5) and *Lohengrin* (1846–8). Before Weber the genre is construed primarily according to subject-matter – medieval, legendary or exotic material in contrast to the Classical orientation of the Metastasian *opera seria* and the operas of Gluck. The paradigmatic work of German Romantic opera, Weber's *Der Freischütz* (1821), drew on recent traditions of *opéra comique* in its combination of popular, sentimental and folk-like material (and dialogue) with more experimental, 'descriptive' elements (the Wolf's Glen Scene) and through-composed finales of a free, additive structure. The folkloristic tradition of *Der Freischütz* and of Marschner's operas, with their admixture of the supernatural and the macabre, is evident in *Der fliegende Holländer*. But perhaps a greater influence was exerted on Wagner's earlier works by Weber's 'grand heroic-Romantic opera', *Euryanthe*, clearly evident in *Die Feen* and still in much of *Tannhäuser* and *Lohengrin*. The earlier two both share the genre designation of *Euryanthe* as 'grosse romantische Oper', while *Lohengrin* (like the *Holländer*) is labelled simply a 'romantische Oper'. A central impulse of this extremely diverse genre can be seen, as Carl Dahlhaus (1986) mentions, in the attempt at musical realization of Friedrich Schlegel's categories of the 'characteristic', the 'striking', and the 'interesting', manifested in a tendency towards melodic fragmentation and the 'emancipation' of instrumental timbres.

Stollen. One of the two stanzas which, followed by a contrasting and somewhat lengthier *Abgesang**, make up the '*Bar* form'* used by Wagner for the various formal song structures in *Die Meistersinger*.

Stabreim. The alliterative verse form used in old Germanic poetry (including Anglo-Saxon), possibly developed as a mnemonic device for oral recitation and transmission. Wagner's use of *Stabreim* in the *Ring* derives, naturally, from his ancient Teutonic sources. Traditionally, *Stabreim* was organized into verse-pairs of two (sometimes three) stresses each, which were unified by alliteration of the first and/or accented syllables.

Having implemented *Stabreim* in the first poetic draft of *Siegfrieds Tod* (1848) Wagner went on to offer an extensive critical defence of it as the necessary and, indeed, only possible verse form for the 'musical drama of the future'. He stresses its ancestry in the 'instinctive' creative impulses of early folk-culture: 'It was this same alliterative verse [*stabgereimter Vers*] in which, inspired by natural speech accents and the most lively sense of rhythm [...], the *Volk* created its poetry, back when the *Volk* was still poet and mythmaker.' (GS IV, 329) In addition he develops a rather speculative argument about the etymological relation of word roots according to consonant 'families' and the significance of this for the natural, immediate communication of semantic and affective content. *Stabreim*, he claimed, reinforced the original relation of music to language as expressive sound-media (GS IV, 137–8).

Throughout the *Ring* Wagner experimented with countless alliterative patterns, often extending beyond the traditional pair of lines. Sometimes the verse-pair will encompass multiple, interlocking alliterations, as in this chiastic pattern from Scene 1 of *Das Rheingold*: 'Mit Händen und Füssen / nicht fasse noch halt' ich', or in the following three verses: 'Feuchtes Nass / füllt mir die Nase – / verfluchtes Niesen!' (as can be seen in the last line, the alliterative syllable may follow a prefix). See also 'Wagner as librettist', pp. 266–7.

Tondichter (tone-poet). See 'Tone-speech'.

Tone-speech (*Tonsprache*). In the Zurich writings and later essays, but above all in *Opera and Drama*, Wagner appealed to familiar analogies between music and language, and to philosophical speculations as to their common roots in the earliest, prehistorical stages of human communication (in this he drew on similar speculative arguments advanced by such 18th-century *philosophes* as Rousseau and Herder). '*Tonsprache* ["tone-speech"] is the beginning and end of *Wortsprache* ["word-speech"]', he proclaims (GS IV, 91). He tries to establish a loose correlation of these two 'linguistic modes' in the phenomenon of *Stabreim**, which highlights the sonorous element of language (*Wortsprache*). *Wortsprache* is the medium of rational thought and the communication of conceptual content, while *Ton-*

sprache remains the vehicle of direct expressive, emotional communication. Hence the poet's instinctive drive towards genuine emotional communication will only be fulfilled, according to Wagner, when he turns to the medium of *Ton*, when spoken language is transformed by music. Wagner also employs the related forms 'word-poet' and 'tone-poet' (*Wortdichter*, *Tondichter*), the latter already having been proudly sported by Beethoven, on occasion.

Total artwork. See '*Gesamtkunstwerk*'.

Transition, art of. In a letter of 29 October 1859, several months after completing the score of *Tristan und Isolde*, Wagner confided to Mathilde Wesendonck that he had recently come to see the 'art of transition' ('*Kunst des Übergangs*') as perhaps his 'finest and deepest art'. He identifies the tendency towards the depiction of emotional extremes as a characteristic he shares with the French Romantics (Victor Hugo, Berlioz), but with the difference that he seeks to mediate between these extremes by means of subtle and gradual transition. The essence of his musical 'fabric' or texture (*Gewebe*) is to be found here. 'My greatest masterpiece in the art of detailed, gradual transition is without a doubt the great scene in Act II of *Tristan und Isolde*. The beginning of the scene presents life at its most ecstatic, the eruption of the most violent emotions – the conclusion, then, the most solemn, inner yearning for death. Those are the pillars [of the scene]: just look, my child, how one gets from one to the other! For that is in fact the secret of my musical form [...].'

Wagner's phrase has been invoked to support a great variety of analytical points. Carl Dahlhaus, for example, points to a subtle overlapping of opposing textual and motivic 'signifiers' in *Tristan* Act II scene 2, where the energetic, jubilant figure accompanying the lovers' meeting continues to echo in the orchestra even after the dialogue has turned towards the sorrows of 'Day'. Wagner's 'art of transition' is most immediately evident in such musical-scenic transitions as those between the scenes of *Das Rheingold* or leading into the Grail temple scenes in *Parsifal*. The gradated transition between emotional extremes that Wagner cites in *Tristan* suggests that he was thinking of large-scale processes, typically accomplished by means of gradually increasing (or decreasing) 'waves' of musical intensity (tempo, orchestral texture, rhythmic and motivic activity, etc.) such as one also finds in the closing scenes of *Die Walküre* or *Siegfried*.

Unendliche Melodie. See 'Infinite melody'.

Verse melody (*Versmelodie*). The concept of 'verse melody' developed in Part III of *Opera and Drama* (GS IV, 116–17) refers to the conjunction of a poetic text and its musical setting in the vocal line of an opera (or, by extension, song). As presented here, the 'verse melody' of the ideal Wagnerian drama is meant to respond closely to the detailed nuances of natural, spoken inflection and accent, while the orchestral accompaniment ('orchestral melody') will provide a sense of the psychological-emotional substratum – that which is left 'unsaid' by the verse melody, although it may be expressed in physical stance, facial expression, gesture, etc. Insofar as this verse melody observes the natural, spoken accents of the poetic lines it will tend to render these as 'prose', overriding the artificial metrical accent of the verse and the implied caesuras of end-rhyme (where it occurs). Verse melody is further imagined as a skiff carried by the 'sounding waves' of the orchestra, representing the harmonic depths of Wagner's metaphorical ocean. According to *Opera and Drama* the 'fundamental motifs' (*Grundmotive**) – recurring, dramatically associative melodic figures (*melodische Momente*) or 'leitmotifs'* – acquire their objective meaning as verse melody in conjunction with significant passages of the dramatic text. They may be anticipated or recollected by the orchestra, but it is in the context of verse melody that their associative meaning is to be communicated most clearly (this overlooks the possibility of generating a semantic 'content' for orchestral motifs by means of gesture or dramatic context alone). Among the nearly synonymous terms used by Wagner are 'song melody', 'word-tone melody', and 'dramatic melody (*Gesangsmelodie, Worttonmelodie, dramatische Melodie*).

Wahn. This elusive concept, enshrined in Hans Sachs's so-called *Wahn* Monologue at the heart of *Die Meistersinger* (Act III scene 1), defies adequate translation. Definitions cited by Ernest Newman (1949) include 'erroneous or false opinion', 'illusion', 'delusion', 'hallucination', 'error', 'monomania', 'folly' and 'madness'. Of these, 'illusion' and 'madness' are the operative meanings in *Die Meistersinger*. Sachs's monologue begins as a meditation on the 'midsummer madness' that had precipitated the previous evening's public brawl. This seemingly innocent bit of local *Wahn* is perceived as a microcosmic manifestation of the violence and instability inherent in human relations through the ages. *Wahn* also connotes here phenomena of mass psychology and collective hysteria. (The more

common word *Wahnsinn* – craziness, insanity, nonsense – echoes this sense of the root word.)

But at the end of the monologue, and in the ensuing scene with Walther, Sachs makes a connection between such hysterical behaviour and the nature of artistic inspiration (Romantically interpreted as a kind of 'divine, poetic frenzy' – Nietzsche's Dionysian principle). Walther reports that a beautiful song has been revealed to him 'in a dream'. Sachs sees it as the mentor's role to 'channel' this subconscious Dionysian creative energy, to 'deftly guide this *Wahn* towards noble works'. Thus he helps adapt Walther's 'natural' musical inspiration to the specific requisites of a *Meisterlied*.

During the genesis of *Die Meistersinger* Wagner expounded the broader implications of *Wahn* in *Über Staat und Religion* (*On State and Religion*, 1864), written for his new royal patron, Ludwig II. In this context *Wahn* takes on a therapeutic, quasi-religious identity: the *Wahn* represented by the arch-Romantic Wagnerian drama will serve to inspire the monarch with a transcendent vision of his own calling. Wagner's enduring fascination with the concept (and his strong identification with the figure of his world-weary poet-musician Hans Sachs) was memorialized in the name for his Bayreuth villa ('Wahnfried') and inscribed, literally, in the motto below the decorative frieze or *sgraffito* adorning the main entrance:

> Hier, wo mein Wähnen Frieden fand
> WAHNFRIED
> Sei dieses Haus von mir benannt.

> Here where my illusions have come to rest,
> Let this house be named by me 'Wahnfried'
> [i.e. peace from illusion or madness]

Word-tone-speech (*Worttonsprache*). One of the plethora of music-aesthetic neologisms of *Opera and Drama*, essentially synonymous with the more consistently used term 'Verse melody'*, which refers to the conjunction of melody and poetic text in the vocal line of the ideal musical drama. More precisely, *Worttonsprache* would be the universal category ('language') of which 'verse melody' represents the particular instance.

Wortsprache. See 'Tone-speech'.

Zukunftsmusik. See 'Music of the future'.

THOMAS S. GREY

Section 11
MUSICAL STYLE

Compositional process   244
Musical language   248

MUSICAL STYLE

THE AVAILABILITY OF Wagner's sketches and drafts suggests that the study of his operas might profitably be founded upon an examination of these documents. Yet sketch study can be employed for various ends: to establish chronology, to verify biographical facts, or to elucidate what is known as 'compositional process'. The section 'Autograph manuscripts' (see pp.196–221) offers some examples of how even undated scraps of paper can sometimes help establish matters of chronology – as, for instance, the fact that the prose sketch for *Das Rheingold* probably preceded that for *Die Walküre*. As regards biography, some scholars have made almost a fetish out of using the manuscripts to disprove or at least seriously challenge certain statements in Wagner's autobiography *Mein Leben* (*My Life*). This can prove an amusing and by no means irrelevant pastime, but its relentless scepticism eventually wears rather thin. Far more productive is the use of sketches and drafts to elucidate compositional process. Knowledge of how a master composer such as Wagner actually went about putting notes on paper is fascinating in its own right; in addition, such knowledge can often aid – and at times even correct – interpretation and analysis.

Because Wagner wrote his own operatic texts, the study of compositional process should really begin with an investigation of how he constructed his libretti. This is explored in the section 'Sketches/drafts (text)' (see pp.196–203), which the reader is invited to consult. The present discussion is thus confined to musical composition. Because Wagner's method of preliminary sketching is outlined in 'Sketches/drafts (music)' (see pp. 203–19), we will focus here upon the next step, the phase that Wagner himself considered the actual act of composition: the writing of the complete draft(s). Wagner's complete pencil draft for *Das Rheingold* is described in some detail in 'Sketches/drafts (music)', and the reader may wish to review that description before continuing with the present account.

The early method

Wagner changed his method of composition several times, with the result that his complete drafts differ in format and complexity. In fact, the first extended manuscripts of *Der fliegende Holländer* and *Tannhäuser* cannot rightly be called 'complete drafts' at all. Working from preliminary sketches, Wagner drafted individual numbers (*Holländer*) or whole scenes (*Tannhäuser*), not necessarily in chronological order. He then assembled these numbers or scenes into proper sequence, producing a more or less continuous manuscript. In the case of *Der fliegende Holländer*, Wagner used this draft, in which he had sketched the accompaniment on two staves, to make an orchestral score. For *Tannhäuser*, however, he made a second complete draft in ink. Whereas the first draft contains only one instrumental stave, the second elaborates the accompaniment on two staves; more important, it was written act by act in chronological order. Thus, only the second of the two *Tannhäuser* manuscripts is a true 'complete draft' of the sort associated with the later operas.

With *Lohengrin*, Wagner began his practice of drafting each act as a whole from beginning to end, starting with the first (he still, of course, worked from preliminary sketches). Thus the first continuous manuscript of this opera can accurately be called a 'complete draft'. It is mostly written on two staves, one for the voice, the other for the accompaniment; but the latter is very sketchy, and the harmonic structure is often merely suggested by a bass line. He then made a second complete draft, in which he elaborated the accompaniment on two staves, using more staves for extra vocal and choral parts; however, he began with Act III, probably because he intended to make some important changes to the text. The oft-quoted statement that Wagner began the composition of *Lohengrin* with Act III is therefore not true, but refers to his preparation of the second complete draft. From this latter document he prepared the score.

Das Rheingold and *Die Walküre*

Working from the preliminary and/or supplementary sketches described in 'Sketches/drafts (music)' (see pp.203–17), Wagner wrote out the complete draft of *Das Rheingold* from beginning to end, in pencil. In many ways, this document (described earlier) resembles the first complete draft for *Lohengrin*. At this stage of the work (and it was really the most important stage), Wagner was primarily concerned with setting the text. He therefore wrote out the vocal line on one staff and the instrumental part on another; however, the latter often amounts to little more than a bass line, sometimes with a sketch of the harmony. Occasionally Wagner elaborated the accompaniment on two staves, especially when he wished to bring in an orchestral melody. In some cases the handwriting suggests that the orchestral part was written first and the vocal line added later, but this is the exception rather than the rule. Wagner worked out purely instrumental passages (such as the orchestral interludes between scenes) on two staves, sometimes having recourse to three. The general sparseness of texture suggests that Wagner fully intended to make a second, more elaborate draft in ink, as he had done for *Lohengrin*.

However, an elaboration of the Prelude, an *auskomponierte* E♭ major triad, would have come so close to being a full score anyway that Wagner decided to go ahead and make one right away. He therefore wrote out an ink score of the Prelude; in doing so, he significantly revised the complete draft version, drawing upon materials from the Erda episode of Scene 4 (see Darcy, 1989, for details). When he reached the beginning of Scene 1, he found that he could not automatically score his complete draft; in addition, the latter was permeated by the figurations of the original Prelude, and these now needed to be replaced by the new Erda arpeggiations. He therefore abandoned his full ink score, and began a pencil sketch of the instrumentation (the so-called 'instrumentation draft' described in 'Sketches/drafts (music)', p.219–20). His general procedure was to write out the vocal line from the complete draft at the top of a page, the bass line (usually assigned to cellos and double basses) at the bottom, then bring in instruments and groups of instruments as needed, in no particular order or arrangement. Sometimes, however, he needed to make a preparatory sketch of a passage's instrumentation. He did this in two places: on unused staves of the instrumentation draft, and in the complete draft itself. Thus many of the instrumental markings and sketches in the complete draft date from the time of scoring, and were not part of Wagner's initial conception. Failure to recognize this fact led Curt von Westernhagen (1973) to many erroneous conclusions about Wagner's compositional process. In addition, some passages in the complete draft needed to be heavily revised, if not actually recomposed. Wagner sometimes reworked a passage in the margins of the instrumentation draft before scoring it; thus, in addition to providing insight into Wagner's method of orchestration, this document also contains instances of actual recomposition, and forms an invaluable link between the complete draft and the full score. However, because the instrumentation draft is not set up like a regular score at all (except for the Prelude), Wagner found it necessary – for the first time in his career – to make a fair copy in ink. Further details may be found in 'Scores' (see pp.219–20).

Before he had completed this fair copy, Wagner started the composition of *Die Walküre*. As with *Das Rheingold*, he began with a complete draft in pencil, working out the entire opera from beginning to end. However, he took care to elaborate this draft to a greater degree than the one for *Das Rheingold*: often the instrumental accompaniment is sketched on two staves rather than one, and even where only one instrumental staff is involved it frequently contains much more detail than had been the case for most of *Das Rheingold*.

The scoring of *Das Rheingold* having thoroughly familiarized Wagner with his new *Ring* orchestra, he found it unnecessary to make an instrumentation draft for *Die Walküre*; he therefore began a full pencil score. However, the composition of this opera had stretched out over a much longer period of time than that for *Das Rheingold*, and Wagner experienced further interruptions and delays while scoring. The result was that often he could not decipher the 'unfamiliar hieroglyphics' of his complete draft, and had to compose some passages all over again. Because of Wagner's need to devote time to purely compositional matters, the scoring of *Die Walküre*, while certainly effective, does not represent much of an advance over that of *Das Rheingold*. The fact that he began his full score in pencil suggests that he had resigned himself in advance to the necessity of making two scores, a pencil draft and a fair copy in ink.

The later method

When Wagner began the composition of *Siegfried*, he was determined not to repeat the mistake he had made with *Die Walküre* — that is, allowing an inordinate amount of time to elapse between his first rough sketch of a passage and its eventual orchestration. His solution to this problem was twofold: first, he would henceforth compose and orchestrate each act at a time before going on to the next. Second, he would return to his earlier procedure of making *two* complete drafts, but this time he would work back and forth between them. His first complete draft for *Siegfried* is in pencil, is similar to that for *Die Walküre*, and about as detailed as the second complete (ink) drafts of *Tannhäuser* and *Lohengrin*. However, his second complete draft for *Siegfried* is a fully developed affair on at least three staves (two instrumental plus one vocal) which works out the musical texture down to the details of its final orchestral setting, including instrumental doublings. Otto Strobel called this document an '*Orchesterskizze*' ('orchestral sketch'), and he also employed this term for the much less detailed second drafts of *Tannhäuser* and *Lohengrin*. However, Strobel's terminology imparts a false sense of consistency to Wagner's compositional method, and 'orchestral sketch' is best replaced by 'second complete draft'.

Wagner's compositional method remained fairly constant from now on: two complete drafts (the first in pencil, the second in ink) plus a score. He would sketch a passage in the first draft and almost immediately elaborate it in the second; orchestration could be done whenever time allowed. At first he still felt the need to make two full scores, a pencil draft and a fair copy. As is well known, Wagner broke off work on the *Ring* after he had completed the second complete draft of *Siegfried* Act II, the pencil score of Act I, and the fair copy of Act I scene 1. He then turned his attention to *Tristan und Isolde*, a work whose conception had been pressing upon him rather insistently. As mentioned in 'Scores' (see p.221), he saw each act of *Tristan* through to the engraving before beginning the next, but after the Prelude to Act I he made only a single ink score. The composition of *Die Meistersinger von Nürnberg* followed. Starting with the second act of this opera, Wagner changed his procedure once again (or, rather, reverted to an earlier procedure), so that he completed the entire opera in his second complete draft before beginning the full score. However, the second complete draft now became extremely elaborate: the instrumental texture occupies two or three staves in the vocal sections, and as many as four or five in the purely orchestral sections. Wagner himself referred to this stage as an '*Orchesterskizze*' (as did Strobel), Bailey calls it an 'orchestral draft', and it is sometimes termed a 'short score' or 'particell', but we may follow the editors of the WWV in considering it a greatly developed second complete draft.

In September 1864 Wagner returned to his fair copy of *Siegfried*, finishing Act I scene 2; in December he began the pencil score of Act II, completing it a year later. In March 1869 he began the composition of Act III, finishing the second complete draft in August; he then completed his ink score, the fully developed second complete draft making two scores of Act III unnecessary. The composition of *Parsifal* followed along the same lines as that of the last two acts of *Die Meistersinger* and the third act of *Siegfried*: two complete drafts written concurrently, followed by a full ink score.

WARREN DARCY

Musical language

WAGNER, IT MIGHT BE ARGUED with some force, did not have a *musical* language at all, in that only very rarely did he compose with no extra-musical concepts in mind. It is certainly true that, in discussing Wagner's musical procedures, we are in danger of producing a distorted picture if we lose sight of the theatrical end towards which the musical means were directed. At the same time, however, the nature of the theatrical events as Wagner conceived them made it increasingly possible for music to seize the initiative in shaping and characterizing those events. In 1851, Wagner was in no doubt that he had mastered 'the language of music' – 'die Sprache der Musik': and yet, 'what can be expressed in the language of music is only *feelings* and *emotions*. [. . .] What remains inexpressible in the language of music by itself is an exact definition of the object of feeling and emotion. [. . .] This it acquires only by being wedded to verbal language' (*Eine Mitteilung an meine Freunde* – *A Communication to my Friends*) (GS IV, 317–18). Wagner attached great importance to that 'exact definition of the object', at least during his first phase of work on the *Ring*. Yet it was the emotion that music brought to that object which he valued above all. As early as 1844, while at work on *Tannhäuser*, he made this famous declaration to Karl Gaillard:

> It is not my practice to choose a subject at random, to versify it then think of suitable music to write for it; – if I were to proceed in that way I should be exposed to the difficulty of having to work myself up to a pitch of enthusiasm on two separate occasions, something which is imposs-ible. No, my method of production is different from that: – in the first place I am attracted only by those subjects that reveal themselves to me not only as poetically but, at the same time, as musically significant. And so, even before I set about writing a single line of the text or drafting a scene, I am already thoroughly immersed in the musical aura of my new creation. (30 Jan 1844)

Three years later, Wagner made his no less celebrated declaration to Eduard Hanslick that 'I have no special ambition to see my poetry overshadowed by my music, but I should be guilty of dismembering myself & exposing an untruth if I were to insist upon doing violence to the music for the sake of the poem. I cannot broach a poetic subject if it is not already conditioned by the music.' (1 Jan 1847) The importance of the eventual musical realization cannot be over-emphasized, even though sketch studies suggest that Wagner did not write down any very elaborate musical materials while producing his libretti; and even though being 'thoroughly immersed in the musical aura' is not the same thing as having a clear and detailed idea of what form those musical materials would ultimately take. Wagner's belief in the unique power of the theatre was expressed through his sense of the unique power of music. 'Wagner took a genre previously half ceremonial pomp, half entertainment, and declared it to be the ne plus ultra of art.' (Dahlhaus 1989a) To make that 'declaration' work in practice required the establishment and development of appropriate musical elements, and those elements would be quite different from those that had obtained in opera as traditionally conceived. While we may rightly be sceptical of Wagner's own attempt to persuade us that he owed everything to Beethoven and nothing to anyone else, therefore, the most fascinating objective in examining Wagner's music is not to establish his sources or define his working methods, but to demonstrate how he responded to the immense challenge presented by his desire to create a new kind of musical theatre: and that demonstration is not simply a matter of identifying the terms, or elements, of the musical language, but of studying its grammar – the way in which the elements are used.

There are obvious musical influences at work in Wagner's early operas: Weber and Marschner in *Die Feen*; Bellini and Auber (among others), in *Das Liebesverbot*. Here the primitive adumbration of what would become the leitmotivic technique serves to establish its provenance in French as well as German opera. Nevertheless, more important than any incipient progressiveness of language (more radically chromatic harmony, for example) in the early operas, including *Rienzi*, is the increasing expansiveness and flexibility of form, the direct result of contact with the world of grand opera. That flexibility may not yet be sufficient to counter the impression of a reliance on monotonously four-square phrase structure, but there is already a quality of memorable melodic economy that is fundamental to the formation of Wagner's mature style.

Anyone who can call the melody of Rienzi's Prayer to mind, and compare it with other characteristic Wagner themes – for example, the Pilgrims' Chorus from *Tannhäuser*, the Wedding March from *Lohengrin*, the Valhalla music that begins Scene 2 of *Das Rheingold*, or the Prize Song from *Die Meistersinger* – may well see some point in the argument that the essence of Wagner's power as a musical dramatist lies in simplicity. There is a directness of emotional utterance that stems from a strong initial shape, self-contained enough to possess a clear identity, but open-ended enough to imply continuation. There is always the sense of something archetypal in Wagner's most prominent motifs, and a sense of something compellingly goal-directed, though not inexorably unified, in the way he builds up forms – periods, scenes, entire acts – from immediate or displaced repetitions, more or less varied, of themes and their evolving transformations. In order to create his new theatre of myth and epic, Wagner needed a language, and a method, which were not so much original (even his later style owed much to Liszt, for example) as of the greatest variety and flexibility in order to sustain and integrate all aspects of the theatrical event. To a considerable extent he seems to have turned for a model (consciously or instinctively) to the great 19th-century image of nature as organically evolving from the simplest, most profound entities to generate the great diversity of the contemporary world. Just as his subject-matter would disdain the ordinary and the everyday, so his musical style would reject the superficial attractions of vocal display and the succession of distinct, tidily structured formal units with their classically balanced phrases. It would offer a constructive critique of the failings of traditional operatic composition by building on symphonic, Beethovenian foundations. Yet just as in developing his subject-matter Wagner found that the idea of new worlds rising bravely from the ruins of old was less neatly Utopian than it at first appeared, so in the creation of his music an initial vision of progress from old arbitrariness to new consistency proved less straightforward in practice. Instead of pithy basic ideas expanding irresistibly to generate integrated forms of unprecedented power and length, the pithiness tended to contrast with the impulse to large-scale formal integration as much as to promote it.

From the purely practical point of view, it is obviously possible for listeners to reach the point where they know Wagner's works well enough to remember what comes next, in word and tone alike. Because they are never at a loss, they can hold in balance the competing claims of the integrative (primarily, the small or larger-scale recurrences of musical material) and the progressive (the changing contexts in which the recurrences occur). There is undoubtedly much aesthetic satisfaction for the listener in sensing that the climactic quality of Lohengrin's 'In fernem Land', or Brünnhilde's final salutation to Wotan and Valhalla in *Götterdämmerung*, owes something fundamental to the fact that in essence the music for these new and decisive events is not being heard for the first time. The musical recyclings embody a formal discipline, in response to the aesthetic principle that coherent progress through a work by means of absolute and constant change is inconceivable. Wagner is therefore using music to constrain the evolutionary potential of his dramatic subject-matter: the plot reaches its crisis, and the sheer momentousness of that crisis can only be conveyed if new and old are brought together in the audience's perception.

Familiar characters are shown in an unprecedented situation, but the music contributes decisively to the sense of impending closure by drawing its own threads together.

The satisfaction of ultimate closure is all the stronger in Wagner because the clear-cut formal divisions of traditional opera – the succession of separate numbers, each ending with an emphatic cadence – are no longer present. In *Don Giovanni* or *The Barber of Seville* these cadences act as structural dividers, interrupting the flow and encouraging the listener to concentrate less on how successive numbers connect than on how they complement each other and contribute to the unfolding of the drama as a sequence of distinct, unrepeatable entities. Yet Wagner's long, continuous acts would offer far less satisfaction to the listener if they were not also subdivided, not simply by the obvious changes of mood and character that go with the succession of events within the act, but by breaks in the musical flow within scenes – breaks that have specific and often subtle dramatic functions, even when they do not conform neatly to the concept of poetic-musical periods presented theoretically in *Oper und Drama* (*Opera and Drama*). The plausible argument that, 'with fundamental motives already in mind, Wagner literally improvised from one moment to the next, often too engrossed in smaller forms and immediate effects to pay much attention to larger formal relationships' (Deathridge, 1977b) does not itself justify the conclusion that continuity within and between those 'smaller forms and immediate effects' mattered more than it did on the largest scale. But it may discourage the glib assumption that Wagner's concern was less with balancing the claims of many different contrasting features than with imposing 'unity', as the sole guarantee of structural and aesthetic coherence.

Matters of large-scale organization will be considered later in this chapter. First, however, it is necessary to define the main elements of Wagner's musical language. In the realm of pitch material, the most basic feature is the tonal system, whose twelve major and twelve minor keys embody a whole nexus of vital concepts to do with degrees of relationship and modes of procedure, within and between keys. Wagner was by no means unusually radical for the second half of the 19th century in regarding a 'key' as embracing both major and minor modes on a given tonic, nor in accepting the principle that a key and its parallel major or minor (A minor and C major, for example) could be brought together within a single harmonic complex. Neither was Wagner particularly ahead of his time when it came to the treatment of tonal harmony's most essential distinction, between consonance and dissonance. Because a dissonance (in effect, any chord other than the basic major or minor triads) had more powerful expressive potential than any consonance, it might be given more emphasis and treated more freely than textbooks allowed. For Wagner, after all, harmonic and tonal relations were means to an end: to provide the most effective context for the musical ideas. It would be a serious distortion to suggest that Wagner's musical ideas were always primarily melodic: very few of his principal motifs do not depend as much on harmonic context as melodic shape for their character, and some – the Tarnhelm motif from the *Ring* is one of the easiest to recall – are more chord than tune. Moreover, that process of continuous melodic evolution, or 'endless melody', so vital to the Wagnerian language, is inconceivable without the controlling, shaping context provided by the harmony. Wagner's own discussions of these matters – for instance, his famous contention in *Opera and Drama* that change of key should always coincide with a significant shift of verbal meaning – tend to be attempts to work out a clear-cut position on technical procedures, rather than the statement of such a position. But it is clear enough, especially from his comments in the late essay *Über die Anwendung der Musik auf das Drama* (*On the Application of Music to Drama*, 1879), that he saw harmony as crucial to the integrative fabric of his music, and as having a role which might well lead to effects that would appear as 'empty sensationalism' if they occurred in a symphony: his example is the emphasis on the transformed version of the Rhinemaidens' song in praise of the gold heard in Hagen's Watch (Act I of *Götterdämmerung*).

The eventual, delayed resolution of dissonance onto consonance that is one fundamental facet of the Wagnerian style is encapsulated with special memorability in the final bars of *Tristan*, where the famous '*Tristan* chord' moves beyond the partial resolution (like that onto the dominant seventh at the work's opening) that has tended to be its lot, onto a full close within the work's ultimate (Plagal) cadence. No less fundamental a feature is the tendency for such dissonant chords not to fit neatly into the prevailing key: even the '*Tristan* chord' – as a so-called 'half-diminished' seventh, a relatively mild dissonance – displays a foreign, chromatic element on its final appearance since one of its four pitches (E$\sharp$) does not belong to the prevailing tonality of B major. General discussions of Wagner's music probably make more of this contrast between diatonic and chromatic than of any other feature: in *Parsifal*, for example, the conflicting significations of chromatic music for the powers of evil and diatonic music for the forces of enlightenment are obvious and consistent, though, as the discussion on pp.260–61 will suggest, such a distinction is only the starting-point for the subtle interplay of musical characteristics and meanings. Simply because chromatic harmony is less stable (and usually more dissonant) than diatonic harmony, it offered Wagner an ideal metaphor for a whole range of dramatic states and situations: in *On the Application of Music to Drama* Wagner used the example of his combination (in Act II of *Die Walküre*) of the Nature and Valhalla motifs from *Das Rheingold* to 'paint a far clearer picture of Wotan's sombre and desperate suffering than his own words ever could' (GS X, 188). Wagner became a master of exploiting the interaction of tendencies towards and away from tonal stability, as well as towards or away from the longer structural spans that such stability made possible. Moreover, he recognized that chromaticism itself was ambiguous, able to change its function from enriching a tonality to undermining it, as the dramatic situation required.

Interaction between contrasting tendencies is also fundamental when the basic elements of Wagner's musical forms are considered. In the Classical and early Romantic styles, phrases were normally built from regular successions of similar units (normally multiples of four or eight bars) organized in conjunction with principles of harmonic progression to generate larger-scale forms which usually elaborated two-part (binary) or three-part (ternary) designs. As Wagner moved away from the clear-cut formal divisions of the number opera (aria, recitative, ensemble, chorus) he increasingly exploited the small-scale contrasts that became possible when phrases built from even or odd numbers of bars are aligned or juxtaposed more consistently than before. As Alfred Lorenz and his followers have shown, there is considerable evidence that Wagner built his formal units, or periods, from ternary structures – 'bridge' or 'arch' forms (ABA), and 'bar' forms (AAB) (see 'A Wagnerian Glossary': *Bar* form, pp.231–2) – but this was never a mechanical process, and other writers have suggested that motivic variation and the use of a refrain or ritornello principle may be no less important, creating a suitably flexible background for the extended dialogues that became Wagner's main means of dramatic exposition. It is also true that without Wagner's skills as an orchestrator, and his innovations in many areas of 19th-century orchestral practice, his progress as a master of formal and harmonic structuring might well seem less imposing in effect than is in fact the case.

The Romantic operas

The remainder of this chapter looks more closely at the working of Wagner's musical language. The very beginning of his first wholly characteristic opera, *Der fliegende Holländer*, illustrates the interplay between simple ideas and more complex contexts: between arresting, immediate statement and the impulse for continuation, to seek an eventual resolution of tension and ambiguity. In the Overture the basic horn-call motif, associated with the Dutchman himself, is presented first in the simplest harmonic context, that formed by its own two principal notes, D and A, the tonic chord of the key of D (minor). After four bars Wagner surrounds the extended restatement of this motif with chromatic scales, and this decorative element (with its strong evocation of marine turbulence) is then rapidly given a fundamental harmonic role (from bar 13) in what is only the second sustained chord in the Overture so far. The chord harmonizes the A of the Dutchman motif with the notes B♯, D♯ and F♯, all of which are foreign to the home key of D minor. Together with A they form that familiar diminished seventh which – at least since the Wolf's Glen Scene in Weber's *Der Freischütz* – is Romantic music's most graphic embodiment of shock and horror: usually because, although not strongly dissonant in itself, it disturbs the more stable musical context into which it intrudes.

Wagner's preparation and presentation of this chromatic chord (which could easily be diatonic to another key – in this case, C♯ minor) might seem from this description nothing more than an incidental detail. What makes it important is the way Wagner uses its initial disruptiveness as the source of the longer-term harmonic organization that serves his expressive and dramatic purposes so much more effectively than mere concentration on the 'local'. This particular diminished seventh is so powerful in its impact because the music's syntax – its phrase structure in terms of numbers of bars – has from the start revealed a tension between 'odd' and 'even', 'irregular' and 'regular'. In essence, there are two preliminary bars to launch the Overture and establish the D–A harmony, then two more bars into which the initial statement of the Dutchman motif is fitted, extended by a further bar as Wagner begins to develop the motif. 'Evenness' is restored at the point where the chromatic scales begin (bar 6): there are four bars of this material. Then the Dutchman's motif is restated with even greater force, and here, as before, the first segment of the phrase is in effect three bars (10–12), leading up to that crucial diminished seventh. So far, then, the music has this basic phrasal framework:

bars:	2 + 3	+	2 + 2 +	3 +	2
motif:	Dutchman motif	extended	Dutchman motif	extended	
harmony:	D + A		chromatic scales		diminished 7th

Representing such a dynamic process as a string of integers may seem not only simple-minded but also positively anti-Wagnerian. Yet in the clearest possible way it illustrates that basic kind of ongoing, cumulative dialogue between 'even' and 'odd' elements whereby Wagner intensifies expectation and motivates the working-out of such dialogues on larger and larger scales. In the first main paragraph of the *Holländer* Overture there is a total of 25 bars, with 12 before the appearance of the diminished seventh, and the remaining 13 devoted to bringing the music safely back to the unambiguous D minor from which it started out. This process of harmonic departure and return is best thought of as enrichment, not modulation (Wagner himself, like most 19th-century writers on music, tended to use 'modulation' for relatively slight shifts of harmonic perspective); and it is paralleled by a simple but highly effective process of thematic development whereby that elemental Dutchman theme is extended, primarily by using its upper note (A) as a neighbour or appoggiatura to G♯, to form an expressive descending semitone that acts as a strong contrast to the ascending leaps of the main part of the theme.

This Overture is a symphonic composition, in which Wagner can work musically without the constraints of a text, even though its expressive relevance to the drama it introduces is never in doubt. But it is clear from the main body of the opera that Wagner is already sensitive to the possibilities which arise when local, immediate surprises are balanced against a strong tendency to create larger-scale continuities, through first delaying, and finally admitting, harmonic resolution. He is already intent on composing links from one 'number' to another, so that, for instance, the Dutchman's Act I aria, 'Die Frist ist um', finishes very quietly, inhibiting disruptive applause, even though it ends with a full harmonic close. Several of the numbers are nevertheless conventional enough to have unobtrusive harmonic accompaniments to melodic lines which are predominantly regular in phrase structure, and have a well-nigh Italianate tendency to introduce ornamentation: Erik's two main solos, for example. Such features persist in both *Tannhäuser* and *Lohengrin*, although there is an increasing contrast between these features and passages in more radical, forward-looking style. In Act II of *Tannhäuser* the conflict between Tannhäuser and the other knights is, to no small extent, a matter of atmosphere: Wagner distances Tannhäuser from Walther and Wolfram more by mood and key than by conflicts between diatonic and chromatic harmony: after all, they are all engaged in performing songs. In Act III, however, the sad incompatibility of Tannhäuser with both Elisabeth and Wolfram is underlined formally and generically by the strong contrast between his 'narration', with its freer form and wider range of harmonic reference, and their 'songs'.

In Act II scene 2 of *Lohengrin*, again, it is almost as if Wagner makes conscious use of 'linguistic' disparity to dramatize the contrast between Elsa's naivety and Ortrud's malevolence. All commentators unite in hailing Act II scene 1 as the scene in which Wagner gives the clearest indication of how his style would develop in the later music dramas. Concentrating as it does on the bitterness and anguish of Ortrud and Telramund, it is certainly a scene of great power, and although its relatively wordy text means that Wagner still relies quite extensively on recitative-like declamation, he maintains a high degree of tension by keeping straightforward tonal cadences to a minimum. For example, Telramund's 'Du Fragst? War's nicht dein Zeugnis' ('You ask? Was it not your witness') first favours one key (A minor), but steps aside from a potentially confirming cadence into a quite different tonality (C minor), then oscillates between the two centres without strongly reinforcing either, before moving away into new regions.

No less important than the harmonic ambivalence prevalent in this scene, and the rhythmic, metric, formal flexibility that goes with it, is the climactic focusing on simple melodic shapes which no longer embody the kind of melodramatic rhetoric found earlier in Telramund's 'aria' of rage – 'Durch dich musst' ich verlieren' ('Through you must I lose [my honour]'). When Ortrud and Telramund sing together in octaves at the end of the scene ('Der Rache Werk' – 'The task of revenge') it is a 'duet' which defies every element of the traditional climactic ensemble, a defiance the stronger since such ensembles are by no means avoided elsewhere in *Lohengrin*. This is a moment of special Wagnerian power, even though it owes much to a similar passage in Weber's *Euryanthe*.

In many respects the triumphs of the three Romantic operas are not to be found in anticipations of later developments but in features more personal to them which would in all probability still be celebrated today had Wagner died in 1850: in *Der fliegende Holländer*, the deeply-felt torments of the Dutchman's Act I aria, the bold juxtapositions of Senta's Ballad, and the remarkably sustained confrontation between humans and spectres in Act III scene 1 (No. 13); in *Tannhäuser*, the profound opposition between the noble breadth of the Pilgrims' Chorus and the hysterical ranting of Tannhäuser's Hymn to Venus, the magically sudden transformation from Venusberg to Wartburg (Act I), and the economical power with which Wagner reworks the confrontation between good and evil at the end of the work; in *Lohengrin*, the style of 'In fernem Land', an eloquent arioso married to a 'symphonic' accompaniment which has – because of its rhyming, regularly scanning text – an intimate yet not inappropriately formal quality not found in the later works. Wagner's triumph over the 'limitations' of his early style, not least in Act III of *Lohengrin*, with its touchingly restrained love music and exuberantly pompous military music, is such as to ensure that these operas have not been rendered artistically obsolete by the splendours of the music dramas which succeeded them.

The music dramas

Although *Das Rheingold* begins with the simplest possible motivic and harmonic material, and the most straightforward form-scheme (successions of four-bar units) the music proclaims a new world. Not even attempts to argue that the orchestral Prelude is 'in essence' a rethinking of the dawn music from *Lohengrin* (Act II scene 3) can detract from its extraordinary originality. The *Lohengrin* music introduces one of Wagner's more routinely protracted choruses of celebration. The *Rheingold* Prelude leads into a scene of unprecedented freshness and freedom, which not only stems from the dramatic situation and its textual embodiment, but which is truly 'made visible' to the ears by the music, in anticipation of the encouragement Wagner would draw from his reading of Schopenhauer to think of music drama as 'musical deeds made visible' (GS IX, 306). This process depends crucially on the sharing of significant, and signifying, material between voices and orchestra. The orchestra does not so much 'accompany' the voices as combine with them in the common purpose of projecting the drama. It is not that every bar of the orchestral music is literally of thematic significance, presenting one of the work's leading motifs. For example, Fricka's words early in Scene 2 – 'Um des Gatten Treue besorgt' ('Concern for my husband's fidelity') – are supported by simple chords quite in the 'old' style, and Wagner may have deliberately reverted to this to symbolize Fricka's conventional conservatism. Yet the passage also underlines the composer's main concern: to convey the dramatic essence as immediately and powerfully as possible, while not creating the kind of exclusive concentration on the moment which he saw as the bane of traditional opera. Fricka's melody is pithy and eloquent, the supporting harmony open-ended rather than closed-off cadentially, the temporary absence of leitmotivic material no hindrance to the ongoing flow of the work.

It is nevertheless in the way it demonstrates Wagner's skill in the new art of motivic transformation and characterization that *Das Rheingold* is most innovatory, allied as this art is to a new formal flexibility. At the end of Scene 1 the motif associated with the World's Wealth alternates in regular two-bar units with the last reminiscences of the Rhine music, as waves become mist. There are three such alternations, spanning twelve bars in all, which serve to clarify and reinforce the prevailing tonality (C). The first two statements of the World's Wealth motif are very similar: the third shifts up a step, and the fourth (after bar 12) starts with the same upper melody note as the third (F). But all else has changed. What belonged to the key of C now belongs to A♭, a harmonic shift of some surprise in this context: and in place of the two-bar alternations there are now eight bars repeating and extending this new version of the World's Wealth motif. The phrase ends on a mild dissonance, and instead of resolving onto the expected tonic (A♭), the harmony moves on one further stage in the tonal system's cycle of keys for the statement (in D♭) of the Valhalla music at the start of Scene 2. The changes – of key, tone-colour and metre – are considerable: but the Valhalla motif is nevertheless a new version of the World's Wealth motif. It forms the basis for the first section of the scene – a clear example, in Lorenz's terms, of an arch-shaped period (ABA) with the 'A' purely orchestral, the 'B' varying A material (the first exchanges between Fricka and Wotan) and the second 'A' a varied repeat of the first, extended to close on tonic rather than dominant harmony and with Wotan's majestic melodic line added. More detailed analysis reveals a subtle interaction of connection and discontinuity even within such an apparently straightforwardly shaped period, and these facets of structure point directly to the inherent semantics. What this music expresses with unmistakable force is not only confidence and contentment, but also the potential for conflict and mutual misunderstanding. The new music for the new music drama would not have been possible, it must be reiterated, without the new, mythic subject-matter and the pithy, alliterative text. And if, in the end, it is impossible for everyone to agree on what the *Ring* is about – or even if it is about one or many things – this is a multivalence of which Wagner's music is entirely worthy.

Commentators on Wagner tend to identify a Schopenhauer-inspired retreat from the relative theoretical purity of the dramas closest to *Opera and Drama – Das Rheingold, Die Walküre –* as musical processes assert their inevitable power, and Wagner even yields to the temptation to readmit such conventional operatic features as the large-scale vocal ensemble. Yet it is less a matter of retreat than of expanding a concept to embrace more elaborate musical processes, and even, on occasion, decorated vocal writing, when justified by the dramatic situation. To the extent that this development sets up a richer sense of tension between formal components (for example, the 'closed' dramatic and musical status of the *Meistersinger* Quintet within the ongoing processes that dominate the third act) it fits well with the tension, no less rich, that becomes apparent between the musical components themselves: as chromatic harmony grows more intense and radical in its reluctance to resolve, so diatonicism is stimulated to fight back, jealously guarding its ultimate right to have the last word. Moreover, within the distinct formal segments, or periods, which it is still possible to detect in the later music dramas, there is a subtle interplay between music whose structure still demonstrates the hierarchic harmonic relations of the tonal tradition, and music which functions more in terms of motivic associations and chordal juxtapositions, lending itself to analytical interpretations emphasizing disjunction and surprise as much as connection and coherence.

Wagner's exploration of diverse facets of his musical language was stimulated by the variety of dramatic subjects that he chose to work on. Stepping aside from the *Ring* to *Tristan* brought a love music more intricate and intense even than that for Siegmund and Sieglinde in *Die Walküre*, and a music of despair and loss (King Mark in Act II, Tristan in Act III) even more extreme and elaborate than Wotan's in *Die Walküre*. The particularly dense symbolism of *Tristan* was then offset by the relative naturalism of *Die Meistersinger*, in which there is a new degree of contrapuntal elaboration that – the Overture clearly suggests – is partly self-mocking (of masterly self-importance). To balance this, *Die Meistersinger* has memorable lyrical directness, appropriate to the more down-to-earth concerns of Walther and Hans Sachs.

Between *Tristan* and *Meistersinger*, Wagner had taken a new look at old material, his partial 'Tristanizing' of *Tannhäuser* intensifying to an almost surreal extent the juxtapositions of erotic intensity and civic rectitude in Act I. After *Die Meistersinger* he returned to the materials of the *Ring*, displaying new richness of development and increased formal flexibility in Act III of *Siegfried* and in *Götterdämmerung*. The statement and combination of motifs may by now have cut loose completely from the precepts of *Opera and Drama*, in that they are not necessarily prompted, more or less directly, by the actual images and references of the text. But, as the Prelude to *Siegfried* Act III makes clear, the motivic process continues to serve the drama, creating a rich and vivid portrait of Wotan's noble anger and despair. Harmonic and formal procedures may determine the music's structure, but dramatic imperatives determine its character.

As a whole, the style of *Siegfried* Act III has an epic grandeur that flirts with blatancy. It may be regretted that more of the pastoral sublimity of Act II does not survive in the long, impassioned love scene with which *Siegfried* ends, but, to no less an extent than in *Tristan*, the need to represent human desire as a phenomenon with shattering consequences means that the potential for a contrasting intimacy of expression is repressed. Here, the most basic objection to Wagner's language – from Debussy and many others – that he shouts when he should whisper, cannot be dismissed out of hand, even if it is a weakness very far from fatal. It might just be possible to imagine the effect Wagner would have achieved in *Siegfried* if, from the point of greatest tenderness, where the *Siegfried Idyll* music is introduced, he had continued in the innocent, almost playful vein of that music and ended Act III in a quiet, rapt E major, complementing the understated ending of Act II in the same key. But the exultant exclamations of the text make such an ending musically implausible; it is also dramatically impossible, given the momentous significance of Brünnhilde's learning to love and Siegfried's learning to fear.

From the standpoint of its musical language, *Götterdämmerung* is a triumphant vindication of the rightness and potency of those basic musical ideas and stylistic elements which Wagner had established at the outset of his epic enterprise. The ending, with its orchestral 'fantasia' on the Valhalla and Rhine motifs, and its final cadence embracing references to Siegfried as hero, the downfall of the gods, and 'redemption through love' ('the glorification of Brünnhilde', according to Wagner in a letter of 1875: see Deathridge 1981–2), does not so much give music the last word as reinforce the intimate relation between staged action and orchestral 'making-visible' when there is no more text. In this final period of *Götterdämmerung*, certain specific, seasoned techniques are employed by Wagner to maximum effect. First, the decisiveness of Brünnhilde's last words do not close the action but initiate its final phase, as Wagner employs his familiar device of cadential evasion: a dominant chord (in D♮ major) followed not by the tonic but by a chromatic alteration of the tonic – D♭, F and A♮. This simple but decisive change launches the music into temporary harmonic limbo, and Wagner sustains and further builds a tension desiring eventual resolution (in the episodes depicting the blazing up of the fire and the burning of Valhalla) by the no less familiar device of ascending sequential repetition – of all his techniques, the one most firmly grounded in Beethovenian precedent. In addition, Wagner complements the cadential evasion of closure (in D♮ major) just described with the understated introduction of the (D♮) tonic chord at the point where the Valhalla motif returns, a device no less effective than the evasion was for suggesting that resolution is still incomplete. In the end, full closure is not achieved by means of a purely diatonic progression at all, but by expanding and enriching a Plagal (subdominant to tonic) cadence with the chromatic Neapolitan chord (D major in the key of D♮). The harmonic scheme is, therefore, subdominant (major turning to minor) for the final statement of the Siegfried theme; Neapolitan chord for the downfall of the gods; tonic (itself enriched by subdominant inflection, major then minor) for the 'glorification of Brünnhilde'. As a scheme, this could be supremely banal, and there is certainly nothing novel about it. But by associating the crucial dramatic event of the gods' downfall with this enrichment of the work's final cadence, Wagner underlines precisely the kind of profound psychological connotations that enabled him time and time again to transcend the commonplace. To achieve such profundity by simple means was his greatest gift, and it is safe to say that no more effective musical means of representing the working through to resolution of dramatic conflicts and tensions has ever been devised.

If the musical language of the *Ring* proves to be the superbly flexible medium for the representation of the drama's epic, mythic qualities, that of *Parsifal* might seem to require a narrower range. Yet the role of religious belief – not the presence of gods, but the presence of a sense of God – creates the need for still greater allusiveness of reference. What is represented in *Parsifal* is not a straightforward fight to the finish between Good and Evil, diatonic and chromatic, consonant and dissonant, but the challenging and undermining of good and evil alike – the demonstration that each is relative. The inherent ambiguities of the interaction between music and drama are evident when we observe that the work's ultimate representation of 'good', as the Knights revere the glowing Grail in Parsifal's raised hands, is accompanied by music which, while it starts from and returns to a secure, diatonic key centre (A♭ major), ranges widely across the chromatic spectrum through sequences of largely consonant harmony. Clearly, there is a distinction between the capacity of chromaticism to suggest an exalted spirituality by enriching a harmonic framework, and the power of chromaticism to suggest the deepest psychic disturbance, as it does in Parsifal's moment of self-realization after Kundry's kiss in Act II. In this Act II music there is also an element of sequential writing, but the harmony is more dissonant, the texture more fragmented, and there is no secure diatonic framework.

Parsifal offers dialogues, and polarities, between different types of chromaticism, and even to an extent between different stylistic manifestations of diatonicism, as demonstrated for example by the contrast between the Knights' march-like hymns and the sinuous flow of Kundry's 'Ich sah das Kind' ('I saw the child'). Ultimately, however, the drama is most memorably shaped by the kind of dialogue demonstrated with surpassing subtlety in the Good Friday Scene (Act III) between projections of the prevailing tonality (Parsifal's delight in the world of nature) and chromatic interruptions of that tonality (Gurnemanz's account of the Crucifixion). So contingent and interdependent are the shifts of mood within each character (basically, between joy and sorrow) that the music moves beyond simple mimesis into realms of inflection whose nuances of meaning resist translation into words. Yet that is not to say that the only thing that matters about the final stages of the Good Friday Scene is its confirmation of its principal tonality (D major) or its demonstration of a particular periodic form (ABA with coda). Even in that 'coda' the motivic allusions to the Flowermaidens and to Amfortas and the spear are the dramatic motivations behind the music's wide perspectives on its central tonality – perspectives which prevent the establishment of strong resolution, and drive the drama on into its final stages.

Musicologists continue to dispute the extent to which it is possible to argue convincingly that a particular Wagnerian process takes place for 'purely' or 'primarily' musical reasons. But whether or not Wagner did succumb to the temptation to pursue musical ideas for their own sake, producing episodes whose musical character is more 'symphonically' organized than those whose prime focus is the declamation of the text, it is impossible to claim that such pursuits are dramatically counter-productive or irrelevant – with the possible exception of the protracted pantomimes in *Die Walküre*, Act I, a work still striving to be faithful to the theories of *Opera and Drama*. It is precisely at that point in the music dramas where there is little or no action to be seen – the curtain may even be down – that the power of music to represent the essences of mood and action in its own language, if not to be literally, consistently referential, is most strongly to be felt.

Wagner transformed the nature of opera as radically as his music transformed early Romantic principles of form and harmonic organization. In place of 'numbers', or the more extended schemes of grand opera, he developed an extraordinary variety of periodic designs in which the continuity or discontinuity of motivic and harmonic processes is the crucial component. And yet, although elaborate, psychologically charged dialogues are at the heart of his musico-dramatic method, he no more escaped associations with older operatic genres (from accompanied recitative to formal aria and ensemble) than he evaded ultimate submission to the authority of resolving dissonances and tonal closure. The language of music changed so rapidly after Wagner as much because of the impossibility of surpassing his supreme balancing act between integrative and disruptive forces within the language of tonality, as from the conscious and positive desire of composers to go beyond the Wagnerian style.

ARNOLD WHITTALL

Section 12
WAGNER AS LIBRETTIST

WAGNER AS LIBRETTIST

THE THEATRICAL ENVIRONMENT in which Wagner grew up predisposed him to drama rather than music, so that his earliest surviving work – the Gothic tragedy *Leubald* – was originally conceived as a stage play. As his interest in music developed, it must have seemed natural to him to write his own libretti, not least in the light of E.T.A. Hoffmann's short story *Der Dichter und der Komponist* (*The Poet and the Composer*), in which the composer Ludwig argues that 'a true opera seems to me to be the one in which the music springs directly from the poem as a necessary product of the same'.

In his earliest libretti Wagner was content to follow Romantic models: *Die Hochzeit, Die Feen, Das Liebesverbot* and *Rienzi* dispense with end-rhyme almost entirely, thereby continuing a process which had been initiated by Hoffmann himself and developed, most notably, by Georg Döring in his libretto for *Der Berggeist* (1825), for which Spohr had specifically requested an unrhymed text. The rejection of end-rhyme was part of a general movement towards heightened prose and a breakdown of formal structures in the interests of psychological realism. Lines of three, four or five feet predominate, alternating, for the most part, for reasons of emotional intensity and change. In many passages the metrical freedom is such that the lines in question might almost have been written as prose.

Der fliegende Holländer, by contrast, reveals a reversion to rhyme in accordance with the work's more 'popular' character and its division into folksong and ballad. Only in moments of heated stichomythia is end-rhyme eschewed. This same development can be observed in *Tannhäuser* and *Lohengrin*. Indeed, so adept had Wagner now become at writing Romantic opera libretti that other composers – Josef Dessauer, Jan Kittl and Ferdinand Hiller – turned to him for texts.

Wagner's own commentary on his early libretti needs to be treated with caution, since it dates from a period when he was already beginning to distance himself from the works in question. Of *Die Feen* he was to write in *Mein Leben* (this passage was dictated in 1865/6):

> As to the poetic diction and the verses themselves, I was almost intentionally careless about them. I was not nourishing my former hopes of making a name as a poet; I had really become a 'musician' and a 'composer' and wanted simply to write a decent libretto, for I now realized nobody else could do this for me, inasmuch as an opera book is something unique unto itself and cannot be easily brought off by poets and literati.

In 1871, while preparing the first volume of his collected writings for publication, he wondered whether to include the poems of *Die Feen* and *Das Liebesverbot*, but dismissed them both as being 'too childish' (CT, 16 Jul 1871). And in *Eine Mitteilung an meine Freunde* (*A Communication to my Friends*) of 1851, he wrote in an equally dismissive vein of *Rienzi*, claiming that 'I certainly took no greater care over the language and prosody than seemed to me necessary to produce a decent *opera text* that was not too trivial.' (GS IV, 259) But in the very same essay he makes the following extravagant claims for *Der fliegende Holländer*:

> The figure of the 'Flying Dutchman' is the mythical poem of the people. [. . .] It was the first popular, national poem that forced its way deep into my heart, inviting me, as an artist, to interpret and recreate it. It is here that my career as a *poet* begins, and with it the end of my career as a mere manufacturer of opera libretti. (GS IV, 265–6)

Interestingly, we can compare this later interpretation of the text with Wagner's own more-or-less contemporary assessment of its poetic worth. In a letter to Karl Gaillard of 30 January 1844 we find him writing:

> I really have no illusions about my reputation as a poet, & I confess that it was only as a last resort that I adopted the expedient of writing my own libretti, since no decent texts were offered me.

(Of course, here, too, there is a reason for Wagner's apparent modesty, since he is anxious to maintain the airs of a literary dandy which he had given himself in his *Autobiographical Sketch* of 1843.) The Romantic primacy of music is explicit in Wagner's suggestion, in the same letter to Gaillard, that he was already imbued with the musical aura of a piece before setting to work on the poem:

> Even before I set about writing a single line of the text or drafting a scene, I am already thoroughly immersed in the musical aura of my new creation, I have the whole sound & all the characteristic motifs in my head so that, when the poem is finished & the scenes are arranged in their proper order, the actual opera is already completed, the moment of actual creativity having already passed.

As a Romantic manifesto this is impressive (it might almost be Hoffmann's composer speaking here), but as an explanation of Wagner's working method it leaves something to be desired. It was clearly immensely inconvenient for Wagner that, in writing his Romantic operas and music dramas, the text always came first, so that the music – which, according to all the Romantic theorists, *ought* to have preceded it – inevitably came second. No amount of theorizing on Wagner's part was able to resolve this difficulty.

When, at the end of the 1840s, Wagner fell under the influence of Ludwig Feuerbach, for whom music was 'the language of feeling [. . .], feeling that communicates itself to another person', he was able to draw on Feuerbach's tuist philosophy to propound an imaginative analogy whereby the Wagnerian music drama was seen as the love-child of (masculine) poetry and (feminine) music

(GS IV, 103). With the discovery, in the autumn of 1854, of that most Romantic of all philosophers, Arthur Schopenhauer, came a renewed insistence upon the primacy of music, and it was this outlook that coloured Wagner's aesthetic for the remainder of his life, even if, as noted above, theory and practice went their separate ways.

Not only did Wagner embrace Feuerbach at the end of the 1840s, he also espoused the *völkisch* ideology that was current among German intellectuals around the middle of the century. Hence his desire to regard himself as the mouthpiece of the *Volk* and hence, too, his justification for using early Germanic metres as the verse-form of the *Ring*.

We shall never know at precisely what point in the 1840s Wagner decided to turn his back on the classical prosody of the Romantic poets and to look instead to the Germanic metres of the early Middle Ages. Other poets, including Fouqué, Rückert, Goethe and Bürger, had used alliterative metres in their stage plays, but Wagner was the first to use *Stabreim* in an opera libretto. His arguments for preferring initial rhyme to end-rhyme may be followed in detail in *Oper und Drama* (*Opera and Drama*), written during the winter of 1850/51. His premiss is Romantically based. The earliest language and most direct expression of individual emotion is said to be music. As the language developed, it moved increasingly away from its poetic origins: the need to describe complex relationships in a society that had lost touch with nature led to the emergence of a language which could express concepts, but which was no longer capable of expressing emotions. In short, the *Volk* or common people spoke the language of the heart. By recreating that language, Wagner hoped to address a direct emotional appeal to the stultified hearts of his 19th-century listeners and arouse within them a sense of the human emotions which he felt had been destroyed by the corrupting influences of modern civilization.

The single most crucial influence on the poetic diction of the *Ring* was Ludwig Ettmüller's *Lieder der Edda von den Nibelungen*, published in Zurich in 1837 and containing modern German alliterative translations of the heroic lays from the Poetic Edda. Alone among early 19th-century Germanists, Ettmüller realized that Old Norse metrical forms were not related to those of Greece and Rome, and that nothing was to be gained by totting up the number of syllables in each line of verse. Instead, Ettmüller analysed the lines in terms of *Hebungen* and *Senkungen*, or 'lifts' and 'dips', noting that there are typically two, occasionally three, lifts per line, with a variable number of dips dividing them. In the following examples, the woodbird warns Sigurd/Siegfried against his foster-father's treachery, first in Ettmüller's translation of the Old Norse *Fáfnismál* and second in Act II of Wagner's *Siegfried*. The lifts are marked by crosses.

x x
Hauptes kürzer lass' er
x x
den haarigen Schwätzer
x x x
fahren hin zur Hel;
x x
ihm dann eigen
x x
wird alles Gold,
x x x
der Hort, den Fafnir hegte.

x x
O traut' er Mime
x x
dem treulosen nicht!
x x x
Hörte Siegfried nur scharf
x x x
auf des Schelmen Heuchlergered';
x x
wie sein Herz es meint,
x x
kann er Mime versteh'n;
x x x
so nützt' ihm des Blutes Genuss.

Lines of two lifts each are linked together alliteratively in pairs: the main stave is located on the first lift of each second half-line, while the two lifts in the preceding half-line are treated as supporting staves, one or both of which must alliterate with the main stave. In the case of lines with three lifts, any two of the staves may alliterate. (Wagner distinguishes the two sorts of line typographically.) For the purposes of alliteration, all vowels and diphthongs may rhyme with one another; initial *h* is disregarded. (It may be mentioned in parentheses that, since Wagner's native Saxon dialect does not distinguish between voiced and voiceless plosives, we occasionally find his characters lapsing into Leipzig regionalisms: the Second Norn's '*D*ämmert der *T*ag schon auf?', for example, suggests that of the three she, at least, may hail from Leipzig.)

Ettmüller advised against secondary alliteration and the coining of pseudo-archaic expressions, but Wagner had no such inhibitions. Indeed, the premiss upon which his argument was based persuaded him that the more insistent the *Stabreim* and the more wilfully archaic the language, the more 'authentic' the text of the *Ring* would be as an expression of 'purely human' emotions. Accordingly, *Stabreim* is also used, albeit to a much more limited extent, in *Tristan und Isolde*, for here too Wagner's aim is to recreate a more primitive form of the legend than that transmitted by his immediate source, Gottfried von Strassburg. None the less, Gottfried's principal contribution to the narrative was his reworking of the tradition in terms of the scholastic *artes*, and traces of that rhetoric are to be found in Wagner's libretto. Wordplay (already a feature of the *Ring*) occurs in lines such as 'Nun hör' wie ein *Held* / Eide *hält*!' ('Now hear how a hero keeps his vows!'); oxymoron transfigures Isolde's cry of 'O Freundesfeindin!' ('O friendly foe!') and King Mark's lament, 'du treulos treuester Freund' ('you faithless faithfullest friend'); and there is prosopopoeia in such verses as 'Im Schweigen der Nacht / nur lacht mir der Quell' ('In the silence of night the fountain alone smiles upon me'). Middle High German semantic usage betrays itself in various ways: in the line 'du wilde, minnige Maid', Wagner was surely thinking of Middle High German *wilt* = 'foreign', while 'blöd' in the line 'Blöde Herzen' has less to do with modern German 'stupid' than with

Middle High German 'weak, cowardly'. Finally, the virtues of medieval chivalry are evident in lines such as 'Von edler Art / und mildem Mut' (*milte* = generous) and 'wohin ist Tugend nun entfloh'n' (*tugent* = knightly excellence). As in the *Ring*, lines of two and three main stresses predominate.

End-rhyme replaced initial rhyme in German verse in the course of the 9th century, and long lines of four main stresses superseded the earlier half-lines of two main stresses each. The number of weakly stressed syllables remained variable until the constraints of classical prosody introduced the metrical regularity missing hitherto. The earlier verse form – four main stresses and an irregular number of weakly stressed syllables – was revived in the 15th and 16th centuries and again in the 18th and 19th centuries, most notably by the historical Hans Sachs, by Goethe in *Faust* and *Hans Sachsens Poetische Sendung* and by Wagner in *Die Meistersinger von Nürnberg*. (The technical term is *Knittelvers*, normally – if unhelpfully – translated into English as 'doggerel verse'.) Wagner's pastiche also extends to his use of *Bar* form, an originally 12th-century form of verse revived by the historical mastersingers in which two metrically identical *Stollen*, together termed the *Aufgesang*, are followed by an *Abgesang* (see 'A Wagnerian Glossary: *Bar* form', p.231). (Strictly speaking, the Renaissance *Bar* may be three, five, seven or more stanzas long, but for Wagner it always meant a tripartite stanza.)

Parsifal is less of a pastiche (although Wolfram's notoriously obscure style has left its mark on some of Wagner's more Byzantine sentence structures) than a summation of all his earlier tendencies. End-rhyme is used only sparingly ('R. talks about his verses, he has not yet used a rhyme; the more natural the music, he says, the less appropriate an end rhyme': CT, 16 Mar 1877), and the number of lifts in each line ranges from one to five. What this metrical freedom achieves most of all is the breakdown of verse into heightened prose, a development which not only harks back to the Romantic aesthetic of his early operas but anticipates the *vers libres* of French and English poets of the 1870s and 1880s.

Although Wagner published his libretti – or 'poems' as he generally preferred to call them – in advance of the actual performance, and in some cases in advance of the musical setting, it was not with a view to having them judged as independent works of poetry. Indeed, he frequently complained at having them so assessed. His aim was simply to prepare audiences for their eventual performance, a need which became all the more pressing following his revolutionary decision in Bayreuth to turn down the houselights during the performance, thus preventing spectators from reading the libretto during the opera, as they had done in the past. In consequence, the composer's libretti should probably not be judged as literature (undeniably poetic though certain passages are), but as an integral part of the musico-dramatic synthesis that Wagner was striving to achieve.

STEWART SPENCER

Section 13
THE MUSIC

Operas   271
Orchestral music   309
Choral music   313
Chamber music   315
Works for solo voices and orchestra   315
Works for solo voice and piano   316
Piano music   318
Projected or unfinished dramatic works   320
Editions and arrangements   322

THE MUSIC

THE NUMBER OF WORKS by Wagner listed in the authoritative *Wagner Werk-Verzeichnis* (to which the following listings are indebted) is 113 – a fact that may surprise those who think of Wagner in terms of thirteen operas and a handful of other works. It is true, on the one hand, that a large number of the non-dramatic works are of secondary significance – and, indeed, of variable quality. But on the other hand they are of more than peripheral interest, not least because they often provide clues about the compositional ambitions of Wagner at different points in his career – ambitions which have generally been glossed over in the presentation of Wagner as he himself approved: a composer destined to continue the Beethovenian tradition by a newly created form, the music drama, uniquely capable of embodying the spiritual needs of the age.

Alongside the central corpus of Wagner's operas or music dramas, then, is a body of work, some of which never reached final form, that throws important light on Wagner as artist and polemicist, as well as affording, in some cases, music of considerable merit and appeal. The non-dramatic works fall into two categories: the early pieces executed in the pursuit of compositional mastery, and the instrumental and vocal works written at different times throughout his life, sometimes in response to specific events or commissions, sometimes simply out of a desire for self-expression in an alternative medium.

The sketches and drafts for the projected and unfinished dramatic works offer fascinating evidence of certain of Wagner's preoccupations that either found no eventual artistic expression, or that were subsumed into one or other of the major works. The years surrounding the Dresden uprisings of 1848–9, for example, produced four different attempts to find a satisfactory vehicle for ideas that achieved final form in the *Ring*: the historical subject of *Friedrich I.* (the 12th-century emperor Friedrich Barbarossa) was abandoned (though not quite as readily as Wagner later suggested, see p.321) in favour of the greater potential afforded by the Nibelung myth, while a three-act drama on the subject of Achilles, with its themes of a free hero and of the gods yielding to humanity, the five-act *Jesus von Nazareth*, with its advocacy of a new religion of humanity, and the 'heroic opera' *Wieland der Schmied* were similarly all superseded by the *Ring*. The Buddhist subject matter of *Die Sieger* (*The Victors*), dealing with the conflict between passion and chastity, preoccupied Wagner from the mid-1850s until the end of his life, but again the theme was treated definitively in another work, *Parsifal*.

Structure of entries

The entries for the operas take the following form: title (with translation where appropriate); WWV number (refers to the entry in the *Wagner Werk-Verzeichnis*: see Select Bibliography, under 'Catalogues/bibliographies', for details); designation of opera with number of acts and primary source; dates of construction of the text, from conception to completion of the libretto; dates of composition of the music, from initial sketches to completion of the score; place and date of first performance; place and date of first UK performance; place and date of first US performance; *dramatis personae*, with voice designations; orchestration; setting; synopsis. This basic information is followed by paragraphs on the literary sources, the genesis of the work, its musical style, alternative versions and revisions, as appropriate.

Entries on the non-dramatic works vary slightly from genre to genre, but take the following basic form: title; WWV number; listing of vocal/instrumental forces; dates of composition and first performance; commentary.

The designation 'frag.' (= 'fragmentary') indicates that a work survives incomplete; cf. 'uncompleted'. 'Prob.' (= 'probably') indicates a greater degree of certitude than '?' (= 'possibly'). In the latter case, where the question mark is *not* closed up to one element in the date or other information it qualifies, the whole date is to be regarded as questionable.

Abbreviations

A	alto
arr.	arranged
B	bass
bass cl	bass clarinet
bass tpt	bass trumpet
bd	bass drum
bn	bassoon
cast	castanets
cl	clarinet
contrabass trbn	contrabass trombone
cor ang	cor anglais

cym	cymbals
db	double bass
double bn	double bassoon
fl	flute
frag.	fragment(ary)
glock	glockenspiel
hn	horn
ob	oboe
oph	ophicleide
orch	orchestra
org	organ
perf.	performed/performance
pf	piano
pic	piccolo
rev.	revised/revision
S	soprano
S,A,T,B	soprano, alto, tenor, bass (solo voices)
SATB	ditto (chorus voices)
sd	side drum
serp	serpent
T	tenor
tamb	tambourine
timp	timpani
tpt	trumpet
trbn	trombone
tri	triangle
va	viola
vc	cello
vn	violin

Operas

THE TEN OPERAS from *Der fliegende Holländer* to *Parsifal* form the accepted canon of Wagner's works: these are the only operas to be performed at the Bayreuth Festival, and the only ones to have entered the regular repertories of opera companies. They were preceded, however, by three by no means negligible operas, whose occasional performances prove them to be slightly more than curios, somewhat less than masterpieces: *Die Feen* (1833–4), *Das Liebesverbot* (1834–6) and *Rienzi* (1837–40). Each of these early works follows different stylistic principles and models – respectively German Romantic opera, Italian/French opera and Parisian grand opera – as Wagner wrestled with the twin imperatives of making a name for himself and forging a convincing personal style.

A wholly characteristic, 'Wagnerian' style emerges in the next group of three so-called 'Romantic operas': *Der fliegende Holländer*, *Tannhäuser* and *Lohengrin*. In these works, the traditional forms of 'number opera' (recitative, aria, chorus and so forth) progressively give way to through-composed structures, and a more malleable vocal line – one that is more sensitive to the accents and expressive nuances of the text (Wagner wrote all his own libretti) – achieves increasing prominence. The advanced stylistic traits of *Lohengrin*, in particular, mark it out as a 'transitional' work to the fully-fledged music dramas of the *Ring* (indeed, the *Holländer*, *Tannhäuser* and *Lohengrin* are all occasionally referred to as 'music dramas' – a practice instigated by Wagner, when he retrospectively accorded them a greater degree of stylistic consistency with the later works than they actually deserve).

'Music drama' (see 'A Wagnerian Glossary', p.236) is the term by which Wagner originally denoted the works from *Das Rheingold* on; he later, in the 1872 essay *Über die Benennung 'Musikdrama'*, (*On the Designation 'Music Drama'*) disowned the expression, but it has continued to be used. The composition of the four operas of the *Ring* extended over a quarter of a century (1848–74), during which *Tristan und Isolde* and *Die Meistersinger von Nürnberg* were also composed and brought to performance. The demands of the *Ring* were always intended by Wagner to outstrip the resources of conventional theatres. After many years of fundraising and artistic preparation, the tetralogy was finally mounted at the specially constructed Festspielhaus in Bayreuth. It was with the unique acoustic qualities of the Festspielhaus in mind that Wagner wrote his last music drama, *Parsifal*.

Die Feen (The Fairies)
WWV 32
Grand Romantic opera in 3 acts, after Carlo Gozzi's *La donna serpente*

Text: Jan/Feb 1833
Music: 20 Feb 1833 – 6 Jan 1834; rev. spring 1834
First perf.: Königliches Hof- und National-Theater, Munich, 29 Jun 1888
First UK perf.: Aston University, Birmingham (The Midland Music Makers Grand Opera Society), 17 May 1969
First US perf.: New York City Opera, New York, 24 Feb 1982 (concert perf.)

The King of the Fairies	bass
Ada	soprano
Zemina } *fairies*	soprano
Farzana	soprano
Arindal, *King of Tramond*	tenor
Lora, *his sister*	soprano
Morald, *her suitor*	baritone
Gernot, *in Arindal's service*	bass
Drolla, *Lora's confidante*	soprano
Gunther, *a courtier at Tramond*	tenor
Harald, *a general in Arindal's army*	bass
Voice of the magician Groma	bass
A messenger	tenor
The two children of Arindal and Ada	mute roles

Fairies, Morald's companions, people, warriors, earth spirits, bronze men, Groma's invisible spirits pic, 2 fl, 2 ob, 2 cl, 2 bn, 4 hn, 2 tpt, 3 trbn, timp, harp, str

On/off stage: 2 fl, 2 cl, 2 tpt, 4 trbn

Synopsis

Arindal, Prince of Tramond, out with his huntsman one day, is spirited away into the magic realm of Ada, who is half fairy, half mortal. She agrees to marry Arindal on condition that he refrains for eight years from asking who she is. Curiosity eventually overpowers him and when he asks the forbidden question the magic realm disappears. Morald and Gernot, from the court of Tramond, find Arindal in a rocky wilderness and persuade him to return home, where on the death of his father he has become king and is needed to repulse the enemy. Ada sends Arindal back to his court; she longs to join him as his wife on earth, but a 'fateful decree' ordains that she is to be punished for marrying a mortal. She makes him promise that whatever happens he will never curse her. He swears, but is ignorant of the fact that their reunion is conditional on his successfully undergoing a series of tribulations to be inflicted by Ada herself. He fails, and goaded beyond endurance curses her. Ada now reveals all and tells Arindal that she is condemned to be turned to stone for a hundred years (in Gozzi's story she becomes a snake). Arindal's despair drives him insane, but following Ada into the underworld he finally restores her to life by singing and playing the lyre. His courage is rewarded with immortality and, renouncing his earthly kingdom, he departs to reign with Ada in fairyland.

Source

For the plot of *Die Feen*, Wagner borrowed a story by the 18th-century Venetian dramatist Carlo Gozzi, *La donna serpente*. Four of the characters' names were taken over by Wagner from his earlier unfinished work *Die Hochzeit* (see 'Projected or unfinished dramatic works', p.321); these names were in turn taken from poems by 'Ossian' and others.

Musical style

The music of *Die Feen* is firmly rooted in the German Romantic tradition (see also 'Musical Background and Influences', pp.66–7), the tradition in which Wagner had been steeped from his boyhood days. In *Mein Leben* he describes with enthusiasm the effect made on his youthful imagination by the spectral setting of Weber's *Der Freischütz*; he also familiarized himself with the score at this stage, and other Weber operas followed before long. Then, when in January 1833 he took up the post of chorus master at the theatre in Würzburg, the operas of Weber and Marschner were among those which it was his duty to rehearse. Marschner's *Der Vampyr*, an extravagant exercise in gothic horror – or *Schauerromantik*, as

it was called in Germany – was an influence on *Die Feen* that Wagner was prepared to acknowledge, at least in terms of the genre.

He was less ready to admit the similarities of another Marschner work, *Hans Heiling*, but although the latter clearly was an influence, it should not be exaggerated. *Hans Heiling* shares with *Die Feen* the theme of a mortal's tragic love for a fairy, but it was a theme that goes back to the Middle Ages, and which had been firmly established in the Romantic imagination by the treatment of Friedrich de la Motte Fouqué in his novella *Undine* (1811), a tale made into an opera by E.T.A. Hoffmann in 1816. Moreover, the Bohemian legend of Hans Heiling itself had been given both narrative and verse form by Theodor Körner (1791–1813). The fateful consequences of mortals falling in love with denizens of the spirit world, and *vice versa*, are given dramatic form in several of Wagner's later works, notably *Der fliegende Holländer*, *Tannhäuser* and *Lohengrin*, and on the evening before he died, Wagner was musing on the similarity between the Undine water-spirits 'who long to have souls' and his own Rhinemaidens. *Die Feen* was well under way, however, before Wagner made the acquaintance of *Hans Heiling*. The libretto was written in January and February 1833 and the first act was already complete in full score by the time Marschner's work was given in Würzburg in the autumn of that year. By coincidence, the premiere of *Hans Heiling* was given in Berlin on 24 May 1833, the very day that Wagner finished the complete draft of Act I, but there is no evidence that he had heard the work before it came to Würzburg. It has been pointed out, however (Warrack, 1979), that in *Hans Heiling* Wagner almost certainly discovered the potentiality of certain technical devices – notably 'the use of sequences as well as reiterated figures to generate tension, the effect of plunging an audience straight into the centre of a drama, and a heightened dramatic use of orchestration' – while the appearance of the Mountain Queen was to be recalled two decades later in the main theme of the Annunciation of Death (*Die Walküre*).

Two *topoi* prominent in *Die Feen* were also to recur in later works of Wagner: redemption and the forbidden question – though it is notable that in the earlier work it is the man rather than the woman who is the agent of redemption and whose human weakness causes him to ask the question.

The stylistic assurance of the twenty-year-old composer is demonstrated convincingly in *Die Feen*, in the imaginative deployment of conventional forms such as aria, recitative, romanza, cavatina and various ensembles such as trio, quartet and septet. Ada's cavatina in Act I, for example, 'Wie muss ich doch beklagen', uses graphically throbbing appoggiatura dissonances to express her sadness at losing Arindal. The final ensemble of the same act, a septet joined by full chorus, is a skilful deployment of multiple voices in celebration of Arindal's oath and the election of Ada as queen.

A glimpse of things to come is afforded by the scene and aria 'Weh' mir, so nah' die fürchterliche Stunde' in Act II (as Ada decides to sacrifice immortality rather than give up Arindal) and that in Act III, 'Halloh!', depicting the torments of Arindal, driven to madness with grief at losing her. The scene and aria is a complex combining recitative, arioso and aria: an opportunity to extend the conventional forms, a principle which Wagner was later to take to its logical conclusion by creating through-composed music dramas. In Arindal's mad scene there is an interesting pre-echo of *Die Walküre*, when he imagines he hears the baying of dogs: the repeated diminished 7ths with acciaccaturas are used in the same way in the later work when Sieglinde fancies she hears the same sound in Act II, scene 3. Arindal's Act III lyre song, with which he regains Ada, is also worthy of note, not least as a precursor of Walther's Prize Song in *Die Meistersinger*, where the resolution of the drama similarly depends on the successful rendering of a musical setpiece. Finally, a comic duet for Drolla and Gernot in Act II is closer to the tradition of *opera buffa* and of the Viennese *Zauberposse* (see 'Musical Background and Influences', p.67) than to that of German Romantic opera, but it is nevertheless one of the most skilfully created numbers in the work. As the lovers quarrel, their vocal lines overlap, while shifts of argumentative stance are reflected in surprise twists of harmony. The scoring is felicitous and the whole piece bubbles with wit and invention.

Wagner's first completed essay in his chosen form, *Die Feen* already benefits from several years of compositional training. Although far from a masterpiece, its apprentice status and its reliance on stylistic models do not preclude many touches of originality. It deserves at least an occasional outing.

Das Liebesverbot, oder Die Novize von Palermo (*The Ban on Love, or The Novice of Palermo*)
WWV 38
Grand comic opera in 2 acts, after Shakespeare's *Measure for Measure*

Text: Prose sketch Jun 1834, poem Aug – Dec 1834
Music: Jan 1835 – early 1836
First perf.: Stadttheater, Magdeburg, 29 Mar 1836
First UK perf. (abridged): Collegiate Theatre, University College, London, 16 Feb 1965

Friedrich, *a German, Regent during the absence of the king of Sicily*		bass
Luzio	*two young noblemen*	tenor
Claudio		tenor
Antonio	*their friends*	tenor
Angelo		bass

Isabella, *Claudio's sister*	*novices in the convent of the order of St Elizabeth*	soprano
Mariana		soprano
Brighella, *police chief*		buffo bass
Danieli, *an innkeeper*		bass
Dorella, *formerly Isabella's chambermaid*	*in Danieli's service*	soprano
Pontio Pilato		buffo tenor

Nuns, judges, policemen, citizens of Palermo of all classes, countryfolk, carnival revellers, a band of musicians

pic, 2 fl, 2 ob, 2 cl, 2 bn, 4 hn, 4 tpt, 3 trbn, oph, timp, bd, cym, tri, cast, tamb, str

On/off stage: bells, military band (2 pic, 5 cl, 4 bn, 4 hn, 6 tpt, 3 trbn, oph, bd, sd, cym, tri)

Setting: Palermo in the 16th century

Synopsis
The Regent Friedrich has outlawed all licentious behaviour – even love itself, it seems, certainly that expressed extra-maritally – on pain of death. Claudio is the first to be condemned under the new law, and his sister Isabella, a novice, is persuaded with some reluctance to make a personal appeal to the Regent. It transpires that Friedrich was once married to Isabella's fellow-novice Mariana but for the sake of ambition repudiated her; in defiance of his own decree, he now offers to set Claudio free in exchange for Isabella's favours. Isabella pretends to agree, but in fact sends Mariana – Friedrich's own wife – to the rendezvous: the fancy-dress carnival forbidden by the Regent himself. Friedrich's lubricious hypocrisy is exposed and although he is willing to accept the penalty, the people set him free and a new era of unfettered sensuality is ushered in by the return of their own king.

Sources
The creative inspiration for *Das Liebesverbot* came to Wagner in June 1834 while he was enjoying a hedonistic summer holiday in Bohemia with his friend Theodor Apel. Under the influence of the radical literary and political movement known as *Junges Deutschland* (Young Germany), which rejected reactionary morality and Catholic mysticism in favour of sensual enjoyment of life, Wagner and Apel indulged themselves with good food and wines and other creature comforts. Two specific literary influences were Heinrich Laube's *Das junge Europa* (*Young Europe*) – a trilogy of novels, of which part 1 had appeared the previous year – and Wilhelm Heinse's *Ardinghello und die glückseeligen Inseln* (*Ardinghello and the Blessed Isles*), which had been published back in 1787. Laube's work propounded liberty in the erotic and political spheres as two inseparable aspects of the same idealistic vision;

273

it also advocated religious toleration and national emancipation, women's liberation and equal rights for Jews.

Laube, a friend of Wagner's, was one of the leading lights of *Junges Deutschland*, whose adherents in turn regarded themselves as heirs of the *Sturm und Drang* writers of the 1770s with their Rousseauesque exaltation of freedom and nature. The author of *Ardinghello*, Wilhelm Heinse (?1749–1803), is identified with the *Sturm und Drang* movement, and the eponymous hero of the novel is a 'universal man', the ideal of the Italian Renaissance. He is an advocate of free love, and eventually after many adventures settles with his followers on the Greek islands of Naxos and Paros; there they proscribe ownership and make possible the development of latent human talents.

It was in the spirit of these two novels that Wagner took as the basis for *Das Liebesverbot* Shakespeare's *Measure for Measure*, transferring the action to Sicily and making the target of his attack not simply hypocritical puritanism but bourgeois morality *per se*.

Musical style
Where, in *Die Feen*, Wagner had drawn on the models of German Romantic opera familiar to him from his youth, in *Das Liebesverbot* he began to give expression to new influences suggested by Young German principles. It was in Laube's periodical *Zeitung für die elegante Welt* that Wagner had his first piece of aesthetic criticism published: the essay *Die deutsche Oper* (*German Opera*) of June 1834. In that piece he turned against what he described as Teutonic 'erudition' and 'pedantry', celebrating instead the virtues of the Italians with their flair for strong, characterful, vibrant melodic lines. Wagner was to express the same idea more pithily in his essay *Bellini* of 1837: 'Song, song, and yet again song, you Germans!' The result of this change of outlook, as far as *Das Liebesverbot* was concerned, was that Wagner now looked towards Italian and French models, notably Bellini and Auber.

The most obvious debt to these models is the light, sparkling quality of the music – a feature not to be repeated in any subsequent Wagner opera – though Italian influence is also to be discerned in the lengthy finales (both well constructed, even if that to Act I is excessively prolix) and in the use of the *banda* (a military-type band playing on or behind the stage). Yet the weight of German tradition can by no means be discounted. Some of the work's most prominent thematic ideas are vigorous, appoggiatura-laden ones typical of Wagner's later works, while there are also echoes of the 'Dresden Amen' (in the nuns' Salve Regina in Act I) and of Beethoven's *Fidelio* (a striking recall of Leonore's climactic 'Töt' erst sein Weib!' at the high point of the trial scene ('Erst hört noch mich')).

Among the most memorable numbers in the work are the Act II trio for Isabella, Dorella and Luzio, which nicely captures the spirit of Luzio's casual gallantry, the duet for Isabella and Claudio, in which the slow middle section depicts the hero's fall from his lofty plane of martyrdom as he realizes that in glorious death he will not enjoy the pleasures of love, and Friedrich's scene and aria (also Act II), in which the puritanical tyrant with a human heart tunefully battles with his conscience.

Das Liebesverbot marks the first sustained use in Wagner's works of the leitmotif technique. Among a number of recurring motifs, the most significant is that associated with Friedrich's ban on love (heard first in the Overture, it begins with an admonitory downward leap and rises through two semitones). Some of the later reappearances of the motif suggest that Wagner could have extracted considerable comic potential from the technique, had he so chosen in his later works. In the Act I finale, for example, a form of the motif sounds ironically on oboes and clarinets as even Friedrich's stony heart is moved by the eloquence of Isabella's pleas for mercy – not to mention the warmth of her breath. The pompous police chief Brighella similarly falls prey to love's charms in the middle of his 'trial' of Dorella, in which he is threatening her with punishment for infringing the new law. The jaunty trilling version of the motif heard then amusingly intimates that it is not exactly the banning of love that is in Brighella's mind.

Early performances
The premiere of *Das Liebesverbot* in Magdeburg on 29 March 1836 was a fiasco, none of the singers having mastered their roles. A violent back-stage marital dispute just before curtain-up prevented the projected second performance from taking place. At Christmas 1866 Wagner presented the score to King Ludwig II with the lines: 'Once I erred and now should gladly atone for it; and how might I absolve myself from that youthful transgression? I humbly lay its work at *your* feet, that your clemency might be its redeemer.' Not until 1923 was *Das Liebesverbot* performed again in Germany – in England not until 1965.

Rienzi, der Letzte der Tribunen (Rienzi, the Last of the Tribunes)
WWV 49
Grand tragic opera in 5 acts, after Edward Bulwer-Lytton's novel of the same name

Text: Prose sketch Jun/Jul 1837, poem completed 5/6 Aug 1838
Music: 7 Aug 1838 – 19 Nov 1840; rev. 1843–4, 1847
First perf.: Königlich Sächsisches Hoftheater, Dresden, 20 Oct 1842
First UK perf.: Her Majesty's Theatre, London (Carl Rosa Opera Company), 27 Jan 1879

First US perf.: Academy of Music, New York (Pappenheim Opera Company), 4 Mar 1878

Cola Rienzi, *papal notary*	tenor
Irene, *his sister*	soprano
Steffano Colonna, *head of the Colonna family*	bass
Adriano, *his son*	mezzo-soprano
Paolo Orsini, *head of the Orsini family*	bass
Raimondo, *papal legate*	bass
Baroncelli, *Roman citizen*	tenor
Cecco del Vecchio, *Roman citizen*	bass
The Messenger of Peace	soprano

Herald, ambassadors from Milan, the Lombard States, Naples, Bohemia and Bavaria, Roman nobles and attendants, followers of Colonna and Orsini, priests and monks of all orders, senators, Roman citizens (male and female), messengers of peace

pic, 3 fl, 2 ob, 3 cl, 3 bn, serp, 4 hn, 4 tpt, 3 trbn, oph, timp, bd, sd, tenor drum, tamb, tri, gong, harp, str

On/off stage: tpt, org, bells. Military band (Act III): 12 tpt, 6 trbn, 4 oph, 10 sd, 4 tenor drums

Setting: Rome, about the middle of the 14th century

Synopsis
Act I opens in a street in Rome. Rienzi's sister Irene is about to be abducted by Paolo Orsini and his followers when they are confronted by their rivals, the Colonnas. Adriano Colonna, in love with Irene, attempts to protect her. Rienzi's arrival quells the fighting; he is urged to take power and bring order to the city. Rienzi has sworn to avenge his brother, murdered by a Colonna. Adriano atones for his family's guilt by pledging himself to Rienzi; in return, he is entrusted with Irene. Rienzi refuses the title of king, but agrees to be the people's tribune.

Act II opens in a great hall in the Capitol, with the patrician youths celebrating the success of their peace mission throughout Italy (the Chorus of the Messengers of Peace). The Colonnas and Orsini, compelled to obey the law just as the plebians do, conspire together against Rienzi. Rienzi receives the foreign ambassadors and claims for the Roman people the historic right to elect the German emperor.

A ballet, allegorizing the union of ancient and modern Rome, is performed. Orsini stabs Rienzi with a dagger, but his assassination attempt is thwarted by Rienzi's steel breastplate. Colonna's men have meanwhile attempted to seize the Capitol. Senators and people demand death for the traitors. Adriano and Irene plead for Colonna's life and Rienzi pardons the nobles.

Act III takes place in a large square in the ancient forum. The nobles are plotting, Adriano agonizing over his divided loyalties. Rienzi, on horseback, leads a grand procession, eventually returning in triumph; the bodies of Orsini and Colonna are borne in on litters. Adriano curses Rienzi and vows revenge.

In a square in front of the Lateran church (Act IV), Baroncelli alleges that Rienzi sought an alliance with the nobles, offering his sister Irene in return. The crowd demands evidence of this treachery and Adriano, throwing off his disguise, endorses the charge. Rienzi enters but Adriano baulks at assassinating him in view of Irene, while the other conspirators are won over by his rhetoric. Rienzi's excommunication is proclaimed; his followers desert him.

The final act opens in a hall in the Capitol. Rienzi prays for strength and leaves to arm himself. Adriano tries to carry away Irene by force, but she resists. In a square outside the Capitol, the people try to stone Rienzi. They set fire to the Capitol and Rienzi and Irene are seen on the balcony, clasped in each other's arms. Adriano tries to reach Irene, but as he approaches, the building collapses, burying him as well as Rienzi and Irene.

Source and composition
The novel used by Wagner as his primary source for *Rienzi* was Sir Edward Bulwer-Lytton's *Rienzi, the Last of the Tribunes* (editions subsequent to the first, published in 1835, were entitled *Rienzi: the Last of the Roman Tribunes*). He read it in Blasewitz, near Dresden, in the summer of 1837 and immediately sketched an outline for an opera – the idea apparently having been implanted earlier by his friend Apel. This brief sketch was followed by a prose draft and, then, the following summer, a verse draft. After making a series of fragmentary composition sketches, Wagner set about a continuous composition draft, the first two acts of which were completed by 9 April 1839. There then followed a short pause, during which Wagner journeyed to Paris. Act III was begun in February 1840 and the work completed in draft, with the Overture being written last, in October 1840, by which time Wagner had also started work on *Der fliegende Holländer*.

Musical style
The break in composition, though short (some ten months), resulted in a palpable stylistic shift during the course of the work. Acts I and II unashamedly imitate the models of Italian and French grand opera, all previous examples of which it was Wagner's intention to outdo 'with sumptuous extravagance'. In Acts III to V, on the other hand, there is some evidence of the new, more progressive style towards which he was working and which came to fruition in the later music dramas. A more imagina-

tive approach to word-setting, for example, breaking down the rigid distinction between recitative and aria, becomes apparent, and the orchestra begins to adopt more of a commentating role.

Nevertheless, there are elements of grand opera throughout both parts of the work: in the spectacular *mises-en-scène* (massive crowd scenes, dramatic excommunications, collapsing buildings and so forth), in the elevated style of Adriano's scene and aria 'Gerechter Gott!' – written with Wagner's idol Wilhelmine Schröder-Devrient in mind – and in the abundance of marches, processions and ballets.

The grandiloquence of the music may perhaps be seen as a reflection of the extravagant pomp and ceremony that were perceived – by an anonymous contemporary biographer of Rienzi – to have been the cause of the demagogue's downfall. The charge of self-aggrandizement was dismissed by Bulwer-Lytton, Wagner's immediate source, yet it seems undeniable that the opera has, intentionally or unintentionally, captured more than a hint of hyper-inflated rhetoric. Nor does the fact that some of the mass effects were not part of the original conception, but were grafted on in order to disguise technical inadequacy, dispose of the claim that the work has fascistic tendencies: the less demagogues have to say, the louder they tend to say it. Certainly it is the case that *Rienzi* made a powerful impact on the young Adolf Hitler: with reference to a performance of the work in 1906 or 1907 he later stated that 'In jener Stunde begann es' ('At that hour it began').

The excessive length of the work – according to *Mein Leben*, the premiere lasted from 6 o'clock to after midnight – did not prevent the occasion from being an enormous success, Schröder-Devrient making a particularly striking impression. Nevertheless, Wagner realized that if the work was to be kept in the repertory, cuts would have to be made. An abridged version was tried and it was also given complete but spread over two evenings, the first part being called *Rienzi's Greatness* and the second *Rienzi's Fall*. Wagner's abridged version was reverted to, but it was a less authentic, and less satisfactory, abridgement, by Cosima Wagner and Julius Kniese, that formed the basis for most performances in the present century. Indiscriminately cutting elements that smacked of grand opera, they tried to turn it into an incipient music drama, in the process losing some of the work's most effective music. The difficulty of producing a complete, 'authentic' version (not least when the composer himself repeatedly changed his mind on the subject) has been increased by the fact that no printed score was ever made from the autograph without cuts being made, and the autograph itself disappeared with Hitler, in whose possession it was. Such an edition was made, however, for a studio performance broadcast by the BBC in 1976, and a critical edition of the full score was published in the collected works (1974–7).

Der fliegende Holländer (*The Flying Dutchman*)
WWV 63
Romantic opera in 3 acts, after Heinrich Heine's *Aus den Memoiren des Herren von Schnabelewopski*

Text: First prose draft 2–6 May 1840, poem 18–28 May 1841
Music: Begun May–Jul 1840, score completed Nov 1841; rev. 1846, 1852, 1860
First perf.: Königlich Sächsisches Hoftheater, Dresden, 2 Jan 1843
First UK perf.: Theatre Royal, Drury Lane, London, 23 Jul 1870 (sung in Italian)
First US perf.: Academy of Music, Philadelphia, 8 Nov 1876 (sung in Italian)

Daland, *a Norwegian sailor*	bass
Senta, *his daughter*	soprano
Erik, *a huntsman*	tenor
Mary, *Senta's nurse*	contralto
Daland's Steersman	tenor
The Dutchman	bass-baritone

Norwegian sailors, the Dutchman's crew, young women

pic, 2 fl, 2 ob, cor ang, 2 cl, 2 bn, 4 hn, 2 tpt, 3 trbn, oph, timp, str

On/off stage: 3 pic, 6 hn, gong, wind machine

Setting: The Norwegian coast

Synopsis
Act I opens to a continuation of the stormy music of the Overture. Daland's ship has just cast anchor. The Steersman, left on watch as the storm subsides, slumbers as it begins to rage again and the Flying Dutchman's ship, with its blood-red sails, heaves into view. The Dutchman, in a monologue, tells how he is permitted to come on land once every seven years to seek redemption from an as yet unnamed curse. Daland comes on deck and is offered vast wealth by the Dutchman in exchange for a night's hospitality. Daland, who cannot believe his ears, is no less delighted by the wealthy stranger's interest in his daughter, Senta, and prepares to lead him back to his house.

Act II takes place in a large room in Daland's house. Urged on by Mary, Daland's housekeeper and Senta's nurse, the women spin to please their lovers who are away at sea. Senta meanwhile gazes at a picture on the wall of a pale man with a dark beard in black, Spanish dress; she sings the ballad of the Flying Dutchman (in which we learn that his curse was laid on him for a blasphemous oath), swearing to be the instrument of his salvation.

Erik, in love with Senta, is horrified to hear her outburst as he enters. He tells her of a dream, in which her father brought home a stranger resembling the seafarer in the picture. He rushes away in despair, leaving Senta to muse on the picture. The door opens and her father appears with the Dutchman, whom Senta recognizes as indeed the subject of the portrait. Left alone with the Dutchman, Senta expresses her desire to bring him redemption; he warns of the fate that would befall her if she failed to keep her vow of constancy. Senta pledges faithfulness unto death. Daland re-enters to ask whether the feast of homecoming can be combined with that of a betrothal. Senta reaffirms her vow.

Act III opens in a bay with a rocky shore. In the background the Norwegian ship is lit up and the sailors are making merry on the deck, while the Dutch ship near by is unnaturally dark and silent. The Norwegian men dance, stamping their feet in time with the music. The women bring out baskets of food and drink and call on the Dutch crew to join them. All appeals are met with a deathly silence. The Norwegians only half-jestingly recall the legend of the Flying Dutchman and their carousing becomes more manic. A storm arises around the Dutch ship and the crew finally burst into unearthly song.

Senta comes out of the house, followed by Erik, who reminds her that she has once pledged to be true to him. The Dutchman, who has overheard, makes to return to his ship and releases Senta from her vow to him. He tells of his terrible fate and how he is saving Senta from the same by releasing her. He boards his ship, but Senta, proclaiming her redeeming fidelity, casts herself into the sea. The Dutchman's ship, with all its crew, sinks immediately. The sea rises and falls again, revealing the Dutchman and Senta, transfigured and locked in embrace.

Sources

Wagner's main source for his opera on the tale of the Flying Dutchman was Heinrich Heine's telling of the legend in *Aus den Memoiren des Herren von Schnabelewopski*, published in 1834; this was a German reworking of a French text published in the *Tableaux de voyages* the previous year (his original brief version had appeared in the *Reisebilder* of 1826). But Heine's developed version is mordantly ironic, with more than a touch of misogyny. It tells how the accursed sea captain is forced to roam the sea until Judgment Day unless he be saved by a woman's devotion. 'The poor Dutchman! He is often only too glad to be rescued from his dear wife and return on board ship in order to recover from feminine loyalty.' At the end, after 'Mrs Flying Dutchman' has made her redemptive leap from the cliff into the sea, Heine appends the cynical, anti-Romantic moral that women 'should beware of marrying a Flying Dutchman; and we men should draw from it the lesson that women at best will be our undoing' – presumably by chaining the wanderer to a marriage he does not really want.

Heine's own possible sources are to some extent a matter of speculation. The legend seems to have grown up during the period of Britain's naval supremacy in the 18th century: England had waged a series of three inconclusive naval and colonial wars against the Dutch republic between 1652 and 1674, and the skirmishes, arising out of trading disputes, which continued to occur in the following century, would have given rise to such sailors' tales, which were passed down from one generation to another.

It was only at the beginning of the 19th century, however, that the legend of the Flying Dutchman achieved literary form, in various English and German versions. A poem of Thomas Moore (1779–1852) alludes to a superstition among sailors about a ghost ship which they call the Flying Dutchman. Sir Walter Scott's pirate poem *Rokeby* (1813), according to its author, relates to 'a well-known nautical superstition concerning a fantastic vessel, called by sailors the Flying Dutchman, and supposed to be seen about the latitude of the Cape of Good Hope. She is distinguished from earthly vessels by bearing a press of sail when all others are unable, from stress of weather, to show an inch of canvas.' The legend crops up too in contemporary German sources, including *Der ewige Segler* (*The Eternal Seafarer*) of 1812, by H. Schmidt; *Das Geisterschiff* (*The Ghost Ship*) of 1832, by Joseph Christian Freiherr von Zedlitz; and a number of popular tales by Wilhelm Hauff, which were almost certainly familiar to both Heine and Wagner.

Wagner never gave his Dutchman a name, but he was given one in an important Scottish source entitled *Vanderdecken's Message Home; Or, the Tenacity of Natural Affection*, printed in the May 1821 issue of Blackwood's *Edinburgh Magazine*. The story, published anonymously but believed to have been written by one John Howison, tells of the appearance of the ghost ship 'scudding furiously before the wind, under a press of canvass [*sic*]' and of the vain attempt by a member of its crew to palm off some letters for delivery to long-dead relatives on land. (This mail-delivery motif, though looming large in many versions of the legend, is relegated to a trifling detail by Wagner.)

While there is no evidence that Wagner had first-hand knowledge of Howison's version, there are notable parallels between the Blackwood's narrative and Heine's. Heine seems therefore to have drawn on Howison, as well as various tales passed on by sailors and fishermen, fleshing out the story with elements from his own imagination. It has occasionally been suggested that Heine was also beholden to Edward Fitzball's play *The Flying Dutchman; or The Phantom Ship*. But this seems most improbable: the play is a farcical trifle, as evidenced by the printer's preface, which congratulates the author on a piece in which 'mirth and moonshine – murder and merriment – fire and fun, are so happily blended!' The central villain (following Howison) is called Vanderdecken, and he himself clambers on board ship in a vain attempt to get his mail delivered. But it is unlikely that either Fitzball's execrable doggerel or his frothy treatment of the nautical yarn, which ends with much waving of the British flag and shouts of 'Huzza!', would have inspired Heine. Moreover, the play closed at the Adelphi Theatre in London a week before Heine arrived in England in 1827 and does not appear to have been published for another two years.

Composition

Notwithstanding the short literary history of the specific Flying Dutchman legend, it contained, for Wagner, a deep mythic resonance. The central figure had been embodied, as he pointed out, in Greek mythology by Ulysses and his longing after home, hearth and wife, and in the Christian tradition in the figure of the Wandering Jew, Ahasuerus (with whom Wagner also identified himself). The possibility of redemption for the tortured wanderer, brought by the selfless love of a woman, made a particular appeal to Wagner. In fact so closely did he identify with the story that he allowed his account of the work's genesis in *Mein Leben* to be coloured by it. Thus he describes the stormy voyage from Riga to London aboard the *Thetis* in July and August 1839, and the sound of the crew's shouts echoing round the granite walls of the Norwegian fjord, as formative experiences on the *Holländer*:

> The sharp rhythm of this call clung to me like a consoling augury and soon shaped itself into the theme of the [Norwegian] sailors' song in my *Fliegender Holländer*. Already at that time I was carrying around with me the idea of this opera and now, under the impressions I had just experienced, it acquired a distinct poetic and musical colour.

The truth is that the opera was originally set not in Norway at all, but in Scotland. Erik and Daland were called 'Georg' and 'Donald' (or 'the Scotsman') and in the prose sketch Senta was 'Anna' (never 'Minna' as sometimes stated). The change of setting, effected just a few weeks before the opera's premiere, when it was already in rehearsal, was no doubt motivated in part by a desire to enhance the autobiographical element. But the change at the same time allowed Wagner to distance himself from Heine's version, which also had a Scottish setting, and, perhaps more urgently, from the operatic version of Pierre-Louis Dietsch (with libretto by Paul Foucher and Bénédict-Henry Révoil), which by an unfortunate coincidence reached the stage of the Paris Opéra in the same month (November 1842) as rehearsals for the *Holländer* began in Dresden. (It is not, however, the case – contrary to popular belief – that Dietsch's librettists based their story on Wagner's scenario; see 'Myths and Legends', p.134.) Having written his poem for the

opera in Meudon, just outside Paris, in May 1841, Wagner turned his attention to the musical setting and had a complete draft ready by 22 August, the full score by 19 November. But three numbers central to the work – Senta's Ballad, the chorus of the Norwegian sailors and the chorus of the Dutchman's crew – had been written already, presumably between 3 May and 26 July 1840, that is between the date on which Wagner informed Meyerbeer that he was about to send the celebrated librettist Eugène Scribe his prose sketch for the work and that on which he announced that the three pieces were ready for audition. Nor is it impossible that some ideas for the music were indeed jotted down in the months following the *Thetis* voyage, though there is no documentary evidence of that.

Musical style

One of the most striking numbers in the work is the Ballad sung by Senta in Act II, which begins with the same bracing open fifths on tremolo strings that began the Overture, and with the 'horn call' figure of the Dutchman heard first as a pounding bass and then in the vocal line itself. (The startling effect of these opening gestures is enhanced, in the version familiar today, by the unprepared drop in tonality from A major to G minor. However, the Ballad was originally in A minor, and Wagner transposed it down at a late date for the benefit of Wilhelmine Schröder-Devrient, who was taking the role.) The strophic structure of Senta's Ballad sets it firmly in the early 19th-century operatic tradition of interpolated narrative songs; indeed, there is a direct link with the song sung by Emmy in Marschner's *Der Vampyr*, which Wagner had prepared for performance in Würzburg in 1833.

Important as Senta's Ballad is, the assertion made by Wagner, a decade after the composition of the work in *Eine Mitteilung an meine Freunde* (*A Communication to my Friends*), that the whole work germinated from the 'thematic seed' planted in the Ballad, should be seen for what it is: a retrospective attempt to represent the *Holländer* as an incipient through-composed music drama rather than an old-fashioned number opera. It is true that elements of the Ballad appear in some of the other central numbers of the work, for example the Dutchman's monologue, Erik's Dream, the duet for Senta and the Dutchman, the finale. It is also true that a melodic idea, which might be called the 'Redemption motif' (sung to 'Ach! möchtest du, bleicher Seemann, sie finden!' in the Ballad), recurs elsewhere in the work. But such recurrences are a far cry from the method of structural organization that characterizes the *Ring*, where large numbers of leitmotifs are subjected to systematic elaboration over a broad canvas.

If *Der fliegende Holländer* is not yet a through-composed music drama, neither is it still a 'number opera' in the old-fashioned sense. The trend of German Romantic opera in the early decades of the

19th century was away from the divisions into numbers with their joining recitatives. Wagner advanced the process with his *Holländer*, which may more accurately be called a 'scene opera', in that the individual acts comprise little groups of connected numbers: no. 4, for example, is called 'scene, duet and chorus'.

Choral ensembles have not yet been banished from the *Holländer*, as they were to be from the mature music dramas – at least theoretically, those that remained being woven seamlessly into the musical fabric. The Sailors' Chorus ending Act I and the Spinning Chorus opening Act II scarcely propel the action forward; nor are they seamlessly integrated into the structure. The extended chorus work in Act III, on the other hand, is more 'progressive' in nature. The rival ensembles of the merrymaking Norwegians and the terrifyingly ghostly Dutch crew are juxtaposed and finally superimposed to wonderfully theatrical effect, their battle for supremacy powerfully reflecting the struggle of the larger work between the spheres of the mundane and the diabolical.

A particularly striking feature of the score is the contrast between the 'exterior', public world of Daland, Erik and the Norwegian sailors and maidens on the one hand, and the 'interior' world of the imagination inhabited by Senta and the Dutchman on the other. The exterior world is characterized by traditional forms and harmonies – the regular two-bar phrases of Erik's third-act cavatina are an extreme example. The interior world, by contrast, makes frequent attempts to break free from the constraints of regular periodic structure: the Dutchman's Act I monologue comes closest to doing so. The only notable exception to this dichotomy is Erik's recital of his dream, 'Auf hohem Felsen', where the irregular, fragmented phrases conjure an appropriately dreamlike atmosphere. See also 'Musical Background and Influences' (pp.74–6).

Versions

In order to stand a better chance of having his work accepted by the Paris Opéra (as a curtain-raiser before a ballet), Wagner originally conceived the *Holländer* in a single act. (The claim, in *Mein Leben*, that it was primarily to focus on the dramatic essentials rather than on 'tiresome operatic accessories' sounds like a retrospective rationalization.) But by the time he came to write the music, the Opéra had rejected his proposal, and he therefore elaborated the scheme in three acts – at this stage to be played without a break. Then, some time after the end of October 1842, when he retrieved his score from the Berlin Opera (and possibly acting on advice from that quarter), he recast it in three discrete acts – the form in which it was given in Dresden and subsequently published. Cosima Wagner, when she introduced the work at Bayreuth in 1901, chose to give it in a single act, the better to

present it as an incipient music drama. Both continuous and separate-act versions therefore have some claim to authenticity.

Revisions

From the time of the first performance to the end of his life Wagner tinkered with the score of the *Holländer*. In 1846 he made some revisions to the orchestration for a projected performance in Leipzig (which did not take place), with the aim of toning down the brassiness he had inherited from French grand opera. More radical revisions were planned in 1852 for performances in Zurich and Weimar, though in the event Wagner contented himself with changes to the scoring and an improved ending to the Overture, declaring that for the rest the 1846 Leipzig version should be considered the authentic one. Then in 1860, when the Overture was included in concerts in Paris, the coda of the Overture was remodelled and the ending of the whole opera adapted in accordance; this remodelling does not, as sometimes stated, date from 1852. The 1860 revision, with its more refined, more intricate textures, reflects Wagner's recent preoccupation with *Tristan* (see Abraham, 1968, and Vetter, 1979 and 1982).

Tannhäuser und der Sängerkrieg auf Wartburg (Tannhäuser and the Singers' Contest on the Wartburg)
WWV 70
Grand romantic opera in 3 acts

Text: first prose draft 28 Jun – 6 Jul 1842, poem completed early Apr 1843
Music: fragmentary and continuous complete drafts summer/autumn 1843 – Dec 1844, full score completed 13 Apr 1845; rev. 1845, 1847, 1851, 1860–61, 1865, 1875
First perf.: Königlich Sächsisches Hoftheater, Dresden, 19 Oct 1845
First UK perf.: Covent Garden, London (Royal Italian Opera), 6 May 1876 (sung in Italian)
First US perf.: Stadt Theater, New York, 4 Apr 1859

Hermann, Landgrave of Thuringia		bass
Tannhäuser		tenor
Wolfram von Eschinbach		bass
Walther von der Vogelweide	*knights and minstrels*	baritone
Biterolf		bass
Heinrich der Schreiber		tenor
Reinmar von Zweter		bass
Elisabeth, *the Landgrave's niece*		soprano
Venus		soprano
A young shepherd		soprano
Four noble pages		soprano, alto

Thuringian knights, counts and nobles, ladies, older and younger pilgrims, sirens, naiads, nymphs, bacchantes. In Paris version, additionally the Three Graces, youths, cupids, satyrs and fauns

pic, 3 fl, 2 ob, 2 cl, bass cl, 2 bn, 2 valve hn, 2 natural hn, 3 valve tpt, 3 trbn, contrabass tuba, timp, bd, cym, tri, tamb, cast (Paris version), harp (4 harps at Paris perfs), str

On/off stage: cor ang, 2 pic, 4 fl, 4 ob, 6 cl, 6 bn, 12 hn, 12 tpt, 4 trbn, tri, cym, tamb

Setting: Thuringia at the beginning of the 13th century

Dresden/Paris versions

The *Wagner Werk-Verzeichnis* (Deathridge, Geck and Voss, 1986) identifies four 'stages' of the work: 1. the original version as given at the Dresden premiere in 1845; 2. the edition published by Meser in 1860, incorporating revisions made (notably to the ending of the work) between 1847 and 1852; 3. the version of 1861 (not published), as performed at the Opéra that year; 4. the version performed under Wagner's supervision in Vienna in 1875, incorporating revisions made subsequently to 1861 (vocal score 1876, full score 1888). There is, however, no reason to abandon the convenient traditional labels of 'Dresden version' (i.e. no. 2) and 'Paris version' (no. 4), provided it is borne in mind that these terms refer not to what was actually heard in Dresden in 1845 or Paris in 1861, but to revised editions of those performances. The major differences between the two versions are described in the synopsis below, and the Paris variants are usefully given in the Dover full score.

Synopsis

One of the primary changes for Paris concerned the opening of the opera, the Bacchanal in the Venusberg (identified by Wagner and others with the Hörselberg in Thuringia) being extended. In the original version, the stage directions prescribed a rocky grotto with bathing naiads, reclining sirens and dancing nymphs. Venus lay on a couch in a rosy light, with Tannhäuser, half-kneeling, nestling his head in her lap. Urged on by bacchantes, the dancers reached a peak of orgiastic excitement. The Paris version adds the Three Graces and cupids, while satyrs and fauns cause a riotous frenzy by chasing the nymphs. Prompted by the Graces, the cupids quell the riot by raining down love-arrows on all below. The Paris Bacchanal is both longer and more frenzied.

Tannhäuser, surfeited with the sensual pleasures of the Venusberg, begs Venus to release him; she eventually yields, and on Tannhäuser's invocation of the Virgin Mary, Venus and her domains instantly disappear. Tannhäuser finds himself in a sunlit valley in front of the Wartburg. A procession of pilgrims passes. Then the Landgrave and minstrels approach and, on recognizing Tannhäuser, greet him warmly. Tannhäuser accedes to their pleas to remain in their company.

Act II opens with Elisabeth's joyous greeting to the Hall of Song in the Wartburg, abandoned by her during Tannhäuser's absence. Tannhäuser and Elisabeth celebrate their reunion. Trumpets sound from the courtyard, heralding the arrival of the guests (knights, counts, their ladies and retinue) for the song-contest. The Landgrave extols the art of song and calls on the minstrels to demonstrate it by singing in praise of love; the worthiest contender will receive his prize from Elisabeth herself. Wolfram uses the image of a fountain to sing of the purity of love; Tannhäuser retorts that the fountain of love fills him only with burning desire. The next singer, Walther von der Vogelweide, warns that the fountain, of which Wolfram sang, bestows grace only so long as fleshly thoughts are banished. Tannhäuser's response makes clear that he has no intention of banishing such thoughts. Biterolf challenges Tannhäuser to a combat of more than vocal prowess, but is scorned by Tannhäuser for his inexperience as regards the joys of true love. There is general consternation and the ladies, with the exception of Elisabeth, leave the hall in shock. The knights round threateningly on Tannhäuser, but Elisabeth urges clemency. Tannhäuser himself is overcome with remorse. The Landgrave tells Tannhäuser that his only hope of salvation is to join the band of pilgrims preparing to make their way to Rome.

In Act III, Elisabeth, seeing that Tannhäuser is not among the pilgrims returning from Rome, sings her Prayer. She leaves and Wolfram sings his celebrated Hymn to the Evening Star. Tannhäuser appears and tells Wolfram, in his Narration, how, as a penitent, he visited the Pope in Rome, only to be condemned: he could no more be forgiven, he was told, than the Pope's staff could sprout green leaves. To Wolfram's horror, Tannhäuser declares his intention of returning to the Venusberg. Venus herself appears in a bright, rosy light, reclining on her couch. (In the original 1845 version Venus did not appear at the end, the Venusberg being suggested by a red glow in the distance; Elisabeth's death was similarly announced only by bells tolling from the Wartburg.) A struggle ensues for Tannhäuser's soul, resolved by an emphatic enunciation of Elisabeth's name by Wolfram. An off-stage chorus announces that Elisabeth has died. But her intercession has redeemed Tannhäuser and Venus disappears, vanquished. Elisabeth's bier is carried on, and Tannhäuser, calling on the saint to intercede for him, falls lifeless to the ground. The final strains of the Pilgrims' Chorus tell of a miracle: the Pope's staff has burst into leaf. Tannhäuser's soul is saved.

Sources

A number of sources were drawn upon by Wagner for *Tannhäuser*, chief among them being: *Der getreue Eckart und der Tannenhäuser* (*Faithful Eckart and Tannenhäuser*), from Ludwig Tieck's collection of fairytales *Phantasus*, which tells the story of Tannhäuser and his cupidinous activities in the Venusberg, his pilgrimage to Rome and his repulsion by the Pope; E.T.A. Hoffmann's story *Der Kampf der Sänger* (*The Singers' Contest*), from his *Serapions-Brüder*, about a song competition at the Wartburg castle; the essay *Elementargeister* by Heinrich Heine, containing a characteristically ironic poem about Tannhäuser; as well as a play by Friedrich de la Motte Fouqué and Eichendorff's story *Das Marmorbild*.

The legends of Tannhäuser (believed originally to have been a crusading knight from Franconia who presumably turned his amatory verses while girding himself to do battle for the next patron) and the song-contest at the Wartburg were traditionally quite separate. But taking his cue from two contemporary writers, Ludwig Bechstein and C.T.L. Lucas, who traced dubious (and anachronistic) connections between them, Wagner conflated the legends to weave a story that gives us not an authentic view of 13th-century ideals and *mores*, but a technicoloured 19th-century one in which the medieval world is refracted through a Romantic lens.

Composition

a) Dresden version

The idea of basing an opera on the Tannhäuser story had already occurred to Wagner during his ill-fated stay in Paris (1839–42), but it was during a summer holiday in Bohemia, shortly after he had returned from France, that the work began to take shape. The first, detailed prose draft (28 June – 6 July 1842) was followed in the spring of 1843 by the libretto itself; then after a number of sketches for individual sections of the work came two complete drafts apparently worked on in tandem (summer/autumn 1843 to January 1845). The first of these two drafts, less developed than the second, exists only in fragmentary form, but it has been painstakingly pieced together by scholars (most, but not all, of the fragments are in the Bayreuth archives). The Overture was written last and the full score completed on 13 April 1845.

b) Paris version

The invitation to Wagner to stage *Tannhäuser* at the Paris Opéra at the beginning of the 1860s came from Emperor Napoleon III himself. But it was well known that the unpopular Princess Pauline Metternich, wife of the Austrian ambassador in Paris, had been instrumental in bringing about the invitation – a fact that had much to do with the demonstrations against the work that eventually brought it off the stage after only three performances. Wagner had declined to humour the white-gloved members of the Jockey Club, who were not in the habit of seeing works through from the beginning: rather they aristocratically decamped from their dining tables in time for the second-act ballet, when their favourite dancers would appear for their delectation. The demand for a ballet did, however, give Wagner the idea for expanding the music of the Venusberg, which had previously opened Act I, into a wild Bacchanal, the better to depict the excesses of the Venusberg from which Tannhäuser wishes to escape.

The members of the Jockey Club were unimpressed and took ruthless revenge on Princess Metternich's protégé by disrupting not only the premiere at the Opéra (13 March 1861) but also two further performances (18 and 24 March) with prolonged baying and blasts on their dog-whistles. Only after this thrice-enacted ordeal for composer and cast was Wagner permitted to withdraw his production – a production that had taken no fewer than 164 rehearsals to bring to the stage.

Musical style

The rival spheres of sensual and spiritual love, represented by the Venusberg on the one hand and by Elisabeth and the Wartburg on the other, are depicted directly in the music. The key of E major is thus associated with the Venusberg, and E♭ major with the pilgrims, holy love and salvation. In Tannhäuser's climactic Rome Narration (Act III scene 3), for example, the E♭ of his audience with the Pope gives way, after a series of modulations, to the E major of the Venusberg, before the final triumphant return to E♭ confirms Tannhäuser's salvation.

But there is also a more fundamental polarity at work which has to be seen in the context of the opera's socio-historical background. Tannhäuser's espousal of worldly, sensual love is a reflection of the hedonistic views of the Young German writers by whom Wagner was influenced in the 1830s. Their contempt for the solid, reactionary virtues of the Biedermeier era and for the bourgeois sexual hypocrisy sustained by the structures of Church and State is evident in Tannhäuser's derisive outbursts at the song-contest. In musical terms, the reactionary Wartburg court is associated with traditional, not to say outmoded, operatic procedures, while the Venusberg is characterized by the new, progressive style of music drama towards which Wagner was steadily moving. The song-contest, for example, is a series of more or less self-contained arias. Elisabeth has two set-piece arias (the Hall of Song aria, 'Dich, teure Halle', opening Act II, and her Prayer, 'Allmächt'ge Jungfrau', in Act III), as well as a conventional duet with Tannhäuser. Wolfram's celebrated aria to the evening star, 'O du mein holder Abendstern', is also highly conservative in its regular eight-bar periods and tonal scheme. More-over, as Carolyn Abbate has pointed out (1984 and 1988), the outline of a traditional 19th-century Italianate finale is still discernible in Act II of *Tannhäuser*; movements that freeze the action alternate with ones that carry it forward, and there is even a classic *coup de théâtre* (Elisabeth's 'Haltet ein!' as she intervenes to protect Tannhäuser from the advancing knights) and closing stretta ('Mit ihnen sollst du wallen'). Elisabeth's dramatic intervention, incidentally, is another direct echo of the comparable moment in Beethoven's *Fidelio*, when Leonore intervenes to protect her husband Florestan (a similar recall occurs in *Das Liebesverbot*; see p.274).

If the music associated with the Wartburg is backward-looking in style, that of Venus is much more radically advanced. Her music in the duet with Tannhäuser (Act I) frequently breaks out of the straitjacket of regular phrase lengths – notably contrasting with Tannhäuser's own more formal utterances. That scene and the preceding Bacchanal are also more progressive in other ways: they are less tightly constructed, the text-setting is more responsive to the drama and there are rudimentary examples of motivic cross-references. All this is true, to some extent, of the original Dresden version, but the Tristanesque protractions and expressive asymmetries of the Paris version (see below) considerably heighten the contrast of styles. These scenes aside, the most advanced writing in *Tannhäuser* occurs in the Rome Narration. Here the narrative is all-important and regular phrase structure therefore gives way to a continuous dramatic recitative or arioso comparable to that of the later music dramas. The nature of the musical line actually changes as the verse describes in turn Tannhäuser's contrite state of mind on beginning his journey, his memory of Elisabeth, the heavily oppressed pilgrims, the mood of adoration in Rome, the grief-stricken penitence and finally the Pope's rebuff. Nor is it simply the vocal line that is noteworthy. The orchestra also assumes a dominant role in the Rome Narration. Its use in a virtually unprecedented manner for expressive, illustrative purposes, as the medium for generating tension and effecting modulations, and in bearing the burden of the dramatic argument, looks forward to the epoch-making innovations of the *Ring* and beyond.

The Paris revisions

Just three weeks before his death, Wagner famously opined that he still owed the world *Tannhäuser* (Cosima Wagner's Diaries, 23 January 1883). In spite of the series of revisions made to the score over the years since its Dresden premiere in 1845 – most recently some small changes made to the Paris version for some performances in Vienna in 1875 – Wagner was still not content that he had produced a definitive score. But it also seems likely that that very tinkering had contributed to the dissatisfaction. It was described above how the score as originally written already contained retrogressive and progressive elements in juxtaposition. Those discrepancies of style were greatly exaggerated when Wagner rewrote sections of the score for the Paris performances, inevitably in a style closer to that of *Tristan*, which he had recently been working on, than to that of his still-developing style in the mid-1840s.

The stylistic incongruity of the Paris version is most apparent in the latter stages of the new Bacchanal and in the newly written scene for Venus and Tannhäuser (Act I scenes 1 and 2). The Bacchanal is not only much longer and more frenzied (castanets and a third timpani being added for Paris): it also contains blatantly Tristanesque ideas and textures – such as the rising chromatic four-note phrase ubiquitous in *Tristan*. The sirens' calls are integrated more voluptuously into the musical fabric, as are Venus's responses to Tannhäuser in scene 2. Where previously her rather plain declamation was simply punctuated by bare chords, now her vocal line is sensually pliable, with richly scored accompaniments.

Venus's characterization is further deepened by the addition of two speeches after Tannhäuser has sung his Hymn to Love. The first ('Sie, die du siegend einst verlachtest') is angry and mocking, the second ('Ha! du kehrtest nie zurück!'), an outburst of genuine despair. Thus the comparatively shallow, one-dimensional Dresden Venus is transformed for Paris, through text and music, into a fully rounded character. The gamut of emotions she runs in attempting to lure back Tannhäuser (quiet incredulity – indignation – seductive charm – fierce anger – despair) is worthy of the resourceful, if schizophrenic, Kundry in Act II of *Parsifal*.

One other major change was made for Paris. Owing to the inadequacy of the tenor due to sing the part, Walther's contribution to the song-contest was removed, Tannhäuser's riposte being made to Wolfram instead. Other, minor revisions were as follows: Act I scene 3, shepherd's song; Act I scene 4, 13 bars rescored immediately before Tannhäuser's 'Zu ihr! zu ihr!'; Act II, final bars slightly amended; Act III, ditto (with addition of harp).

Lohengrin
WWV 75
Romantic opera in 3 acts

Text: prose draft completed 3 Aug 1845, poem completed 27 Nov 1845
Music: first complete draft finished 30 July 1846, second complete draft finished (Prelude) 29 Aug 1847, score 1 Jan – 28 Apr 1848
First perf.: Grossherzogliches Hof-Theater, Weimar, 28 Aug 1850
First UK perf.: Covent Garden, London (Royal Italian Opera), 8 May 1875 (sung in Italian)

First US perf.: Stadt Theater, New York, 3 Apr 1871

King Henry	bass
Lohengrin	tenor
Elsa of Brabant	soprano
Duke Gottfried, *her brother*	mute role
Friedrich von Telramund, *a count of Brabant*	baritone
Ortrud, *his wife*	mezzo-soprano
The King's Herald	bass
Four noblemen of Brabant	tenor, bass
Four pages	soprano, alto

Saxon and Thuringian counts and nobles, Brabantine counts and nobles, noblewomen, pages, vassals, ladies, serfs

pic, 3 fl, 3 ob, cor ang, 3 cl, bass cl, 3 bn, 4 hn, 3 tpt, 3 trbn, contrabass tuba, timp, cym, tri, tamb, harp, str

On/off stage: pic, 3 fl, 3 ob, 3 cl, 3 bn, 4 hn, 12 tpt, 4 trbn, org, harp, timp, cym, tri, tenor drum

Setting: Antwerp. First half of the 10th century

Synopsis

Act I opens in a meadow on the banks of the Scheldt near Antwerp. King Henry (the historical Henry the Fowler) has come to Antwerp to exhort the Brabantines to join him in defending Germany against the imminent invasion from the Hungarians in the east. The Herald summons the Brabantines to arms, but one of their counts, Friedrich von Telramund, accuses Elsa of murdering her brother Gottfried, the heir to the dukedom of Brabant; he claims the succession for himself.

Urged to defend herself, Elsa can only relay a vision of a knightly champion. The King and bystanders are much moved, but Telramund is unimpressed. He demands judgment through combat; Elsa invokes her visionary champion. Herald and trumpeters twice sound the call, but there is no response. Elsa sinks to her knees in prayer and in the distance appears a knight in a boat drawn by a swan. Lohengrin offers himself as Elsa's champion, but makes her promise that she will never ask his name or origin. They pledge themselves to each other and Telramund, ignoring entreaties to desist, braces himself for battle.

Lohengrin defeats Telramund but spares his life. Ortrud wonders who the stranger is that renders her magical powers useless. Telramund, crushed and humiliated, falls at her feet.

Act II takes place at the fortress at Antwerp. Telramund upbraids Ortrud for his disgrace; she tells him that Lohengrin's power would be nullified if Elsa were to ask him his name and origin. Ortrud calls up to Elsa, who has appeared on the balcony, and hypocritically appeals to her generous nature. As Elsa disappears to descend to ground level,

Ortrud invokes the pagan gods. Affectedly prostrating herself before Elsa, Ortrud gradually instils the poison, commenting darkly on Lohengrin's mysterious origins and appearance.

The Herald announces that Telramund is banished. The stranger sent by God, he continues, wishes to take as his title not Duke, but Protector of Brabant; today he celebrates his wedding, tomorrow he will lead them into battle. The wedding procession is interrupted first by Ortrud and then by Telramund, who vehemently accuses Lohengrin of sorcery. His demand that the knight reveal his name is brushed aside by Lohengrin. No king or prince can command him, he replies, only Elsa. But as he turns to his bride, he sees with dismay that she is agitated. As Elsa and Lohengrin reach the top step of the minster, she looks down to see Ortrud raising her arm in a gesture of triumph.

Act III begins in the bridal chamber. Elsa urges Lohengrin to share his secret, and despite his alternate warnings and protestations of love, eventually asks outright who he is. Telramund and his henchmen at that moment break into the chamber. Lohengrin fells Telramund and orders his body to be taken to the King's judgment seat; there he will answer Elsa's question.

Scene 3 returns to the banks of the Scheldt. Telramund's covered body is brought in. Then Elsa enters, followed by Lohengrin, who tells the King that he can no longer lead his troops into battle. He explains how he killed Telramund in self-defence and goes on to denounce Elsa for breaking her vow. Now he is forced to reveal his origins. In his Narration, he tells how he came as a servant of the Grail; such knights are granted invincible power on condition of anonymity. Now his secret is revealed, he must return to Monsalvat. His father is Parzival and his name is Lohengrin. The swan appears, drawing an empty boat. Lohengrin tells Elsa that had they lived together for just a year, her brother Gottfried would have been restored to her. He entrusts her with his sword, horn and ring, to be given to Gottfried should he return one day. Ortrud declares that she recognizes the swan, by the chain round its neck, as Gottfried, whom she bewitched; now he is lost to Elsa for ever. Lohengrin kneels silently in prayer. A white dove descends and hovers over the boat. Seeing it, Lohengrin loosens the chain round the swan, which sinks. In its place appears a boy in shining silver: Gottfried. Lohengrin lifts him to the bank, proclaiming him Duke of Brabant. Ortrud falls to the ground. As Lohengrin vanishes from sight, Elsa falls lifeless to the ground.

Sources

Wagner first became acquainted with the Lohengrin legend in the winter of 1841–2, when he encountered it in the form of a synopsis and commentary in the annual proceedings of the

Königsberg Germanic Society. He then pursued his study of the sources while taking the waters at Marienbad, in the summer of 1845. He had with him editions by Simrock and San-Marte of *Parzival* and *Titurel* by the poet Wolfram von Eschenbach (*c.* 1170 – shortly after 1220), as well as Johann Joseph von Görres' edition of the anonymous epic *Lohengrin*. According to Wagner's later account in *Mein Leben*, his opera 'stood suddenly revealed before me, complete in every detail of its dramatic construction', and indeed the prose draft which he had worked out by 3 August of that year did not require radical reshaping when he came to elaborate it on his return to Dresden.

Composition
Departing from the method of composition he had employed in *Der fliegende Holländer* and *Tannhäuser*, Wagner made for *Lohengrin* a through-composed draft for the whole work, though it consisted of only two staves (one for the voice, one indicating harmonies, often just by a bass) and amounting to little more than 'a very hasty outline', as he later described it. This work was done between May and July 1846, after which Wagner elaborated the instrumental and choral parts in a second complete draft, which he began on 9 September 1846 and finished, with the Prelude, on 29 August the following year.

Various changes were made to the poem during the course of composition, especially in Act III, which probably accounts for the fact that the second complete draft for this act was made, unusually, before those for Acts I and II. This reversal of order has led to the oft-repeated, but incorrect, statement that the opera itself was composed in that order (i.e. beginning with Act III): the first complete draft, in which the work was set down in a detailed outline, was written in conventional order. Wagner made his full score between 1 January and 28 April 1848.

Musical style
The 'associative' use of tonality, described above in connection with *Tannhäuser* (see p.281), is again evident in *Lohengrin*. The central character and the sphere of the Grail are represented by A major, the key of the work's beginning and conclusion, and of Lohengrin's important Narration, 'In fernem Land', in Act III. Just as in *Tannhäuser* Wagner chose keys a semitone apart (E and E♭) for his principal contrasts, so in *Lohengrin* he sets Elsa's A♭ major (and minor) against Lohengrin's A, with the result that some adroit – though undeniably effective – manoeuvring between the two is required. Act I scene 2 (the entry of Elsa to answer the charge against her) opens in A♭, minor and major; her account of her dream, 'Einsam in trüben Tagen', is principally in A♭ too. But Elsa's anticipation of Lohengrin's arrival in a swan-drawn skiff lifts the tonality by a semitone: it is a transfiguring moment,

in which the music graphically reflects the radiant expression that comes over Elsa's face. A major is then firmly established as Lohengrin's tonality both by the choral acclamation and by his farewell to the swan. But, as he enters Elsa's sphere, by offering himself as her champion, the music switches back to A♭, only for it to return swiftly to A as Elsa acknowledges him as her protector.

The relative minor of Lohengrin's A major is F♯ minor, which is the key primarily associated with Ortrud and her evil attributes. But whereas in *Tannhäuser* the reactionary nature of the Wartburg is reflected in regressive stylistic features (see pp.281–2), in *Lohengrin* the reverse at first appears to be the case. Ortrud is the representative not only of evil but also of the old pagan gods; her malignant magical powers are finally overcome by Lohengrin's benign spirituality. It may therefore seem paradoxical that the most progressive passage in the work, in stylistic terms, is the scene for Ortrud and Telramund (Act II scene 1), in which the former shows the latter how the powers of darkness can prevail over Lohengrin and Elsa. In this scene, the vocal lines are liberated from four-square phrase structures and project the sense of the words with something of the immediacy that was to characterize the subsequent music dramas. The explanation of the paradox lies in the fact that for Wagner the struggle in *Lohengrin* was not essentially one between benighted paganism and enlightened Christianity. In the essay *Eine Mitteilung an meine Freunde* (*A Communication to my Friends*, 1851) he is at pains to make clear that the Lohengrin myth inspired him not because of its 'leanings towards Christian supernaturalism', but because it penetrated to the core of human longings. The 1840s was the decade in which Young Hegelians such as David Friedrich Strauss and Bruno Bauer issued challenges to the tenets of conventional religion, and in which the humanist ethics of Ludwig Feuerbach had enormous influence on German intellectuals of the day (see 'Intellectual Background', pp.59–60). Even though Wagner appears not to have read Feuerbach for himself until after the revolution, there seems little doubt that he was influenced by some of the ideas prevalent in the radical circles of cities such as Dresden. The figure of Lohengrin appealed to Wagner, therefore, not primarily as some kind of divine protector or saviour, but as a 'metaphysical phenomenon' whose contact with human nature could end only in tragedy; the Christian trappings of the legend, as in *Parsifal*, were of essentially symbolic value to him. Thus, as in *Tannhäuser*, it is the sphere counterposed to orthodox religion that evokes the most progressive writing.

Vestiges of the old-fashioned number form are still to be found throughout *Lohengrin*: recitatives, arias, duets and choruses. Even the progressive scene for Ortrud and Telramund mentioned above (Act II scene 1) ends with a conventional revenge duet, the voices in unison. The vocal lines here, however, depart from the regular two- or four-bar phrase structures that otherwise dominate the work. There are also significant deviations from the norm in Elsa's Dream and Lohengrin's Narration, whose opening phrases balanced in the conventional fashion give way to less tightly organized patterns as the numbers proceed. The shift in each case serves a dramatic purpose: the stiff formality typical of the beginning of a public address yields to a looser structure as both teller and listener are swept along by the flow of the narrative.

The technique of the leitmotif was still to be fully developed by Wagner, but there is a striking anticipation of it in *Lohengrin*: the motif of the Forbidden Question. First heard sung to the words 'Nie sollst du mich befragen' ('Never shall you question me') in Act I scene 3, it reappears as a constant reminder of Lohengrin's stern injunction to Elsa not to enquire after his name or origin. Undoubtedly its most dramatic reappearance is in the closing bars of Act II, when the wedding procession is interrupted by Elsa's terror at Ortrud's menacingly outstretched arm: the motif rings out on trumpets and trombones, its F minor colouring casting a sombre shadow over the prevailing C major. The gesture anticipates a similar moment in the closing bars of Act II of *Götterdämmerung*, where the wedding procession is halted by an action of Hagen, whose baleful motif likewise rings out *fortissimo*. (The interrupted ceremonial, a trope of grand opera, is also used earlier in the same act of *Götterdämmerung*: see 'Musical Background and Influences', p.77.) For all its dramatic effect and forward-looking tendency, the Forbidden Question motif, like others in *Lohengrin*, is different in kind from typical leitmotifs in the *Ring* and serves a different structural function. Whereas the motifs of *Lohengrin* are generally fully-rounded themes with complementary phrases, the characteristic *Ring* leitmotif is short, pithy and capable of infinite transformation (though more elaborate melodic ideas are also to be found there). And where the motifs of the *Ring* are developed in such a way as to determine the shape of whole paragraphs, even scenes, those of *Lohengrin* have only an illustrative or dramaturgical purpose – they do not provide the building blocks of the structure.

Revisions and cuts

Unlike *Tannhäuser*, with which he was never entirely satisfied, *Lohengrin* was not subjected to substantial revision by Wagner. He did, however, request Liszt, who conducted the premiere in Weimar in the absence of the composer (who was in exile in Switzerland) to make a significant excision in Lohengrin's Narration. The second part of that Narration, the cutting of which has been observed by tradition following Wagner's instructions, went on to explain that the knights in Monsalvat had heard Elsa's plea and taken the swan (the spell-bound Gottfried) into service: one year's service for the Grail frees a victim from a magic curse. Thus the deleted passage explains Lohengrin's reference shortly after to 'one year by your side', after which Elsa would have had Gottfried restored to her. There is some new and worthwhile music there, but the only commercial recording to restore the passage (that conducted by Erich Leinsdorf) rather confirms Wagner's judgment that its inclusion has an anti-climactic effect.

Two other cuts often made in performance are less desirable. The omission of the double male-voice chorus 'In Früh'n versammelt uns der Ruf' in Act II involves the sacrifice of some imaginative antiphony, while a cut traditionally made after Lohengrin's Narration (from Elsa's swoon to 'Der Schwan!') is particularly regrettable in that it gives Elsa no chance to express remorse.

Der Ring des Nibelungen (*The Ring of the Nibelung*)
WWV 86
Stage festival play for three days and a preliminary evening

'In my view a setting of the Nibelung opera would indeed be a step forward, and I believe the composer who could accomplish this task in an adequate manner would become the man of his era.' That prophetic challenge was issued in 1845 by Franz Brendel, the editor of the influential periodical *Neue Zeitschrift für Musik*, at a time when enthusiasm for the medieval epic poem the *Nibelungenlied* had reached fever pitch in Germany. Already at the beginning of the 19th century the Nibelung saga had begun to enjoy a surge of popularity; by the 1840s it had become a potent symbol in the struggle for German unification. Wagner's was not the first or the only operatic treatment of the subject to appear, but it was by far the most influential and it could indeed be said to have made him 'the man of his era'.

Though originally conceived as a single drama, the *Ring* expanded into a vast tetralogy: a cycle of operas occupying four evenings and consisting of more than fourteen hours' music (timings vary considerably, but Hans Richter took fourteen and a half hours at the first performances in 1876). The composition of the work occupied Wagner, with interruptions, for twenty-six years, from the first prose sketch in 1848 to the final touches on the score of *Götterdämmerung* in 1874.

Contrary to Wagner's claim that he turned away from historical subjects on discovering the potentialities of myth for his future music dramas, myth and history were interwoven in the *Ring* from the beginning. Not only was he working on his historical drama *Friedrich I.*, begun in 1846, as late as 1848–9, but he was also making speculative connections between the stories of the Hohenstaufen emperor and the Nibelung hoard. Those supposed connections were formulated in the essay *Die Wibelungen: Weltgeschichte aus der Sage* (*The Wibelungs: World History from Legend*). And although it was previously supposed that *Die Wibelungen* preceded the initial prose résumé and libretto for what became the *Ring*, it is now considered more likely that it succeeded them, probably *c.* mid-February 1849 (Deathridge, Geck and Voss, 1986).

Sources

The chief sources drawn on by Wagner for the *Ring* are as follows: the Poetic (or Elder) Edda, the *Völsunga Saga*, and the Prose Edda by Snorri Sturluson (all three of which were compiled in Iceland, probably in the first half of the 13th century); *Das Nibelungenlied*, an epic poem written in Middle High German *c.*1200; and *Thidreks Saga af Bern*, a prose narrative written *c.*1260–70 in Old Norse. Wagner also read copiously around the subject and was indebted to the work of such scholars as Karl Lachmann, Franz Joseph Mone, Ludwig Ettmüller and the Grimm brothers.

Greek drama was a major influence too, not least in its use of mythology, its life-affirming idealism and the religious aura surrounding its performance. The *Oresteia* suggested not only the structure of a trilogy (*Rheingold* was merely a 'preliminary evening') but also the confrontations of pairs of characters, the possibility of linking successive episodes with the themes of guilt and a curse, and perhaps even the leitmotif principle (in Aeschylus' use of recurrent imagery). There are also important parallels between the *Ring* and the *Prometheus* trilogy, especially as reconstructed by its German translator, Johann Gustav Droysen.

Construction of the libretto

Wagner outlined a prose résumé for his drama, dated 4 October 1848, which in his collected writings he called *Der Nibelungen-Mythus: Als Entwurf zu einem Drama* (*The Nibelung Myth as Sketch for a Drama* – the original manuscript is headed *Der Nibelungensage (Mythus)*). In this résumé the drama centres on Siegfried's death, and at the conclusion, Brünnhilde purges the guilt of the gods by an act of self-immolation, allowing the gods to reign in glory instead of perishing. The story at this stage largely follows the order familiar from the finished work, but Wagner next, in autumn 1848, compiled a libretto for *Siegfrieds Tod* (originally spelt *Siegfried's Tod*). This created so much back-narration of earlier events, however, that he subsequently, in 1851, wrote *Der junge Siegfried* (originally *Jung-Siegfried*), and finally *Die Walküre* and *Das Rheingold* (1851–2). Returning to revise *Der junge Siegfried* and *Siegfrieds Tod* in the light of the whole cycle, Wagner replaced Siegfried as the central figure by Wotan, and altered the ending so that the gods and Valhalla are all destroyed by fire. *Der junge Siegfried* and *Siegfrieds*

Tod were eventually renamed *Siegfried* and *Götterdämmerung*. Thus the libretti of the constituent parts of the *Ring* cycle were written in reverse order, though the original conception was in the 'correct' order, as was the composition of the music.

The drama

The *Ring* is a complex, contradictory work whose 'meaning' has never yet been – and probably cannot be – adequately formulated: as with any great work of art, successive generations continue to find in it insights and resonances, not all of which may have been clearly perceived by the composer himself. At the heart of the work lies the conflict between love and power: humankind's progress towards self-knowledge and compassionate understanding of others is constantly threatened by the desire for power and by the compromises we are forced to negotiate in our daily lives.

The world-view propounded in the *Ring* is generally characterized as Schopenhauerian, that is to say essentially renunciatory, accepting that human desires are intrinsically evil and the 'will to live' reprehensible. But before Wagner discovered Schopenhauer – and even after – he was deeply influenced also by the philosophy of Ludwig Feuerbach. For Feuerbach, the essence of human nature and the source of its morality was the 'I-you' relationship. Only in conjunction with another could an individual attain both happiness and a consciousness of social responsibility. Wagner's own interpretation of the *Ring*, as it evolved in the 1850s and 60s, may indeed have inclined more towards the Schopenhauerian view, but he never entirely relinquished the joyous, affirmative concept of love he took from Feuerbach.

Feuerbach was in turn influenced by Hegel, and it has recently been demonstrated (Corse, 1990) that the *Ring* actually owes a great deal more to Hegel's philosophy than previously assumed. A number of Hegelian concepts are relevant here: self-realization (the attaining of enlightenment or self-awareness as the result of experiences undergone by the individual), mutual recognition (an individual identifying something of him- or herself in the loved one), the master/slave relationship, necessity as the moving spirit of history.

Wagner's notion of free, unconditional love also owes a great deal to the French writer Pierre-Joseph Proudhon. True love could not be subjugated to the law or to the institution of marriage – the mere establishment and perpetuation of property rights – declared Wagner, echoing both Proudhon and Feuerbach. All the marriages depicted or referred to in the *Ring* are loveless. That of Wotan and Fricka, for example, is both loveless and sterile. Sieglinde is held in bondage by Hunding, while his kinsmen, according to Siegmund's narration, treat their womenfolk with little more respect. True love, on the other hand, is found only outside marriage – as with Siegfried and Brünnhilde – or even between brother and sister (Siegmund and Sieglinde).

Wagner's critique was directed, of course, not only against feudal sexual relations in mythological times, but also against the situation obtaining in his own day, as is quite clear from his various writings of the time. Similarly, the *Ring* contains a critique of production relations, of the destructive, alienating power of capital, and of exploitation and oppression in both industrial and social spheres. Not merely a tale about the adventures of gods, giants, dwarves and dragons, it is an allegory of the conflicts that arise when civilization and power politics obtrude on the innocent world of nature. Social contracts and institutions, based invariably on property rights and hierarchies of power, contaminate the natural order of things.

Das Rheingold (*The Rhinegold*)
WWV 86A
Preliminary evening of *Der Ring des Nibelungen* in 4 scenes

Text: prose sketch autumn (probably Oct) 1851, prose draft entitled *Der Raub des Rheingoldes./Vorspiel. (oder: das Rheingold)?* 23 – 31 Mar 1852, verse draft 15 Sep – 3 Nov 1852, final text probably Dec 1852/ Jan 1853
Music: first complete draft 1 Nov 1853 – 14 Jan 1854, draft of full score 1 Feb – 28 May 1854, fair copy of full score 15 Feb – 26 Sep 1854
First perf.: Königliches Hof- und National-Theater, Munich, 22 Sep 1869; first perf. as part of cycle, Festspielhaus, Bayreuth, 13 Aug 1876
First UK perf.: Her Majesty's Theatre, London, 5 May 1882
First US perf.: Metropolitan Opera, New York, 4 Jan 1889

Gods:

Wotan	bass-baritone
Donner	bass-baritone
Froh	tenor
Loge	tenor

Nibelungs:

Alberich	bass-baritone
Mime	tenor

Giants:

Fasolt	bass-baritone
Fafner	bass

Goddesses:

Fricka	mezzo-soprano
Freia	soprano
Erda	contralto

Rhinemaidens:

Woglinde	soprano
Wellgunde	soprano
Flosshilde	mezzo-soprano

Nibelungs

pic, 3 fl, 3 ob, cor ang, 3 cl, bass cl, 3 bn, 8 hn, 2 tenor tubas, 2 bass tubas [i.e. 'Wagner tubas', played by 4 of the hn players], 3 tpt, bass tpt, 4 trbn, contrabass trbn [= 4th trbn], contrabass tuba, timp, cym, tri, gong, 6 harps, 16 1st vn, 16 2nd vn, 12 va, 12 vc, 8 db

On/off stage: 18 anvils of various sizes, 1 hammer, 1 harp

Synopsis
Prelude and Scene 1
The action opens at the bottom of the Rhine. The three Rhinemaidens, Woglinde, Wellgunde and Flosshilde, are disporting themselves in the waves, teasing and trying to catch each other. Flosshilde chides her sisters for failing to watch over the 'sleeping gold'. Meanwhile, the dwarf Alberich has climbed out of a dark chasm lower down and after watching the Rhinemaidens at play, calls out to them. They initially recoil at his loathsome appearance, but then decide to reward his lubricious advances by teaching him a lesson. Woglinde invites him to come closer; as he does so, he slithers on the rocks and sneezes as water fills his nostrils. He tries to embrace her, but she slips away, first to one rock then to another. He gives up Woglinde and turns his attentions to Wellgunde, who appears to lead him on but then mocks his hairy, hunchbacked body. She likewise eludes him, but the third maiden, Flosshilde, seems to offer consolation, and flatters him by praising his sweet singing and physical charms. Holding him in her arms, she mutters endearments about his bristly hair, toad-like appearance and croaking voice. Alberich now realizes he has been duped, and moans in injured frustration. The Rhinemaidens continue to tease him and he makes a final desperate effort to catch hold of them. As he looks up, speechless with rage, a bright light shines through the waters from high above, illuminating the rock in the middle with a golden gleam, which is reflected in the waters all around. The Rhinemaidens greet the glowing gold and swim round the rock in joyous abandon. Alberich, mesmerized by the sight, asks what it is. He is told that it is the Rhinegold, from which a ring can be made that will confer limitless power. Only he who forswears the power of love can fashion the ring, adds Woglinde – in which case they have nothing to fear from the lascivious dwarf. But Alberich has been paying close attention and, as they watch, he climbs to the top of the central rock, declares his curse on love, and wrests the gold away with terrible force. He scrambles away with it, deaf to the lamenting cries of the Rhinemaidens.

Scene 2
Wotan, the ruler of the gods, and his consort Fricka are asleep on an open space on a mountain height. Behind them, a magnificent fortress gleams in the light of dawn. Fricka, awaking first, sees the fortress and rouses her husband. Wotan sings a paean to the

completed work, but Fricka reminds him that it was her sister, Freia, the goddess of love, who was rashly offered to the giants in payment. Wotan brushes aside her fears. It was she who asked for the fortress, he says; her reply is that her wish was to bind them more closely. She chides him for trading love and the virtues of woman in exchange for power and dominion. Reminding her that he once pledged his only remaining eye to court her (a pledge he was not called upon to fulfil), Wotan says that he never had any intention of giving up Freia.

Then protect her now, Fricka replies, and even as she speaks, Freia enters in terrified haste, followed closely by the giants Fasolt and Fafner. Wotan wonders what has detained Loge, the fire god, on whom he had been relying to disengage him from the contract. Fasolt demands their fee for the work done, but when he insists on Freia as the agreed payment, Wotan tells him that some other reward must be asked. Fasolt indignantly reminds Wotan that the runes on his spear symbolize his contractual agreements and it is they that legitimize his power. Fafner is less interested in Freia for her beauty, but realizes that if she is abducted, the gods, denied her youth-perpetuating apples, will wither and die.

As the giants prepare to take Freia away, her brothers Froh and Donner (the god of thunder) rush in to protect her. Wotan prevents Donner from exercising force and is relieved to see Loge arrive at last. Loge reports that he has been testing the workmanship of the giants, but Wotan demands to know from him what he is to offer them in payment. Loge relates how he has circled the world attempting to find out what men hold dearer than the virtues of womankind. No one would give up love, except one man, a Nibelung dwarf, who stole the Rhinegold after suffering the rejection of his sexual advances. Loge calls on Wotan to secure the return of the gold to the custody of the Rhinemaidens. Fasolt and Fafner have been listening with interest and they ask what is the use of the gold. When Loge explains that a ring forged from it would give absolute power, Wotan begins to lust after it. Fricka too, desiring the gold for ornaments, urges Wotan to acquire it. Loge suggests that it be obtained by theft, and Fafner demands that it then be handed over in payment. Meanwhile they will hold Freia hostage.

As the giants trudge away, dragging Freia behind them, a mist descends on the gods, who, denied Freia's golden apples, begin to wilt. Wotan, accompanied by Loge, descends through a sulphur cleft in pursuit of the gold.

Scene 3
In the depths of Nibelheim, Alberich is tormenting his weaker brother Mime, and demands the magic Tarnhelm that he has forced Mime to make. The Tarnhelm renders its wearer invisible, and Alberich proves its efficacy by disappearing and raining blows on the defenceless Mime. Alberich eventually

leaves, and Wotan and Loge arrive. Loge, offering to help Mime, hears from him how the carefree race of Nibelung blacksmiths has been held in thrall by Alberich since he forged a ring from the Rhinegold.

Alberich returns, driving his slaves with whip-lashes to pile up the gold. He brandishes the ring and they scatter in all directions. Alberich now turns his attention to the strangers. Wotan flatters him, but Loge at first is driven to remind him that it was the warmth of his fire that once comforted Alberich. The dwarf scornfully dismisses that earlier false friendship. Alberich boasts about the power he now wields, obtained by relinquishing love, and threatens one day to vanquish the gods and force his favours on their women. Now Loge begins to flatter him, but asks, mighty as he is, how he would protect himself against a thief in the night. Alberich shows him the Tarnhelm and Loge asks for a demonstration. Alberich turns himself into a dragon and Loge pretends to be terrified. That was truly impressive, he says, but is Alberich clever enough to turn himself into something small like a toad? Alberich duly does so, and is trapped by the gods. They tie him and drag him up to the surface.

Scene 4
Back on the mountain heights, Loge and Wotan deride Alberich and his pretensions to world domination. If he wants to be set free, they tell him, he will have to give up the gold. Intending to keep the ring, which he knows he can use to generate more wealth, Alberich agrees to hand over the gold. His right hand is untied and he summons the Nibelungs with the ring. The Nibelungs drag in the gold, while Alberich, fuming with the disgrace of being seen by his slaves in captivity, threatens them with punishment if they don't return to work immediately. He kisses the ring and they scatter in terror.

Alberich demands the return of the Tarnhelm, but Loge adds it to the pile of gold. He can still have another made, Alberich thinks, but then, to his horror, Wotan demands the ring on his finger. 'My life, but not the ring!', pleads Alberich. Wotan is unmoved, and tells him that in any case it was stolen from the Rhinemaidens. Alberich bitterly lays bare Wotan's hypocrisy, claiming that he too would have stolen the gold if he had known how to forge it into a ring. Moreover, he, Alberich, has sinned only against himself; if Wotan now stole the ring from him, he would be sinning against everything that was, is and shall be.

Wotan violently tears the ring from Alberich's finger and gloats in his possession of it. Alberich, crushed, is untied. But before he goes, he lays a curse on the ring. It will bring anxiety and death to whoever owns it; those who possess it will be racked with torment, those who do not will be consumed with envy.

Donner, Froh and Fricka welcome back Wotan and Loge, who show them Freia's ransom: the pile of gold. The air lightens as Freia returns with the giants. Fasolt is reluctant to relinquish Freia and insists that the gold be piled up so as to hide her from sight. Loge and Froh pile up the treasure, filling up all the gaps. But Fafner can still see Freia's hair: the Tarnhelm has to be thrown on the heap. Fasolt, too, can see her shining eyes through a chink, and Fafner demands that the ring on Wotan's finger be used to stop the gap. Loge suggests that Wotan will be returning it to the Rhinemaidens, but Wotan silences them all: he will not give up the ring. The giants threaten to take away Freia again, and the other gods all beg him to relent. Wotan remains impervious, until Erda, the earth goddess, appears in a blue light from a rocky cleft. She warns Wotan that possession of the ring condemns him to irredeemable dark perdition. A dark day is dawning for the gods: he should give up the ring.

Erda disappears from sight and Wotan decides to yield. He tosses the ring on the pile and Fafner begins to stow it away. When Fasolt demands his share, Fafner retorts that he was more interested in Freia. Wotan refuses to get involved, but Loge advises Fasolt to let go the treasure and keep the ring. There is a struggle for the ring and Fafner clubs his brother to death. Wotan realizes with horror the power of the curse.

The gods prepare to enter the fortress. Donner swings his hammer and there is thunder and lightning. Suddenly the clouds lift and a rainbow bridge is visible, stretching across the valley to the fortress. Wotan invites his wife to follow him into the fortress, which he now calls Valhalla. As the couple walk to the bridge, followed by Froh, Donner and Freia, Loge looks on nonchalantly. The wail of the Rhinemaidens, lamenting their lost gold, rises out of the valley. Wotan ignores them and leads the gods over the bridge as the curtain falls.

Composition

It is perhaps appropriate that the genesis of the music for the *Ring* is shrouded in the mists of myth. According to Wagner's own account in *Mein Leben*, the initial inspiration for *Das Rheingold* – rushing arpeggio figures in E♭ major – came to him as he lay in a trance-like state in an inn at La Spezia. Doubt has been cast on the likelihood of such a 'vision', but Warren Darcy (1989; see also 'Autograph manuscripts', p.217) has argued that the documentary evidence neither supports nor contradicts Wagner's account. Discounting a handful of musical jottings, the composition proper of *Rheingold* was begun on 1 November 1853, with the first complete draft, a continuous setting of the poem that occupied Wagner until 14 January 1854. In view of the unprecedented problems of writing for the *Ring*'s expanded forces (including quadruple woodwind), he elaborated the orchestration in a draft of a full score (a procedure he was not to repeat). The final stage was a fair copy of the full score, written out

between 15 February and 26 September 1854. (For more details of the drafts and of Wagner's procedures see 'Autograph manuscripts', pp.196–221, and 'Compositional process', pp.244–8.)

Musical style

As the first dramatic work to appear in the wake of the theoretical essays of 1849–51, *Das Rheingold* exhibits a number of advances over its predecessors. In the first place, regular phrase patterns give way to fluid arioso structures in which the text is projected in a vocal line that faithfully reflects its verbal accentuations, poetic meaning and emotional content. Occasionally in *Rheingold*, it has to be admitted, the rigorous attempt to match poetic shape with musical phrase results in somewhat pedestrian melodic ideas: this was a technique that Wagner truly mastered only in the next opera of the cycle, *Die Walküre*. In scenes 2 and 4, in particular, there are passages that revert to an old-fashioned *recitativo* style of writing, with abrupt and sustained chords alternating in the orchestra in the 18th-century manner.

Whereas in *Lohengrin* characteristic musical motifs were deployed for dramatic purposes, in the *Ring* the leitmotif (see 'Glossary', pp.234–5) takes on a structural function in addition. That is to say, motifs are recalled not only for referential purposes – as when the Curse motif rings out at the murder of Fasolt – but also in order to be subjected to quasi-symphonic development. The pictorial references of leitmotifs are still at their most literal in *Rheingold*: there is rarely any doubt as to why they occur when they do. By the end of the cycle (*Siegfried* Act III and *Götterdämmerung*) associations have become more abstruse, not to say tenuous: motifs appear in such profusion and are combined with such contrapuntal virtuosity that it is clear that the strict principles of *Oper und Drama*, governing the deployment of motifs, are no longer being adhered to. (For more on motivic transformation, see 'Musical Style', pp.256–61; for the historical precedents of the leitmotif, see 'Musical Background and Influences', pp.79–82.)

In *Tannhäuser* and *Lohengrin*, individual characters are often associated with specific tonalities. In the *Ring*, however, those associations are with groups of characters. Thus the Nibelungs' key is B♭ minor and the entire Nibelheim Scene (scene 3) of *Rheingold* is dominated by that tonality; it even interrupts Loge's A major music as Alberich boasts of world domination. Certain motifs, too, have specific tonal associations: the Curse and the Tarnhelm both with B minor, Valhalla with D♭ major, the Sword with C major. Not every appearance of these motifs is in the 'correct' key, but it is remarkable how the tonal orientation of whole paragraphs, even scenes, is often determined by such associations.

Die Walküre (*The Valkyrie*)
WWV 86B
First day of *Der Ring des Nibelungen* in 3 acts

Text: Prose sketch autumn (probably Nov) 1851, prose draft 17–26 May 1851, verse draft 1 Jun – 1 Jul 1852, final text probably Dec 1852/Jan 1853
Music: first complete draft 28 Jun – 27 Dec 1854, draft of full score Jan 1855 – 20 Mar 1856, fair copy of full score 14 Jul 1855 – 23 Mar 1856
First perf.: Königliches Hof- und National-Theater, Munich, 26 Jun 1870; first perf. as part of cycle, Festspielhaus, Bayreuth, 14 Aug 1876
First UK perf.: Her Majesty's Theatre, London, 6 May 1882
First US perf.: Academy of Music, New York, 2 Apr 1877

Siegmund	tenor
Hunding	bass
Wotan	bass-baritone
Sieglinde	soprano
Brünnhilde	soprano
Fricka	mezzo-soprano

Gerhilde		
Ortlinde		
Waltraute		
Schwertleite	*Valkyries*	sopranos and
Helmwige		contraltos
Siegrune		
Grimgerde		
Rossweisse		

Orchestration as for *Das Rheingold* (above), but with 2 pic [= 3rd fl], tenor drum and glock

On/off stage: cow horn, thunder machine

Synopsis
Prelude and Act I
The orchestral Prelude depicts a violent thunderstorm. It has begun to abate as the curtain rises on the interior of Hunding's hut. Siegmund enters and throws himself down, exhausted, on a bearskin rug, where he is found by Hunding's wife Sieglinde. She brings him water and, fascinated by Sieglinde's face, he asks where he is. 'This house and this woman both belong to Hunding', she replies. Her husband has nothing to fear, he says, as he is unarmed and wounded. Sieglinde anxiously asks to see his wounds, but he brushes her fears aside. His body is strong, he assures her, and if only his spear and shield had been as sturdy, he would not have needed to flee from his enemies. But they smashed them and pursued him.

Sieglinde now fetches him a horn of mead. As he drinks, he finds himself increasingly drawn to her. But fearing that he brings her ill luck, he abruptly makes to depart. 'Who are your pursuers?', she asks. 'Everywhere I am pursued by misfortune', he replies, and walks to the door. 'Then stay', she exclaims. 'You cannot bring misfortune where it already lives.' For a long while they gaze at each other, deeply moved. Then Hunding arrives and curtly demands to know who the stranger is. She explains his plight and Hunding roughly extends his own hospitality. As Sieglinde serves the two men a meal, Hunding notices with distaste and suspicion how like his wife the stranger is. He asks what drove him there and Siegmund replies evasively that he was driven by storms and direst need. What is his name then, Hunding persists. As Sieglinde too evinces interest, Siegmund says he should be called Woeful, describing how one day he returned from hunting with his father, Wolfe, to find their home burnt down, his mother murdered and his twin-sister brutally abducted. Siegmund goes on to tell how he lost track of his father and how he always found himself at odds with society. He went to the aid of a young woman forced into a loveless marriage, he continues; he killed her savage kinsmen, but with spear and shield hacked from his arms, he was unable to protect the woman. She died in front of his eyes and he had to flee from the mob. Hunding now realizes that the men attacked by Siegmund were his kinsmen and that he is harbouring the enemy in his house. The laws of hospitality compel him to give Siegmund shelter for the night, but in the morning he will have to fight for his life.

As she prepares Hunding's night drink, Sieglinde drugs it; she leaves the room with a lingering gaze at Siegmund, indicating a spot on the trunk of the ash tree around which the room is constructed. Siegmund, left alone, meditates on the fever of excitement stirred up by Sieglinde, and on his weaponless plight, adding that his father had once promised that he would find a sword in the hour of his need. The light of the fire catches the spot on the trunk of the tree, where the hilt of a buried sword is now visible.

Sieglinde re-enters and narrates how at the wedding of Hunding and herself, a stranger dressed in grey, with a hat pulled down over one eye, interrupted the festivities, thrusting a sword into the tree trunk. Not even the strongest men could move it an inch. Embracing Sieglinde passionately, Siegmund exclaims that both sword and wife will be his: she is everything he has yearned for. Suddenly the main door flies open, revealing a glorious spring night with full moon. Siegmund speaks of Spring and Love as brother and sister, to which Sieglinde replies that he is the spring for whom she has so longed. The remainder of the act is an ecstatic declaration of their love. He admits that Woeful is now no longer an appropriate name. She renames him Siegmund ('guardian of victory') and to her delight he pulls the sword out of the tree. She tells him that he has won both sister and bride with the sword. They embrace rapturously and the curtain – at least in traditional productions – falls with decorous swiftness.

Act II

On a wild, rocky mountain ridge Wotan instructs his daughter Brünnhilde, the Valkyrie of the title, to ensure that Siegmund wins the ensuing battle over Hunding. She revels in the Valkyrie battlecry, but warns him that he has another battle on hand: his wife Fricka is furiously approaching in a ram-drawn chariot. Brünnhilde disappears and Fricka enters angrily but with dignity. As the guardian of wedlock, she has been appealed to by Hunding, who has called on her to punish the adulterous Volsung pair. Wotan asks what wrong they have done: they are simply united in love. To her complaint that they have flouted the vows of marriage, he replies that he has no respect for vows that compel union without love.

Fricka turns her attack to the incestuous nature of the twins' relationship, demanding to know whether he cares nothing for the values that hold the race of the gods together. The gods have need of a hero, replies Wotan – one free from their protection who will be able to do the deed they are prevented from doing. If Siegmund needs no protection, then take the sword from him, says Fricka. Wotan's weak insistence that it was won by Siegmund himself in his hour of need is crushed by Fricka's observation that he created the need for Siegmund just as he provided the sword. She makes him promise that neither he nor his Valkyrie daughter will give Siegmund protection in his coming fight. Brünnhilde's warcry is heard approaching as, forced to accept the strength of Fricka's arguments, Wotan, in utter despair, gives his oath.

Left alone with his daughter, Wotan gives vent to his anger and shame. Brünnhilde presses him to confide in her. He hesitates, fearing it would be a sign of weakness. But when Brünnhilde suggests that in speaking to her, he is speaking to his own will, he relents and embarks on his great narration. He begins by describing how, when the youthful delights of love waned in him, he began to lust after power. He mastered the world, but in the process became embroiled in contracts. While he then began to yearn for love again, Alberich, the Nibelung dwarf, renounced love in order to acquire the Rhinegold. The ring he made from it was stolen by Wotan himself, but instead of returning it to the Rhinemaidens, he used it to buy off the giants.

Then he visited Erda, the source of ancestral wisdom, in the bowels of the earth. He learned her secrets and she bore him Brünnhilde. She was brought up with her eight Valkyrie sisters (who, incidentally, are apparently not daughters of Erda; see 'Myths and Legends', pp.136–7); together they gather dead heroes from the battlefield to serve Wotan in Valhalla. Those heroes will, Wotan believes, protect him against the forces being raised by Alberich, though the ring must at all costs be kept out of his hands. Wotan therefore now urgently desires to regain the ring from its current holder –

the giant Fafner, who has transformed himself into a dragon, the better to guard his treasure. Yet Wotan knows that his strength would fail him if he were to attack Fafner, because of the contract once concluded with him. This is why he needs a special hero, one who could act as a free agent, but who would be fighting for the same ends as those to which he aspires.

Is not Siegmund, the Volsung, such a hero, asks Brünnhilde. Fricka saw through that self-deception, replies Wotan. Now he must abandon what he loves most; he longs only for an end to all his suffering. He has heard that Alberich has fathered a son; 'may he inherit that which I deeply loathe', Wotan bitterly declares. Brünnhilde must now protect not Siegmund in the coming battle, but Hunding. She tries to change his mind, but he is implacable and threatens the severest punishment if she disobeys. Siegmund and Sieglinde enter breathlessly. She, tormented by guilt, begs him to abandon her, but he merely vows to avenge the wrong that was done her by killing Hunding. Horns are heard echoing round the forest, and Sieglinde, feverishly imagining Hunding's dogs tearing at Siegmund's flesh, falls into a faint. There follows a scene of key significance in the cycle: the Annunciation of Death. Brünnhilde appears, announcing to Siegmund that he must follow her to Valhalla. There he will find not only the great Warfather (Wotan), but also his own father and will be tended by Wishmaidens. When he hears that he cannot take his sister-bride, Siegmund determines not to go to Valhalla. Brünnhilde tells him that his fate is unalterable. She is distressed by his evident devotion to Sieglinde and when he even threatens to kill her, rather than be separated, Brünnhilde relents and promises to protect him, in defiance of Wotan's command. Siegmund bends lovingly over the sleeping Sieglinde.

Hunding's horn is now heard, and in the ensuing fight Brünnhilde attempts to protect Siegmund with her shield, only for Wotan to appear and shatter Siegmund's sword with his spear. Hunding kills Siegmund, but is himself despatched by Wotan in a gesture of bitter anger. Wotan then sets off in pursuit of Brünnhilde.

Act III

In the Prelude and Ride of the Valkyries the warmaidens gather, on the summit of a rocky mountain, collecting their heroes for Valhalla. They notice that Brünnhilde is missing, but eventually she is sighted carrying on her saddle not a hero, but a woman. Brünnhilde begs her sisters to protect both herself and Sieglinde, whom she rescued from the battlefield, from the fury of Wotan. None of her sisters will risk helping her. Sieglinde longs to die, but on being told that a Volsung stirs in her womb, she implores Brünnhilde to protect her. She is urged to make her escape to the forest in the east and is given the fragments of Siegmund's sword from which one day his son will forge a new weapon.

Wotan storms in and the Valkyries attempt to shield Brünnhilde from his rage. He scorns their feeble spirit and tells of her 'crime' of disloyalty and disobedience. Brünnhilde presents herself for punishment and is told that she can no longer be a Valkyrie; moreover, she is to be confined in sleep on the mountain top, a prey to the first man to find her. The Valkyries protest in horror, but, under threat of the same punishment if they interfere, they separate and scatter.

Left alone with Wotan, Brünnhilde begs him to be merciful to his favourite child. She recounts how the Volsung touched her heart and how she decided to protect him, knowing that that was Wotan's innermost wish. Wotan is deaf to her pleas and angered by being reminded of the Volsungs. He intends to leave her sleeping on the rock, to be claimed by the first man to find her. Brünnhilde pleads that at least she be spared the disgrace of an ignoble union: let her be surrounded by a circle of fire that will deter all but the bravest of heroes. Deeply moved, Wotan raises Brünnhilde from her knees and embraces her. He sings passionately of the inspiration of her shining eyes and laying her down on a rock, he kisses them closed. He summons Loge and points with his spear to where he should blaze round the rock. Wotan sorrowfully departs.

Composition

The first musical sketches for *Die Walküre* date from the summer of 1852, and include an early version of the Spring Song. The first complete draft was made between 28 June and 27 December 1854. Unlike the comparable draft for *Rheingold*, which for the most part consisted of one vocal stave plus one instrumental, that for *Walküre* shows some degree of orchestral elaboration, often with one vocal stave plus two instrumental. In spite of the difficulties he experienced – on account of many delays and interruptions – in expanding that first draft into score, Wagner did not find it necessary to make a second draft as for *Rheingold*, since he was now familiar with the expanded orchestral forces. Instead he went straight into a draft of the full score (January 1855 – 20 March 1856); the fair copy was made in parallel between 14 July 1855 and 23 March 1856.

Musical style

Whereas in *Rheingold*, the rigour with which Wagner applied his theoretical principles resulted in occasionally undistinguished melodic lines, in *Walküre* he achieved equality of status for words and music without any such sacrifices. In Act I, especially, Wagner's musico-poetic synthesis is demonstrated at its finest: the text is set with natural word stresses and to a melodic line that registers every nuance while remaining musically interesting in its own right. Acts II and III are no less masterly, though there are already perceptible signs in these acts of

Wagner's subsequent shift away from absolute equality of poetry and music. The encounter, at this very time, with the philosophy of Schopenhauer – who elevated music above all other forms of art – may well have been largely responsible for the shift.

In Act II scene 2 occurs one of Wagner's great narrations: that for Wotan beginning with the lines 'Als junger Liebe Lust mir verblich' ('When the delights of young love had waned in me'). It is often said that by conceiving his cycle in reverse order (see p.286) Wagner subsequently rendered his back narrations redundant. But that is to reckon without the significance attached to the narrative mode by Wagner – Greek drama was, after all, one of the antecedents of the music drama. In any case, to criticize such narrations for holding up the action, or for repeating what we, the audience, already know, is to miss the point. Strictly speaking, no story told, or opera heard, more than once offers any real surprise in terms of plot. What a narration can offer is the chance to reflect on past events, to see them through the eyes of another character. And it is a device that lends itself perfectly to Wagner's technique of leitmotif, because not only can the interaction of characters, objects and ideas all be represented by the juxtaposition of the relevant musical motifs, but the transformation of those motifs can express subtle nuances and psychological depths more powerfully than any words.

In the case of Wotan's narration, the god is persuaded to lay bare his soul to his favourite daughter and her sympathy encourages him to articulate and come to terms with his dilemma. Wotan begins the exchange by confessing how he attempted to fill the vacuum of lovelessness in his life by acquiring power. His hushed reliving of the story ('Als junger Liebe') is the closest thing in the whole work to pure recitative, but it is by no means oblivious to the *Oper und Drama* principles of word-setting and in any case it acquires a special aura of suspense from the accompaniment – double basses alone, *pianissimo*. The characteristic motifs appear as Wotan recalls the theft of the gold, the building of Valhalla, the ring. Other motifs come to the fore, notably those of the Curse and the Sword, which drive the narration to a tremendous climax: Wotan looks for only one thing – 'das Ende' ('the end').

Siegfried
WWV 86C
Second day of *Der Ring des Nibelungen* in 3 acts

Text: First prose sketches for *Jung-Siegfried* (the opera's original title, subsequently changed to *Der junge Siegfried*) probably 3–24 May 1851, prose draft 24 May – 1 Jun 1851, verse draft 3–24 Jun 1851, poem revised Nov–Dec 1852, 1856
Music: preliminary sketches 1851, first complete draft 1856 (probably early Sep) – 14 Jun 1869,

second complete draft 22 Sep 1856 – 5 Aug 1869, first full score 11 Oct 1856 – 5 Feb 1871, second full score (Acts I and II only) 12 May 1857 – 23 Feb 1869. For clarification see 'Composition' below.

First perf.: Festspielhaus, Bayreuth, 16 Aug 1876
First UK perf.: Her Majesty's Theatre, London, 8 May 1882
First US perf.: Metropolitan Opera, New York, 9 Nov 1887

Siegfried	tenor
Mime	tenor
The Wanderer	bass-baritone
Alberich	bass-baritone
Fafner	bass
Erda	contralto
Brünnhilde	soprano
Woodbird	soprano (originally designated 'boy's' voice')

Orchestration as for *Das Rheingold* (above), but with 2nd pic (doubling as 3rd fl), 4th fl (doubling as pic), 4th ob (doubling as cor ang), 4th cl (doubling as bass cl) and glock

On/off stage: cor ang, hn, forging hammer, thunder machine

Synopsis
Prelude and Act I
Act I is set in a cave in the rocks in the forest. The Prelude opens with a soft roll on the timpani and a repeated two-note motif on a pair of bassoons suggestive of the dark forest and the scheming Nibelung dwarf, Mime, it harbours. Other motifs associated with the Nibelungs and the ring are heard, as well as an unexpected sounding of the Sword motif, before the curtain rises on Mime hammering away at an anvil. He curses his wearisome labour and his hopeless attempts to forge a sword that the boy Siegfried cannot break in two. If only he had the skill to weld together the fragments of Nothung, the sword of Siegfried's father, Siegmund: that would withstand any blow. The giant Fafner has transformed himself into a fierce dragon, Mime continues, the better to guard the Nibelung treasure. If he, Mime, could only forge Nothung, Siegfried might kill the dragon with it and the ring would come to Mime.

Siegfried comes in from the forest leading a huge bear on a rope. He sets it on Mime and laughs as the bear chases the dwarf round the cave. He demands to see what Mime has forged, but scorns his latest effort and smashes it on the anvil. Siegfried, demanding to know the truth of his parentage, is told that Mime once took pity on a woman whimpering out in the wood and brought her into the cave. She died in giving birth to Siegfried and he, Mime, has carried out her wishes in bringing him up.

Siegfried asks, and is told, his mother's name:

Sieglinde. But Mime withholds the name of the boy's father. Siegfried demands proof of this story and Mime fetches the fragments of Nothung, which were left in his custody. Siegfried excitedly instructs Mime to recreate Nothung by forging the pieces together and, happy at the prospect of the freedom it will bring, he rushes off into the forest. Mime sits dejectedly at the anvil, despairing of fashioning the fragments into an invincible sword.

The Wanderer (Wotan in disguise) appears at the door of the cave; he is wearing a large hat whose brim covers his missing eye, and he carries a spear. He stakes his head on answering any questions Mime may ask. The dwarf first asks the name of the race that lives in the earth and is answered: the Nibelungs, lorded over by Alberich. Then he asks who lives on the face of the earth. The giants, comes the answer. The third question is about the inhabitants of the cloudy heights. There live the gods, the Wanderer replies, ruled by Wotan. As his spear touches the ground, a clap of thunder is heard.

Demanding the same bargain in turn, the Wanderer asks first the name of the tribe treated harshly by Wotan, though dearest to him. The Volsungs, replies Mime confidently. The second question concerns the name of the sword to be wielded by the hero Siegfried. Nothung, replies Mime. But when the Wanderer asks who will forge the sword, Mime jumps up in alarm: he has no idea. The Wanderer rebukes Mime for failing to ask the question he should have; the answer, he says, is 'one who has never known fear'. He leaves Mime's head forfeit to the fearless one and departs.

Mime, left in an agitated state, is terrified by the fire, seeing in it the shape of the dragon. Siegfried returns and the dwarf, realizing that his head is forfeit to the fearless Siegfried, determines to teach the boy fear. Siegfried demands the sword fragments and begins to do the forging himself, starting by filing the pieces into splinters. Mime looks on aghast. Siegfried, on being told the name of the sword, launches his Forging Song with it. Mime plots how he will offer Siegfried a drugged drunk after his tussle with the dragon, and then kill him with his own sword. At last the forging is done, and Siegfried crashes the sword down on the anvil, splitting it in two.

Act II
Alberich, keeping watch over Fafner's cave deep in the forest, is surprised by the appearance of the Wanderer. He bitterly recalls how, as Wotan, he stole the ring from him. Alberich taunts the Wanderer with his ambitions for world supremacy, but the latter remains quietly philosophical and even warns Alberich of the approach of Siegfried and Mime. He surprises Alberich further by arousing Fafner on his behalf and asking him to yield up the ring. The dragon is unmoved. After further friendly advice, the Wanderer disappears into the forest.

Mime arrives with Siegfried and describes to him the fearsome dragon, whose venom is poisonous and tail deadly. Siegfried is concerned only to know where is the dragon's heart, so that he can plunge in his sword. Mime leaves Siegfried alone and to the music of the Forest Murmurs, the boy expresses his relief that the ugly dwarf is not his father after all.

He is saddened by the thought that his mother died in giving birth to him. Hearing the song of the woodbird, he tries to imitate it, in the hope that he will understand the song. He makes a pipe from a reed, but after cutting it in vain this way and that, he gives up. He blows his horn instead and a somnolent Fafner drags himself out of the cave. After an exchange of banter, Siegfried stabs Fafner in the heart with Nothung. Fafner, in his last gasp, tells Siegfried his history. In withdrawing his sword from the dragon's heart, Siegfried smears his hand with blood; it burns and he involuntarily puts his hand to his mouth. As he tastes the blood, he understands at last the song of the woodbird: it tells him to take the ring and tarnhelm from the cave.

As Siegfried disappears into the cave, Mime and Alberich appear from opposite sides. They argue angrily about the rightful ownership of the treasure. Mime offers to relinquish the ring, provided he be allowed the tarnhelm. Their argument is halted by the reappearance of Siegfried with both items. The woodbird tells him to beware Mime, who now cajoles Siegfried, though his actual words keep betraying his real intention. Siegfried, in an access of revulsion, kills him with a blow of the sword.

He tosses Mime's body into the cave and drags Fafner's over its mouth. Lying down under the lime tree, he listens again to the song of the woodbird and asks its advice. The bird tells him of the bride that awaits him on a mountain top surrounded by fire. Siegfried jumps up and follows the bird as it leads the way.

Act III

The Wanderer appears at the foot of a rocky mountain and summons Erda, the earth goddess, from her slumber. He wishes to know more of the earth's secrets. First she tells him to ask the Norns as they weave the rope of destiny; then she suggests he ask the daughter she bore him, Brünnhilde. When he tells Erda that Brünnhilde is being punished for her disobedience, she expresses surprise that the one who taught defiance is now punishing it. Erda wishes to return to her sleep, but the Wanderer demands to know how to overcome his anxieties. He goes on to tell her that he no longer fears the end of the gods: indeed, it is what he desires. His inheritance is bequeathed to the Volsung hero, who will defeat Alberich's evil ambitions by the goodness of his nature. Erda sinks back into the earth.

As the Wanderer waits by the cave, Siegfried comes into view, led by the woodbird. Their exchange becomes increasingly heated until finally the Wanderer tries to block Siegfried's path by stretching out his spear; it is shattered by a stroke of Siegfried's sword. The Wanderer vanishes and Siegfried confronts the wall of fire.

The scene changes to the rocky summit of the end of *Die Walküre*. Siegfried climbs to the top and notices the form of the sleeping Brünnhilde under the trees. Her face is covered and he takes her for a man, even after removing her helmet. As he loosens the breastplate with his sword, he realizes that it is a woman. He feels weak and dizzy and invokes his mother. Now for the first time he has been taught fear, yet he longs to waken her. In desperation he kisses her on the lips, at which she opens her eyes and slowly raises herself to a sitting position.

She greets the daylight and they both bless the mother who gave birth to him. She tells him that she has always loved him, even before he was conceived. Siegfried wonders if she is in fact his mother, but she tells him how she shielded him against Wotan's wishes and was confined on the rock. When Siegfried embraces her passionately, she pushes him away in terror, conscious of her vulnerability. Though frightened, she looks fondly at him; yet she begs him not to destroy the purity of their love. Gradually she is won over by the intensity of Siegfried's passion and is able to accept her new mortal status. They embrace in ecstasy and Brünnhilde bids farewell to the world of the gods. Transformed by each other's love, they invoke 'laughing death'.

Composition

Some preliminary musical sketches were made for the work under its original title *Der junge Siegfried* in 1851, but the composition proper was begun in 1856 (probably early September) with the first complete draft. To avoid the problems he had experienced with *Die Walküre*, Wagner took each act through from first draft to score before embarking on the next. He also worked in tandem between the first complete draft (in pencil) and the second (in ink, on at least three staves – two instrumental plus one vocal – elaborating details of the orchestral texture). In June 1857 he broke off work on the drafts, with Siegfried resting under the linden tree (Act II), partly because the *Ring* was becoming a drain on his financial resources, partly because he wished to try out his increasingly chromatic style on the subject of Tristan. Nevertheless, he briefly took up again the composition of Act II shortly after, finishing the first complete draft on 30 July 1857 and the second on 9 August. Not until 27 September 1864 was the task of making a fair copy of the score of Act I resumed and between 22 December of that year and 2 December 1865 the scoring of Act II was undertaken. Work on Act III began on 1 March 1869, after the fair copy of the Act I and II scores had been finished. The scoring of the whole work was completed on 5 February 1871.

Musical style
The twelve-year gap between finishing the composition of Acts I and II (all except for the scoring) and starting Act III inevitably resulted in some discrepancies of style. Acts I and II are closer to the style of *Rheingold* and *Walküre* in their use of predominantly short, pithy motifs. In Act III, however – as in *Götterdämmerung* – motifs are more often expansive melodic ideas. Even when motifs of the former type recur, they are combined with a new freedom, and serve less of a referential function than before. Now motifs frequently aspire to a life of their own, and their constant interplay produces a much denser, more closely worked texture, one that is clearly influenced by the concentration on musical values in the intervening *Tristan*.

The new maturity is signalled immediately at the start of Act III. First comes the orchestral Prelude: a masterly symphonic development of a number of the major motifs, notably the dotted rhythm pervading the Prelude, associated with Wotan, the Valkyries and their riding; the Erda motif and its inversion, the Twilight of the Gods; the flattened mediant harmonies of the Wanderer; the falling semitone associated in *Rheingold* with Alberich and the baleful power of his ring; and the Magic Sleep. The curtain rises and the Wanderer appears. His scene with Erda, the earth goddess, takes the form of a dialogue in which the characteristic material of each is subjected to variation. Powerfully conceived vocal lines completely abandoning recitative in favour of heightened arioso are supported by an orchestral texture of unprecedented richness and motivic density. The form threatens to disintegrate as the emotional temperature rises, until a climax is reached with the Wanderer's announcement that he now looks forward to the end of the gods. The gravity of the moment is signalled with a noble new motif; leitmotifs of such expansiveness and autonomy are henceforth to play a major role in the *Ring*.

Götterdämmerung (*Twilight of the Gods*)
WWV 86D
Third day of *Der Ring des Nibelungen* in a Prologue and 3 acts

Text: First prose draft of *Siegfrieds Tod* (the opera's original title) dated (at end) 20 Oct 1848, verse draft 12–28 Nov 1848, rev. 1848/9, 1852, 1856
Music: preliminary sketches summer 1850, first complete draft 2 Oct 1869 – 10 Apr 1872, second complete draft (short score) 11 Jan 1870 – 22 Jul 1872, full score 3 May 1873 – 21 Nov 1874
For clarification see 'Composition' below.
First perf.: Festspielhaus, Bayreuth, 17 Aug 1876
First UK perf.: Her Majesty's Theatre, London, 9 May 1882
First US perf.: Metropolitan Opera, New York, 25 Jan 1888 (Norn and Waltraute scenes omitted)

Siegfried	tenor
Gunther	bass-baritone
Alberich	bass-baritone
Hagen	bass
Brünnhilde	soprano
Gutrune	soprano
Waltraute	mezzo-soprano
First Norn	contralto
Second Norn	mezzo-soprano
Third Norn	soprano
Woglinde	soprano
Wellgunde	soprano
Flosshilde	mezzo-soprano

Vassals, women

Orchestration as for *Das Rheingold* (above), but with tenor drum and glock

On/off stage: cow horns, horns, 4 harps

Synopsis
Prologue
The setting is the Valkyrie rock, as at the end of *Siegfried*. The Three Norns, daughters of Erda, are weaving the rope of destiny. The First Norn tells how, long ago, when she was spinning at the World Ash Tree, Wotan came to drink at the Well of Wisdom, sacrificing an eye as forfeit. He had cut a spear from the trunk of the tree, which had later withered and died. The Second Norn tells how a brave hero broke Wotan's spear in battle; the god then sent heroes from Valhalla to chop down the World Ash. The Third Norn describes how the chopped logs of the World Ash have been piled round Valhalla; one day they will be ignited and the entire hall will be engulfed in flames. Gods and heroes are awaiting that day. The First Norn sees fire burning round the Valkyrie rock and is told that it is Loge fulfilling Wotan's command. A vision of Alberich and the stolen Rhinegold causes the Norns anxiety: their rope breaks.

They descend into the earth, day dawns and Siegfried and Brünnhilde come out of the cave to which they retired at the end of *Siegfried*. Brünnhilde sends Siegfried off on deeds of glory, urging him to remember their love. Siegfried gives her the ring as a token of his faithfulness; in exchange, Brünnhilde offers him her horse, Grane. The pair sing of their indivisible love and Siegfried embarks on his journey down the Rhine.

Act I
Gunther, the chief of the Gibichungs, sits on a throne in his palace with his sister Gutrune. He asks his half-brother Hagen whether his reputation is high. Hagen replies that it would be higher if Gunther were to find a wife and Gutrune a husband. He tells Gunther about Brünnhilde, how she lies on a rock encircled by fire, and how only the hero Siegfried

can win her. He tells him about Siegfried's slaying the dragon and suggests that Siegfried would win the bride for Gunther if Gutrune had won him first. Hagen reminds them of a potion they have that would make Siegfried forget any other women.

Siegfried's horn is now heard and hospitality is extended to him. Hagen asks about the Nibelung treasure and Siegfried says he left it lying in a cave, taking only the piece of metalwork they see dangling from his belt. Hagen, recognizing the tarnhelm, explains that it renders its wearer invisible; when Siegfried says that he gave the ring from the treasure to a glorious woman, Hagen breathes Brünnhilde's name to himself. Gutrune appears with the drugged potion and Siegfried, in a gesture pregnant with irony, drinks to the memory of Brünnhilde and their love. He is immediately drawn to Gutrune, whose name he asks of her brother, and loses no time in offering himself as her husband.

Siegfried then offers to win Gunther a wife and as he is told about Brünnhilde high on a rock surrounded by fire, it is clear that he has only the faintest memory of her. He proposes to use the tarnhelm to disguise himself as Gunther in order to bring back Brünnhilde. They swear an oath of blood brotherhood, from which Hagen abstains. Siegfried sets off up the river again, followed by Gunther. The dour Hagen sits guarding the palace, contemplating the satisfactory progress of his scheme to win power.

Back on the Valkyrie rock, Brünnhilde sits outside her cave, happily meditating on the ring left her by Siegfried. There is thunder and lightning and her sister Waltraute approaches on a winged horse. So delighted is Brünnhilde to see her that she fails to notice Waltraute's agitation: has Wotan, perhaps, forgiven her? Waltraute has broken Wotan's command in coming, she says, but sadly Wotan is no longer to be feared. Waltraute then narrates how Wotan, as the Wanderer, returned to Valhalla with his spear shattered, how he ordered the heroes to pile up logs from the World Ash Tree, how the gods sit there in fear and dread, and how Wotan longs for the ring to be given back to the Rhinemaidens; it is to persuade Brünnhilde to do this that Waltraute has come.

Brünnhilde is stunned by this narration, but Waltraute begs her to throw the ring away. Brünnhilde refuses to entertain the idea of throwing away Siegfried's pledge and sends her sister back to Valhalla to tell the gods as much. Waltraute departs in a thundercloud which passes to reveal a calm evening sky. Then the flames leap up again round the rock and Brünnhilde hears Siegfried's horn. She rushes excitedly to the edge of the cliff and is horrified to find a stranger (Siegfried disguised as Gunther). The stranger claims her as wife, violently snatches the ring from her finger and forces her into the cave for the night. He places his sword symbolically between them.

Act II

Hagen, sitting outside the Gibichung hall in a halfsleep, is visited by his father, Alberich. He is urged to acquire the ring and intends to do so, but will swear faithfulness only to himself. Dawn breaks and Siegfried returns, now in his own form once more. Gunther is following with Brünnhilde, he says, and he tells Hagen and Gutrune how he braved the fire again and overpowered Brünnhilde. He secretly changed places with Gunther and, using the tarnhelm's magic, returned in an instant. Gunther's boat is seen in the distance and Gutrune asks Hagen to call people together to celebrate the wedding.

Hagen summons his vassals with blasts on his horn. They rush in from all directions and are intemperately amused when they find out that Hagen has summoned them not for battle but for celebration. Clashing their weapons together, they hail Gunther, who leads Brünnhilde forward, her eyes cast down. He greets Siegfried and hands her over to Gutrune. When Brünnhilde hears Siegfried's name, she reacts in violent amazement. Has he forgotten his bride, she asks? Brünnhilde sees the ring on Siegfried's hand and asks how he got it, as it was seized from her by Gunther. There is much confusion among the bystanders; Siegfried says he simply won it by slaying a dragon. Brünnhilde rages against the gods for allowing Siegfried to betray her; Siegfried is her husband, she announces. Siegfried tells how he won Brünnhilde for Gunther and claims that his sword lay between them during the night. Brünnhilde asserts that Nothung hung on the wall as its master wooed her. Siegfried, pressed by Gunther and the onlookers to declare his innocence, swears on the point of Hagen's spear that he has kept faith with his 'blood-brother'. The enraged Brünnhilde swears on the same spear-point that Siegfried has perjured himself. Siegfried calls everyone to the wedding-feast and leads Gutrune into the palace.

Brünnhilde, left alone with Gunther and Hagen, laments Siegfried's treachery. At first she scorns Hagen's offer to avenge her; the hero would soon make him quake, she says. But then she confides that Siegfried's back would be vulnerable; she gave him no protection there as he would never turn it on an enemy. Gunther bemoans his own disgrace, but initially reacts with horror to Hagen's proposal to strike Siegfried dead. He is persuaded by the promise of obtaining the ring and it is decided to tell Gutrune that Siegfried was killed by a boar while out hunting. Siegfried and Gutrune reappear from the palace and a wedding procession forms.

Act III

The setting is wild woodland and a rocky valley by the bank of the Rhine. The Rhinemaidens are playing in the river, singing of the lost gold. Hearing Siegfried's horn, they hope that he may be coming to return the ring to them. Siegfried, having lost his way, stumbles on the Rhinemaidens. They playfully ask him for the ring on his finger, but he refuses. Then he relents, but when the Rhinemaidens tell him of the dangers the curse-laden ring brings, Siegfried says he will not succumb to threats. The Rhinemaidens leave the 'fool' and swim out of sight, leaving Siegfried to meditate on the oddness of women's behaviour.

Hagen's voice is heard and Siegfried calls the hunting party over. He tells them that the only game he has seen was three wild water-birds, who told him he would be murdered that day. Siegfried drinks jovially from a horn, but Gunther can see only Siegfried's blood in his. Siegfried is asked to tell the story of his life and he begins with his upbringing by the ill-tempered dwarf Mime. The dwarf taught him smithing, but it was his own skills that enabled him to forge Nothung, with which he killed the dragon Fafner. He tells how the taste of the dragon's blood enabled him to understand the song of the wood-bird, who told him about the ring and tarnhelm inside the dragon's cave. The bird then warned him of Mime's treachery and he despatched the evil dwarf. Hagen hands him a drink which he says will help him to remember what happened next. Siegfried then recalls how he was led to a high rock surrounded by fire. There he found the sleeping Brünnhilde, whom he awoke with a kiss. On hearing this, Gunther jumps up in alarm. Two ravens fly overhead and as Siegfried looks up, Hagen plunges his spear in his back. Siegfried dies with Brünnhilde's name on his lips and his body is carried off in a solemn funeral procession.

The scene changes to the hall of the Gibichungs. Gutrune comes out of her room into the palace. She thinks she hears Siegfried's horn, but he hasn't returned. She has seen Brünnhilde walking towards the Rhine and is anxious. Hagen is heard approaching and Siegfried's corpse is brought in. Gutrune collapses over the body. She accuses Gunther of killing him, but her brother puts the blame on Hagen, who claims to have killed him for committing perjury; Hagen steps forward to seize the ring and when Gunther stands in his way, he is murdered by Hagen. Hagen tries again to take the ring, but as he approaches Siegfried, the dead man's hand rises into the air, to the horror of all.

Brünnhilde enters, now calm, and tells how Siegfried swore her an eternal oath. Gutrune curses Hagen and leans again over Gunther's body, where she remains, motionless, until the end. Brünnhilde orders logs to be gathered to make a funeral pyre worthy of the hero. She sings of her betrayal by this noblest, most faithful of men. Addressing Wotan in Valhalla, she says that Siegfried's death has atoned for his guilt and has brought her enlightenment through sorrow. She takes Siegfried's ring, promising that it will be returned to the Rhinemaidens. Taking a blazing torch from one of the bystanders, she hurls it on to the pile of logs which immediately ignites. She greets her horse Grane, mounts it and

rides into the flames. The whole building seems to catch fire and the men and women press to the front of the stage in terror. Suddenly the fire dies down and the Rhine bursts its banks, flooding the entire space. On the appearance of the Rhinemaidens, Hagen leaps into the water in pursuit of the ring. The Rhinemaidens drag him down into the depths and hold up the ring in triumph. The water-level falls again and from the ruins of the palace, which has collapsed, the men and women watch a burst of firelight as it rises into the sky. Eventually it illuminates the hall of Valhalla, where gods and heroes are seen assembled. Valhalla is engulfed in flames: the long-awaited end of the gods has come to pass.

Evolution of text and music
The first draft of *Siegfrieds Tod* (originally spelt *Siegfried's Tod* and later renamed *Götterdämmerung*) is dated (at the end) 20 October 1848. This draft begins in the hall of the Gibichungs, but having been persuaded that too much background knowledge to the story was presupposed, Wagner added a Prologue some time before 12 November. He undertook the versification of *Siegfrieds Tod* between 12 and 28 November, but then put aside the drama, perhaps unsure how to reconcile its diverging strands: divine myth and heroic tragedy. In the summer of 1850 he made some preliminary musical sketches for the Prologue and began a composition draft, which was discontinued after the opening of the leavetaking scene for Siegfried and Brünnhilde. Having then added a preliminary drama, *Der junge Siegfried* (1851), and *Die Walküre* and *Das Rheingold* (1851–2), Wagner found it necessary to subject *Siegfrieds Tod* to revision: Siegfried had already been replaced as the central figure of the cycle by Wotan; the ending was altered so that the gods and Valhalla are all destroyed by fire; the Norns' Scene was completely rewritten; a confrontation between Brünnhilde and the rest of the Valkyries was compressed into the dialogue for Brünnhilde and Waltraute (Act I scene 3); and several passages of narrative now rendered superfluous by *Die Walküre* and *Das Rheingold* were removed.

In this 1852 version of the text, the following lines were added:

Nicht Gut, nicht Gold,	Not wealth, not gold,
noch göttliche Pracht;	nor godly splendour;
nicht Haus, nicht Hof,	not house, not court,
noch herrischer Prunk; . . .	nor overbearing pomp; . . .
selig in Lust und Leid	blessed in joy and sorrow
lässt – die Liebe nur sein. –	only love may be. –

Because of the evident influence of the philosopher Ludwig Feuerbach (see 'Intellectual Background', p.59–60) – particularly in the elevation of love above material possessions – this ending has come to be known as the 'Feuerbach ending'.

In 1856, however, following his momentous

discovery of the philosophy of Schopenhauer (see 'Intellectual Background', pp.54–5) and his coterminous interest in Buddhism, Wagner changed his concluding text yet again. In the 'Schopenhauer ending', Brünnhilde, the 'enlightened one', sees herself as redeemed from the endless cycle of suffering and rebirth; made wise by the 'deepest suffering of grieving love', she enters the state of non-being, or Nirvana:

> Führ' ich nun nicht mehr
> Nach Walhalls Feste,
> wiss't ihr, wohin ich fahre?
> Aus Wunschheim zieh' ich fort,
> Wahnheim flieh' ich auf immer;
> des ew'gen Werdens
> off'ne Tore
> schliess' ich hinter mir zu:
> nach dem wunsch- und wahnlos
> heiligstem Wahlland,
> der Welt-Wanderung Ziel,
> von Wiedergeburt erlös't,
> zieht nun die Wissende hin.
> Alles Ew'gen
> sel'ges Ende,
> wiss't ihr, wie ich's gewann?
> Trauernder Liebe
> tiefstes Leiden
> schloss die Augen mir auf:
> enden sah ich die Welt. –

> Were I no longer to fare
> to Valhalla's fortress,
> do you know whither I would fare?
> I depart from the home of desire,
> I flee for ever from the home of delusion;
> the open gates
> of eternal becoming
> I close behind me:
> to the holiest chosen land,
> free from desire and delusion
> the goal of world-wandering,
> redeemed from rebirth,
> the enlightened one now goes.
> The blessed end
> of all things eternal,
> do you know how I attained it?
> Grieving love's
> deepest suffering
> opened my eyes:
> I saw the world end. –

Sustained work on the music of *Götterdämmerung* was initiated with the first complete draft, begun on 2 October 1869 and finished on 10 April 1872. The second complete draft (short score) was made, as with *Siegfried*, in parallel, between 11 January 1870 and 22 July 1872. The full score was finished in Wahnfried on 21 November 1874.

(For more on the genesis of *Siegfrieds Tod* and its subsequent development, see 'Autograph manuscripts', pp.199–219.)

Musical style

Götterdämmerung continues the process initiated in *Siegfried* Act III, whereby motifs are deployed and combined with a freedom scarcely envisaged in *Oper und Drama*. Whereas the earlier operas of the cycle tie motivic statements fairly closely to the text, the score of *Götterdämmerung* is characterized by congeries of motifs drawn on for a brief thematic development. And yet, in various ways *Götterdämmerung* represents a stylistic regression too. The trio of conspirators in Act II, for example, with its verbal duplications, ensemble singing and its mode of declamation in general, is often likened to the gestures of conventional grand opera. The paradox can be accounted for, in part, by the fact that the libretto for *Götterdämmerung* was written more than twenty years before the music, at a time when the theories of the music drama had not yet been formulated.

Similarly regressive is the chorus of the vassals in Act II scene 2: a C major ensemble (though with augmented-triad coloration under the baleful influence of Hagen) in a somewhat old-fashioned style. It is undeniably rousing in the theatre, however, and it evidently made a forceful impression on the young Schoenberg, for it is alluded to extensively in his *Gurrelieder*.

For all its backward-looking tendencies, the stylistic integrity of *Götterdämmerung* is scarcely compromised. The disparate elements are welded together with a technical skill and a dramaturgical conviction that sweeps petty criticisms aside. The length and complexity that preclude frequent performance of the work also ensure that when it is staged – usually as the climax to the *Ring* cycle as a whole – the event is a special one.

Tristan und Isolde
WWV 90
Drama in 3 acts

Text: prose sketch (lost) Oct 1854, prose scenario begun 20 Aug 1857, poem completed 18 Sep 1857
Music: earliest dated surviving sketch 19 Dec 1856, first complete draft 1 Oct 1857 – 16 Jul 1859, second complete draft 5 Nov 1857 – 19 Jul 1859, full score completed 6 Aug 1859
First perf.: Königliches Hof- und National-Theater, Munich, 10 Jun 1865
First UK perf.: Theatre Royal, Drury Lane, London, 20 Jun 1882
First US perf.: Metropolitan Opera, New York, 1 Dec 1886

Tristan	tenor
King Mark	bass
Isolde	soprano
Kurwenal, *Tristan's servant*	baritone
Melot, *a courtier*	tenor

Brangäne, *Isolde's maid*   soprano
A shepherd   tenor
A steersman   baritone
A young sailor   tenor

Sailors, knights and esquires

pic, 3 fl, 2 ob, cor ang, 2 cl, bass cl, 3 bn, 4 hn, 3 tpt, 3 trbn, bass tuba, timp, cym, tri, harp, str

On/off stage: cor ang, 6 hn (more if possible), 3 tpt, 3 trbn

Synopsis
Act I
The first act is set at sea, on the deck of Tristan's ship, during the crossing from Ireland to Cornwall. The curtain rises to reveal a construction like a tent on the foredeck of a ship; Isolde is seen on a couch, her face buried in the cushions. A young sailor sings, 'as if from the masthead', an unaccompanied song about the Irish lover he has left behind. Isolde, who is being brought from Ireland to Cornwall by Tristan as a bride for his uncle, King Mark, starts up, assuming that the reference to an 'Irish maid' is an insult to her. When her maid and confidante Brangäne tells her that they are soon to land in Cornwall, Isolde launches into a furious outburst against her own 'degenerate race' who have succumbed so easily to the enemy. Brangäne attempts in vain to calm her.

For the second scene the whole length of the ship becomes visible; in the stern stands Tristan thoughtfully, his faithful retainer Kurwenal reclining at his feet. Isolde tells Brangäne to instruct Tristan to attend on her. Brangäne's timid request to Tristan is courteously turned aside by him, but when she repeats Isolde's command, Kurwenal makes his own bluntly negative reply. He goes on to revel in the slaying by Tristan of Morold, Isolde's betrothed, who came from Ireland to exact tribute from Cornwall.

Brangäne returns in confusion to Isolde who is barely able to control her anger (scene 3). Isolde's Narration tells how the wounded Tristan, disguised as 'Tantris', came to her to be healed and how she recognized him as Morold's killer. Isolde's determination to slay Tristan in revenge dissolved as he looked pitifully into her eyes, but now she bitterly regrets that she let the sword drop. Brangäne reminds Isolde of her mother's magic potions; Isolde, however, has only vengeance in mind and she selects the draught of death. Kurwenal boisterously calls the ladies to make ready (scene 4), but Isolde insists on speaking to Tristan before they land, in order to 'forgive' him. Tristan approaches. Isolde tells him that she saw through his disguise as 'Tantris' and demands vengeance. Tristan offers her his sword, but Isolde signals to Brangäne for the potion. Isolde hands Tristan the cup. Tristan lifts the cup and drinks. Fearing further betrayal, Isolde

wrests the cup from him and drinks in her turn: Brangäne, in desperation, has substituted the love for the death potion. Tristan and Isolde embrace ecstatically, while Brangäne looks on in horror. Land has been reached, and the conflicting emotions are registered against a background of fanfares and general rejoicing.

Act II
The curtain rises to reveal a garden with high trees in the garden of King Mark's castle in Cornwall; Isolde's chamber is to one side and a burning torch stands at the open door. A volley of horn calls gradually receding into the distance signifies the departing hunt of King Mark and his courtiers. The cautious Brangäne warns her mistress that the horns are still audible, but all Isolde can hear are the sounds of the balmy summer night. Brangäne further warns Isolde that in her impatience to see Tristan she should not be oblivious to the devious Melot, Tristan's supposed friend, who, she alleges, has arranged the nocturnal hunt as a trap. Isolde brushes these fears aside and requests Brangäne to extinguish the torch: the signal for Tristan to approach. Brangäne demurs, bewailing her fateful switching of the potions. Isolde throws the torch to the ground and sending Brangäne to keep watch, she waits impatiently for Tristan. He finally bursts in (scene 2) and they greet each other ecstatically.

Tristan draws Isolde to a flowery bank for their central love duet, which is punctuated by Brangäne's Watchsong from the tower. The surging passion of the music leaves little to the imagination, but at the critical juncture a scream is heard from Brangäne in the watchtower, as King Mark, Melot and the courtiers burst in on the scene. King Mark, much moved, addresses Tristan and receiving no direct answer, embarks on a long monologue of questioning reproach. To King Mark's questions there can be no reply, Tristan responds. He feels that he no longer belongs to this world and invites Isolde to follow him into the realm of night; she assents and he kisses her on the forehead. At this, Melot, whose actions, according to Tristan, have been motivated by his jealous love for Isolde, draws his sword. Tristan also draws, but allows himself to be wounded.

Act III
The curtain rises on Tristan's castle in Brittany. Tristan is seen lying asleep under a lime tree, with Kurwenal bending over him griefstricken. A melancholy shepherd's song is heard on the cor anglais offstage. The shepherd appears over the castle wall. Kurwenal tells him to play a merry melody if Isolde's ship should come into sight. 'Öd und leer das Meer!' ('Empty and desolate the sea!') responds the shepherd and continues with his mournful tune. To the joy of Kurwenal, Tristan revives and asks where he is. Kurwenal replies that he is in his family castle, Kareol. Tristan returns slowly and painfully

to consciousness. He is dimly aware that he has been brought back from the distant realm of endless night, where he had glimpsed oblivion. Isolde remains in the bright light of day, but he looks forward to the final extinction of the torch and their union.

Kurwenal tells him that he has sent for Isolde, and Tristan, in his fevered imagination, sees the ship approaching. Tristan's frantic cries to Kurwenal to look for the ship are answered by the cor anglais playing the mournful shepherd's song. In the next phase of his delirium, Tristan remembers how he heard that song in his childhood, when his mother and father died. He sinks back in a faint. Kurwenal listens anxiously for signs of life. Tristan revives and in the final, sublime phase of his delirium, he imagines Isolde coming to him across the water. This time a sprightly tune on the cor anglais confirms that the ship has indeed been sighted. Kurwenal rushes to the watchtower and reports on its progress. He sees Isolde come ashore and goes down to assist (scene 2). Tristan, meanwhile, anticipates her arrival in feverish excitement, tearing the bandages from his wounds.

Isolde enters in haste, but Tristan expires in her arms. The shepherd tells Kurwenal that a second ship is arriving (scene 3); they try to barricade the gate. Brangäne appears and then Melot, whom Kurwenal strikes dead. King Mark and his followers also appear and, oblivious to the king's pleas, Kurwenal sets upon them, sustaining a fatal wound; he dies at Tristan's feet. King Mark, who had come to yield Isolde to Tristan, laments the scene of death and destruction. In her Liebestod (or Transfiguration, as Wagner preferred to call it) Isolde sinks, as if transfigured, on to Tristan's body, mystically united with him at last.

Sources
The ancient Tristan legend, probably of Celtic origin, achieved its first literary form in the 12th century. The version used by Wagner as the basis for his drama was that of Gottfried von Strassburg (fl. 1200–20). Three characters in Gottfried are fused into the single figure of Melot in the opera, and Wagner introduced the subsidiary characters of the sailor, shepherd and steersman. His chief characters, however, remain as he found them, from which we can assume that Tristan is little more than eighteen years old, and Isolde similarly 'of tender years'. The custom of the period dictated that the companions of noble offspring should be of a like age. Kurwenal and Brangäne are also, therefore, probably in their teens, while King Mark, described by Eilhart von Oberge in an earlier version of the story as 'the young king', is generally held to be in his thirties.

Composition
Inspired, according to *Mein Leben*, by a flawed attempt of his friend Karl Ritter to dramatize the Tristan legend, Wagner conceived the idea of an opera on the subject in the October of 1854. The *Mein Leben* account suggests that a prose sketch was made at this time, though a letter to Liszt (16? December 1854) is more ambiguous: 'I have planned in my head a *Tristan* and *Isolde*, the simplest, but most full-blooded musical conception'. If a prose sketch was indeed made at this time, it has not survived. The earliest dated surviving sketch (an elaboration of two fragments) is from 19 December 1856, at which point Wagner was still engaged on Act I of *Siegfried*.

The prose scenario was begun the following summer, on 20 August 1857, and the poem was completed on 18 September. Like *Siegfried* – but unlike all the other music dramas – each act was drafted and elaborated, in sequence, the full score being reached before the next act was embarked on in sketch. Indeed, because Breitkopf & Härtel were eager to have the new work ready for public consumption, the score was actually engraved one act at a time. The fair copy of the full score of Act I was completed on 3 April 1858 in Zurich, of Act II on 18 March 1859 in Venice, and of Act III on 6 August 1859 in Lucerne.

The drama
Tristan und Isolde is the musical depiction of a passion so intense, a yearning so inextinguishable, that its consummation can be experienced only in death. As such, it is generally acknowledged to be one of the most voluptuous scores ever written. Nor did the composer make any concessions to bourgeois taste: one writer (Wilfrid Mellers) refers to the 'orgiastic ecstasy' of the music, while Virgil Thomson claimed that in the Act II duet 'the lovers ejaculate simultaneously seven times', and that these moments are 'clearly marked in the music'.

Yet this is only half the story. It is no coincidence that the work took shape in Wagner's mind at precisely the time when he was responding to the abnegatory ideals of Schopenhauer and to the Buddhist concept of renunciation. Schopenhauer believed that suffering and striving were inevitable in this life, that the only escape lay in denial of the will, in attaining the state of Nirvana, or cessation of individual existence. Wagner, however, succeeded in reconciling parts of that philosophy with his own inclination towards sensual indulgence: the pathway to the pacification of the 'will to live' lay through love, he declared, and specifically the sexual love between a man and a woman.

The love of Tristan and Isolde thus reaches beyond the purely physical, beyond material existence, to a metaphysical plane. Shedding their physical, 'phenomenal' forms (that is the forms in which they appear to the outside world), the lovers merge their identities in the realm of inner consciousness, the ultimate reality, symbolized by 'death' and 'night'.

Musical style

The phrase of Wagner's most often quoted in connection with *Tristan* is 'deeds of music made visible'. It is a definition of music drama that hints at the ascendancy of music over text – a hierarchy more apparent in *Tristan* than in any other of Wagner's works. The influence of Schopenhauer's aesthetic, elevating music over all the other arts, is clear: Wagner's discovery of Schopenhauer occurred only a month before the 'full-blooded musical conception' of *Tristan* in 1854. Nevertheless, the work by no means abandons the prescriptions of *Oper und Drama*: the organic relationship of music and poetry is still very much in evidence, even if the subtleties of the word-setting are often obscured by the increased opulence of the orchestral textures.

Appropriately, therefore – but also because *Tristan* unfolds on a metaphysical plane quite different from the social world of the *Ring* – leitmotifs are generally not, in this work, tied to specific objects or states of mind. Where, in the *Ring*, there are motifs clearly associated with the sword or the gold (even if those associations become somewhat tenuous as the cycle proceeds), in *Tristan* one association merges into another as rapidly as the motifs themselves undergo thematic metamorphosis. A system that attempts to label the descending chromatic motif that opens the work, for example, will soon come to grief, for it is identified with various qualities or states of mind at different points in the drama. It is, moreover, so closely related to several other definable motifs in the work that at times they become indistinguishable.

The musical language of *Tristan* is characterized by its dislocation of tonality and extreme chromaticism in both line and harmony. Never before had the Classical tonal system been so stretched: dominant sevenths and other discords are constantly left unresolved, cadences remain uncompleted, and both melodies and harmonies are consistently heightened by chromatic alteration. All these devices are employed, of course, for expressive effect: everything is geared to the generation and intensification of tension – the tension of promised but evaded fulfilment. The result was something that irreversibly affected the course of music history. With *Tristan* began in earnest the emancipation of harmony from the Classical tonal system.

For more on the antecedents to the musical language of *Tristan*, see 'Musical Background and Influences', pp.84–8.)

Die Meistersinger von Nürnberg (The Mastersingers of Nuremberg)
WWV 96
Music drama in 3 acts

Text: first prose draft July 1845, second prose draft ?14–16 Nov 1861, third prose draft 18 Nov 1861,

poem completed 25 Jan 1862
Music: begun Mar/Apr 1862, first complete draft finished 7 Feb 1867, second complete draft finished 5 Mar 1867, full score finished 24 Oct 1867
First perf.: Königliches Hof- und National-Theater, Munich, 21 June 1868
First UK perf.: Theatre Royal, Drury Lane, 30 May 1882
First US perf.: Metropolitan Opera, New York, 4 Jan 1886

Hans Sachs, *cobbler*		bass-baritone
Veit Pogner, *goldsmith*		bass
Kunz Vogelgesang, *furrier*		tenor
Konrad Nachtigal, *tinsmith*		bass
Sixtus Beckmesser, *town clerk*		bass
Fritz Kothner, *baker*	Mastersingers	bass
Balthasar Zorn, *pewterer*		tenor
Ulrich Eisslinger, *grocer*		tenor
Augustin Moser, *tailor*		tenor
Hermann Ortel, *soapmaker*		bass
Hans Schwarz, *stocking weaver*		bass
Hans Foltz, *coppersmith*		bass
Walther von Stolzing, *a young knight from Franconia*		tenor
David, *Sachs's apprentice*		tenor
Eva, *Pogner's daughter*		soprano
Magdalene, *Eva's nurse*		soprano
A Nightwatchman		bass

Citizens of all guilds and their wives, journeymen, apprentices, young women, people

pic, 3 fl, 2 ob, 2 cl, 2 bn, 4 hn, 3 tpt, 3 trbn, contrabass tuba, timp, bd, cym, tri, glock, harp, lute, str

On/off stage: org, cow horn, horns, trumpets, tenor drums

Synopsis
Act I
The act opens inside St Katharine's Church, with the congregation singing a sturdy C major chorale (of Wagner's invention). Walther is urgently trying to communicate with Eva. At the end of the service, the church empties and Walther addresses Eva. He wishes to know whether she is betrothed, and though Eva sends away her nurse Magdalene to find first her handkerchief, then the clasp, and then her prayer-book, she never quite manages to stem Walther's impassioned flow with an answer. Magdalene finally tells him that Eva will marry the mastersinger that wins the song-contest to be held the next day. Walther is left to be instructed in the rules of the mastersingers by David, Sachs's apprentice, with whom Magdalene is in love.

In scene 2 David, after some ribbing from his fellow apprentices, proceeds to initiate Walther into the secrets of his own master's art: a properly fashioned song is, after all, he says, like a well-made pair of shoes. His catalogue of the tones that have to be learned, along with the appropriate rules (most taken by Wagner from Wagenseil's Nuremberg Chronicle) overwhelms Walther, but he sees that his only hope of winning Eva is by composing a mastersong in the approved manner. The apprentices, who have erected the wrong stage, put up the right one under David's supervision.

Eva's father, Pogner, now enters with the town clerk, Beckmesser (scene 3). Pogner assures Beckmesser of his good will and welcomes Walther to the guild, surprised as he is that Walther wishes to seek entry. Kothner calls the roll and Pogner then announces the prize he intends to award to the winner of the song-contest the next day. He tells how burghers such as they are regarded in other German lands as miserly, and he proposes to counter this slander by offering all his goods, as well as his only daughter, Eva, to the winner of the song-contest. His proviso that she must approve the man is not welcomed by all the masters. Sachs's proposal, however, that the winner be chosen by the populace, as a means of renewing the traditional rules with the good sense and natural instincts of the common people, is laughed out of court.

Walther is introduced by Pogner and asked about his teacher. His reply, 'Am stillen Herd' ('By the quiet fireside'), is that he learned his art from the poetry of Walther von der Vogelweide and from nature itself. Beckmesser withdraws into his Marker's box, ready to pass judgment on the young knight's formal attempt to enter the guild. The rules of the *Tabulatur* are read out by Kothner.

For his Trial Song, Walther takes up the command of the Marker: 'Fanget an! So rief der Lenz in den Wald' ('Begin! Thus cried the spring through the wood'). A passionate celebration of the joys of spring and youthful love, it again fails to find favour with the masters. Beckmesser's critical scratching of chalk on slate provokes an angry outburst from Walther about envious Winter lying in wait in the thorn-bush (for the significance of this, see below, p.304).

Beckmesser leads the chorus of opposition to Walther; only Sachs admires his originality. Walther mounts the singer's chair (a gross breach of etiquette) to complete his song. The hubbub increases as he does so: the masters, by an overwhelming majority, reject his application to the guild, while the apprentices revel in the commotion. With a gesture of pride and contempt, Walther strides from the stage, leaving Sachs to gaze thoughtfully at the empty singer's chair.

Act II

The curtain rises to reveal a street and a narrower adjoining alley in Nuremberg. Of the two corner houses presented, Pogner's grand one on the right is overhung by a lime tree and Sachs's simpler one on the left by an elder. The apprentices are tormenting David once again. Magdalene asks him how Eva's paramour fared at the Song School and is vicariously disconsolate at the bad news. Sachs arrives and instructs David to set out his work for him by the window. Pogner and Eva return from an evening stroll and sit on a bench under the lime tree. Pogner belatedly realizes that Eva's questions about the knight are no idle curiosity.

As Eva follows her father inside, Sachs has his work bench set up outside his workshop. Sachs's relishing of the scent of the elder in his solo, 'Was duftet doch der Flieder', has given it the name of the '*Flieder*' Monologue: it develops into an exquisite evocation of the joys of spring.

Eva approaches Sachs's workshop (scene 4) and, in a long, delicately woven exchange, tries to elicit from him the likely winner of the next day's contest. Sachs playfully parries her questions until Magdalene enters to tell her that her father is calling, and that Beckmesser intends to serenade her.

Walther now turns the corner (scene 5) and an impassioned duet ensues. They are at a loss as to how to obviate her father's conditions for obtaining her hand. Walther suggests eloping, but he gets carried away by his loathing of the masters' pedantry until he is interrupted by the sound of the Nightwatchman's horn. Eva has meanwhile followed Magdalene into the house and now re-emerges, having changed clothes with her.

Eva and Walther are about to make their escape when Sachs, who has realized what is afoot, allows his lamp to illuminate the alley they are in. They hesitate and are then pulled up short by the sound of Beckmesser tuning his lute. Walther is for settling his score with the Marker and has to be restrained by Eva: 'What trouble I have with men!', she sighs. She persuades him to sit quietly under the lime tree until Beckmesser has finished his song. But Sachs has other ideas, launching into a noisy, vigorous song of his own: 'Jerum! Jerum!' Sachs's song is permeated with references to the biblical Eve and to shoemaking that are not entirely lost on the listeners. But Beckmesser has less time for the poetic subtleties; seeing what he believes to be the object of his wooing come to the window (in fact Magdalene in Eva's clothes), he begs Sachs to stop his clattering. Reminding him that he had been critical of his workmanship earlier in the day, Sachs suggests that both would make progress if Beckmesser were to serenade while he, Sachs, marked any faults with his cobbler's hammer. The commotion caused by Sachs's hammering and Beckmesser's attempts to make himself heard above it brings the populace out on to the streets. A riot ensues (scene 7), during which David cudgels Beckmesser, under the impression that he is courting Magdalene. At the height of the pandemonium, the Nightwatchman's horn is heard again. Everybody disperses and by the time he arrives on the scene the streets are empty; he rubs his eyes in disbelief.

Act III

The final act opens in Sachs's workshop. David enters the workshop. Sachs, deep in thought, at first ignores him, but then asks him to sing the verses he has learnt for the festival of St John, celebrated on midsummer's day. His mind still on the events of the previous evening, David begins his ditty to the tune of Beckmesser's Serenade and has to start again. David belatedly realizes that it is also his master's name day (Hans = Johannes). When the apprentice has left, Sachs resumes his philosophical meditation on the follies of humanity: 'Wahn! Wahn! Überall Wahn!' (The concept of *Wahn*, which includes the notions of illusion, folly and madness, lies at the heart of *Die Meistersinger*: by the 1860s, Wagner had come to believe that all human endeavour was underpinned by illusion and futility, though art, he considered, was a 'noble illusion'.)

Walther appears and tells Sachs of a wonderful dream. Sachs urges him to recount it as it may enable him to win the master's prize. (Wagner had readily become a convert to the Schopenhauerian view that creativity originated in the dream-world.) Walther's resistance to the demands of the masters is overcome in the name of love, and he embarks on his Morning Dream Song – what is to become the Prize Song: 'Morgenlich leuchtend im rosigen Schein' ('Radiant in the roseate glow of morning'). He produces one *Stollen* or stanza, and then, at Sachs's bidding, another similar, followed by an *Abgesang* (after-song). Under Sachs's instruction, Walther goes on to produce another three stanzas.

In the third scene, Beckmesser appears alone in the workshop. After his beating the night before, he is limping and stumbling, and prey to nightmarish memories and imaginings. Picking up Walther's freshly penned song, he pockets it on Sachs's re-entry. He adduces it as proof that Sachs means to enter the song-contest, but Sachs denies such a plan and offers him the song. Beckmesser's suspicions are eventually allayed, and he delightedly retires in order to memorize the song.

Eva enters (scene 4) and under the cover of a complaint about the shoes Sachs has made for her, she expresses her anxieties about Walther and the coming contest. Sachs affects not to understand, and pretends not to notice Walther's arrival, in spite of Eva's passionate cry and a thrilling tonal shift in the orchestra. Walther delivers the final section of his song and Eva, moved to tears, sobs on the shoulder of Sachs, until the latter drags himself away, complaining about the lot of the cobbler. Eva, emotionally torn between the avuncular shoemaker and her younger lover, draws Sachs to her again. Sachs reminds her of the story of Tristan and Isolde and says he has no wish to play the role of King Mark. Magdalene and David arrive, and Sachs, with a cuff

on his ear, announces David's promotion to journeyman, in time to witness the baptism of 'a child'. The progeny turns out to be Walther's new song, which is blessed in the celebrated quintet.

The setting changes to an open meadow on the Pegnitz (scene 5). The townsfolk are all gathered and, to the accompaniment of fanfares on stage, greet the processions of the guilds: first the shoemakers, then the tailors and bakers. A boat brings 'maidens from Fürth' and the apprentices begin dancing with them; David, at first reluctant, is drawn in.

At last the masters arrive. Sachs is hailed by the populace to the words with which the historical Sachs greeted Luther and the Reformation: 'Wach auf, es nahet gen den Tag' ('Awake, the day draws near'). Sachs modestly acknowledges the homage and exhorts people and masters to accord the coming contest and prize their due worth. Beckmesser, who had frantically been trying to memorize Walther's song, is led first to the platform. His rendering of the song, to the tune of his own Serenade, is marked by grotesque misaccentuations and violations of metre, but it is his garbling of the words, producing an absurd, tasteless parody of the original, that provokes a crescendo of hilarity in the audience. He presses on in confusion, but only makes a greater fool of himself. Finally he rushes from the platform, denouncing Sachs as the author.

Sachs refutes that honour and introduces the man who will make sense of it for them. Walther sings his song and is awarded the prize by general consent. When Pogner proffers the master's chain to Walther, he impetuously refuses, and Sachs delivers a homily about the art that the masters have cultivated and preserved throughout Germany's troubled history. Sachs's address concludes with a celebration of the sovereignty of the German spirit; that spirit, it is proposed, can never be exterminated so long as the great German art that sustains it is respected. The chorus join in a final apostrophe to Sachs and 'holy German art'.

Sources:
Much of the historical background of Wagner's 1845 prose draft for *Die Meistersinger* was based on Georg Gottfried Gervinus's *Geschichte der poetischen National-Literatur der Deutschen* (*History of the Poetic National Literature of the Germans*) of 1835–42. Other volumes in Wagner's Dresden library include Jacob Grimm's *Über den altdeutschen Meistergesang* (*On the Old German Meisterlieder*) (1811), J.G. Büsching's edition of Hans Sachs's plays (1816–19), and Friedrich Furchau's life of Sachs (1820). For the later drafts J.C. Wagenseil's Nuremberg Chronicle of 1697 proved a particularly rich source of information on the ancient crafts and guilds and on other aspects of Nuremberg. Also evident are motifs from such contemporary stories as E.T.A. Hoffmann's *Meister Martin der Küfner und seine Gesellen* (*Master*

Martin, the Cooper, and his Journeymen), which is set in 16th-century Nuremberg.

Composition

The original idea for *Die Meistersinger* was that it should be a comic appendage to *Tannhäuser*, rather like a satyr play followed the tragedy in Greek drama. Even as late as October 1861, shortly before he made the second and third prose drafts, Wagner was describing the projected work to his publisher Schott as a 'thoroughly light and popular' opera – one calling, moreover, for only modest resources and thus remaining within the reach of smaller houses. The orchestra was indeed restricted to double wind (as opposed to the triple of *Tristan* or the quadruple of the *Ring*), but the work that eventually emerged was anything but modest in scale. In sheer length alone (some 4¼ hours) it dwarfs most operas in the repertory.

According to Wagner's account in *Mein Leben*, he was inspired to start work on *Die Meistersinger* after viewing Titian's *Assumption of the Virgin* while visiting Otto and Mathilde Wesendonck in Venice at the beginning of November 1861. A letter to Schott of 30 October, however, announcing his intention of beginning work on the new opera, suggests that any initial inspiration must have been somewhat less prosaic than Titian. Work began in earnest the following March or April, but a series of delays meant that the first complete draft was not completed until 7 February 1867. The second complete draft was prepared in parallel, though the nature of it changed between the first and second acts. For the second act Wagner produced a far more elaborate draft, often using three, or as many as four or five, staves; furthermore, he did not begin the full score of the second and third acts until he had completed them both in draft (cf. *Tristan*, where the score was actually engraved one act at a time). The full score was completed on 24 October 1867.

The drama

The philosophical world-view expounded in *Die Meistersinger* is as paradoxical as that of any of Wagner's works. On one level it is a glorious affirmation of humanity and the value of art, as well as a parable about the necessity of tempering the inspiration of genius with the rules of form. Walther, the natural, untrained genius, despises the pedantry of the masters and has to be taught that while great art may be conceived in visionary dreams, it nevertheless has to be subjected to the regulation of formal structure. His teacher is the cobbler-poet Hans Sachs, whose mastery and wisdom in the artistic sphere are matched by his benevolent insights into the follies of human nature. His liberal, tolerant attitude towards the ardour of youth and modern trends provides a benchmark for the other masters and populace alike.

For too long, however, this humane world-view has been taken to be the sole impulse of *Die Meistersinger*. The truth is that the work has also a dark underside, for it may be regarded at the same time as the artistic component in Wagner's ideological crusade of the 1860s: a crusade to revive the 'German spirit' and purge it of alien elements, chief among which were the Jews. It can further be argued that anti-Semitism is woven into the ideological fabric of the work and that the representation of Beckmesser carries, at the very least, overtones of anti-Semitic sentiment. This can be seen clearly by comparing Wagner's characterization of Beckmesser with his image of the Jew (not least in his inability to create, or to match words and music) as represented in the notoriously anti-Semitic essay *Das Judentum in der Musik* (*Jewishness in Music*), which the composer had reprinted at the time of the *Meistersinger* premiere. In addition, the characterization of the town clerk and critic who becomes a social outcast draws on the parody Jewish language of *mauscheln* and on the stereotypical Jewish comic persona of the schlemiel.

The accumulation of evidence (see Millington, 1991) makes the thesis irresistible, but one series of references in particular puts it beyond doubt: namely the references to, and parallels with *Der Jude im Dorn* (*The Jew in the Thorn-bush*), the archetypal anti-Semitic folk-tale of the Grimm brothers. Towards the end of Act I, as Beckmesser's scratching of chalk is heard from his box, interrupting Walther's Trial Song, Walther bursts out angrily with an image of envious Winter lying in wait in the thorn-bush. Wagner even describes Winter as 'Grimm-bewehrt', an elaborate pun suggesting both 'guarded with anger' and 'authenticated by Grimm' ('Grimm-bewährt'), and nobody familiar with Wagner's literary style can seriously suggest that the pun is a coincidence. Beckmesser is thus unmistakably identified with the crabbed Jew in the story; moreover, Walther returns to his idea of the thorn-bush after Beckmesser has filled his Master's slate. In the Grimm tale a bird flies into the thorn-bush; in Walther's song it flies out in an image of liberation. There is also a parallel in the *mise-en-scène*. The boy in the tale stands on the steps of the gallows and looks down on judge, Jew and everybody dancing wildly as he plays his fiddle; Walther, having jumped onto the Singer's chair, looks down on the commotion among the Masters as he sings his song.

The nationalistic and anti-Semitic sentiments expressed in *Die Meistersinger* do not, as already suggested, exclusively circumscribe the work. However, they are an intrinsic element of it, and need to be confronted in any attempt to come to terms with the opera in its entirety.

Musical style

Central to the story of *Die Meistersinger* are the songmaking rules of the masters and in particular the creation of a mastersong, consisting of two identical *Stollen* and a contrasting *Abgesang*: AAB (see 'Bar, bar form' in 'A Wagnerian Glossary', pp.231–2). Unsurprisingly, therefore, this *Bar* form occurs frequently, often modified, during the course of the score. It is not necessary to take this observation to the extremes of the German musicologist Alfred Lorenz, who in 1930 contrived to impose the *Bar* form on the entire work. Rather it is clear that Wagner is more often simply alluding to the form in jest. In his Act I aria 'Am stillen Herd', for example, Walther responds to a question about his educational background with a structure that is clearly a mockery of *Bar* form. Similarly, much fun is had at the expense of Beckmesser and his conservative colleagues in the delivery of Walther's Trial Song (see 'Bar, bar form', p.231–2).

Such self-contained songs, together with choruses, processions, marches and dances, are a feature of *Die Meistersinger*, and Wagner's unashamed exploitation of all these traditional forms indicates just how far he has moved from the theoretical principles laid down in *Oper und Drama*. This is no stylistic regression to the trappings of grand opera, however; rather Wagner has now succeeded in integrating traditional forms into the structure of the music drama.

Something similar happens in the sphere of tonality. The previous opera, *Tristan und Isolde*, took chromaticism to its furthest limits, but the *Meistersinger* Prelude is a monument to the staying power of diatonicism: its insistent assertions of C major are a powerful reaffirmation of the virtues of the Classical tonal system. Yet there is more to this C major than meets the eye. In the first place, it is flanked both by sudden tonal shifts (to E and E♭ major in the Prelude, for example) and, throughout the work, by secondary triads, which give the music an archaic, modal flavour. Thus the opera's tendency towards nostalgic retrospection is indulged while at the same time traditional tonality is revivified by being recast in a new context. In the second place, as Warren Darcy (forthcoming) has shown, the reattainment of C major at the end of the opera has ideological implications. The social stability represented by the final strains of C major comes at the price of loss of individuality: all those who have threatened the complacency of Nuremberg society are ultimately absorbed into a massive, undifferentiated C major sonority.

Parsifal
WWV 111
Sacred stage festival play in 3 acts

Text: first prose sketch Apr 1857, first prose draft 27–30 Aug 1865, second prose draft completed 23 Feb 1877, poem completed 19 Apr 1877
Music: first complete draft Sep 1877 – 16 Apr 1879, second complete draft 25 Sep 1877 – 26 Apr 1879, full score finished Jan 1882
First perf.: Festspielhaus, Bayreuth, 26 July 1882
First UK perf.: Royal Opera House, Covent Garden, 2 Feb 1914 (first to be staged; a concert performance took place at the Royal Albert Hall, London, on 10 Nov 1884)
First US perf.: Metropolitan Opera, New York, 24 Dec 1903 (first to be staged; a concert performance took place, also at the Metropolitan Opera House, on 4 Mar 1886)

Amfortas	baritone
Titurel	bass
Gurnemanz	bass
Parsifal	tenor
Klingsor	bass
Kundry	mezzo-soprano
First and second knights of the Grail	tenor and bass
Four esquires	soprano, tenor
Voice from above	contralto
Klingsor's flowermaidens	6 soloists (soprano) and 2 semi-choruses (soprano and contralto)
The brotherhood of knights of the Grail	tenor, bass
Youths and boys	tenor, alto, soprano

pic, 3 fl, 3 ob, cor ang, 3 cl, bass cl, 3 bn, double bn, 4 hn, 3 tpt, 3 trbn, contrabass tuba, timp, 2 harps, str

On/off stage: 6 tpt, 6 trbn, tenor drum, bells, thunder machine

Synopsis
Act I
The act opens in a forest clearing in the domain of the knights who guard the sacred relics of the Grail: the cup used at the Last Supper, and the spear that pierced Christ's side on the Cross. Gurnemanz rouses two of the esquires from sleep and together they kneel and pray. He bids them prepare the bath for Amfortas, the son of Titurel, and now the ailing guardian of the Grail. Kundry, the accursed 'wild woman', rushes in with balsam from Arabia for Amfortas, who is now brought in on a litter. Amfortas intones the formula of the 'pure fool made wise by suffering', whom he has been promised as a saviour. He is given Kundry's balsam and carried away to his bath.

Gurnemanz reprimands the esquires for their harsh words about Kundry; she is perhaps atoning with good deeds for a past sin, he says. Their taunt that she should be sent in quest of the missing spear draws from Gurnemanz an emotional recollection of how Amfortas was seduced and dealt his terrible wound, losing possession of the sacred spear to the magician Klingsor. The esquires enquire how Gurnemanz knew Klingsor, and he begins his Narration proper. The sacred relics had been given into the care of Titurel, then guardian of the Grail, he tells them. The brotherhood of the Grail, assembled by Titurel to guard the relics, was closed to Klingsor on account of some unnamed sin. Desperate to quell his raging passions, Gurnemanz continues, Klingsor even castrated himself, but was still rebuffed. To avenge himself, he turned to magic and created a garden of delights, where he lies in wait for errant knights, seducing them with 'devilish lovely women'. The aging Titurel sent his son Amfortas to defeat Klingsor, with the consequences already described. Gurnemanz ends his narrative with a recollection of the divine prophecy concerning a 'pure fool'.

A young man wielding a crossbow (Parsifal) is suddenly dragged in by the knights; he has shot down a swan on the holy ground. Gurnemanz's rebuke fills him with remorse and he breaks his bow. To Gurnemanz's questions about his name and origins, however, he professes ignorance. The two are left alone with Kundry, and Parsifal tells what he knows about himself: his mother's name was Herzeleide (Heart's Sorrow), he had strayed from home in search of adventure and had made his own arms for protection. When Kundry, who clearly knows more about him than he does himself, announces that his mother is dead, Parsifal attacks her and has to be restrained.

In the distance, the knights and esquires are seen bearing Amfortas back to the Grail castle. As the processional music starts, Gurnemanz offers to lead Parsifal there. Bells ring out in the Transformation Scene, as the action moves from forest to castle. Gurnemanz and Parsifal enter the Grail hall. Amfortas is borne in, and the Grail, still covered, placed on a marble table. Amfortas, reluctant to accede to Titurel's request for him to uncover the Grail, breaks into a tormented monologue; he seeks atonement for his sin. At Titurel's insistence, the cover is removed from the golden shrine and the crystal Grail chalice taken from it. Amfortas consecrates the bread and wine and they are distributed to the knights; the Grail's guardian is borne out again, his wound gaping anew. Parsifal, who had convulsively clutched his heart at Amfortas's cry of agony, is unable to tell Gurnemanz what he has seen and is roughly shepherded out. A voice from above (contralto solo) repeats the prophecy, answered by other voices in the dome.

Act II

From a tower of his castle, surrounded by magical and necromantic apparatus, the sorcerer Klingsor watches over his domains. Seeing Parsifal approach, he summons Kundry, who groans monosyllabically. Attempting to resist Klingsor's instructions to seduce Parsifal, she taunts her master with his self-enforced chastity. Klingsor watches Parsifal as he fells one guard after another. The tower suddenly

sinks and in its place appears a luxuriant magic garden.

Flowermaidens rush in from all sides, and as Parsifal appears, they vie for his attention. Just as Parsifal manages to free himself from their caresses, he is stopped in his tracks by the sound of his long-forgotten name. It is Kundry, now transformed into an enchanting beauty, who calls. At her command the flowermaidens reluctantly disperse.

Kundry tells Parsifal how she saw him as a baby on his mother's breast. His mother watched over him lovingly, but one day he broke her heart by not returning and she died of grief. Deeply distressed at the news, Parsifal is consoled by Kundry, who urges him to show her the love he owed his mother. A prose sketch for the work suggests that when Parsifal first heard Kundry invoking his name, he thought it was his mother calling. As Kundry caresses him ever more intimately, the confusion in Parsifal's mind between the maternal love he once enjoyed and the sexual love he is now offered is explored by Wagner with Freudian insight. Kundry bends right over Parsifal, presses her lips to his mouth, and delivers, during eight long bars of music, a far from maternal kiss. Parsifal leaps up, clutching his heart. His cry 'Amfortas! Die Wunde!' ('Amfortas! The wound!') indicates his first real identification with Amfortas's suffering, and his first step on the road to self-knowledge. Falling into a trance, he hears Christ the Redeemer himself call on him to save him from 'guilt-tainted hands' and cleanse the polluted sanctuary.

He repels Kundry, but she appeals to him to use his redemptive powers to save her: for her blasphemous mockery of Christ she has wandered the world for centuries. One hour with him would bring her release, she says. But Parsifal, recognizing that salvation for them both depends on his withstanding her allurements, resists her. She attempts to block his way to Amfortas and calls to Klingsor. The magician appears and hurls his spear at Parsifal. Parsifal seizes the spear and as he makes the sign of the Cross with it, the castle collapses and the magic garden disappears.

Act III

The curtain rises on an open spring landscape in the domains of the Grail. Gurnemanz, grown very old and dressed as a hermit, emerges from his hut and uncovers Kundry, whose groans, as she lies stiff and lifeless in the undergrowth, he has heard. He revives her, but receives no thanks: Kundry's only utterance in the entire act is 'Dienen . . . Dienen!' ('Let me serve . . . serve!'). A man approaches in a suit of armour bearing a spear. A sober variant of the motif associated with Parsifal tells us both the stranger's identity and that he is a changed man. Gurnemanz welcomes him but bids him divest himself of his weapons: it is Good Friday and this is holy ground. As Parsifal does so, Gurnemanz recognizes the man whom he once roughly turned away.

He also recognizes the spear, which, Parsifal tells him, he has guarded safely throughout his troubled wandering. Gurnemanz hails its recovery, and tells Parsifal that his return with the healing spear is timely. Amfortas, longing for death, has refused to reveal the Grail, the brotherhood has degenerated, and Titurel has died. Parsifal is almost overcome with remorse. His feet are bathed by Kundry, and Gurnemanz sprinkles water from the spring on his head. Kundry then anoints his feet and dries them with her hair. The hesitant reminiscence of the flowermaidens' music suggests that Parsifal may now be aware of Kundry's *alter ego*.

Gazing on the beautiful meadows, Parsifal says that on Good Friday every living thing should only sigh and sorrow. Gurnemanz replies that on this day repentant sinners rejoice at the Redeemer's act of self-sacrifice and nature herself is transfigured. In a Transformation Scene similar to that in the first act (but in the reverse direction), Gurnemanz now leads Parsifal and Kundry to the Grail hall. There one group of knights bears Titurel in his coffin, while a second group carries Amfortas on a litter. When Titurel's coffin is opened, all break into a cry of woe. Amfortas refuses to uncover the Grail, and when the knights become threateningly insistent, he merely invites them to plunge their swords into his heart.

Parsifal has meanwhile appeared unobserved; he holds out his spear and with its point touches Amfortas's wound. Amfortas is miraculously healed, and he yields his office as lord of the Grail to the new redeemer. Parsifal takes the Grail from the shrine and it shines softly, then radiantly as light falls from above. Kundry sinks lifeless to the ground, redeemed at last. Parsifal waves the Grail in blessing over the worshipping knights. A white dove descends to hover above his head.

Sources

Wagner's main source for his last music drama was the epic poem *Parzivâl* by Wolfram von Eschenbach (*c*.1170–*c*.1220), written during the early years of the 13th century and just a few years after Chrétien de Troyes had left unfinished his *Li contes del Graal*, which Wagner also read. Chrétien conceived of the Grail as a dish, Wolfram as a stone with miraculous powers. Neither identified it with either the chalice used by Christ at the Last Supper or the vessel in which Joseph of Arimathea caught the blood of Christ as he hung on the Cross. These associations were made for the first time in the early years of the 13th century by the Burgundian poet Robert de Boron and the first of the anonymous poets to continue Chrétien's story.

In addition to these Christian and pagan sources, Wagner was strongly influenced both by Buddhism and by the philosopher Schopenhauer, many of whose ideas are closely related to oriental thought. Fellow-suffering and renunciation are key Schopen-

hauerian concepts, while the Buddhist doctrine of metempsychosis, or transmigration of the soul, is evident in Kundry's centuries-long journeying through the world, during which she assumed the forms of the Nordic Gundryggia and the biblical Herodias. The second act of *Parsifal* recalls a pivotal event in Buddha's life, where, in a state of deep meditation, he expects the ultimate enlightenment that will make him a Buddha, or Enlightened One. There is a similar parallel in the immediately preceding episode in the Buddha's reported life, when the tempter Mara tries to lead him astray by letting loose on him his seductive daughters and armed warriors. In the opera it is Klingsor who tries to tempt Parsifal with his seductive flowermaidens.

Composition

Wagner's autobiographical account of the genesis of *Parsifal* in 1857 is coloured, in characteristic fashion, by poetic licence (see 'Myths and Legends', pp.135–6). The prose sketch made at that time has not survived. The prose draft made in Munich in 1865 does more than merely outline the story: it contains a great deal of detailed commentary on the characters and themes of the drama, which is invaluable for an understanding of the work. (The draft is reproduced, in an English translation, in the Brown Book (see Bergfeld, 1975/80.)

The two drafts of the music were made in Wagner's now customary fashion: side by side, the second, in ink, elaborating the pencilled setting of the text in the first. The Prelude was orchestrated in the autumn of 1878 and the remainder of the score between August 1879 and January 1882.

First performances

Wagner's debt of 98,634 Marks to the Bavarian Court incurred at the first Bayreuth Festival was discharged by an agreement of 31 March 1878, giving Ludwig II certain rights over Wagner's works in exchange for a 10 per cent royalty. One of the clauses of this agreement stipulated that the first performance of *Parsifal* (whether in Bayreuth or Munich) should be given with the orchestra, singers and artistic personnel of the Munich Court Theatre; it was this provision that obliged Wagner to accept the Jewish Hermann Levi as the conductor of the first performance. *Parsifal* was, however, specifically conceived by Wagner in terms of the Bayreuth Festspielhaus and that special relationship, which came to acquire a quasi-religious aura after the composer's death, was enshrined in a thirty-year embargo of the work's performance outside Bayreuth.

Apart from the private performances mounted for Ludwig in Munich after Wagner's death, the work was therefore generally heard, for three decades, only in concert performances. Joseph Barnby, for example, conducted two in London in 1884. The work was, however, staged in Amsterdam for members of the Wagner Society in 1905 (and again in 1906 and 1908). Although this venture was not popular with the Bayreuth circle, it attracted nothing like the bitter antipathy aroused by the New York Metropolitan Opera's staging of 1903. The Metropolitan's manager, Heinrich Conried, determined to break the embargo, instituted a civil suit in New York and obtained a ruling that performances could not be prevented in the USA, because no copyright agreement existed between that country and Germany.

The drama

As the range of sources for the work would indicate (see 'Sources' above), *Parsifal* represents a rich cross-fertilization of ideas and beliefs: Christian and pagan, Buddhist and Schopenhauerian. Although it is the Christian symbolism that is most often associated with the opera, it was Buddhism by which Wagner was more affected at the time of the genesis of *Parsifal*. In April 1855 he reported to Mathilde Wesendonck that he was reading Adolf Holtzmann's *Indische Sagen* (*Indian Legends*). Soon after, Eugène Burnouf's *Introduction à l'histoire du bouddhisme indien* inspired him to sketch a drama based on a Buddhist legend of passion and renunciation: *Die Sieger* (*The Victors*) was never completed, but its preoccupations were absorbed into *Parsifal*.

The Buddhist concept of fellow-suffering is related specifically to *Parsifal* in an important letter from Venice to Mathilde Wesendonck, dated 1 October 1858. Describing Wagner's horror at the cruel treatment by a poulterer of a live hen, it suggests that the only purpose of such suffering can be 'to awaken a sense of fellow-suffering in man'. Wagner goes on to indicate that this theme will be treated in the Good Friday scene in Act III of *Parsifal*.

Renunciation is another Buddhist concept with which Wagner was already familiar through the philosophy of Schopenhauer. Human existence, for Schopenhauer, was a meaningless round of suffering and striving; the only escape lay in denial of the will, in extinction or Nirvana (the cessation of individual existence). The apparent renunciation of sexuality in *Parsifal* should be seen against this philosophical background. It is not so much that sexuality itself is repudiated but that self-enlightenment, or 'redemption', is a process of liberation from self-centredness. Renunciation or self-denial can thus be seen not primarily as a question of chastity but as the acceptance of moral responsibility.

In Christian terms, the Grail represents both the profession of atonement through Christ's blood, celebrated at the Last Supper, and the promise of eternal life and God's presence among men and women. It was these elements that came to the fore when Wagner produced his expanded prose draft in 1865. In this lengthy exposition of the work, much of

which was cut from the final libretto, are elaborated some of the Christian elements that are merely alluded to in the text itself: the sacredness of the Grail and of the Saviour's blood caught in it, the plea of the Saviour for the cup to be delivered from impure hands. Wagner was far from a conventional Christian, even in his latter days, but he believed that the function of art was to salvage the essence of religion 'by grasping the symbolic value of its mythic symbols' (*Religion und Kunst*, 1880; GS X, 211); by such a representation, truths that lay concealed in the literal observance of religion might be revealed. Hence, in *Parsifal*, the Christian imagery of the chalice, the spear that pierced Christ's side, Good Friday, baptism and the Eucharist.

A further aspect of *Parsifal* remains to be mentioned. The opera was written at a time in Wagner's life when he had become obsessed with ideas about 'racial purity' and the supposed necessity for 'regeneration' of the human race. The essential idea was that humankind had degenerated because of its departure from a natural vegetable diet, leading to corruption by the blood of slaughtered animals. Even the most degenerate races, however, could be purified and thus redeemed by the blood of Christ. Included in those degenerate races were, of course, the Jews. So much of the story of *Parsifal* revolves around the elite company of knights – the 'race chosen to guard the Grail', as Wagner significantly called them – the decline and feared extinction of that race, and the redeeming qualities of pure, uncontaminated blood, that it can scarcely be argued that the work is untainted by the pernicious racist ideology of the composer's latter years.

Musical style

The subject matter of *Parsifal*, taken with the fact that it was the only work of Wagner's to be written specifically with the atmosphere and acoustic of the Bayreuth Festspielhaus in mind, ensures that the score is strikingly different from any other of the composer's. To begin with, the ritualistic conception of at least Acts I and III of the work generates a vertical, hierarchically ordered organization, evident even from the layout on the printed page. In that sense the score contrasts markedly with that of *Tristan*, where the motifs interweave more horizontally, the lines more sensually. *Parsifal* nevertheless has its own form of voluptuousness: an exquisitely refined, lingering sensuousness that again contrasts with the phallic aggression of *Tristan*, where the very nature of the thematic material dictates a thrusting, penetrating, goal-orientated musical discourse.

The score of *Parsifal* has qualities frequently associated with Impressionism: its play of light and shade, its sense of floating weightlessness, its substance constantly on the point of dissolution into atmosphere, its enveloping mystical energy. It was qualities of this kind that induced Debussy to suggest that the score sounded as though 'lit from behind', and that also appealed so strongly to the Symbolist and Decadent artists of the 1880s and 90s (see 'The Birth of Modernism', pp.396–7 and 399–400).

Orchestral music

Overture in B♭ major ('Drum-beat Overture') (lost)
WWV 10
Summer 1830; first perf. Leipzig, 25 Dec 1830
Nickname derives from loud timpani stroke on second beat of every fifth bar

Political Overture (lost and prob. uncompleted)
WWV 11
Prob. Sep 1830
Inspired by the revolutionary outbreaks in Paris and Dresden in Jul and Sep 1830

Overture to Schiller's *Die Braut von Messina* (?lost)
WWV 12
Summer or autumn 1830
Possibly inspired by perfs of the play in Leipzig in May and Jun 1830. See WWV 13 below.

Orchestral work in E minor (frag.)
WWV 13
2 fl, 2 ob, 2 cl, 2 bn, 4 hn, 2 tpt, oph(?), timp, str
Prob. 1830
Possibly to be identified with the lost Overture to Schiller's *Die Braut von Messina* (see WWV 12 above): the work has a programmatic character and, in particular, a funeral march as in the Schiller play.

Overture in C major (in 6/8 time) (lost)
WWV 14
End 1830
Mentioned briefly in Cosima Wagner's Diaries (15 Dec 1878): 'R. talked about his overture in C major, in 6/8 time, which he regrets having lost; he says it was not all that bad, and it contained the *Holl[änder]* chord (interrupted cadence).'

Overture in E♭ major (lost and prob. uncompleted)
WWV 17
Early 1831

Overture in D minor (Concert Overture no.1)
WWV 20
2 fl, 2 ob, 2 cl, 2 bn, 4 hn, 2 tpt, timp, str
summer/autumn 1831; first perf. Leipzig, 25 Dec 1831
Probably begun while Wagner studying with Müller in the summer of 1831. Score subjected to

revision by the composer, the second version (entitled 'Concert Overture') being dated 4 Nov 1831.

Overture in E minor and incidental music to Ernst Raupach's play *König Enzio*
WWV 24
2 fl, 2 ob, 2 cl, 2 bn, 4 hn, 2 tpt, timp, str [overture]
Winter 1831–2; first perf. Leipzig, 17 Feb 1832
Overture, and probably more music by Wagner, played at perfs of the Raupach in the Königlich Sächsisches Hoftheater, Leipzig, in Feb and Mar 1832. Only the Overture, however, survives.

Entreactes tragiques, no. 1 in D major, no. 2 in C minor
WWV 25
2 fl, 2 ob, 2 bn, 2 hn, 2 tpt, timp, str [no.1]
Prob. early 1832
Little is known about these pieces as they are not mentioned either in Wagner's autobiographical writings or in his letters. Possibly conceived as entr'actes for Raupach's play *König Enzio*, since they are contemporaneous with the Overture WWV 24 (see above).

Concert Overture no. 2 in C major
WWV 27
2 fl, 2 ob, 2 cl, 2 bn, 4 hn, 2 tpt, 2 trbn, timp, str
Mar 1832; first perf. Leipzig, prob. end Mar 1832
Possibly originated as some kind of apprentice work; given several perfs by Wagner.

Symphony in C major
WWV 29
2 fl, 2 ob, 2 cl, 2 bn, double bn, 4 hn, 2 tpt, 3 trbn, timp, str
Prob. Apr–June 1832; first perf. Prague, Nov 1832
Wagner's only completed symphonic work. It was written, in a period of six weeks according to Wagner, under the influence of Beethoven's symphonies, especially the Third, Fifth and Seventh. The work is full of Beethovenian gestures: indeed the ten orchestral hammerblows that open the symphony may be seen as at once a recollection of the *Eroica* and an attempt to outdo it. In later life, Wagner said that the slow movement of his work would probably never have seen the light of day without the Andante of Beethoven's Fifth and the Allegretto of the Seventh; certainly the thematic reminiscences of both those movements are striking. The finale, on the other hand, owes something to Mozart, in particular the finale of K.551, the *Jupiter* Symphony, in the same key. Notwithstanding these influences, the symphony is a strongly characteristic work, in which the young composer's mastery of the medium is impressively demonstrated. Wagner maintained a lifelong affection for the work and conducted it in a private performance at La Fenice, Venice, to celebrate Cosima's birthday in 1882.

Symphony in E major (uncompleted)
WWV 35
Aug–Sept 1834; first perf. Munich, 13 Oct 1988
Only the first movement completed. The second
movement, which borrows the secondary subject
from Wagner's own A major Piano Sonata, breaks
off after 29 bars. Wagner suggests, in *Mein Leben*,
that the models for the symphony were the Seventh
and Eighth Symphonies of Beethoven, but closer
resemblances are discernible to the *Pastoral*, in terms
of the process of symphonic development, and to the
overtures of Weber. The fragmentary symphony
was until recently lost. Wagner's own manuscript
remains so, but a score in the hand of Felix Mottl
resurfaced in Munich in the late 1980s.

**Overture (E♭ major) and incidental music to
Theodor Apel's play *Columbus***
WWV 37
pic, 2 fl, 2 ob, 2 cl, 2 bn, 4 hn, 6 tpt, 3 trbn, contrabass
tuba, timp, str
Dec 1834 – Jan 1835; first perf. Magdeburg, 16 Feb
1835
Wagner was instrumental in having his friend
Theodor Apel's five-act historical drama *Columbus*
put on at the Stadt-Theater in Magdeburg. Of the
music he wrote to accompany its performance, only
the Overture survives. Wagner was undoubtedly
influenced by Mendelssohn's overture *Calm Sea and
Prosperous Voyage*, which he conducted in Magdeburg on 13 January 1835, the month in which his
Columbus score was completed. Mendelssohn's trumpet fanfare, similarly depicting the sighting of land,
was imitated by him and there are also structural
parallels between *Columbus* and the overtures of
Mendelssohn.

***Polonia* Overture (C major)**
WWV 39
2 pic, 2 fl, 2 ob, 2 cl, 2 bn, 4 hn, 4 tpt, 3 trbn, oph,
timp, bd, sd, tenor drum, cym, tri, str
May–Jul 1836; first perf. Königsberg, ? winter
1836–7
Since the *Polonia* Overture followed five years after
the uprising of the Poles against the Russians, it is
possible that Wagner's sympathy for the refugees
was rekindled by that of his friend Heinrich Laube,
whom he saw frequently during his stay in Berlin in
May and June 1836. The Overture, which is broadly
in sonata form, contains Polish allusions that add
local colour.

**Incidental music to J. Singer's play *Die
letzte Heidenverschwörung in Preussen***
(frag.)
WWV 41
Prob. Feb 1837; first perf. Königsberg, prob. 17 Feb
1837
Neither Singer's play nor Wagner's score survives. A
sketch indicates choruses of priests and of young men

and women, but it is not known whether more music
was written.

***Rule Britannia* Overture (D major)**
WWV 42
2 pic, 2 fl, 2 ob, 3 cl, 2 bn, double bn, serp, 4 hn, 4 tpt,
3 trbn, oph, timp, bd, sd, cym, tri, str
Mar 1837: first perf. Riga, prob. 19 Mar 1838
Conceived, along with the *Polonia* Overture (WWV
39) and an unexecuted one depicting the exploits of
Napoleon, as a trilogy. The score was sent, unavail-
ingly, to Sir George Smart of the Philharmonic
Society in London in the hope of a performance. The
work is flatulent and overscored, the triangle
sounding like an untended burglar alarm. But it is
impossible not to warm to a work that so blatantly
attempts to outstrip Wagner's idol Beethoven: a
series of false endings, with increasingly emphatic
tonic and dominant chords, creates an unintentionally comic effect.

A *Faust* Overture (D minor)
WWV 59
pic, 2 fl, 2 ob, 2 cl, 3 bn [1st version: 4 bn], 4 hn, 2 tpt,
3 trbn, contrabass tuba [1st version: serp], timp, str
Dec 1839 – Jan 1840, rev. Jan 1855; first perf.
Dresden, 22 Jul 1844 (1st version), Zurich, 23 Jan
1855 (2nd version)
Conceived as first movement of a *Faust* Symphony,
but designation changed to 'Overture' presumably
to increase likelihood of performance. The primary
influence was probably not Beethoven's Ninth
Symphony (*pace Mein Leben*) but Berlioz's *Roméo et
Juliette*, with which Wagner became acquainted at
the time of composition, and which he viewed as a
potential solution to the problem of reconciling
literary inspiration with abstract symphonic form.
The work was subjected to a series of revisions,
reaching its final form when it was eventually
published in 1855.

***Trauermusik*, on motifs from Weber's
*Euryanthe***
WWV 73
5 fl, 7 ob, 20 cl, 10 bn, 14 hn, 6 tpt, 9 trbn, 4
contrabass tubas, 6 muffled drums
Nov 1844; first perf. Dresden, 14 Dec 1844
Wagner was a moving spirit behind the campaign to
have Weber's remains transferred from London to
Dresden. The final stage of the journey, to the
Friedrichstadt cemetery, was accompanied by a
torchlight procession, for which Wagner composed
the *Trauermusik (Funeral Music)*, based, in homage to
Weber, on two themes from *Euryanthe*, one from the
overture and the other Euryanthe's cavatina 'Hier
dicht am Quell'. Wagner's model was Berlioz's
Grande symphonie funèbre et triomphale for a wind band
of 200 players.

Symphonies (uncompleted)
WWV 78
1846–7
Sketches exist for at least two symphonies from the years 1846–7, a period when Wagner was engaged in the composition of *Lohengrin* in Dresden, as well as making assiduous preparations for the performance of Beethoven's Ninth Symphony at the traditional Palm Sunday concert in the old opera house in the same city. This major undertaking was one of the high points in Wagner's career as a Kapellmeister and it is probable that his close study of the Ninth stimulated this brief burst of symphonic inspiration. See also WWV 107.

Huldigungsmarsch (E♭ **major**)
WWV 97
2 pic 4 fl, 23 cl, bass cl, 2 bn, 8 hn, 12 tpt, 3 flugelhorns, 3 alto hn, 2 tenor hn, 2 baritone hn, 6 trbn, 6 contrabass tubas, timp, bd, sd, cym, tri [version for military band]

pic, 2 fl, 2 ob, 2 cl, bass cl, 2 bn, 4 hn, 3 tpt, 3 trbn, contrabass tuba, timp, bd, sd, cym, tri, str [orchestral version]

Aug 1864; first perf. Munich, 5 Oct 1864 [version for military band], Vienna, 12 Nov 1871 [orchestral version]
Composed to celebrate the birthday of King Ludwig on 25 Aug 1864, though the first performance had to be postponed until October. Wagner appears to have begun an arrangement for full orchestra as early as February 1865, but it was finally completed by Joachim Raff and not performed until 1871. Approximately 70 or 71 bars of the March, about one-third of its total length, were orchestrated by Wagner. The March is an attractive work with characteristic Wagnerian touches; it unfolds in a single movement rather than as a conventional March and Trio.

Romeo und Julie (uncompleted)
WWV 98
Apr–May 1868
Two fragmentary sketches from the spring of 1868 are the only notated evidence of Wagner's intention to write a work on the Romeo and Juliet theme. But it was an idea that recurred throughout the 1870s (see Cosima Wagner's Diaries for 3 May 1873, 26 Oct 1876, 8 Mar 1879 and 19 Apr 1879).

Siegfried Idyll (E **major**)
WWV 103
fl, ob, 2 cl, bn, 2 hn, tpt, str
End Nov–Dec 1870; first perf. Tribschen, 25 Dec 1870
Conceived as a birthday present for Cosima, and first performed on the staircase in the house at Tribschen on Christmas Day 1870 (Cosima's birthday was actually on 24 December, but she modestly

celebrated it on the 25th). Wagner had been making secret preparations for some time, and Hans Richter had learnt the trumpet specially for the occasion. In her Diaries (25 Dec 1870), Cosima tells how she woke on the morning in question, hearing the music outside her room as though in a dream. When it had finished, Wagner, who had been conducting, entered the room with the five children and put into her hands the score of the 'Symphonic Birthday Greeting'. The entire household was reputedly in tears. After breakfast, the orchestra reassembled and gave another performance, followed by the wedding march from *Lohengrin* and Beethoven's Septet. The *Siegfried Idyll* was then given for a third time.

As the tone of Cosima's diary entry confirms, the work both reflected and set the seal on the couple's new-found domestic bliss (after years of uncertainty and misery they were at last happily, and legally, united at Tribschen – Cosima had finally moved in on 16 November 1868, but they had not been able to marry until 25 August 1870). The *Idyll* was also a retrospective celebration of the birth of their son Siegfried (on 6 June 1869) and of the composition of Act III of *Siegfried* also the previous year. The private significance of the work for the couple caused them to resist publication as long as possible, but financial necessity eventually made it inevitable: 'the secret treasure is to become public property', Cosima wrote in her Diaries (19 Nov 1877).

In spite of its intimacy, the *Siegfried Idyll* was not intended for a small chamber ensemble: the size of the band for the first performance (fifteen players – according to WWV, following Fehr, 1953 – rather than the oft-cited thirteen) was dictated more by the width of the staircase at Tribschen than by aesthetic considerations. For a later private performance in Mannheim on 20 December 1871, Wagner requested a considerably larger body of strings: 6–8 first violins, 7–8 seconds, 4 violas, 4 cellos and 2–3 double basses (there had been eight string players altogether at the first performance). And in her Diaries (14 Jan 1874) Cosima reports a later intention of Wagner's (not realized) to arrange the *Idyll* for 'a large orchestra'.

The relevance of the *Idyll* to Wagner's symphonic ambitions is confirmed both by this information and by the phrase 'symphonic birthday greeting' in the original inscription. Moreover, in spite of the lyrical melodies and pastoral pedal-points, the work itself is in a broadly based (modified) sonata form, in which the subsidiary material is represented by the lullaby 'Sleep, baby, sleep', noted down in the Brown Book on New Year's Eve 1868, and in which new thematic ideas are given out in place of an orthodox development.

The full inscription on the title-page of the autograph reads, somewhat enigmatically: '*Tribschen Idyll* with Fidi-Birdsong and Orange Sunrise, presented as a symphonic birthday greeting to his Cosima by her Richard, 1870.' Fidi was their pet-name for Siegfried; the 'Orange Sunrise' refers to the 'incredibly beautiful, fiery glow' (CT 6 Jun 1869) caused by the blazing of the sun on the orange wallpaper in the bedroom – nature's own tribute to his first son, Wagner assumed. The title *Siegfried Idyll* appears to date from around the time of a performance in Meiningen on 10 March 1877.

For the mythical 'Starnberg Quartet', supposedly related to the *Siegfried Idyll*, see 'Myths and Legends', (pp. 137–8).

Kaisermarsch (B♭ major)
WWV 104
unison 'people's chorus' [Volksgesang] ad lib, pic, 2 fl, 3 ob, 3 cl, 3 bn, 4 hn, 3 tpt, 3 trbn, contrabass tuba, timp, bd, sd, cym, tri, str
Feb – mid-Mar 1871; first perf. Berlin, 14 Apr 1871
The *Kaisermarsch* (*Imperial March*) was composed in the fever of nationalism following the proclamation of the Second Reich and the German victory in the Franco-Prussian War. In a postscript to *Was ist deutsch?*, published in 1878, Wagner tells how he offered to write music for a memorial service – or alternatively a march, with chorus – to celebrate the return of the troops in 1871. The offer was declined and Wagner made his March into a concert piece.

It was originally scored for a military band, but subsequently arranged by the composer himself for a full orchestra. The optional verses, which all too clearly reflect Wagner's rabid jingoism at the time of the Franco-Prussian War – they are aptly described as 'tumid doggerel' by Ernest Newman – were also added later. Wagner's suggestion was for the singers not to be positioned on a platform but dispersed among the audience, who should be supplied with copies of both words and music.

A moving struggle of aesthetic purity over material considerations is recorded, with reference to the *Kaisermarsch*, in Cosima Wagner's Diaries (16 Mar 1871): 'At lunch he had also considered whether he could not send his march to the London exhibition, replacing "*Ein' feste Burg*" with "*God Save the King*". "That would mean 50 pounds, but it would spoil the March."'

The jingoistic spirit embodied in the piece scarcely produces music of the highest order. The March's principal theme is a fairly promising inspiration, but the persistent interpolation of Luther's *Ein' feste Burg* – a reflection of the Hohenzollerns' staunch Protestantism – sounds increasingly bombastic. As Wagner himself recognized, four-square march tunes do not lend themselves ideally to symphonic development, and the working out of these ideas is unconvincing; a sense of desperation is only accentuated by insistent side-drum rolls and trilling of the triangle.

Plans for overtures and symphonies (uncompleted); themes and melodies
WWV 107

1874–83

Overtures
From January 1874 to February 1875 Wagner played with the idea of writing a set of orchestral overtures, none of which ever materialized. On 23 January 1874 he wrote to his publisher Schott asking for an advance of 10,000 gulden ('to complete his house and garden'), in exchange for which he promised to deliver, at six-monthly intervals, 'six large orchestral works, each of the dimensions and importance of a large overture'; the first was to be delivered by the end of the present year at latest. Cosima Wagner's diary entry for the following day gives three of the projected titles: *Lohengrin's Ocean Voyage*, *Tristan the Hero* and *Dirge for Romeo and Juliet*. A later entry (CT, 10–16 Feb 1874) records that Schott sent the 10,000 gulden and that Wagner began to reflect on the overtures, five of which are now entitled: *Lohengrin's Journey*, *Tristan*, *Epilogue to Romeo and Juliet*, *Brünnhilde* and *Wieland the Smith*. The works are mentioned again in a letter to Schott of 14 October 1874 and in diary references for 14 December 1874 and 3 January 1875, but on 17 February 1875 Cosima recorded Wagner's wish to break with Schott and make an agreement with Peters, 'who is offering him three times as much for an overture'. Nothing more is heard of this project, and with the possible exception of a sketch that may have been intended for *Tristan the Hero* (see WWV 107) there is no good reason for supposing that any of the random sketches dating from this period relate to the projected overtures.

Symphonies
Between autumn 1877 and his death in February 1883, Wagner gave frequent consideration to the possibility of composing symphonies; none progressed beyond the sketching stage. The earliest mention in Cosima Wagner's Diaries is on 8 October 1877, when she records: 'In the evening he plays me a splendid theme for a symphony and says he has so many themes of this kind, they are always occurring to him, but he cannot use such merry things in *Parsifal*.' Some of these bursts of inspiration were followed by sketches; in other cases, connections between CT references and surviving sketches – even when they are dated – cannot be traced (for details see WWV 107).

It is clear that Wagner saw such symphonies as continuing the Beethovenian tradition. He believed, however, that 'since Beeth[oven] one can no longer write symphonies in four movements, for they just look like imitations' (CT, 19 Nov 1878). Wagner's intended solution was a single-movement structure (*loc. cit.*) In one diary entry he proposes to call the pieces 'symphonic dialogues' because they would consist of theme and countertheme in conversation with one another (CT, 22 Sep 1878). Elsewhere, he exhorts Liszt: '"If we write symphonies, Franz, then let us stop contrasting one theme with another, a method Beeth[oven] has exhausted. We should just spin a melodic line until it can be spun no farther".' (CT, 17 Dec 1882) This idea is picked up in a later diary reference (CT, 30 Jan 1883), in which Wagner tells Cosima that 'he can still imagine a type of symphonic work, like the *Kaisermarsch*, for example, in which themes are not contrasted, but each emerges out of another.'

Themes and melodies
A considerable number of other sketches were made at this time, apparently unconnected to the plans for overtures and symphonies. One melody in particular has given rise to confusion. A sketch in E♭, with falling fifths, was inscribed by Cosima as 'Melodie der Porazzi!'; this theme evidently dates from the Wagners' stay at the Piazza dei Porazzi in Palermo (2 Feb – 19 Mar 1882) and it is this, rather than the plangent fragment in A♭ (WWV 93), that is the true 'Porazzi Theme'. A further theme, in C major and marked 'Tempo di Porazzi', also dates from this time.

Grosser Festmarsch (*Centennial March*) (G major)
WWV 110
pic, 3 fl, 3 ob, 3 cl, 3 bn, double bn, 4 hn, 3 tpt, bass tpt, 3 trbn, contrabass trbn, timp, bd, sd, cym, tri, gong, str
Feb–Mar 1876; first perf. Philadelphia, 10 May 1876
Composed to a commission to celebrate the hundredth anniversary of the American Declaration of Independence, the overture's full title is 'Grand festival march for the inauguration of the hundredth anniversary commemoration of the American Declaration of Independence'. Wagner was approached in December 1875 by Gottlieb Federlein, on behalf of the conductor Theodore Thomas, who had been entrusted by the festival committee in Philadelphia with the musical arrangements for the celebrations. In a letter to Thomas of 8 February 1876 Wagner accepted the commission, for which he requested 5000 dollars. Notwithstanding his flirtation with the idea of emigrating to the USA, Wagner found it difficult to muster the enthusiasm or inspiration he needed for the composition of the march. On 14 February Cosima recorded: 'R. still working, complains of being unable to visualize anything to himself in this composition; it had been different with the *Kaisermarsch*, he says, even with *Rule Britannia*, where he had thought of a great ship, but here he can think of nothing but the 5000 dollars he has demanded and perhaps will not get.'

In respect of the fee, at least, Wagner was not disappointed, but the march remains an undistinguished composition. The principal theme is a strong one, but the working out, in a *Meistersinger*-like mode, is – as was the case with the *Kaisermarsch* – unconvincing, resorting to what sounds like mere padding in place of genuine development.

Choral music

Vocal fugues
WWV 19
4-part chorus *a cappella*
Autumn 1831 – winter 1831/2
These two fugues, the first of which is set to the words 'Dein ist das Reich, von Ewigkeit zu Ewigkeit' ('Thine is the glory, for ever and ever'), date from the period of Wagner's study with the Leipzig cantor Christian Theodor Weinlig. The second fugue, for which no text has been set, is a double fugue.

Incidental music for Wilhelm Schmale's one-act allegorical play *Beim Antritt des neuen Jahres 1835*
WWV 36
chorus (SATB), pic, 2 fl, 2 ob, 2 cl, 2 bn, double bn, 4 hn, 2 tpt, 3 trbn, timp, bd, sd, cym, tri, str
On/off stage: 2 fl, 2 ob, 2 cl, 2 bn, 4 hn
End Dec 1834; first perf. Magdeburg, 1 Jan 1835
Schmale was the stage director of the theatrical troupe in Magdeburg to which Wagner was attached from 1834 to 1836. His festival play to celebrate the new year required incidental music, and Wagner reported in a letter to his friend Theodor Apel (27 Dec 1834) that he had had to turn out five numbers in a very short space of time: an overture, choruses and 'allegorical music'. For Wagner's 60th birthday celebrations in 1873, the music was reset to a new text by Peter Cornelius.

Nicolay (anthem for the birthday of Tsar Nicholas)
WWV 44
S or T solo, chorus (SATB), pic, 2 fl, 2 ob, 2 cl, 2 bn, double bn, 4 hn, 4 tpt, 3 trbn, oph, timp, bd, sd, cym, tri, str
Autumn 1837; first perf. Riga, 21 Nov 1837
Dating from Wagner's period in Riga, the 'Volks-Hymne' (national anthem) was commissioned for the birthday celebrations of Tsar Nicholas; the text was by Harald von Brackel. In *Mein Leben* Wagner says he tried to give it 'as despotic and patriarchal a colouring as possible'. It achieved a measure of success and was apparently performed on the same day in subsequent years.

Gesang am Grabe (*Funeral Dirge*) (lost)
WWV 51
Between 29 Dec 1838 and 4 Jan 1839; first perf. Riga, 4 Jan 1839
Dirge composed to a text by Harald von Brackel for the funeral of Julie von Holtei, the actress wife of Karl von Holtei, the director of the theatre in Riga. The chorus is lost, but a surviving sketch, if it was indeed intended for this piece, suggests that it would have been for a male chorus in four parts.

Descendons gaiment la courtille (chorus for the vaudeville *La descente de la courtille* by Marion Dumersan and Dupeuty)
WWV 65

Prob. Jan 1841; first perf. prob. Paris, 20 Jan 1841
chorus (SSTB), pic, fl, 2 ob, 2 cl, 2 bn, 2 hn, 2 tpt, 3 trbn, timp, bd, sd, cym, tri, tamb, castanets, str
On/off stage: cornett

Chorus in B♭ (text possibly by Dumersan) written to be interpolated in the two-scene vaudeville *La descente de la courtille*, which had its first performance at the Théâtre des Variétés in Paris on 20 January 1841.

Der Tag erscheint (*The Day Appears*)
WWV 68

May 1843; first perf. Dresden, 7 Jun 1843
male chorus (TTBB) *a cappella*

Composed, as part of Wagner's official duties as Kapellmeister to the Saxon court, for a ceremony at which a memorial to King Friedrich August I was unveiled. The text was by Christoph Christian Hohlfeld. The chorus was sung *a cappella* on that occasion, but Wagner also made a version, probably at about the same time, for male chorus and brass instruments (4 hn, 4 tpt, 3 trbn, contrabass tuba).

Das Liebesmahl der Apostel (*The Love-Feast of the Apostles*) ('Biblical scene')
WWV 69

chorus of youths (3 choruses, each TTBB), Apostles (12 B), voices from on high (16 T, 12 first B, 12 second B), pic, 4 fl, 4 ob, 4 cl, 4 bn, serp, 4 hn, 4 tpt, 3 trbn, contrabass tuba, 4 timp, harp(s), str [in 1st edition of score only 2 fl, 2 ob, 2 cl, no harp(s)]
Apr–Jun 1843; first perf. Dresden, 6 Jul 1843

Composed during the period of Wagner's Kapellmeistership in Dresden. In January 1843 he became conductor of the Dresden Liedertafel, a male-voice choral society, whose leading light, a Professor Löwe, decided to organize a gala performance in which all the male choral societies in Saxony would participate. Wagner was given the job of writing a work for male chorus of half an hour's duration; *Das Liebesmahl der Apostel* was the result.

He attempted to obviate the potential tedium by dividing his chorus into various groups: one, consisting of forty specially picked tenors and basses, was to sing from the cupola of the dome; another, representing the Apostles, was a group of twelve basses; and the chorus of youths was subdivided into three choruses each consisting of tenors and basses in two parts. At the first performance, in the Dresden Frauenkirche, the massed singers – some 1200 in all – occupied almost the whole of the nave, with an orchestra of 100 players seated behind them.

The text of the work, written by Wagner himself, deals with the events of the first Pentecost, at which the Holy Ghost descended on the Apostles. That descent is depicted in dramatic terms: after twenty-five minutes of *a cappella* singing, the orchestra enters with whispering tremolando strings low down at the words 'Welch' Brausen erfüllt die Luft?' ('What rushing fills the air?') To ensure that pitch was maintained in the unaccompanied section, Wagner employed – both in the rehearsals and in the performance itself – a pair of harps to sound the keynote from time to time. The performance was enthusiastically received, though Wagner himself was disappointed with the 'comparatively feeble effect' of such a large body of amateur singers, and vowed never to involve himself in such an undertaking again.

Gruss seiner Treuen an Friedrich August den Geliebten (*Greeting to the Beloved Friedrich August from his Loyal Subjects*)
WWV 71

male chorus (TTBB), pic, 3 fl, 2 ob, 8 cl, 2 bn, 6 hn, 4 tpt, 6 trbn, 2 contrabass tubas [a version for voice and piano was made in the same month as the windband version]
Early Aug 1844; first perf. Dresden, 12 Aug 1844

Composed to celebrate the return of King Friedrich August II of Saxony from England. The composition was not an official obligation but a spontaneous expression of affection towards the monarch. Indeed, by breaching protocol in organizing the tribute, Wagner incurred the wrath of his superior, Lüttichau, and of the senior Kapellmeister Reissiger. Wagner soothed the latter by inviting him to conduct, taking his own place among the tenors in the chorus. The display of loyalty seems to have given as much pleasure to Wagner as to the king, especially when the composer was able to organize a dramatically effective recessional (the king had requested a repeat performance, but on account of a severe toothache had asked for it to be shortened). The refrain combines two melodic ideas shortly to be used in Act II of *Tannhäuser*: the grand march and the phrase 'Sei mir gegrüsst!' from Elisabeth's Hall of Song Aria.

An Webers Grabe (*At Weber's Grave*)
WWV 72

male chorus (TTBB)
Early Nov 1844; first perf. Dresden, 15 Dec 1844

Wagner had been instrumental in having the remains of his idol Carl Maria von Weber transferred from London to his home town of Dresden. After much procrastination, the ceremony took place on 14 December 1844, with a torchlight procession and funeral music written by Wagner (see *Trauermusik*, WWV 73). On the following morning, by the graveside, in the Catholic Friedrichstadt cemetery, Wagner gave an oration and conducted his chorus, set to his own words: 'Hebt an den Sang, ihr Zeugen dieser Stunde' ('Lift up your voices, ye witnesses to this hour').

Wahlspruch für die deutsche Feuerwehr (Motto for the German Fire Brigade)
WWV 101
male chorus (TTBB)
Early Nov 1869
A short (9-bar) chorus in four parts, to a text by Franz Gilardone. Cosima refers to it in her diary entry for 9 November 1869: 'R. is asked for a tribute to the firemen, which he immediately drafts.' Wagner's score, however, is dated 8 November.

Kinder-Katechismus (A Children's Catechism)
WWV 106
children's voices (soloists and unison chorus), pf [rev. version for orchestral accompaniment of fl, ob, 2 cl, bn, 2 hn, str]
Dec 1873; first perf. Bayreuth, 25 Dec 1873 (rev. version 25 Dec 1874)
Chorus composed as a surprise birthday present for Cosima in 1873. The autograph is inscribed 'Kinder-Katechismus zu Kosel's Geburtstag' ('A Children's Catechism for Kosel's birthday'). 'Kosel' or 'Cosel', one of Wagner's pet-names for Cosima, was derived from the verb kosen ('to caress'). Wagner's verse, which is in question-and-answer form (hence the 'catechism'), makes a word-play on the roses that bloom in May and the Kose that blooms at Christmastime; Cosima refers to it in her Diaries (25 Dec 1873) as the 'Kose- und Rosenlied'.

The chorus was performed outside Cosima's bedroom in Wahnfried on Christmas Day 1873 (the day on which she celebrated her birthday – actually the 24th) by her four daughters (perhaps also son); Siegfried then recited the poem to her at her bedside. The following December Wagner made a new version, in which he made use of the orchestra he had assembled in order to serenade Cosima with the Siegfried Idyll and excerpts from his operas. For this version he added a postlude, weaving in the 'glorification of Brünnhilde' motif from the end of Götterdämmerung, which he had completed a month before.

Willkommen in Wahnfried, du heil'ger Christ (Welcome to Wahnfried, Holy Christ)
WWV 112
children's voices
24 Dec 1877; first perf. Bayreuth, 24 Dec 1877
Short (8-bar) chorus composed spontaneously on Christmas Eve 1877 and performed in Wahnfried for Cosima by the children. Cosima's Diaries record: 'When he came home and saw the house and "all its joys", it had occurred to R. that Christ was not only a "bringer of salvation", but a "bringer of joy" as well! Under Lulu's [Daniela's] supervision the children learned the words at once and sang them very nicely.' (24 Dec 1877) Wagner may have improvised an accompaniment on the piano.

Ihr Kinder, geschwinde, geschwinde (Children, Hurry, Hurry)
WWV 113
children's voices
Prob. Dec 1880; first perf. Bayreuth, 25 Dec 1880
This lighthearted chorus, described as an 'antique choral song', was performed in Wahnfried by the children as a birthday present for Cosima on Christmas Day 1880. At the same time, Wagner presented her with a casket that included his transcription of Beethoven's Ninth Symphony, made fifty years previously. The casket was inscribed with the words 'Geschreibsel, Gebleibsel für lieb' gut' Weibsel' ('Scribbles and scraps for my good little wife').

Chamber music

String Quartet in D major (lost)
WWV 4
Autumn 1829
One of Wagner's first compositions, but like the Sonatas WWV 2 and 5 it has not survived. The dating of autumn 1829 follows the Red Pocketbook rather than Mein Leben, where it is assigned to the summer.

String Quartet (the 'Starnberg' Quartet)
No evidence survives of such a work. See 'Myths and Legends', pp.137–8.

Adagio for Clarinet and String Quintet
Formerly attributed to Wagner; in fact by Heinrich Joseph Baermann (1784-1847), belonging to his Clarinet Quintet, op.23.

Works for solo voice and orchestra

Aria (lost)
WWV 8
S, orch
? early 1830
According to Mein Leben the aria for soprano, which he scored 'with great care', was composed as a result of obtaining the score of Mozart's Don Giovanni. It is mentioned in the context of the 'pastoral opera', WWV 6 (see 'Projected or unfinished dramatic works', p.321), of which it may or may not have been intended to be a part. The dating is from the Red Pocketbook, rather than Mein Leben, which implies summer 1829.

Scene and aria (lost)
WWV 28
S, orch
Early 1832; first perf. Leipzig, 22 Apr 1832

Described in *Mein Leben* as a quite substantial aria for soprano and orchestra, this piece was sung by Henriette Wüst in the theatre at Leipzig, where the theatre bill described it as a 'Scene and Aria'. Gerald Abraham's thesis (1969) that the aria was in fact the first version of Ada's second-act aria 'Ich sollte ihm entsagen' in *Die Feen* has been discounted (Deathridge, 1978). The nature of the text and its author remain unknown.

'Doch jetzt wohin ich blicke' (new allegro section for aria in Marschner's *Der Vampyr*)
WWV 33
T, 2 fl, 2 ob, 2 cl, 2 bn, 2 hn, 2 tpt, timp, str
Sep 1833; first perf. Würzburg, 29 Sep 1833
The influence of his brother Albert secured a job for Wagner as chorus master at the theatre in Würzburg in 1833. One of his first tasks was to drill the chorus for performances of Marschner's *Der Vampyr*, for which he also wrote this new concluding *allegro* section for Aubry's aria 'Wie ein schöner Frühlingsmorgen'. The new ending, with scalic runs and arpeggios, proved an effective display piece for Albert, who played the part of Aubry.

'Sanfte Wehmut will sich regen' (aria for Carl Blum's comic opera *Mary, Max und Michel*)
WWV 43
B, pic, fl, 2 ob, 2 cl, 2 bn, 4 hn, 2 tpt, timp, sd, str
Aug 1837; first perf. Riga, 1 Sep 1837
Taking up his post as music director of the theatre in Riga, Wagner opened the season with a performance of Carl Blum's comic opera *Mary, Max und Michel*, for which he composed an extra bass aria (text by Karl von Holtei) consisting of 'a sentimental introduction together with a military rondo' (*Mein Leben*).

Bass aria for Joseph Weigl's 'lyrical opera' *Die Schweizerfamilie* (lost)
WWV 45
Prob. Dec 1837; first perf. Riga, prob. 22 Dec 1837
This aria, like 'Sanfte Wehmut', WWV 43 (see above), was composed for insertion in another composer's opera, in this case Joseph Weigl's 'lyrical opera' *Die Schweizerfamilie*. The aria is lost, but according to *Mein Leben* it took the form of a *Gebet* (prayer) and 'bore witness to the great changes taking place in my musical development'.

'Norma il predisse, O Druidi' (aria for Bellini's *Norma*)
WWV 52
B, male chorus (TB), pic, fl, 2 ob, 2 cl, 2 bn, serp, 4 hn, 2 tpt, 3 trbn, timp, bd, cym, str
End Sep/beginning Oct 1839
Composed in the hope of making an impression in Paris, in the early days of Wagner's period there

(not, *pace Mein Leben*, towards the end when all else had failed). Wagner's idea was for it to be sung by the celebrated bass Luigi Lablache, who took the role of Oroveso in Bellini's opera. Lablache politely declined to include the aria on the grounds that 'it was quite impossible to insert it at this late date in an opera given as frequently as Bellini's'.

Works for solo voice and piano

Songs
WWV 7
1828–30
This small group of songs appears not to have proceeded beyond the stage of sketches and drafts. They may possibly have been intended either for the 'pastoral opera', WWV 6 (see 'Projected or unfinished dramatic works', p.321), or for theatrical performances involving Wagner's sisters, especially Rosalie.

Aria (lost)
WWV 3
1829
According to *Mein Leben* the aria was arranged for a wind band by one Flachs and played in Kintschy's Swiss Chalet.

Seven pieces for Goethe's *Faust*
WWV 15
No. 1   Soldier's Song: 4-part male chorus, pf
No. 2   Peasant under the lime tree: S, T, 4-part chorus, pf
No. 3   Brander's Song: B, unison male chorus, pf
No. 4   Mephistopheles' Song: B, unison male chorus, pf
No. 5   Mephistopheles' Song: B, pf
No. 6   Gretchen at the Spinning Wheel: S, pf
No. 7   Melodrama: speaking role (Gretchen), pf
Early 1831
These pieces for Goethe's *Faust*, possibly written in conjunction with a performance of the play in Leipzig, date from the beginning of 1831, several months before Wagner began his lessons with Weinlig; they therefore count among his first compositions.

Glockentöne (also entitled *Abendglocken*) (lost)
WWV 30
12 Oct 1832
Song composed by Wagner to a text by his friend Theodor Apel, beginning with the line 'Glockentöne hör' ich klingen' ('I hear the sound of bells ringing'). It was written at Pravonin, near Prague, where Wagner was staying with Count Pachta and his two nubile daughters in the autumn of 1832.

Der Tannenbaum (*The Fir Tree*)
WWV 50
Prob. autumn 1838
One of a group of songs Wagner sent to August
Lewald, editor of *Europa*, in the hope of making a
name for himself in Paris. *Der Tannenbaum*, to a text
by Georg Scheurlin, was probably written in Riga in
autumn 1838, rather than in Königsberg as stated in
Mein Leben. The E♭ minor tonality and slow-moving
melodic line reflect the brooding melancholy of the
text.

Dors mon enfant (*Sleep, my child*)
WWV 53
Autumn 1839
Wagner's friends in Paris, Anders and Lehrs, urged
him to write some songs which could be offered to
celebrated singers for inclusion in their concerts.
The text for *Dors mon enfant* was provided by a young
poet friend of Anders; it was the first French text
Wagner had set. The contralto Widmann sang the
song 'tenderly' for Wagner but not in public. *Dors
mon enfant* was published by Lewald in *Europa* in
1841, and together with *Mignonne* and *Attente*, as '3
Mélodies' by Durand, Schoenewerk et Cie in Paris
in 1870.

Extase (*Ecstasy*) (frag.)
WWV 54
Autumn 1839
This song, to a text by Victor Hugo, survives only in
fragmentary form and it is assumed that it was never
completed.

Attente (*Expectation*)
WWV 55
Autumn 1839
Composed in the same circumstances as *Dors mon
enfant*, WWV 53 (above). *Attente*, a setting of a poem
by Victor Hugo (from his *Les Orientales*), was first
published by Lewald in *Europa* in 1842. The
breathless expectation of the poem is depicted in
rapidly repeated notes in the accompaniment,
supporting a vocal line full of appoggiatura sighs.

La Tombe dit à la rose (*The Tomb Says to the Rose*) (frag.)
WWV 56
Autumn 1839
Like *Extase*, WWV 54 (see above), this song exists
only in fragmentary form, and was presumably
never completed. The text is by Victor Hugo, from
his collection of poems entitled *Les Voix intérieures*.

Mignonne
WWV 57
Autumn 1839
Composed in the same circumstances as *Dors mon
enfant*, WWV 53, and *Attente*, WWV 55 (see above).
Mignonne, to a text by the 16th-century French poet

Pierre de Ronsard, was first published by Lewald in
Europa in 1843. It is a flowing, compound-time
ballad, rather in the manner of Mendelssohn.

Tout n'est qu'images fugitives (*Soupir*) All is but fleeting images (*Sigh*)
WWV 58
Autumn 1839
Mentioned neither in Wagner's letters nor in his
autobiographical writings, this song was written at
approximately the same time as the other French
settings, but not published until 1914. *Soupir* is the
title of the poem by Jean Reboul, but it does not
appear in Wagner's manuscript. The 'fleeting
images' of the poem are suggested by an 'agitato'
semiquaver accompaniment, but each of the three
stanzas ends with an effective broadening out
(arpeggios in the accompaniment), as mundane
activity is contrasted with the immensity of the sky.
The first line of the third stanza, 'Navigateur d'un
jour d'orage' ('Sailor on a stormy day'), is anticipated by turbulent demisemiquaver figuration in
the accompaniment.

Les Deux Grenadiers (*The Two Grenadiers*)
WWV 60
Dec 1839 – beginning 1840
Setting for baritone of a French translation of the
poem by Heinrich Heine describing the return from
Moscow of two defeated soldiers. Heine's Napoleonic sympathies would have been gratified by the
appearance of the *Marseillaise* towards the end, as
one soldier fantasizes about his resurrection from the
grave to defend the emperor. Curiously, Schumann
adopted the same device when he made his own
setting of the poem a few months later, though that
composer's ironic five-bar postlude for the piano has
no parallel in Wagner. Wagner had the song
published at his own expense in July 1840; the title-
page was adorned with a poignant lithograph by his
friend Kietz.

Adieux de Marie Stuart
WWV 61
Mar 1840
Composed probably for the soprano Julie Dorus-
Gras, who participated in the audition of numbers
from *Das Liebesverbot* in 1840, this song is on a much
grander, more expansive scale than any of the others
of Wagner's Paris years. Pierre de Béranger's poem
evokes the tearful farewell from France of Mary
Queen of Scots, and Wagner seizes the opportunity
for some grand operatic gesturing (he was in the
middle of *Rienzi* at the time). The vocal line swoops
down through a whole octave, for example, on the
words 'patrie' and 'Marie', while cadenza-like
flourishes later in the song become even more
extravagant. Delivered with panache and conviction, the song makes a considerable dramatic effect.

Wesendonck Lieder
WWV 91
End Nov 1857 – May 1858 (1st version)
Dec 1857 – Oct 1858 (2nd version)
Early Oct 1858 (3rd version)
First perf. Laubenheim, near Mainz, 30 Jul 1862
Published under the title 'Fünf Gedichte für eine Frauenstimme' ('Five Poems for a Female Voice') in the following order (the order in which they are generally performed today): *Der Engel* (*The Angel*), *Stehe still!* (*Stand Still!*), *Im Treibhaus* (*In the Greenhouse*), *Schmerzen* (*Sorrows*), *Träume* (*Dreams*). The texts, written by Mathilde Wesendonck, with whom Wagner was having an affair at the time, are imbued with Schopenhauerian and Tristanesque sentiments and language. The heat of passion seems not to have blinded Wagner to the amateurishness of the texts, however, for the title of the second version originally described them as 'dilettante poems'. Two of the songs were designated by Wagner 'studies for *Tristan und Isolde*' (the first two acts of which he was engaged upon at the same period): *Im Treibhaus*, which anticipates the bleak Prelude to Act III, and *Träume*, which looks forward to the Act II duet.

Each of the songs was amended, in detail rather than substance, either once or twice; all these versions were for voice and piano. Within the first version of *Schmerzen* Wagner tried three different endings before he was satisfied: the first concludes the song with a simple three-bar cadence; the second expands the cadence to six bars; and the third (the familiar one, as published) adds a further bar, with the inscription 'One more ending. It must be ever more beautiful.' The five songs were first performed at Schott's villa near Mainz, by the soprano Emilie Genast, accompanied by Hans von Bülow on the piano.

As a birthday present for Mathilde, Wagner arranged *Träume* for solo violin and chamber orchestra (2 cl, 2 bn, 2 hn, 2 first vn, 2 second vn, 2 va, 1 vc) and conducted it at the Wesendoncks' villa in Zurich on 23 December 1857. The orchestral version of the songs generally performed today is by Felix Mottl.

On the spelling of Mathilde Wesendonck's surname, and hence the title of the set of songs, see 'Who's Who', p.33.

Es ist bestimmt in Gottes Rat (God has decreed) (draft)
WWV 92
Prob. Jan 1858
Wagner refers to the first lines of this song, 'God has decreed that man must leave that which he holds dearest', in a letter to Liszt written from Paris in January 1858. This was the time when he was obliged to leave Zurich briefly on account of the 'neighbourly confusion' (as the Annals delightfully refer to it) arising from his infatuation with Mathilde Wesendonck. The clear autobiographical connection makes it almost certain that this 13-bar draft (first stanza only) dates from that time. The text is by Baron Ernst von Feuchtersleben.

Schlaf, Kindchen, schlafe (Sleep, Baby, Sleep)
End Dec 1868
Brief (10-bar) lullaby headed 'New Year's Eve 68–69' using a theme that was to reappear in the *Siegfried Idyll*.

Der Worte viele sind gemacht (Much is Promised)
WWV 105
Apr 1871
Song composed for and dedicated to Louis Kraft, the proprietor of the hotel in Leipzig who accommodated Wagner and Cosima in the royal apartments on their visit there in April 1871. The title by which the piece is often referred to, *Kraft-Lied*, is not authentic.

Piano music

Sonata in D minor (lost)
WWV 2
Summer 1829
One of Wagner's earliest pieces, dating from the year after his first harmony lessons with Müller, and his first attempt to teach himself the principles of composition.

Sonata in F minor (lost)
WWV 5
Autumn 1829
Another early work that has not survived. The F minor Sonata dates from the year after Wagner's first lessons with Müller (autumn 1828). It is mentioned in the Red Pocketbook both in connection with that study and with the String Quartet in D major, WWV 4.

Sonata in B♭ major for four hands (lost)
WWV 16
Early 1831
Wagner tells us in *Mein Leben* that he practised this duet sonata with his sister Ottilie, and because it pleased them so much he also orchestrated it. Neither the original nor the orchestrated version has survived.

Sonata in B♭ major, op. 1
Autumn 1831
The earliest surviving piano sonata of Wagner's, described as 'op.1' by Breitkopf & Härtel when it was published in 1832. The work dates from the period of Wagner's study with Weinlig, and accord-

ing to *Mein Leben*, his teacher's instruction was for a piano sonata which 'should be constructed on the most insipid harmonic and thematic principles, as a model for which he recommended one of the most childlike sonatas of Pleyel'. It would appear, however, from the lack of an obvious prototype and from the evidence of the work itself, that Wagner took as his model not Pleyel but Beethoven and possibly Mozart also to some extent. Though little more than a pale imitation of Beethoven, the Sonata has considerable inventive wit and a vivacity that is impressively sustained.

Fantasia in F♯ minor
WWV 22
Autumn 1831
The Fantasia (the published title – the fair copy of the autograph has 'Fantasie') followed shortly after the B♭ Sonata, WWV 21 (see above). As a reward for following the Classical formal discipline in the Sonata, Wagner tells us in *Mein Leben*, Weinlig allowed him to compose a piece in a less structured form. The Fantasia was the result, and a quirky individuality is evident in the uneven phrases, abrupt rhythms and frequent stops and starts. An undeniable atmosphere of dark brooding is also created, notably by means of an insistent motif that rises and falls through a minor third, in an uncanny prefiguration of Tannhäuser's Narration. The influence of Beethoven is once again evident, but no less strong is the pull of Bellinian bel canto, an early manifestation of an influence that was to be of some importance.

Polonaise in D major [op.2]
WWV 23A: version for two hands
WWV 23B: version for four hands
End 1831 – early 1832
Evidently inspired by the wave of sympathy for the Polish refugees, following the unsuccessful uprising against the Russians in 1831, the Polonaise adopts the traditional features of the dance: the strong, dotted, martial rhythms; thrusting melodic lines; and characteristic delayed cadences. The four-handed arrangement is a revised, improved version of the original for two hands.

Sonata in A major, op.4 (Grosse Sonate)
WWV 26
Early 1832
Beethoven is the undoubted influence on this sonata, the title of which, 'Grand Sonata', proclaims its aspirations. Typically Beethovenian is the opening three-note motif and its ubiquitous reappearance in the first movement. The slow movement, with its long-drawn bel canto line over sombre low-pitched chords in the bass, recalls the slow movements of two of Beethoven's piano sonatas: the *Hammerklavier*, op.106, and the Sonata in A♭, op.110. A three-part fugue of 41 bars was struck out of the autograph

manuscript by Wagner himself, who probably concluded that it was too much in the nature of an academic exercise.

Albumleaf in E major ('Song Without Words')
WWV 64
Prob. Dec 1840
The albumleaf originated as a short piece in an indeterminate form dedicated to a particular person and presented to him or her in a folio or album. In the 19th century the term came to be used more generally, though the notion of dedication often remained. Wagner's Albumleaf in E major has no title in the autograph, but it appears to have been written at the same time as an affectionate poem to his friend Ernst Benedikt Kietz, who was about to leave on a journey. A phrase in the poem – 'words are lacking' – seems to have given rise to the title 'Lied ohne Worte' ('Song Without Words') that accompanied the composition on its first publication in 1911. The title, even if inauthentic, is an apt one, for the piece has the eloquent lyricism and triplet accompaniment characteristic of Mendelssohn's celebrated works in the genre.

Polka
WWV 84
End May 1853
The piece is untitled in the only surviving autograph source (a first draft), but there can be little doubt that it is identifiable with the 'few bars of a polka' that according to Wolfgang Golther, the editor of the correspondence with Mathilde Wesendonck, accompanied a note from Wagner of 29 May 1853. The note read: 'Hier Geschmolzenes für das Gefrorene von gestern' – rendered neatly by Ashton Ellis as 'Here's syrup, for yesterday's ice.' The 23-bar trifle is indeed a confection, but not a sentimental one; rather, the humorous tone of this pseudo-Straussian polka has a parodistic edge.

Eine Sonate für das Album von Frau M[athilde] W[esendonck]
WWV 85
June 1853
Composed immediately after the Polka (see above), the Album Sonata for Mathilde Wesendonck is, by contrast, the most substantial of the series of dedicatory works Wagner wrote for the piano. The sonata and the Polka were the first works to be composed since Wagner completed *Lohengrin* in 1848.

The sonata is in one movement, but rather than following the model of Liszt's recently composed B minor Sonata (several movements integrated into one), it is one of the rare examples in the 19th century of a single sonata-form movement. Other unconventional features include the four subsidiary themes beginning in the mediant (rather than the dominant) and the reversal of the order of the subjects in the recapitulation, so that the main theme of the work is the last to appear back in the home key.

The sonata, which bore the oracular inscription 'Wisst ihr wie das wird?' ('Do you know what will happen?' – an echo from the Norns' Scene in *Götterdämmerung*), was finally given the title as above, which Wagner felt made it clear that the work was of an occasional nature. The first performance was probably that given by Wilhelm Tappert for the Berlin Wagner-Verein on 29 September 1877.

Züricher Vielliebchen-Walzer (Zurich Philippina Waltz)
WWV 88
End May 1854

This short (32-bar) piece was written for Mathilde Wesendonck's sister, Marie Luckemeyer, who frequently visited the Wesendonck Villa in Zurich. The inscription reads, in part: 'Zurich Philippina Waltz, Polka or whatever . . . dedicated to Marie of Düsseldorf by the best dancer in Saxony, called Richard the Waltzmaker.' The tone of the piece, with its frequent cross-rhythms, is endearingly skittish. 'Philippina' alludes to the dinner-party game 'in which each of two persons eats a twin kernel of a nut, and one pays a forfeit to the other on certain conditions' (*Chambers Twentieth Century Dictionary*). The German formula for claiming the gift made as a forfeit is 'Guten Morgen, Vielliebchen' ('Good morning, beloved').

Theme in A♭ major
WWV 93
Prob. 1858; rev. 1881

Incorrectly known as the 'Porazzi Theme' and suggested to be Wagner's 'last musical thought'. The plangent A♭ theme in fact dates almost certainly from 1858: the appearance of its first draft on the reverse side of a sheet containing a sketch for Act II scene 2 of *Tristan*, which can probably be dated to December 1858, suggests that the theme also dates from about that time. Wagner revised the theme, extending it from eight to twelve bars, probably at the time of his visit to Palermo (November 1881). The purpose of the theme is unclear. It may originally have been intended for *Tristan*, but its later continuation suggests a more self-contained statement. For the true 'Porazzi Theme', see under 'Themes and melodies', p.313.

In das Album der Fürstin M[etternich]
WWV 94
Jun 1861

An albumleaf in C major (for 'albumleaf', see WWV 64 above) dedicated to Princess Pauline Metternich, the wife of the Austrian ambassador in Paris. The princess had helped to secure the production of *Tannhäuser* in Paris in March 1861 – a dubious service in view of the fiasco that ensued – and the albumleaf was Wagner's token of gratitude.

Ankunft bei den schwarzen Schwänen (Arrival at the House of the Black Swans)
WWV 95
Jul 1861

This albumleaf in A♭ major was dedicated to Countess Pourtalès. To the count and countess Wagner owed his stay, in the summer of 1861, in a guesthouse belonging to the Prussian Embassy in Paris. A letter to Mathilde Wesendonck of 12 July describes the view: 'I have in front of me a garden with beautiful tall trees and a pool with two black swans; beyond the garden is the Seine, and beyond the Seine is the Garden of the Tuileries'. The charged atmosphere recalls *Tristan und Isolde* (in particular the Act III Prelude at the beginning), though it is 'Sei mir gegrüsst' from Elisabeth's Hall of Song aria in *Tannhäuser* that emerges in a magical transformation to the major.

Albumleaf in E♭ major
WWV 108
Jan – 1 Feb 1875

Dedicated to Betty Schott, the wife of Wagner's publisher. The composer indicated his intention of writing an albumleaf for Frau Schott as early as 16 January 1872, the day after receiving back from the publisher the manuscript of his youthful arrangement of Beethoven's Ninth Symphony. It was not until January 1875, however, that the promise was fulfilled. The piece was dispatched on 2 February; Frau Schott died soon after, on 5 April. In its relative harmonic and rhythmic freedom the albumleaf cautiously reflects Wagner's later style.

Projected or unfinished dramatic works

Leubald
WWV 1
Tragedy in 5 acts
1826–8

The adolescent Wagner's first dramatic conception was an ambitious one, drawing, as he later reported in *Mein Leben*, on *Hamlet*, *Macbeth* and *King Lear*, as well as Goethe's *Götz von Berlichingen*. The grisly plot, which involved ghosts, insanity and multiple murders, made a less than favourable impression on Wagner's family, but he determined to write incidental music for the 'vast tragic drama' in the style of Beethoven's *Egmont*. If any music was written specifically for *Leubald*, it has not survived.

Pastoral opera (unnamed)
WWV 6
? early 1830
This youthful pastoral poem of Wagner's (now lost) was modelled on Goethe's *Die Laune des Verliebten* 'as far as form and content were concerned'. The dating of early 1830 is from the Red Pocketbook, though *Mein Leben* implies that it was written in 1829 and taken to Magdeburg that summer. According to Wagner's account, he composed a scene for three female voices and tenor aria.

Die Hochzeit (*The Wedding*)
WWV 31
Opera in ?3 acts
Oct/Nov 1832 – 1 Mar 1833
Opera conceived by Wagner in the autumn of 1832 while he was staying with the Pachta family in Pravonin, near Prague. As with *Leubald*, the subject was one of murder and revenge, but treated in more 'refined' fashion, the youthful composer felt. The poem is lost, and of the music only an introduction, chorus and septet were written.

Die hohe Braut, oder Bianca und Giuseppe (*The Noble Bride, or Bianca and Giuseppe*)
WWV 40
Grand opera in 4 acts (5 in original prose sketches)
Prob. Jul 1836 and Aug 1842
Wagner most probably sketched his prose scenario for *Die hohe Braut* while in Königsberg in July 1836, attempting to secure a conductor's post there. He sent it to Eugène Scribe in Paris, in the hope that the celebrated librettist might develop it into a text which Wagner could then be commissioned to set to music for the Paris Opéra. *Die hohe Braut* was eventually elaborated into a libretto not by Scribe, however, but by Wagner himself in Dresden, in 1842; it was offered first to Karl Reissiger, the senior Kapellmeister at Dresden, and then to Ferdinand Hiller, but was finally set to music by Jan Bedřich Kittl.

Männerlist grösser als Frauenlist, oder Die glückliche Bärenfamilie (*Man's Cunning Greater than Woman's, or The Happy Bear Family*)
WWV 48
Comic opera in 2 acts
Prob. summer 1838
Based on a story from *The Arabian Nights*, this was intended as a comic opera, in the form of a Singspiel, with prose dialogue and individual numbers. Two numbers were composed for it, but according to the *Autobiographical Sketch*, Wagner broke off the composition when he realized it was turning out like Auber. The project almost certainly dates from the summer of 1838, rather than the 1837 given in *Mein Leben*.

Die Sarazenin (*The Saracen Woman*)
WWV 66
Opera in 5 acts
Prob. 1841, early 1843
This projected five-act opera, on the subject of the Hohenstaufen prince Manfred, son of Friedrich II, and a mysterious Saracen prophetess, Fatima, was conceived almost certainly in Paris, late in 1841. Wagner subsequently elaborated his draft in Dresden, in 1843, but proceeded no further, and wrote no music for it.

Die Bergwerke zu Falun (*The Mines of Falun*)
WWV 67
Opera in 3 acts
Feb–Mar 1842
This aborted project also dates from Wagner's Paris years. A libretto was requested from him by a Bohemian composer called Josef Dessauer, who was temporarily resident in Paris. Wagner based his prose draft on a story by E.T.A. Hoffmann set among a mining community in the Swedish town of Falun. He abandoned the project when the idea was turned down by the Paris Opéra. In Dresden he gave the scenario to August Röckel, who appears to have intended to set it to music.

Friedrich I.
WWV 76
?Opera in 5 acts
Oct 1846, winter 1848–9
Wagner made his first sketch for this five-act work (probably intended to be an opera) in Dresden in 1846. The subject was the 12th-century Hohenstaufen emperor Friedrich Barbarossa. Wagner subsequently claimed that he abandoned the idea as soon as he realized the superior potential of the Nibelung myth, but the existence of a sketch for the second act, written in Roman script (indicating a date of winter 1848–9, since Wagner abandoned Gothic script only in mid-December 1848), shows that this cannot have been the case, for it postdates the writing of the poem for *Siegfrieds Tod* (later *Götterdämmerung*).

Jesus von Nazareth
WWV 80
?Opera in 5 acts
Jan–Apr 1849
Jesus von Nazareth, which followed immediately after *Friedrich I.* was abandoned, reached the stage of a complete five-act scenario before being aborted, and the existence of a musical sketch strongly suggests that an opera was intended. The scenario, depicting Jesus as a social revolutionary, betrays the influence of Feuerbach, Proudhon and the Young Hegelians David Friedrich Strauss and Bruno Bauer.

Achilleus
WWV 81

?Opera in 3 acts
Early 1849, Feb–Jul 1850
Only prose sketches exist for this project, and it was later described by Wagner to King Ludwig as a 'purely dramatic poem', but it was also probably one of the 'five operas' Wagner told Ferdinand Heine (letter of 19 Nov 1849) he was considering. As with *Friedrich I.*, the themes of the projected Achilles drama – a free hero, the gods yielding to humanity – were subsumed into the *Ring*.

Wieland der Schmied (*Wieland the Smith*)
WWV 82
Heroic opera in 3 acts
Dec 1849 – Mar 1850
For this projected opera only prose drafts exist, dating from the winter of 1849–50. The story, which concerns a smith who soars on self-made wings above the world that has held him in bondage, contains many pre-echoes of the *Ring* and other works. Wagner's original plan was that the opera could be performed in Paris, but he eventually decided that the Germanic hero Wieland could never be translated into a French context, and consequently abandoned the project.

Die Sieger (*The Victors*)
WWV 89
Opera in ?3 acts
May 1856
Wagner made his short prose sketch for this projected opera in between finishing the score of *Die Walküre* and taking up work on *Siegfried*. Nothing came of the project, but it continued to haunt Wagner for the rest of his life. Its Buddhist subject dealt with the themes of passion and chastity, renunciation and redemption, all of which informed Wagner's later works, especially *Parsifal*, with which *Die Sieger* has much in common. Wagner believed that the notion of reincarnated souls might lend itself to his recently developed technique of motivic reminiscence.

Luthers Hochzeit (*Luther's Wedding*)
WWV 99
Drama
Aug 1868
This project dates from 1868, the year celebrated as the 350th anniversary of the Reformation and marked by the erection of a Luther memorial at Worms. Treating one of the decisive acts of the Reformation – Luther's rejection of his priestly celibacy and his marriage to Catharina von Bora – *Luthers Hochzeit* also reflected an acute conflict in Wagner's own life in the late 1860s: Wagner was by this time cohabiting with Cosima von Bülow, and wished her first to obtain a divorce from her husband, and second to renounce her Catholicism. Only prose sketches exist; Wagner appears not to have attempted to compose any music, and ten years later he was considering writing a prose play on the subject (CT, 5 Jul 1878).

Ein Lustspiel in 1 Akt (*A Comedy in 1 Act*)
WWV 100
End Aug 1868
Prose draft for a frivolous, satirical comedy on a theatrical theme. Nothing came of the project, though a reference to it in Cosima Wagner's Diaries several years later (19 Apr 1879) as a *Posse* (i.e. farce) may suggest that some musical treatment was originally intended.

Eine Kapitulation (*A Capitulation*)
WWV 102
Comedy in the antique style
Nov 1870
The heavy-handed farce and dubious taste of *Eine Kapitulation* make it probably the least attractive of Wagner's works, completed or otherwise. The action is set in Paris in the autumn of 1870, and the 'capitulation' of the title refers to the expected surrender of the Parisians, at that time under siege in their own city. Wagner's underlying theme, however, is the supposed 'swamping' of German culture by meretricious French or French-inspired works. Wagner did not set the text himself, but he may have tinkered with the setting undertaken by Hans Richter, which has not survived (possibly destroyed by Richter himself).

Editions and arrangements

Beethoven, Symphony no. 9, arr. for pf
WWV 9
Summer 1830 – Easter 1831
Wagner submitted the transcription of the Choral Symphony to Schott, who declined to publish it.

Haydn, Symphony no. 103 in E♭, arr. for pf
(lost)
WWV 18
Summer 1831
Wagner submitted his transcription of Haydn's *Drumroll* Symphony to Breitkopf & Härtel (letter of 14 Aug 1831), offering at the same time to arrange all the other Haydn symphonies published by Breitkopf. The offer was declined.

Bellini, cavatina from *Il pirata*, orchestrated from pf score (lost)
WWV 34
Nov–Dec 1833
Arrangement made at request of Wagner's brother, Albert, who wanted to insert an aria from *Il pirata* (for which the score was not available) into another

work of Bellini's: *La straniera*. Wagner admitted that the arrangement was not a success, and it was not used.

Bellini, *Norma*, retouching of orchestration
WWV 46A
Prob. Dec 1837
Minor retouching of brass in score of *Norma*, for performance of the opera in Riga on 11 December 1837.

Rossini, 'Li marinari' from *Les Soirées musicales*, orchestration of piano accompaniment
WWV 47
Prob. early 1838
The arrangement of Rossini's duet was presumably made specially for the performance conducted by Wagner himself in Riga on 19 March 1838.

Meyerbeer, *Robert le diable*, harp part of cavatina 'Robert toi que j'aime' transcribed for strings
WWV 46B
Prob. Nov 1838
Transcription made probably for performance at Wagner's benefit concert in Riga on 30 November 1838.

Weber, *Euryanthe*, reorchestration of hunting chorus
WWV 46C
Prob. Jan 1839
Wagner's reorchestration, increasing Weber's 4 horns and contrabass trombone to 12 horns, was made probably for the subscription concert in Riga on 17 January 1839.

Various composers, suites for the *cornet à pistons* (operatic excerpts) (lost)
WWV 62A
Prob. autumn 1840
According to *Mein Leben*, Wagner was commissioned by the Parisian publisher Maurice Schlesinger to write fourteen suites for the then fashionable *cornet à pistons*, consisting of excerpts from popular operas of the day; Schlesinger sent him no fewer than sixty opera scores for the purpose. Wagner was relieved of the commission mid-stream, however, on account of his ignorance of the instrument's capabilities.

Various composers, vocal scores and arrangements
WWV 62B, C, D, E and F
1840–42
Notwithstanding his failure with the suites for *cornet à pistons* (see above, WWV 62A), Wagner was commissioned by Schlesinger to make a series of arrangements of Donizetti's *La Favorite* (WWV 62B). Wagner lists them in *Mein Leben*: 'complete vocal

score, piano score (without words) for two hands, ditto for four hands, complete arrangement for quartet, the same for two violins, ditto for *cornet à pistons*'. With the possible exception of the last, all these were completed by Wagner and published by Schlesinger, together with a volume of excerpts with piano accompaniment. The arrangement for *cornet à pistons* may possibly have appeared under another name.

WWV 62C consists of an arrangement for piano duet of the *Grande fantaisie sur 'La Romanesca'* by Henri Herz.

WWV 62D consists of arrangements of Halévy's opera *Le Guitarrero*: of the overture for piano four hands, and for piano with flute or violin ad lib; and of excerpts for string or flute quartet, and for two violins.

WWV 62E consists of arrangements of Halévy's opera *La Reine de Chypre*: vocal score; piano score; excerpts with piano accompaniment; arrangements for quartet and for two violins.

WWV 62F consists of arrangements of Auber's opera *Zanetta* for flute quartet.

Spontini, *La Vestale*, retouching of orchestration
WWV 74
Prob. Nov 1844
Minor alterations to score made in connection with new production of *La Vestale* (29 November 1844) under Spontini's own direction.

Gluck, *Iphigénie en Aulide*, rev. version
WWV 77
Prob;. Dec 1846 – beginning Feb 1847
Wagner undertook this revision of Gluck's score for the production he mounted in Dresden in February 1847. The arias and choruses were linked by means of preludes, postludes and transitions, using Gluck's material as far as possible. The orchestration was similarly retouched – with discretion and highlighting features of Gluck's own score. Wagner's chief alteration was to eliminate what he regarded as the predictable and sentimental marriage of Achilles and Iphigenia at the end; in order to effect this return to the spirit of Euripides it was necessary to introduce a new character (Artemis) as well as some recitatives.

Palestrina, Stabat Mater, rev. version
WWV 79
Prob. Feb – beginning Mar 1848
This arrangement was made for a performance of the work in Dresden under Wagner's direction on 8 March 1848. The antiphonal character of the original is generally preserved, though occasionally the two choirs are combined. Characteristically 19th-century dynamic, expression and tempo indications are added.

Mozart, *Don Giovanni*, rev. version (lost)
WWV 83
Beginning Nov 1850
This arrangement was made for a series of three performances of the work under Wagner's own direction at the Stadt-Theater in Zurich (premiere 8 November 1850). The existing orchestral parts had to be corrected in places and missing parts supplied. Some of the recitatives were translated into German, and the scenic arrangements simplified.

Gluck, *Iphigénie en Aulide*, concert ending for overture
WWV 87

Prob. Feb – beginning Mar 1854
Made for performances in Zurich under Wagner's direction; that on 7 March 1854 was the first.

Johann Strauss the Younger, *Wine, Women and Song* waltz, reorchestration
WWV 109
May 1875
The new scoring, for a large symphony orchestra, is indicated by markings in a piano score. The arrangement may have been heard at the concert given on Wagner's birthday, 22 May 1875, at Wahnfried, though Cosima's report of the occasion to King Ludwig mentions only a string orchestra.

BARRY MILLINGTON

Section 14
THE PROSE WORKS

THE PROSE WORKS

This list includes most of Wagner's writings, reviews, speeches, open letters and letters on specific subjects published (not always with complete justification) in SS; occasional poems and dedications as well as prose drafts and texts of the stage works in GS and SS are excluded. The list does not claim to be complete. Wagner wrote a great deal that was published in obscure newspapers and periodicals that are often difficult to obtain today; he also published many essays, reviews and speeches anonymously or under a pseudonym. Included here, however, are a number of unpublished writings listed by J.-J. Nattiez in the skeleton catalogue published in his *Wagner androgyne* (Paris, 1990; Eng. trans. in preparation). A more detailed catalogue by Nattiez is in preparation.

The entries are listed in chronological order (within as well as between years) according to the date of writing. The precise form of the title, which occasionally varies from edition to edition, is taken from the Volksausgabe of the writings (Leipzig, 1911–16), except that all titles of journals and musical and literary works are rendered in italics.

(For abbreviations GS, SS and PW, see p.412)

Title, date	GS, SS	PW
Die deutsche Oper, 1834	xii	viii
Pasticcio, 1834	xii	viii
Eine Kritik aus Magdeburg, 1835	xvi	—
Aus Magdeburg, 1836	xii	—
Berliner Kunstchronik von Wilhelm Drach, 1836 [lost]	—	—
Bellinis *Norma*, 1837 [review of perf. in Magdeburg first pubd in F. Lippmann: 'Ein neu entdecktes Autograph Richard Wagners', *Musicae scientiae collectanea: Festschrift Karl Gustav Fellerer* (Cologne, 1973)	—	—
Der dramatische Gesang, 1837	xii	—
Note for the concert of 13 November, 1837	—	—
Bellini: ein Wort zu seiner Zeit, 1837	xii	viii
Theater-Anzeige, 1837 [perf. of *Norma* in Riga]	xvi	—
Wagner's announcement of the concert of 19 March, 1838	—	—

Title, date	GS, SS	PW
Konzert-Anzeige, 1839	xvi	—
Wagner's programme for the concert of 14 March, 1839	—	—
Ein Tagebuch aus Paris, 1840	xvi	—
Über deutsches Musikwesen, 1840	i	vii
Über Meyerbeers *Hugenotten*, ?1840	xii	—
Stabat mater de Pergolèse, arrangé . . . par Alexis Lvoff, 1840	xii	vii
Der Virtuos und der Künstler, 1840	i	vii
Eine Pilgerfahrt zu Beethoven, 1840	i	vii
Über die Ouvertüre, 1841	i	vii
Ein Ende in Paris, 1841	i	vii
9 Paris reports for the Dresden *Abend-Zeitung*, 1841	xii	viii
Pariser Amüsements, 1841	xii	viii
Der Künstler und die Öffentlichkeit, 1841	i	vii
Ein glücklicher Abend, 1841	i	vii
Der Freischütz: an das Pariser Publikum, 1841	i	vii
Le Freischütz in Paris: Bericht nach Deutschland, 1841	i	vii
Pariser Fatalitäten für Deutsche, 1841	xii	viii
Rossinis *Stabat Mater*, 1841	i	vii
Bericht über eine neue Pariser Oper (*La Reine de Chypre* von Halévy), 1841	i	vii
Ein Pariser Bericht für Robert Schumanns *Neue Zeitschrift für Musik*, 1842	xvi	viii
Halévy und die französische Oper, 1842	xii	viii
La Reine de Chypre d'Halévy, 1842 [continuation of above]	xii	—
Autobiographische Skizze, 1842–3	i	i
Das Oratorium *Paulus* von Mendelssohn-Bartholdy	xii	—
Zwei Schreiben an die Dresdener Liedertafel: i, Aufruf, 1843; ii, Niederlegung der Leitung, 1845	xvi	—
Zwei Erklärungen über die		

Title, date	GS, SS	PW	Title, date	GS, SS	PW
Verdeutschung des Textes der Komposition *Les Deux Grenadiers*: i, Verwahrung; ii, Erklärung. 1843	xvi	—	SS, but possibly by Röckel]	xii	viii
			Die Revolution, 1849 [included in SS, but authorship unproven]	xii	viii
Rede an Webers letzter Ruhestätte, 1844 [preceded in GS by report of the reburial of Weber's remains, extracted from *Mein Leben*]	ii	vii	Die Kunst und die Revolution	iii	i
			Flüchtige Aufzeichnung einzelner Gedanken zu einem grösseren Aufsatze: das Künstlertum der Zukunft, 1849	xii	viii
Die königliche Kapelle betreffend, 1846	xii	—	Das Kunstwerk der Zukunft, 1849	iii	i
Zu Beethovens Neunter Symphonie, 1846	xii	viii	Zu *Die Kunst und die Revolution*, 1849	xii	viii
Programme note for Beethoven's Ninth Symphony, 1846 [preceded in GS by report on 1846 perf. in Dresden, extracted from *Mein Leben*]	ii	vii	Das Kunstwerk der Zukunft: dedication to Feuerbach, 1850	xii	—
			Kunst und Klima, 1850	iii	i
Künstler und Kritiker, mit Bezug auf einen besonderen Fall, 1846	xii	viii	Vorwort zu einer 1850 beabsichtigen Herausgabe von *Siegfrieds Tod*, 1850	xvi	—
Eine Rede auf Friedrich Schneider, 1846	xvi	—	Das Judentum in der Musik, 1850, rev. 1869	v	iii
Notes concerning the Dresden concerts of 1847–8	—	—	Vorwort zu der 1850 beabsichtigen Veröffentlichung des Entwurfs von 1848 *Zur Organisation eines deutschen National-Theaters für das Königreich Sachsen*, 1850	xvi	—
Entwurf zur Organisation eines deutschen National-Theaters für das Königreich Sachsen, 1849	ii	vii	Eine Skizze zu *Oper und Drama*, 1850	xvi	—
Wie verhalten sich republikanische Bestrebungen dem Königtum gegenüber, 1848	xii	iv	Oper und Drama, 1850–51	iii, iv	ii
			Über die musikalische Direktion der Züricher Oper, 1850	xvi	—
Vier Zeitungs-Erklärungen [i and ii from *Dresdener Anzeige*, iii from *Europe artiste*, iv from *Ostdeutsche Post*], 1848–61	xvi	—	Zur Empfehlung Gottfried Sempers, 1851	xvi	—
			Über die musikalische Berichterstattung in der *Eidgenössischen Zeitung*, 1851	xvi	—
Trinkspruch am Gedenktage des 300jährigen Bestehens der königlichen musikalischen Kapelle in Dresden, 1848	ii	vii	Beethovens *Heroische Symphonie* [programme note], 1851	v	iii
Der Nibelungen-Mythus: als Entwurf zu einem Drama, 1848	ii	vii	Ein Theater in Zürich, 1851	v	iii
			Über die 'Goethestiftung': Brief an Franz Liszt, 1851	v	iii
Deutschland und seine Fürsten, 1848	xii	—	Eine Mitteilung an meine Freunde, 1851	iv	i
Zwei Schreiben aus dem Jahre 1848 [i, to Franz Wigand; ii, to Lüttichau], 1848	xvi	iv	Über musikalische Kritik: Brief an den Herausgeber der *Neuen Zeitschrift für Musik*, 1852	v	iii
Die Wibelungen: Weltgeschichte aus der Sage, ?1849, rev. 1850	ii	vii	Wilhelm Baumgartners Lieder, 1852	xii	—
Über Eduard Devrients *Geschichte der deutschen Schauspielkunst*, 1849	xii	viii	Beethovens Ouvertüre zu *Coriolan*, 1852 [programme note]	v	iii
Theater-Reform, 1849	xii	viii	Zum Vortrag Beethovens, 1852 [letter to Uhlig]	xvi	—
Nochmals Theater-Reform, 1849	xii	—	Ouvertüre zu *Tannhäuser*, 1852 [programme note]	v	iii
Der Mensch und die bestehende Gesellschaft, 1849 [included in			Über die Aufführung des		

Title, date	GS, SS	PW	Title, date	GS, SS	PW
Tannhäuser: eine Mitteilung an die Dirigenten und Darsteller dieser Oper, 1852	v	iii	Justizminister Behr, 1858	xvi	—
Vieuxtemps, 1852	xvi	—	Nachruf an L. Spohr und Chordirektor W. Fischer, 1859	v	iii
Über die Aufführung der *Tannhäuser*-Ouvertüre, 1852	xvi	—	Aus der *Europe Artiste* [newspaper correction], 1859	xvi	—
Bemerkungen zur Aufführung der Oper: *Der fliegende Holländer*, 1852	v	iii	*Tristan und Isolde*: Vorspiel, 1859 [programme note]	xii	—
Vorlesung der Dichtung des *Ringes des Nibelungen*, 1853 [invitation]	xvi	—	Ein Brief an Hector Berlioz	vii	iii
Vorwort zu der Veröffentlichung der als Manuskript gedruckten Dichtung des *Ringes des Nibelungen*, 1853	xii	—	'Zukunftsmusik': an einen französischen Freund (Fr. Villot) als Vorwort zu einer Prosa-Übersetzung meiner Operndichtungen, 1860	vii	iii
Ankündigung der im Mai 1853 zu veranstaltenden Konzerte, 1853	xii	—	Bericht über die Aufführung des *Tannhäuser* in Paris	vii	iii
Ouvertüre zum *Fliegenden Holländer*, 1853 [programme note]	v	iii	Vom Wiener Hofoperntheater, 1861	xii	—
Zu *Tannhäuser*: i, Einzug der Gäste auf der Wartburg; ii, Tannhäusers Romfahrt, 1853 [programme notes]	xvi	—	*Gräfin Egmont* ballet by Rota, 1861 [review pubd under pseud. in *Oesterreichische Zeitung*, 8 Oct 1861 and in E. Kastner: *Wagner-Catalog*, 1878]	—	—
Vorspiel zu *Lohengrin*, 1853 [programme note]	v	iii	Drei Schreiben an die Direktion der Philharmonischen Gesellschaft in St. Petersburg, 1862–6	xvi	—
Zu *Lohengrin*: i, Männerszene und Brautzug; ii, Hochzeitsmusik und Brautlied, 1853 [programme notes]	xvi	—	Vorwort zur Herausgabe der Dichtung des Bühnenfestspiels *Der Ring des Nibelungen*, 1863	vi	iii
Über die programmatischen Erläuterungen zu den Konzerten im Mai 1853, 1853 [prefatory remarks]	xvi	—	Richard Wagner über die ungarische Musik, 1863 [pubd in *Pesther Lloyd* (Budapest), no. 188, and *Niederrheinische Musik-Zeitung*, 29 Aug 1863]	—	—
Glucks Ouvertüre zu *Iphigenia in Aulis*, 1854	v	iii	Das Wiener Hof-Operntheater, 1863	vii	iii
Empfehlung einer Streichquartett-Vereinigung, 1854	xvi	—	Die Meistersinger von Nürnberg: Vorspiel, 1863 [programme note]	xii	—
Beethovens Cis moll-Quartett (Op.131), 1854 [programme note]	xii	—	*Tristan und Isolde*: Vorspiel und Schluss, 1863 [programme note]	xii	—
Dante–Schopenhauer, 1855 [letter to Liszt]	xvi	—	Über Staat und Religion, 1864	viii	iv
Bemerkung zu einer angeblichen Äusserung Rossinis, 1855	xii	—	Zur Erwiderung des Aufsatzes 'Richard Wagner und die öffentliche Meinung' [by O. Redwitz], 1865	xii	—
Über die Leitung einer Mozart-Feier, 1856	xvi	—	Bericht an Seine Majestät den König Ludwig II. von Bayern über eine in München zu errichtende deutsche Musikschule, 1865	viii	iv
Über Franz Liszts Symphonische Dichtungen, 1857 [letter to Marie Sayn-Wittgenstein]	v	iii	Einladung zur ersten Aufführung von *Tristan und Isolde*, 1865 [letter to F. Uhl]	xvi	viii
Metaphysik der Geschlechtsliebe, 1858 [frag. letter to Schopenhauer]	xii	—	Ansprache an das Hoforchester in München vor der Hauptprobe zu *Tristan und*		
Entwurf eines Amnestiegesuches an den Sächsischen					

Title, date	GS, SS	PW
Isolde am Vormittag des 11. Mai 1865, 1865	xvi	—
Mein Leben, 1865 (see 'Autobiographical writings', pp.182–6	xiii–xv	—
Dankschreiben an das Münchener Hoforchester, 1865	xvi	—
Was ist deutsch?, 1865, rev. 1878	x	iv
Ein Artikel der Münchener *Neuesten Nachrichten* vom 29. November 1865, 1865	xvi	—
Preussen und Österreich, 1866	—	—
Zwei Erklärungen im *Berner Bund*, 1866	xvi	—
Deutsche Kunst und deutsche Politik, 1867	viii	iv
Censuren, i: W.H. Riehl: *Neues Novellenbuch*, 1867	viii	iv
Censuren, ii: Ferdinand Hiller: *Aus dem Tonleben unserer Zeit*, 1867	viii	iv
Vorwort zu der Buchausgabe der Aufsätze *Deutsche Kunst und deutsche Politik*, 1868	xvi	—
Zur Widmung der zweiten Auflage von *Oper und Drama*: An Constantin Frantz, 1868	viii	ii
Zum Andante der Es dur-Symphonie von Mozart, 1868 [letter to H. von Bülow]	xvi	—
Meine Erinnerungen an Ludwig Schnorr von Carolsfeld (+1865), 1868	viii	iv
Censuren, iii: Eine Erinnerung an Rossini, 1868	viii	iv
Censuren, v: Aufklärungen über *Das Judentum in der Musik* (An Frau Marie Muchanoff, geborene Gräfin Nesselrode), 1869	viii	iii
Censuren, iv: Eduard Devrient: *Meine Erinnerungen an Felix Mendelssohn-Bartholdy*, 1869	viii	iv
Vier Erklärungen in den *Signalen für die musikalische Welt*, 1869–71 [concerning i, Hans von Bülow; ii, *Rienzi*; iii, Paris; iv, Wagner's letter to Napoleon III]	xvi	—
Fragment eines Aufsatzes über Hector Berlioz, 1869	xii	—
Fünf Schreiben über das Verhältnis der Kunst Richard Wagners zum Auslande, 1869–80 [i, to Judith Gautier (probably written by Cosima); ii, to Champfleury; iii, to ed.		
of *American Review*; iv, to Professor Gabriel Monod; v, to the Duke of Bagnara (written by Cosima)]	xvi	—
Zum *Judentum in der Musik* [letter to Tausig]	xvi	—
Das Münchener Hoftheater: zur Berichtigung, 1869	xii	—
Über das Dirigieren, 1869	viii	iv
Persönliches: warum ich den zahllosen Angriffen auf mich und meine Kunstansichten nichts erwidere, 1869	xii	—
Die Meistersinger von Nürnberg: Vorspiel zum dritten Akt [programme note; Ger. trans. of letter to Judith Gautier], 1869	xii	—
Zur *Walküre*: i, Siegmunds Liebesgesang; ii, Der Ritt der Walküren; iii, Wotans Abschied und Feuerzauber. 1869 [programme notes]	xvi	—
An den Wiener Hofkapellmeister Heinrich Esser, 1870	xvi	—
Draft of response to *Allgemeine Zeitung* (unpubd), 1870	—	—
Beethoven, 1870	ix	v
Ein nicht veröffentlichter Schluss der Schrift *Beethoven*, 1870	—	—
Vorwort zu *Mein Leben*, 1870	—	—
Offener Brief an Dr. phil. Friedrich Stade, 1870	xvi	—
Über die Bestimmung der Oper, 1871	ix	v
Rede anlässlich des Banketts im Hôtel de Rome in Berlin, 1871	—	—
Ansprache an das Orchester in der Singakademie, 1871	—	—
Über die Aufführung des Bühnenfestspieles: *Der Ring des Nibelungen* und Memorandum über Aufführung des *Ring* in markgräflichen Opernhaus Bayreuth, 1871	—	—
Ankündigung der Festspiele, 1871	xvi	—
Aufforderung zur Erwerbung von Patronatsscheinen, 1871	xvi	—
Vorwort zur Gesamtherausgabe, 1871 [foreword to GS], 1871	i	i
Einleitung, 1871 [introduction to vol.i of GS], 1871	i	vii
Das Liebesverbot: Bericht über eine erste Opernaufführung, ?1871 [draws on notes for *Mein Leben* about perf. of 1836]	i	vii

Title, date	GS, SS	PW	Title, date	GS, SS	PW
Einleitung, 1871 [introduction to vol.ii of GS], 1871	ii	vii	über die Oper *Theodor Körner* von Wendelin Weissheimer, 1872	xvi	—
Einleitung zum dritten und vierten Bande, 1871 [introduction to vols iii and iv of GS]	iii	—	An Friedrich Nietzsche, 1872	ix	v
Erinnerungen an Auber, 1871	ix	v	Zwei Berichtigungen im *Musikalischen Wochenblatt*, 1872–3 [i, second report of the Academic Wagner Society, Berlin; ii, Brockhaus Konversationslexikon]	xvi	—
Brief an einen italienischen Freund [Boito] über die Aufführung des *Lohengrin* in Bologna, 1871	ix	v	Über Schauspieler und Sänger, 1872	ix	v
Epilogischer Bericht über die Umstände und Schicksale, welche die Ausführung des Bühnenfestspiels *Der Ring des Nibelungen* bis zur Veröffentlichung der Dichtung desselben begleiteten, 1871	vi	iii	Schreiben an den Bürgermeister von Bologna, 1872	ix	v
			Über die Benennung 'Musikdrama', 1872	ix	v
			Brief über das Schauspielerwesen an einen Schauspieler, 1872	ix	v
Ein später fortgelassener Schluss des Berichtes an den deutschen Wagner-Verein, 1871	xvi	—	Ein Einblick in das heutige deutsche Opernwesen, 1872–3	ix	v
Rede, gehalten in Mannheim am 20. Dezember 1871	—	—	Zwei Reden gehalten anlässlich eines Banketts auf der Brühlschen Terrasse in Dresden am 14. Januar 1873, 1873	—	—
An den Intendanten von Loën in Weimar über die Wagner-Vereine, 1871	xvi	—	Einleitung zu einer Vorlesung der *Götterdämmerung* vor einem ausgewählten Zuhörerkreise in Berlin, 1873	ix	v
Eine Mitteilung an die deutschen Wagner-Vereins, 1871	xvi	—	An den Vorstand des Wagner-Vereins Berlin, 1873	xvi	—
Ankündigung für den 22. Mai 1872, 1872 [laying of foundation stone in Bayreuth]	xvi	—	Zum Vortrag der neunten Symphonie Beethovens, 1873	ix	v
Ankündigung der Aufführung der Neunten Symphonie für den 22. Mai 1872, 1872	xvi	—	Das Bühnenfestspielhaus zu Bayreuth: nebst einem Bericht über die Grundsteinlegung desselben, 1873	ix	v
An die Patrone, 1872	—	—	Schlussbericht über die Umstände und Schicksale, welche die Ausführung des Bühnenfestspieles *Der Ring des Nibelungen* bis zur Gründung von Wagner-Vereinen begleiteten, 1873	ix	v
Zirkular an die Patrone über ihre Anwesenheit bei der Grundsteinlegung, 1872	xvi	—			
Instruction, ?1872	—	—			
Erinnerungen an Spontini, 1872 [preceded by appreciation of 1851]	v	iii	An die Patrone der Bühnenfestspiele in Bayreuth, 1873 [letter of 30 August]	xii	—
Einleitung zum fünften und sechsten Bande, 1872 [introduction to vols v and vi of GS]	v	iii	An die Patrone der Bühnenfestspiele in Bayreuth, 1873 [letter of 15 September]	xvi	—
Censuren: Vorbericht, 1872	viii	iv	Zwei Erklärungen (i, Notgedrungene Erklärung; ii, Die 'Presse' zu den 'Proben'), 1874, 1875	xii	—
Dank an die Bürger von Bayreuth nach der Grundsteinlegung am 22. Mai 1872, 1872	xvi	—	Über eine Opernaufführung in Leipzig: Brief an den Herausgeber des *Musikalischen Wochenblattes*, 1874	x	vi
Bruchstück einer Danksagung, 1872	xvi	—			
Zwei Erklärungen in der Augsburger *Allgemeinen Zeitung*					

Title, date	GS, SS	PW	Title, date	GS, SS	PW
Einladungs-Schreiben an die Sänger für Proben und Aufführungen des Bühnenfestspiels *Der Ring des Nibelungen*, 1875	xvi	—	Programmen der (1.) 6. Konzerte in London, 1877	—	—
An die Orchester-Mitglieder, 1875	xvi	—	Entwurf: veröffentlicht mit den Statuten des Patronatvereines, 1877 [proposal of music school for Bayreuth]	x	vi
Zur *Götterdämmerung*: i, Vorspiel; ii, Hagens Wacht; iii, Siegfrieds Tod; iv, Schluss des letzten Aktes, 1875 [programme notes]	xvi	—	Ansprache an die Abgesandten des Bayreuther Patronats, 1877	xii	vi
Ankündigung der Festspiele für 1876, 1875	xvi	—	Aufforderung zur Anmeldung für die Stilbildungsschule, 1877	—	—
Über Bewerbungen zu den Festspielen, 1875	xvi	—	Ankündigung der Aufführung des *Parsifal*, 1877	xii	vi
An die Künstler, 1875	xvi	—	Zur Einführung (*Bayreuther Blätter*, erstes Stück), 1878	x	vi
Austeilung der Rollen, 1875	—	—	An die geehrten Vorstände der noch bestehenden lokalen Wagner-Vereine, 1878	xvi	—
Voranschlag der 'Entschädigungen', 1876	—	—	Modern, 1878	x	vi
Skizzierung der Proben und Aufführungen 1876, 1876	—	—	Erläuterung des *Siegfried Idylls* für S.M. den König, 1878	—	—
An die Orchestermitglieder (Einladung), 1876	xvi	—	Publikum und Popularität, 1878	x	vi
An die Sänger (Einladung), 1876	xvi	—	Das Publikum in Zeit und Raum, 1878	x	vi
Für die Patrone, 1876	xvi	—	Ein Rückblick auf die Bühnenfestspiele des Jahres 1876, 1878	x	vi
An die Ehrenpatrone, 1876	—	—	Metaphysik. Kunst und Religion. Moral. Christentum [frags.], 1878–82	xii	viii
Verzeichnis der Ehrenpatrone und Freikarten-Empfänger, 1876	—	—	Ein Wort zur Einführung der Arbeit Hans von Wolzogens *Über Verrottung und Errettung der deutschen Sprache*, 1879	x	vi
Circular, die 'Costümproben auf der beleuchteten Bühne' betreffend, 1876	—	—	Wollen wir hoffen?, 1879	x	vi
Anordnung der Proben zu den Aufführungen des Bühnenfestspieles *Der Ring des Nibelungen* in Bayreuth im Jahre 1876, 1876	—	—	Über das Dichten und Komponieren, 1879	x	vi
Über den Gebrauch des Textbuches, 1876	xvi	—	Erklärung an die Mitglieder des Patronatvereines, 1879	x	vi
Über den Hervorruf, 1876	xvi	—	Über das Operndichten und Komponieren im Besonderen, 1879	x	vi
Für das Orchester, 1876	xvi	—	Über die Anwendung der Musik auf das Drama, 1879	x	vi
Letzte Bitte an meine lieben Genossen! Letzter Wunsch, 1876	xvi	—	Offenes Schreiben an Herrn Ernst von Weber, Verfasser der Schrift: *Die Folterkammern der Wissenschaft*, 1879	x	vi
Ansprache nach Schluss der *Götterdämmerung*, 1876 [authenticity uncertain]	xvi	—	Zur Einführung in das Jahr 1880, 1879	x	vi
Abschiedswort an die Künstler, 1876 [authenticity uncertain]	xvi	—	Religion und Kunst, 1880	x	vi
Gedanken über Zahlung des Defizits und Fortführung der Festspiele, 1876	xvi	—	An König Ludwig II. über die Aufführung des *Parsifal*, 1880	xvi	—
An die geehrten Patrone der Bühnenfestspiele von 1876, 1876	xii	—	'Was nützt diese Erkenntnis?': ein Nachtrag zu: *Religion und Kunst*, 1880	x	vi
Entwürfe und Notizen zu den			*Parsifal*: Vorspiel, 1880 [programme note]	xii	viii

Title, date	GS, SS	PW
Zur Mitteilung an die geehrten Patrone der Bühnenfestspiele in Bayreuth, 1880	x	vi
Gedanken zur Fortführung der Festspiele, 1880	—	—
Ausführungen zu *Religion und Kunst*: i, 'Erkenne dich selbst'; ii, Heldentum und Christentum, 1881	x	vi
Zur Einführung der Arbeit des Grafen Gobineau: *Ein Urteil über die jetzige Weltlage*	x	vi
Einladung der Sänger, 1882	—	—
Austeilung der Partien, 1882	—	—
Begleitschreiben zur 'Austeilung' der Partien sowie Plan der Proben und Aufführungen, 1882	—	—
Sketch of rehearsal plan, 1882	—	—
Brief an H. v. Wolzogen, 1882	x	vi
Offenes Schreiben an Herrn Friedrich Schön in Worms, 1882	x	vi
Rede, gehalten in Wahnfried anlässlich der Hochzeit Blandine von Bülows, 1882	—	—
Danksagung an die Bayreuther Bürgerschaft, 1882	xvi	—
Das Bühnenweihfestspiel in Bayreuth 1882, 1882	x	vi
Bericht über die Wiederaufführung eines Jugendwerkes: an den Herausgeber des *Musikalischen Wochenblattes*, 1882	x	vi
Brief an H. v. Stein, 1883	x	vi
Über das Weibliche im Menschlichen [inc.], 1883	xii	vi

Anthologies, other editions

E.L. Burlingame, ed. and trans.: *Art, Life and Theories of Richard Wagner Selected from his Writings* (New York, 1875, 2/1909)

C.F. Glasenapp and H. von Stein: *Wagner-Lexikon: Hauptbegriffe der Kunst- und Weltanschauung Richard Wagners in wörtlichen Anführungen aus seinen Schriften* (Stuttgart, 1883)

C.F. Glasenapp: *Wagner-Encyclopädie: Haupterschein-ungen der Kunst- und Kulturgeschichte im Lichte der Anschauung Richard Wagners* (Leipzig, 1891)

J. Kapp. ed.: *Der junge Wagner: Dichtungen, Aufsätze, Entwürfe 1832–1849* (Berlin, 1910)

W. Golther, ed.: *Richard Wagner: Gesammelte Schriften und Dichtungen in 10 Bänden* (Berlin, 1913) [incl. prefatory life and works, suppl. vol. of notes and commentary]

E. Bücken, ed.: *Richard Wagner: Die Hauptschriften* (Leipzig, 1937, rev., abridged 2/1956 by E. Rappl)

A. Lorenz, ed.: *Richard Wagner: Ausgewählte Schriften und Briefe* (Berlin, 1938)

M. Gregor-Dellin, ed.: *Richard Wagner: Mein Leben* (Munich, 1963, 2/1976; Eng. trans., Cambridge, 1983) [1st authentic edn.]

A. Goldman and E. Sprinchorn, eds.: *Wagner on Music and Drama: a Compendium of Richard Wagner's Prose Works* (New York, 1964) [trans. W.A. Ellis]

C. Dahlhaus, ed.: *Wagners Aesthetik* (Bayreuth, 1972; Eng. trans. 1972)

R. Jacobs and G. Skelton, eds. and trans.: *Wagner Writes from Paris: Stories, Essays and Articles by the Young Composer* (London, 1973)

C. Osborne, ed.: *Richard Wagner: Stories and Essays* (London, 1973) [Eng. trans. W.A. Ellis, rev. Osborne]

D. Mack, ed.: *Ausgewählte Schriften* (Frankfurt am Main, 1974) [with essay by Ernst Bloch]

J. Bergfeld, ed.: *Das braune Buch: Tagebuchaufzeich-nungen 1865–1882* (Zurich, 1975; Eng. trans., London, 1980) [contains frags., sketches, etc. and the Annals (autobiographical notes for 1846–68)]

E. Voss, ed.: *Schriften eines revolutionären Genies* (Munich, 1976)

M. Gregor-Dellin and D. Mack, eds.: *Cosima Wagner: die Tagebücher 1869–1883* (Munich, 1976–7; Eng. trans., London and New York, 1978–80)

E. Voss, ed.: *Schriften: ein Schlüssel zu Leben, Werk und Zeit* (Frankfurt am Main, 1978)

R. Jacobs, ed. and trans.: *Three Wagner Essays* (London, 1979)

G. Strobel and W. Wolf, eds.: *Die rote Brieftasche*, ed. in *Richard Wagner: Sämtliche Briefe*, i (Leipzig, 1979) 81–92 [autobiographical notes for 1813–39]

M. Gregor-Dellin, ed.: *Mein Denken* (Munich, 1982)

D. Borchmeyer, ed.: *Dichtungen und Schriften* (Frankfurt am Main, 1983)

K. Kropfinger, ed. : *Richard Wagner: Oper und Drama* (Stuttgart, 1984)

BARRY MILLINGTON

Section 15
ORCHESTRATION

ORCHESTRATION

WAGNER INHERITED an orchestra scarcely larger than the Classical forces employed by Beethoven, and gradually developed it into a vast sonorous instrument of unparalleled power and flexibility. Richard Strauss (in his 1904 revision of Berlioz's treatise on instrumentation) considered that 'Richard Wagner's scores [. . .] embody the only important progress in the art of instrumentation since Berlioz'; Theodor Adorno (1952) believed that Wagner's subtle handling of orchestral colour was something entirely new: 'there was no art of orchestration before Wagner'. In fact Wagner was an extremely practical musician brought up in a tradition of serviceable if unexciting operatic instrumentation with occasional 'dramatic' touches of colour, derived from Weber and Meyerbeer, as the orchestration of *Der fliegende Holländer* plainly illustrates. But he could see beyond the limitations of each instrument or section of the orchestra and grasp its potential for colour and expression; he was fortunate to be working at a time when rapid advances were being made in both instrumental construction and playing technique, and eagerly seized on each new development, adding some of his own and even inventing new instruments as he perceived the need for them. He utilized the tone colours of his mature orchestral palette in linear polyphony designed to support the singing voice without drowning it; lines are doubled in subtle combinations so that individual instruments do not assert themselves unless for a specific purpose – announcing a leitmotif, delineating a mood or association of ideas, portraying a bird or a dragon.

In the Festspielhaus at Bayreuth, Wagner succeeded in burying the orchestra beneath the stage in the famous covered pit, thus ensuring that the singers would not be overwhelmed, however vast the orchestral sound. But the 'invisible orchestra' was not necessarily the ideal solution to all Wagner's problems of balance and scale; Strauss (1953) felt that it was effective only in *Parsifal*, *Tristan* and the *Ring*, and that in *Die Meistersinger* too much detail was lost. Each of the mature operas inhabits a different sound-world: the rough and ready conventionality of *Rienzi* and the *Holländer* gives way to the featuring of solo instruments in *Tannhäuser* and the subtleties of woodwind scoring in *Lohengrin*, the magnificent variety of resources in the *Ring*, the atmospheric layered polyphony of *Tristan*, the refreshing simplicity of *Die Meistersinger*, and finally the hieratic massiveness of *Parsifal*, whose glowing colours seemed to Debussy 'illuminated as from behind'.

Strings

For Wagner, the orchestral strings constitute a powerful, flexible instrument capable of great subtlety of shading and mood whilst never taking the limelight from the singers (Strauss calls it a 'deep velvet carpet'). Wagner requires a very large body of strings: 16 first violins, 16 seconds, 12 violas, 12 cellos and 8 double basses for the *Ring* – too large for most orchestra pits or opera-house budgets. On the rare occasions when he lets the full strings loose on their own, they can build up a tremendous head of steam, as in the storm at the beginning of *Die Walküre*; conversely, the soft muted strings as Beckmesser sneaks a look at the manuscript of the Prize Song in *Die Meistersinger* convey an uncanny sense of the two-dimensional notes on the page..

More usually, Wagner achieves his results by delicate handling of the repertory of string techniques, as in the accompaniment to the Spinning Chorus in *Der fliegende Holländer*, in which measured tremolandi in the violas are combined with fluttering figures on second violins and pizzicato cellos and basses to convey just the right atmosphere of vacuous busyness; or the brittle, urgent sound of the bowed (or 'broken') measured tremolando in the *Ring* at the Valkyries' 'Hojotoho!' or as Siegfried tastes the dragon's blood. The unmeasured string tremolando, *fortissimo*, makes a striking appearance at Siegmund's 'Wälse! Wälse! Wo ist dein Schwert?' in *Die Walküre*; more unusual effects include bowing *col legno* (with the back of the bow) for Mime's giggles in *Siegfried*, and the tremolo 'am Steg' (*sul ponticello* – on the bridge) as a shiver introducing the clarinet solo before Isolde's appropriate words 'Sorgende Furcht beirrt dein Ohr' ('Anxious fear deceives your ear') near the beginning of Act II of *Tristan*. The hushed sensuous sound of muted strings sets a contrasting mood for the love duet, 'O sink' hernieder', in the following scene.

Wagner's use of massed violins can be uniquely exciting; for the Magic Fire Music in *Die Walküre*, the dense demisemiquaver figuration is actually too fast to be playable by an individual violinist, even assuming the 'concerto' standard of execution Wagner took for granted, but the sound of thirty-two players battling to achieve an approximation – termed by Strauss a 'fresco' technique – results in a dazzling, glittering effect. At Brünnhilde's awakening in *Siegfried*, unison first violins sustain a vast unbroken melodic span, ranging over three and a half octaves, almost entirely unaccompanied for twenty-six bars, conveying exactly the mood of concentration, wonder and discovery in Siegfried's 'Selige Öde auf wonniger Höh'!' A different kind of rapt stillness is evoked by the opening of *Lohengrin*, with four high solo violins hovering above a shimmering background of the remaining violins divided in four parts. Wagner reserves the sound of a single solo violin for special moments of intimacy; Richard Strauss quotes only one instance, accompanying Fricka in *Das Rheingold* 'to unveil the innermost secrets of a woman's heart'.

In the unison violin line in *Siegfried* mentioned above, Wagner appears to set his violinists an impossible task with a series of overlapping slurs over fourteen bars, suggesting the need for a bow several yards long; however, his slurs are not bowing marks but indications of phrasing, and he leaves it to the players (or their leader) to allocate up- and down-bows so that the dovetailed phrases *sound* seamless. He sets the same problem for the chamber players in the *Siegfried Idyll*, with an opening violin phrase of five slow bars in one 'bow'.

Cecil Forsyth (1935) writes: 'With the advent of Wagner the Viola began to be written for as it deserved. [...] His Violas have to play acres of "filling-up" stuff, but their prominence when it comes, is a prominence urgently demanded by the special character of the music.' Forsyth quotes as illustration the soaring chromatic viola solo in *Tristan* as Brangäne produces the love-potion. In Act I of *Siegfried*, the violas seem to mock Mime with the ostinato Forging motif as he tells Wotan the story of Nothung. Divided violas add a particular richness to inner harmony; in Lohengrin's Act III Narration, Wagner uses four-part *divisi* violas in unison with divided first and second violins to add an extra magical glow.

The cello is the soul of the string section, and Wagner makes fine use of its voice in all registers. The opening of Act III of *Die Meistersinger* is an effective use of the cello's moody lower depths. In the *Siegfried Idyll* it sings in its middle register; and surely no other instrument could convey the infinite yearning of the soaring opening phrases of the *Tristan* Prelude, launched into the darkness by cellos in their high register. In Act I of *Die Walküre*, Wagner uses an ensemble of solo cellists, a device perhaps suggested to him by Rossini's *William Tell* Overture.

The double basses are rarely heard as a presence in their own right, mainly confining themselves to providing a solid foundation for the orchestral tutti or supporting the cellos in dark or sombre moods; indeed, the flexibility of Wagner's string writing partly consists of knowing when to leave them out. In the first sixty-five bars of the *Parsifal* Prelude, the basses contribute only two tellingly placed isolated pizzicato notes. It comes as a surprise to realize that Wagner could not take the lowest notes of the bass for granted; the extra fifth string, down to low C, was a rarity (and is far from universal even today), and the extension mechanism for adding the lower notes to the E string was not invented until the turn of the century. In consequence, although Wagner does write down to the low C (in the Act III Procession in *Parsifal*, for instance), he assumes at the beginning of *Das Rheingold* that his basses have only four strings, since he instructs the lower players to tune their 'lowest string' to E♮.

Harps

The great Broadway arranger Robert Russell Bennett (1975) has criticized Wagner's harp writing:

> More fine arrangers have written badly for the harp than for any other instrument – or so they say. Among the most prominent of these are the two great Richards, Wagner and Strauss, who wrote as though harpists played with five fingers on each hand. They don't. The number is four.

However, Strauss (who does cite a harp passage from *Tannhäuser* as being 'practically impossible to execute') records Wagner's realistic approach to the problem when confronted by the harpist August Tombo, who declared his part in *Das Rheingold* to be unplayable:

> Wagner said to the excellent artist, 'You cannot expect me to be able to play the harp; you see what effects I want to achieve; now arrange your part as you like.' (Berlioz/Strauss, 1948)

Wagner uses the harp sparingly but with telling effect; for example, the impact of its entry in Isolde's Liebestod at the end of *Tristan* is the more striking because it has been almost totally silent since the love music of Act II. The most notorious instance is the Rainbow Bridge Music at the end of *Das Rheingold*, for which Wagner requires six harps, each of which has a separate part – occupying so many staves that their parts have to be relegated to an appendix in the score.

Woodwind

Der fliegende Holländer is scored for a 'Classical' woodwind section of pairs of flutes, oboes, clarinets and bassoons, with the addition of a piccolo (and a cor anglais played by the second oboist); Wagner steadily augmented his woodwind, adding permanent third players on third flute or piccolo, cor anglais, bass clarinet and third bassoon (but not double bassoon) for *Tannhäuser* and *Lohengrin*, and further increasing the strength to quadruple woodwind (though only three bassoons) for the *Ring*. He curbed this extravagance for *Tristan* (triple woodwind) and *Die Meistersinger* (double, plus piccolo/third flute), but reverted to mainly quadruple forces for *Parsifal*: three flutes (with the third player momentarily doubling on piccolo), three oboes plus cor anglais, three clarinets and bass clarinet, three bassoons and – at last – a double bassoon.

Strauss (1953) remarks on the soloistic nature of the wind writing in *Tannhäuser*, a score 'partly still imbued with Weber's spirit'. Referring to an 1891 Bayreuth performance, he writes:

> Only a conductor steeped in the poetic content of the drama like Felix Mottl could, assisted by the members of the orchestra, almost conjure up before the eye of the listener in his rendering of the clarinet melody in the overture or the oboe solo passages in the preludes to Act II and III the *very characters* whose fate, as portrayed on the stage, was to compel the sympathy of the listener and to move and elate him profoundly.

Adorno (1952) remains unmoved ('Neither the *Dutchman* nor *Tannhäuser* contains any great instrumental intuitions'), but concurs with Strauss and Liszt in hailing the subtlety of the woodwind writing in *Lohengrin*. Claiming somewhat cryptically that 'The particular place of the woodwinds and woodwind combinations in *Lohengrin* is linked to the poetic idea of the wedding that dictates the style of the entire opera', he proceeds to analyse an eight-bar passage at the beginning of Act I scene 2 in terms of the homogeneity resulting from the woodwind doublings: Wagner's precise choice of unison instruments submerges individual timbres to achieve an overall blend, with smoothly 'cemented' transitions between phrases. Strauss praises the delicate woodwind passage when Elsa appears on the balcony (Act II scene 2); also noteworthy is the start of Act II scene 4, thirty-one bars of triple woodwind in inexhaustible flowing lines, unaccompanied except for occasional support from the horns.

Wagner's use of the flute is restrained, partly to avoid obscuring the soprano voice with a competing tone in the same register. Memorable flute solos occur either for pictorial effect (the fluttering of the flag on Isolde's ship, Act III of *Tristan*) or in purely orchestral passages (in *Lohengrin*, the 'balcony' passage mentioned above; in *Die Meistersinger*, the first appearances of the *ausdrucksvoll* phrase in the Overture, and the staccatissimo figuration just before the curtain falls on an empty stage at the end of Act II; in *Tristan*, the solo in the Prelude to Act II). Despite Wagner's interest in advances in instrument technology, he seems to have preferred the older conical-bored German flute to the louder and more agile cylindrical Boehm flute introduced in 1847. The German flute would have been made of wood, with a metal or ivory head, with twelve or thirteen keys, often descending to the low *b* – a note used in *Lohengrin*, but unavailable on the standard modern Boehm flute.

Unlike the other 'extra' woodwind instruments, the piccolo appears in the earliest scores, a legacy of the crude orchestration Wagner inherited from grand opera. Its use in the sailors' choruses of *Der fliegende Holländer* is chirpy but entirely conventional; however, Wagner's addition of three extra piccolos in their highest register to depict the unearthly wind whistling through the sails of the Dutchman's ship in Act III is a wonderful stroke of sonic imagination. Wagner evidently hoped that he might have at least six extra piccolos at his disposal, since a footnote in the score reads (as translated in the Fürstner edition): 'If more than one piccolo can be got for each of the 3 parts, they should be placed on the stage, near the Dutchman's ship; if however there be only one player to each part, they must sit in the orchestra.' In the later scores, the piccolo is reserved for lighthearted characterizations (the tailors and apprentices in *Die Meistersinger*) or for coloristic effects such as the glittering sparks of the Magic Fire Music in *Die Walküre* (two piccolos).

Wagner uses the oboe in the earlier operas for conventional expressions of pathos, its plaintive tones giving voice both to

Senta's pity for the Dutchman as she shows Erik the portrait in Act II of *Der fliegende Holländer*, and to Erik's own suffering in his Cavatina in Act III. In later works the oboe is featured sparingly but with more sensitivity, notably in *Tristan*, to the delight of Leon Goossens and Edwin Roxburgh (1977):

> Within its pages the oboists and cor anglais players can discover some of the most rapturous music ever composed for the instruments, by a master who had precise ideas about the sounds he desired to hear, but at that time, few players who could muster these qualities.

In contrast, Forsyth (1935) merely remarks: 'In the more significant works of his middle and later life Wagner seems to have used the Oboe less. [. . .] Perhaps he did not like the German Oboe-players.' As with the flute, the preferred instrument would have been the German oboe, thicker, rounder and less flexible in tone than its French counterpart which gained the ascendancy in Germany only after Wagner's death. Goossens would have played *Tristan* on his 'sweet-toned Lorée'.

The cor anglais brings to the oboe section not only added weight but an inescapable air of sadness and longing; hence its prominence in *Tristan*, and its absence from *Die Meistersinger*. In *Parsifal*, its melancholy tone colours the orchestral tutti, even darkening the unison theme of the opening bars of the Prelude. Wagner had an alto oboe specially constructed for use in the *Ring* and *Parsifal*, in place of the cor anglais, which he considered too weak; but the new instrument failed to establish itself permanently.

Wagner's most striking use of the cor anglais is for the 'shepherd's pipe' in Act III of *Tristan*, a mournful unaccompanied offstage solo of more than forty bars (plus several later entries) as Tristan waits longingly for Isolde's ship; Wagner asks that this should be performed by the same 'accomplished artist' who plays the cor anglais in the pit. To herald the arrival of the ship, the 'shepherd' plays a contrastingly merry solo, still labelled *Englisch Horn* although a footnote calls for the effect of 'a powerful natural instrument (like the Alphorn)'; if reinforcement of the cor anglais by oboes and clarinets is insufficient, Wagner suggests that a wooden instrument should be constructed, which because of its simplicity should be 'neither difficult nor expensive'. Hans Richter tried a single-reed Hungarian tarogato, used also at Covent Garden; other expedients include the *tiple* or treble shawm, soprano saxophone, muted trumpet, and the Heckelclarina, an instrument expressly designed for the purpose (though possibly never built) by the bassoon-maker Wilhelm Heckel. Wagner's own suggestion is used at Bayreuth and elsewhere: a straight wooden trumpet with a single valve.

By Wagner's day, the clarinet was already fully developed in range and technique, enabling him to write parts of great brilliance and fluency, right up to the (written) high c'''' – almost as high as the flute. He employs only the clarinets in B♭ and A (according to the prevailing tonality), ignoring the shriller C clarinet; occasionally he adds the higher clarinet in D, in *Tannhäuser* and for the Magic Fire Music and Ride of the Valkyries in *Die Walküre*.

Cecil Forsyth maintains that, in contrast to the oboe ('apparently not one of his favourite instruments'), 'The Clarinets were undoubtedly great favourites with Wagner. He understood them thoroughly.' Quoting two wide-ranging *dolce* solo phrases from Act II of *Die Meistersinger*, as Pogner invites Eva to sit down beside him, Forsyth calls the effect 'a sort of aural-optical suggestion of the little eddies of dust and straw that are whirled up by the wind at a street-corner', though Strauss thinks it represents the song of a blackbird.

Berlioz felt that the clarinet tone had a feminine quality; Wagner confirms this by associating it with Brünnhilde (her exit in Act II of *Die Walküre*, and the entr'acte before Act I scene 3 of *Götterdämmerung* – an extended duet for two clarinets) and with Kundry ('the embodiment of demonic sensuality', according to Strauss).

The bass clarinet had first been heard in Meyerbeer's *Les Huguenots* (1836); Wagner adopted it enthusiastically, realizing that it provided a more sonorous, flexible and discreet bass to the woodwind choir than the bassoons. As a solo instrument its tone is dignified and mournful; Wagner uses it for Elisabeth's Prayer in *Tannhäuser*, and for King Mark's Monologue in Act II of *Tristan*. He writes for bass clarinet in both B♭ and A; the instrument in A is now virtually extinct, necessitating not only awkward transpositions but also an extra key to enable the B♭ instrument to reach the written low E in the *Tristan* solo.

Having largely relieved the bassoons of their traditional function as bass to the woodwind section, Wagner tends to use them as middle-harmony instruments in the tenor register, or as honorary extra 'horns' (as in the Introduction to Act III of *Die Meistersinger*). Their rare solo appearances exploit the bassoons' hollow tone, as in the variants of the Ring motif in thirds associated with Mime in the *Ring*, or parodistically for the hobbling Beckmesser in Act III scene 3 of *Die Meistersinger*.

The *Meistersinger* solo contains a top c''; in the *Tannhäuser* Overture (Dresden version), Wagner recklessly writes up to the high e'', although this is safely covered by string doubling. The bottom note of the standard bassoon is B♭′, but in the *Ring* Wagner writes some low As for the third bassoon, with a footnote that if this note is unavailable it should be supplied by a double bassoon; in *Tristan* he writes down to low A without comment. A bassoon with low A extension was made for Wagner by the woodwind manufacturer Wilhelm Heckel; Wagner was a frequent visitor to Heckel's workshops at Biebrich, eagerly observing the development of the modern German bassoon, which had its antecedents in the efforts of Carl Almenraeder in the 1820s to improve the faulty intonation and weak tone of the eight-keyed classical bassoon by resiting holes and enlarging the bore. Heckel refined the coarse tone of Almenraeder's instrument and added more keywork for increased chromatic agility; the perfected Heckel bassoon was launched at Bayreuth in 1879.

Heckel also developed an efficient *Kontrafagott* or double bassoon, an octave below the bassoon; Wagner felt the need for a solid 'double bass' to the woodwind section, but earlier double bassoons (as used by Handel, Haydn and Beethoven) were inadequate for his purposes. Wagner heard Heckel's double bassoon in October 1879 and included a part for it in *Parsifal*, unusually notating it at sounding pitch rather than an octave higher.

Wagner also suggested to the indefatigable Heckel that he should design a bass oboe, thus providing the woodwind section with complete 'families' of oboes as well as clarinets and bassoons; but Wagner did not live to see the completed 'Heckelphone', which made its début in Strauss's *Salome* in 1905.

Horns

According to Richard Strauss:

> The introduction and improvement of the valve horn has undoubtedly inaugurated the greatest advance in the technique of the modern orchestra since Berlioz. To demonstrate the truly protean nature of this instrument I should have to go through the scores of the great magician bar after bar, beginning with *Rheingold*. (Berlioz/Strauss, 1948)

Berlioz knew of the existence of valve horns, but the first composer to utilize them was Halévy, who wrote for a pair of valve horns alongside a pair of natural horns in *La Juive* (1835), an example quickly followed by Wagner for *Rienzi* (1834–40), as also by Schumann in *Genoveva* (1847–9). Wagner's principal horn at the Dresden Opera was Josef-Rudolf Lewy, younger of two famous brothers who were pioneers of the valve horn in the 1820s; the elder brother Eduard-Constantin is thought to have played the notorious fourth horn part in an early first performance of Beethoven's Ninth Symphony, and Schubert wrote the chromatic obbligato horn part to the song *Auf dem Ström* for Josef-Rudolf in 1828. Wagner continued to write for pairs of natural horns (*Waldhörner*) and valve horns (*Ventilhörner*) in *Der fliegende Holländer* and *Tannhäuser*; *Lohengrin* uses four valve horns, confusingly notated as if they were natural horns. A 'real' natural horn would need a gap of several bars to remove one length of tubing and insert a longer or shorter one to play natural harmonics in a lower or higher key; in *Lohengrin*, Wagner may leave only a crotchet or so for the horns to change, for example, from playing 'in D' to 'in G' and then 'in E', suggesting that he was thinking of the valve horn as a natural horn with an instantaneous ability to change crooks. Wagner was also aware of the difference in tone between 'open' notes (natural harmonics) and hand-stopped notes, as well as between crooks of different lengths; even as late as 1865 he felt it necessary to append a note to the score of *Tristan*:

> The composer desires to draw special attention to the treatment of the horns. This instrument has undoubtedly gained so greatly by the

introduction of valves as to render it difficult to disregard this extension of its scope, although the horn has thereby indisputably lost some of its beauty of tone and power of producing a smooth legato. On account of these grave defects, the composer (who attaches importance to the retention of the horn's true characteristics) would have felt himself compelled to renounce the use of the valve-horn, if experience had not taught him that capable artists can, by specially careful management, render them almost unnoticeable[. . .]. Pending the inevitable improvement in the valve-horn that is to be desired, the horn-players are strongly recommended most carefully to study their respective parts in this score, in order to ascertain the crooks and valves appropriate to all the requirements of its execution. [. . .] (trans. W.F.H. Blandford, quoted in Morley-Pegge, 1973)

This advice would have been superfluous to Wagner's principal horn in Munich, Franz Strauss, who played in the premieres of both *Tristan* and *Die Meistersinger* and whose technique and tone were unsurpassable, although according to his son Richard Strauss (1953) there was no love lost between composer and performer:

Wagner once went past the horn player, who was sitting in his place in moody silence, and said, 'Always gloomy, these horn players', whereupon my father replied: 'We have good reason to be'.[. . .] Wagner [once paid him] the compliment of saying: 'Strauss is an unbearable fellow, but when he plays his horn, one cannot be cross with him.'

Wagner's most characteristic horn writing is close to the spirit of the natural horn; fanfare motifs abound, as for Freia's golden apples in *Das Rheingold*, a horn duet entirely playable on natural horns. Erik's Dream in *Der fliegende Holländer* is heralded by a fanfare in which the two natural horns are joined by a valve horn playing open notes until a diminished seventh chord requires the use of the valves. Even the thirty-nine bars of Siegfried's Horn Call contain only one note which would be totally unplayable on a natural horn, and one phrase (the Hero motif) which would require hand-stopping.

The four horns of the early operas are augmented to eight in the *Ring*, an extravagance immediately justified in the opening bars of *Das Rheingold*, as each of the eight horns in turn rises in a slow arpeggio from the depths of the Rhine; in Act III of *Siegfried*, Wagner can use four horns in harmony for the Fire motif while the other four play Siegfried's horn call in unison. *Tristan*, like *Tannhäuser*, calls for six horns offstage ('more if possible') as well as the four in the pit. The *Siegfried Idyll* uses only two, involving the hapless second player in notoriously long held notes (seventeen bars without a breath).

The muting of horns was an effect known to Beethoven and Weber but fully exploited only by Wagner. Single notes would be hand-stopped (*gestopft*), as in the chilling chords (with bassoons supplying the minor third) in Act III of *Der fliegende Holländer* as the Dutchman's ghostly crewmen fail to respond to the shouts of Daland's sailors; longer passages require a cardboard or fibre mute inserted into the bell of the instrument, as for the unforgettably spooky Tarnhelm motif on six muted horns in *Das Rheingold*.

'Wagner tubas'

As part of his expansion of tonal resources in the *Ring*, Wagner calls for a quartet of additional instruments, usually referred to as 'Wagner tubas' but marked in the score only as *Tenortuben* and *Basstuben*: they are played by the second quartet of horn players (V to VIII), using horn mouthpieces. Various experimental varieties of middle-register brass instruments already existed, made by Cerveny, Sax, Mahillon, Distin and others; in his quest for a new voice to give weight to the brass, Wagner was exploratory but hardly revolutionary. He had been impressed by Adolphe Sax's instruments – presumably saxhorns – which he had seen in Paris in 1853, and it was only when he was unable to procure either these or a suitable substitute that he 'invented' the new instruments. Exactly what was used for the Munich premiere of *Das Rheingold* in 1869 is uncertain; Wagner later asked Hans Richter, himself a horn player, to commission a German maker (probably Moritz of Berlin) to supply a set of tubas for the Bayreuth premiere in 1875.

The tenor tubas are pitched in F, the bass tubas in B♭, although in *Die Walküre* and *Siegfried* Wagner notates them, in the score but not the parts, in B♭ and E♭ respectively, 'because the composer believed this way easier to read'. In the Prologue to *Götterdämmerung* he tries yet another notation, in F and B♭ but an octave higher, all in the treble clef, before reverting to the *Walküre/Siegfried* format: 'An unholy muddle', as Forsyth comments.

The distinctive, portentous sound of the four tubas is first heard in *Das Rheingold* as Woglinde tells Alberich of the need to forswear love to obtain the gold. Wagner uses them, with the contrabass trombone and orchestral tuba, as a sonorous chorale representing Valhalla; they are also prominent at the close of Act II of *Die Walküre*, where Strauss describes their 'hoarse and rancorous tone' as symbolizing 'the swelling vein of fury on Wotan's forehead'.

Trumpets, trombones, bass tuba

For the *Ring*, Wagner enlarged the size and range of his brass section, not simply for sheer power but to enable him to utilize the distinct colours of families of instruments (horns, tubas, trumpets, trombones). He is remarkably restrained in his writing for the brass tutti, reserving its full majesty only for orchestral declamations (as in the Overture to *Rienzi* and the Prelude to *Parsifal*) or climaxes such as the end of *Das Rheingold* or *Die Meistersinger*, otherwise being content to keep the players silent for long stretches except for significant solo utterances of leitmotifs or gentle chordal touches to underpin an atmosphere or characterization. He generally avoids using trumpets and trombones alone to support voices, although they convey an appropriate sense of raw animality for Hagen's

'Starke Stiere sollt' ihr schlachten' in Act II scene 3 of *Götterdämmerung*.

Wagner uses three trumpets in his mature works (only two in *Der fliegende Holländer*, but an improbable six in the early *Columbus* Overture of 1835); after *Rienzi* these would have been fully chromatic valve trumpets, although in *Lohengrin* Wagner has the same notational quirk as for the horns, writing as if for natural trumpets with instantaneous crook-changes. The standard instrument would have been the 'long' trumpet in F or E♭, but in *Parsifal* Wagner writes a solo marked *sehr zart* up to written g″, sounding c‴, a hazardous twelfth harmonic on the F trumpet, which suggests that his players were already using the smaller modern B♭ or C trumpet. In the *Meistersinger* Overture, Wagner writes for first and second trumpets in F, plus a part for third trumpet in C which is almost entirely on open notes, perhaps as a deliberate archaism.

As with the horns, Wagner writes traditionally conceived parts for the trumpets, using them to announce the many triadic motifs in the *Ring*, such as the Gold and the Sword, as well as for rhetorical touches like the triplet figures accompanying the Valhalla theme or the many fanfares and fanfare-like phrases in *Lohengrin* and *Die Meistersinger*. The entry of the single trumpet in the *Siegfried Idyll*, for which Hans Richter had to learn the instrument specially, is no less characteristic.

Speaking of the use of mutes for the trumpets, Forsyth asserts that 'it was Richard Wagner who first found this particular brand of tone-colour where it was lying in the dust of the cellar, and brought it upstairs to stimulate the jaded palates of the musical world. The vinegary "tang" of this vintage is well suited to both Mime and Beckmesser.' In Act III of *Die Meistersinger* Wagner asks for muted trumpets to convey 'bei starkem Anblasen' ('by blowing hard') the humorous sound of children's toy trumpets.

Another of Wagner's innovations for the *Ring* was the bass trumpet, although as with the tubas there were existing precedents in military bands. Wagner's initial proposal was for an instrument pitched an octave below the long E♭ trumpet; this would have been a vast and unwieldy creation, larger than a bass trombone, and Wagner settled for a smaller but still majestic instrument crooked in C, D or E♭, built for him by Moritz. Wagner gives the bass trumpet appropriately portentous triadic motifs, most notably as Siegmund prepares to draw the sword from the tree in Act I of *Die Walküre*.

The sound of trombones in Wagner calls to mind such heroic unison tunes as the Prelude to Act III of *Lohengrin* or the Ride of the Valkyries, but these moments are rare. Equally characteristic is the menacing voice of trombones singly or in unison announcing the (non-triadic) Curse motif in the *Ring*. Wagner was concerned to achieve a full but noble tone in the trombone section, capable of soft radiance as well as power; for homogeneity and range, he asks for the 'so-called tenor-bass trombone' for the upper instruments (not the narrow-bored alto on top) with a 'genuine bass trombone' on the third part. For the *Ring*, however, he requires three tenor-bass instruments plus yet another 'new invention', the contrabass trombone, to complete the family. Deep trombones, too, already existed in military bands; Wagner's contrabass is pitched an octave below the tenor, with doubled tubing for the slide so that the extensions remain within the player's reach. Its effect is unforgettable, whether providing a full-throated bass to the Valhalla motif at the end of *Das Rheingold* or marching inexorably down the Spear motif for over two octaves, all the way down to '16-foot' E'.

In *Rienzi*, Wagner had followed convention in using the rawtoned and now obsolete ophicleide as the bass to his brass section; he later turned to the bass tuba, but soon felt that its tone was not satisfactory as a bass to the trombones – hence his adoption of the contrabass trombone in the *Ring*, in which he prefers to use the deep contrabass tuba as a bass to the horns and Wagner tubas. The tuba is occasionally heard as a noble solo voice, as at the opening of the *Faust* Overture; for the dragon Fafner in *Siegfried*, the contrabass tuba plays in octaves with a 'normal bass tuba' in C, apparently played by the fourth Wagner tuba player. In the *Meistersinger* Overture, the bass tuba carries an important line independently of the trombones – complete with famous trill.

Timpani and percussion

Wagner is obliged to write quite conventionally for timpani, as the 'machine drum' with tuning by pedal or a single screw handle was not developed until the turn of the century; to change the pitch of the drum involved retensioning several individual screws around the rim of the drumhead by hand. Wagner could not even expect his player to have more than two drums, although he advises three for *Tristan*; in *Parsifal*, the *Ring* and the Venusberg Music of *Tannhäuser* he writes for two players on two pairs of timpani, largely to provide different tunings. Nevertheless, Wagner's writing for timpani is always atmospheric, whether in the pomp of the *Meistersinger* Overture, the expectant roll which opens Act II of *Lohengrin*, or the sinister single drum taps (described by Strauss as 'an anxious pulse beat') in Siegmund's Monologue and the Annunciation of Death in *Die Walküre*. At the beginning of Act II of *Siegfried*, the two drums are tuned a tritone apart, a sinister effect borrowed from the Introduction to Act II of Beethoven's *Fidelio*.

Wagner's use of tuned orchestral percussion is limited almost entirely to the bright metallic ring of the glockenspiel in the Forest Murmurs in *Siegfried* and the Dance of the Apprentices in *Die Meistersinger*. He employs untuned percussion equally sparingly, dispensing with the conventional operatic bass drum and cymbals even in *Der fliegende Holländer*, which calls only for a few well-placed strokes on the gong; *Tristan* requires only cymbals and triangle. The castanets in the *Tannhäuser* Bacchanal produce an untypically vulgar, if appropriate, effect. In the *Ring*, Wagner's percussion colours include the tenor drum in the Ride of the Valkyries; a *pianissimo* roll with timpani sticks on suspended cymbal in *Das Rheingold* to symbolize the glitter of the gold; and – Strauss's favourite example of 'the wise application of the triangle' – a single triangle stroke at the end of Act II of *Siegfried*.

'Special effects'

This heading covers the numerous onstage and offstage instruments called for by Wagner for dramatic purposes, such as the 'echo' horns in *Der fliegende Holländer*, the thirteen-piece offstage orchestra of woodwind, horns and harp in the Venusberg Music of *Tannhäuser*, stage trumpets in *Lohengrin*, Beckmesser's lute in *Die Meistersinger*, and the one-note 'cow horns' (*Stierhörner*) in *Die Walküre*, *Götterdämmerung* and *Die Meistersinger*. In *Das Rheingold* (1853 – the same year as Verdi's Anvil Chorus in *Il Trovatore*), Wagner represents the labours of the Nibelungs by no fewer than eighteen anvils, carefully notated in three groups at different pitches and in different rhythms. Less problematic 'noisemakers' include the wind machine in *Der fliegende Holländer* and the thunder machine for Klingsor's collapsing castle in *Parsifal*.

The four deep bells (C, G, A, E) for the Grail Ceremony scenes in *Parsifal* pose a major problem. Conventional tubular bells are too high in pitch; real church bells would be too large and heavy to install. Barry Millington (1984) reproduces a photograph of the 'bells' used at the premiere, looking like vast beer-barrels on gun carriages; according to Forsyth (1935), Felix Mottl devised a machine of 'somewhat startling' appearance – 'as if an amateur carpenter had been trying to convert a billiard-table into a grand piano' – which struck six pianoforte strings for each note, but was not loud enough and had to be reinforced by five gongs and a bass tuba. Other expedients have included a piano playing in tritones, extra large tubular bells (played from the top of a ladder), and suspended brass plates; modern theatres sometimes use a synthesizer. Nothing sounds quite right.

Wagner's orchestra

The vast and varied orchestral resources developed by Wagner in the service of the drama have created a magnificent and flexible instrument for composers of later generations; the full orchestra of Bruckner, Mahler, Strauss, Schoenberg and Berg as well as Debussy, Ravel, Stravinsky, Messiaen and Tippett is basically Wagner's orchestra. Wagner's 'new' instruments have survived outside Bayreuth. Bruckner, Strauss and Schoenberg use the quartet of Wagner tubas; the bass trumpet reappears in Strauss's *Macbeth* and *Elektra* (which also uses the contrabass trombone) and Stravinsky's *The Rite of Spring*. Wagner's legacy also includes the Heckelphone, which he 'invented' but did not live to see or hear.

Later composers have not always followed Wagner's example

of acute sonic imagination and economy of resources. Strauss (Berlioz/Strauss, 1948) recommends that the student of orchestration

> should compare Wagner's eleven scores with each other. Let him observe how each of these works has its own combination of instruments, its own orchestral style; how each says what it wants to say in the simplest possible way, and how this noble moderation in the use of means is to be found in all of them.

JONATHAN BURTON

Section 16

PERFORMANCE PRACTICE

The orchestra   350
Conducting   352
Singing   354
Wagner and the early music movement   358

PERFORMANCE PRACTICE

FOR NO COMPOSER of the 19th century is the concept of 'authentic' performance practice more problematical than it is in the case of Wagner. To be sure, the performances – and attitudes toward performance – to which Wagner and his contemporaries were accustomed differed considerably from those we encounter today, and many of those differences can be discovered or inferred from surviving evidence. On the other hand, Wagner was thoroughly dissatisfied with many features of the performing style of his day and was one of the leading agitators for its reform; certainly when he supervised or took part in performances he did his best to transform the habits of the participants so that their contributions might demonstrate the persuasiveness of conviction and under-standing of the work at hand rather than reliance on a mode of performance characterized by predictability or routine. (Of course, such an attitude itself implies certain stylistic characteris-tics.) To this hybrid style, consisting of an uneasy relationship between conditions which Wagner could take for granted and those which could be wrung from performers in his lifetime only by great effort on a case-by-case basis, there must also be added an assessment of the actual achievement of the best Wagner perfor-mances of the composer's own day, which were usually the 'model' presentations on which he exerted a supervisory influence. Altogether, these vantage-points and other considerations suggest that any attempt to recreate the performing style of Wagner's day in our own may be even less advisable than it is possible, and that Wagner's chief aim was for performances of his works to create effects and address larger aesthetic issues that transcend any narrow definition of correct style. Nevertheless, a close examin-ation of conditions and practices prevailing in Wagner's day and the ways in which he attempted to alter those assumptions can provide insight into the way in which style in his day affected the perception of his works.

IN WAGNER'S YOUTH and early career as a conductor and composer the art of musical performance in Germany was in a dismal state. Orchestras were usually small, their numbers overworked, under-rehearsed, underpaid, and not always in a condition to give of their best. It is not surprising that Wagner was dissatisfied with this state of affairs. Nevertheless, this was the environment in which he grew up and developed his enthusiasm for music and drama, and so it is equally unsurprising that he retained an enthusiasm for certain

The orchestra

elements of these surroundings. In particular, where the orchestra was concerned, he found the tonal qualities of some instruments – especially the winds and brass – preferable before they developed over the course of the century. In some cases he objected to the greater power they later attained; for example, he especially disliked the 'cannons' into which flutes evolved. In the case of horns – which originally changed tuning by means of manually replaced crooks of different lengths but, with the introduction of valves, were able to reach all the notes of the chromatic scale more easily – Wagner stated in his preface to the score of *Tristan und Isolde* that the nobility of tone and smooth legato of which the earlier instrument was more capable should be emulated on the valved instrument. The vast 'improvement' of most instruments during Wagner's lifetime, in short, did not meet with his consistent approval, even though his works were among those which necessitated some of those changes. (Incidentally, metal strings were generally adopted only well after Wagner's death.)

Wagner's ideal orchestra was much larger than that standard in his youth. This expansion was due not only to the need for more strings to maintain a proper balance with wind and brass instruments which had gained in power, but also to the fact that in his search for more refined shades for his timbral palette Wagner made new instruments permanent members of the orchestra. After writing prominent solos for cor anglais and bass clarinet in *Tannhäuser*, he made these instruments and the piccolo part of the triple woodwind of *Lohengrin*, and finally of the quadruple woodwind in the *Ring*. Brass instruments too became more numerous in his scores; the introduction of a quartet of so-called 'Wagner tubas' to be played when called for by the fifth to eighth horn players as well as a bass trumpet and a fourth trombone in the *Ring* suggests the size to which Wagner's scoring extended, although *Parsifal* represented a retrenchment to smaller forces, and *Tristan* and *Meistersinger* are content with only pairs of some woodwinds. Ironically, this sheer volume of sound forced Wagner himself to propose and have constructed more powerful versions of some instruments (for example, in the mid-1870s Wagner sponsored the development of an alto oboe which boasted more power and projection than the cor anglais of the day, and proposed that this new instrument should be used in place of the cor anglais in all his scores – a suggestion which was almost universally ignored), and his correspondingly large string section – sixteen first violins, sixteen second violins, twelve violas, twelve cellos and eight basses – was intended to give a proper balance to this operatically unprecedented contingent of winds and brass.

Such extravagant scoring threatened the audibility of singers, and Wagner was led to search for a new solution to the balance between singers and orchestra. His idealistic enthusiasm for rendering the orchestra invisible had its practical side as well: covering the orchestra decreased its volume, and consequently those theatres which adopted this arrangement, namely the

Festspielhaus at Bayreuth and later the Prinzregententheater in Munich, were considered ideal Wagner theatres in part because difficulties of balance were considerably ameliorated.

The style according to which instruments were played represents another area in which 19th-century performances differed from those we hear today. It must be suggested that Wagner's influence on modern conceptions of orchestral sound – not just orchestral scoring – has been profound; but it was in an effort to achieve his new ideal of sostenuto string playing – full bows and seamless sound – that later accretions such as a free and frequent use of portamento (by now long since abandoned) and continuous vibrato were introduced into his scores and into orchestral playing generally. That continuous vibrato was not always used in string playing emerges clearly from the first phrase of the veteran Joseph Joachim's 1903 recording of Brahms's Hungarian Dance in G minor. Unlike later performances in which vibrato is used liberally to intensify the pathos and character of the passage and thereby causes the non-vibrato quality of the final g – which can only be attained by an open string – to leap out of context, Joachim's style of playing features no such disjunction of tonal quality. In fact, most 19th-century writers viewed vibrato as a special effect to be used sparingly. Portamento, it has been argued, was more liberally applied several decades after Wagner's death than it was during his lifetime. Although this seems likely, these later excesses can be attributed at least in part to an attempt to cope with Wagner's emphasis on sostenuto playing without the availability of his guidance in determining appropriate limits.

Conducting

WAGNER'S PRIMARY CONTRIBUTION to the art of interpretation had to do with his conception of the role of the conductor. In the operatic performances of Wagner's youth the singer might achieve an inspiring dramatic portrayal of a given role, but the context in which the portrayal took place was usually sadly unfocused. This state of affairs is made tangible to modern sensibilities by the fact that the conductor was placed between the stage and the pit, and was required to turn to either one group of the performers or the other to obtain their special attention – and in any case he relied on the leader (concertmaster) for securing ensemble in the orchestra. In the absence of an overriding conception of the work among performers, and given that it was through the performances of leading singers that successful operatic performances were achieved, it was a stylized conception of roles, dramatic situations and musical functions which enabled operatic performance to take place with any efficiency.

Wagner's testimony concerning the standard style of orchestral performances in his youth and early career must be understood as a less than sympathetic view of the status quo rather than as an accurate stylistic description. Nevertheless, his perception of the change wrought by his own approach to orchestral and operatic performance has unavoidably characterized the prevailing style at the time of his advent as tending towards uniform, comfortably quick tempi (the better to cover up flaws of orchestral execution partly attributable to inadequate rehearsal) and a constricted dynamic range devoid of extremes. The style which Wagner himself espoused, both as a conductor and as a writer, notably in *Über das Dirigieren* (*On Conducting*), placed a greater value on overt expressiveness than this prevailing style allowed, and was consequently much more heavily inflected in both pacing and dynamics. In this respect Wagner caused orchestral performance to emulate the more flexible techniques of expression associated with the new breed of Romantic instrumental virtuosi. Not surprisingly, those who used the old style as a yardstick against which to evaluate Wagner's performances regarded them as eccentric or even misguided.

It seems clear that Wagner's conducting technique differed from that which characterized virtuoso conductors who emerged in response to the new paths his example suggested – how else can his thrice unsuccessful attempt to launch the *Fliegender Holländer* Overture during his 1877 London visit (Klein, 1903) be explained? Instead, the performing conditions with which he was acquainted in his early years caused him to rely on the leader (concertmaster) to secure ensemble while he, the conductor, suggested the expression. Even in his best days it seems clear that, especially when he could not obtain adequate rehearsal time, ragged ensemble sometimes plagued his performances. For many listeners, however, Wagner's conducting provided unprecedented clarification of the expressive or dramatic content of the works he directed. By the time his conducting enjoyed its greatest renown, it was heard primarily in his own works, and consequently Wagner's conducting style came to be regarded as an integral part of his dramatic conception.

The increased dynamic range over which Wagner's performances played soon came to be a standard technique of virtuoso conductors and orchestras and is a linchpin of modern performance style. Far more controversial – and long extinct – is the kind of tempo modification which Wagner adopted in practice and encouraged in his writings. Wagner insisted that each theme contains a specific expressive quality which implies its own tempo, and consequently his performances shunned the regular beat which characterized orchestral performance of his youth and which today has become still more rigid. Wagner's preferred means of bridging the gap between a quick prevailing tempo and the slower pace which encased a lyrical theme seems to have been that of introducing a substantial ritardando before establishing the new tempo. Evidence concerning his tactic for moving in the other direction is less conclusive, but a systematic, incremental, gradual increase in speed over a long span of time seems unlikely for a performer so preoccupied with the immediate melodic quality of the music he led.

One is tempted to imagine that Wagner's performances exhibited qualities not unlike some with which we are familiar. Certainly the celebrated tempo modifications of Wilhelm Furtwängler appeal to many as a manifestation of Wagner's influence. Insofar as Wagner's style can be reconstructed from evidence, however, it must be argued that in his own music, at any rate, the level on which Wagner's manipulations of tempo operated was much more detailed than anything Furtwängler attempted. One of the most revealing documents of Wagner's conducting style in his own music is Richard Strauss's 1928 recording of the *Tristan* Prelude. Willi Schuh has found documentary evidence (Schuh, 1982) in which Strauss confirms that he learned his conception of this work from his erstwhile mentor Hans von Bülow, who not only conducted the first performances of the Prelude itself and of the complete opera, but was thoroughly familiar with Wagner's own conducting style and can be shown to have embodied it in many important respects in the 'model' Wagner performances at Munich in the 1860s. What Strauss's performance enshrines is a style of conducting in which the varied tempi which Wagner urged for symphonic works are applied to brief motifs even when densely intertwined melodic fragments would seem to preclude such an approach. In Strauss's performance of the *Tristan* Prelude – a passage which today is understood as a grand symphonic sweep describing a single arc – the drastic hairpin of acceleration and deceleration for the 'Glance' motif in bars 17–22 is astonishingly detail-oriented. Even more illuminating is the series of abrupt shifts between two plateaus of tempo in bars 63–73, so that the numerous statements of the ascending chromatic motif first introduced in bar 2 serve as solemn foils to the exulting upward runs that urge the Prelude towards its climax. This performance is so unlike Strauss's otherwise streamlined approach to the conducting of both Wagner and other composers that one can be forgiven for suspecting that the conception does indeed stem at least from Bülow, and probably from Wagner. The magnetic power that Wagner exerted over orchestras becomes comprehensible from such an example: when the expressive *topos* of each moment may differ from the one that came before through the application of this gestural style, attention and emotional involvement become necessary components of the orchestral musician's role.

Singing

WAGNER DESCRIBES IN *Mein Leben* how a singer, Wilhelmine Schröder-Devrient, provided him with a formative theatrical experience (see 'Myths and Legends', p.133). Though his intuitive genius for drama drove him to create works which have an endless fascination and innumerable facets, it can be argued that on a fundamental level the impetus for bringing them into being was an attempt to recreate in permanent form the kind of overwhelming dramatic experience that Wagner himself had received from

Schröder-Devrient's artistry. And because he portrayed the performance of a singer as the vehicle for his own dramatic epiphany, Wagner always maintained that the intended effect of his work could be most directly realized by an overpowering dramatic impersonation of the leading roles. What he considered to be such a performance can be described to a certain extent. But 'performance practice' becomes an extremely problematical notion in any attempt to codify ways in which such an effect could be achieved. After all, Wagner made every attempt to obtain performances like those he imagined from the singers with whom he worked, and yet was unable to elicit on a regular basis the effect he desired. That effect still eludes simple technical definition, since achieving it has little to do with the external trappings of style; rather, Wagner's aim is attained when singers discover a mode of utterance which can absorb and subsume even the densest and most expressive musical fabric into heightened verbal expression. 'R. complains about how insensitive the singers are to all there is in [the Parsifal/Kundry scene in *Parsifal*, Act II], and he thinks of Schröder-Devr., how she would have uttered the words "So war es mein Kuss, der hellsichtig dich machte." Now the music has to do it all', writes Cosima in her diary (CT, 9 Jul 1882). Only in the case of Ludwig Schnorr von Carolsfeld did Wagner encounter a singer whose performance of his own roles moved him to more than the kind of praise that is common coin in theatrical circles. Given that Wagner himself was unable to find and develop the kind of singing and dramatic acting that he envisioned, 'performance practice' in this case cannot focus on recreating a style that actually existed but rather on attempting to define a style that Wagner only imagined.

The differences between the singing Wagner knew and that which we hear today are nevertheless considerable. In his day, the best singing was far from straight-toned: it possessed a sympathetic vibration that helped projection of the voice and provided it with tonal allure. But it must be emphasized that the continuous heavy vibrato – or, technically speaking, tremolo – which has long been an automatic element in present-day operatic singing was entirely foreign to the singing Wagner knew. One can only speculate as to how he would have reacted to it, but since he called for vibrato in certain moments which are either highly charged or, by contrast, opportunities for caricature, it seems that he thought of vibrato as a special effect not to be used indiscriminately. Further, since the motivation for continuous vibrato is a preconceived notion of strictly musical beauty, and since in practice it inhibits dramatic abandon and a suitably vivacious pronunciation of the text, Wagner's displeasure would no doubt be considerable. At the very least, it can be voluminously demonstrated that well-trained singers of Wagner's time employed a style which did not incorporate the tonal ideal that is mandated by a large, regular vibrato.

The extent to which Wagner desired the use of vocal portamento is a vexed question. First, the sign he used for indicating its use – a slur – is imprecise because it can be used to indicate so many things: which notes in a melismatic passage are to be sung on a certain syllable, which notes should be phrased together in one breath (or an illusion thereof), and so on. Second, portamento itself embraces a number of different effects – the smooth legato connecting a phrase which describes a rising or descending line marks one aspect of the term, while the long glissando which connects two pitches between which there is a large interval represents another. But hesitancy to apply the effect because of such uncertainty – some singers have been reluctant to employ the glissando for fear of being thought tasteless – should be overcome in certain instances. Any pair of notes slurred together in which the second is set to a new word or syllable is a clear request for portamento ('ich hört' *ihn fern* hin hallen' from the first paragraph of Elsa's Dream in *Lohengrin*, Act I, is a fine example). And certain passages in which slurs might be – and sometimes are – rationalized away as a mere text-setting convention are clearly to be sung as portamenti (the octave leaps in Brünnhilde's Battle Cry, or 'Seine Raben beide sandt' er auf *Reise*' in Waltraute's Narration). Considerations peculiar to each situation ought to be employed in an attempt to justify the use of portamento. In the Battle Cry, for instance, the fact that portamento is required between the first two syllables of 'Hojo-toho!' establishes a characteristic quality of freedom which is breached by a clean jump from one note to the other on the last syllable, while in Waltraute's words the slow tempo, the precarious quality of the interval, the meaning of the word in which the slur appears, and the fact that the previous leap of the same interval (between the two syllables of 'Raben') does not ask for such an effect conspire to suggest that Wagner desired a portamento at this point. In general, large upward leaps so slurred ask for portamento of the glissando type, culminating in a brief anticipation of the second pitch. But in any case, reserving portamento for slurs expressly connecting two notes can aid the singer in realizing the expressive syntax in Wagner's vocal writing.

Other markings too bring that syntax into clearer focus – accents, for example, are used at points where a special clarity of verbal enunciation is appropriate. Up to *Lohengrin* Wagner's vocal lines are increasingly adorned with articulations, dynamic markings and other musical symbols suggesting how to shape words, lines and phrases; thereafter a rather more plain notational style becomes the norm. This change in notational strategy should not be construed to suggest that the vocal parts of Wagner's later works are to be inflected with less detail, but rather that the act of projecting the text in conjunction with the musical line will result in a richness of such inflections that could not be achieved with musical symbols.

It is unfortunate that the term 'singer' is the one generally adopted to designate the person who appears on stage in Wagner's works. 'Singer' often connotes a performer who is responsible first and foremost for producing an aesthetically pleasing musical sound, and in whom any departure from an abstract ideal of beautiful vocalism is to be censured. Wagner's momentous encounter with Schröder-Devrient, however, found him enthusing over a 'singer' whose 'singing' was denigrated by those who were qualified to judge that endeavour as defined narrowly. The English critic Henry F. Chorley, for example, did not scruple to call her a 'nature-singer', by which one is led to understand that she had not developed the technique of cultivating careful breathing and sustaining a beautiful line of tone. Those who insist that Wagner valued beautiful singing – and then interpret beautiful singing to mean singing as practised by the great international (i.e., non-German) stars around the turn of the century – read Wagner's writings out of context. Indeed, the record of his enthusiasms causes one to wonder whether the art of 'singing' was one for which Wagner had much use. Of the singers who were especially associated with him in major roles, indeed, only Joseph Tichatschek, his leading tenor at Dresden, seems to have been consistently able to emit an unbroken stream of sound in a way that might have found the approval of a connoisseur of fine singing. Many of the other singers with whom Wagner worked and to whom he entrusted his major roles were typical of German singers of the time – they were poorly trained and possessed unsophisticated techniques.

Although he wrote appreciatively of singing that cultivated beautiful tone, Wagner's primary concern in his vocal writing was to develop a vehicle for flexibility and conviction of utterance that simulated heightened speech. In order to achieve this effect, however, the singers of his day needed to overcome their habit of partitioning the music they sang into either recitatives or arias, which they sang with sloppy freedom and benign musicality, respectively. Wagner's parlando vocal writing seemed to most singers to resemble recitative, and consequently, if not directed otherwise, they sang this music with the uncomprehending overlay of distortions that was routinely expected in recitative. Wagner's writings and comments throughout his life discuss in various ways his desire that the note values of his vocal lines be learned with strict accuracy and his text enunciated with clarity, since he could count on vivacious delivery of the music; only by channelling their innate energy into a precise rendering of his vocal lines could the correct spoken inflection of the words reveal itself to the performers of his day. Even at the Bayreuth *Ring* production of 1876 his last advice to his singers included the words 'Distinctness! The big notes will take care of themselves; the little notes and the text are the chief things.' Wagner's hope was that, after mastering the notes and durations of his vocal lines, singers would 'proceed with discretionary freedom, showing animation rather than reserve' in order to 'produce the impression of an impassioned and poetical mode of delivery'. While Wagner's concern for accuracy required greater concentration and an unusual mastery of the part for singers of his day, the challenge for singers of today is to achieve the other side of his equation – to exhibit 'discretionary freedom', to show 'animation rather than reserve', and thereby to produce 'an impassioned and poetical mode of delivery'.

A word about what Wagner's singers actually achieved is in order. Given the questionable and widely various technical abilities of most German singers of his day, it is scarcely surprising that their performances were seldom lauded by those accustomed to different conceptions of beautiful singing. It seems, too, that Wagner's coaching had different levels of success in causing singers to overcome the 'corrupt' styles in which they were steeped. Success stories include Anton Mitterwurzer as Wolfram and Schnorr as Tristan (Wagner's essay *Erinnerungen an Ludwig Schnorr von Carolsfeld* (*Recollections of Ludwig Schnorr von Carolsfeld*) idealizes this singer and, through Schnorr's example, outlines the qualities Wagner's ideal singers would possess). Those singers who met his requirements were exceptions in that, in addition to having intelligence and talent, they were flexible and devoted enough to Wagner to be pliable and receptive to his suggestions – and seemed grateful to the composer once he had shown them the correct way. But the tenor Albert Niemann, whose effect in Wagner roles made an impact on his contemporaries that could be compared to Schröder-Devrient's on Wagner, even though he had a stormy relationship with Wagner both personally and on artistic grounds, demonstrates that the singing style Wagner sought could be conceived in different terms from those on which the composer insisted. Hanslick assigned to Niemann the same label with which Chorley branded Schröder-Devrient, 'nature-singer', but also described his singing as the 'complete fusion of word and tone, of poem and composition'. While Wagner's desire for tractable singers was perpetuated and made into a virtue at Bayreuth after his death, it was Niemann's singing and acting which exerted influence as the first long-lived model of a great Wagner singer. The paradox that the 'best' and most influential Wagner singer of his day offered interpretations to which the composer took exception has two divergent implications for performance practice: either the attempt to understand the most successful performers of Wagner during his lifetime might focus on those of whom the composer disapproved, or else the discipline will continue to advocate a style that Wagner never succeeded in establishing more than provisionally.

Wagner and the early music movement

As THE SO-CALLED 'early music' or 'period instrument' movement has made incursions into the standard 19th-century repertory, it is clear that the music of Wagner too will ultimately come to be performed more frequently under the influence of these ideals. The opportunity of hearing Wagner's music with instruments like those he knew or admired is one which few interested in his music will deny themselves, and in other respects too such performances have the potential to be enlightening. One consideration which militates against thoroughgoing realizations of Wagner's music according to these criteria is that the perennial shortage of singers of Wagnerian calibre makes it unlikely that singers able to meet Wagner's demands of projection and endurance will adopt a style of singing and expression so unlike that which prevails in the more numerous mainstream Wagner productions. At this stage of performance history, in any case, it would be extremely difficult – and even more undesirable – to reproduce the kinds of technical limitations and shortcomings which singers of Wagner's day demonstrated.

If, on the other hand, the aim of the movement is to achieve performances which Wagner himself might have considered ideal, the primary difficulty would appear to be that of rediscovering the expressive urgency of Wagner's conception of performance, which involves such spontaneity, encompasses such extremes, and is so dependent on a now unfashionable show of subjectivity that it can hardly be achieved in an age where musicians are expected and trained to produce performances of cosmetic perfection. An early effort in applying 'early music' principles to Wagner, Roger Norrington's 1988 recording of the Overture to *Der fliegende Holländer*, founders on the adoption of inflexible tempi in which the 'fast' passages seem staid, the 'slow' ones brittle and breathless. The early music movement has here succeeded in recreating (in modern terms) an essential part of the style against which Wagner reacted with passionate disdain; will its adherents have the flexibility of approach necessary to dispense with some of its most cherished characteristics – in this case, inviolable continuity of a prevailing tempo – in order to approximate the freedom that was the starting-point for Wagner's revolution in performance style? Time will tell.

DAVID BRECKBILL

Section 17

WAGNER IN PERFORMANCE

Singing	362
Conducting	368
Staging	374

WAGNER IN PERFORMANCE

COMING TO TERMS WITH the history of Wagner's works in performance is vital background for considering the ways in which they have been received and assessed through the years. Any given Wagner performance consists of a complex interaction between many artistic parameters, and this fact would seem to militate against a strict partitioning of topics such as that adopted here. Nevertheless, singing, conducting and staging – each a significant artistic enterprise encompassing a number of more detailed performance issues – have all undergone extensive development in relation to Wagner's works, and each element deserves to be described on its own terms. Before launching these partially independent histories, however, it might be useful to propose a general overview of the history of Wagner performance by means of a three-part periodization. First, in the era following Wagner's death, a variety of solutions to Wagner's unprecedented musical demands were proposed and refined while the spirit of Wagner's staging went largely unchallenged in practice. Second, in the course of an era lasting a couple of decades (roughly between 1920 and 1940), the most important musical approaches from the earlier era achieved a synthesis which in some important ways yielded the most consistently satisfying results ever heard in this repertory. At the same time, new theatrical principles infused Wagner's works with additional layers of meaning during the demise of traditional – by this point often routine – productions. Third, since 1945, increasingly experimental and 'interpretative' staging has caused production eventually to take over from music as the primary issue in Wagner performance. The course of this large-scale interaction between different components of the synthesis of the arts which Wagner's works represents suggests that the point at which we have arrived in the 1990s is not the final stage in this intriguing history.

Singing

WAGNER'S EARLY WORKS entered the repertory gradually and had been assimilated into the standard German repertory both stylistically and statistically by the time of his death. A chronicle of the operatic performances on twenty-eight leading German stages in 1885 (Kürschner, 1886) shows that Wagner's Romantic operas were performed more often than any group of works of comparable scale by other composers. Mozart's three most popular masterpieces (*Le nozze de Figaro*, *Don Giovanni* and *Die Zauberflöte*), for example, achieved 194 performances, while *Der fliegende Holländer*, *Tannhäuser* and *Lohengrin* tallied 305 and were respectively the ninth, third and second most frequently performed operas during that calendar year. (The most popular work was Nessler's one-year-old *Der Trompeter von Säckingen*, which in the short term enjoyed such a vogue that it alone received 300 performances.) German singers had come to view Wagner's early works as old friends, and had learned to project this music, once thought to be of insuperable difficulty, by means of a style which the regular presence of these works in the repertory had helped to shape, to some extent, but which also had served to blunt the direct expressiveness Wagner imagined them to possess.

When Wagner's later works began to be performed frequently in the late 1870s and 1880s (in our sample year of 1885, *Die Walküre* led this group in popularity by a large margin, with 71 performances on German stages), their status as music dramas was thought to demand a different performing style from that which was customarily applied to traditional operas, among which were now counted Wagner's own early works. In Germany, at any rate, this perception stemmed from the belief that Wagner's music was essentially symphonic in nature. The singer, in such a conception, was more important as a vehicle through which the text was conveyed and as an actor in whom the symphonic component achieved dramatic crystallization than as a singer in traditional terms, and this sentiment was exacerbated by the commonly held and entirely erroneous assumption that Wagner's vocal writing (in the post-*Oper und Drama* works) was an awkward afterthought in the compositional process. Many singers were understandably nonplussed by this attitude and found ways of channelling Wagner's music through standardized expressive affects with which they were already familiar, although the erratic rhythms and pitches of the vocal lines were often allowed to coarsen the musicianship applied to Wagner singing.

This *laissez-faire* attitude occupied an interpretative middle ground between two apparently contradictory ideologies of Wagner singing which emerged in the late 19th century: that of projecting the words and that of singing the music. Most German singers who strayed from a vague, intuitive style embraced the former aim, and claimed the singing of Albert Niemann as a model. Unfortunately, few who emulated the model rivalled Niemann's artistic magnetism; the inexpert approximation of his style which achieved general circulation in the 1880s and 90s featured sloppy, imprecise, often choppy singing at a monotonously forthright dynamic level which it was thought would make the words more comprehensible.

Despite the ugly vocalism to which they were generally subjected, Wagner's works had become extremely fashionable by the 1890s. Managements of international houses soon found it to their advantage to produce these works, but some of the more perceptive members of the audience objected to the stark contrast in the quality of singing between the best practitioners of French and Italian opera on the one hand and that which prevailed in

Wagner on the other. (Indeed, Wagner's early operas had become staples of the Italian and, to a lesser extent, French repertory since the 1870s; in those contexts, Wagner's vocal writing was adapted to national styles of singing which did not recognize the split between singing and projecting the text that troubled German singers.) Critics such as G.B. Shaw and W.J. Henderson encouraged their favourites to attempt the mature Wagner in German while obeying inviolable laws of good singing, and singers such as Lilli Lehmann, Lillian Nordica and Jean and Edouard de Reszke obliged with a singing approach to Wagner which was considered ideal in international circles but insufficiently inflected and overly 'operatic' in Germany.

Bayreuth under the direction of Wagner's widow Cosima offered an alternative to this dichotomy. Her insistence that realizing the drama of Wagner's works was the chief aim of Bayreuth productions aligned her with those who favoured a clear recitation of the text – indeed, she was in the forefront of those who developed that aesthetic principle. Consequently, the often unpleasant singing that reached the stage of the Festspielhaus during her tenure was sometimes perceived as a dry-toned, brittly enunciated caricature of singing. Cosima's Bayreuth is with some justice accused of being a graveyard for voices, of encouraging undue emphasis on consonants, and not only of failing to appreciate good singing *per se* but of mistrusting it as an operatic excess. Nevertheless, some singers – among them Ernestine Schumann-Heink and Anton Van Rooy – were appreciated both at Bayreuth and on the great international stages. Their work, along with that of some of their Bayreuth colleagues, suggests that Cosima was groping towards a style in which singing enhanced the expression of a vibrantly detailed recitation of the text. Recorded examples of this style at its best – Luise Reuss-Belce's outburst as Ortrud on a Mapleson cylinder of 1903, Schumann-Heink's abridged 1929 account of Waltraute's Narration, Otto Briesemeister's 1904 recording of Loge's Narration, and recordings by Alfred von Bary, Felix von Kraus and others – suggest that it embraced a wide variety of technical procedures in order to convey a highly charged level of discourse. Line, for example, assumed in major international centres to be a supreme virtue to be maintained at all times, was not cultivated with anything resembling regularity at Bayreuth (although it was used as a special effect in certain situations). Instead, a series of phrases, or even of words, was likely to emerge in a like number of clearly differentiated expressive/technical procedures. As a synthesis of the two ideological extremes in turn-of-the-century Wagner singing – or, better, as a detailed enhancement of verbal expression through vocal means – the Bayreuth style was poorly understood in its own day and had little positive influence on succeeding styles.

By the early 20th century, numerous geographical styles of Wagner singing persisted in Germany – one concerned with sweet lyricism and accurate musicianship in Dresden, one which continued the earlier German style in Munich, a more poised but less colourful style in Berlin, one predicated on luxuriating in luscious voices in Vienna, and so on. These coexisting styles began to merge as leading exponents of each were exposed to a wider stylistic array of Wagner singing, especially in London and at the annual Munich Wagner Festival. Even more broadly, the enormous impact of the singing of Enrico Caruso in Germany meant that more lyrical methods were soon to be incorporated into German singing generally. By the end of World War I, a synthesis of the word-based German Wagner style and the best lyrical standards of international operatic singing was at hand in the work of Frida Leider, Lotte Lehmann, Lauritz Melchior, Friedrich Schorr and numerous others. These singers were notable for both energy and stamina, but memorable because their singing was capable of achieving a range of expressive characterization through strictly vocal (which includes enunciatory) means. Melchior, for example, strides meatily through Siegfried's Forging Songs with exuberant vigour and almost nonchalant security, but is then able to deliver Siegfried's Death with achingly slow portamenti which fill out both the line of the music and the complexity of the character. Leider's remarkable account of Brünnhilde's Battle Cry shows a highly differentiated series of expressive affects rubbing shoulders in a brief excerpt: the sword-like thrust of the octave-deep portamenti and the exuberance of a real trill are linked and underpinned by vivacious enunciation, bright tone and a secure, direct tempo. A tempo brisk by later standards causes Leider's recording of the Immolation Scene from *Götterdämmerung* to achieve the effect of heightened speech – natural rhythms and inflections accrue to the words as they pass in review. Lehmann's acoustical recording of Sieglinde's 'Der Männer Sippe' – even more vivid than the same passage in her celebrated recording of *Die Walküre* Act I with Melchior, Emmanuel List and Bruno Walter – similarly reveals a happy instance of a singer moulding the music to a direct expression of the words. These commercial recordings are not always true reflections of actual performance standards: live recordings from the period suggest that Melchior in particular was a careless singer who in the theatre infused his vivid enunciation with lyricism rather less often than might be considered ideal, while the upper reaches of Schorr's voice were sadly frayed even by the mid-1930s. At their best, however, these singers, along with a number of others (including Germaine Lubin, Maria Müller, Karin Branzell, Kerstin Thorborg, Franz Völker, Max Lorenz, Herbert Janssen, Rudolf Bockelmann and Alexander Kipnis), who were secondary only to these remarkable performers, achieved a Wagner style which has been widely regarded as a yardstick against which to measure subsequent Wagner singers.

The Metropolitan Opera début of the Norwegian soprano Kirsten Flagstad in 1935 launched the career of the most celebrated Wagner singer of her time; the renown she enjoyed engrained in the general consciousness the notion that Wagner singing enjoyed its halcyon years during that period. Nevertheless, Flagstad's perceived pre-eminence in this repertory signalled a change in perspective which was ultimately to bring to an end the unique stylistic synthesis that had flourished in the inter-war period. On the one hand, Flagstad was if anything a more impressive vocal athlete than Leider, and was blessed with a bigger, richer voice and remarkable stamina; further, in the often chaotic live performance recordings of the 1930s she maintains poise with utterly reliable musicianship and preparation. On the other hand, her singing was a less comprehensive synthesis of musical and textual values than was that of the great quartet. Her strengths were musical and vocal virtues, and it is worth noting that her great acclaim as a Wagner singer came in the English-speaking world, before audiences less able to appreciate the eloquent but subtle verbal inflections of a Leider. Further, Flagstad's dramatic demeanour, although capable of considerable intensity, tended toward unruffled matronliness, a quality enhanced, in vocal terms, by a habit of settling into many notes from below. Scooping would be too strong a word to describe this technique, at least as handled by Flagstad, but its prevalence in her singing became influential for later singers. Despite the jarring stylistic elements which Flagstad introduced, her wartime departure from the scene in 1941 spelled the end of a period which boasted what with hindsight can be called the most unified and consistently outstanding Wagner singing that has so far emerged.

At first the post-war era seemed only to lack the exceptional voices boasted by Flagstad and Melchior in their prime. When important Wagner singers did emerge, however, the tendencies they displayed seemed to stem from the less desirable traits of Flagstad. Some of the singers associated with the Bayreuth of Wieland Wagner – notably Wolfgang Windgassen, Hans Hotter and Astrid Varnay – adopted Flagstad's approximate attack and less visceral attitude, and a split between musical and verbal expression began to emerge. Often the musical values seemed to be gaining the upper hand, but without some of the vocal presence and ease which made Flagstad's singing so remarkable. That ease had also given some the idea that the weighty format of such a voice required slower tempi and more mellifluous (in practice, indistinct) enunciation – a hypothesis that is frankly contradicted by Flagstad's rhythmic alertness when her conductors (primarily in the 1930s) chose fast tempi.

German was no longer the native language of an increasing number of leading Wagner singers of the 1950s and 60s – George London, Jess Thomas, James King, Jon Vickers, Thomas Stewart and Claire Watson were all born in North America, for example. As a consequence of this fact, those capable of achieving in audible fashion Wagner's detailed interaction between word and tone became ever fewer. Not coincidentally, this inaugurated an era of self-conscious vocalism in Wagner. The pre-eminent Wagner singer of this era was Birgit Nilsson, whose powerful, steely voice and comparatively ungenerous use of portamento – which she sometimes omitted even when Wagner composed it, as in Brünnhilde's Battle Cry – gave Wagner singing a more energetic feeling than that which had predominated in the 1950s. At the same time, this effect sprang not so much from the words, as was the case in the inter-war period, as from visceral musical considerations. Before long the conductor Herbert von Karajan challenged the practice of casting only vocal supermen and -women in leading Wagner roles by presenting lighter voices in his Salzburg Wagner productions, but these singers and their kind, although they dominated the 1970s (in part because of their ability to act convincingly in increasingly experimental and topical productions), did not receive anything resembling universal approbation even in their own day. In the 1980s, singers like Gwyneth Jones, René Kollo, Peter Hofmann, Hildegard Behrens and James Morris enjoyed great vogue in Wagner roles, although their vocal achievements have, sadly, been of inconsistent quality.

One of the most objectionable features of Wagner singing since the Flagstad era has been the heavy wobble or tremolo which afflicts many of the singers we hear. This condition is not a new one – it has sometimes appeared in worn voices, and singers with a wide, unvarying vibrato which persists regardless of context can be found in Wagner recordings as early as 1923 (in a recording of Waltraute's Narration by Hedwig Fichtmüller). It is since Flagstad, however, that the combination of excessive vibrato and a striving toward an artificially heavy vocal format has resulted in a reign of soggy, rhythmically imprecise singing. A comparison between the singing of Göta Ljungberg and Walter Widdop in their 1927 HMV recording of *Die Walküre* Act I scene 3 with that of Jeannine Altmeyer and Peter Hofmann (in the 1980 Philips *Walküre* recording from Bayreuth) is instructive. By staying abreast of the beat at the urgent tempi (which today would be regarded as frantic) set by Albert Coates, the former pair cannot avoid seeming rhythmically and dramatically alert; for them the challenge, which they mostly succeed in meeting, is that of maintaining vocal composure in a context of frenetic energy and dynamic propulsion. In the later performance the orchestral background unfolds more neutrally, even though under Pierre Boulez there is an unerringly projected rhythmic profile. Although the conductor's approach invites rhythmic and tonal precision, the singers' style is founded on an invariably enormous and lethargic vibrato. This vocal format encompasses slow-speaking tone and soupy portamenti, both of which cause the singers to be rhythmically approximate and late for even the most important downbeats. While perhaps an extreme example, this latter recording embodies a tendency found in too many of today's most admired Wagner singers (Gwyneth Jones and, to a lesser extent, Hildegard Behrens among them).

Another way in which post-war Wagner singing has lost definition is in the abandonment of stylized conceptions of the major Wagner roles. Many regard the 'heroic' *topos* as incapable of revealing the complexity of character which resides in a Tristan, a Wotan, or a Kundry; consequently, productions which reveal Wagner's characters in a distinctive, flexible and innovative light have come to be expected. The diversity and plurality of interpretations to which Wagner's works have been subjected in productions since 1951, however, has resulted in the discovery of 'non-traditional' personality traits in Wagner's characters, which in turn discourages prospective Wagner singers from finding value in establishing a vocal type which embraces a number of Wagner roles. Consequently the breed once known as Wagner singer seems to have died out, since a well-defined impersonation of any given role sometimes does not translate from one production to another, much less from one Wagner role to another. Any gain in visual and histrionic delineation of character in Wagner performances of recent decades has been offset by the lack of stylistic authority the singers bring to their tasks. Since singers cannot draw upon an innate stylistic reservoir, Wagner has become just another composer in the operatic mainstream. The only remaining hope for effective musical portrayals of his leading characters is for singers to meet specific demands on a role-by-role basis; and, given that recent years have seen the emergence of such impersonations as James Morris's Wotan and Waltraud Meier's Kundry, there are reasonable grounds for continued optimism.

DAVID BRECKBILL

Conducting

THE TASK CONFRONTING Wagner performers in the years following the composer's death was that of promptly developing a practicable means of performing regularly the music dramas which just then were taking the musical world by storm. These new works moved far beyond the seemingly traditional demands of their predecessors. Conductors in particular were affected by these new challenges, since the widespread belief that the scores of Wagner's music dramas were essentially symphonic in nature elevated the position of opera conductor from that of a mechanical facilitator to that of an interpreter whose contribution was every bit as essential to a successful performance as were those of the singers. The status and function of operatic conductors were thus enhanced as a result of these works, and the solutions which various gifted conductors proposed through their examples have considerably affected the performance history of Wagner's works.

Of the Wagner conductors who became leading figures in the years following the composer's death, the one most like Wagner in temperament and in his concern with all aspects of a performance was Anton Seidl. After presiding over Angelo Neumann's touring *Ring* production in 1881–3, Seidl settled in New York, where he established an enviable Wagner tradition at the Metropolitan Opera. Renowned for his extremely high artistic standards, and more specifically for the harmonious ensemble he secured between stage and pit, as well as the tireless energy he devoted to non-musical matters on the stage, Seidl obtained fiery, flexible and sensitive playing from his orchestra; on encountering the enchanting expressivity and discreet delicacy of Seidl's Wagner conducting, the lyric tenor Jean de Reszke viewed the final obstacle to his undertaking the heavy Wagner roles as having been overcome. Today we would regard the cuts Seidl imposed on Wagner's works when they appeared in regular repertory as excessive; some scenes – for example, the Norns' and Waltraute scenes in *Götterdämmerung* – were simply omitted in Seidl's Metropolitan performances in an effort to prevent the works from lasting more than four hours (including intermissions). In this draconian practice Seidl merely obeyed the Master's own suggestion for how to present the works in non-festival settings, however, and his perpetuation of Wagner's own gestural approach to the music, which underlined the immediate expressivity of each moment, was an ideal conductorial style for such heavily abridged performances.

Seidl did not conduct at Bayreuth until a year before his death in 1898. In his place, others whose piety towards Wagner included at least some degree of artistic deference to Cosima Wagner (who succeeded her late husband as director of the festival) filled this post. Among them were Hermann Levi (the first conductor of *Parsifal*), Felix Mottl, Richard Strauss, Karl Muck and Siegfried Wagner. All of these men ultimately developed distinct interpretative profiles which it would be irresponsible to link too closely. While under the influence of Cosima at Bayreuth, however, they adopted and progressively intensified a tendency toward slow tempi, which not only reflected Cosima's ideology but dovetailed nicely with the seamlessly sustained sonority which the acoustical properties of the Festspielhaus seem to encourage. Mottl in particular excited comment for his performances, both at Bayreuth and elsewhere, which seemed slower and more distended than was common practice, and this approach is reflected in the tempo indications and modifications he provided in editions of some of Wagner's works. (Interestingly enough, the timings of individual acts and operas under different conductors kept by members of the Bayreuth orchestra through the years demonstrate that the way in which a performance moves through time often has little to do with how much time it occupies.) At their best, these conductors, like Seidl, were concerned to integrate proceedings on stage and in the pit to an uncommon degree. The gestural style was still in evidence, but marked differentiations between the themes and motifs of different characters became subsumed in the larger flow of symphonic texture; the result was a gently undulating weave of sound which often became its own justification. This style of Wagner conducting can best be heard in the recordings of Muck, the highlights of whose discography are portions of the Grail Scene from Act I of *Parsifal* made at Bayreuth in 1927 and a nearly complete recording of Act III from the same work made in Berlin a year later. Karl Elmendorff and more recently Horst Stein have been later exponents of this style.

Because Wagner chose him as the conductor for the 1876 Bayreuth *Ring*, Hans Richter enjoyed unique prestige, becoming an institution in Vienna and especially London (at Covent Garden he produced the *Ring* in English in 1908–9 as a kind of valedictory culmination of his close relationship with the British public). A frequent conductor of *Die Meistersinger* and the *Ring* at Bayreuth until 1912, Richter nevertheless encountered an undercurrent of resistance there for two reasons. First, after the 1876 *Ring* Wagner had complained to both Cosima and King Ludwig II that Richter was unsure of the tempi, and naturally Wagner's private reservation prevented Cosima from adopting the public's automatic admiration for Richter. Second, public perception of him as Wagner's chosen conductor prevented Cosima from dismissing him for an attitude of personal and musical autonomy which she did not allow in her other conductors. Richter kindly but completely ignored Cosima's attempts to influence his musical interpretations but, on the other hand, did not meddle in her work with the rest of the production. The result was a noticeably different kind of performance from that otherwise encountered at turn-of-the-century Bayreuth. Richter's performances possessed an imposing musical grandeur which, far from working toward the kind of unified utterance at which Wagner and Bayreuth aimed, implied a diversified artistic approach in which each artistic parameter was allowed to achieve its own logic, on its own terms. At any rate, the symphonic quality – that is, an inherent musical logic in the orchestral writing – of Wagner's scores was especially prominent in Richter's performances. It might even be suggested that this quality was present in at least a preliminary form in the *Ring* performances of 1876 and that Wagner's dissatisfaction had as much to do with the composer's inability to perceive or accept Richter's interpretative aims as with any indecisiveness on Richter's part. (Interestingly enough, Hans von Bülow – Wagner's conductor of choice before Cosima left Bülow for Wagner – seems also to have concentrated on musical leadership at the expense of a more all-encompassing dramatic conception.)

Each era of Wagner performance has had to tolerate a certain amount of uninspired conducting, and so one might suppose that the new demands made by the music dramas left many conductors at the turn of the century groping for solutions that never came. Apart from some of the leading figures associated with Wagner or Bayreuth, however, it is difficult to obtain an overview of 'average' Wagner conducting before 1925 (the year in which electrical recordings were introduced). One window on this era opens through the Mapleson cylinder recordings made during Wagner performances at the Metropolitan Opera in 1901–3. The leading Wagner conductor on these recordings is Alfred Hertz, whose first season at the Met was 1902–3. His memoirs reveal that he realized his conducting to be aggressive and enthusiastic rather than subtle, and indeed there is a kind of blunt urgency in these recordings which corresponds to his reputation at the time. Significantly, however, the meandering quality of Walter Damrosch's conducting in recorded excerpts in earlier Maplesons does not stem from noticeably more cautious tempi. In short, quick tempi seem to have prevailed in the early years of the century among those who were not beholden to any of the styles so far mentioned. This approach derived from Wagner's own gestural style, in which manipulations of tempo took place against a moderately quick background pace, but such conducting soon lost the expressive flexibility of the gestural styles and concentrated instead on a sleek propulsion through the Wagner scores. Conductors of later days who adopted this approach were Albert Coates, Artur Bodanzky (who additionally inflicted extensive cuts on the works during his Metropolitan tenure from 1915 to 1939) and Karl Böhm.

Gustav Mahler and Arturo Toscanini were two important conductors with no personal connection to Wagner who continued Seidl's practice of working for performances in which the musical results were merely one part of an integrated dramatic presentation. Ironically, however, as celebrated conductors in the concert hall as well as the theatre, their musical interpretations often received inordinate attention, especially since their standards of execution guaranteed outstanding orchestral playing; consequently, the results they achieved were often construed to represent a symphonically conceived realization of Wagner's music. Although both of these men were noted for the intensity of their interpretations, the overlay of interpretative cohesion which their performances implied ultimately rendered unfashionable the more impulsive heirs of the gestural style – such as Coates and Bodanzky – and caused a re-evaluation of more traditional German conducting styles, so that the approaches of Bruno Walter, Hans Knappertsbusch (an assistant and stylistic legatee of Richter), Leo Blech and others gained an interpretative prestige which their Wagner performances would not have enjoyed several decades before.

Five strains in Wagner conducting have so far been enumerated: those exemplified by Seidl, Bayreuth conductors, Richter, those who favoured a fast pace, and the Mahler/Toscanini legacy of symphonic intentionality. Most subsequent Wagner conductors can be linked to one or more of these approaches even if no direct line of influence from the respective progenitors can be drawn. Not surprisingly, the central figure in the history of Wagner conducting, Wilhelm Furtwängler, can only be adequately understood as one who synthesized many of these styles. Like those of Richter (and Artur Nikisch, whom Furtwängler admired immensely), Furtwängler's conceptions were recognized as having little to do with the intentional integration of drama and music practised by Seidl and Bayreuth conductors. Like those of Toscanini and Mahler, his interpretations possessed the trappings of a symphonic logic. Like the Bayreuth conductors, Furtwängler favoured a seamless sonority and moulded it into large-scale structures by employing flexible tempo – which the Wagner–Bülow–Seidl school applied to motifs and phrases – on a much larger level: in his hands Wagner's scores achieved a sense of direction and purpose which enables the listener to perceive the dramatic and structural context of any given moment by means of the ebb and flow of tempo. To speak of Furtwängler's Wagner conducting as a style, however, is misleading. For example, the sostenuto style of the Bayreuth conductors of his day – Muck, Elmendorff and others – is only one of many techniques at Furtwängler's command for constructing an unbroken span. The challenge of integrating a caesura which interrupts the texture, generally solved by the Bayreuth practitioners by means of gentle endings and beginnings surrounding the silence, elicits more varied solutions from Furtwängler. Notice his treatment of the pause after Waltraute's quotation of Wotan in Act I of *Götterdämmerung* (especially in the 1953 Rome *Ring*): by emphasizing the clarinet statement of the Ring motif (at 'Des tiefen Rheines Töchtern') and quickening the tempo slightly, he creates a feeling of uneasiness around the reiterated figures in the subsequent Valhalla motif, thereby preventing the pause before 'Da sann ich nach' from lapsing into the enervated reverie which has since become customary. This way of searching out and emphasizing continuity in musical – dare one say analytical? – terms makes for surprising and uniquely appropriate dramatic revelations and felicities. In the end, Furtwängler's Wagner goes far towards convincing us that a coherent, organic realization of Wagner's *music* provides an appropriate approximation of Wagner's own *dramatic* aims as well as a justification of the composer's claim that his works were 'deeds of music made visible'.

Although in the years since World War II Wagner conducting has continued many of the strains found previously, the prevailing style has come from combining two of them. To begin with, the grandly weighty tempi of Richter were perpetuated by Knappertsbusch (who conducted at Bayreuth nearly annually from the reopening of the Festival in 1951 until 1964) and still later by Reginald Goodall, whose carefully wrought productions (among them the *Ring* in English) with the English National Opera in the 1970s and 80s were widely hailed as supreme poetic achievements, even though to some the tempi seemed too distended to provide a sufficient impetus for the drama. Nevertheless, on the authority of Knappertsbusch and Goodall, recent Wagner conductors often seem to believe that the slower the pace the more profound the effect. Unfortunately, the style with which this approach has been combined in recent decades has been the Mahler/Toscanini strain, which treats the orchestra as a single instrument to be manipulated by the conductor. Knappertsbusch's slow tempi were successful because he revelled in the massive, many-stranded nature of Wagner's orchestral sonority which is not easily achieved through more precise orchestral execution. In any case, many of the slow tempi favoured by present-day conductors (James Levine, Giuseppe Sinopoli and so on) founder into lethargy and stasis – a failing which can be at least partially explained by the insistence of the production-minded that the music should illustrate certain psychological states.

Furtwängler's importance has been recognized, and his interpretative ideals occasionally found an echo in the performances of his successor Herbert von Karajan, whose best performances (on records *Das Rheingold* and the last two acts of *Die Walküre*) preserved a sense of the long line that was so marked in Furtwängler's Wagner. Karajan's later recordings, however, are increasingly marred by somnolence due to calculation (something which could not have been predicted from his Bayreuth *Tristan* of 1952, which blazes with energy), and by a complacency of conception which cheapens important moments in *Tristan* and *Parsifal* in particular. Daniel Barenboim too has attempted to perpetuate Furtwängler's approach without always convincing listeners of the appropriateness of his particular applications of tempo modification; more successful fluctuations of tempo occur in the *Tristan* of Carlos Kleiber.

Perhaps the most insidious influence on modern Wagner conducting has been the role of recordings in shaping conceptions of how Wagner's works should sound. Historically, the greatest Wagner conductors were those who had developed compelling solutions to the difficulties of pacing and structuring Wagner's large spans, or of shaping the orchestral contribution so that it helped to create convincing dramatic discourse. All that changed with the introduction of the long-playing record. The first great complete Wagner performance released on records – Knappertsbusch's *Parsifal* – represented a composite of rehearsals and stage performances at Bayreuth (1951), and was thus a reasonable reflection of how Knappertsbusch dealt with the work in the theatre. The only commercial Wagner recording of the 1950s of comparable quality was Furtwängler's *Tristan*, and although it remains a very great performance, the alchemy of the recording studio altered the nature of Furtwängler's usual advocacy of the work. As is revealed in extended excerpts from the 1947 Berlin *Tristan* revival, and as can be inferred from his other live Wagner recordings, Furtwängler's *Tristan* was generally a more urgent and varied affair than the achingly sustained but more abstractly structural studio recording would suggest.

Soon recorded interpretations rather than live performance became normative. Perhaps the most influential Wagner conductor of the last thirty years has been Sir Georg Solti, but his greatest achievements have been recordings (he was the first – and so far only – conductor to have made commercial recordings of all ten canonical Wagner operas) which have consistently been more admired than his Wagner performances in the theatre. Solti's greatest strength is that of filling each moment with dramatic urgency, and recording methods ensure that a conductor's intentions for such moments can be achieved with precision. The aural image thereby created is a potent lure, and the temptation to try to match these localized effects has caused many younger conductors to cease investigating ways of shaping and projecting larger units of time convincingly, just as Solti's recordings lack a large-scale interpretative profile. In short, modern Wagner conducting seems torn between admiration for slow tempi and exciting detail; the attempt to wed the two has resulted in the abandonment of both convincing overall structure and the feeling of large-scale momentum that was originally a prerequisite for slow tempi.

DAVID BRECKBILL

Staging

THE HISTORY OF THE STAGING of Wagner's operas reflects a contradiction inherent in the works themselves. The aesthetic tradition to which Wagner considered himself the heir was that of Goethe and Schiller, in which art was elevated above the mundane, sordid realities of everyday life. Yet Wagner's works, with their insistent social critiques and dissolving of regular metrical patterns into freely expressive 'musical prose', themselves exemplify the new spirit of realism, which came to pervade all branches of the arts in the 19th century. The characteristic deployment by Wagner of myths and symbols is the perfect embodiment of that contradiction: underlying social realities are thereby objectified in the sphere of fantasy. In the *Ring*, for example, we are presented, at the surface level of plot, with gods, dragons and sleeping beauties. It does not require exceptional perspicacity to realize that such types are merely the dramaturgical representations of the plutocrats, labourers and other products of the bourgeois capitalist society so detested by Wagner.

And yet the implications of this have only comparatively recently been grasped as far as theatrical staging is concerned. In the first decades of Wagner production the contradiction was glossed over by the prevailing theatrical mode of Romantic naturalism. But gradually throughout the 20th century, more radical approaches have come to dominate the Wagnerian stage, some explicitly political, though a strand of traditionalism has also continued to find favour.

The sets for the first *Ring* at Bayreuth in 1876 were made by the Brückner brothers after designs by Josef Hoffmann. Hoffmann's drawings, which are all that remain, suggest a Romanticized view of nature, with gnarled tree-trunks and spookily angled branches like woodland scenes by Caspar David Friedrich. The actual sets were almost certainly less detailed than these drawings; in any case, Wagner was deeply disappointed by them, while accepting that they had been executed as convincingly as possible in the difficult economic circumstances.

'Natural' expression also took the place of traditional stock histrionics, and singers were encouraged to ignore the audience and respond only to fellow performers on the stage. Wagner also placed strong emphasis on the role of improvisation and inspiration in stage blocking.

Unfortunately, any such spark of creativity in performers was effectively stifled by Cosima Wagner, the composer's widow, when she assumed control of the festival after his death. Cosima had a natural dramatic talent and continued the progressive tendency of naturalistic acting she had observed at the first festivals, but her determination to reproduce every gesture, every movement as she remembered it, led to uninspired, over-prescriptive stage choreography. The so-called 'Bayreuth style' (both of stagecraft and *mise-en-scène*) held sway at the Festspielhaus until the 1930s and provided a model for other houses too, for example the Metropolitan, New York, where the pre-World War I sets of the Kautsky brothers continued to be used right up until 1939.

But radical developments were under way elsewhere. The Swiss designer Adolphe Appia turned away from traditional pictorialism, seeking the essence of Wagner's music dramas in a new, anti-naturalistic way: psychologically determined, with the action much simplified and stylized, and with colour and light accorded a primary role. Appia's own *Ring* in Basle was discontinued after *Die Walküre* in 1925, but his influence was enormous. His theories of opera production, expounded in a series of essays, were reflected, before and after the years of World War I, in the work of such directors as Gustav Wunderwald in Berlin, Alfred Roller in Vienna, Hans Wildermann in Cologne, Dortmund and Düsseldorf, and Ludwig Sievert in several German cities. In Bayreuth, however, it was not until after World War II that his theories were triumphantly realized in the productions of the composer's grandson, Wieland Wagner. In the Bayreuth ruled by Cosima, Appia's ideas were anathema. Her judgment, delivered to Houston Stewart Chamberlain in 1896, is a classic piece of reactionary fetishism: 'Appia appears not to know that the *Ring* was performed here in '76; consequently, in respect of scenery and staging, there is nothing more to be discovered.'

A celebrated production of *Der fliegende Holländer* at the Kroll Opera, Berlin, directed by Jürgen Fehling in 1929, exemplified the provocative new wave of realism espoused there. It was a style of realism rooted in the anti-Romantic functionalism of the Bauhaus, and the *Holländer* was typical in its starkly lit stage compositions drawing on principles of Cubist abstraction.

Meanwhile, even Bayreuth was beginning to feel the winds of change, ironically at the very time that the Nazis, not known for their avant-garde artistic predilections, were coming to power. The festival had been run by Wagner's son Siegfried after Cosima's retirement through ill-health, in 1906. Between 1924, when the festival reopened after the war, and his death in 1930, Siegfried made a sustained attempt to introduce solid three-dimensional sets and other cautious innovations more in tune with the times. Then came Siegfried's most forward-looking production, that of *Tann-*

häuser in 1930, after which the reign of Heinz Tietjen as artistic director of the festival, with Emil Preetorius as his scenic designer, ushered in an era of less than decisive reform, admittedly at precisely the time when the Nazis were halting all progressive experimentation in dramaturgy in Germany.

Preetorius's dilemma, caught as he was between the demands of the rigid Bayreuth orthodoxy and a desire for moderate reform, probably accounts for the confused argumentation in his essay *Wagner: Bild und Vision (Wagner: Stage Picture and Vision)*. Preetorius here argues simultaneously for on the one hand a faithful, even reverential recreation of the many natural effects in Wagner's works, which, he said, 'must be rendered clearly and with complete illusion', and on the other for a recognition that the works were conceived essentially as allegories. The latter insight justified his own use of symbolism, reflecting that of the composer himself, and like Appia he favoured the reduction of stage props and the imaginative use of lighting.

Under Hitler's enthusiastic patronage, the Bayreuth Festival prospered in the 1930s: the size of the chorus was increased to an unprecedented extent. Yet there seems to have been little actual interference from the authorities on artistic matters: Tietjen and the new administrator, Siegfried's widow Winifred, had far greater problems with the old guard associated with Bayreuth itself. And certainly Bayreuth produced nothing comparable to the blatant Nazi propaganda of Benno von Arent's *Meistersinger* in Berlin, prepared under Hitler's direct supervision. The final festival scene, with its massed ranks of participants and banners, resembled a Nazi party rally and provided a model for opera houses elsewhere in Germany too.

The signing of the Non-aggression Pact between Germany and Russia in 1939 prompted Stalin, as a friendly gesture to Hitler, to stage *Die Walküre* at the Bolshoy in Moscow. The director chosen was the film-maker Sergey Eisenstein, who, believing that Wagner's highly pictorial music demanded a specific visual shaping, introduced some interesting innovations. He used a 'mimic chorus', a group of extras, to play out the events of Sieglinde's Act I narration in pantomime, and to shadow the singers in the Ride of the Valkyries. His enacting of the events of the Prelude has subsequently become something of a commonplace, as has his idea of having Hunding accompanied by a gang of henchmen. Unfortunately for Stalin, Eisenstein's conception of the work was avowedly anti-fascist and the production was hastily withdrawn.

When the Bayreuth Festival reopened after the Second World War, in 1951, the need for a clean break from all the dubious associations of the past led Wagner's grandson, Wieland, to a series of productions whose ideological basis was similarly anti-fascist, even if that ideology was frequently disguised by the subtlety and imagination of his dramaturgy. His new *Ring*, for example, rejected the trappings of Germanic saga in order to present the work as a timeless moral drama. All the pictorial sets, foliage, rocks and winged helmets were jettisoned and the *mise-en-scène* reduced to bare essentials. The entire action was set on a circular platform or disc which, symbolic of the ring, acted as a satisfying unifying device for the cycle. Valhalla was projected cinematically as a dreamlike vision, and the disc became obscured as Wotan became increasingly enmeshed in his contracts. After the final conflagration, the disc returned to its original state. Wieland's less than reverential attitude towards the composer's specific instructions was justified by the drawing of a distinction between the stage directions, which remained bound to 19th-century theatrical modes, and the timeless ideas of the works themselves, which demand constantly new representations. The stage directions, in other words, he regarded as inner visions rather than practical demands.

Walter Felsenstein's commitment, in his work at the same period at the Komische Oper in East Berlin, to 'realistic music theatre', bore most fruit, as far as Wagner productions were concerned, in the work of his followers. Directors such as Götz Friedrich, Joachim Herz and Harry Kupfer fused Felsenstein's principles of psychological and social realism, and his emphasis on role identification, with the quite contrary ones of Brechtian theory to establish the fundamentals of an approach that dominated the stages of Europe, in a variety of contrasting forms, throughout the sixties, seventies and eighties. Brecht's so-called 'alienation effect' was used conspicuously by Friedrich in his two *Ring* cycles, where, for example, he caused Loge, Alberich and Wotan to step outside the framework of the drama to address the audience directly. Such techniques gave the work of this generation of East German directors a sharp ideological edge to which western capitalist audiences and critics took time to adjust.

Herz's socially critical Leipzig *Ring* of 1973–6 set a number of trends. Beginning the second act of *Die Walküre* inside Valhalla instead of on the rocky pass was to become a popular idea, for example. Herz's intention in setting the action in a bourgeois palatial home was presumably to remind the audience that Wotan's dilemma arises from the conflict between natural instincts and materialist society. Another historically significant *Ring* production of the period was that of Ulrich Melchinger, mounted at Kassel from 1970. Its *Star Wars* images and pop art references, unintegrated into any coherent unity, set the action not in the present but in some timeless sphere.

A landmark in the history of Wagner staging was reached with Patrice Chéreau's *Ring* at Bayreuth in 1976. Chéreau's demythologization of the tetralogy entailed an anti-heroic view of the work, as essayed by Wieland Wagner, Friedrich and Herz, and his setting of the action in an industrialized society, with a hydroelectric dam taking the place of the free-flowing Rhine, along with occasional 20th-century costumes and props, suggested a continuity between Wagner's time and our own. Chéreau's production was no less ground-breaking in its sheer theatricality: scene after scene was recreated in a series of powerful images that have lingered in the memory, and which have been echoed, but rarely surpassed, in subsequent stagings.

Other directors too have emphasized the relevance of the *Ring* to the world of the late 20th century. The ecological aspect was forcefully engaged by Harry Kupfer in his 1988 production at Bayreuth, the entire action taking place in a world already ravaged by a catastrophe, presumably nuclear. Kupfer's reading highlighted the message of the *Ring* that the abandonment of love and humanity's finer sensibilities in favour of territorial aggrandizement and enhanced material possessions leads to the despoliation of nature and ultimately global extinction.

Nikolaus Lehnhoff's 1987 production of the *Ring* for Munich similarly concerned itself with the 'immorality and perversion of human values' engendered by the pursuit of political power and ambition. Erich Wonder's designs, though visually striking, were outstripped by those of Axel Manthey for Ruth Berghaus's *Ring* in Frankfurt (1985–7), in which a constant succession of bizarre, shocking images and of references and gestures derived from the Theatre of the Absurd overturned all expectations based on the tradition of naturalism. Such references have also informed the work of the younger generation of directors, notably Richard Jones, whose witty, imaginative *Rheingold* of 1989 initiated a *Ring* for Scottish Opera.

Throughout these decades of radical experimentation, a conservative tradition has also been maintained. The futuristic tendency of Ralph Koltai's abstract, symbolic designs for the Sadler's Wells *Ring* in the early 1970s was mitigated by the unobtrusiveness of the production, while Peter Hall's naive fairytale representation (Bayreuth, 1983) and Otto Schenk's picture postcard exercise in nostalgia (Metropolitan, 1986–8) were enjoyed primarily by those who regard opera houses as a refuge from cerebral activity.

In a postmodernist age, where multiplicity of styles is the order of the day, radical and traditional approaches seem likely to continue to hold the stage together.

BARRY MILLINGTON

Section 18
RECEPTION

Contemporary assessments   380

Posthumous reputation and influence   384

The Bayreuth legacy   389

The birth of modernism:

    Wagner's impact on the history of music   393

    Wagner's impact on literature   396

    Wagner's impact on the visual arts   398

Wagner literature:

    Biographies   402

    Analysis and criticism   404

    Miscellaneous   408

RECEPTION

'NO MATTER WHERE ONE GOES,' complained Karl Marx in 1876, 'one is plagued with the question "What do you think of Richard Wagner?"' It was a question to which most of the composer's contemporaries could give very definite answers, for Wagner – far more than any other 19th-century artist – had managed to make himself into a figure of endless and impassioned contention. He achieved this distinction (if that is what it was) not simply through his art, but through the grandiose claims he made for that art, through his changeable but always stridently expressed political views, and finally through a life which was filled with as much pathos and bathos as the melodramatic opera plots he so despised. (It was Wagner's curse to live a life that imitated Meyerbeer's art.) Even today it is difficult for most people to think about Wagner the musician without contemplating Wagner the man; this was all the more the case when the man was still alive, constantly adding fuel to the fires of controversy burning around him.

Contemporary assessments

Fellow musicians

Even artists like Wagner who eventually became legends in their own time must of course begin on a humbler footing, struggling to generate enthusiasm for their work. In Wagner's case the most important early assessments of his art came from fellow-musicians, some of whom later learned that they had better try to separate the music from the musician. A crucial early backer was the wildly popular operatic composer Giacomo Meyerbeer, who thought enough of Wagner's work to smooth the way for the young composer first in Paris, then in Dresden and Berlin. Yet Wagner's failure quickly to achieve the level of success enjoyed by Meyerbeer convinced him that his benefactor was in fact thwarting his career, and he turned venomously against him.

One of Wagner's earliest attacks on Meyerbeer was published in Robert Schumann's *Neue Zeitschrift für Musik*. In opening his influential journal to Wagner, Schumann registered his confidence in Wagner's judgment as critic and theoretician, encouraging him to embark on an aspect of his professional career that might better have been nipped in the bud. At any rate, Schumann soon alienated Wagner by commenting that the latter's *Höllander* score seemed to betray 'echoes of Meyerbeer', to whom Wagner felt immensely superior.

Wagner might think himself a great musician, but had not Franz Liszt agreed with this assessment, the budding Master would certainly have had a much harder time making his presence felt on the European operatic stage. As the most popular and celebrated musical virtuoso of his day, Liszt was in a very good position to promote Wagner's work. Liszt probably did not understand much of Wagner's theoretical writings, but he was captivated by his music, which struck him as allied to his own pioneering efforts in chromaticism and tone-painting.

Wagner profited from the support rendered not only by musical giants like Schumann and Liszt, but also by lesser-known musicians who truly believed that Wagner's work was 'the music of the future'. Theodor Uhlig, a violinist in the Dresden court orchestra, became one of the composer's most zealous disciples, writing essays about him in musical reviews, searching out performance opportunities, and enlisting other musicians on his behalf. Karl Klindworth, a pupil of Liszt who emigrated to London in 1854, worked hard to advance Wagner's cause in England, where the composer conducted a series of concerts one year later.

When Wagner reached the height of his influence by launching the Bayreuth Festival in 1876, some of Europe's leading musicians were on hand to assess the significance of this monumental undertaking. Of *Das Rheingold*, Pyotr Tchaikovsky wrote: 'Musically, it is inconceivable nonsense, in which here and there occur beautiful and even captivating moments.' After hearing more of the tetralogy, however, Tchaikovsky concluded that he could not fully assess Wagner's music without intensive study, though he was prepared to admit that as a whole the '*Ring* made an overwhelming impression on me not so much through its musical beauty (which it possesses in perhaps too great an abundance) but rather through its gigantic proportions.' And he declared, prophetically: 'One thing is certain, that something has happened at Bayreuth, something which our grandchildren and great-grandchildren will remember.' Edvard Grieg had some criticisms ('ceaseless modulations and wearying chromaticism of the harmonies') but agreed with Tchaikovsky that the *Ring* premiere was an extraordinary accomplishment. 'Yesterday,' he wrote, 'I came face to face with the greatest that the music drama of our century has given us. I can now understand Liszt's assessment of the great Wagner when he says it rises above all our epoch's art like Mont Blanc over the Alps.'

The production of *Parsifal* in Bayreuth a few years later had a similarly powerful effect on Wagner's musical colleagues, particularly on the younger ones like Gustav Mahler, Hugo Wolf and Anton Bruckner. After first hearing *Parsifal* in 1883, Mahler wrote: 'Emerging speechless from the Festspielhaus, I realized that I had undergone the greatest and most soul-wrenching experience in my life, and that I would carry this experience with me for the rest of my days.' Wolf (who heard the work the previous year) wrote that *Parsifal* was 'by far the most beautiful and sublime work in the whole field of art. My whole being reels in the perfect world of this wonderful work, as if in some blissful ecstasy, becoming ever more enraptured and blessed.' For Bruckner *Parsifal* simply confirmed an infatuation with Wagner that had begun when he heard *Tristan* in 1865, and that lasted the rest of his life.

Though Wagner's music by no means always had such a galvanic effect on the famous musicians of his day – neither Berlioz nor Mendelssohn had been swept away by his earlier works – even non-Wagnerian musicians were often obliged to admit the power of his art. In this context one might recall that Wagner's great rival Giuseppe Verdi confessed to an interviewer that he stood 'in wonder and terror' before *Tristan*.

Music critics

In general, Wagner was judged more severely by the professional music critics of his day than by his fellow musicians. Perhaps this was partly because Wagner claimed competence as a critic himself, expounding at length in his prose works on the virtues and deficiencies of other composers past and present. Critics were also irritated by the ambitious claims Wagner made for his music and by his propensity to accompany his compositions with elaborate philosophical explanations. Many would have agreed with the music critic of London's *Saturday Review*, who thanked the author of a new book on Wagner 'for not having wearied us with the philosophical theories Wagner amused himself by spinning when he was not seriously occupied with composition'.

To some of Europe's most influential music critics, however, Wagner's worst offence was his alleged relegation of music to a subordinate status behind the text in his music dramas. In 1852 the Belgian critic François-Joseph Fétis launched a polemic against Wagner in the *Revue et Gazette Musicale*, charging that in Wagner's mind music was 'only secondary', no more than an 'aid to expression'. Fétis' point was quickly taken up by the influential Viennese critic Eduard Hanslick, who, having praised earlier Wagnerian works like the *Holländer* and *Tannhäuser*, came to regard the mature music dramas as a threat to the musical conventions set down by Mozart, Beethoven, Weber and Schumann (see 'Dealings with critics', p.127). Undoubtedly, Hanslick failed fully to understand what Wagner was about, but this did not prevent his argument from becoming a central rallying-cry for anti-Wagnerian critics in the late 19th century.

While Fétis and Hanslick were Wagner's most authoritative detractors on the Continent, James Davison of *The Times* assumed that role in England. After Wagner's conducting premiere in London in 1855, Davison wrote that the German musician was unfit as a conductor, that the *Tannhäuser* and *Lohengrin* selections played by the Old Philharmonic were dull and uninspired, that Wagner's obvious incompetence as a musician made him hardly fit to condemn the works of other composers. 'Admirers of Mendelssohn', huffed Davison, 'may console themselves with the reflection that nothing such a mushroom musician as Herr Wagner can possibly say against his compositions will rob them of their value.'

Toward the end of his career Davison came to soften his view of Wagner, and indeed he had considerable praise for the *Ring* on its premiere in Bayreuth. So did the *Daily Telegraph* critic Joseph Bennett, who debunked the town of Bayreuth as 'a tenth-rate Versailles, crossed with a sleepy provincial borough', but liked most of the music he heard there, especially *Die Walküre* and *Siegfried*, which he called 'a grand addition to the world's store of beauty'. Two years later, a considerably more passionate Wagnerian, the German-born critic Francis Hueffer, joined *The Times* and helped make Wagner widely acceptable to British tastes. When Wagner died in 1883, *The Times* pronounced him 'the greatest musician of our time'.

Living legend

Whether or not one agreed with *The Times*'s assessment, Wagner had been for some time such a dominant figure on Europe's cultural scene that people who claimed an elevated cultural status for themselves felt obliged to comment on this phenomenon. A few samples of the verdicts rendered by Europe's *culturati* will suffice to show that there was only one common ingredient in their assessments: extreme partisanship, for or against.

Upon first hearing a Wagner concert, the poet Charles Baudelaire told friends that he had had 'the most joyous musical experience' of his life. His literary colleague Jules Champfleury wrote an essay that hailed the German composer as a divine gift to music. The young Parnassian Villiers de l'Isle-Adam proclaimed that Wagner was 'a genius such as appears on earth once every thousand years'. Houston Stewart Chamberlain, who was to marry Wagner's eldest daughter and become a central figure in the Bayreuth Circle, said that he experienced 'seraphic bliss' upon first entering the Festspielhaus in 1883. Yet Leo Tolstoy found *Siegfried* so 'artificial and stupid' that he could not sit it out, while William Morris thought it a 'desecration' to bring a profound subject like the Nordic sagas under 'the gaslights of an opera: the most rococo and degraded of all forms of art'. He hated the idea of some 'sandy-haired German tenor tweedledeeing over the unspeakable woes of Sigurd'. John Ruskin thought *Die Meistersinger* the most 'bête, clumsy, blundering, boggling, baboon-blooded stuff [he] ever saw on a human stage'.

Undoubtedly, the last word on Wagner from some of his more illustrious contemporaries should be left to Friedrich Nietzsche, that tortured philosopher who wrestled more intensely with the Wagner phenomenon than anyone else in the 19th century. In his *Richard Wagner in Bayreuth*, Nietzsche, who clearly idolized Wagner and wanted to see him as the embodiment of everything pure and noble, hailed the Master as an uncompromising genius who used his great gift to improve 'that part of the world which has been recognized as still susceptible to change'. Yet it was not long before Nietzsche became disgusted by Wagner's calculated embrace of the new German Empire, and by his apparent abandonment of Dionysian sensuality for Schopenhauerian quietism and Christian pity – this last quality most clearly exemplified in *Parsifal*, which Nietzsche denounced as an espousal of 'slave morality'. Now he viciously attacked Wagner as an 'arch deceiver' who had come to represent the worst of the German nation. And yet, even as he poured venom on his erstwhile idol he retained a deep love for his music. This was true even of *Parsifal*, of whose beautiful Prelude he could write: 'It was as if someone were speaking to me again, after many years, about the problems that disturb me.' In *Ecce Homo*, one of his last works, he claims Wagner as 'the greatest benefactor of my life'. Nietzsche's refusal to discount the power of Wagner's art despite a profound distaste for many of his social and aesthetic ideas would be echoed by legions of Wagnerians in the century to come.

DAVID C. LARGE

Posthumous reputation and influence

WE SPEAK OF 'WAGNERISM' but not of Mozartism, Beethovenism, or Brahmsism. Wagner's influence, especially during the peak period of Wagnerism in the late 19th and early 20th centuries, reached far beyond the world of music and theatre, embracing most of the other arts, as well as philosophy, social theory and politics. The main reason for this is that Wagner, perhaps regrettably, always considered himself more than a mere musician. He put himself forward as an all-purpose messiah come to redeem not just opera, but the sorry state of European culture and society.

It is astounding how many *fin-de-siècle* artists and intellectuals believed that Wagner's multifaceted legacy could be of use in enhancing their work, not to mention their lives. But since they generally employed what they took from Wagner as springboards for their own flights of fancy, Wagner's influence ultimately took on a life of its own, its radically differing manifestations often only distantly related to their source. And since the various Wagner disciples tended to believe that they alone understood the true meaning of the Master's word, the Wagner movement became as rigidly sectarian as it was protean. Needless to say, the enthusiasm of the Wagnerians also helped to generate an equally passionate anti-Wagnerian sentiment. George Bernard Shaw, himself a claimant to true Wagnerian wisdom, exaggerated only slightly when he observed that 'the wars of religion were not more bloodthirsty than the discussions of the Wagnerians and anti-Wagnerians'.

Given the many-sidedness of Wagner's posthumous influence and reputation, no tidy summary of this subject will be attempted here. But it might be useful to highlight the diversity of Wagner's legacy in the three or four decades following his death by examining some of the ways it was used and abused in those countries where it had the greatest impact. This will serve to remind us that the man who once called himself 'the most German of beings' had an influence that was nothing if not international.

France

The cultural historian Jacques Barzun once insisted that late 19th-century Paris was 'almost more Wagnerian than the home of the Master'. This was an exaggeration, but it is true that Wagner remained surprisingly popular in the French capital despite bitter memories of the Franco-Prussian War and Wagner's own crude Francophobia. After a brief hiatus in the 1870s, conductors such as Edouard Colonne and Charles Lamoureux made Wagner's music an integral part of Paris's orchestral repertory in the 1880s, though it took somewhat longer to revive the music dramas at the national Opéra. In the decade after Wagner's death, Frenchmen proved more loyal pilgrims to Bayreuth than the fickle Germans; without the French, Bayreuth might have folded.

France, and particularly Paris, was also an important centre of literary Wagnerism. A seminal work in this domain was Joris-Karl Huysmans's novel *A rebours* (*Against the Grain*), first published in 1884. The protagonist is a world-weary aesthete who seeks refuge from bourgeois mediocrity and ugliness in the music of Wagner, as well as in other sensuous delights. Through Huysmans – and later a host of epigones – Wagner's name became a byword for 'decadence' – for the pursuit of personal fulfilment via a combination of sensualism and mysticism. Wagner's influence among the French literati was further enhanced by the appearance in 1885 of a new journal, the *Revue Wagnérienne*. Though this journal survived only until 1888, it contributed significantly to the dissemination of Wagner's influence by publishing translations of his writings, reviews of books about him, analyses of the music dramas, and reports on the ongoing efforts to mount his operas in Paris. The *Revue* was less successful in its attempts to apply Wagnerian aesthetic principles to the production of Symbolist poetry, for this effort was based on little direct contact with Wagner's music dramas and on an imprecise understanding of Wagnerian concepts such as 'endless melody' and 'synthesis of the arts' (see also 'Wagner's impact on literature', pp.396–8).

Whatever the shortcomings of literary Wagnerism in France, the French were instrumental in spreading Wagner's influence far beyond their own country. Unburdened by the extreme nationalism that increasingly characterized German interpretations of Wagner, French Wagnerians from Baudelaire to Mallarmé made this legacy 'exportable' throughout Europe.

Italy

In Italy, the world capital of Romantic opera, Wagner's music dramas inevitably presented a threat to entrenched cultural traditions. A production of *Lohengrin* at Milan's venerable La Scala in 1873 elicited outraged cries of 'Viva Rossini!', 'Viva Verdi!' and 'Death to Wagner!' Yet this country, like France, produced impassioned partisans of Wagner who did their best to spread his influence in their own country and elsewhere, especially after he was safely dead. Wagnerians in the towns of Bologna and Turin took the lead in this enterprise, partly because it was a good way of poking a cultural stick in the eye of their old rival Milan. After giving the Italian premieres of *Lohengrin* in 1871 and *Tannhäuser* in 1872, Bologna mounted those of *Der fliegende Holländer* in 1877, *Tristan und Isolde* in 1888, and *Parsifal* in 1914. Turin attempted to stage an Italian *Ring* in 1891, but was prevented from doing so by Giulio Ricordi of Milan, a staunch Verdi defender who happened to own the Italian rights to the work. Bologna's small but committed Wagnerian community established an Italian chapter of the International Richard Wagner Society in 1893, which among other contributions published a journal called *Cronaca Wagneriana*, a register of all Wagnerian events in Italy. Bologna and Turin also sponsored regular pilgrimages to Bayreuth so that the faithful from these outposts of Latin Wagnerism could dutifully worship at the Mother Shrine.

But Wagner's influence in Italy went well beyond local enthusiasms and communal rivalries. It achieved true national significance when it was taken up in the 1890s by artists and intellectuals who saw Wagnerism as an effective weapon against the desiccated bourgeois liberalism that set the political tone in post-Unification Italy. Most prominent among this faction was the 'warrior-poet' Gabriele D'Annunzio, who applied some of Wagner's social and political ideals to the cause of 'integral nationalism', which demanded the triumph of 'heroic activism' over parliamentary squabbling and irresolution. D'Annunzio's short-lived rule over the island of Fiume in 1919 betrayed a certain Wagnerian quality in its heady combination of exalted rhetoric, stirring music and mass choreography – a style of politics that would soon be appropriated by Mussolini (and later by Hitler).

Russia

If it seems somewhat odd that Wagner would have found such an enthusiastic following in Italy, it seems perhaps even stranger that his work would ultimately have a yet more significant impact on Russia, a country he only briefly toured in 1863 – apart from his youthful posting in Riga. But Wagner's message proved highly attractive to the *fin-de-siècle* Russian intelligentsia, which was turning away from utilitarian positivism and toward more spiritually compelling ideals and aesthetic forms. In fact, Wagner's protean legacy spawned a number of quite divergent schools or tendencies among his Russian followers: most prominently a Symbolist-aesthetic school strongly influenced by French Wagnerians; a mystical-religious persuasion; and (oddly enough) an anarcho-communist wing. Although these groups differed significantly in what they found essential or usable in Wagner's work, they were united in their willingness to impose on it a distinctly Russian flavour. Sergey Diaghilev's Ballets Russes, for example, amounted to a kind of Russification of the *Gesamtkunstwerk* (synthesis of the arts): its motivating idea was the employment of Wagner's aesthetic principles in a campaign to unify Russian culture. The Wagnerians associated with the Ballets Russes produced a journal, *Mir iskoustva* (*The World of Art*), which dutifully translated the major French and German interpretations of Wagner's works. Its focus, however, was on the uses to which this legacy could be put in the cultural renovation of Russia.

The same can be said for the Russian application of Wagner's legacy to revolutionary politics. Wagner himself, of course, had once hoped that his work might serve just such a purpose, especially in his native land of Germany, but he had eventually grown disillusioned with the prospects for combining cultural and political revolution. The political idealism inherent in his early career found practical application not in Germany, but in distant Russia, where radical Wagnerians such as Vyacheslav Ivanov, Georgi Chulkov, Aleksandr Blok and Anatoli Lunacharsky mixed Wagnerian aesthetics into their own distinctly Russian blend of mysticism, neo-populism and revolutionary activism.

Great Britain

In Great Britain the idea of Wagner turned out to be as protean in influence and application as in Russia. Here, there was an 'aesthetic' or decadent direction inspired largely by the French, and which found in Wagner's work a celebration of 'art pour l'art', as well as an escape from the constraints of Victorian moral conventions. This was certainly the case with Aubrey Beardsley's version of the *Tannhäuser* myth, *Venus and Tannhäuser*, which was too pornographic to be published in Beardsley's lifetime. Oscar Wilde, like Huysmans, made Wagner a code word for the cultivation of forbidden pleasures, but also, in an intriguing anticipation of Thomas Mann, a symbol of self-destruction. Thus we have his most famous fictional character, Dorian Gray, 'listening in rapt pleasure to *Tannhäuser* and seeing in the prelude to that great work of art a presentation of the tragedy of his own soul' (*The Picture of Dorian Gray*).

Wagner's legacy served a much different purpose for the group of disciples clustered around a journal called *The Meister*. These apostles found in Wagner a comprehensive value-system that might serve as an alternative to the Victorian belief in technological progress. The journal's editor, William Ashton Ellis, summed up this impulse and Wagner's importance to it when he asserted that the Master's music and ideas would help to liberate mankind 'from the tightening grip of crushing scientific materialism', because 'at no time [had] there been such a widespread desire to search all things, and to bring forth some of the hidden secrets of that which is above and beyond matter'.

Ellis's brand of Wagnerism found little favour with Britain's most famous Wagnerite, George Bernard Shaw. Shaw dismissed *The Meister* as a fount of pious claptrap, devoid of any appreciation of Wagner's socialistic critique of the capitalist system. It was such a critique which Shaw found to be the essence of the *Ring* cycle, which he treated as a political parable of capitalist greed and self-destruction. Shaw's interpretation of the *Ring* had little influence on turn-of-the-century Wagnerism, but it was to enjoy something of a revival in Patrice Chéreau's controversial Bayreuth *Ring* of 1976, which treated Wagner's work as an allegory on the evils of capitalism and industrialization.

Germany

The history of Wagner's posthumous influence in his own country is a testament to the wisdom of Nietzsche's dictum that artists and intellectuals should be wary of attracting disciples. His most zealous followers – the so-called Bayreuth Circle (see 'The Bayreuth legacy', p.390–91) – were so convinced that they alone had a legitimate claim to his legacy that they tried to control or limit the production of his works outside Bayreuth. The most infamous case of this was Cosima Wagner's unsuccessful legal battle to prevent New York's Metropolitan Opera from producing *Parsifal* in 1903. As Wagner's literary executor, Cosima also controlled access to his voluminous papers, welcoming only those Wagner students who (like the 'official' biographer, Carl Friedrich Glasenapp) echoed her own cramped views on the meaning of Wagner's works. Bayreuth's house journal, the *Bayreuther Blätter*, was equally narrow-minded, opening its pages almost exclusively to writers and critics who toed the conservative-nationalist line of the editor, Hans von Wolzogen. Thus it is not surprising that neither Nietzsche nor Thomas Mann, Germany's most brilliant but quite imperfect Wagnerites, ever appeared in the *Blätter*; nor, indeed, did any other German writer of the first rank, save for Theodor Fontane.

Wagner's Bayreuth disciples helped to ensure that his posthumous influence in Germany would be closely connected to the forces of Wilhelminian nationalism. Kaiser Wilhelm II, an admirer of Houston Stewart Chamberlain, the English-born *völkisch* guru who became Wagner's son-in-law, saw Wagner's music as the perfect accompaniment to Germany's quest for world power. Unlike his grandfather, Wilhelm I, he visited Bayreuth regularly and tithed 1000 thalers annually to this shrine of Germanic worship. He also helped to design a characteristically pompous Wagner monument in Berlin and had his automobile horn tuned to the motif of Donner's thunder from *Das Rheingold*.

Less amusingly, the Reich's superpatriots constantly invoked Wagner's legacy in defending Germany's 'sacred mission' in World

War I. A typical product of this enterprise was Richard Sternfeld's *Richard Wagner und der heilige deutsche Krieg*, which found justification for Germany's imperialist aspirations in Wagner's music dramas (especially in *Lohengrin*) and in his prose writings. When passages from *Parsifal* were played in a concert for German soldiers in occupied Lille's Cathedral of St Quentin, the *Liller Kriegszeitung* gushed: 'Here the musical celebration of the pure fool; out there [on the front] the heroic deeds of the pure sword of the Germans.' Even Prussian generals found uses for Wagner's legacy, naming German military positions on the front after Wotan, Siegfried, Brünnhilde and Hunding.

Adolf Hitler, of course, would emulate this last practice in World War II, but it should be clear that Wagner's legacy had been thoroughly appropriated by German nationalists well before the Führer exploited Wagner's works as the theme music for the Third Reich. In this context, we might recall that Nietzsche had already observed in 1888: 'It is full of profound significance that the arrival of Wagner coincides with the arrival of "the Reich": both events prove the same thing – [the need for] obedience and long legs.'

DAVID C. LARGE

The Bayreuth legacy

LIKE RICHARD WAGNER HIMSELF, the festival theatre he founded in Bayreuth generated over the years a complex legacy rife with contradictions. While the central purpose of the summer festivals remained that of mounting Wagner's music dramas in an ideal setting, the name 'Bayreuth' came to connote much more than Wagnerian musical theatre. Virtually from the outset, the festivals took on a cargo of ideological and political baggage that grew more ponderous with the years and eventually almost crushed the entire enterprise. Contemporary Bayreuth is still struggling to come to terms with the implications of its burdensome past.

Wagner's selection of Bayreuth as the site for his projected festival theatre was not based entirely – or even primarily – on aesthetic considerations. In the wake of Prussia's victory over Austria in 1866, Wagner had come to see that North German kingdom as the potential saviour not just of Germany, but of his own artistic ambitions. Though the town of Bayreuth lay in Bavarian territory (an important consideration, for Wagner hoped to continue to tap King Ludwig II of Bavaria for financial support), it had formerly been a Prussian seat. In the 18th century it was the residence of Margravine Wilhelmine, Friedrich the Great's favourite sister. It was she, in fact, who had built the local opera house that Wagner initially thought might serve as a suitable stage for his music dramas, but which on closer inspection turned out to be unsatisfactory. At any rate, a move to Bayreuth might connote Wagner's staking a claim to the Prussian-backed German nationalist movement, and perhaps even to the largesse of the ascendant Hohenzollern house. Moreover, Bayreuth had no ongoing theatrical operation of its own that might have competed with Wagner's enterprise. Indeed, it had no prominent cultural or social institutions of any kind – save perhaps for the local lunatic asylum, which some Wagner detractors would eventually consider a haven of sanity in comparison to the Festspielhaus. Bayreuth, in other words, was a place where Wagner could be king, a place he could put on the map as the new capital of German art. It might become, as he put it, 'a sort of Art-Washington D.C.'

The achievement of German unity in 1871 under Prussian hegemony convinced Wagner that his own artistic destiny lay with the new Reich. For the next few years he courted Germany's new rulers, especially Bismarck, unctuously seeking financial backing from Berlin for his planned theatre. In exchange for imperial funding, he proposed to stage the premiere of his *Ring* tetralogy as 'a quinquennial celebration to mark the victory over France in 1871'. Alas, Bismarck, who could not abide Wagner, was not enticed by this generous offer, and he made sure that the Bayreuth project received no financial support from the Reich.

The Iron Chancellor stayed away from the first Bayreuth Festival in 1876, as did generals Roon and Moltke, the architects of Germany's victory over France. Kaiser Wilhelm I consented to make an appearance, but he left early to attend a military manoeuvre. Wagner was thus forced to recognize that he had failed to make his Bayreuth Festival the 'artistic sister of German Unification', the theatrical symbol of Germany's national consciousness and ascendant military power. He responded to this affront as his ardent disciple Adolf Hitler would later react to Germany's impending defeat in World War II: by deciding that the German people were not worthy of him. In his growing disillusionment with the fatherland, he even contemplated emigrating to Minnesota, whose German–American citizens had offered to subsidize a New World Festspielhaus. It is a shame that he did not make this move: a New World Bayreuth in the American Middle West would certainly have had a more wholesome influence on the evolution of Wagner's legacy. ·

In the hands of the composer's widow, Cosima, the Wagner festivals prospered commercially, as Wagnerians from around the world streamed to the 'Green Hill' in Bayreuth to witness competent, albeit narrowly conservative and stultifyingly unvarying productions of the music dramas. Though at heart a chauvinist, xenophobe and racist, Cosima was careful not to offend the foreign visitors upon whose money Bayreuth depended. Nevertheless, under Cosima the Festspielhaus became a pilgrimage goal for extreme German nationalists. They flocked there not just because they loved Wagner's music, but also because they saw the annual festivals as opportunities for patriotic communion that might lend a greater sense of unity and cohesion to a nation still sharply divided along regional, religious and class lines.

Bayreuth became central to the evolution of German nationalism in the Wilhelminian era also because it was the home of the so-called 'Bayreuth Circle' – a small coterie of Wagner disciples who invariably interpreted his complex work in a *völkisch* vein. This group, whose most prominent representative was the naturalized Englishman and Wagner son-in-law Houston Stewart Chamberlain, took Wagner's problematical prose writings as seriously as his music. They celebrated their idol as a great philosopher whose ideas could be appropriated as an antidote to the foreign and 'racially alien' influences they believed were corrupting the German people. Their journal, the barely readable *Bayreuther Blätter*, became a repository of 'idealist' anti-Semitism and pan-German megalomania.

During the years of the Weimar Republic (1918–33), famous for its spirit of artistic experimentation, Bayreuth became something of a cultural backwater. Richard Wagner's son Siegfried, who administered the festivals between 1907 and his untimely death in 1930, declared that 'Bayreuth [was] not there for any sort of hyper-modern vogues. This would contradict the style of the works, which after all were not written and composed as Cubist, Expressionist, or Dadaist.' Siegfried accordingly hewed close to the traditionalist line in most of his productions, though occasionally employing some new stage designs and lighting innovations that irritated the old Bayreuth guard, who wanted to see nothing but sets 'upon which the Master's eyes had once rested'. Siegfried invited Toscanini to conduct a new *Tannhäuser* production in 1930, but did not live to witness what amounted to a genuine though temporary accommodation of more contemporary tastes.

On the political front, Siegfried's Bayreuth betrayed that same strained dualism between cosmopolitanism and Germanic nationalism that it had developed so strongly in the Wilhelminian era. This dualism was starkly evident at the first post-war festival in 1924, when a group of Nazis stood up at the end of *Die Meistersinger* and sang the *Deutschlandlied*. Siegfried, though himself sympathetic to the Nazi cause, promptly placed a banner over the Festspielhaus entrance that proclaimed: 'Hier gilt's der Kunst!' ('Our Aim Is Art!'). As if to underscore this ideal, Siegfried made a point of employing Jewish singers and musicians at Bayreuth, a practice that caused Hitler later to observe that Siegfried had been 'somewhat in the hands of the Jews'.

But whatever Siegfried's claims regarding the festival's 'unpolitical' mission, art was no more the sole aim of Bayreuth in the 1920s than it had been in the Wilhelminian era, or for that matter in Richard Wagner's own day. At Siegfried's request, Hitler stayed away from the festivals between 1926 and 1933, but the Nazi spirit was very much evident in the town. The Bayreuther Bund der deutschen Jugend, founded in 1925, emphasized in its official programme 'the deep interrelationship between the great German [. . .] cultural ideas of Adolf Hitler and the work of Bayreuth'. In a fundraising drive for the new *Tannhäuser* production in 1930, Bayreuth described itself as the 'last bastion of the German spirit and character'.

When Hitler assumed power in Germany in 1933, Wagner's

Festspielhaus finally became something like a German national theatre. The Führer, who had very close ties to Bayreuth's new mistress, Siegfried's English-born widow Winifred, graced the summer festivals with his presence and supported them with generous subsidies from the Reich treasury. So close was the relationship between Hitler and Winifred that Bayreuth managed to maintain a certain independence from the Nazi cultural bureaucracy, successfully resisting Goebbels' efforts to bring the festivals under the control of his Reich Cultural Chamber. But this did not alter the fact that Bayreuth was now clearly an instrument of Nazi propaganda and increasingly a cultural shrine visited primarily by Germans. During the war, indeed, the Festspielhaus was filled almost exclusively with Nazi officials, arms-factory workers, and wounded soldiers brought in via the 'Strength through Joy' programme. (No doubt many of the soldiers found this a particularly sadistic form of 'Rest and Recreation'.) The Nazis insisted that these wartime festivals amounted to a realization, at long last, of Wagner's original ideal of making Bayreuth into a popular festival open to all 'friends of his art', regardless of financial means. Though it is doubtful that these sleeping party officials and restless soldiers were exactly what Wagner had in mind, it is true that they were less privileged than the aristocratic and upper-bourgeois patrons of the past – and, for that matter, less well-off than the Wagnerian frequent-fliers who would set the tone at Bayreuth in the late 20th century.

The admonition 'Our Aim Is Art' again greeted visitors to the revived Bayreuth Festival in 1951. Now, however, art really did take precedence, and the interpretations of Wagner's art were, for a change, refreshingly heretical by the standards of Old Bayreuth. Richard Wagner's grandsons Wieland and Wolfgang were determined to treat their grandfather's work not as a relic to be carefully preserved against change, but as a heritage requiring constant reassessment and rejuvenation. Yet for all their concern with evolving a new aesthetic, they realized that the challenge they faced was moral and political as well as artistic. Hence Wieland Wagner interpreted *Die Meistersinger* in 1956 as a warning against German delusions of grandeur, and mounted the *Ring* in 1965 as an allegory on fascism. In taking this line Wieland argued that he was bringing his grandfather's originally progressive intentions up to date. But in trying to deploy 'true' Wagnerian ideals against what he regarded as their perversion by extreme nationalists and racists, he was also waging a struggle against the Wagnerian legacy he and his brother had inherited from the previous administrators of Bayreuth.

DAVID C. LARGE

The birth of modernism: Wagner's impact on the history of music

WAGNER'S IMPACT ON the history of music has been all-pervading in the sense that historians may continue to categorize the major composers born between the mid-1850s and the end of the century – from Elgar, Sibelius and Richard Strauss to Schoenberg, Stravinsky and Bartók – as 'post-Wagnerian', or even 'anti-Wagnerian'. Historians in search of a conveniently reductive formula may still attempt to offer general interpretations of musical developments since the 1880s as if those developments were determined entirely by responses to specific challenges thrown down by Wagner, about the role of music (and drama) in society, the status of the composer, and the need to adopt a progressive approach to harmony, tonality, form and rhythmic organization. Connected with this is the argument that Wagner's impact was felt less through his music than through the ideas and actions of his immediate followers, reflecting the degree to which his prose works and life-style were more explicitly influential than his compositions. This position has been developed by William Weber, as part of his thesis that 'Wagnerism' was a notably potent cultural force in the years immediately after Wagner's death:

> The followers of Wagner launched the first movement that saw itself as a musical avant-garde, an intellectual cadre supporting works that it claimed were progressive and, by definition, controversial. In so doing, Wagnerism laid the intellectual and social ground-work for the rise of the self-contained cultural world of new music, which today devotes itself primarily to contemporary works. (Large and Weber, 1984)

In Weber's terms, Wagner himself was not an archetypal 'Wagnerian'; he was concerned simply to make sure that his works were performed in the most appropriate manner. It was his followers who sought to lay down the guidelines for what has become known as 'musical modernism', and Weber finds important evidence for this development in the Vienna of the 1890s and the feud between Brahmsians and Wagnerians, with Hugo Wolf the most prominent activist in the Wagnerian camp. The subject of the emergence of a concept of the avant garde in music is a complex one, and Carl Dahlhaus has claimed that it 'is an historical category which arose in the 18th century together with the notion of originality and the idea of the autonomous work' (Dahlhaus, 1987). Yet Wagnerism undoubtedly did encourage the specific qualities we associate with post-Wagnerian modernism. In Weber's terms, the arch-modernist is Arnold Schoenberg, and so it is important to recognize that Wagner's music was as important a source of Schoenberg's development as a composer as was the position of the Wagnerites on the appropriate social role for an avant-garde composer.

Very little music of significance that recalls Wagner's own style closely and sustainedly has survived, and that which has – Humperdinck's *Hänsel und Gretel*, certain works by Dvořák – is far from slavishly imitative. Yet it would be historically blinkered to limit the legitimacy of the Wagnerian impact to such direct associations. Dahlhaus has contended that 'Wagner's impact [. . .] was almost equally as strong in the symphony and symphonic poem, in chamber music and lied [. . .] as on the musical stage', and for two associated reasons: first, because Wagner's later espousal of a Schopenhauerian aesthetic promoted that elevation of music 'for its own sake', and therefore an emphasis on non-vocal concert music, that Wagner had originally scorned; second, because 'in the official Bayreuth view [. . .] legitimate Wagnerianism lay in avoiding the overwhelming presence of Wagner's legacy by seeking refuge in musico-theatrical genres considered peripheral by Wagner himself' (Dahlhaus, 1989a). It is in such terms that the possibility of Wagner's music having a strong impact on Schoenberg should be considered. Schoenberg himself acknowledged Wagner as one of the most important sources of his own development as a composer, declaring that he had learned from Wagner

i. The way it is possible to manipulate themes for expressive purposes and the art of formulating them in the way that will serve this end.
ii. Relatedness of tones and chords.
iii. The possibility of regarding themes and motives as if they were complex ornaments, so that they can be used against harmonies in a dissonant way. (Schoenberg, 1975)

It seems clear that Schoenberg saw Wagner as, above all, a precursor of the kind of total thematicism in which linear and motivic features were all-pervading, and chords were in essence simply the vertical aggregate of motivic tones. It can also be argued that the principle of 'musical prose' adumbrated by Wagner in *Oper und Drama* reaches its evolutionary apotheosis in such works of Schoenberg as the fifth of the op. 16 Orchestral Pieces ('The obbligato recitative') and the monodrama *Erwartung*, in which form consists of a succession of brief, period-like segments each dominated by a distinctive, motif-like idea. In this way it can be claimed that Wagner's most personal and essential formal principle exercised a far greater influence on subsequent developments in composition than either his life-style or his musical style as such, and that these developments have continued, through Schoenberg, to affect avant-garde composers of later generations, like Pierre Boulez and Peter Maxwell Davies. Boulez, in particular, who became one of the most prominent conductors of Wagner's music dramas in the 1970s, has commented on the 'constant mobility' of material in the *Ring*, and the 'perpetual evolution' at work in *Parsifal*, revealing obvious links between his understanding of Wagner and his own avant-garde concerns as a composer (Boulez, 1986). Moreover, like Schoenberg, Boulez has nailed his avant-garde colours to the mast in his championship of new music.

Attempts to consider Wagner's impact in terms of certain kinds of musical atmosphere may nevertheless promote 'connections' so broad as to be meaningless: for example, between the Dionysiac, ritual spirit often evident in Wagner's work (especially in *Tristan*) and a comparable quality in Stravinsky's *The Rite of Spring*. As is the case with Debussy's *Pelléas et Mélisande*, resistance to, and even rejection of, Wagner may be difficult to disentangle from awareness of, or stimulation by, Wagner; and it may indeed be true that if Stravinsky had not been so deeply bored by *Parsifal* at Bayreuth in 1912 he would not have composed *The Rite of Spring* in quite the way he did. Yet there is little or nothing to be gained, even from the perspectives of cultural history, in considering that masterpiece alongside, or in relation to, Wagner's means of expressing the 'Dionysiac, ritual spirit'. By contrast, there are plenty of composers who have adopted and developed Wagner's technical or aesthetic concepts – even, in Skryabin's case, that of the *Gesamtkunstwerk*. As for the leitmotivic technique, this has flourished in the context of utterly unWagnerian styles – Britten's, for example; while the English composer Rutland Boughton, whose Arthurian cycle of five operas (1908–45) is frequently labelled 'Wagnerian' on account of its evident desire to emulate the Master of Bayreuth, actually wrote a very different kind of music, reacting against the more truly Wagnerian manner of his own earlier work rather than continuing that manner.

In more recent times, when 'Wagnerian' tends to be synonymous with anything large-scale and epic (pretentious) in character, it is well to be even more cautious in identifying evidence of 'impact'. Yet the avant-garde aesthetic has continued to promote the operatic treatment of myth and ritual, as in Stockhausen's seven-opera cycle in progress, *Licht*; and Berio has adopted a Wagnerian perspective in describing what he sees as opera's failure to come to terms with the genre of 'Handlung', which, he believes, Wagner invented in *Tristan*. Berio says of his own attempt at such a work, *Un re in ascolto* (1984), that it is 'the musical processes that are primarily responsible for the narration' (Berio, 1989), and whether or not this is an accurate interpretation of Wagner's procedure in *Tristan*, it demonstrates that Wagner's own critique of traditional opera continues to influence the thinking and techniques of later composers.

The most obvious evidence for Wagner's continued presence in music over the years since his death comes in the direct quotation (or parodied recomposition) of his own musical ideas. As Debussy, Berg and Britten have demonstrated, the '*Tristan* chord' could be used as a metaphor for the spirit of desire and longing in ways that could be mocking or intensely serious, according to context. Hans Werner Henze, in his *Tristan* for piano, tapes and orchestra (1973), used quotation and allusion as the starting-point for a work that seeks to drain every last drop from the potent brew which is created when all that is associated with various manifestations of the Tristan story confront the manipulative resources of the modern composer. Robin Holloway, by contrast, has moved from the network of quotations and allusions found in his opera *Clarissa* (1976) to something closer in spirit to the piano-duet parodies of Fauré–Messager and Chabrier. *Wagner Nights* for orchestra (1990) is an expression of what Holloway sees as the need to acknowledge Wagner's unique impact on music, an impact which will never be completely lost:

> Such figurative power of expression [as that arising from a leitmotivic texture], its directness and impact uninhibited by verbal limitation, is the part of music's intrinsic possibilities first unloosed by Wagner. I believe that composers a hundred years later owe just as much to him, albeit obliquely, as in the decades after his death when his direct *influence* was well-nigh inescapable. (Holloway, 1990)

ARNOLD WHITTALL

Wagner's impact on literature

'WAGNER HAS HAD a greater influence than any other single artist on the culture of our age' (Magee, 1968): the impingement of Wagner on literature is our concern here, an impingement, in William Blissett's words, both profound and persuasive. That a musician should have had such an overwhelming effect on literature is remarkable indeed, but Wagner dramatically accelerated that shift towards music in the arts which the late 19th century exemplified, and provided imaginative writing with an enormous enrichment. His protean abundance meant that he could inspire the use of the literary leitmotif in many a novel employing interior monologue; the yearnings of the mythmakers increasingly took his music dramas as a fecund source; the Symbolists saw him as a mystic hierophant; the Decadents found many a frisson in his work. The composer who provided a common source for *symboliste* subtleties, for mystagogues and psychologists must have been of uncommon stature, and European culture would have been immeasurably impoverished without him.

The *symbolistes* were the first to see in Wagner a powerful stimulus, being preoccupied by the nature of music and its relations to poetry: art was to be symbolical rather than representational and an attempt was to be made in writing to 'musicalize' the inner universe. A poet of the stature of Mallarmé feared that the literary mode would become jejune and limited if it could not emulate musical patterns, and by 'musical' he meant Wagnerian. Verlaine's demand that all art be subordinate to music, and Mallarmé's suspicions that poetry might have become the lesser achievement both derive from an awed devotion to Wagner. The foundation of the *Revue Wagnérienne* in 1885 showed how central Wagner had become to the French *symbolistes*, who used Wagner as a mirror and an image of their own theories and aspirations. Mallarmé's contribution to this journal, 'Richard Wagner: Rêverie d'un poëte français', is an act of homage, half article, half prose poem. The description of Wagner's ideal and work is set forth in religious and ritualistic terms: the theatre is to become a temple and the spectacle a ceremony in which the masses were to participate in a sacred rite. Mallarmé's 'Notes sur le théâtre', contributed to the *Revue Indépendante*, continued to stress the need for an ideal, symbolic drama; naturalism is deplored, and the formulation of spiritual attitudes, imaginative vision and timeless states of soul are encouraged.

Symbolism and inwardness, leitmotif and stream of consciousness – the Wagnerian presence looms large. The tendency for the modern novel to reject definite plot and subject matter, and to concentrate on the consciousness of the main character (frequently to the exclusion of everything else) is well known. The writer Théodore de Wyzewa insisted in 1895 that the novelist of the future would erect a single consciousness which he would imbue with life; through it images would be perceived, themes would be resolved, emotions would be felt. Wyzewa had been an active contributor to the *Revue Wagnérienne*: what is more important is the fact that the founder of that journal, Edouard Dujardin, had published in 1887 his novel *Les Lauriers sont coupés* (*The Laurels are Cut*), which was revolutionary in that the reader is suspended in the consciousness of a single character throughout. Dujardin pointed out the analogy between musical motifs and the short, direct phrases of interior monologue and admitted that his novel was written with the intention of transposing Wagnerian procedures into literary devices. It was to be James Joyce who would perfect this technique, a writer who knew his Wagner intimately. With Joyce the stream of consciousness technique reached its finest flowering, and in the hands of a master like Proust the leitmotif would also be used with an amazing subtlety and complexity. *A la recherche du temps perdu* may be seen as a literary counterpart to Wagner's *Ring*, a vast fabric of themes constantly modulating and repeating, constantly cross-referring until all sense of linear development has been suspended. The name of Virginia Woolf is important here: she had visited Bayreuth in August 1909 and recorded her 'Impressions at Bayreuth' for *The Times*. Her novel *The Waves*, conceived and composed musically, relegates both character and plot to the background: a pulsating fabric of symbols and motifs, derived incontrovertibly from Wagner, takes precedence.

That which may be called the symbolical novel owes much to him: that bizarre offshoot of French Symbolism – decadence – equally exults in his presence. The sultry religiosity of *Parsifal*, the death-intoxicated eroticism of *Tristan und Isolde* and the glorification of incest in *Die Walküre* could not fail to enrapture, and it became *de rigueur* for the generation of the *décadents* to invoke his name. Verlaine's *Parsifal* sonnet (later quoted by Eliot in *The Waste Land*), Huysmans's *Ouverture de Tannhäuser*, Beardsley's *Under the Hill*, Thomas Mann's *Wälsungenblut*, D'Annunzio's *Il trionfo della morte* (*The Triumph of Death*), Maurice Barrès's *La Mort de Venise*, Vernon Lee's *A Wicked Voice* – the list is long of those works which delighted in portraying Wagner's apparent sensuality, dubious morality and unsettling blandishments: Nietzsche had prepared the way.

More important, however, are those works which are indebted to Wagner's exemplary handling of myth. Claude Lévi-Strauss has seen in Wagner the father of the structural analysis of myth, going so far as to claim that those strange words of Gurnemanz, 'You see, my son, time here becomes space', were the most profound definition of myth in general. Wagner's treatment of mythical, archetypal situations and of themes handed down from ancient legends represented a stimulating antidote to sterile urban writing: a vast body of literature sprang up after him in which mythical patterns became paramount. His prose writings had emphasized the life-enhancing quality of myth, and passages from *Das Kunstwerk der Zukunft* (*The Artwork of the Future*) are a remarkable anticipation of the work of D.H. Lawrence. *The Trespasser* is suffused by Wagnerian references (*Tristan* above all); *Women in Love* is full of love, death, blood brotherhood and the collision between life and the destructive urges of an industrial society. Mythical reverberations are also perceptible in Joseph Conrad, whose writing is enriched by Wagnerian parallels, *Nostromo* above all (the images of the fearful mine and the wall of metal built between human beings); the sombre knitters of the *Heart of Darkness* hint at the Norns. George Moore is another name to add to the list, but his countryman James Joyce is the supreme novelist for whom myth was paramount. Wagner references abound in his work, with *Finnegans Wake* providing an amusing compendium of Wagnerian puns. Another great recipient was Thomas Mann, who never ceased to praise Wagner's fusion of myth and psychology, seeing him as the man who, long before Freud, explored oedipal situations. Mann's vast oeuvre owes an enormous debt to Wagner, yet Mann was not blind to the manner in which Wagner had fallen into the hands of unscrupulous mythmakers in the Third Reich.

More recent writing has preferred parody (Anthony Burgess's *The Worm and the Ring*, for example, with its portrayal of 'Albert Rich' in his pursuit of three giggling schoolgirls through the rain), but Wagner's stature has not diminished. The literature of the last century, it has been said, contains more references to the man and his work than to any other artist (see 'Myths and Legends', p.132). He has conquered vast areas of the world's mind, and the canon of modern classics is beholden to his hegemony.

RAYMOND FURNESS

'I AM READING a book on Wagner', wrote Vincent van Gogh to his brother Theo in June 1888. 'What an artist – one like that in painting would be something. It *will come*.' Wagner's influence on the visual arts was then at its zenith. It went far beyond the use of subjects from the operas, although that was important. Indeed, its very diffuseness is a problem in tackling the subject, for artists were not principally attracted by the dramatic, psychological or philosophical complexities of the works, and very few had any technical grasp of the music. Instead, they were drawn by a loosely understood notion of 'Wagnerism'. That meant an admiration of

Wagner's impact on the visual arts

Wagner himself as the type of the heroic artist; a belief that his use of an abstract medium to convey pictorial effects and powerful emotions was a justification for the visual arts using a symbolic, synaesthetic or abstract language; and a strong interest in the *Gesamtkunstwerk*, albeit with a more prominent role for the visual arts than Wagner, notoriously indifferent to painting, sculpture or architecture, would have envisaged.

It is ironic, given Wagner's Francophobia, that his influence over artists was felt most emphatically in France. The few German-speaking artists of distinction who had been drawn into Wagner's circle, such as the Swiss Arnold Böcklin, who declined invitations to work on the designs of the *Ring* and *Parsifal*, were cool about the Bayreuth phenomenon. Those German or Austrian artists who were later influenced by Wagnerian ideas, such as Max Klinger or Gustav Klimt, derived their interest principally from the Parisian avant garde. French enthusiasm for Wagner had begun with Baudelaire's celebrated essay on *Tannhäuser* of 1861. Artistic theorists of the next generation were deeply affected by his championing of the composer, which was reinforced by ideas expressed in his essay on the Salon of 1846 about the inherent musicality of colour. Such notions were current among the artists and critics who met throughout the 1860s at the Café Guerbois and were to be known as the Impressionists. Despite the famous comparison between Wagner's music and Impressionist techniques made by the poet and critic Jules Laforgue, direct use of Wagnerian motifs was rare in the Impressionists' work, although Auguste Renoir painted two overdoor panels illustrating scenes from *Tannhäuser*. An unenthusiastic listener to Wagner's music, Renoir was none the less intrigued by the man, whose portrait he painted in Palermo in 1882. His memories of that occasion include a tantalizing reference to Wagner discussing 'Impressionism in music'.

The Franco-Prussian War delayed the full burgeoning of Wagnerism in Paris, which came in the 1880s, remembered by Edouard Dujardin in 1908 as the movement's 'époque héroïque'. Dujardin was one of the founders in 1885 of the *Revue Wagnérienne*, an avant-garde journal devoted to promulgating ideas supposedly derived from Wagner about 'correspondences' between the arts. Its attitude towards painting was elaborated in an article of 1886 by Dujardin's fellow editor, Théodore de Wyzewa, who praised certain artists exhibiting at the 1885 Salon – mostly those now thought of as 'Symbolists' – for being 'Wagnerian'. This meant that they depicted 'not a direct vision of things but – as a consequence of age-old associations between images and feelings – a world of living, blissful emotion'. These artists included Gustave Moreau, Odilon Redon – whose first Wagnerian lithograph, *Brünnhilde*, appeared in the *Revue* in 1885 – and Henri Fantin-Latour, who had been producing lithographs and paintings illustrating Wagner's operas since 1862. Thanks largely to the *Revue*, Wagnerism permeated the philosophy of Symbolist and Decadent artists throughout the 1880s and 90s. Its influence was felt even in England, where Aubrey Beardsley's interest in Wagner culminated in a superb set of illustrations for *Das Rheingold* (1896).

In 1890 the *Revue Wagnérienne*'s synaesthetic ideals received their fullest and most coherent expression in Maurice Denis's influential *Définition du néo-traditionnisme*. A mark of how far such ideas had been disseminated is the number of references to Wagner in Van Gogh's letters during the summer of 1888, when he wrote to Theo that 'I made a vain attempt to learn music, so much did I already feel the relation between our colour and Wagner's music'. Paul Gauguin's response was even more intense. Thanks to the Symbolists, he conceived a strong belief in 'l'union féconde de tous les arts'. His so-called *Texte Wagner* (now in the Bibliothèque Nationale), a scrapbook of quotations by and about Wagner, documents the composer's influence during the time Gauguin was developing a theory of non-representational art. However, Wagner's influence over the generation of artists later to be loosely known as the 'Post-Impressionists' was not due solely to the Symbolists, for the young Paul Cézanne (with his close friend Emile Zola) had joined a Wagner Society in Marseilles as early as the mid-1860s. Cézanne's principal tribute was the several versions of the painting of a young woman at the piano, entitled *Overture to 'Tannhäuser'*, but it has been suggested (by Mary Tompkins Lewis, 1989) that depictions of the Venusberg by Fantin-Latour and Delacroix are among the sources for Cézanne's first paintings of bathers.

Despite the interest of Post-Impressionist painters in synaesthetic ideas, their complete dedication to one art alone suggests that the broad theory of the *Gesamtkunstwerk* made little headway in France. Yet in other countries it was to be of some importance in the development of 20th-century art. In his *Reminiscences* (1913), Wassily Kandinsky recorded the two events of his early years in Moscow which were to leave their stamp on his entire life: an exhibition of Impressionist paintings and a performance of *Lohengrin*. Significantly, he saw Wagner's music as a challenge to his art, for it seemed to him that it conveyed intense visual experience more powerfully than any painting. Although he later distanced himself from Wagner's 'materialism' and nationalism, the composer, with Skryabin, was a powerful influence as late as the *Blauer Reiter* period of Kandinsky's career. Between 1908 and 1912 he experimented with combining dance, drama and music in a *Bühnengesamtkunstwerk* ('total work of art for the stage') and it is clear that French ideas about Wagnerian 'correspondences' between the arts influenced his subsequent move into abstraction.

None of the visual arts has a better chance of realizing the *Gesamtkunstwerk* ideal than architecture. However, the Modern Movement's doctrinaire insistence on rationalism and eschewal of symbolism and nationalism were not fertile ground for Wagnerian ideas. It is only now that reappraisal of late 19th-century styles is leading to a realization that Wagner's influence was felt by architects also, although no attempt has yet been made to trace the Wagnerian element in, for instance, the fantasy designs of Expressionist architects such as Hermann Finsterlin. In America, however, explicitly Wagnerian buildings were actually erected.

Louis Sullivan was swept away by hearing Wagner concerts in Chicago, 'revealing anew, refreshing as dawn, the enormous power of man to build, as a mirage, the fabric of his dreams'. This Whitmanesque vision was given theoretical shape by the writings of an older Chicago architect, John Root, notably 'The Art of Pure Color' (1883). He added to mid-19th-century concerns for architectural polychromy an emotionally affective and symbolic function for colour that was explicitly derived from an analogy with Wagner's music. In Sullivan's early buildings this was realized principally by mural painting; later, in such masterpieces as the National Farmers' Bank in Owatonna, Minnesota (1906–8), he used abstract colour and architectural ornament to create a 'color tone poem', as he called it, designed to evoke emotion and the appearance of the natural world.

Once Wagner's works and ideas had moved from avant-garde status into the mainstream of artistic thought and practice, it was inevitable that his explicit influence would become fragmentary. It is more a matter of individual paintings, such as Salvador Dali's evocation of the ravings of the dying Tristan in *Le Bateau – Mad Tristan* of 1944, than of any sustained engagement with the works. Yet there were delayed surprises. A painting from the mid-1880s by the American artist Albert Pinkham Ryder, which depicts the Flying Dutchman's ship tossed by a storm, had a late offspring in the young Jackson Pollock's *Seascape* of 1934. This has led Robert Rosenblum (1975) to suggest that a Romantic evocation of natural forces coloured by a response to Wagner's music may be an ancestor of Abstract Expressionism.

The one exception to the absorption of Wagner's influence is in Germany, where artists still have to reclaim many of the traditions appropriated by the Nazis. In the 1970s Anselm Kiefer made a controversial start in a series of works on mythological themes that focuses closely on Wagner. *Notung* (1973) depicts the blood-stained sword thrust into the bare boards of an empty wooden room (Kiefer's attic studio at Hornbach in the Odenwald). Inscribed with Siegmund's words 'Ein Schwert verhiess mir der Vater' ('A sword was promised me by my father'), it is both a reminder of what is lying ignored in the lumber-room of German culture and an enigmatically threatening suggestion of a pledge still awaiting fulfilment.

MICHAEL HALL

MUSICAL BIOGRAPHY is a relatively recent phenomenon. Whereas the lives of saints and monarchs have a long and distinguished pedigree, it was not until the artist developed an independent identity during the Renaissance that accounts of painters' lives, pioneered by Vasari, first began to appear. Not until the 18th century, however, were the lives of musicians accorded necrological status, perhaps because, as Herta Blaukopf has suggested (Blaukopf, 1991), audiences, in their constant desire for musical novelty, regarded music as a fashionable recreation without any lasting value: until the 19th century, the musical repertory lacked the historical dimension that we nowadays take for granted.

The hagiographical origins of biography continued to leave their mark on 19th- and even 20th-century lives of composers and, although not even Wagner's most fervent apologists were able to gloss over every aspect of his turbulent and turpitudinous life, they succeeded at least in placing a *cordon sanitaire* around his Art.

The earliest full-length biographies of Wagner were written by two members of the Bayreuth praetorian guard, Carl Friedrich Glasenapp (1876–7) and Houston Stewart Chamberlain (1896), and paved the way for many later lives of the composer, with Glasenapp concentrating exclusively on the 'facts' of Wagner's life, while Chamberlain examined both life and works, convinced that the latter transfigured the former. Glasenapp's biography, originally published in two volumes, was later expanded to six, and, although the author clearly had access to information not otherwise available, his uncritical tone was such that, having embarked on an English translation of it, William Ashton Ellis found himself radically rewriting the text from the third volume onwards, before finally abandoning the enterprise altogether, with Wagner's life still incompletely told.

Chamberlain's golden rule was that, for the Wagner scholar, 'Wagner's writings, with his letters and his works[!], will always be the most important, I might more properly say the *only* source from which we shall be able to derive a deeper knowledge of this extraordinary man.' (quoted Lippert, 1930) Later biographers have been more sceptical – though often more so in theory than in practice; but as long as those sources themselves remained corrupt or at least suspect, any life of the composer which relied upon them was unlikely to stand the scrutiny of time.

It was to Ernest Newman's credit that, refusing to accept received opinion, he probed with inquisitional zeal beneath the superficial facts of Wagner's life. His four-volume life of Wagner (Newman, 1933–47) has always been held in high regard and there is no doubt that, in its day, it did sterling service in encouraging a common-sensical approach to Wagner, while at the same time offsetting wartime prejudice against the composer. Equally, the Newman of the four-volume life is much to be preferred to the frivolous, philistine writer of the earlier books on Wagner (Newman, 1899, 1914, 1931). But his obsessional loathing of Liszt disfigures his writings on Wagner as surely as it does his 1934 monograph on the Hungarian composer, while his disinterest in the philosophical background derives from an attitude amounting to what Bryan Magee quite rightly terms 'hostility' (Magee, 1990). Finally, Newman's refusal to face up to the issues raised by the essays of Wagner's final years results in what Robert Gutman has called 'sentimental evasions' (Gutman, 1968).

Gutman's own biography of Wagner was itself not free from prejudice, but at least it brought a welcome blast of fresh air to the incense-laden sanctum of the Bayreuth Circle, as ministered by Westernhagen, Kraft and others. (Westernhagen's 1956 monograph of Wagner's life and thought is superior in every way to his 1968 study (Eng. trans. 1978), which represents a reversion to the purblind adulation and uncritical acceptance of the Master's word that typified the old Bayreuthians.) In a sense Gutman was in advance of his time, since the demythologized view of Wagner which his biography advances was only later confirmed by the publication of important primary sources such as the Brown Book and Cosima Wagner's Diaries. At the same time, his insistence on seeing links between Wagner's life and art and in interpreting both against the wider 19th-century background was bound to seem unfashionable in the days of the New Criticism.

Acclaimed in Germany at the time of its appearance in 1980, Martin Gregor-Dellin's life of Wagner fared less well at the hands of English critics, partly because the English translation amounted to edited highlights of the original but mainly because his *biographie romanesque*, with its preoccupation with the phallic stage in Wagner's development, was bound to disturb an English audience versed in Newman and a more nominalist approach to musical biography. (For other recent examples of this factional approach see Dieckmann, 1983 and 1989, and Schneider 1989.)

Among recent English lives of Wagner, the ones by Ronald Taylor (1979) and Barry Millington (1984) are particularly good: the former is distinguished by its elegant grasp of the literary and intellectual background of the 19th century, the latter by its incorporation of the latest Wagnerian research, including the findings of the *Wagner Werk-Verzeichnis*.

Among biographical writings which have concentrated on shorter periods in Wagner's life, the most valuable are Walter Lange's account of Wagner's association with Leipzig (Lange, 1921), Woldemar Lippert's monograph on Wagner's years in exile (Lippert, 1927; Eng. trans. 1930), Max Fehr's authoritative study of Wagner's period in Switzerland (Fehr, 1934–54), Elmar Arro's sketch of Wagner's spell in Riga (Arro, 1965), Helmut Kirchmeyer's monumental documentation of Wagner's years in Dresden (Kirchmeyer, 1967–) and Geoffrey Skelton's account of Wagner's relationship with his second wife (Skelton, 1982). Wagner's years in Paris, Vienna and Munich, together with his visits to England and Russia, remain inadequately documented.

It remains to be asked whether we need a biography of Wagner at all. Does a knowledge of Wagner's life further our understanding of his music dramas? A biography may be valuable as a document of social, literary or musical history; and the circumstances of the individual's life may be worth retelling for their own intrinsic interest – certainly, few composers have led such enthralling lives as the Behemoth of Bayreuth. But, until such time as the creative process is more adequately understood (see Vetter, 1992), it is difficult to know what light a biography can throw on an artist's works. If those works are interpreted simply as a reflection of the artist's life, there will not be anything new in (say) Wagner's life that we did not already know from his art: the latter, to paraphrase the composer, will simply be 'acts of biography made visible' (cf. GS IX, 306). Perhaps the answer is provided by Wagner himself in a letter to Theodor Uhlig of 12 January 1852: 'I cannot help feeling that, if we had *life*, we'd have no need of *art*. Art begins at precisely the point where life leaves off: when all around us ceases to exist, we call out in art, "I wish". I simply do not believe that a *truly happy* individual could ever hit upon the idea of creating "art".' Wagner's music dramas might be regarded, therefore, not as slices of life but as the composer's attempt to propose a solution to the problems which beset him and, in particular, to the problem why his relations with other people so frequently ended in failure. The alternatives which he advanced – love, death, art, compassion – do not necessarily form a codifiable philosophical system, but they may go some way towards explaining the ability of the Wagnerian music drama not only to have survived the immediate philosophical, political and biographical conditions which brought it into existence but to continue to lay so powerfully emotional a hold on the 20th-century listener.

STEWART SPENCER

THE GERMAN THEORIST Alfred Lorenz saw his work on Wagner's music dramas as laying bare the 'secret of form'. In four volumes published between 1924 and 1933, volumes which for good or bad are still considered as a watershed in the history of Wagner analysis, he resolved the 'endless melody' of the *Ring*, *Tristan*, *Die Meistersinger* and *Parsifal* into discrete poetico-musical 'periods'. There were different kinds of periods which could be heard simply or in various combinations – strophes, arches, double arches, bars, rondos and refrains; and he dealt with their harmony and tonality in terms derived from the German theorist Hugo Riemann. He also discussed proportion and rhythm, where he laid special emphasis on prosody and the persistence within the newly fluid musical idiom of symmetric groupings (for example, of units of 4 + 4 bars); and in dealing with thematicism, he inevitably drew upon a tradition of analysis of leitmotifs (short, characteristic figures which wove themselves through the symphonic web in the way that the older, less malleable 'motifs of reminiscence' could not do, and which often found their definitive statements in the vocal parts) – a

Analysis and criticism

tradition inaugurated by Hans von Wolzogen in 1877. Although Lorenz placed himself in a line of about twenty critics, including Otakar Hostinsky, Karl Grunsky, August Halm and Christian von Ehrenfels, his attempt to reveal the stitching behind the 'symphonic fabric' explicitly laid the ghost of 'formlessness' which had haunted Wagnerian criticism ever since the time of Eduard Hanslick.

More recent scholars, though, have asked whether the secret of Wagnerian music drama really does lie in form, at least as Lorenz described it. Most prominent among the new sceptics has been the editor of the Wagner Edition, Carl Dahlhaus, now, even after his death, one of the most influential of late 20th-century music critics. Through many publications, including his study of Wagner's music dramas (1971a), he argued that the real issue lay in the nature of the musical idea in Wagner. This had contracted from the extended symphonic arches of Classicism to short, pregnant motifs with determinate extra-musical meanings. The givens were no longer the (dance-derived) four- and eight-bar units characteristic of Beethoven; nor was tonality centripetal, integrating into a single centre all other keys, however remote (each of Lorenz's periods was ascribed a 'tonic'). Rather, a new musical prose joined tonalities 'like links in a chain', with no necessary connection between, for example, a first link and a third. Each tonality was to be celebrated for the moment to which it belonged and no more. And this attitude allowed Wagner to approach the most essential features of drama with a flexibility previously found only in the most marginal aspects of traditional ('number') opera: in *Wagners Konzeption des musikalischen Dramas* (1971c), he argued for the centrality of dialogue as a determinant of form. Indeed, one might add that according to this view, the musical materials – themes and tonalities – became simply agents in a theatre which constantly alluded to the past and the future as well as the present, and where flexibility of cross-reference was paramount.

Challenging though Dahlhaus's views are, and fascinating though their dialectical method is, they tend towards a certain extremism. A precedent for a middle way, though, lies in the work of the Swiss musicologist Ernst Kurth, who, between 1920 and 1923, published three editions of his *Romantische Harmonik und ihre Krise in Wagners 'Tristan'*. Here he offered a quite different approach to harmony from that adopted by Lorenz and Riemann. He saw its 'luminosity and darkness' deriving from the alterations of chords through chromatic inflection, addition of auxiliaries, and purely chromatic connections. The chords could be celebrated for their relation to a tonic, for their relationship one to another, and also for their inherent character. Harmony, thus, could look back to dependence on stable keys (integration) on the one hand, and forward to autonomy and liberation (disintegration) on the other. Even keys could be viewed according to this twofold perspective. Kurth argued not only that this ambiguity was central to *Tristan*, but that the idea of the expansion of tonal coherence over wide arches had to be reviewed. Kurth made special studies of the Preludes to the first and third acts of *Tristan*, and in the latter, especially, demonstrated that the broadly ranging harmony could be accommodated within a tonic F minor, once the harmonic 'pillars' were identified: he saw nothing but an expansion of simple cadential relations onto a large scale.

Similar issues were addressed by the followers of Heinrich Schenker, the doyen of radically conservative tonal analysis. Schenker himself had discussed Wagner's music sympathetically in his *Harmonielehre* of 1906, but later condemned music drama precisely because of the overwhelmingly destructive tendencies noted by Kurth. In his final work *Der freie Satz* (1935) he criticized Wagner for his 'inability' to achieve the large arches of song sustained by the great Classical composers, and for being driven into 'overexpressiveness' as a consequence. Later Schenkerians implicitly disagreed. Adele Katz, in *Challenge to Musical Tradition* (1945) not only found large-scale harmonic integration in the Preludes to *Tristan*, *Die Meistersinger* and *Parsifal*, but in other excerpts showed how chromatic harmonies too could be the basis of expansion. In his influential *Structural Hearing* (1953), Felix Salzer applied similar precepts to the Act I interlude from *Parsifal*. Later, William Mitchell (1967) provided an elaborate A minor/major context for the Prelude to Act I of *Tristan*, though this view was countered by Milton Babbitt (1973) and Benjamin Boretz (1972), who found that atonal procedures, especially those based on extensions of diminished harmonies, held the key to integration. While the merit of all these writings was to demonstrate the continuing power of traditional procedures in music drama, it is noticeable that they all dealt with orchestral material, or short, manifestly 'closed' entities, whose continuing presence in the apparently seamless symphonic web no commentator has denied. Schenker's sense that the heartland of Wagner's writing – Dahlhaus's dialogues – invited newer, more local and disruptive ways of hearing may still represent a surer indication of where the composer's 'challenge to tradition' actually lay.

Katz also wrote that 'there are many aspects of Wagner's treatment of the leitmotif that suggest how strongly the psychological element coloured his musical expression'. The Wagnerian psychological, and psychoanalytical, literature as it relates to the man and the texts, dates back to the early years of this century (Carl Jung, Max Graf, Otto Rank and Thomas Mann): but the integration of a Jungian interpretation with a psychologically orientated study of leitmotivic interrelationships came only with Robert Donington's *Wagner's 'Ring' and its Symbols* (1963). This book, which touches on musical concerns also explored by Deryck Cooke, prompted few direct successors. But a new pragmaticism has certainly been the hallmark of the most recent generation of mainly American critics, who have moved between music and text, on both small and large scales, with a refreshing ease.

Robert Bailey (1977–8) traced the growth of the *Ring* through sketches and drafts. To the discussion of tonality he brought rhetorical principles, which, though familiar in themselves, had not always been acknowledged by earlier writers. Increased tension, for example, can be indicated by an upward shift of a semitone (and vice versa), and in the early 'operas' these semitonal relations could sometimes be used for characterizing large-scale dramatic oppositions: in *Tannhäuser*, E major is associated with Venus, E♭ with the Pilgrims. In the *Ring*, some of these associations and conflicts still endure: for example, B minor for the Valkyries and B♭ minor for the Nibelungs; D♭ major for Valhalla 'raised' to the D minor which frames two acts of *Die Walküre*, and the D major to which Siegfried reforges Nothung. In a study of Act II scene 3 of *Die Walküre*, he shows how, from a thematic point of view, the intensification of the exchange between Brünnhilde and Siegmund (a 'psychological' development) is reflected in the progressive diminutions of the rhythmic values of the Annunciation motif.

Four years later, Anthony Newcomb (1981–2) published an 'essay in Wagnerian formal analysis'. Also pitting himself against Lorenz, and finding support not only in Dahlhaus, but in Voss, Stephan, Kunze and Brinkmann too, he redresses the previous excesses by concentrating on the tonal 'build' of various scenes from the *Ring*. Identifying three principles of form – the architectural (including large-scale and local symmetries), the musical process (the principle of gradual transformation within scenes and acts), and extra-musical processes (the dramatic events articulated by the music) – he identified, after *Tristan* Act II scene 1, a shift away from scrupulous attention to detail towards larger symphonic sweeps. Within the 'processes', Wagner mixes highly structured and loosely structured types, although the highly structured units (of the kind described by Lorenz) may be left incomplete, as in the first scene of *Siegfried* Act III; contrasts of tempo and instrumentation assume a new importance; proportions move in regular and irregular phases; the stage events help to articulate structure; and (leit)motifs, which are used either for form-building purposes or for cross-reference, powerfully engage in their own processes of transformation.

From this climate several other initiatives have developed. In a full study of *Siegfried* (1982), based on sources, Patrick McCreless necessarily confronts the differences in formal structure before and after the point at which Wagner broke off composition (the end of Act II). In the later 'symphonic' mode of Act III, he demonstrates in particular the operation of underlying complexes of keys – C, E A♭ – and complexes operating within that complex. Later, in two chapters from *Reading Opera* (1988) dealing with Wagner's narratives-within-narratives, Carolyn Abbate compares Erik's dream from *Der fliegende Holländer* with Tannhäuser's account of his journey to Rome – issues expanded in her *Unsung Voices* (1991) – and Christopher Wintle discusses the large-scale musical consequences of the mythmaking effected by Siegfried's Funeral March. There have been many other post-war studies too, notably those by

Kunze (1970), Stephan (1970), Brinkmann (1972, 1978, 1982, 1984), Holloway (1979), Breig (1980), Whittall (1981, 1983b, 1990) and Darcy (1989–90, 1990). Although the analytic reception of Wagner has undergone many vicissitudes in the last century or so, and shows emphases different from those implicit in Wagner's own 'manifesto', *Oper und Drama*, the very richness of the works themselves suggests that its lines of enquiry are far from exhausted: the 'earnestness' of which Wagner spoke in his own preface lives on in the seriousness of modern scholarship.

CHRISTOPHER WINTLE

Miscellaneous

INTELLECTUAL PANTOPHAGIST that he was, Wagner straddles a multiplicity of disciplines; or, as Dieter Borchmeyer has put it, 'Just as Wagner wanted to set the whole world talking, the whole world now demands to have its say in turn.' (Borchmeyer, 1991) The chief implication of this is that no one person has either the time or qualifications to read and comment on everything that has ever been written about Wagner. Even within Wagner's lifetime, Nikolaus Oesterlein had already catalogued 10,180 publications on the subject of the composer, and that number has grown immeasurably in the meantime. (There is, however, no truth in the claim that more has been written about Wagner than any other human being except Christ and Napoleon: see 'Myths and Legends', p.132.) On the other hand, much that has been written in the past about Wagner by authors lacking even a modicum of sanity and common sense, let alone a knowledge of the musical and philosophical background, is simply not worth cataloguing. Academically qualified writers have always treated Wagner with scarcely concealed suspicion, no doubt fearing the same fate as Nietzsche. Even today – notwithstanding the pioneering work of Dahlhaus in Germany and Deathridge in England – a scholarly interest in Wagner is regarded as somehow unprofessional. From that point of view one can only echo Goethe's words: 'Amerika, du hast es besser!' Jack Stein, Robert Bailey, Anthony Newcomb, Patrick McCreless, Warren Darcy, Carolyn Abbate, Thomas S. Grey and David Breckbill are only some of the American scholars who have made important contributions to Wagner studies since 1960.

Among the earliest writings on Wagner are those which deal with his medieval literary sources. Indeed, with rare exceptions (Magee, 1990), the earlier the article or monograph, the more informative it is likely to be, since 20th-century medievalists have largely lost sight of the first generation of German Romantic scholars whose writings left their mark on Wagner's oeuvre. By contrast, the 19th-century literary and ideological background has not received the degree of attention that it deserves (but see Borchmeyer, 1982; Hollinrake, 1982; Suneson, 1985; Kreckel, 1986; and especially Corse, 1990). Far too often Wagner has been wrenched from his context, thereby allowing the writer in question to foist on the hapless composer whatever anachronistic ideas he or she might happen to harbour. This is a particular problem with Wagner's nationalism and anti-Semitism but, whereas the former remains largely misunderstood (see Magee, 1992), the latter has recently come in for more scholarly treatment by a number of Jewish historians (see Poliakov, 1975; Katz, 1985; and Rose, 1990 and 1992). Rose advances the thesis that revolutionary anti-Semitism was a part of Wagner's ideological make-up from the very outset rather than a belated, reactionary stance adopted during the latter half of his life. Meanwhile Nattiez (1987) and Millington (1991) have lent musicological weight to Rose's (and Adorno's) belief that the composer's anti-Semitism also finds expression in his music dramas.

An inescapable part of the ideological background is the role that has been played by the 'Bayreuth Circle', a term used by Winfried Schüler (Schüler, 1971) to describe those writers whose self-appointed task it was to preserve what they saw as Wagner's nationalist legacy. The *Bayreuther Blätter*, founded by Wagner to promulgate the ideology underlying *Parsifal*, degenerated under its editor, Hans von Wolzogen, into an openly propagandist organ, while many of the other publications emanating from Wahnfried were tendentiously aimed at cultivating a particular image of Wagner and his works. Not even the writings of the otherwise admirable Wahnfried archivist, Otto Strobel, can escape this charge entirely. (For studies of the Bayreuth ideology, see also Zelinsky, 1976; Prieberg, 1982; and Wessling, 1983.) The Bayreuth centenary in 1976 produced a series of monographs on the first hundred years of the Festival: not all the titles originally advertised finally saw the light of day and none has been translated into English, but the series contains authoritative studies by Dahlhaus (1971), Karbaum (1976), Mack (1976), Voss (1976) and Baumann (1980).

Although post-war Bayreuth programme booklets cannot be accused of nationalist bias, they have failed, none the less, to turn themselves into a forum for state-of-the-art Wagnerian scholarship and contented themselves, on the whole, with publishing essays of a journalistic nature. In consequences, Wagner studies, as a literary discipline, may be said to lack a focal point: non-musicological scholars with something to say on the subject are reduced to having their articles published in out-of-the-way periodicals, often unaware that they are merely repeating other scholars' findings. (Other journals have proved too short-lived or too parochial to make any real impression on the subject.)*

The lack of an adequate bibliography of writings on Wagner, together with deficient editions of Wagner's prose works and letters, are problems which serious Wagner scholars have to

* A notable exception, however, is *Wagner*, the periodical of the Wagner Society, which since 1980 has provided an invaluable forum for Wagner scholarship (see Spencer, 1980–) (Ed.).

confront even before they set foot on their chosen field of study. From this point of view, the general reader may be better served than the scholar. Useful introductions to the individual operas and music dramas are published in a series of Opera Guides edited by Nicholas John (similar series exist in Germany and France), and more Wagnerian titles are promised in the Cambridge Opera Handbooks series to add to Lucy Beckett's excellent monograph on *Parsifal* (Beckett, 1981). The *Ring* continues to provoke the most widespread interpretations, many of them influenced by the '-ism' of the day, be it socialism (Shaw, 1898), Jungian psychology (Donington, 1963), anthroposophy (Winkler, 1974), structuralism (Ingenschay-Goch, 1982) or feminism (Zurmühl, 1984).

Recent interest in the libretto as a literary genre has spawned a series of studies by Just (1978), Groos/Parker (1988), Abbate/ Parker (1989), Nieder (1989) and Abbate (1991), while valuable work on Wagner's aesthetic writings has been done by Stein (1960), Borchmeyer (1982), Franke (1983) and Nattiez (1990).

The reception of Wagner's works is so vast a field of enquiry that any single study is bound to incur the charge of selectivity. Perhaps the most useful additions to the subject are those which are purely documentary (Kirchmeyer, 1967–) or limited to a particular discipline, such as Wagner and his literary influence (Jäckel, 1931– 2; Koppen, 1973; Furness, 1982). Attempts to grapple with Wagner's impact on an entire nation's culture – Wagner and Italy (Jung, 1974; Rostirolla, 1982), England (Sessa, 1979), Flanders (Wauters, 1983) and France (Kahane/Wild, 1983) – have been less satisfactory, although two anthologies of essays on Wagner's cultural influence in general show what can be achieved by an interdisciplinary approach (Large/Weber, 1984; Müller and others, 1984). Production studies have been dominated by Bayreuth – each new staging of the *Ring* there precipitates an avalanche of books on the subject – but mention should none the less be made of contributions by Skelton (1965), Petzet (1970) and Bauer (1982), each of which has tried, in its way, to set Wagnerian productions in their historical context. And yet their failure to convince the majority of Wagnerian readers of the inevitability of historical change is not only disturbing in its own terms but symptomatic of a frame of mind on the part of many Wagnerites which views with suspicion any attempt to dismantle the hallowed Wagnerian icon.

STEWART SPENCER

SELECT BIBLIOGRAPHY
LIST OF ILLUSTRATIONS
THE CONTRIBUTORS
INDEX

SELECT BIBLIOGRAPHY

The titles under 'Editions', 'Writings', 'Diaries/notebooks', 'Letters' and 'Catalogues/bibliographies' are listed broadly in chronological order, but with priority given to major editions. The entries in the main list, however ('Books/articles'), are arranged alphabetically by author's surname, and chronologically under each surname. Where two or more publications by the same author appeared in the same year – and where these are referred to in the text – the entries are distinguished by a letter suffixed to the year of publication.

Editions

Richard Wagners Werke, ed. M. Balling (Leipzig, 1912–29; repr. New York, 1972). Only 10 vols appeared.

Sämtliche Werke, gen. eds C. Dahlhaus and E. Voss (Mainz, 1970–). Critical edition planned in 31 vols.

Die Musikdramen (Hamburg, 1971; Munich, 1978). Texts of the music dramas, with introduction by J. Kaiser.

Writings

Gesammelte Schriften und Dichtungen, 10 vols (Leipzig, 1871–83). The first edition of Collected Writings, prepared under Wagner's own supervision. 4th edition (Leipzig, 1907, repr. Hildesheim, 1976). [GS]

Sämtliche Schriften und Dichtungen, 16 vols (Leipzig, 1911–16). The most complete edition available. [SS]

Richard Wagner's Prose Works, 8 vols, ed. and trans. W. A. Ellis (London, 1892–9; repr. 1972). [PW]

Mein Leben, ed. M. Gregor-Dellin (Munich, 1963, 2/1976); Eng. trans. A. Gray, ed. M. Whittall (Cambridge, 1983). First authentic edition.

Diaries/notebooks

Die rote Brieftasche, in *Sämtliche Briefe*, ed. G. Strobel and W. Wolf, i (Leipzig, 1967), 79–92. Wagner's Red Pocketbook, containing brief biographical notes for the years 1813 to 1839.

Das Braune Buch: Tagebuchaufzeichnungen 1865 bis 1882, ed. J. Bergfeld (Zurich and Freiburg im Breisgau, 1975); Eng. trans. G. Bird (London, 1980)

Cosima Wagner: Die Tagebücher 1869–1883, 2 vols, ed. M. Gregor-Dellin and D. Mack (Munich, 1976–7); Eng. trans. G. Skelton (London, 1978–80)

Letters

Sämtliche Briefe, ed. G. Strobel, W. Wolf, H.-J. Bauer and J. Forner (Leipzig, 1967–). Complete edition.

Briefe von Richard Wagner an seine Zeitgenossen: 1830–1883, ed. E. Kastner (Berlin, 1897)

Richard Wagners Briefe nach Zeitfolge und Inhalt, ed. W. Altmann (Leipzig, 1905; repr. 1971). Index of 3143 of Wagner's letters arranged chronologically, with résumé of contents and quotation of selected extracts.

Richard Wagners Gesammelte Briefe, ed. J. Kapp and E. Kastner, 2 vols (Leipzig, 1914)

Richard Wagners Briefe, selected and annotated by W. Altmann, 2 vols (Leipzig, 1925); Eng. trans. London and Toronto, 1927

The Letters of Richard Wagner to Anton Pusinelli, ed. E. Lenrow (New York, 1932)

König Ludwig II. und Richard Wagner: Briefwechsel, ed. O. Strobel, 5 vols (Karlsruhe, 1936–9)

Briefe: Die Sammlung Burrell, ed. J. Burk (Frankfurt am Main, 1953); Eng. trans. *Letters of Richard Wagner: The Burrell Collection* (London, 1951)

Richard Wagner: Briefe, ed. H. Kesting (Munich and Zurich, 1983). Selection of 206 letters.

Richard Wagner: Briefe 1830–1883, ed. W. Otto (Berlin, 1986)

Selected Letters of Richard Wagner, trans. and ed. S. Spencer and B. Millington (London, 1987). Selection of 500 letters.

Catalogues/bibliographies

Kastner, E.: *Wagner-Catalog: chronologisches Verzeichniss der von und über Richard Wagner erschienenen Schriften, Musikwerke* (Offenbach, 1878; repr. 1966)

Oesterlein, N.: *Katalog einer Richard Wagner-Bibliothek: nach den vorliegenden Originalien zu einem authentischen Nachschlagebuch durch die gesammte insbesondere deutsche Wagner-Literatur bearbeitet und veröffentlicht* (Leipzig, 1882–95; repr. 1970)

Catalogue of the Burrell Collection (London, 1929)

Barth, H., ed.: *Internationale Wagner-Bibliographie: 1945–55* (Bayreuth, 1956); *1956–60* (1961); *1961–6* (1968); *1967–78* (1979)

Klein, H.F.G.: *Erst- und Frühdrucke der Textbücher von Richard Wagner: Bibliographie* (Tutzing, 1979)

Bott, G., ed.: *Die Meistersinger und Richard Wagner: die Rezeptionsgeschichte einer Oper von 1868 bis heute* (Nuremberg, 1981) [catalogue of exhibition at Germanisches Nationalmuseum, Nuremberg]

Kahane, M., and Wild, N., eds: *Wagner et la France* (Paris, 1983)

Klein, H.F.G.: *Erstdrucke der musikalischen Werke von Richard Wagner: Bibliographie* (Tutzing, 1983)

Richard Wagner und die politischen Bewegungen seiner Zeit [catalogue of exhibition mounted by the Bundesarchiv, Koblenz] (Koblenz, 1983)

Eger, M., ed.: *Wagner und die Juden: Fakten und Hintergründe* [documentation accompanying exhibition in the Richard-Wagner-Museum, Bayreuth] (Bayreuth, 1985)

Deathridge, J., Geck, M., and Voss, E., eds: *Wagner Werk-Verzeichnis: Verzeichnis der musikalischen Werke Richard Wagners und ihrer Quellen* (Mainz, 1986)

Spencer, S.: 'The Stefan Zweig Collection' [includes annotated list of Wagner MSS in BL], *Wagner*, viii (1987), 4–13

Books/articles

Abbate, C.: *The 'Parisian' Tannhäuser*, diss. Princeton U., 1984

——: 'Erik's Dream and Tannhäuser's Journey', in *Reading Opera*, ed. A. Groos and R. Parker (Princeton, NJ, 1988), 129–67

——: 'Orpheus and the Underworld: the Music of Wagner's "Tannhäuser"', in *Opera Guide 39: Tannhäuser*, ed. N. John (London, 1988), 33–50

——: 'Opera as Symphony, a Wagnerian Myth', in *Analyzing Opera: Verdi and Wagner*, ed. C. Abbate and R. Parker (Berkeley, CA, 1989), 92–124

——: 'Wagner, "On Modulation", and *Tristan*', *Cambridge Opera Journal*, i (1989), 33–58

——: *Unsung Voices: Opera and Musical Narrative in the Nineteenth Century* (Princeton, NJ, 1991)

——, and Parker, R., eds: *Analyzing Opera: Verdi and Wagner* (Berkeley, CA, 1989)

Aberbach, A.D.: *The Ideas of Richard Wagner* (Lanham, MD, 1984, 2/1988)

Abraham, G. : *A Hundred Years of Music* (London, 1938, 4/1974)

——: *Slavonic and Romantic Music* [esp. chap. 'Wagner's Second Thoughts'] (London, 1968)

——: 'A Lost Wagner Aria', *Musical Times*, cx (1969), 927

Adorno, T.W.: 'Wagner, Nietzsche and Hitler' [review of Newman's *Life*, vol. iv], *Kenyon Review*, ix (1947), 155–62

——: *Versuch über Wagner* (Berlin and Frankfurt am Main, 1952); Eng. trans. as *In Search of Wagner* (London, 1981)

Amerongen, M. van: *De buikspreker van God* (Amsterdam, 1983); Eng. trans. as *Wagner: a Case History* (London, 1983)

Arro, E.: 'Richard Wagners Rigaer Wanderjahre: Über baltische Züge im Schaffen Wagners', *Musik des Ostens*, iii (1965), 123–68

Ashbrook, W.: 'The First Singers of *Tristan und Isolde*', *Opera Quarterly*, iii/4 (wint. 1985–6), 11–23

Babbitt, M.: 'Since Schoenberg', *Perspectives of New Music*, xii/1 (1973), 33

Bailey, R.: 'Wagner's Musical Structures for *Siegfrieds Tod*', in *Studies in Music History: Essays for Oliver Strunk*, ed. H. Powers (Princeton, NJ, 1968), 459–94

——: *The Genesis of 'Tristan und Isolde' and a Study of Wagner's Sketches and Drafts for the First Act*, diss. Princeton U., 1969

——: 'The Structure of the *Ring* and its Evolution', *19th Century Music*, i (1977–8), 48–61

——: 'The Method of Composition', in *The Wagner Companion*, ed. P. Burbidge and R. Sutton (London, 1979), 269–338

——, ed.: *Richard Wagner: Prelude and Transfiguration from 'Tristan and Isolde'* (Norton Critical Score) (New York, 1985)

Baines, A.: *Woodwind Instruments and their History* (London, 1957, 3/1967)

——: *Brass Instruments: Their History and Development* (London, 1976)

Barth, H., ed.: *Bayreuther Dramaturgie: Der Ring des Nibelungen* (Stuttgart, 1980)

——, Mack, D., and Voss, E., eds: *Wagner: sein Leben, sein Werk und seine Welt in zeitgenössischen Bildern und Texten* (Vienna, 1975); Eng. trans. as *Wagner: A Documentary Study* (London, 1975)

Barzun, J.: *Darwin, Marx and Wagner* (Boston, MA, 1941)

Bauer, O.G.: *Richard Wagner: die Bühnenwerke von der Uraufführung bis heute* (Berlin, 1982); Eng. trans. New York, 1983

Baumann, C.-F.: *Bühnentechnik im Festspielhaus Bayreuth* (Munich, 1980)

Becker, H.: 'Giacomo Meyerbeer: On the Occasion of the Centenary of his Death', Leo Baeck Institute, Year Book IX (London, 1964), 178–201

Beckett, L.: *Richard Wagner: 'Parsifal'* (Cambridge, 1981)

Bekker, P.: *Richard Wagner: das Leben im Werke* (Stuttgart, 1924); Eng. trans. London, 1931

Bennett, R.R.: *Instrumentally Speaking* (New York, 1975)

Bergfeld, J.: see under 'Diaries/notebooks' above

Berio, L.: 'Eco in Ascolto: Luciano Berio interviewed by Umberto Eco', *Contemporary Music Review*, v (1989), 1–8

Berlioz, H.: *Treatise on Instrumentation*, rev. and enlarged edn by R. Strauss, Eng. trans., New York, 1948

Bermbach, U.: 'Die Destruktion der Institutionen: Überlegungen zum politischen Gehalt von Richard Wagners "Ring des Nibelungen"', *Bayreuther Festspiele: Programmheft III. Die Walküre* (Bayreuth, 1988; Eng. trans.), 13–66

——, ed.: *In den Trümmern der eigenen Welt: Richard Wagners 'Der Ring des Nibelungen'* (Berlin, 1989)

——: 'Wagner und Lukács: über die Ästhetisierung von Politik und die Politisierung von Ästhetik', *Bayreuther Festspiele: Programmheft II. Lohengrin* (Bayreuth, 1990; Eng. trans.), 1–27

Biddiss, M.D.: *Father of Racist Ideology: the Social and Political Thought of Count Gobineau* (London, 1970)

——: 'The Founder of Aryan Racism' [on Gobineau], *Times Higher Education Supplement*, 8 Oct 1982, p.11

Blaukopf, H.: 'Wozu biographische Forschung?', in *Das Gustav-Mahler-Fest Hamburg 1989*, ed. M.T. Vogt (Kassel, 1991), 125–32

Blissett, W.: 'D.H. Lawrence, D'Annunzio, Wagner', in *Wisconsin Studies in Contemporary Literature*, vii (1966), 34ff

Bloom, P.: 'The Fortunes of the Flying Dutchman in France', *Wagner*, viii (1987), 42–66

Blunt, W.: *The Dream King: Ludwig II of Bavaria* (London, 1970)

Borchmeyer, D.: *Das Theater Richard Wagners: Idee – Dichtung – Wirkung* (Stuttgart, 1982); Eng. trans. as *Richard Wagner: Theory and Theatre* (London, 1991)

——, ed.: *Wege des Mythos in der Moderne: Richard Wagner: 'Der Ring des Nibelungen'* (Munich, 1987)

——: 'Wagner literature', *Wagner*, xii (1991), 51–74 and 116–37

Boretz, B.: 'Meta-variations, Part IV: Analytic Fallout (II)', *Perspectives of New Music*, xi/2 (1973), 156–203

Boulez, P.: *Orientations: Collected Writings*, ed. J.-J. Nattiez (London, 1986); originally published in French as *Points de repère*, Paris, 1981

Branscombe, P.: 'Wagner as Poet', in *Richard Wagner: The Ring* (trans. A. Porter) (London, 1976), pp.xxix-xl

Breig, W.: 'Der "Rheintöchtergesang" in Wagners "Rheingold"', *Archiv für Musikwissenschaft*, xxxvii (1980), 241–63

Breithaupt, R.: 'Richard Wagners Klaviermusik', *Die Musik*, iii (1903–4), 108–34

Brinkmann, R.: '"Drei der Fragen stell' ich mir frei". Zur Wanderer-Szene im 1. Akt von Wagners "Siegfried"', *Jahrbuch des Staatlichen Instituts für Musikforschung Preussischer Kulturbesitz* (Berlin, 1972), 120–62

——: 'Mythos – Geschichte – Natur: Zeitkonstellationen im "Ring"', in *Richard Wagner: Von der Oper zum Musikdrama*, ed. S. Kunze (Berne and Munich, 1978), 61–77

——: 'Richard Wagner der Erzähler', *Österreichische Musikzeitschrift*, xxxvii (1982), 299–306

——: 'Sentas Traumerzählung', *Bayreuther Festspiele: Programmheft I. Der fliegende Holländer* (Bayreuth, 1984; Eng. trans.), 1–17

Brod, M.: 'Some Comments on the Relationship between Wagner and Meyerbeer', Leo Baeck Institute, Year Book IX (London, 1964), 202–5

Brown, H.M.: *Leitmotiv and Drama: Wagner, Brecht, and the Limits of 'Epic' Theatre* (Oxford, 1991)

Burbidge, P., and Sutton, R., eds: *The Wagner Companion* (London, 1979)

Burrell, M.: *Richard Wagner: his Life & Works from 1813 to 1834* (London, 1898)

Cagli, B.: 'Verdi and the Business of Writing Operas', in *The Verdi Companion*, ed. M. Chusid and W. Weaver (New York, 1979), 106ff

Carnegy, P.: 'Damming the Rhine' [review of H. Mayer's *Richard Wagner in Bayreuth*], *Times Literary Supplement*, 10 June 1977, 707–8

Chamberlain, H.S.: *Richard Wagner* (Munich, 1906, 3/1911); Eng. trans. London, 1897

Chancellor, J.: *Wagner* (London, 1978)

Cicora, M.A.: *'Parsifal' Reception in the 'Bayreuther Blätter'* (Frankfurt am Main, Berne and New York, 1987)

Coleman, A.: 'Calderón/Schopenhauer/Wagner: the Story of a Misunderstanding', *The Musical Quarterly*, lxix (1983), 227–43

Conrad, H.: 'Absturz aus Klingsors Zaubergarten: ein biographischer Beitrag zu den letzten Lebensjahren Richard Wagners', *Fränkischer Heimatbote* (monthly suppl. to *Nordbayerischer Kurier*), 11. Jahrgang (1978), no.8

Cook, P.: *A Memoir of Bayreuth 1876* ('related by Carl Emil Doepler including illustrations of his costume designs for the first production of the "Ring"') (London, 1979)

Cooke, D.: *I Saw the World End: a Study of Wagner's 'Ring'* (London, 1979)

——: 'Wagner's Musical Language', *The Wagner Companion*, ed. P. Burbidge and R. Sutton (London, 1979), 225–68

Corse, S.: *Wagner and the New Consciousness: Language and Love in the 'Ring'* (Cranbury, NJ, 1990)

Culshaw, J. *Reflections on Wagner's 'Ring'* (New York and London, 1976)

Dahlhaus, C., ed.: *Das Drama Richard Wagners als musikalisches Kunstwerk* (Regensburg, 1970)

——: *Die Musikdramen Richard Wagners* (Velber, 1971a); Eng. trans. Cambridge, 1979

——, ed.: *Richard Wagner: Werk und Wirkung* (Regensburg, 1971b)

——: *Wagners Konzeption des musikalischen Dramas* (Regensburg, 1971c)

——: *Wagner's Aesthetics* [selection of Wagner's writings with introductory essays] (Eng. trans., Bayreuth, 1972)

——: 'Wagners Stellung in der Musikgeschichte', in *Richard-Wagner-Handbuch*, ed. U. Müller and P. Wapnewski (Stuttgart, 1986), 60–85; Eng. trans. Cambridge, MA, 1992

——: *Schoenberg and the New Music* (Eng. trans., Cambridge, 1987)

——: *Nineteenth-Century Music* (Eng. trans., Berkeley and Los Angeles, 1989a)

——: 'What is a Musical Drama?', *Cambridge Opera Journal*, i (1989b), 95–111

Dahlhaus, C., and Voss, E., eds: *Wagnerliteratur – Wagnerforschung: Bericht über das Wagner-Symposium München 1983* (Mainz, 1985)

Darcy, W.: 'The Pessimism of the *Ring*', *Opera Quarterly*, iv/2 (1986), 24–48

——: ' "Alles was ist, endet!" Erda's Prophecy of World Destruction', *Bayreuther Festspiele: Programmheft II. Das Rheingold* (Bayreuth, 1988), 67–92

——: '*Creatio ex nihilo*: the Genesis, Structure, and Meaning of the *Rheingold* Prelude', *19th Century Music*, xiii (1989–90), 79–100

——: 'A Wagnerian *Ursatz*; or, Was Wagner a Background Composer After All?', *Intégral*, iv (1990), 1–35

——: 'In Search of C Major: Tonal Structure and Formal Design in Act III of *Die Meistersinger*', Proceedings of 1989 *Meistersinger* symposium in Seattle, ed. A. Porter and B. Millington (publication forthcoming)

——: *Wagner's 'Das Rheingold': Its Genesis and Structure* (publication forthcoming)

Daube, O.: *'Ich schreibe keine Symphonien mehr': Richard Wagners Lehrjahre nach den erhaltenen Dokumenten* (Cologne, 1960)

Dean, W.: 'French Opera', in *New Oxford History of Music*, ed. G. Abraham, viii (1982), 14–46

Deathridge, J.: 'The Nomenclature of Wagner's Sketches', *Proceedings of the Royal Musical Association*, ci (1974–5), 75–83

——: *Wagner's 'Rienzi': a Reappraisal Based on a Study of the Sketches and Drafts* (Oxford, 1977a)

——: 'Wagner's Sketches for the "Ring"', *Musical Times*, cxviii (1977b), 383–9

——: 'Eine verschollene Wagner-Arie?', *Melos/Neue Zeitschrift für Musik*, iv (1978), 208–14

——: Review of Wagner publications, *19th Century Music*, v (1981–2), 81–9

——: 'Wagner "literature" and Wagner "research"', *Wagner*, viii (1987), 92–114

——: 'Through the Looking Glass: Some Remarks on the First Complete Draft of *Lohengrin*', in *Analyzing Opera*, ed. C. Abbate and R. Parker (Berkeley, CA, 1989), 56–91

——, and Dahlhaus, C.: *The New Grove Wagner* (London, 1984)

Del Mar, N.: *Anatomy of the Orchestra* (London, 1981)

Dennison, P., ed.: *The Richard Wagner Centenary in Australia* (Adelaide, 1985)

Dieckmann, F.: *Richard Wagner in Venedig: eine Collage* (Darmstadt and Neuwied, 1983)

——: *Wagner – Verdi: Geschichte einer Unbeziehung* (Berlin, 1989)

DiGaetani, J.L., ed.: *Penetrating Wagner's 'Ring': an Anthology* (Cranbury, NJ, 1978)

——: *Richard Wagner and the Modern British Novel* (Cranbury, NJ, 1978)

Donington, R.: *Wagner's 'Ring' and its Symbols: the Music and the Myth* (London, 1963)

Eger, M.: 'Richard Wagner und König Ludwig II.', in *Richard-Wagner-Handbuch*, ed. U. Müller and P. Wapnewski (Stuttgart, 1986), 162–73; Eng. trans. Cambridge, MA, 1992

——: *'Wenn ich Wagnern den Krieg mache...': der Fall Nietzsche und das Menschliche, Allzumenschliche* (Vienna, 1988)

Ellis, W.A.: *Life of Richard Wagner*, 6 vols (London, 1900–08) [vols i–iii are a trans. of C.F. Glasenapp's biography]

Emslie, B.: 'Woman as Image and Narrative in Wagner's *Parsifal*: a Case Study', *Cambridge Opera Journal*, iii (1991), 109–24

Erismann, H.: *Richard Wagner in Zürich* (Zurich, 1987)

Ewans, M.: *Wagner and Aeschylus: The 'Ring' and the 'Oresteia'* (London, 1982)

——: 'The Bayreuth Centenary *Ring*', in *The Richard Wagner Centenary in Australia*, ed. P. Dennison (Adelaide, 1985)

Fehr, M.: *Richard Wagners Schweizer Zeit*, 2 vols (Aarau and Leipzig, 1934 [vol. I], Aarau and Frankfurt am Main, 1953 [vol. II])

Fischer-Dieskau, D.: *Wagner und Nietzsche* (Stuttgart, 1974); Eng. trans. New York, 1976

Forsyth, C.: *Orchestration* (London, 1914, 2/1935)

Franke, R.: *Richard Wagners Zürcher Kunstschriften: Politische und ästhetische Entwürfe auf seinem Wege zum 'Ring des Nibelungen'* (Hamburg, 1983)

Fricke, R.: *Bayreuth vor dreissig Jahren: Erinnerungen an Wahnfried und aus dem Festspielhause* (Dresden, 1906); Eng. trans. in *Wagner*, xi (1990), 93–109, 134–50, and xii (1991), 3–24 [diary kept by production assistant at first Bayreuth Festival]

Furness, R.: *Wagner and Literature* (Manchester, 1982)

Gal, H.: *Richard Wagner: Versuch einer Würdigung* (Frankfurt am Main, 1963); Eng. trans. London, 1976

Garten, H.F.: *Wagner the Dramatist* (London, 1977)

Gay, P.: *Freud, Jews and Other Germans: Masters and Victims in Modernist Culture* (New York, 1978), esp. chap. IV: 'Hermann Levi: a Study in Service and Self-Hatred', 189–230, which originally appeared as 'Hermann Levi and the Cult of Wagner', *Times Literary Supplement*, 11 April 1975, pp. 402–4

Geck, M.: *Die Bildnisse Richard Wagners* (Munich, 1970)

——: 'Parsifal: a Betrayed Childhood', *Wagner*, ix (1988), 75–88

Gillespie, I.: 'The Theory and Practice of "Wahn"', *Wagner*, v (1984), 79–95

——: 'Wagner and the Twilight of the Muse', *Wagner*, v (1984), 114–21

——: 'Anti-Semitism, Sacred or Profane', *Wagner*, vi (1985), 18–28

Glasenapp, C.F.: *Richard Wagners Leben und Wirken* (Cassel, 1876/7, rev. and enlarged 3/1894–1911 as *Das Leben Richard Wagners*); Eng. trans. of 3rd edn ed. W.A. Ellis, London, 1900–08 [vols iv-vi by Ellis alone]

Glass, F.W.: *The Fertilizing Seed: Wagner's Concept of the Poetic Intent* (Ann Arbor, 1983)

Goossens, L., and Roxburgh, E.: *Yehudi Menuhin Music Guides: Oboe* (London, 1977)

Goslich, S.: *Die deutsche romantische Oper* (Tutzing, 1975)

Gregor-Dellin, M.: *Wagner-Chronik: Daten zu Leben und Werk* (Munich, 1972)

——: *Richard Wagner: Sein Leben, Sein Werk, Sein Jahrhundert* (Munich, 1980); Eng. trans. (abridged) London, 1983

——: *Richard Wagner: eine Biographie in Bildern* (Munich, 1982)

——: 'Neue Wagner-Ermittlungen (Das Geheimnis der Mutter)', *Bayreuther Festspiele: Programmheft II. Parsifal* (Bayreuth, 1985); Eng. trans. 21–32

Grey, T.S.: *Richard Wagner and the Aesthetics of Musical Form in the Mid-19th Century (1840–1860)*, diss. U. of California, Berkeley, 1988

——: 'Wagner, the Overture, and the Aesthetics of Musical Form', *19th Century Music*, xii (1988–9), 3–22

Groos, A.: 'Appropriation in Wagner's *Tristan* Libretto', in *Reading Opera*, ed. A. Groos and R. Parker (Princeton, NJ, 1988), 12–33

——, and Parker, R., eds: *Reading Opera* (Princeton, 1988)

Gutman, R.: *Richard Wagner: the Man, His Mind, and His Music* (London, 1968)

Habel, H.: *Festspielhaus und Wahnfried* (Munich, 1985)

Hakel, H.: *Richard der Einzige: Satire, Parodie, Karikatur* (Vienna, Hanover and Berne, 1963)

Hanslick, E.: *Vom Musikalisch-Schönen: ein Beitrag zur Revision der Ästhetik der Tonkunst* (Leipzig, 1854); Eng. trans. as *The Beautiful in Music*, New York, 1969

——: *Vienna's Golden Years of Music: 1850–1900*, ed. H. Pleasants (New York, 1950, rev. 1969) [trans. of selected writings]

Hartford, R.: *Bayreuth: the Early Years. An Account of the Early Decades of the Wagner Festival as seen by the Celebrated Visitors & Participants* (London, 1980)

Hollingdale, R.J.: *Nietzsche: the Man and his Philosophy* (London, 1965)

Hollinrake, R.: *Nietzsche, Wagner, and the Philosophy of Pessimism* (London, 1982)

Holloway, R.: *Debussy and Wagner* (London, 1979)

——: 'Wagner and Holloway: the Composer, Robin Holloway, in Conversation with David Allenby', *Wagner News*, no. 77 (1990), 1–5

Hurn, P.D., and Root, W.L.: *The Truth about Wagner* (London, 1930)

Ingenschay-Goch, D.: *Richard Wagners neu erfundener Mythos: Zur Rezeption und Reproduktion des germanischen Mythos in seinen Operntexten* (Bonn, 1982)

Jäckel, K.: *Richard Wagner in der französischen Literatur*, 2 vols (Breslau, 1931–2)

John, N., ed.: *Opera Guides 6 (Tristan), 12 (Holländer), 19 (Meistersinger), 21 (Walküre), 28 (Siegfried), 31 (Götterdämmerung), 34 (Parsifal), 35 (Rheingold), 39 (Tannhäuser)* (London, 1980–)

Jung, U.: *Die Rezeption der Kunst Richard Wagners in Italien* (Regensburg, 1974)

Just, K.G.: 'Richard Wagner – ein Dichter? Marginalien zum Opernlibretto des 19. Jahrhunderts', in *Richard Wagner: Von der Oper zum Musikdrama*, ed. S. Kunze (Berne and Munich, 1978), 79–94

Kahane, M., and Wild, N.: see under 'Catalogues/bibliographies' above

Kapp, J.: *Richard Wagner und die Frauen* (Berlin, 1929); Eng. trans. London, 1932

Karbaum, M.: *Studien zur Geschichte der Bayreuther Festspiele (1876–1976)* (Regensburg, 1976)

Katz, A.: *Challenge to Musical Tradition: a New Concept of Tonality* (New York, 1945)

Katz, J.: *Richard Wagner: Vorbote des Antisemitismus* (Königstein, 1985); Eng. trans. as *The Darker Side of Genius*, Hanover and London, 1986

Kerman, J.: 'Opera as Symphonic Poem', chap. 7 in *Opera as Drama* (New York, 1956)

——: 'Wagner and Wagnerism', *New York Review of Books*, 22 December 1983, 27–37

Kester, S.: *An Examination of the Themes of Love, Power and Salvation in Richard Wagner's 'The Ring of the Nibelung': a Study of a Failed Individuation Process* (diss., U. of Western Australia, 1984)

Kinderman, W.: 'Dramatic Recapitulation in Wagner's *Götterdämmerung*', *19th Century Music*, iv (1980–81), 103–4

——: 'Das Geheimnis der Form in Wagners "Tristan und Isolde"', *Archiv für Musikwissenschaft*, xl (1983), 174–88

Kirchmeyer, H.: *Situationsgeschichte der Musikkritik und des musikalischen Pressewesens in Deutschland dargestellt vom Ausgang des 18. bis zum Beginn des 20. Jahrhunderts: IV. Teil: Das zeitgenössische Wagner-Bild. Vol. I: Wagner in Dresden* (Regensburg, 1972); Vols II-VI: *Dokumente* (Regensburg, 1967–)

Klein, H.: *Thirty Years of Musical Life in London, 1870–1900* (New York, 1903)

Knapp, R. : 'The Tonal Structure of *Tristan und Isolde*: a Sketch', *Music Review*, xlv (1984), 11–25

Koppen, E.: *Dekadenter Wagnerismus: Studien zur europäischen Literatur des Fin de siècle* (Berlin and New York, 1973)

Kreckel, M.: *Richard Wagner und die französischen Frühsozialisten* (Frankfurt am Main, 1986)

Kropfinger, K.: *Wagner und Beethoven: Untersuchungen zur Beethoven-Rezeption Richard Wagners* (Regensburg, 1975); Eng. trans. Cambridge, 1991

Kunze, S.: 'Über Melodiebegriff und musikalischen Bau in Wagners Musikdrama', in *Das Drama Richard Wagners als musikalisches Kunstwerk*, ed. C. Dahlhaus (Regensburg, 1970), 111–48

——: *Der Kunstbegriff Richard Wagners* (Regensburg, 1983)

Kürschner, J., ed.: 'Theatralische Aufführungen', *Richard Wagner-Jahrbuch*, i (1886), 435–65

Kurth, E.: *Romantische Harmonik und ihre Krise in Wagners 'Tristan'* (Berne and Leipzig, 1920, 2/1923)

Lange, W.: *Richard Wagner und seine Vaterstadt Leipzig* (Leipzig, 1921)

Langwill, L.G.: *The Bassoon and Contrabassoon* (London, 1965)

Large, D.C.: 'The Political Background of the Foundation of the Bayreuth Festival, 1876', *Central European History*, xi (1978), 162–72

——, and Weber, W., eds: *Wagnerism in European Culture and Politics* (Ithaca, 1984)

Laudon, R.T.: *Sources of the Wagnerian Synthesis: a Study of the Franco-German Tradition in 19th-Century Opera* (Munich and Salzburg, 1979)

Lenrow, E.: see under 'Letters' above

Lewin, D.: 'Amfortas's Prayer to Titurel and the Role of D in *Parsifal*', *19th Century Music*, vii (1983–4), 336–49

Lewis, M.T.: *Cézanne's Early Imagery* (Berkeley, CA, 1989)

Lippert, W.: *Richard Wagners Verbannung und Rückkehr 1849–1862* (Dresden, 1927); Eng. trans. as *Wagner in Exile*, London, 1930

Lippmann, F.: '*Die Feen* und *Das Liebesverbot*, oder die Wagnerisierung der diverser Vorbilder', in *Wagnerliteratur – Wagnerforschung: Bericht über das Wagner-Symposium München 1983*, ed. C. Dahlhaus and E. Voss (Mainz, 1985), 14–46

Lloyd-Jones, H.: 'Wagner and the Greeks', *Times Literary Supplement*, 9 January 1976, pp.37–9; rev. version in *Blood for the Ghosts* (London, 1982)

Lorenz, A.: *Das Geheimnis der Form bei Richard Wagner*, i: *Der musikalische Aufbau des Bühnenfestspieles Der Ring des Nibelungen* (Berlin, 1924, repr. 1966); ii: *Der musikalische Aufbau von Richard Wagners 'Tristan und Isolde'* (Berlin, 1926, repr. 1966); iii: *Der musikalische Aufbau von Richard Wagners 'Die Meistersinger von Nürnberg'* (Berlin, 1930, repr. 1966); iv: *Der musikalische Aufbau von Richard Wagners 'Parsifal'* (Berlin, 1933, repr. 1966)

Löw, R.: 'Ein Dogma wankt', *Deutsches Ärzteblatt*, lxxxiii (1986), 3475–7 and 3480

McClatchie, S.: 'The warrior foil'd: Alfred Lorenz's Wagner analyses', *Wagner*, xi (1990), 3–12

——: *Alfred Lorenz as Theorist and Analyst* (diss., U. of Western Ontario, in preparation)

McCreless, P.: *Wagner's Siegfried: Its Drama, History, and Music* (Ann Arbor, 1982)

Machlin, P.S.: 'Wagner, Durand and "The Flying Dutchman": the 1852 Revisions of the Overture', *Music & Letters*, lv (1974), 410–28

——: 'A Sketch for the "Dutchman"', *Musical Times*, cxvii (1976), 727–9

Mack, D.: *Der Bayreuther Inszenierungsstil 1876–1976* (Munich, 1976)

——, ed.: *Theaterarbeit an Wagners Ring* (Munich, 1978)

——, ed.: *Cosima Wagner: das zweite Leben: Briefe und Aufzeichnungen 1883–1930* (Munich, 1980)

Magee, B.: *Aspects of Wagner* (London, 1968, enlarged Oxford, 2/1988)

——: *The Philosophy of Schopenhauer* (Oxford, 1983)

——: 'Newman Nods', *Wagner*, xi (1990), 27–30

——: 'Is Wagner's Work Really Chauvinistic?', in Proceedings of 1989 *Meistersinger* symposium in Seattle, ed. A. Porter and B. Millington (publication forthcoming)

Magee, E.: *Richard Wagner and the Nibelungs* (Oxford, 1990)

Mann, E., ed.: *Wagner und unsere Zeit* [essays and letters of Thomas Mann] (Frankfurt am Main, 1963); Eng. trans. as *Pro and Contra Wagner*, London, 1985

Marek, G.R.: *Cosima Wagner* (New York, 1981)

Martin, S.: *Wagner to 'The Waste Land': A Study of the Relationship of Wagner to English Literature* (London, 1982)

Mayer, H.: *Richard Wagner in Bayreuth: 1876–1976* (Stuttgart, 1976); Eng. trans. London, 1976

——: *Richard Wagner: Mitwelt und Nachwelt* (Stuttgart, 1978)

Millington, B.: 'Did Wagner Really Sell his "Dutchman" Story? A Re-examination of the Paris Transaction', *Wagner*, iv (1983), 114–27

——: *Wagner* (London, 1984, 2/1992)

——: '"The Flying Dutchman", "Le vaisseau fantôme" and other Nautical Yarns', *Musical Times*, cxxvii (1986), 131–5

——: '"Parsifal": a Wound Reopened', *Wagner*, viii (1987), 114–20

——: '"Parsifal": a Work for our Times', *Opera*, xxxix (1988), 13–17

——: 'An Introduction to the Paris "Tannhäuser"', *Tannhäuser* (DG 427 625-2, 1989), 25–33 [record notes]

——: 'Nuremberg Trial: Is There Anti-semitism in *Die Meistersinger*?', *Cambridge Opera Journal*, iii (1991), 247–60

——, and Spencer, S., eds: *Wagner in Performance* (New Haven, 1992)

Mitchell, W.: 'The Tristan Prelude: Techniques and Structure', *Music Forum*, i (1967), 162–203

Morley-Pegge, R.: *The French Horn* (London, 1960, 2/1973)

Müller, U., Hundsnurscher, F., and Sommer, C., eds: *Richard Wagner 1883–1983: die Rezeption im 19. und 20. Jahrhundert* (Stuttgart, 1984)

Müller, U. and U., eds: *Richard Wagner und sein Mittelalter* (Anif, Salzburg, 1989)

Müller, U., and Wapnewski, P.: *Richard-Wagner-Handbuch* (Stuttgart, 1986); Eng. trans. Cambridge, MA, 1992

Murray, D.R.: 'Major Analytical Approaches to Wagner's Musical Style: a Critique', *Music Review*, xxxix (1978), 211–22

Nattiez, J.-J.: *Tétralogies – Wagner, Boulez, Chéreau: Essai sur l'infidélité* (Paris, 1983)

——: 'Le Ring comme histoire métaphorique de la musique', in *Wagner in Retrospect*, ed. L.R. Shaw, N.R. Cirillo and M.S. Miller (Amsterdam, 1987), 44–9

——: *Wagner androgyne* (Paris, 1990); Eng. trans. 1992

Neumann, A.: *Erinnerungen an Richard Wagner* (Leipzig, 3/1907); Eng. trans. London, 1909

Newcomb, A.: 'The Birth of Music out of the Spirit of Drama: an Essay in Wagnerian Formal Analysis', *19th*

Century Music, v (1981–2), 38–66

——: 'Those Images that Yet Fresh Images Beget', *Journal of Musicology*, ii (1983), 227–45

——: 'Ritornello Ritornato: a Variety of Wagnerian Refrain Form', in *Analyzing Opera: Verdi and Wagner*, ed. C. Abbate and R. Parker (Berkeley, CA, 1989), 202–21

Newman, E.: *A Study of Wagner* (London, 1899)

——: *Wagner as Man and Artist* (London, 1914, 2/1924)

——: *Fact and Fiction about Wagner* (London, 1931)

——: *The Man Liszt: a Study of the Tragi-Comedy of a Soul Divided against Itself* (London, 1934)

——: *Wagner Nights* (London, 1949) [as *The Wagner Operas*, New York, 1949]

——: *The Life of Richard Wagner*, 4 vols (London, 1933–47)

Nieder, C.: *Von der 'Zauberflöte' zum 'Lohengrin': das deutsche Opernlibretto in der ersten Hälfte des 19. Jahrhunderts* (Stuttgart, 1989)

Nietzsche, F.: *Der Fall Wagner* (Leipzig, 1888); see also *Friedrich Nietzsche: Kritische Studienausgabe in 15 Bänden*, ed. G. Colli and M. Montinari (Munich, 1988), VI, 9–53; Eng. trans. New York, 1968

Osborne, C.: *The Complete Operas of Richard Wagner* (London, 1990)

Petzet, D. and M.: *Die Richard Wagner-Bühne Ludwigs II.* (Munich, 1970)

Piston, W.: *Orchestration* (New York, 1955)

Poliakov, L.: *The History of Anti-Semitism*. Vol.III: *From Voltaire to Wagner* (London, 1975)

Porges, H.: *Die Bühnenproben zu den Bayreuther Festspielen des Jahres 1876* (Leipzig, 1877, 2/1896); Eng. trans. Cambridge, 1983

Porter, A.: 'How Many Children had Erda?', *About the House*, v/3 (1977), 50–51

——, and Millington, B.: Proceedings of 1989 *Meistersinger* symposium in Seattle (publication forthcoming)

Prieberg, F.K.: *Musik im NS-Staat* (Frankfurt am Main, 1982)

Rather, L.J.: *The Dream of Self-Destruction: Wagner's 'Ring' and the Modern World* (Louisiana, 1979)

——: *Reading Wagner: a Study in the History of Ideas* (Baton Rouge, LA, 1990)

Rayner, R.: *Wagner and 'Die Meistersinger'* (London, 1940)

Reeser, E.: 'Die literarischen Grundlagen des "Fliegenden Holländer"', *Offizieller Bayreuther Festspielführer* (Bayreuth, 1939), 73–81; repr. in *Bayreuther Festspiele: Programmheft Der fliegende Holländer* (Bayreuth, 1959), 47–54

Rendall, F.G.: *The Clarinet* (London, 1954, 3/1971 by P. Bate)

Richardson, J.: *Judith Gautier: a Biography* (London, 1986)

Rose, P.L.: *Revolutionary Antisemitism in Germany from Kant to Wagner* (Princeton, NJ, 1990)

——: *Wagner: Revolution and Race* (London, 1992)

Rosenblum, R.: *Modern Painting and the Northern Romantic Tradition* (London, 1975)

Rosselli, J.: *The Opera Industry in Italy from Cimarosa to Verdi* (Cambridge, 1984)

Rostirolla, G.: *Wagner in Italia* (Turin, 1982)

Rothstein, W.: *Phrase Rhythm in Tonal Music* (New York, 1989)

Sabor, R.: *The Real Wagner* (London, 1987)

Salzer, F.: *Structural Hearing: Tonal Coherence in Music* (New York, 1952, 2/1962)

Samama, G., ed.: *L'avant-scène opéra*, 6–7 (*L'Or du Rhin*), 8 (*La Walkyrie*), 12 (*Siegfried*), 13–14 (*Le Crépuscule des dieux*) (Paris, 1976–8)

Schenker, H.: *Harmonielehre* (Stuttgart, 1906); Eng. trans. 1954

——: *Der freie Satz* (Vienna, 1935, 2/1956); Eng. trans. 1979

Schneider, R.: *Die Reise zu Richard Wagner* (Vienna and Darmstadt, 1989)

Schoenberg, A.: *Style and Idea* (Eng. trans., London, 1975)

Schuh, W.: *Richard Strauss: a Chronicle of the Early Years* (Eng. trans., Cambridge, 1982)

Schüler, W.: *Der Bayreuther Kreis von seiner Entstehung bis zum Ausgang der Wilhelminischen Ära: Wagnerkult und Kulturreform im Geiste völkischer Weltanschauung* (Münster, 1971)

Sessa, A.D.: *Richard Wagner and the English* (Rutherford, NJ, 1979)

Shaw, G.B.: *The Perfect Wagnerite: a Commentary on the Niblung's Ring* (New York, 1967; repr. of 4/1923)

Shaw, L.R., Cirillo, N.R., and Miller, M.S., eds: *Wagner in Retrospect: a Centennial Reappraisal* (Amsterdam, 1987)

Shirer, W.: *The Rise and Fall of the Third Reich* (New York, 1960)

Skelton, G.: *Wagner at Bayreuth: Experiment and Tradition* (London, 1965, enlarged 2/1976)

——: *Wieland Wagner: the Positive Sceptic* (London, 1971)

——: *Richard and Cosima Wagner: Biography of a Marriage* (London, 1982)

——: *Wagner in Thought and Practice* (London, 1991)

Spencer, S.: 'Tannhäuser: mediävistische Handlung in drei Aufzügen', *Wagner 1976: a Celebration of the Bayreuth Festival* (London, 1976), 40–53

——, ed.: *Wagner 1976: a Celebration of the Bayreuth Festival* (Wagner Society, London, 1976)

——, ed.: *Wagner*, the periodical of the Wagner Society, London. New series (1980–)

——: '"Zieh hin! Ich kann dich nicht halten!"', *Wagner*, ii (1981), 98–120

——: 'Wagner in London (1)', *Wagner*, iii (1982), 98–123 [incl. previously unpubd material]

——: 'A Wagnerian Footnote', *Wagner*, iv (1983a), 90

——: 'Wagner Autographs in London', *Wagner*, iv (1983b), 98–114; v (1984), 2–20, 45–52 [24 previously unpubd letters, with Eng. trans., from the BL collection]

——, ed.: '"Die hohe Braut": an Unpublished Sketch', *Wagner*, iv (1983c), 13–26

——, ed.: '"Die hohe Braut": an Unpublished Draft', *Wagner*, x (1989), 50–65

——: 'Nineteenth-century Attitudes to Nuremberg', *Cambridge Opera Journal*, iv (1992)

Srocke, M.: *Richard Wagner als Regisseur* (Berlin, 1988)

Stein, J.M.: *Richard Wagner & the Synthesis of the Arts* (Detroit, 1960)

Stephan, R.: 'Gibt es ein Geheimnis der Form bei Richard Wagner?', in *Das Drama Richard Wagners als musikalisches Kunstwerk*, ed. C. Dahlhaus (Regensburg, 1970), 9–16

Stern, F.: *The Politics of Cultural Despair* (Berkeley, CA, 1961)

Strauss, R.: *Betrachtungen und Erinnerungen*, ed. W. Schuh (Zurich, 1949); Eng. trans., London, 1953

Strobel, O.: *Richard Wagner: Skizzen und Entwürfe zur Ring-Dichtung* (Munich, 1930)

Strobel, 1936–9: see under 'Letters' above

Strohm, R.: '"Rienzi" and Authenticity', *Musical Times*, cxvii (1976), 725

——: 'On the History of the Opera "Tannhäuser"', *Bayreuther Festspiele: Programmheft III. Tannhäuser* (Bayreuth, 1978), 21–9

Suneson, C.: *Richard Wagner och den indiska tankevärlden* (Stockholm, 1985); Ger. trans. 1989

Tanner, M.: 'The Total Work of Art', *The Wagner Companion*, ed. P. Burbidge and R. Sutton (London, 1979), 140–224

Taylor, R.: *Richard Wagner: his Life, Art and Thought* (London, 1979)

Thomson, J.L.: 'Giacomo Meyerbeer: the Jew and his Relationship with Richard Wagner', *Musica Judaica*, i (1975–6), no.1, pp.54–86

Turing, P.: *New Bayreuth* (London, 1969)

Turner, R.: '"Die Meistersinger von Nürnberg": the Conceptual Growth of an Opera', *Wagner*, iii (1982), 2–16

Tusa, M.C.: 'Richard Wagner and Weber's *Euryanthe*', *19th Century Music*, ix (1985–6), 206–21

Umbach, K., ed.: *Richard Wagner: ein deutsches Ärgernis* (Reinbek bei Hamburg, 1982)

Vaget, H.R.: 'Erlösung durch Liebe: Wagners "Ring" und Goethes "Faust"', *Bayreuther Festspiele: Programmheft VI. Götterdämmerung* (Bayreuth, 1985; Eng. trans.), 14–31

Vermeil, E.: *Germany's Three Reichs* (London, 1945)

Vetter, I.: 'Der "Ahasverus des Ozeans" – musikalisch unerlöst? Der fliegende Holländer und seine Revisionen', *Bayreuther Festspiele: Programmheft II. Der fliegende Holländer* (Bayreuth, 1979; Eng. trans.), 70–79

——: '*Der fliegende Holländer' von Richard Wagner: Entstehung, Bearbeitung, Überlieferung* (diss. Technical University, Berlin, 1982)

——, ed.: '"Leubald. Ein Trauerspiel": Richard Wagners erstes (erhaltenes) Werk', *Bayreuther Festspiele: Programmheft VII. Die Meistersinger* (Bayreuth, 1988; Eng. trans.), 1–19, 95–208 [incl. transcription of complete text]

——: 'Wagner in the History of Psychology', in *Wagner Handbook*, ed. J. Deathridge (Cambridge, MA, 1992)

Vogel, M.: *Nietzsche und Wagner: ein deutsches Lesebuch* (Bonn, 1984)

Vogt, M.T.: 'Taking the Waters at Bayreuth', in *Wagner in Performance*, ed. B. Millington and S. Spencer (New Haven, 1992)

Voss, E.: *Studien zur Instrumentation Richard Wagners* (Regensburg, 1970)

——: *Die Dirigenten der Bayreuther Festspiele* (Regensburg, 1976)

——: *Richard Wagner und die Instrumentalmusik: Wagners symphonischer Ehrgeiz* (Wilhelmshaven, 1977)

——: 'Noch einmal: das Geheimnis der Form bei Richard Wagner', in *Theaterarbeit an Wagners 'Ring'*, ed. D. Mack (Munich, 1978), 251–67; Eng. trans. in *Wagner*, iv (1983), 66–79

——: 'Wagners "Sämtliche Briefe"?', *Melos/Neue Zeitschrift für Musik*, iv (1978), 219–23

——: *Richard Wagner: Dokumentarbiographie* (Mainz and Munich, 1982a) [rev. and enlarged edn of Barth, Mack and Voss, eds, 1975]

——: 'Wagnerliteratur und Wagnerforschung', *Wolfenbütteler Forschungen*, xv (1982b), 75–9

——: 'Von Notwendigkeit und Nutzen der Wagnerforschung', *Bayreuther Festspiele: Programmheft I. Lohengrin* (Bayreuth, 1987; Eng. trans), 16–41

——: 'Auch eine Unvollendete: Richard Wagners wiederaufgefundenes Sinfonie-Fragment in E-Dur WWV 35', *Neue Zeitschrift für Musik*, (Nov. 1988), 14–18

Walker, A.: *Franz Liszt: the Weimar Years 1848–1861* (London, 1989)

Wapnewski, P.: *Der traurige Gott: Richard Wagner in seinen Helden* (Munich, 1978)

Warrack, J.: *Carl Maria von Weber* (London, 1968, 2/1976)

——: 'The Musical Background', *The Wagner Companion*, ed. P. Burbidge and R. Sutton (London, 1979), 85–112

——: 'The Influence of French Grand Opera on Wagner', in *Music in Paris in the Eighteen-Thirties*, ed. P. Bloom (Stuyvesant, NY, 1987), 575–87

Watson, D.: *Richard Wagner: a Biography* (London, 1979)

Wauters, K.: *Wagner en Vlaanderen 1844–1914* (Ghent, 1983)

Wessling, B.W.: *Bayreuth im Dritten Reich: Richard Wagners politische Erben* (Weinheim and Basel, 1983)

Westernhagen, C. von: *Richard Wagner: Sein Werk, sein Wesen, seine Welt* (Zurich, 1956)

——: *Vom Holländer zum Parsifal: Neue Wagner-Studien* (Zurich, 1962)

——: *Richard Wagners Dresdener Bibliothek 1842–1849* (Wiesbaden, 1966)

——: *Wagner* (Zurich, 1968, 2/1978); Eng. trans. Cambridge, 1978

——: *Die Entstehung des 'Ring', dargestellt an den Kompositionsskizzen Richard Wagners* (Zurich, 1973); Eng. trans. Cambridge, 1976

——: 'Wagner's Last Day', *Musical Times*, cxx (1979), 395–7

Weston, J.L.: *The Legends of the Wagner Drama: Studies in Mythology and Romance* (London, 1896)

White, D.A.: *The Turning Wheel: a Study of Contracts and Oaths in Wagner's 'Ring'* (Selinsgrove, PA, 1988)

Whittall, A.: 'The Music', chap. in *Richard Wagner: 'Parsifal'*, ed. L. Beckett (Cambridge, 1981)

——: 'The Music: a Commentary', in *Opera Guide 19: The Mastersingers of Nuremberg*, ed. N. John (London, 1983a), 15–26

——: 'Wagner's Great Transition? From Lohengrin to Das Rheingold', *Music Analysis*, ii (1983b), 269–80

——: 'Wagner's Later Stage Works', in *New Oxford History of Music*, ed. G. Abraham, ix (1990), 257–321

Winkler, F.: *For Freedom Destined: Mysteries of Man's Evolution in the Mythology of Wagner's Ring Operas and Parsifal* (New York, 1974)

Wintle, C.: 'The Numinous in *Götterdämmerung*', in *Reading Opera*, ed. A. Groos and R. Parker (Princeton, NJ, 1988)

Wolzogen, H. von: *Thematischer Leitfaden durch die Musik zu Richard Wagners Festspiel 'Der Ring des Nibelungen'* (Leipzig, 1876); Eng. trans. London and Leipzig, 1882

——: *Richard Wagner's Tristan und Isolde: ein Leitfaden durch Sage, Dichtung und Musik* (Leipzig, 1880); Eng. trans., 1884

——: *Thematischer Leitfaden durch die Musik zu R. Wagner's Parsifal* (Leipzig, 1882); Eng. trans., 1889

Wörner, K.: 'Beiträge zur Geschichte des Leitmotivs in der Oper', *Zeitschrift für Musikwissenschaft*, xiv (1931–2), 151

Wynn, M.: 'Meister Wolfram', *Wagner* (old series), lxxxiv (June 1980), 2–4

Zelinsky, H.: *Richard Wagner: ein deutsches Thema: eine Dokumentation zur Wirkungsgeschichte Richard Wagners 1876–1976* (Frankfurt am Main, 1976, 3/1983)

——: 'Die "feuerkur" des Richard Wagner oder die "neue religion" der "Erlösung" durch "Vernichtung"', in *Wie antisemitisch darf ein Künstler sein?*, ed. H.-K. Metzger and R. Riehn (Munich, 1978), 79–112

Zuckerman, E.: *The First Hundred Years of Wagner's Tristan* (New York, 1964)

Zurmühl, S.: *Leuchtende Liebe, lachender Tod: Zum Tochter-Mythos Brünnhilde* (Munich, 1984)

LIST OF ILLUSTRATIONS

Frontispiece Lorenz Gedon, bronze cast of Wagner, 1880–83. Nationalgalerie, Staatliche Museen zu Berlin.

1 Photograph of Wagner by Joseph Albert, 1864. Thüringer Museum, Eisenach, photograph by R.M. Kunze.

2 Anonymous, silhouette of Wagner, 1835. The Burrell Collection, Curtis Institute of Music, Philadelphia.

3 Ernst Benedikt Kietz, drawing of Wagner, 1840–42. Nationalarchiv der Richard-Wagner-Stiftung, Richard-Wagner-Gedenkstätte, Bayreuth.

4 Clementine Stockar-Escher, watercolour of Wagner, 1853. Nationalarchiv der Richard-Wagner-Stiftung, Richard-Wagner-Gedenkstätte, Bayreuth.

5 Photograph of Wagner by Pierre Petit & Trinquart, Paris, 1860. Nationalarchiv der Richard-Wagner-Stiftung, Richard-Wagner-Gedenkstätte, Bayreuth.

6 Friedrich Pecht, oil painting of Wagner, 1864–5. Metropolitan Museum of Art, New York, Gift of Frederick Loeser, 1889.

7 Photograph of Wagner by Franz Hanfstaengl, 1865. Thüringer Museum, Eisenach, photograph by R.M. Kunze.

8 Photograph of Wagner by Franz Hanfstaengl, 1871. Nationalarchiv der Richard-Wagner-Stiftung, Richard-Wagner-Gedenkstätte, Bayreuth.

9 Franz von Lenbach, oil painting of Wagner, 1871. Nationalarchiv der Richard-Wagner-Stiftung, Richard-Wagner-Gedenkstätte, Bayreuth.

10 Anton Scharff, bronze cast of Wagner, 1872. Reproduced by kind permission of Professor Martin Geck.

11 Photograph of Richard and Cosima Wagner by Fritz Luckhardt, 1872. Nationalarchiv der Richard-Wagner-Stiftung, Richard-Wagner-Gedenkstätte, Bayreuth.

12 Viennese caricature by Karl Klic, 1873.

13 Photograph of Wagner with his son Siegfried, 1880. Nationalarchiv der Richard-Wagner-Stiftung, Richard-Wagner-Gedenkstätte, Bayreuth.

14 Caricature of Wagner with Aeschylus and Shakespeare in the *Berliner Ulk*, 1876.

15 Caricature of Wagner in *Figaro*, London, 1876.

16 Gustav Adolph Kietz, plaster cast of marble relief of Wagner, 1881. Thüringer Museum, Eisenach, photograph by R.M. Kunze.

17 Lorenz Gedon, bronze cast of Wagner, 1880–83. Nationalgalerie, Staatliche Museen zu Berlin.

18 Photograph of Wagner by Joseph Albert, 1882. Nationalarchiv der Richard-Wagner-Stiftung, Richard-Wagner-Gedenkstätte, Bayreuth.

19 Caricature of Wagner in *Der junge Kikeriki*, Vienna, 1883.

20 Paul von Joukowsky, drawing of Wagner dated 12 February 1883. Nationalarchiv der Richard-Wagner-Stiftung, Richard-Wagner-Gedenkstätte, Bayreuth.

21 Wagner's piano transcription of Beethoven's Ninth Symphony, beginning of last movement, 1830–31. Nationalarchiv der Richard-Wagner-Stiftung, Richard-Wagner-Gedenkstätte, Bayreuth.

22 *Faust* Overture, first page of autograph score, 1839–40. Nationalarchiv der Richard-Wagner-Stiftung, Richard-Wagner-Gedenkstätte, Bayreuth.

23 *Trauermusik*, on motifs from Weber's *Euryanthe*, first page of autograph score, 1844. Staatsbibliothek zu Berlin, Stiftung Preussischer Kulturbesitz, Music Department, Berlin.

24 *Lohengrin*, opening of Act I, first complete draft, 1846. Nationalarchiv der Richard-Wagner-Stiftung, Richard-Wagner-Gedenkstätte, Bayreuth.

25 *Lohengrin*, opening of Act I, second complete draft, 1847. Nationalarchiv der Richard-Wagner-Stiftung, Richard-Wagner-Gedenkstätte, Bayreuth.

26 *Siegfrieds Tod*, first page of autograph of the poem, 1848. Nationalarchiv der Richard-Wagner-Stiftung, Richard-Wagner-Gedenkstätte, Bayreuth.

27 *Die Meistersinger von Nürnberg*, sketch for the Prize Song, 1866. Nationalarchiv der Richard-Wagner-Stiftung, Richard-Wagner-Gedenkstätte, Bayreuth.

28 *Kaisermarsch*, first page of autograph score, 1871. Nationalarchiv der Richard-Wagner-Stiftung, Richard-Wagner-Gedenkstätte, Bayreuth.

29 *Parsifal*, sketch for the Flowermaidens' music, Act II, 1876. Nationalarchiv der Richard-Wagner-Stiftung, Richard-Wagner-Gedenkstätte, Bayreuth.

30 Wagner's handwritten notice posted at the Bayreuth Festspielhaus on 13 August 1876. Nationalarchiv der Richard-Wagner-Stiftung, Richard-Wagner-Gedenkstätte, Bayreuth.

THE CONTRIBUTORS

KONRAD BUND — Historian and medievalist. Deputy Director of the Stadtarchiv, Frankfurt am Main. Director of the Deutsches Glockenmuseum, Greifenstein/Hessia. Editor of the *Jahrbuch für Glockenkunde*.

DAVID BRECKBILL — Writer, teacher and pianist. Doctoral dissertation on *The Bayreuth Singing Style around 1900*. Comprehensive critical discography of acoustical vocal Wagner recordings in progress.

JONATHAN BURTON — Music Librarian for English National Opera; formerly part-time lecturer at Goldsmiths' College, University of London. Surtitle translator, bassoonist and arranger.

WARREN DARCY — Professor of Music Theory at Oberlin College, Ohio. Book on the genesis and structure of *Das Rheingold* shortly to be published.

RAYMOND FURNESS — Professor of German, University of St Andrews. Author of *Wagner and Literature*.

THOMAS S. GREY — Assistant Professor at Stanford University, California. Doctoral dissertation *Richard Wagner and the Aesthetics of Musical Form in the Mid-19th Century (1840–1860)* due to be published in revised form.

MICHAEL HALL — Architectural Writer and Editor, Applied Arts, for *Country Life*.

ROGER HOLLINRAKE — Musical scholar. Author of *Wagner, Nietzsche, and the Philosophy of Pessimism*.

DAVID C. LARGE — Professor of History at Montana State University. Co-editor of *Wagnerism in European Culture and Politics*.

HUGH LLOYD-JONES — Former Regius Professor of Greek at Oxford University.

STEWART SPENCER — Writer and translator. Editor of *Wagner* magazine. Co-editor of *Selected Letters of Richard Wagner* and *Wagner in Performance*.

RONALD TAYLOR — Writer and translator. Former Professor of German at the University of Sussex. Author of books on modern and medieval German literature and culture, and of biographies of Wagner, Schumann, Liszt and Weill.

JOACHIM THIERY — Researcher at the Institut für Klinische Chemie, Ludwig-Maximilians-Universität, Munich.

ULRICH TRÖHLER — Director of the Institut für Geschichte der Medizin, Georg-August-Universität, Göttingen.

WILLIAM WEBER — Professor of History at California State University, Long Beach, California. Co-editor of *Wagnerism in European Culture and Politics*.

ARNOLD WHITTALL — Professor of Musical Theory and Analysis at King's College, London; has written widely on 19th- and 20th-century music, especially Wagner, Schoenberg, Britten and Tippett.

CHRISTOPHER WINTLE — Lecturer at King's College, London. Member of the Editorial Board of *Music Analysis*. Writes and lectures on analytical and psychoanalytical aspects of 19th- and 20th-century music.

INDEX

INDEX

Compiled by Dorothy Groves

Italics refer to plate numbers.

Page numbers in **bold** indicate the principal references.

ABBATE, CAROLYN 282, 407, 408, 410
Abend-Zeitung (Dresden) 13, 73
Abraham, Gerald 137, 316
absolute melody 230
absolute music 230
Adam, Adolphe 70
Adorno, Theodor W. 334, 338, 409
Aeschylus 150, **158–61**, *14*
Agoult, Countess d' 140
Albert, Joseph 104, *1*, *18*
albumleaf 319
Alsace-Lorraine 47
Altmann, Wilhelm 126, 192, 193
Altmeyer, Jeannine 367
Ambros, A.W. 235
America
  American Wagner scholars 408
  Wagnerian buildings 401
  see also Chicago, New York, Minnesota, Seattle
Anders, Gottfried Engelbert **22**, 317
anti-Semitism
  historical background 41–2, 161–2
  growth in Wagner's time 42, 45, 49
  Siegfried Wagner and Jewish employees 391
  Wagner's *see* Jews *under* Wagner
anticipation, motifs of 231, 238, 239
Apel, Theodor **22**, 119, 134–5, 273, 275, 310, 313, 316, 344
Appia, Adolphe 375
Arent, Benno von 376
Aristophanes 158
Arro, Elmar 403
Artwork of the Future, The see Kunstwerk der Zukunft, Das under Wagner, WRITINGS
Auber, Daniel-François-
  Esprit **22, 71**, 72, 75, 77, 249, 274, 321
  Wagner's arrangements of 323
  works rehearsed or conducted by Wagner 69, 70
Austria 38, 40, 44, 45–6
  Austro-Prussian War 141
  see also Metternich
Avenarius, Eduard **22**

BABBITT, MILTON 406
Bach, Johann Sebastian 85
Baermann, Heinrich Joseph 315
Bailey, Robert 203, 218, 248, 406–7, 408
Bakunin, Mikhail **22**, 57, 140–41, 144
Balling, Michael 222
Balzac, Honoré de 150
Bar, Bar form **231–2**, 268
Barenboim, Daniel 373
Barnby, Joseph 307
Barrès, Maurice 397

Barth, Herbert 97, 98, 99
Bary, Alfred von 364
Barzun, Jacques 385
Basle 375
Battle of the Nations 36, 94, 140
Baudelaire, Charles 383, 399
Bauer, Bruno 54, 144, 321
Bauer, Hans-Joachim 192
Bauer, Oswald G. 410
Baumann, C.-F. 409
Bayreuth **389–92**
  choice of town 170, 389–90
  conception and planning 123, 148, 154, **167–70**
  concert at foundation-stone laying 101
  Cosima as director *see under* Wagner, Cosima
  Cosima's Diaries as source of information on 190
  1876 Festival 370, 374, 381, 383, *30*
  finances 92, 101, 117, 142, 307
  1882 Festival
    ostracized 143
    Parsifal 101, 305
  and Hitler 376
  post-war reopening and productions 366–8, 376–8, 392
  singing style, 'Bayreuth' 364
  Wagner archive material 187, 188–9, 192, 196
  see also Bayreuth Circle; *Bayreuther Blätter*
Bayreuth Circle 128, 383, 390–91, 403, 409
Bayreuther Blätter 142, 145, 148, 175, 177, 186, 188, 388, 391, 409
Bayreuther Bund der deutschen Jugend 391
Beardsley, Aubrey 387, 397, 400
Bebel, August 46
Bechstein, Ludwig 281
Becker, Nikolaus 43
Beckett, Lucy 410
Beethoven, Ludwig van 65–6, 73, **82–5**, 100, **151–3**, 309, 310
  Fidelio 66, 69, 70, 133, 274, 345
  Ninth Symphony 65, 73, 74, 83, 101, 133, 151, 152, 230, 235, 311, 341
    W.'s piano arrangement 65–6, 125, 208, 315, 322, *21*
  Wagner writes on 83, 116, 133, 152
  and Wagner's piano music 319
Behrens, Hildegard 367
Bekker, Paul 73
Bellini, Vincenzo **22**, 69, 70, 71, 173, 249, 319
  Wagner impressed by Schröder-Devrient in 67–8, **133**
  Wagner's arrangements of 322–3
  Wagner's essay on 274
  Wagner's operatic inserts for 222, 316

Benda, Georg 80
Benedictus, Louis (Ludwig) **22**
Bennett, Joseph 383
Bennett, Robert Russell 337
Béranger, Pierre de 317
Berg, Alban 346, 395
Bergfeld, Joachim 187
Berghaus, Ruth 378
Bergson, Henri 55
Berio, Luciano 395
Berlin 13, 17, 18, 38, 44, 70, 90, 101, 126, 142, 143, 231, 365, 375, 377
Berlioz, Hector **22**, 73–4, 78, 82, **85–6**, 151, 340, 341, 382
  and *Faust* Overture 133–4, 310
  influence on Wagner's *Trauermusik* 310
  as model for Wagner's writing 115
  Wagner's ambivalence towards 85, 172
  Wagner's open letter to 237
Betz, Franz **22**, 88
Bilz(-Planer), Natalie **22**, 98, 119
biographies of Wagner 402–4
Bird, George 187
Bischoff, Ludwig 237
Bismarck, Otto von **22–3**, 46, 48, 49, 60, 61, 141, 142, 170, 178, 390
  references in Cosima's Diaries 188
  Wagner's relations with 142–3
Bizet, Georges 173
Bizonfy, Franz 145
Blech, Leo 371
Blissett, William 396
Blok, Aleksandr 387
Blum, Carl
  W.'s operatic insert for 67, 222, 316
Bockelmann, Rudolf 365
Böcklin, Arnold 399
Bodanzky, Artur 371
Böhm, Karl 371
Boieldieu, Adrien 69, 70, 75
Bologna 386
Bonfantini, G.A. (publisher) 185
Borchmeyer, Dieter 150, 190, 195, 408, 410
Boretz, Benjamin 406
Boughton, Rutland 395
Boulez, Pierre 367, 394
Bozman, M.M. 193
Brackel, Harald von 313
Brahms, Johannes **23**, 68, 127, 151, 153, 173, 393
Brandt, Carl **23**
Branzell, Karin 365
Brecht, Bertolt 377
Breckbill, David 408
Breig, Werner 408
Breitkopf & Härtel 125, 126, 221–2, 225, 226, 300, 318, 322
Brendel, Franz **23**, 84, 285

Breslau 16, 100
Briesemeister, Otto 364
Brinkmann, Reinhold 408
Britten, Benjamin 395
Brockhaus, Friedrich
  (brother-in-law) 23, 135
Brockhaus, Luise, *née* Wagner
  (sister) 23, 64, 97
Brockhaus, Ottilie, *née*
  Wagner (sister) 23, 97, 318
Brückner brothers (sets) 374
Bruckner, Anton 173, 346, 381–2
Brückner, Gotthold 23
Brückner, Max 23
Brückwald, Otto 170
Brunswick 18
Büchner, Ludwig 57
Budapest 16, 18, 100
Buddhism 54, 145, 147–8, 298, 300, 307,
  308, 322
Bühnenfestspiel 232
Bühnenweihfestspiel 232
Bülow, Cosima von *see* Wagner, Cosima
Bülow, Hans von 23, 72, 84, 87, 318, 354,
  370
  and Cosima 120, 123, 189
  and New German School 23, 173
  Nirwana 88, 173
  on Wagner's anti-Semitism 163
Bulwer-Lytton, Edward 149, 275, 276
Bürger, Gottfried August 266
Burger, Theodor (publisher) 185
Burgess, Anthony 398
Burnoul, Eugène 147, 308
Burrell, Mary 185
  Burrell Collection 191, 193
Büsching, J.G. 303
Byron 150

Cage, John 115
Calderón de la Barca, Pedro 150, 151
capital and capitalism 48, 118, 374, 388
Carlsbad Decrees 41
Caruso, Enrico 365
Cassel (Kassel) 90, 377
Cervantes, Miguel de 150
Cézanne, Paul 400
Chabrier, Emmanuel 395
Chamberlain, Eva, *née* Wagner 187, 188–9
Chamberlain, Houston Stewart 188, 375,
  383, 388, 391, 402
Champfleury, Jules 383
Chateaubriand 150
Chéreau, Patrice 377–8, 388
Cherubini, Luigi 69, 70, 75, 80
Chezy, Helmine von 78
Chicago 401
Chopin, Frédéric 172
Chorley, Henry F. 357
Chrétien de Troyes 307
Christianity
  Catholicism and *Tannhäuser* 126
  Christian symbolism in *Parsifal* 308
  Hegelian view of 53–4
  see also religious beliefs *under* Wagner
Chulkov, Georgi 387
church *see* religion
Coates, Albert 367, 371
Cologne 101, 375
Colonne, Edouard 385
commissions and royalties 90–92, 117
composers, contemporary
  view of Wagner 380–82
  Wagner's attitude to 170–74

see also names of composers
Comte, Auguste 55
conducting and conductors 352–4, 368–74
  Wagner as *see under* Wagner
  Wagner's influence on 101, 353
Conrad, Joseph 398
Conried, Heinrich 308
Constantin of Saxe-Weimar-Eisenach,
  Prince 95
Cooke, Deryck 406
Cooper, James Fenimore 134
copyright laws 90–91
Corder, Frederick 226
Corneille, Pierre 151
Cornelius, Peter 23, 90, 99, 173
Corse, Sandra 408
critics and critical analysis
  contemporary 382–4
  later 404–8
Cronaca Wagneriana 386

Dahlhaus, Carl 64, 85, 194, 195, 223, 232,
  239, 240, 249, 393, 394, 405, 406, 408, 409
Dahlmann, Friedrich 55
Dahn, Felix 58
Daily Telegraph 383
Dali, Salvador 401
Damrosch, Walter 371
Dannreuther, Edward 23
D'Annunzio, Gabriele 386, 397
Dante 150
Darcy, Warren 135, 217, 305, 408
Darwin, Charles and Darwinism 60, 157
Daube, Otto 65
Davies, Peter Maxwell 394
Davison, James W. 382–3
Dean, Winton 80
Deathridge, John 182, 185, 188, 194, 203,
  217, 251, 259, 286, 316, 408
Debussy, Claude 259, 308, 334, 346, 395
Decadents 396, 397, 399
Deinhardstein, J.L. 171
Delacroix 400
Denis, Maurice 400
Dessauer, Josef 264, 321
Devrient, Eduard Philippe 23
Diaghilev, Sergey 387
Dieckmann, F. 403
Dietsch, Pierre-Louis 23–4, 134, 278
Doepler, Carl Emil 24
Donington, Robert 406, 410
Donizetti, Gaetano 73, 173, 323–4
Döring, Georg 264
Dorn, Heinrich 24, 70, 75, 90
Dortmund 375
Dorus-Gras, Julie 317
Draeseke, Felix 84
Dresden 12, 14, 16, 57, 58, 70, 74, 77, 83, 89,
  90, 99, 100, 143, 152, 158, 165, 167,
  274, 276, 279, 315, 364
  Liedertafel (choral society) 314
  Palm Sunday concerts 311
  uprisings 45, 184, 270, 309
  Wagner's library in 149–50
Droysen, J.G. 55, 158, 160, 286
Düfflipp, Lorenz von 24
Dühring, Eugen 164
Dujardin, Edouard 397, 399
Dumersan, Marion 314
Du Moulin Eckart, Richard 188
Dupeuty 314
Duponchel, Charles Edmond 74
Durand, Schoenewerk & Cie 317

Düsseldorf 375
Dvořák, Antonín 393

Early music movement 358–9
Edinburgh Magazine 277
Ehrenfels, Christian von 405
Eichendorff, Joseph von 281
Eisenstein, Sergey 376
Eiser, Otto 24
Eliot, T.S. 397
Ellis, William Ashton 195–6, 319, 387–8,
  402
Elmendorff, Karl 370, 372
Engels, Friedrich 44, 60, 146
Ettmüller, Ludwig 165, 266–7, 286
Eulenburg, Ernst (publishers) 226–7
Euripides 159
Europa 317
Evangelischer Bund 61
Ewans, Michael 159
Expressionism 401

Falk, Adalbert 61
Fantin-Latour, Henri 399, 400
Fauré, Gabriel 395
Federlein, Gottlieb 235
Fehling, Jürgen 375
Fehr, Max 403
Felsenstein, Walter 377
Fétis, François-Joseph 382
Feuchtersleben, Ernst von 318
Feuerbach, Ludwig 24, 53, 54, 57, 143–4,
  146–7, 148, 183, 230, 231, 232, 265–6,
  286, 321
  The Essence of Christianity 24, 54, 59–60
  'Feuerbach ending' to *Götterdämmerung*
  297
Feustel, Friedrich 24, 88, 123
Fichte, Johann Gottlieb 52, 54, 59, 143
Fichtmüller, Hedwig 367
Finsterlin, Hermann 401
Fitzball, Edward 277–8
Flagstad, Kirsten 365–6
Flaxland, Gustave (publisher) 91
Flotow, Friedrich von 81, 171
Fontane, Theodor 58, 388
Forner, Johannes 192
Förster, Bernhard 163
Forsyth, Cecil 336, 339, 340, 343, 346
Foucher, Paul 134, 278
Fouqué, Friedrich de la Motte 56, 266, 272,
  281
France 40, 41, 42, 44, 49
  Wagner's Francophobia 142, 156, 385,
  399
  Wagner's posthumous influence 385
  see also Franco-German relations; French
  influences; French Revolution; Paris
Franck, Hermann 24, 127
Franco-German relations 37–8, 39–44,
  46–7
Franco-Prussian War 17, 142, 190, 312,
  390, 399, *see also Kaisermarsch*
Frankfurt 14, 378
Frantz, Constantin 24, 141, 142
French influences on Wagner 70–74, 76–7,
  79
French Revolution 39, 40, 42, 47
Freud, Sigmund 55
Freytag, Gustav 150
Friedrich August I, King of Saxony 314
Friedrich August II, King of Saxony 140,
  314

Friedrich Barbarossa 321
Friedrich the Great 38, 156, 157
Friedrich Wilhelm III, King of Prussia 59
Friedrich Wilhelm IV, King of Prussia 44, 45, 59, 231
Friedrich, Götz 377
Fritzsch, Ernst Wilhelm **24**
Fröbel, Julius **24**
Frommann, Alwine **24-5**
Furchau, Friedrich 303
Furness, Raymond 410
Fürstner, Adolph 224, 225, 226
Furtwängler, Wilhelm 354, **371-2**, 373

GAILLARD, KARL **25**, 248, 265
Gasperini, Auguste de **25**
Gauguin, Paul 400
Gautier, Judith **25**, 113, 120, 189
Gay, Peter 164
Geck, Martin 104
Gedon, Lorenz 104, *17*
Genast, Emilie 318
German Confederation 41, 45, 46, 60
Germany
    1848 Revolution 44-5
    Bayreuth and German nationalism 390-92
    unification and founding of the Reich (1871) 47
    Wagner's posthumous influence on 388-9
    see also anti-Semitism, nationalism *under* Wagner, Nazism
Gervinus, Georg Gottfried 165, 303
Gesamtkunstwerk 65, 127, 161, **232-3**, 387, 395, 399, 400
    Kandinsky's *Bühnengesamtkunstwerk* 400
Geyer, Ludwig **25**, 56, 64, 94-5, 95-6
Gibbon, Edward 150
Gilardone, Franz 315
Glasenapp, Carl Friedrich **25**, 188, 388, 402
Gläser, Franz 69, 75
Gleizès, Jean Antoine 178
Gluck, Christoph Willibald 78, 100, 323, 324
Glyn, Margaret H. 226
Gobineau, Joseph-Arthur de **25**, 164, 190
Goebbels, Joseph 392
Goethe, Johann Wolfgang von 56, 127, 150, 159, 374, 408
    source for unfinished Wagner works 56, 320, 321
    verse form 266, 268
    Wagner's pieces for *Faust* 316
    see also Faust Overture
Goldmark, Karl 173
Goldoni, Carlo 151
Goldstein, Max 145
Goldwag, Bertha **25**, 99, 190
Golther, Wolfgang 186, 195, 319
Goodall, Reginald 372
Goossens, Leon 339
Görres, Johann Joseph von 284
Goslich, S. 89
Göttling, Carl Wilhelm 165
Gounod, Charles 173
Gozzi, Carlo 56, 151, 272
Graf, Max 406
grand opera 72-3, *see also* Romantic opera
Gray, Andrew 186
Great Britain, Wagner's influence on 387-8
    see also Glasgow, London
Gregor-Dellin, Martin 95, 96, 186, 189, 403
Greive, Hermann 49
Grétry, André-Ernest-Modeste 79-80

Grey, Thomas S. 408
Grieg, Edvard 381
Grillparzer, Franz 58
Grimm brothers (Jacob and Wilhelm) 57, 165, 286, 303, 304
Groos, Arthur 410
Grundmotiv 233
Grunsky, Karl 405
Gutman, Robert 113, 163, 403
Gutzkow, Karl **25**, 57, 149

HABENECK, FRANÇOIS 73, 152
Habsburg Empire 44, *see also* Holy Roman Empire
Hagen, Friedrich Heinrich von der 165
Halévy, Jacques-François-Fromental **25-6**, 69, 70, 72, 73, 76, 82, 171
    first to use valve horns 341
    Wagner's arrangements of 323-4
Hall, Peter 378
Halm, August 405
Hamburg 101
Hanfstaengl, Franz 104, *7, 8*
Hanover 18, 90
Hanslick, Eduard **26**, 74, 127, 230, 249, 358, 382, 405
Hartmann von Aue 164
Hauff, Wilhelm 134, 277
Haydn, Franz Joseph 65, 66, 322
Hebbel, Friedrich 58
Heckel, Emil **26**, 88
Heckel, Wilhelm 339, 340-41
Hegel, Georg Wilhelm Friedrich **52-3**, 54-5, 59, 143, 145, 150, 230
Heim, Ignaz **26**
Heine, Ferdinand **26**, 322
Heine, Heinrich **26**, 57, 143, 149, 165
    and Flying Dutchman story 134, 183, **277-8**
    Les Deux Grenadiers 125, 317
    and *Tannhäuser* 281
Heinse, Wilhelm 57, 273-4
Henderson, W.J. 364
Henze, Hans Werner 395
Herder, Johann Gottfried 150, 240
Hérold, Ferdinand 67, 69, 70, 71-2
Herwegh, Georg **26**, 141, 144
Herz, Joachim 377
Hesse, Sophie Friederice 95
Hey, Julius **26**
Heyse, Paul 58
Hiller, Ferdinand 77, 237, 264, 321
Hill, Karl **26**
Hitler, Adolf 221, 276, 376, 389, 390, 391, 392
Hoffmann, Ernst Theodor Amadeus **56**, 65, 67, 80, 149, 165, 264, 321
    and motifs 231
    source for *Die Feen* 272
    source for *Die Meistersinger* 303
    source for *Tannhäuser* 281
Hoffmann, Josef **26**, 374
Hoffmann von Fallersleben 43
Hofmann, Peter 367
Hohenstaufen dynasty 77, 165, 321
Hohenzollern dynasty 58, 60, 312, 389
Hohlfeld, Christoph Christian 314
Holbach, Paul 147
Hollinrake, Roger 408
Holloway, Robin 395-6, 408
Holtei, Julie von 313

Holtei, Karl von 313
Holtzmann, Adolf 150, 308
Holy Roman Empire 36-9, 40, 41, 47
Homer 150, 158
Hostinsky, Otakar 405
Hotter, Hans 366
Howison, John 277
Hueffer, Francis 383
Hugo, Victor 150, 317
Hülsen, Botho von **26**
Humperdinck, Engelbert 221, 393
Hurn, Philip Dutton 95, 185-6
Husserl, Edmund 55
Huysmans, Joris-Karl 385, 397

IDEALISM 52-5, 59, 143
Impressionists 308-9, 399
Industrial Revolution 42, 45, 47-8
infinite melody 233-4
influence, Wagner's 384-9, 393-401
    on conducting style 101, 353
    on history of music 393-6
    on literature 396-8
    on orchestra and orchestration 346-7
    on visual arts 398-401
Isouard, Nicolò 75
Italy
    family visits 18, *see also* Venice, Palermo
    Italian influences on Wagner 70-72
    Wagner's influence on 385-6
Ivanov, Vyacheslav 387

JACHMANN-WAGNER, JOHANNA (niece) 97
Jähns, F.W. 235
Janssen, Herbert 365
Jenkins, Newell Sill **26**
Jews *see* anti-Semitism
Joachim, Joseph 351
John, Nicholas 410
Jones, Gwyneth 367
Jones, Richard 378
Joukowsky, Paul von **26**, 104, 179, 20
    Journal des Débats 237
Joyce, James 397, 398
Jung, Carl 406
Junges Deutschland see Young German movement

KANDINSKY, WASSILY 400
Kant, Immanuel 52, 54, 59, 143
Kapp, Julius 192, 195
Karajan, Herbert von 367, 373
Karbaum, Michael 409
Karlsruhe 16, 100
Kassel *see* Cassel
Kastner, Emerich 192
Katz, Adele 406
Katz, Jacob 157, 409
Kautsky brothers (sets) 375
Keller, Gottfried 58
Kiefer, Anselm 401
Kierkegaard, Søren 59
Kietz, Ernst Benedikt **26-7**, 104, 168, 317, 319, 3
Kietz, Gustav Adolph 104, *16*
King, James 366
Kipnis, Alexander 365
Kirchmeyer, Helmut 403, 410
Kirchner, Theodor F. **27**
Kittl, Jan 264, 321
Kleiber, Carlos 373
Kleist, Heinrich von 150

Klic, Karl *12*
Klimt, Gustav 399
Klindworth, Karl **27**, 86, 381
Klinger, Max 399
Klink, Gustav 224
Knappertsbusch, Hans 371, 372, 373
Kniese, Julius 276
Kollo, René 367
Koltai, Ralph 378
Königsberg 13, 70, 99, 100, 321
Körner, Theodor 272
Kraft, Louis 318
Kraft, Zdenko von 403
Kraus, Felix von 364
Kreckel, M. 408
Kreutzer, Conradin 67, 75
Kropfinger, Klaus 83, 84, 152
Kulturkampf 48, 49, 61
Kunstreligion see religion
Kunze, Stefan 408
Kupfer, Harry 377, 378
Kurth, Ernst 405–6

LABLACHE, LUIGI 316
Lachmann, Karl 165, 286
Lachner, Franz 81, 90
Laforgue, Jules 399
Lamoureux, Charles 385
Lange, Walter 403
Large, David C. 410
Lassalle, Ferdinand 46
Laube, Heinrich **27**, 57, 135, 143, 149, 182, 273–4, 310
Laudon, R.T. 156
Laussot, Jessie (née Taylor) **27**, 119, 120
Lawrence, D.H. 398
Lee, Vernon 397
Lehmann, Lilli 364
Lehmann, Lotte 365
Lehnhoff, Nikolaus 378
Lehrs, Samuel **27**, 149, 158, 165, 317
Leibniz, Gottfried Wilhelm von 52, 59
Leider, Frida 365, 366
Leipzig 12, 13, 17, 18, 69, 89, 100, 133, 140, 143, 377
leitmotif 79–82, **234–5**, 252, 270–309
  Aeschylus's use of recurrent themes 159
  critical analyses 404, 406
  first sustained use 274
  influence on later composers and writers 395–7
  see also anticipation, reminiscence, *Grundmotiv* and musical style under each opera
Lemoyne, J.B. 80
Lenbach, Franz von **27**, 104, *9*
Lenrow, Elbert 118
Leo XIII, Pope 61
Lessing, Gotthold Ephraim 41, 150
Levant Treaty 42
Lévi-Strauss, Claude 397–8
Levi, Hermann **27**, 164, 225, 307, 369
Levine, James 372
Lewald, August 317
Lewis, Mary Tompkins 400
Lewy, Eduard-Constantin 341
Lewy, Josef-Rudolf 341
Liller Kriegszeitung 389
Lindpaintner, Peter Joseph von 75, 81
Lippert, Woldemar 402, 403
Lippmann, Friedrich 71
List, Emmanuel 365
Liszt, Franz **27**, **86–8**, 98, 169, 202, 250, 312–13, 380–81, 402

as conductor of Wagner 90, 168, 285
criticizes Wagner's humanism 147
and *Lohengrin* 285, 338
references in Cosima's Diaries 188
Wagner's opinion of his music 172
and *Zukunftsmusik* 237
literature and literary influences **55–8**
literature on Wagner 402–10
  biographies 402–4
  see also critical analysis
Ljungberg, Göta 367
Lloyd-Jones, Hugh 55, 159
Loewe, Carl 171
Logier, J.B. 65
London 13, 15, 83, 100, 101, 126, 140, 339, 353, 365, 370, 372, 378
London, George 366
Lorenz, Alfred 232, 238–9, 305, 404–5
Lorenz, Max 365
Lortzing, Albert 67, 81, 171
Louis XIV of France 37
Louis-Napoléon 141
Louis-Philippe of France 140
Löwenberg 100
Löwe, Professor 314
Lubin, Germaine 365
Lucas, C.T.L. 165, 281
Luckemeyer, Marie 320
Luckhardt, Fritz 104, *11*
Ludwig II, King of Bavaria **27–8**, 88, 91, 92, 98–9, **121–4**, 141, 148, 177, 186, 187, 190, 389
  acquires rights and manuscripts 221
  birthday music 311
  essay *Über Staat und Religion* written for 234
  and festival theatre plans 169–70
  Das Liebesverbot dedicated to 274
  ostracizes second Bayreuth Festival 143
  triggers *Mein Leben* and diaries 183
  and Wagner's appeal for music school 116, 155
  Wagner's attitude to 156
  Wagner's letters to 193
Lunacharsky, Anatoli 387
Luther, Martin 312, 322
Lüttichau, August von **28**, 314

McCRESS, PATRICK 407, 408
Mach, Ernst 55
Mack, Dietrich 189, 409
Magdeburg 13, 69, 89, 99, 100, 273, 274
Magee, Bryan 132, 162, 396, 403, 408, 409
Mahler, Gustav 346, 371, 381
Maier, Mathilde **28**, 121
Mainz 16
Mallarmé, Stéphane 396
Mannheim 100
  performance of *Siegfried Idyll* 311
Mann, Thomas 36, 40, 58, 97, 388, 397, 398, 406
Manthey, Axel 378
Marbach, Rosalie, *née* Wagner (sister) **28**, 64, 97, 316
Marienbad 135
Marryat, Captain 134
Marschner, Heinrich **28**, 66–7, 69, 73, 75, 77, 81, 90, 171
  influence on *Höllander* 239, 278
  influence on *Die Feen* 249, 272
  Wagner's operatic insert for 222, 316
Marx, Karl 44, 46, 47, 53, 54, 60, 144, 380
Materna, Amalie **28**
Mauro, Seraphine 121

Mazzini, Giuseppe 154
medieval literature and
  ideals **164–7**
  poetic metres 266–8
  writers on Wagner's medieval sources 408
Méhul, Etienne-Nicolas 70, 75, 80
Meier, Waltraud 368
Meister, The 387–8
Melchinger, Ulrich 377
Melchior, Lauritz 365
Mellers, Wilfrid 300
Mendelssohn-Bartholdy, Felix **28**, 41, 171–2, 231, 310, 382
Mendelssohn, Moses 41
Mendès-Gautier, Judith *see* Gautier, Judith
Mendès, Catulle **28**
Meser, C.F. 91, 125, 224
Messager, André 395
Metternich, Clemens von 41, 44, 57
Metternich, Princess Pauline **28**, 281, 320
Metzdorf 144
Meyerbeer, Giacomo **28–9**, 68, **72–3**, 134, 334, 380
  L'Africaine 173
  Les Huguenots 72–3, 75, 76, 82, 126, 340
  Le Prophète 77, 82, 122, 232
  Robert le diable 69, 70, 71, 76, 323
  and royalties 91, 122
  Wagner's hostility to 72, 74–5, 157, 162–3, 171, 193, 232, 380
Meyer, Conrad Ferdinand 58
Meyer, Friederike 121
Meysenbug, Malwida von **29**, 98, 174
Middle Ages *see* medieval
Milan, La Scala 386
Miller, Marion 154
Minnesang 166
Minnesota 390, 401 *Mir iskoustva* (*The World of Art*) 387
Mitchell, William 406
Mitleiden (compassion), concept of 174
Mitterwurzer, Anton **29**, 358
Molière (Jean-Baptiste Poquelin) 150, 151
Moltke, Helmuth von 61, 390
Mommsen, Theodor 55
Mone, Franz Joseph 165, 286
Monnais, Edouard **29**, 74
Moore, George 398
Moore, Thomas 277
Moreau, Gustave 399
Moritz (brass instrument maker) 343, 344
Morris, James 367, 368
Morris, William 383
Moscow 16, 100, 376, 400
Mosenthal, S.H. (librettist) 173
Mottl, Felix 225, 310, 318, 337, 346, 369
Mozart, Wolfgang Amadeus 66, 67, 69, 70, 126, 309, 315, 319, 362
  reminiscence motifs 80
  Wagner's version of *Don Giovanni* 100, 324
Mrazéck, Anna 29
Mrazéck, Franz 29
Muck, Karl 369, 372
Müller, Gottlieb **29**, 65, 318
Müller, Hermann 91, 224
Müller, Maria 365
Müller, U. 410
Müller, Wenzel 80
Muncker, Theodor **29**, 123
Mundt, Theodor 57
Munich 16–17, 18, 89, 90, 121, 122, 123, 124, 137, 169, 271, 287, 290, 298, 301, 352, 354, 365, 378
music drama **236–7**, 271
  analyses 404–8

effect on conductors 368
its enduring power 404
and performing style 363
symphonic nature 368
Music of the future **237**, *see also Zukunftsmusik*
under WRITINGS
'musical modernism' 393
'musical prose' 374, 394
musico-poetic synthesis 83, 240, 248–9, 252, 301

NAPOLEON I (Bonaparte) W.'s planned
overture 310
Napoleon III 46, 47, 281
Napoleonic wars 36, 41, 94, 140, 156, 165
Nattiez, J.-J. 409, 410
Nature motif **237**
Nazism 375–6
and Bayreuth 391–2
Neefe, C.G. 80
Nessler, Viktor E. 363
Neue Zeitschrift für Musik 116, 125, 126, 195, 285, 380
Neumann, Angelo **29**, 91, 143, 368
'New German School' 85, 173
New York Metropolitan Opera 308, 365, 368, 369, 370, 371, 375, 378, 388
Newcomb, Anthony 407, 408
Newman, Ernest 113, 137, 241, 312, 402–3
Das Nibelungenlied poem 285, 286
Nicholas I, Tsar 313
Niederrheinische Musik-Zeitung 237
Niemann, Albert **29**, 358, 363
Nietzsche, Friedrich **29**, 49, 55, 60, 388
friendship with Wagner 58, 158, 383–4
writings on Wagner 65, 94, 143, 145, 185, 383–4, 389, 397
Nikisch, Artur 371
Nilsson, Birgit 367
Norddeutscher Bund 46
Nordica, Lillian 364
Norrington, Roger 359
Norse Sagas: sources for *Ring* cycle 286
North German Confederation 142
Novalis (Friedrich von Hardenberg) 57
Nuitter, Charles 226
Nuremberg 69

OESTERLEIN, NIKOLAUS 408
Ollivier, Blandine (sister-in-law) **29**, 121
Ollivier, Emile (brother-in-law) 142
Olmütz, Treaty of 45, 60
opera-going public:
attitudes and traditions 153–4
orchestra, 'invisible' 234, 334, 351–2
orchestras in Wagner's day 350–51
Oxenford, John 54

PACHTA FAMILY 316, 321
Paer, Ferdinando 69
Paisiello, Giovanni 69
Palermo 19, 137, 320
Palestrina 323
Paris 13, 15, 16, 72–3, 89, 100, 133–5, 140, 158, 163, 186
and *Tannhäuser* 281, 282
uprisings (1830) and Political Overture 309
Parker, Roger 410
patronage, systems of 88–90, 118
Wagner's patrons *see under* Wagner
Pätz, Dorothea Erdmuthe (grandmother) 95
Pätz, Johann Gottlob (grandfather) 95

Pätz, Johanna *see* Wagner, Johanna
Pecht, Friedrich 97, 104
Perfall, Karl von **29**
performance fees 91–2
performance, Wagner in *see* singers and singing, conducting, staging
Peters, C.F. (publishers) 125, 225, 226
Petit, Pierre, & Trinquart 104, *5*
Petzet, D.and M. 410
Pfistermeister, Franz von **30**, 122
Pfordten, Ludwig von der **30**, 122
Pillet, Léon **30**, 74, 134
Pius IX, Pope 60
Planer, Minna *see* Wagner, Minna
Planer, Natalie *see* Bilz (-Planer)
Plato 150, 158
Pleyel, Ignaz 319
poetic intent 238
poetic-musical period 238–9, 251, 404
Poliakov, Léon 409
Pollock, Jackson 401
'Porazzi Theme' 313, 320
Porges, Heinrich **30**, 99, 164, 225, 235
portamento (instrumental) 351
portamento (vocal) 355–6, 367
Porter, Andrew 136
Post-Impressionists 400
Pourtalès, Count and Countess 320
Praeger, Ferdinand Christian Wilhelm **30**
Prague 12, 13, 16, 100
Prague, Peace of 142
Preetorius, Emil 376
Prieberg, Fred K. 409
Pringle, Carrie 121, 189
Proudhon, Pierre-Joseph 57, 140–41, 143, 146, 178, 232, 286, 321
Proust, Marcel 397
Prussia 38–47, 40, 42, 44–5, 46, 47, 58
Hegel on 53
publishers **124–6**, *see also* names of publishers
Pusinelli, Anton **30**, 91, 98, 118, 184

RACINE, JEAN 151
Raff, Joachim 90, 173, 311
Raimund, Ferdinand 67
Ranke, Leopold von 55
Rank, Otto 406
Raupach, Ernst 309
Reboul, Jean 317
recordings **373–4**
early 365, 366, 367, 370, 371
effect on interpretations 373–4
Strauss's 354
Redon, Odilon 399
Reissiger, Karl Gottlieb **30**, 78, 81, 314, 321
religion 36–7, **58–60**
churches against Jews 49
German church-state relationships 48–9
Kunstreligion **234**
see also Buddhism, Christianity, anti-Semitism
Rellstab, Ludwig 126
reminiscence motif 79–82, 238, **239**, 404
Renoir, Auguste 399
Reszke, Edouard de 364
Reszke, Jean de 364, 369
Reuss-Belce, Luise 364
Révoil, Bénédict-Henry 134, 278
Revue et Gazette Musicale 73, 115, 382
Revue Indépendante 396
Revue Wagnérienne 58, 385, 396, 397, 399–400
Rheinbund 40
rhyme **264–8**, *see also Stabreim*

Richter, Hans **30**, 101, 221, 322, 339, 343, 372
and Bayreuth 169, 285, **370**
and *Siegfried Idyll* 311
Riemann, Hugo 404
Riga 13, 70, 89, 99, 100, 169, 403
Ritter, Emilie 135
Ritter, Julie **30**
letters from Wagner 119, 120
Ritter, Karl **30**, 300
Robert de Boron 307
Röckel, August **30**, 121, 140, 144, 166, 195, 321
Roller, Alfred 375
Romantic movement 149, 165
Romantic opera 74, 75, **239**
Ronsard, Pierre de 317
Roon, Albrecht von 61, 390
Root, John 401
Root, Waverley Lewis 95, 185–6
Rose, Paul Lawrence 164, 409
Rosenblum, Robert 401
Rosselli, John 90
Rossini, Gioachino 69, 70, 71, 81, 170, 173, 230, 336
Wagner's arrangements of 323
Rousseau, Jean-Jacques 52, 115, 150, 240
Roxburgh, Edwin 339
royalties and commissions 90–92, 117
Rubinstein, Anton 90, 173
Rubinstein, Joseph **30–31**, 164, 172, 221
Ruge, Arnold 53, 144
Ruskin, John 383
Russia, Wagner's influence on 386–7
see also Moscow, Riga, St Petersburg
Ryder, Albert Pinkham 401

SACHS, HANS (historical figure) 150, 171, 268, 303
St Petersburg 16, 100
Salzburg 367
Salzer, Felix 406
Sand, George 150
Saturday Review 382
Sax, Adolphe 343
Sayn-Wittgenstein, Princess Carolyne **31**, 192
Scharff, Anton 104, *10*
Schelling, Friedrich Wilhelm Joseph von 52, 59, 143
Schenk, Johann Baptist 69
Schenk, Otto 378
Schenker, Heinrich 406
Scheurlin, Georg 317
Schiller, Johann Christoph Friedrich von 39, 40, 150, 309, 374
Schlegel, Friedrich 57, 149, 239
Schleiermacher, Friedrich Ernst Daniel 52
Schleinitz, Marie von **31**
Schlesinger, Maurice **31**, 323
Schleswig-Holstein 46
Schmale, Wilhelm 313
Schmidt, H. 277
Schneckenburger, Max 43
Schnorr von Carolsfeld, Ludwig **31**, 355, 358
Schnorr von Carolsfeld, Malvina **31**
Schoenberg, Arnold 236, 346, **393–4**
Schopenhauer, Arthur **31**, 54, 57, 135, **144–5**, **147–8**, 153, 178, 185, 190, 266, 300–01, 307, 308
'Schopenhauer ending' to *Götterdämmerung* 298

Schopenhauerian character of the *Ring* 286

Schorr, Friedrich 365

Schott (publishers) 66, 91, 117–18, **124–6**, 132, 205, 225, 226, 312

Sämtliche Werke 223–5

Schott, Betty 320

Schröder-Devrient, Wilhelmine **31**, 67–8, 133, 233, 276, 278, 354–5, 357

Schubert, Franz 66, 172, 341

Schuh, Willi 354

Schüler, Winfried 409

Schumann-Heink, Ernestine 364

Schumann, Robert **31**, 43, 81, 172, 317, 341 and Wagner's annoyance at 'Meyerbeerian' charges 72, 74, 380

see also Neue Zeitschrift für Musik

Scott, Sir Walter 134, 150, 277

Scribe, Eugène 22, 71, 77, 134, 232, 278, 321

Seattle 198

Seidl, Anton **31**, 221, 368–9

Semper, Gottfried **31**, 169, 170

Sessa, A.D. 410

Shakespeare, William **56**, 150, 151, 233, 239, *14*

source for *Das Liebesverbot* 274

source for *Leubald* 320

Shaw, George Bernard 364, 388, 410

Sievert, Ludwig 375

Simrock, Karl 165

Singer, J. 310

singers and singing 154, 155, 157, 354–8, **362–8**, *see also* individual names

Sinopoli, Giuseppe 373

Skelton, Geoffrey 189, 403, 410

Skryabin, Alexander 395, 400

Smart, Sir George 310

Solti, Sir Georg 373–4

Sophocles 150

Spencer, Stewart 188, 193, 409n.

Spielhagen, Friedrich 58

Spitzer, Daniel 190–91

Spohr, Louis **32**, 73, 77, 80, 171, 237, 264 as exponent of Wagner 32, 90

Jessonda 69, 70, 75

and reminiscence motif 81

Spontini, Gaspare 70, 72, 73, 77, 78, 171, 323

Stabreim 200, 235–6, **240**, 266, 267

staging Wagner **374–8**

'Bayreuth style' 375

Stalin, Joseph 376

Standhartner, Joseph **32**

Stein, Horst 370

Stein, J.M. 408, 410

Stephan, R. 408

Sternfeld, Richard 195, 389

Stewart, Thomas 366

Stirner, Max 54, 144

Stockar-Escher, Clementine 104, *4*

Stocker, Jakob **32**

Stocker, Vreneli *see* Weidmann, Vreneli

Stockhausen, Karlheinz 395

Strassburg, Gottfried von 166, 267, 300

Strauss, David Friedrich 53, 144, 321

Strauss, Franz 342

Strauss, Johann the Younger 324

Strauss, Richard 341, 354, 369 on Wagner's orchestration 334–46 *passim*

Stravinsky, Igor 346, 395

Strobel, Gertrud 192

Strobel, Otto 182, 186, 187, 192, 203, 247, 409 and Eva Wagner 188–9

transcription of *Ring* text manuscripts 201

Strohm, Reinhard 222, 223–4, 224

Sturluson, Snorri 286

Süddeutsche Presse 141

Sullivan, Louis 401

Sulzer, (Johann) Jakob **32**

Suneson, Carl 408

Switzerland 17, 409, *see also* Zurich

Sybel, Heinrich von 55

Symbolism 385, 386, **396–7**, 399–400

TAPPERT, WILHELM 320

Taubert, Wilhelm 90

Tausig, Carl **32**

Taylor, Ronald 403

Tchaikovsky, Pyotr 156, 381

Teplitz 94

Thirty Years' War 37

Thomas, Jess 366

Thomas, Theodore 313

Thomson, Virgil 300

Thorborg, Kerstin 365

Tichatschek, Joseph **32**, 123, 357

Tieck, Ludwig 56, 58, 149, 150, 165, 231, 281

Tiersot, Julien 191

Tietjen, Heinz 376

Times, The 382, 383, 397

Titian 304

Tolstoy, Leo 383

Tombo, August 337

Toscanini, Arturo 188, 371, 391

Treitschke, Heinrich von 55

Turin 386

Tusa, Michael C. 78

UHLIG, THEODOR **32**, 120–21, 168–9, 172, 191, 202, 381

Unger, Georg **32**

VAN GOGH, VINCENT 398, 400

Van Rooy, Anton 364

Varnay, Astrid 366

VEB Deutscher Verlag für Musik (publishers) 192

Vega, Lope de 151

Venice 16, 19

Verdi, Giuseppe 90, 91, 172–3, 346, 382

Verlaine, Paul 396, 397

Véron, Louis 89

Vetter, Isolde 224, 404

vibrato (instrumental) 351

vibrato (vocal) 355, 367

Vickers, Jon 366

Vienna 16, 18, 38, 44, 58, 67, 89, 100, 101, 127, 365, 370, 375, 393

Vienna, Congress of 41, 42

Villiers de l'Isle-Adam, Auguste 32, 383

Vischer, F.Th. 58

Vogl, Heinrich **32**

Vogt, Matthias Theodor 169

Völker, Franz 365

Völkl, Lisbeth 121

Völkl, Marie 121

Volksblätter 140, 195

Voltaire 52

Voltz and Batz (agents) 88

Voss, Egon 192, 195, 223, 223–4, 224–5, 409

WAGENSEIL, J.C. 303

Wagner, Adolf (uncle) 56, 64, 97

Wagner, Albert (brother) **32**, 64, 66, 97, 316

Wagner, Cäcilie (sister) 94, 96, 97

Wagner, Carl Friedrich (father?) 94, 95

Wagner, Carl Julius (brother) 97

Wagner, Clara *see* Wolfram, Clara

Wagner, Cosima, *formerly* von Bülow, *née* Liszt 15–19, **32–3**, 114, 120, 121, 123, 150, 170, 311, 312

birthday celebrations 101, **315**

Siegfried Idyll 311–12

and Brown Book 186–7

character 390

diaries 56, 78, 83, 85, 128, 136, 137, 158, 164, 172, 173, 178, **188–90**, 403

as Festival director 276, 279, 364, 369, 375, 388, 390

and *Mein Leben* 184, 185, 187, 187–8

and 'Porazzi Theme' 137, 313

publishes Wagner's letters 191

and 'Starnberg Quartet' 137–8

and von Bülow 32, 120, 123, 189

Wagner, Eva *see* Chamberlain, Eva

Wagner, Franziska (niece) 33

Wagner, Johanna Rosine, *née* Pätz (mother) 14, 94–7, 146

Wagner, Johanna (niece) *see* Jachmann-Wagner

Wagner, Luise *see* Brockhaus, Luise

Wagner, 'Minna', *née* Planer 13–17, **33**, 96, 97, 98, **119–20**, 190,

Wagner, Ottilie *see* Brockhaus, Ottilie

Wagner, Richard

calendar of life **12–19**

and animals 145, **174–7**, 177–8, *see also* vegetarianism

appearance and dress 97–8, 99, 113

and Beethoven *see* Beethoven

birth and baptism 94

capitalism *see* finances *below*

character 98–9, 128–9, 149, 190, *see also* finances, relationships with women

concert tours 15, 16, 18, 100, 173

as conductor 69–70, 83, **99–102**, 352–4

and contemporary composers **170–4**

as critic 382, *see also* WRITINGS

and critics **126–8**

death 19, 121

early life and training 64–7, 94, 158

early operatic repertory 69–70

family **94–7**

finances and attitude to money 98, **116–18**, 124–5

anti-capitalism 118, 374, 388

payments from Ludwig II 122, 123

Francophobia 142, 156, 385, 399

and Greek literature 57, 78, **158–61**, 167–8, 231, 232, 286

health 19, 97, 190

influence on the arts *see* influence (main entry)

Jews, attitude to

anti-Semitism 156–7, **161–3**, 190

literature on 409

Schopenhauer's influence 145

in his works 163–4, 304, 308

fear of own Jewishness 95, *13*

and individual Jews 162–3, 164, 171–2, 307, *see also* Meyerbeer, nationalism *below*, and *Was ist deutsch?* and *Das Judentum in der Musik* under WRITINGS

as librettist 203, **264–8**

sketches and drafts **196–202**

literary influences and tastes 55–8, **149–51**, *see also* Greek literature *above*

and medical practice **174–7**, 177–9, 178

myths about 132–8

nationalism 143, **155–7**, 312
  and Bayreuth 389–90
  developing 141
  literature on 409
  and operatic reform **153–8**, see also Bayreuth
paternity **94–5**
patrons 88–90
  for Bayreuth 170
  see also Friedrich August II, Ludwig II, Otto Wesendonck
philosophical outlook **143–6**, 168, see also Feuerbach, Schopenhauer
political and social attitudes **140–43**, 155, 168–9, 178, see also nationalism above
printed editions 222–7
and publishers **124–6**
quantity of literature on 132
relationships with women **118–21**
  Jessie Laussot 119
  Mathilde Wesendonck 120
  mother **96–7**, 119
  see also Wagner, 'Minna', Wagner, Cosima
religious beliefs **146–9**, 157–8, 161, 308
  see also essays Über Staat und Religion, Religion und Kunst under WRITINGS
residences
  'Asyl' (Zurich) 102, 113, 117, 120, 135–6
  Munich 121, 137, 141
  Tribschen 102, 113–14, 122, 150, 187, 188, 190, 311
  Venice 102
  Wahnfried 17, 150, 172, 190, 241, 315
  Zeltweg (Zurich) 136
as scapegoat 128–9
and science and technology 174–7, 177–9
Vaterlandsverein speech 140
vegetarianism 157, 174, 178
and vivisection **174–7**, 178
working routine 102, **113–14**

MUSIC
autograph manuscripts **196–203**, 203–6, 217–23
  fair copies 221
  fair copies (text) 201–2
  scores **219–21**
  sketches and drafts (music) 203–6, 217–19
  sketches and drafts (text) 196–202
compositional process **244–8**
  letters as valuable source of information on 193
  see also autograph manuscripts above
editions **221–7**
  Dover full-size scores 225–6
  Eulenburg pocket scores 225–6
  study scores 226–7
musical language 248–61, 405, 407
  'associative tonality' 281, 284, 289, 407
  chromatic/diatonic polarity 252–3, 258, 260, 405–6
  flexibility of forms 252–3
  the music dramas 256–61
  the Romantic operas **253–6**
  tonal system 251–2
  musico-poetic synthesis 292
orchestration 70–71, **334–47**, 350–52
  harps 337
  horns 341–3
  'special effects' 346
  strings 335–6
  timpani and percussion 345–6

trumpets, trombones, bass tuba 343–5
  'Wagner tubas' 343, 351
  woodwind 337–41
    proposed alto oboe 351
  see also compositional process
performance practice **350–59**
  conducting 352–4
  orchestra 350–52
  singing and singers 354–8
  staging 374–5
transition **240**

WORKS
1. Operas and music dramas
2. Orchestral music
3. Choral music
4. Chamber music
5. Works for solo voice and orchestra
6. Works for solo voice and piano
7. Piano music
8. Projected/unfinished dramatic works
9. Editions and arrangements

1. OPERAS AND MUSIC DRAMAS **270–309**
form 405, 407
stylistic categories 270–71
Die Feen 66, 67, 221, 222, **271–3**
  influences 239, 249
  libretto 264, 265
  source 272
Der fliegende Holländer **276–9**
  compositional process 114, 219–20, 224, 244–5, 276, 279
  editions 224, 225, 226
  failure of Overture in London 353
  French version 134
  influences on text 158
  libretto 264, 265
  musical language 253–5, 256, 278–9
  Norrington's Overture recording 359
  orchestration 71, 334–46 passim
  philosophy 183
  popularity 362
  productions 126, 276, 375, 386
  publication 125
  rights and royalties 90, 91
  Romantic influences and style 65, **74–6**, 85, 239
  Schumann on 380
  sources 277–8
  story of conception 134, 278
Götterdämmerung **295–8**
  compositional process 221, 295, 297–8
  musical influences 77, 81, 84
  musical language 259–60, 298
  orchestration 340, 344, 346
  philosophical influences 297–8
  productions 143, 295
  see also Ring
Der junge Siegfried 202, 286, see also Siegfried, Siegfrieds Tod
Das Liebesverbot 66, 89, **273–4**
  autograph score 221
  edition 222
  libretto 264, 265
  musical influences 68, 249
  musical language 274
  orchestration 70–71
  productions 273, 274
  sources 149, 273–4
Lohengrin **282–5**
  compositional process 208, 219, 245, 282–3, 284, 24, 25
  editions 222, 225, 226
  and German imperialism 389

influences on text 158
libretto 264
musical language 255–6, 284–5
orchestration 81, 334–46 passim
philosophy 183
popularity 362
productions 123, 168, 282, 386, 400
publication 125
Romantic influences and style 74, 76, 77, 78, 239
royalties 91
sources 165, 283–4
Wagner conducts 100, 101
and Wagner's religious beliefs 146
Die Meistersinger von Nürnberg **301–5**
  anti-Semitism 304
  Bar forms and rhyme 231–2, 268, 305
  compositional process 114, 208, 217, 221, 247–8, 301, 304, 27
  editions 226
  Hanslick as Beckmesser 127
  musical influences 84, 85, 87
  musical language 258, 304–5, 406
  nationalism 39, 40, 43, 304
  orchestration 334–46 passim
  philosophical ideas 304
  philosophy 58
  productions 301, 376, 391, 392
  publication 125
  and racial purity 164
  royalties and rights 91, 124, 125
  Ruskin on 383
  sources 56, 165, 303–4
  Wahn 167, **241**
  and Weinlig 65
Parsifal **305–9**
  and art of transition 240
  compositional process 114, 187, 208, 221, 248, 307, 29
  editions 226
  and Euripides 159
  first major recording of a Wagner opera 373
  and German imperialism 389
  its impact 58, 384, 394, 397
  and Ludwig II 123–4
  musical influences 81, 85, 86
  musical language 260–61, 406
  orchestration 334–46 passim
  philosophical and religious content 145, 147–9, 158
  productions 305, 307–8, 369, 373, 381, 386, 388, 395
  publication 125
  and racial purity 163–4
  reception 381
  rhyme and metre 268
  sources 165, 305
  story of conception 135–6
  Wagner as conductor 101
  Wagner on singers' insensitivity 355
  and Wagner's vivisection theory 176
Das Rheingold **287–9**
  Beardsley's illustrations 400
  compositional process 205–6, 217, **218–21**, 245–6
  editions 224–5
  musical influences 78, 84
  musical language 256–7
  Nature motif 237
  orchestration 335–46 passim
  productions 123, 287
  publication 125
  transitions 240

Wagner's supposed vision 135
see also Ring
Rienzi 67, 68, **274–6**
  compositional process 275
  editions 223–4, 276
  fate of autograph manuscripts 224, 276
  libretto 264, 265
  musical influences 71, **72–3**, 78
  orchestration 334, 341, 343, 345
  political and philosophical ideas 140,
    183
  productions 74, 274
  publication 125
  rights and royalties 90, 91
  source 275
  Wagner conducts 100
Der Ring des Nibelungen **285–7**
  advice to Bayreuth singers 357
  as allegory on capitalism 118, 388
  Bayreuth: plans for staging 167–70
  and Beethoven 152
  Boulez on 394
  editions 225–6
  Eine Mitteilung an meine Freunde on 183
  orchestration 334–46 *passim*
  philosophical and religious influences
    144–7
  productions 142–3, 357, **374–8**, 392
  thwarted in Italy 386
  prose outline *Der Nibelungen-Mythus*
    140, 144, 146, 199, 286
  publication 125
  rights and royalties 91, 117–18
  Schopenhauer's aversion to 145
  sources and early studies of the myth
    57–8
  Stabreim 240
  studies and analyses 407, 410
  text
    compositional process 196–203
    first printed 202
    influence of Aeschylus **159–61**
    other literary influences 165, 266–7
  Valkyries as daughters of Erda 136–7
  Wagner's account of inspiration 135
  Wagner's letters as source of infor-
    mation 193
  and Wagner's own marriages 119
  Wotan's eye 136
  see also Bayreuth
Siegfried **292–5**
  compositional process 113, 114, 205,
    206, 217, 221, 247, 248, 292, 294
  musical influences 81, 87
  musical language 258–9, 295
  and Old Norse verse 266–7
  orchestration 335, 336, 342, 343, 345,
    346
  productions 292
  Starnberg theme, possible use of 137–8
  Tolstoy on 383
  see also Ring
Siegfrieds Tod 140, 168, 199, 200–01, 202,
  204, 208, 240, 286, *26*, *see also*
  Götterdämmerung
Tannhäuser **279–82**
  Baudelaire's essay on 399
  compositional process 219–20, 244–5,
    279
  and critics 126, 127
  'Dresden' and 'Paris' versions 280–81,
    282
  editions 222, 224, 225, 226
  Eine Mitteilung an meine Freunde on 183
  historical character 167, 281

  musical influences and Romanticism
    74, 76–7, 81, 85, 239
  musical language 255, 256, 407
  orchestration 334–46 *passim*
  Oscar Wilde on 387
  popularity 362
  productions 279, 376, 386, 391
  publication 125
  religion, incidental references to 146
  rhyme 264
  rights and royalties 90, 91
  Romanticism 239
  sources 165, 166–7, 281
  textual influences 158
  Wagner conducts 100
Tristan und Isolde **298–301**
  analyses 405–6
  Berio on 395
  Berlioz on 237
  compositional process 102, 114, 120,
    217, 218, 221, 298
  editions 226
  its impact 394, 395, 397
  melody and 'form' 233–4, 235
  musical influences 81, 84, 85–6, 87
  musical language 252, 258, 301
  'Tristan chord' 80, 252, 395
  orchestration 334–45 *passim*
  productions 298, 386
  publication 125
  and racial purity 164
  recordings
    Furtwängler 373
    R. Strauss, Prelude 354
  sources and textual influences 57, 145,
    159, 165, 166
  transition 240
  use of *Stabreim* 267
  Verdi on 382
  Wesendonck Lieder as studies for 318
Die Walküre 261, **290–92**
  compositional process 220–21, 246–7,
    290, 292
  influence on Decadents 397
  musical influences 87
  musical language 292
  orchestration 335–46 *passim*
  popularity 363
  productions 123, 290
  see also Ring
2. ORCHESTRAL MUSIC **309–13**
  Entractes tragiques 309
  Grosser Festmarsch (*Centennial March*) 208,
    313
  Huldigungsmarsch 141, **311**
  incidental music to *Die letzte Heidenversch-*
    wörung in Preussen (J. Singer) 310
  Kaisermarsch 125, 142, 208, 222, **312**, *28*
  Orchestral work in E minor 309
  overtures
    B♭ major ('Drum-beat') 309
    C major (in 6/8 time) 309
    Concert Overture No. 1 in D minor 65,
      309
    Concert Overture No.2 in C major 309
    E♭ major 309
    E♭ major and incidental music to
      Columbus (Apel) 310, 344
    E minor and incidental music to *König*
      Enzio (Ernst Raupach) 309
    Faust Overture 65, 74, 208, 222, **310**,
      345, *22*
      story of origin 133
    Political 309
    Polonia 310

  'Porazzi Theme' 313
  Rule Britannia 310
  to Schiller's *Die Braut von Messina* 309
  uncompleted 312
  Romeo und Julie 311
  Siegfried Idyll 101, 222, **311–12**
    orchestration 336, 342, 344
    so-called Starnberg theme 137–8
  symphonies
    C major 309
    E major (uncompleted) 310
  Trauermusik, on motifs from Weber's *Eur-*
    yanthe 208, 310, *23*
  plans for uncompleted works 312–13
3. CHORAL MUSIC **313–15**
  An Webers Grabe (*At Weber's Grave*) 314
  Descendons gaiment la courtille (chorus for
    vaudeville) (Dumersan and Dupeuty)
    314
  Gesang am Grabe (*Funeral Dirge*) 313
  Gruss seiner Treuen an Friedrich August den
    Geliebten (*Greeting to the Beloved Friedrich*
    August from his Loyal Subjects) 315
  Ihr Kinder, geschwinde, geschwinde (*Children,*
    Hurry, Hurry) 315
  incidental music for *Beim Antritt des neuen*
    Jahres 1835 (W. Schmale) 314
  Kinder-Katechismus (*A Children's Catechism*)
    315
  Das Liebesmahl der Apostel (*The Love-Feast*
    of the Apostles) 222, 314
  Nicolay anthem 313
  Der Tag erscheint (*The Day Appears*) 314
  vocal fugues 313
  Wahlspruch für die deutsche Feuerwehr (*Motto*
    for the German Fire Brigade) 315
  Willkommen in Wahnfried, du heil'ger Christ
    (*Welcome to Wahnfried, Holy Christ*) 315
4. CHAMBER MUSIC **315**
  Adagio for Clarinet and String Quintet
    (spurious) 315
  String Quartet in D major 315
  String Quartet (the 'Starnberg' Quartet
    137–8, 315
5. WORKS FOR SOLO VOICE AND ORCHESTRA
  315–16
  Aria 315
  Aria (bass) for Weigl's *Die Schweizerfamilie*
    316
  'Doch jetzt wohin ich blicke' (for
    Marschner's *Der Vampyr*) 316
  'Norma il predisse, O Druidi' (aria for
    Bellini's *Norma*) 316
  'Sanfte Wehmut will sich regen' (for
    Blum's *Mary, Max und Michel*) 316
  Scene and aria 315–16
6. WORKS FOR SOLO VOICE AND PIANO 222,
  316–18
  Abendglocken see Glockentöne
  Adieux de Marie Stuart 317
  Aria 316
  Attente (*Expectation*) 317
  Dors, mon enfant (*Sleep, my child*) 317
  Es ist bestimmt in Gottes Rat (*God has decreed*)
    318
  Extase (*Ecstasy*) 317
  Glockentöne (*Abendglocken*) 316
  La Tombe dit à la rose (*The Tomb Says to the*
    Rose) 317
  Les Deux Grenadiers (*The Two Grenadiers*)
    125, 317
  Mignonne 317
  Schlaf, Kindchen, schlafe (*Sleep, Baby, Sleep*)
    318
  Seven pieces for Goethe's *Faust* 316

6. WORKS FOR SOLO VOICE AND PIANO cont.
Songs (1828–30) 316
Der Tannenbaum (The Fir Tree) 317
Tout n'est qu'images fugitives (Soupir) (All is but fleeting images (Sigh)) 317
Wesendonck Lieder 318
Der Worte viele sind gemacht (Much is Promised) 318
7. PIANO MUSIC **318–20**
Albumleaf in E♭ major 320
Albumleaf in E major ('Song Without Words') 319
Ankunft bei den schwarzen Schwänen (Arrival at the House of the Black Swans) 320
Fantasia in F♯ minor 319
In das Album der Fürstin M[etternich] 320
Polka 319
Polonaise in D major 319
Eine Sonata für das Album von Frau M[athilde] W[esendonck] 319–20
Sonata in A major (Grosse Sonate) 310, **319**
Sonata in B♭ major for 4 hands 318
Sonata in B♭ major, op.1 125, 318–19
Sonata in D minor 318
Sonata in F minor 318
Theme in A♭ major 320
Züricher Vielliebchen-Walzer (Zurich Philippina Waltz) 320
8. PROJECTED/UNFINISHED DRAMATIC WORKS **320–22**
Die Bergwerke zu Falun (The Mines of Falun) 321
Achilleus 144, 321–2
Friedrich I. 77, **321**
Die Hochzeit (The Wedding) 222, 321
libretto 264
Die hohe Braut, oder Bianca und Giuseppe (The Noble Bride, or Bianca and Giuseppe) 321
Jesus von Nazareth 119, 144, 146–7, 175, 321
Eine Kapitulation (A Capitulation) 142, 187, 322
Leubald 56, 65, **320**
Ein Lustspiel in 1 Akt (A Comedy in 1 Act) 322
Luthers Hochzeit (Luther's Wedding) 322
Männerlist grösser als Frauenlist, oder Die glückliche Bärenfamilie (Man's Cunning Greater than Woman's, or The Happy Bear Family) 321
Pastoral opera (unnamed) 321
Die Sarazenin (The Saracen Woman) 77, **321**
Die Sieger (The Victors) 147, 308, 322
Wieland der Schmied (Wieland the Smith) 322
9. EDITIONS AND ARRANGEMENTS **322–4**
Beethoven, Symphony no. 9
Bellini, *Il pirata*, orchestration of cavatina 322–3
Bellini, *Norma*, retouching of orchestration 323
Gluck, *Iphigénie en Aulide*, revised version 323
Gluck, *Iphigénie en Aulide*, concert ending for overture 324
Haydn, Symphony no. 103 arr. for piano 322
Meyerbeer, *Robert le diable*, transcription of harp part of cavatina 323
Mozart, *Don Giovanni*, revised version 100, 324
Palestrina, Stabat Mater, revised version 323
Rossini, *Les Soirées musicales*, orchestration of duet accompaniment 323

Spontini, *La Vestale*, retouching of orchestration 323
Strauss, Johann the Younger, *Wine, Women and Song* waltz, reorchestration 324
various composers, suites for the *cornet à pistons* 323
various composers, vocal scores and arrangements 323
Weber, *Euryanthe*, reorchestration of hunting chorus 323

WRITINGS
chronological list 326–32
anthologies and other editions 332
collected writings 115, **193–6**
autobiographical works **182–6**
Annals 150, 182, 187
Autobiographische Skizze 140, 182–3, 265
Mein Leben **183–6**
Brown Book as basis for 182
challenge to scholars 244
Cosima to continue 187
Nietzsche reads 94
publication 185–6
story of *Holländer* origin 134, 278
story of genesis of *Faust* Overture 133
story of inspiration for *Parsifal* 135
story of *Ring* vision 135, 289
story of Schröder-Devrient and *Fidelio* 133
Eine Mitteilung an meine Freunde 64, 70, 125, 155, 183, 233, 235, 248, 265, 278, 284
Red Pocketbook 182, 318
diaries **186–8**
Brown Book 182, 186–7, 187, 307, 311, 403
essays, articles and open letters 67, **114–16**
Beethoven 133, 153
Bellini 274
Berlioz, open letter to 237
Deutsche Kunst und deutsche Politik 141, 156, 157
Die deutsche Oper 195, 274
Ein Ende in Paris (novella) 74
Entwurf zur Organisation eines deutschen Nationaltheaters für das Königreich Sachsen 167, 194
Erinnerungen an Auber 71
Erinnerungen an Ludwig Schnorr von Carolsfeld 358
Heldentum und Christentum 148, 157–8
on *Les Huguenots* 72–3
Das Judentum in der Musik 45, 74, 115, 156, 162–3, 172, 304
Die Kunst und die Revolution 116, 141, 232
Das Kunstwerk der Zukunft 116, 144, 146, 152, 155, 196, **231**, 398
Der Mensch und die bestehende Gesellschaft 195
Der Nibelungen-Mythus 140, 144, 146, 199, 286
Die Not (political poem) 140
Offenes Schreiben an Herrn Ernst von Weber **174–6**, 177, 178
Oper und Drama
attack on Meyerbeer 72, 74
on Beethoven's Ninth Symphony 152
on motifs 234–5, 239
on musical prose 394
on musico-poetic synthesis 240, 252, 301
on orchestral melody 238

on poetic intent 238
on poetic-musical periods 238, 251
on public attitudes 154
on rhyme 266
Pasticcio 195
Eine Pilgerfahrt zu Beethoven (novella) 83, 133, 152
Religion und Kunst 145, 177, 178, 179, 308
Die Revolution 195
Ein Theater in Zürich 116, 155
Über die Anwendung der Musik auf das Drama 153, 173, 235, 236, 252
Über die Benennung 'Musikdrama' 271
Über die Bestimmung der Oper 157, 233, 239
Über das Dichten und Komponieren 172, 173
Über das Dirigieren 68, 83, 353
Über Franz Liszts Symphonische Dichtungen 86
Über musikalische Kritik 126
Über das Opern-Dichten und Komponieren im Besonderen 239
Über Schauspieler und Sänger 233
Über Staat und Religion 141, 234, 241
Der Virtuoso und der Künstler 115
Was ist deutsch? 141, 148, 156
Die Wibelungen 77, 148, 194, 286
Wie verhalten sich republikanische Bestrebungen dem Königtum gegenüber 140
Wollen wir hoffen? 141
'Zukunftsmusik' 152–3, 233, 234, 237
Zum Vortrag der neunten Symphonie Beethovens 83, 152
letters 98, 128, **190–93**, 195
correspondence with publishers 125–6
open letters see essays
'pink drawers' letter 121
ruse letter to Apel 134–5
to mother 96
Wagner, Rosalie see Marbach, Rosalie
Wagner, Siegfried (son) 33, 311, 369, 375–6, 391, *13*
Wagner, Wieland (grandson) 366, 375, 376–7, 392
Wagner, Winifred (daughter-in-law) 376, 392
Wagner, Wolfgang (grandson) 392
Wagner Societies 100, 142, 170, 196, 308, 320, 386, 400
Wagner (Wagner Society periodical) 409n.
Wahn 241
Wahnfried archives 185, 191, 409
Wahnfried (home) see residences under Wagner
Walter, Bruno 365, 371
Warrack, John 82
Wars of Liberation see Napoleonic Wars
Wartburg Festival 41
Watson, Claire 366
Weavers' Uprising (1844) 43
Weber, Carl Maria von 73, 75, **239**, 249, 272, 334, 342
Euryanthe 66, 68, 69, 78–9, 82, 239, 256, 310
Wagner's reorchestration of hunting chorus 323
Der Freischütz 64–5, 69, 70, 76, 80, 239, 253, 272
Oberon 66, 69, 70
overture construction 80
Preciosa 70
reminiscence motif 80–81, 82
Wagner's funeral music for 310, 314, *23*

Weber, Ernst von **33**, **174–6**, 177
Weber, William 115, 393, 410
Weidmann, Vreneli (Verena) **33**
Weigl, Joseph 69, 70, 233, 316
Weimar 15, 90, 168, 169, 282
Weingartner, Felix 224, 225, 226
Weinlig, Christian Theodor **33**, 65, 313, 318, 319
Weissheimer, Wendelin 33
welsch 39
Wesendonck, Mathilde **33**, 102, 118, 120, 184, 186, 304
   inking of Wagner's manuscripts 218
   music composed for 318–20
Wesendonck, Otto **33–4**, 91, 117–18, 304
Wessling, B.W. 409
Westernhagen, Curt von 136, 217, 218, 246, 403
Whittall, Arnold 408
Widdop, Walter 367
Widmann (contralto) 317
Wienbarg, Ludolf 57
Wildenbruch, Ernst von 58

Wilde, Oscar 136, 387
Wildermann, Hans 375
Wilhelm I, Kaiser 44, 142, 388, 390
Wilhelm II, Kaiser 61, 388
Wilhelmine, Margravine 389
Wille, Eliza **34**, 97–8
Windgassen, Wolfgang 366
Winkler, Franz 410
Winter, Peter von 70, 80
Wintle, Christopher 407
Wölfel, Friedrich 220, 224
Wolf, Hugo 381–2, 393
Wolfram von Eschenbach 135, 164, 268, 284, 307
Wolfram, Clara, *née* Wagner (sister) **34**, 64, 97, 120
Wolf, Werner 192
Wolzogen, Hans von **34**, 68, 78, 188, 195, 235, 388, 405, 409
Wonder, Erich 378
Woolf, Virginia 397
Wunderwald, Gustav 375
Würzburg 13, 66, 69

Wüst, Henriette 316
Wynn, Marianne 151
Wyzewa, Théodore de 397, 399

Young German movement 55, 57, 67, 68, 143, 145, 149, 273, 274
Young Hegelians **53–4**, 55, 59, 143–4, 145, 161, 232, 321

Zedlitz, Joseph Christian von 277
Zeitung für die elegante Welt 182, 195, 274
Zelinsky, Hartmut 163, 409
Zellner, L.A. 237
Zola, Emile 400
Zollverein (Customs Union) 42
'Zukunftsmusik' 144
   Wagner's essay on 152–3, 233, 234, 237
Zurich 15–16, 57, 100, 145, 168, 183
   political circle in 141, 144
Zurmühl, S. 410